VEFA ALEXIADOU

GREECE

-

THE COOKBOOK

INTRODUCTION
ΕΙΣΑΓΩΓΗ

Isagogi

Greece: The Cookbook contains hundreds of traditional recipes collected from all over Greece. From the delicious fish dishes of the coast, to the huge variety of pies and breads from rural mountain villages, they reveal the mouthwatering variety of Greek cooking. They also show a remarkable continuity from the dishes of antiquity to those cooked today. There are many dishes here that citizens of ancient Greece might recognize, and the culture and history of Greece are deeply embedded in the recipes. In fact, even the briefest look into the history of Greek cuisine reveals a gastronomic tradition not just a few centuries old, but with roots reaching back to the dawn of Western civilization, which began on the shores of the Aegean archipelago.

The development of Greece's cuisine was influenced by many factors, the most important being its remarkable geography and topography. High mountain ranges, isolated valleys and a long coastline create Greece's unique microclimates, which account for the wide diversity of ingredients and local variations in the traditional diet and cuisine. The staples of Greece today are the same as they have been for centuries: cereals, beans, greens, herbs, the olive and its oil, figs, grapes, wine, and cheese. Greeks ate very little meat until the second half of the twentieth century. For thousands of years meat was consumed only during feasts and festivals in honor of the many gods and goddesses of the Greek pantheon, and, later, Christian saints and martyrs. In addition, the long history of fasting in the Greek Orthodox religion, which insisted upon abstention from animal products for almost a third of the year, has resulted in a rich tradition of vegetable dishes cooked with olive oil.

Mediterranean food as we know it today was born in Greece. In the eighth century BC, the Hellenic Greeks began to settle in other areas of the Mediterranean basin (in what is now Spain, Sicily and southern Italy, France, and Turkey). They planted vineyards and olive trees and made wine and olive oil. Their colonies became wealthy centers of commerce and culture, and oil, cereals, and wine—the holy trinity of the Greek diet—became the fundamentals of the diet of civilized man. According to some food historians, the ancient Greeks were also the first to recognize and record the excellence of local food specialties. This unique idea eventually led to the appellation of origin regulations of modern European wines, cheese and other products. This is possibly the most important culinary legacy of ancient Greece, whose impact is still felt throughout Western gastronomy.

The ancient Greek writer Athenaeus compiled a vast amount of information on food and eating, quoting over 1,000 sources on the gastronomic practices of the ancient world. In his epic work, *The Deipnosophists* (or *Wise Men at Dinner*), he describes how all fish, meat and herbs have different properties at different times of year, showing that, even very early in their history, Greeks valued the seasonal character of their foods. Even today, Greeks prefer fresh seasonal produce to ingredients that are out of season, or frozen foods. The traditional Greek diet (the word itself is derived from the ancient Greek *dieta*, meaning "way of life"), based on olive oil, high-fiber fruits, vegetables and grains, natural cheese, nuts, more poultry and fish and less red meat, is also being promoted by nutritionists the world over as one of the healthiest. During the past twenty years, olive oil has been making culinary and scientific headlines. The world has discovered that it is not only delicious, but also good for the health.

Just as they did in ancient times, Greek cooks still rely on the natural qualities and flavor of fresh vegetables and fruit, extra-virgin olive oil, cheeses made from sheep's and goat's milk, fish and shellfish fresh from the Aegean, and meat and poultry from animals that have spent their lives in the open. They use herbs and spices judiciously, never excessively. Depending on where they live, they may reach for hot pepper or cumin or grab a handful of mint from a patch in the garden. Regional differences abound, and here the recipe titles indicate when a dish is associated with a particular region. Many dishes are also traditionally prepared at certain times of year to celebrate religious festivals or special occasions. These culinary traditions are an essential part of Greek culture.

Today, the mother of Mediterranean cuisine continues to evolve, while remaining tightly bound to the sparse soil and the blue sea. The survival of the ageless characteristics of the cuisine—simple, wholesome ingredients combined and prepared to enhance flavor and aroma—is impressive. Greek cooking offers healthy, tasty dishes designed to be savored slowly with good wine in pleasant company. Traditional Greek cuisine continues to encompass a way of life that transcends ingredients, chefs, and historic origins. Its timeless philosophy is eloquently expressed by Nikos Kazantzakis in his novel *Zorba the Greek*:

I at last realized that eating was a spiritual function and that meat, bread and wine were the raw materials from which the mind is made.

Wishing you *kali orexi*, or *bon appétit*!

Vefa Alexiadou

REGIONS

-

ΠΕΡΙΟΧΕΣ

-

Periohes

NORTHERN GREECE
ΒΟΡΕΙΑ ΕΛΛΑΔΑ
Voria Ellada

The famous dish named after Macedonia—*macédoine de fruits*, a preparation of chopped mixed fresh fruit—is so called because its namesake region of Greece is such a diverse mixture of language groups and nationalities. In antiquity, southern Macedonia (the part that is now united with Greece) formed a land bridge with Thrace between Constantinople in the east and Rome in the west, as well as between the inner Balkans and the Aegean. Over the centuries it has attracted emperors and tradesmen alike, and under the Byzantines, Franks, and Ottomans it rivaled only Constantinople in size and influence. Its landscape matched the variety of its people, and a wide range of produce came from its forests, plains, rivers, and coastline. Towns and cities sprang up at key locations, the most important of which was Thessaloniki, which quickly became a microcosm of the ethnically diverse population of the region as a whole. Influences from countries such as Turkey, Bulgaria, Armenia, and Serbia have all contributed to a cuisine of unusual complexity.

Thessaloniki could be called the gastronomic capital of Greece, and its markets and restaurants reflect the intricate roots of its people, as well as the traditions and products of its hinterland. There is no such thing as Macedonian cooking per se, rather a number of gloriously dissimilar components. A wide variety of seafood is harvested from all along the coast from below Olympus, up and down the three fingers of Chalkidiki, and as far as Kavala, appearing on the table in the form of plump mussels, squid, octopus, and both large and small fish of many kinds, all prepared in dozens of different ways. The preponderance of available ingredients and cooking methods may have given birth to the mezedes culture, whereby numerous little dishes can be cooked or ordered and shared at a party or taverna. Everyone gets to taste everything, a concept quite different from the French approach of a series of courses. The mezedes culture, already established throughout Asia Minor and the Middle East, was strengthened in the early twentieth century by refugees from Constantinople and Smyrna, who introduced a series of foods now thought of as quintessentially Hellenic. They stuffed any vegetable that could be used as a container with meat, rice, or both, seasoned it with exotic spices such as cumin, added luxury ingredients like raisins, pine nuts, and pistachios, and a pinch of sugar to bring out the taste of savory dishes. Their recipes often involved laborious techniques, not just the slow, one-pot cooking of a few ingredients. For example, when they made an elaborate Anatolian dish such as moussaka, they gave it a French touch by topping it with a nutmeg-scented béchamel sauce.

With street food, from the gyro (doner kebab) to dolmades (subtly fragrant stuffed grape (vine) leaves with egg-lemon sauce), the Constantinople and Smyrna Greeks left an indelible imprint on Greek

MACEDONIA
ΜΑΚΕΔΟΝΙΑ
Makedonia

cuisine. To them we also owe the vast range of phyllo (filo) pastry desserts and confectionery stuffed with nuts or dried fruit and dripping with honey, which have made Thessaloniki the dessert capital of Greece.

Inland, there is a wealth of other culinary traditions. Western Macedonia, for example, is Greece's lake district. The waters of the Prespes lakes are home to freshwater fish such as carp and trout, and their shores are planted with endless rows of beans, which end up in *fasolada* or bean soup (considered by some to be the Greek national dish), *gigantes plaki* (baked giant beans), and casseroles. Many of them contain the sweet, long red peppers of Florina, an indispensable accompaniment to almost any meal in that area. Chiles also play a major role in Macedonian cooking. Dried and crumbled into flakes called *boukovo*, a name with Slavic origins, they appear in many dishes, along with sweet and hot paprika, and cabbage. In the cold, mountainous north, cabbage forms the basis of many hearty meals, as a wrap for ground (minced) meat, or in stews and pies. Pickled cabbage, or sauerkraut, is also a great favorite in these parts. Other warming dishes rely on leeks, onions, and nettles, while pork is the most common meat.

The district of Kozani in the south is purple with millions of crocus blooms. Their coral stigmas, three to a flower, are collected, dried, and sold as the most expensive spice in the world. It takes 200,000 of them to fill a 2¼-lb (1-kg) bag. Surprisingly, however, only a couple of Greek recipes call for saffron, and these are breads from the southern Cyclades. Between Kozani and Thessaloniki lies Macedonia's orchard belt, which provides a substantial amount of Greece's fruit, including cherries, peaches, apricots, plums, and quinces. Used both fresh and dried, they are often combined with meat, vegetables, and even fish in dishes such as leeks with prunes, plums, and tomatoes, veal with apples, or lamb with quinces. Southern Greeks would shudder at the very notion of mingling sweet and savory flavors. In this area, especially around Naousa, one of the country's foremost wine producers, recipes often incorporate wine-making by-products, such as verjuice (unfermented grape juice) or *petimezi* (grape must molasses or syrup) as well as its signature red wine. In fact, almost every corner of Macedonia has its own local specialties, from Drama's spicy meatballs to Kerkini's clay-baked water buffalo, and Chalkidiki's delicious wrinkled olives.

THRACE
ΘΡΑΚΗ
Thraki

The long, narrow region of Thrace is the handle connecting Greece to the East, forming a corridor and a bridge used by tribes, armies, and merchants, who brought both commodities and ideas. Romans, Byzantines, Slavs, Crusaders, Ottomans, and modern Europeans have all left their mark on the countryside, whether in the form of castles, roads, churches, or the railroad (railway). There is still a remarkable cultural mix in Thrace, partly the result of the Treaty of Lausanne, which in 1923 provided for the separation of the Greek and Turkish populations, excluding western Thrace and what was then known as Constantinople. It is especially apparent in the approach to food in the region. On every main street, kabob (kebab) houses alternate with tiny stores selling slices of *bougatsa*, a delicious flaky pastry with a sweet cream filling. Tavernas offer dishes with Turkish names like *giaourtlou, tourlou,* and *sarmas*: rich, spicy combinations of meats, vegetables and sauces. In some neighborhoods, settled by relatively recent refugees from the Caucasus, some restaurants feature Russian-style dishes like *borscht, piroski,* and *manti* (varieties of stuffed pasta similar to ravioli), pickles, and red cabbage. Bulgur wheat and cracked corn are much more popular than rice, as is buttermilk and a kind of thick yogurt, both fresh and dried for winter use. Thrace's version of *trahana* (a type of rough homemade pasta) is laced with sweet and hot peppers, and dough is also treated in unusual ways, such as broiling (grilling) phyllo (filo) sheets and noodles (pasta) before folding them into pies.

Most of Thrace's towns are no more than thirty minutes from the sea, so fish features prominently on local menus, usually simply broiled (grilled). They are smoked, pickled, salted, preserved in oil, and even made into *pastourma* with the paprika-garlic crust normally reserved for beef, but most of all they are served fresh. Perhaps the most popular shellfish is the mussel, and in both Macedonia and Thrace there are dozens of mussel recipes, from crispy deep-fried versions with garlic sauce, to *saganaki* with cheese and tomato.

Thracian desserts have an Eastern flavor, including *samali,* semolina flavored with mastic and honey syrup; *ekmek,* bread soaked in syrup and topped with a thick wedge of clotted cream as firm as butter; and mastic-scented *kaimaki* ice cream, not to mention the full spectrum of crisp phyllo (filo) pastries stuffed with chopped nuts or dried fruit, beloved from Athens to Damascus. *Loukoumia* is another popular treat consisting of gelatinous squares scented with rosewater, mastic, or orange blossom, sometimes concealing pistachios or almonds. In Komotini, special ovens in the old town roast sesame seeds before they are ground into sesame paste or halva. Sometimes they are left whole and mixed with honey to make brick-like slabs of tooth-wrenching *pasteli.* Komotini is also famous for its *stragalia* or roasted garbanzo beans (chickpeas), a favorite snack in the days before popcorn.

The valleys of Thrace are white with cotton, yellow with tobacco, or green with asparagus. Great rivers, the Nestos and the Evros, flow down from Bulgaria, while the Rodopi Mountains separating Greece from Bulgaria contain vast stretches of dense forests of willow, oak, beech, and fir, a haven for wild boar, deer, wolves, bears, and other animals, although most of the game served in Greek restaurants actually comes from Thracian game farms. The region also supplies a good deal of the country's domestic meat, especially pork, and boasts almost as many types of sausage as Germany. These range from Xanthi's horseshoe-shaped *petala,* to the long ropes that dangle like giant beaded curtains in every butcher's store in the Byzantine town of Didymoteicho. They often contain both pork and beef, and can be seasoned with leeks, cumin, and, of course, red and black pepper. Another specialty of this district is *kavourmas,* a plump pâté-like sausage reminiscent of the *rillettes* of France. All in all, Thrace offers a fascinatingly different dimension to the gastronomic culture of Greece.

EPIRUS
ΗΠΕΙΡΟΣ
Ipiros

Epirus has a strong history of cheese production because of the legacy of its nomadic shepherds, who used to walk their flocks of sheep and goats from the plains where they wintered up into the high mountain pastures, where the grass was always green. Some of the best cheeses come from Dodoni, the site of the ancients' oldest oracle, and a sanctuary dedicated to Zeus. Dodoni feta and *graviera* are sold all over Greece, but you'd have to go to Epirus to taste *galotiri*, more like a tangy dip than a cheese, which is delicious with chunks of the unrefined local bread. The region's *manouri*, on the other hand, is a widely-available, solid, smooth white cheese, whose sweetness complements fresh fruit perfectly. Travel across the mountains and you come to Metsovo, an alpine town where the local cheeses have made the residents rich. Among them is a *graviera* made exactly like Swiss Gruyère, smoked Metsovone, similar to Italy's provolone, and a delicate goat's cheese studded with black peppercorns. Although not Greek in origin, they have become Greek classics. Apart from dairy products, other Metsovites are at work on other traditional foods, such as *hilopites* (homemade egg noodles or pasta) and *trahana*, a kind of rustic pasta found all over the Balkans and Turkey. The latter, made from flour or cracked wheat boiled with fresh or sour milk, is left to dry in the sun, and stored as dry pellets or clusters of pellets, and forms the basis of many soups and stews. It is also an ideal way of condensing nutritious but perishable milk into a food that is easy both to cook and to carry.

Much of Epirus' cuisine reflects its nomadic origins. Take the region's most characteristic food: the *pita*, or pie. As portable as a sandwich, it can be filled with just about anything and there are almost as many local recipes for pies as there are cooks making them. While the most elaborate can contain as many as twenty sheets of hand-rolled phyllo (filo), the simplest involves a milky batter, a sprinkling of cornmeal, or no pastry crust at all. Fillings include cheese with wild greens, garden vegetables, lentils, or *trahana*, and so basic were pies to the locals' existence that they came to be known simply as *trofi*, or "food." There are also more lavish concoctions stuffed with chicken, game, or meat, eggs, and a mix of cheeses, designed for eating on special occasions. To make the simpler pies and other foods on the move, the *gastra*, a portable metal baking pan with a tight-fitting, dome-shaped lid that can be heated over an open fire, was invented in Epirus. Anything cooked in it simmers evenly and emerges tender and tasty, and nowadays many tavernas in Epirus advertise meats slow-roasted in the *gastra*, having turned a traditional necessity into an exotic utensil.

Generally speaking, the flavors of Epirus resemble those of the Balkans more than those of the rest of Greece. Butter, rather than olive oil, is the cooking medium, while sauces are red with paprika rather than tomatoes. As in Macedonia, there are many recipes for soups and

stews thickened with yogurt or ground walnuts and garlic. The region's many lakes and rivers yield freshwater fish, while the lakeshore tavernas at Ioannina, Epirus' largest city, specialize in crayfish and frogs' legs. Many years of Turkish rule have left their mark on Ioannina's atmosphere and food, and it has an extensive repertoire of Middle Eastern sweetmeats. Perhaps the most characteristic is the *gianiotiko*, a type of baklava oozing honey and nuts and wrapped in *kataifi* pastry. Perhaps surprisingly, Epirus can also claim high quality seafood. The Amvrakikos (or Ambracian) Gulf consists of twenty-four lagoons, natural fisheries that have been exploited since Roman times and are home to delectable blue-veined shrimp (prawns), dozens of species of fish, and the country's largest eel population. The mullet caught here in the late summer are among those that produce the sea's most luxurious product, *avgotaraho*, the cured, salted roe of the gray mullet.

Thessaly is Greece's great plain, a three-color patchwork of wheat, corn, and cotton that separates Macedonia from the southern half of the country. If you half-close your eyes, you can imagine it as the vast lake it was hundreds of thousands of years ago. In that distant past, a violent earthquake sundered Mount Olympus from Mount Ossa, and with the earthquake the water surged into the Aegean, draining the lake but leaving a bed of soil that was wonderfully fertile. The plain of Thessaly became Greece's main bread-producing area, vital to the country's nourishment. Surprisingly, though, much of this region's approach to food is similar to those of infertile, mountainous Epirus and Sterea Ellada, because it has similar nomadic pastoral roots. The farming communities around the edge of the vast plain grew into cities as the shepherd clans who wintered there built permanent homes. Even though fewer and fewer of them take their flocks west to pastures in the Pindos mountains in summer, they still enjoy the traditional dishes.

Many of these traditional dishes contain cheese. Towns like Larisa, Trikala, Farsala, and Karditsa are among the country's foremost cheese producers. Renowned for their feta, *kaseri*, a sweet, soft yellow cheese, and *graviera*, similar to Gruyère, they also produce a range of engagingly sour, spreadable white cheeses that remain relatively unknown. One of the best is *katiki* from Domokos near the southern border of the region. Many of these cheeses find their way into pies, for Thessaly, like Epirus and Sterea Ellada, is at the core of Greece's *pita* culture. An inventory of the different types of crust, shapes, and fillings would need a book in itself. Some of the simpler ones originated as a portable meal for shepherds on the move, but there are also many more complex versions for special occasions. With more elaborate fillings, often containing sumptuous mixtures of meat or poultry, vegetables, and milk or cheese, these rank among the masterpieces of Greek cuisine.

One characteristic sets the food of Thessaly apart from much of the rest of Greece, and that is a fondness for beef. The plain is large and flat enough to support cattle, and the locals have many recipes for beef and veal, whether stewed, pot-roasted, or even made into sausages. They also enjoy pork, lamb, and goat in every form, roasted whole on the

THESSALY
ΘΕΣΣΑΛΙΑ
Thessalia

spit, skewered in chunks, or in thick chops grilled over charcoal. Tripe soup is a favorite comfort food to restore body and soul after a night of drinking and dancing. Organ meats (offal) are highly prized, and no part of an animal is ever thrown away. As for desserts, the cornstarch (cornflour) halva from Farsala with its caramelized sugar topping is spectacular and can be sampled from roadside stands outside the town.

At the eastern end of Thessaly, two mountains rise above the Aegean: Pelion and the lesser-known Ossa (also known as Kissavos). Pelion was the traditionally the centaurs' mountain, and it is still so wooded and filled with healing herbs that you might be only mildly surprised to see Chiron, teacher of Achilles and of Asklepios (the god of medicine) canter out of a thicket. Today, Pelion and Ossa supply most of Greece's apples and many of its chestnuts, cherries, kiwis, and other fruits and nuts. One indigenous type of apple, the *firiki*, oval in shape and smaller than other apples, has a particularly delicate flavor and is preserved in various ways, often candied whole at Christmas. Volos, Thessaly's capital and the port from which Jason set off in search of the Golden Fleece, is located at Pelion's base, and its food combines the best of sea and mountain. *Spetsofai*, a spicy stew of sausages, hot and sweet peppers, and tomatoes, is its best-known dish, but there are also recipes for beef and chicken stews with unusual flavorings, such as raisins and cinnamon, sweet paprika, or even *spetsofai* with fish. Seafood mezedes menus can run to many pages in the neighborhood tavernas. The locals tuck into them with a tiny glass of *tsipouro*, a distillation similar to ouzo but without ouzo's licorice flavor, similar to the Cretan raki.

STEREA ELLADA (ROUMELI)
ΣΤΕΡΕΑ ΕΛΛΑΔΑ (ΡΟΥΜΕΛΗ)
Sterea Ellada (Roumeli)

Before Greece declared independence in 1821, the name Roumeli had come to refer to all the Greek lands from the Gulf of Corinth to Macedonia in the north and from Epirus to the gates of Constantinople. Now a much smaller region, it covers the territory secured by the Revolution that was considered "solid" (*sterea*), or belonging to the mainland, as even the Peloponnese was considered an island in those days—hence the name Sterea Ellada. An area of high mountains and nomadic shepherds, it was once the center of Greek life, for Delphi (the navel of the world in ancient times) and the oracle at Pythia, are located here. Above it looms the legendary Mount Parnassos, sacred to Apollo and the Muses, and to Dionysos and his maenads.

The area can claim some of modern Greece's most beloved culinary traditions, such as the spit-roasted Easter lamb. In Thiva (Thebes), Delphi, or Livadia on Easter Sunday, whole streets are turned into barbecue pits, with dozens of lambs rotating over smoldering coals. Fifty years ago, this quintessentially Greek custom was rarely found in other parts of Greece, where oven-roasted, stuffed lamb was preferred. Now families all over the country cook lambs in their backyards. The local cuisine has also produced great taverna favorites like *kokoretsi*, *gardouba*, and *splinantero*, all dishes of organ meats (offal) prepared in ways that make even the squeamish forget their origins.

There is also an array of pies made with greens, cheese, yogurt, and milk. As in Epirus and Thessaly, the pie appears here in endless variations. Along with a host of foraged and cultivated greens, they may contain one or more of the region's exceptional cheeses, including *psomotiri* and *formaela,* which, dusted in flour and quickly fried, becomes *saganaki,* a popular meze. *Psomotiri,* which translates literally as "bread cheese" (perhaps because the two are such good partners), is a creamy, tangy thickened yogurt that has been salted and fermented for about three weeks.

The rural talent for making foods that can be stored and transported is another feature shared with many of the country's regions. Virtually every pantry is stocked with homemade dough and pasta products, all made in the summer and stored for the winter. In the more remote mountain districts they are cooked with butter, not olive oil, even though the southern part of Sterea Ellada is one of Greece's foremost oil-pro-ducing areas. Below Delphi, the olive grove of Amfissa is a sea of silver-leaved trees that fills the plain between the foot of Parnassos and the Gulf of Corinth. From here come the large round green or purple-black olives that compete with the pointed Kalamata variety for the title of Greece's most delicious. Further westward along the coast is Galaxidi, where the pastry stores (shops) behind the port specialize in cookies (biscuits) flavored with the local firewater, *tsipouro,* orange zest, and walnuts. The Vardousia and southern Pindos mountains are still home to much of the country's game, while the area around Karpenisi has recently started to produce the mainland's first prosciutto. Further south, Missolonghi is lagoon country, where fish, not meat, is king. Fishermen camp in reed-roofed wooden shacks balanced on stilts and punt through the shallows in flat-bottomed boats. Among the catch are clams, crabs, tiny squid, eel, bream, and mullet, but the real delicacy for which Missolonghi is famous is *avgotaraho* (the salted roe of the gray mullet), one of the most expensive foods produced in Greece. Finally, Agrinio, to the north of Missolonghi, is a rice-producing center, which traditionally produces long-grain rice for pilafs, the smaller-grained *nihaki* rice, which lends itself to stuffings for vegetables, meats, and poultry, and *glase* rice for soups and desserts.

The Peloponnese is the birthplace of the godlike heroes and heroines whose names are almost as familiar to Greeks as their own: Herakles, Helen, Agamemnon, Clytemnestra, Orestes, Nestor. On this mulberry leaf-shaped peninsula, named after Pelops (the founder of the ill-fated house of Atreus), the distinction between myth and history blurs with a host of associations from *The Iliad, The Odyssey,* and the stories of Herakles' Twelve Labors. The Peloponnese region is more than a vast open-air museum, however. Although it is relatively small in area, its landscape is incredibly varied. In the north, a band of dense green citrus and other fruit trees separates the Gulf's pebbly beaches from a range of high, fir-clad mountains. The Mani is a spur of rock home to the prickly pear, but Messinia just northwest of it is an immense olive grove. It is the country's leading producer of olives for the table, the black, tear-shaped, succulent Kalamata variety, and for oil, the Koroneiki or Lianolia variety. It's no wonder that dishes here contain what a non-

THE PELOPONNESE
ΠΕΛΟΠΟΝΝΗΣΟΣ
Peloponnisos

Mediterranean might consider an excessive amount of olive oil. The Peloponnese produces more oil than any other region in Greece: 100,000–120,000 tons per year, and 95 percent of it is extra virgin. Butter is rarely used, except in a few festive cakes.

To temper the richness of their oil-based dishes, Peloponnesian cooks rely on two main acidic ingredients, tomatoes and lemons, sometimes both in the same dish. They also have a fondness for garlic, with as many as three whole bulbs sometimes called for in recipes for rabbit or beef stew. The locals generally have a limited taste for spices. Cinnamon is paired with tomato sauce, and allspice and cloves flavor sausages, but spices rarely turn up in other combinations. Even common herbs such as parsley, dill, and mint are used more sparingly than in the rest of Greece, although two kinds of chervil (*mironia* and *kafkalithra*) give soups and stews a delicate aroma not found elsewhere. Generally, though, Peloponnesian one-pot dishes rely on the quality of their ingredients for flavor. In Corinth, for example, currants and raisins complement the tartness of the lemons. This is a major grape-growing area, and the word "currant" may even be derived from Corinth. The Venetians and the British both had a passion for them, and in previous centuries the British engaged in the profitable trade of bartering currants for salt cod. The preserved fish became popular in mountain villages that had no other source of fish, and gave rise to some unusual but delicious recipes combining salt cod with currants, unique to the region. Another by-product in this land of vines is vinegar, which is valued more than wine as a cooking medium. In the Argolis, the Mycenaean heartland, the artichoke is king, and the globe, purple-leaved, and spiny varieties probably account for more dishes here than in the rest of the country put together. Much of the area is dark green with citrus orchards as far as the eye can see. Orange zest is a favorite ingredient in sausages from Arkadia to the Mani and Messinia, while orange juice flavors many doughs and cakes.

The west coast of the Peloponnese is backed by greenhouses, where some of Greece's tastiest strawberries, melons, watermelons, pumpkins, and garden vegetables are grown. The mountains of Arkadia soar behind it, where cheese-makers still produce what is considered Greece's best feta, aged in wooden barrels instead of packed into rectangular cans. As for baking, the Peloponnese boasts a rich tradition of festive breads, including *hristopsomo* for Christmas, dense with nuts and raisins, and buttery *vasilopita* for New Year. Decorated ring-shaped loaves to commemorate rites of passage such as births, deaths, and marriages, similar to those in Crete and the Dodecanese, are also traditional. Fried *diples* are drenched in honey and sprinkled with chopped nuts, and served at weddings and festivals. The signature dessert of the region is *pasteli*, a kind of sesame brittle. It is eaten all over Greece, but the versions from Kalamata are particularly crisp. Finally, this fascinating region produces many successful wines from vineyards near Patras, Pyrgos, Nemea, and Mantineia.

ISLANDS
ΝΗΣΙΑ
Nisia

The five islands in the north Aegean (Limnos, Samos, Ikaria, Lesvos, and Chios) have throughout their history led a life quite distinct from that of mainland Greece. In the seventh and sixth centuries BC, they formed alliances with cities in Asia Minor, founded colonies, and gave birth to such legendary figures as Sappho, Aesop, Homer, and Pythagoras. Later, the islands alternated between Athens or Sparta and the influence of foreign powers, and Venice and Genoa, Italy's rival trading empires, fought bitterly over them until the Ottomans threw both out and ruled the islands until the 1920s.

Except for steep, wild Ikaria, each island is known for a few specialties that rank among the best of their kind in Greece. All the islands share a love of wild fennel as a seasoning, goat's milk cheeses, both fresh and aged, and pumpkin as the star ingredient in vegetable ragouts. Otherwise, both gastronomically and culturally, they have developed separate identities, distinct from the other island chains and from each other. Limnos is the flattest of the five. Its volcanic soil produces the largest durum wheat and barley crops of any Greek island. The inhabitants of Limnos make several kinds of pasta unknown elsewhere, in the shapes of ears, curls, and knots, as well as the more usual varieties. Grapes are also grown, including an ancient variety known as Limnio, used to make an excellent dry, aromatic white wine, and sweet Muscat. Limnos abounds in fish and also boasts an immense variety of shellfish. Two foods are unique to the island: *trahana* made with garbanzo beans (chickpeas), tomatoes, onions, and flour instead of the more usual cracked wheat and sour milk, and *melipasto*, a goat's·milk cheese that is sun-dried and then washed in the sea.

Lesvos, curled like a huge bean around a deep bay, is Greece's third largest island and one of its biggest olive groves. There are reportedly 11½ million trees, some growing on impossibly tiny terraces on almost perpendicular slopes. It is said that the oil of each district has its own unique flavor. Lesvos' ouzo is extremely popular all over Greece, although much of it is distilled from sugar beet rather than the more usual lees left after wine pressing. The local sardines and anchovies, fresh or salted for up to a day, are a delicious accompaniment for the ouzo. Cans of them, packed in salt, are standard stock in almost every grocery in the country. The island's signature cheese is *ladotiri*, hard, yellow, and made with sheep's milk. Stored in olive oil rather than brine, it has a piquant bite that increases with age.

Most of Chios is so inhospitably rocky that its most profitable profession is shipping. However, it also happens to possess a natural phenomenon that grows here uniquely: the mastic tree. Mastic, the tree's crystallized resin, is used as a natural gum and a flavoring agent, and it was so highly valued during the Renaissance that Columbus traveled across the

THE NORTH AEGEAN ISLANDS
ΝΗΣΙΑ ΒΟΡΕΙΟΥ ΑΙΓΑΙΟΥ
Nisia Voriou Egeou

Atlantic to find another source, or so the locals claim. Although similar trees do exist in the Caribbean and elsewhere, only in southern Chios do they shed their aromatic "tears" of resin. As well as chewing gum, mastic is used to flavor an ouzo-like drink, desserts, and breads, and a sticky white candy (sweet) beloved of Greek children. Chios is also known for jewel-like preserves made with local fruit, which are eaten on their own or with ice cream or yogurt rather than a slice of bread. A fiery fermented cheese, *kopanisti*, a spectacular range of pickles, and strands of whole sun-dried tomatoes are other Chios delicacies, along with homemade pasta and a wealth of shellfish.

Samos, lush and green, consists largely of vineyards, pine forests, and beach resorts. Famous since antiquity, Samos Muscat wines are naturally sweet and have enjoyed considerable popularity. Fragrant herbs from the hillsides flavor all sorts of dishes, from bean salads to elaborate stuffed Easter lamb, oven-roasted rather than spit-roasted. Although Samos has a booming tourist industry, it has not sacrificed its traditions. One very unusual dish still served at church festivals is *kiskesi*, or crushed wheat cooked with meat in a cauldron until it becomes like porridge. The same dish can be found across the sea in coastal Turkey.

THE IONIAN ISLANDS
ΙΟΝΙΑ ΝΗΣΙΑ
Ionia Nisia

For much of their history, the Ionian islands were separate from the rest of Greece. Although small to the point of insignificance if viewed on a map of the Mediterranean, they held the key to some of its major shipping routes until the opening of the Suez Canal in 1869. By the end of the fourteenth century, all the islands were part of the Republic of Venice, and would remain part of Venice's realm for the next 400 years. The long centuries of Venetian occupation left an indelible mark on almost every aspect of Ionian life, including the landscape of the two main islands of Corfu and Zakynthos, where they planted olive trees and currant vines. Just as fundamental was the mark the Venetians left on the islanders' cuisine. In their capital, Corfu, for example, many of the best-known dishes have Italian-derived names like *bourdeto, pastitsada, sofrito,* and *bianco*. Similar though these dishes may sound, they differ subtly from their Venetian counterparts. *Bourdeto* (fish stew) and *pastitsada* (cockerel or veal simmered in tomato sauce with noodles or pasta) are both spiked with hot paprika, something not found on any of the other islands. *Sofrito* calls for handfuls of chopped parsley and garlic sandwiched between layers of sliced veal moistened with vinegar, while *bianco* simply means fish cooked without tomato. The Corfiots love tomatoes so much they even combine them with artichokes, rabbit, and *tsilihourda*, their version of the traditional Easter soup, dishes more commonly seasoned with lemon juice in the rest of Greece.

Paxoi and Antipaxoi share the culinary traditions of Corfu. Lefkada's food, on the other hand, reflects its proximity to the mainland and the large shallow lagoon on its north coast that acts as a natural fishery. Apart from fish and shellfish, its specialties include delicate lentils, a robust salami, cornmeal, and excellent honey from its mountainous green interior. Ithaca and Kefallonia, far less fertile than their neighbors, produced many generations of seafarers, who brought back recipes for exotic shrimp (prawn) curries and squid ink risottos from their travels. Kefallonia, the largest in the Ionian chain, lacks arable land, but its people have always had the reputation of being the wittiest, cleverest, and most eccentric of all Greeks. They make the Ionian's finest wine, (Robola), its creamiest feta, and its most pungent garlic sauces. Their best-known dish is a hearty two- or three-meat pie baked with rice—an Ionian idiosyncrasy—and *kefalotiri* cheese. Both Ithaca and Kefallonia have a host of casseroles slow-cooked in a clay pot called a *tserepa*.

Zakynthos, gentle and vine-clad, has a number of wonderful dishes not found elsewhere. Some have a Venetian accent, like *saltsa*, a rich garlicky stew of beef, tomatoes and a piquant local cheese called *ladotiri*, and *skartsoseta*, veal stuffed with two cheeses and cooked with wine and tomatoes. Garlic, beloved of all the islanders, figures prominently in another favorite, *melitzanes skordostoubi*, or eggplants (aubergines) baked in a vinegary tomato sauce with a whole bulb of chopped garlic. Zakynthos also exports sweet pink-white onions, melons, and strawberries.

The Ionian islands' few desserts also have Italian influences. In Corfu, there are derivatives of *zabaglione*, *pan di spagna* (sponge cake), and *pasta flora* (fruit tart with a thick crust), but the housewives' old cookery notebooks also contain dozens of recipes for English puddings. Variations on a theme of eggs, milk, and bread, combined with currants, candied citrus peel, apples, caramel, or other flavorings, they are a relic of fifty years of British rule in the nineteenth century, and inherited along with them is Corfu's unique *tzitzibira,* or ginger beer, the drink of preference while watching a cricket match in the town's main square. Other distinctive sweetmeats are the *madolato* (nougat) and *pasteli* (sesame seed bars) of Zakynthos, the *madoles* or candied almonds of Kefallonia, Ithaca's *rovani*, a rice-based, honey-saturated cake usually made with semolina, and *sykomaida*, a very ancient thick paste of dried figs, ouzo, black pepper, orange zest, and fennel seeds. There is no doubt that the Ionian islands have contributed some of Greece's most delicious and original dishes.

THE CYCLADES
ΚΥΚΛΑΔΕΣ
Kiklades

A blue dome against a cloudless sky, meringue-white cubes on a tawny, treeless mountainside, and wine-dark waves lapping at the hull of a red *kaiki*. These are some of the images conjured up by the Cyclades, those quintessentially Greek islands arranged in a loose circle around the sacred island of Delos in the middle of the Aegean. Among the most famous are Santorini, Mykonos, Delos, and Naxos, and although the islands share a common history and many culinary traditions, every one also has its own distinctive food specialties. Linking them is the reliance on olive oil and olives, often grown among tiny patches of wheat and barley on terraces carved out of steep hillsides. The scarcity of fertile soil resulted in numerous dishes using foraged ingredients, such as capers, wild fennel, and the wild greens so popular all over Greece. Many families raised—and still raise—sheep and goats, and there are even cows on Andros, Tinos, Naxos, Syros, and Kea. This means that virtually all the Cyclades produce cheese. Some of these are variations of well-known cheeses, such as the delicious, nutty *gravieras* made in Tinos and Naxos. Others are quite unusual, and among them are the pungent, fermented *kopanisti* of Mykonos, the *manouri* of Sifnos, which is aged in red wine lees, a hard, yellow cheese called *arseniko* in Naxos, and a mild creamy white cheese called *hloro* in Folegandros.

The cuisine of the Cyclades is similar to its architecture, in that it is deceptively simple, straightforward, and memorable. Containing a minimum of ingredients, the dishes there might consist of the freshest of broiled (grilled) fish seasoned with nothing but oil, lemon, and oregano; octopus seared over charcoal; a peasant salad of juicy tomatoes, crisp bell peppers, cucumbers, and sweet onions, sprinkled with purslane, capers, salicornia (samphire), and marjoram; or a chicken stewed slowly with tomatoes and served with homemade egg noodles (pasta). Santorini and Milos are famous for fritters made with intensely flavored tomatoes grown without water on their volcanic soils. The young plants receive two or three waterings in their infancy and then produce their fruit nourished only by the dew. The cooks of Tinos make delicious croquettes with wild fennel (*maratho*), grated potatoes, zucchini (courgettes), or eggplants (aubergines) seasoned with herbs and cheese. Others contain legumes (pulses), such as the yellow split pea fritters of Santorini or the garbanzo bean (chickpea) patties of Sifnos. These two islands make great use of legumes in dishes like *pantremeni fava* (split pea purée with caramelized onions) or *revithada*, a dish of garbanzo beans baked for hours in a clay pot.

As elsewhere in Greece, lamb and beef were luxuries for special occasions, but most families raised a pig each year. The fall (autumn) pig slaughter became a festive event, with feasting and dancing to accompany sausage making and meat curing. Lean Mykonos sausages, seasoned with savory, are renowned throughout Greece, while Tinos and Syros boast an air- or wine-cured peppery fillet called *louza* that tastes like spiced ham. At Easter, lamb comes into its own and on the islands it was traditionally baked and stuffed rather than roasted on a spit. As well as these and many more savory dishes, the Cyclades produce a wide range of delicious sweet treats. Perhaps the best known are the *loukoumia* of Syros, sticky squares scented with rosewater, mastic, and pistachio that were introduced by refugees from Chios in the early nineteenth century. Others to look out for are *pasteli* (honey and sesame seed bars) from Andros, preserves, macaroons (*pastitsakia*), and several variations on the little cheese pie with honey, whose origins can be traced back to Homer. Perhaps the most unusual is the pizza-like watermelon pie from Milos.

THE DODECANESE
ΔΩΔΕΚΑΝΗΣΑ
Dodekanisa

Broadly speaking, the Dodecanese can be divided into two groups. First, there are the islands that have been fertile enough for people to live off the land: Rhodes, Kos, Karpathos, Leros, and Nisyros. Then there are those whose inhabitants have been obliged to look to the sea for a living: Kalymnos and Symi (the sponge-fishers' islands), Kasos, and Astypalaia. The former developed unusual ways of preserving their foods, such as dried grape (vine) leaves, while the latter invented interesting

ways of preserving fish, including drying tiny pickerel or lobster tails, or even pickling shellfish in seawater. Although they are extremely varied, the Dodecanese share a common heritage because of their position on the trade routes that linked three continents. There have been few Mediterranean powers that have not attempted to settle, conquer, or control them. The two that had the most impact were the Knights of Saint John of Jerusalem, who ruled for about 200 years until 1522, and the Italians, who occupied them in the first half of the twentieth century. However, the strongest influence on the Dodecanese is simply the Aegean, and nowhere more so than in its cuisine. Octopus tentacles and fresh fish are grilled over charcoal and sprinkled with olive oil and lemon juice, salads are tossed with wild greens or succulent tomatoes, dishes are seasoned with pungent oregano, thyme, and fennel picked from the hillsides, casseroles are slow-cooked, and Easter lambs are stuffed with rice and herbs and baked in a clay pot.

Some flavors are well-rooted in the Dodecanese. One of these is cumin, a favorite spice that probably originated in Asia Minor and spread throughout the Middle East and North Africa. Rather too exotic for many Greeks, it occurs frequently in the meat and vegetable recipes of these islands, but not in those of their Cycladic cousins. A liberal sprinkling of dried chili on Symi's tiny fried shrimp (prawns) makes them memorably delicious. Moreover, the islanders have a great fondness for tahini (sesame paste), whose distinctive nutty taste turns up in breads, pies, and even a sauce for fish. This preference may have come from contact with Cyprus and Egypt. Another Dodecanese culinary trait is sweet caramelized onions, which often appear as a topping to liven up pasta, legumes (pulses), and many other dishes.

In fact, pasta, bulgur wheat, and legumes (pulses) are all staples in the local diet. Nisyros, especially, is known for its fava (broad) beans, yellow split peas, and garbanzo beans (chickpeas), which are the basis of a wealth of soups, salads, dips, and fritters. As on Crete, there is a rich repertoire of breads for special occasions and rites of passage, decorated with dough symbols denoting love, prosperity, and fertility, such as birds, snakes, and flowers. Also shared with the Cretans is an appreciation of *paximadia*, rusk-like cookies (biscuits) with dozens of possible flavorings. Some things are more surprising by their absence. For example, the Dodecanese have none of the yellow cheeses—*graviera*, *kefalograviera*, *kefalotiri*, and others—which are produced all over Greece as well as in the Cyclades. Instead, the southern islanders tend to make their sheep's and goat's milk into butter and their cream into *sitaka*, similar to Cretan *staka*. There are fresh white cheeses, however, and Kos is also famous for its cheese marinated in red wine.

Crete, Greece's largest island, is the proverbial land of plenty. Legend has it that when Zeus was born on its highest mountain, Mount Idi, he was nursed by the goat Amaltheia. From her horns poured an endless abundance of good things—fruit, vegetables, fish, and meat—which, along with her milk, nourished the young god. Upon her death, he placed her cornucopia among the stars as a constellation, and through

CRETE
KPHTH
Kriti

the ages Crete has continued to produce wonderful ingredients. Today, the island exports fruit and vegetables to northern Europe and the rest of Greece. Citrus, kiwi, and avocado groves fill the plain between the sea and the White Mountains to the west, and the Lasithi plateau is a vast apple and pear orchard. Wild Cretan greens are known for their variety and nutritional content, and for all fruit and vegetables a Cretan stamp of origin is synonymous with flavor and quality. However, they are recent additions compared with Crete's olive and vine plantations: the olive was cultivated here as early as the third millennium BC, and Crete now produces 30 percent of Greece's total olive oil output.

Cretan vineyards are similarly prolific. One fifth of all Greek wine comes from the island, ranging from light whites from around Siteia in eastern Crete to deep reds from Arkhanes and Peza in the hills above Irakleio. In Classical and Roman times, Cretan wines were so prized that many Romans preferred them to their own vintages. Later, fostered by the Venetians, a sweet red called Malvasia was shipped all over Europe, reaching England as Malmsey and Portugal as Madeira. Cretans are also partial to *tsikoudia*, a potent grappa-like alcohol made from the skins, branches, and seeds of grapes after the initial pressing. They drink it at any time of the day or night, always accompanied by a simple meze to mitigate the effects. Perhaps because of the just-picked freshness of their local products, Cretan cooks aim for simplicity in their recipes. Rather than resorting to artifice and spices, they rely on herbs to enhance flavor. Mint is a particular favorite, turning up in such diverse dishes as sweet and savory cheese pies, meat dishes, stuffed vegetables, and many more, followed closely by wild fennel tips, often accompanied by green olives and generous amounts of parsley. The only exception to the use of spices is cumin, which is so beloved in eastern Crete that residents sometimes refer to "cumin and pepper" instead of "salt and pepper."

Cretan cuisine is also distinctive for imaginative and unusual pairings of ingredients in dishes like grouper with okra, fish with artichokes, or meat (usually lamb, goat, or pork) with green almonds. Some 1,800 species of plants grow on the island, of which 300 are edible. It is not uncommon to find cooks using up to twenty varieties in a stew or pie, judiciously selecting them for their balance of flavors as well as for their healthy properties. When the Romans occupied Crete, they thought of it as their medicine chest and some forty of the plants that the great naturalist Dioscurides identified at that time are still valued by local healers. Cretans rate some greens as the greatest of delicacies. A spiny thistle known as *askolibrous* fetches an even higher price than *filet mignon* (beef fillet) on the market.

A favorite way of cooking greens is in pies, and Crete may boast the most versions in all Greece. They can be squares or triangles, coiled like a sultan's turban, with layers of phyllo (filo) or a simple crust, with or without yeast, baked in a pan for a crowd, or pan-fried and bite-size, containing one or a dozen ingredients. The possibilities can seem endless. Even the dough, when homemade, is rarely a simple mixture of flour and water; instead, it may incorporate raki, orange juice, lemon juice, wine, milk, eggs, or vinegar. Crete also produces a prodigious amount of cheese, mainly from sheep's or goat's milk. The best known is *graviera*, which has a nutty flavor similar to Gruyère, but they also include incredibly fresh, soft *malaka* and the white, soft whey cheeses *anthotiri* and *mizithra*, tangy *xinomizithra*, and hard, piquant *kefalotiri*. Unique to western Crete and the southern Dodecanese is *staka*, a sheep's milk cream cooked with a little flour. This process separates it into *stakovoutiro* (clarified butter), and the luscious, rich-tasting *staka* itself, which is often added to celebratory pilafs and meat pies for extra richness on special occasions.

A catalog of Cretan specialties would not be complete without mention of its breads, or more precisely its rusks. In the past, baking bread in large quantities—a month's supply of thirty loaves at a time—was standard practice to save on the firewood needed to heat the oven. However, because bread could not stay fresh for long, it was baked twice, sliced and returned to a low oven to dry out completely into hard rusks that could last indefinitely. From thick brick-like slabs of barely refined barley to dainty finger-size cookies (biscuits) flavored with cinnamon, coriander seeds, red wine, and almonds, the rusks of Crete are the most delicious in Greece.

Although Crete succumbed to waves of invaders—Romans, Arabs, Byzantines, Venetians, Ottoman Turks—the diet of the islanders remained very similar to that of their Minoan ancestors, and consisted mostly of shellfish and snails, greens awash with olive oil, honey, nuts, goat's and sheep's milk cheeses, legumes (pulses), and small amounts of meat on holy days and at celebrations, augmented over the centuries by imports like potatoes and tomatoes. It would take four years of terrible deprivation during World War II for this natural diet to be recognized as the clue to health and longevity. After the war, American scientists seeking to aid the long-suffering population discovered that, although hungry, they were virtually unscathed by heart disease or cancer. Thus the now-famous Mediterranean diet was "discovered," something that the Cretans had known all along.

The Republic of Cyprus has always contributed its own influence to Hellenic culture, whether in terms of ceramics, art, or cooking. Every power that has roamed the Mediterranean has laid claim to this strategically-positioned island, including the Assyrians, Egyptians, Persians, Alexander's Greeks, Romans, Byzantines, Arabs, Crusaders, Venetians, Turks, and even the British. Given this history it is remarkable that Cyprus has retained much semblance of "Greekness" at all. The influence of these disparate groups is revealed in various elements of Greek Cypriot cuisine. For example, the ceramic cooking pot known as *giouvetsi* in Greek is called *tavas* locally, a Persian word for skillet or frying pan; a kind of pasta filled with cheese, egg, and mint is called *ravioles*, indicating a possible Venetian origin; and several dishes on the Cyprus mezedes menu are clearly Middle Eastern. These include hummus, a puréed garbanzo bean (chickpea) dip flavored with tahini,

CYPRUS
ΚΥΠΡΟΣ
Kipros

and *koupes* or *kibbeh,* meatballs with a coating of fine bulgur wheat, which are rarely found in Greece. A predilection for crushed or ground coriander seeds—particularly in dishes with pork, mushrooms, artichokes, or potatoes—is a legacy from the Byzantines, but it has all but vanished from mainland cooking. *Koupepia,* the local name for dishes of for stuffed leaves of various kinds, is also a Byzantine inheritance. Greek Cypriots share with Greeks their fondness for legumes (pulses), green wild and cultivated vegetables, egg-lemon sauces, rusks, dishes cooked with tomatoes, and oven-baked casseroles. Where they differ radically from their neighbors is in the frequent use of corn oil rather than olive oil as a cooking medium.

There are also dozens of foods the Greek Cypriots can call their own. A well-known example is halloumi, a rubbery braided (plaited) cheese usually made with sheep's milk, which is delicious fried or broiled (grilled) and sprinkled with lemon juice. Its origins have been traced to tenth-century Egypt. A by-product of halloumi, the whey cheese *anari,* is the Greek Cypriot version of *mizithra,* a ricotta-like soft cheese. Favorite seasonings for stews of all kinds are cinnamon and cloves, which even turn up in squid and octopus dishes. Other specialties to look for are *seftalia,* ground (minced) meat wrapped in caul and then broiled (grilled); *loutza* (smoked pork loin, spiced and soaked in wine); strawberries doused with rosewater; *elioti,* a delectable olive bread; *kolourka,* pasta with a meat filling; and, strangest of all, *kolokasi,* a kind of tuber similar to taro, called colocasia in English. Naturally, variations on the kabob (kebab) abound, and, continuing in that tradition, a Greek Cypriot meal can begin with as many as thirty plates of different mezedes. A wedding feast would not be complete without *resi,* a dish of wheat cooked in a broth made from two lambs or piglets and five to six chickens, while pastitsio is a standard at Christmas and New Year, along with a roast. Finally, Greek Cypriot desserts run the whole gamut of phyllo (filo) pastries with nuts and honey, including festive treats like *melomakarona, vasilopita,* and *kourabiedes,* preserves, and several confections made from a grape must molasses (syrup) known as *petimezi.* All in all, the cuisine of Cyprus is as interesting and complex as its history.

BASIC RECIPES AND SAUCES

-

ΒΑΣΙΚΕΣ ΣΥΝΤΑΓΕΣ ΚΑΙ ΣΑΛΤΣΕΣ

-

Vasikes sintages ke saltses

VEGETABLE STOCK
ΖΩΜΟΣ ΛΑΧΑΝΙΚΩΝ
Zomos lahanikon

Put all the ingredients except the wine (if using) and peppercorns into a large pan and pour in 6 cups (1.5 litres / 2½ pints) water. Bring to a boil, reduce the heat, cover, and simmer for 10–20 minutes. Add the wine and peppercorns and simmer for 15 minutes more. Remove the pan from the heat and let cool, then strain the stock through a fine strainer into a bowl. Use immediately or store in the refrigerator for 3–4 days. Alternatively, freeze in small quantities in plastic containers or bags for up to 2 months. A chopped tart green apple simmered with the vegetables adds body to the stock.

Makes about 6 cups (1.5–1.8 litres / 2½–3¼ pints)
Preparation time 15 minutes
Cooking time 30 minutes

- 1 large onion, sliced lengthwise
- 1 large carrot, thinly sliced
- 1 leek, white part only, chopped
- 5 fresh parsley sprigs
- 1 small celery stalk, chopped
- 3 garlic cloves (optional)
- 2 bay leaves (optional)
- 3 fresh thyme sprigs or ½ teaspoon dried thyme
- 1 small red bell pepper, seeded and chopped (optional)
- 2 teaspoons salt
- ½ cup (120 ml / 4 fl oz) dry white wine (optional)
- 10 black peppercorns
- 1 tart green apple, chopped (optional)

FISH STOCK
ΖΩΜΟΣ ΨΑΡΙΟΥ
Zomos psariou

Put the fish bones, onion, celery, carrot, leek, garlic, and a pinch of salt into a large pan, pour in 4 cups (1 litre / 1¾ pints) water, and bring to a boil over low heat. Skim off the scum that rises to the surface, then add all the remaining ingredients. Cover and simmer for 40 minutes. Remove from the heat, strain through a fine strainer into a bowl, and let cool. Use immediately or store in the refrigerator for up to 3 days. To freeze, measure 1 cup (250 ml / 8 fl oz) stock into each of four heavy-duty freezer bags or plastic containers, seal, and freeze for up to 2 months.

Makes 4 cups (1 litre / 1¾ pints)
Preparation time 30 minutes
Cooking time 50 minutes

- 1 lb 2 oz (500 g) bones from flounder, plaice or other flat fish, fins and tails removed
- 1 onion, sliced
- 1 celery stalk, cut into pieces
- 1 carrot, cut into pieces
- 1 small leek, white part only, thickly sliced
- 1 garlic clove (optional)
- salt
- 1 cup (250 ml / 8 fl oz) dry white wine
- 1 tablespoon freshly squeezed lemon juice
- 6 fresh parsley sprigs
- 1 bay leaf
- 6 black peppercorns

- 2¼ lb (1 kg) veal or beef knuckle bones
- 2¼ lb (1 kg) veal trimmings, such as neck, shank or rib tips
- 2¼ quarts (4 litres / 7 pints) water
- 2 onions
- 3 cloves
- 4 large carrots, halved
- 1 small celery root (celeriac), quartered
- 1 leek, halved
- 4–5 fresh parsley sprigs
- 1 garlic bulb
- 1 bay leaf
- salt

MEAT STOCK
ΖΩΜΟΣ ΚΡΕΑΤΟΣ
Zomos kreatos

Put the meat and bones into a large, heavy, nonstick pan and pour in enough of the water to cover. Bring to a boil over medium heat and skim off the scum that rises to the surface. Continue skimming, occasionally adding the remaining cold water, until no more scum rises. Meanwhile, stud one of the onions with the cloves. Add all the remaining ingredients and continue skimming, until the stock comes back to a boil. Reduce the heat and simmer gently for 5–7 hours, occasionally skimming the scum from the surface. Remove from the heat and strain through a very fine strainer into a bowl. Let cool, then chill in the refrigerator overnight. Remove and discard the solidified fat from the surface. Use the stock immediately or store in the refrigerator for up to 1 week. To freeze, divide the stock into 1–2 cup (250–450 ml / 8–16 fl oz) portions, place in heavy-duty plastic bags or containers, and seal. Freeze for up to 6 months.

Makes 8 cups (1.8 litres / 3¼ pints)
Preparation time 12¼ hours (including chilling)
Cooking time 7 hours

Note: To make chicken stock, substitute chicken wings, backs and necks for the meat bones and meat.

- 9 cups (1 kg / 2¼ lb) black olives
- ½ cup (100 g / 3½ oz) sea salt

SALTED BLACK OLIVES
ΕΛΙΕΣ ΣΤΑΦΙΔΩΤΕΣ
Elies stafidotes

Mix fresh ripe black olives with sea salt in a bowl, allowing ½ cup (100 g / 3½ oz) salt for every 9 cups (1 kg / 2¼ lb) olives. Put them into a woven bag and place it in a basket. Put a weight on top of the bag and hang the basket in a cool place, such as a cellar. Put a large bowl underneath to collect the juices. Leave for 2 weeks, or until the olives are ready to eat.

Makes 9 cups (1 kg / 2¼ lb)
Preparation time 2 weeks

SUN-DRIED TOMATOES
ΛΙΑΣΤΕΣ ΝΤΟΜΑΤΕΣ
Liastes domates

Rinse firm ripe tomatoes and pat dry. Cut them in half and place side by side on a board, cut sides up. Sprinkle coarse salt over the cut surfaces to cover them completely and put in a sunny place. Protect the tomatoes from rain or damp. The drying process takes 15–20 days, depending on the weather, during which time the tomatoes will shrink and wrinkle. Thread on a strong string and hang up in the sunshine, with a bowl underneath to catch any remaining juice, until they are completely dried. The drying process can be speeded up initially by placing the tomatoes in a very low oven for 15–20 minutes and then stringing them. When they are completely dried, store them in cheesecloth (muslin) bags hanging in a cool, dark, well-ventilated place. To use the tomatoes, rinse under cold running water. Place them in a bowl, add warm water to cover, and let soak for several hours, until they swell. Rinse and drain well. Sun-dried tomatoes can be used in pasta sauces, salads, vegetable stews, and bread. Coated with flour, dipped in a thin batter (p 47), and fried in hot olive oil, sun-dried tomatoes make a delicious meze.

PHYLLO DOUGH (FILO PASTRY)
ΖΥΜΗ ΓΙΑ ΦΥΛΛΟ
Zimi gia filo

Lightly dust a baking pan with flour and set aside. Sift together the flour, salt, and baking powder into a bowl. Make a well in the center and pour in the oil, vinegar, and water. Using your hands, gradually draw the flour from the sides of the well into the liquid and mix well. Knead lightly to form a soft, elastic dough, adding a little more water if necessary. Divide into small balls, according to the number of phyllo sheets required and the size of the pan. Place the balls side by side in the pan, cover with plastic wrap (cling film) or a damp dish towel, and let rest for 1–2 hours. Roll out each ball on a surface lightly dusted with cornstarch, then roll each one around the rolling pin, pressing lightly and rolling to a thickness of ⅛ inch (3 mm) or less. To prevent it from sticking, sprinkle the surface with a little cornstarch as you work. Phyllo for pies can be made more easily by flattening the dough into 8-inch (20 cm) rounds, spreading each generously with oil or melted butter before stacking in threes, one on top of the other, and rolling them out into one large round sheet. Sometimes five sheets are rolled out together to make one large thick sheet of phyllo used to make the vlakiki pie famous in the villages of the Epirus region. When baked, the dough separates into layers because of the fat trapped between them, resulting in a very flaky, crisp pastry, like a rustic puff pastry.

Makes about 1 lb 2 oz (500 g)
Preparation time 1½–2½ hours (including resting)

- 4½ cups (500 g / 1 lb 2 oz) all-purpose (plain) flour, plus extra for dusting
- 2 teaspoons salt
- 2 teaspoons baking powder
- 2 tablespoons olive oil
- 1 tablespoon red wine vinegar
- 1 cup (250 ml / 8 fl oz) warm water
- cornstarch (cornflour), for dusting

BATTER FOR FRYING
ΧΥΛΟΣ ΓΙΑ ΤΗΓΑΝΙΣΜΑ
Hilos gia tiganisma

- 1 cup (120 g / 4 oz) all-purpose (plain) flour
- salt and pepper
- 1 tablespoon olive oil
- 1 cup (250 ml / 8 fl oz) beer or club soda (soda water)
- 2 egg whites

Sift the flour with a pinch of salt and pepper into a bowl. Make a well in the center and pour in the oil and beer or club soda. Gradually stir into the flour until a smooth, thin batter forms. Avoid over-mixing. Add a little more flour, if a thicker batter is required. Let stand for about 1 hour. When ready to use, beat the egg whites until they form soft peaks, then gradually fold into the batter.

Makes about 2 cups (450 ml / 16 fl oz)
Preparation time 1 hour

BASIC PASTRY DOUGH
ΖΥΜΗ ΤΑΡΤΑΣ
Zimi tartas

- 1⅓ cups (165 g / 5½ oz) all-purpose (plain) flour, plus extra for dusting
- 2 tablespoons superfine (caster) sugar
- salt
- ½ cup (120 g / 4 oz) white vegetable fat or clarified butter, chilled and diced
- 3 tablespoons iced water or 1 egg yolk beaten with 1–2 tablespoons water
- 1 teaspoon vanilla extract or grated lemon zest

Preheat the oven to 400°F (200°C / Gas Mark 6). Sift together the flour, sugar, and a pinch of salt into a bowl. Add the fat and rub it in with your fingertips until the mixture resembles coarse bread crumbs. Sprinkle the water or egg yolk mixture and the vanilla or lemon zest over the mixture and mix lightly until it just begins to come together. The dough should feel crumbly. Gather the crumbs into a ball, pressing them together with your hands, but do not knead. Roll out the dough on a lightly floured work surface to an 11-inch (28-cm) round. (It is better to roll it out on a lightly floured cloth to prevent it from sticking. You can use the cloth to help lift the dough into the tart pan.) Lift the dough into an ungreased 9-inch (23-cm) tart pan, easing it into the base and side. Pierce it all over with a fork. Bake for about 15–20 minutes, until crisp and golden. The unbaked dough can also be stored in a sealed plastic bag in the refrigerator for up to 3 days, or in the freezer for up to 3 months.

Makes one 9-inch (23-cm) tart shell
Preparation time 15 minutes
Cooking time 15 minutes

RICH PASTRY DOUGH
ΖΥΜΗ ΤΑΡΤΑΣ ΜΕ ΑΥΓΑ
Zimi tartas me avga

Sift together the flour and baking powder into a bowl. Beat together the butter and sugar in another bowl with an electric mixer until the mixture is pale and fluffy. Beat in the egg yolks, one at a time, then the brandy and lemon zest or vanilla. Gradually fold in the flour mixture, a little at a time, until a light, smooth dough forms. Do not overwork it or the dough will become tough when baked. Roll out the dough as described for Basic pastry dough (see p 47) and use it to line large or individual tart pans for tarts with jam and dried fruits. Alternatively, it can be used to make crunchy, melt-in-your-mouth cookies (biscuits).

Makes two 9-inch (23-cm) tart shells
Preparation time 30 minutes

- 3 cups (350 g / 12 oz) all-purpose (plain) flour
- 1 teaspoon baking powder
- 1 cup (225 g / 8 oz) butter
- ⅓ cup (70 g / 2¾ oz) superfine (caster) sugar
- 2 egg yolks
- 2 tablespoons brandy
- 1 tablespoon grated lemon zest or 1 teaspoon vanilla extract or other flavor of choice

---

PUFF PASTRY DOUGH
ΖΥΜΗ ΣΦΟΛΙΑΤΑ
Zimi sfoliata

Sift together the flour and salt into a bowl. Dice a quarter of the butter and add it to the flour mixture. Using two knives or a pastry blender, cut the butter into the flour with a rapid crisscross movement until the mixture has a coarse and mealy texture. Add just enough water to bind the ingredients and work them with your fingertips, gathering the crumbs together to form a ball. Wrap the dough in plastic wrap (cling film) and chill in the refrigerator for 45 minutes or in the freezer for 25 minutes. Meanwhile, place the remaining butter between two sheets of baking parchment and, using a rolling pin, flatten it into a 6-inch (15-cm) square. Chill in the refrigerator for 30 minutes. Roll out the dough on a lightly floured, cold work surface into an 8 x 14-inch (20 x 35-cm) rectangle. Peel off the top sheet of baking parchment from the butter and invert the butter over center of the dough, then peel off the second sheet. Lightly brush the edges of the dough with water and fold the two short sides over the butter to meet in the center, pressing the edges together to seal. Fold the dough in half and roll out into a rectangle, pressing evenly so as not to squeeze out the butter. Fold in half again, lightly moistening the edges and pressing them together. Wrap the dough in plastic wrap and chill in the refrigerator for 30 minutes. Repeat the rolling and folding process twice more, chilling the dough in the refrigerator for 30 minutes in between. Sprinkle the surface of the dough with flour, brushing the excess away carefully before each rolling to prevent it from sticking. The dough will keep in the refrigerator for 2–3 days and in the freezer for up to 6 months.

Makes 2¼ lb (1 kg)
Preparation time 3–4 hours (including chilling)

- 4½ cups (500 g / 1 lb 2 oz) all-purpose (plain) flour, plus extra for dusting
- 1 teaspoon salt
- 2¼ cups (500 g / 1 lb 2 oz) butter
- ⅔ cup (150 ml / ¼ pint) iced water

- 1 oz (25 g) fresh yeast
  or 1 tablespoon dried yeast
- 2 tablespoons sugar
- 1 cup (250 ml / 8 fl oz)
  lukewarm milk
- 4½ cups (500 g / 1 lb 2 oz)
  strong white bread flour, plus
  extra for dusting
- 1 teaspoon salt
- 2 tablespoons vegetable oil
- 2 eggs
- 2¼ cups (500 g / 1 lb 2 oz)
  butter, softened

LEAVENED PUFF PASTRY DOUGH
ΖΥΜΗ ΣΦΟΛΙΑΤΑ ΜΕ ΜΑΓΙΑ
Zimi sfoliata me magia

If using fresh yeast, dissolve the sugar in the milk in a bowl, add the yeast, and mash well with a fork until smooth. If using dried yeast, dissolve the sugar in the milk in a bowl, sprinkle the yeast over the surface, and let stand for 10–15 minutes, until frothy, then stir to a smooth paste. Sift together the flour and salt into a large bowl, make a well in the center, and pour in the oil and the yeast mixture. Add the eggs. Using your hands, break the egg yolks and mix the liquid ingredients together, then gradually incorporate the flour from the sides of the well to make a loose dough. Knead the dough for about 10 minutes, until it is soft and easy to handle, adding more flour if necessary. Cover and let rise for 1½–2 hours, until doubled in volume. Punch down the dough with your fist and knead for 5 minutes. Roll out on a lightly floured work surface into a rectangle about ½ inch (1 cm) thick. Using a spatula, spread one-third of the butter over half its length, leaving a ¾-inch (2-cm) wide margin around the edges. Brush the margin with a little water and fold the dough in half, enclosing the butter. Lightly press the edges to seal. Lightly roll out the dough again into a rectangle and repeat the procedure using half the remaining butter. Let the dough rest for a short while, then repeat the procedure once more using the rest of the butter. Sprinkle the surface of the dough with flour, carefully brushing off the excess before each rolling to prevent it from sticking. Prick the dough in the center with a skewer to release any trapped air. Seal it in a large, plastic bag, leaving enough room for expansion, and chill in the refrigerator for 1 hour. The dough is now ready for shaping, rising, and baking.

Makes about 2¼ lb (1 kg)
Preparation time 3–5 hours (including rising)

SIMPLE PUFF PASTRY DOUGH
ΣΦΟΛΙΑΤΑ ΣΠΙΤΙΚΗ
Sfoliata spitiki

- 2¼ cups (250 g / 9 oz) all-purpose (plain) flour, plus extra for dusting
- ½ teaspoon salt
- generous 1 cup (250 g / 9 oz) butter, chilled
- ½ cup (120 ml / 4 fl oz) iced water

Sift together the flour and salt into a bowl. Using a knife or a pastry blender, cut the butter into the flour until the mixture resembles coarse bread crumbs. Alternatively, grate it into the flour and mix lightly. Add just enough water to bind and lightly work the dough with your fingers, gathering the crumbs together to form a ball. Wrap in plastic wrap (cling film) and chill in the refrigerator for 45 minutes or in the freezer for 25 minutes. Roll out the dough on a lightly floured, cold work surface into a rectangle 3 times longer than it is wide. Lightly flour the top of dough and fold the bottom third up over to the middle, and then fold the top third down to cover it. Give the dough a quarter turn and roll out again into a rectangle. Repeat the folding, turning, and rolling procedure four more times. Wrap in plastic wrap (cling film) and chill in the refrigerator for 30 minutes. Repeat the procedure twice more, chilling for 30 minutes each time. The dough can be kept in the refrigerator for 2–3 days and in the freezer for 3–6 months.

Makes 1 lb 2 oz (500 g)
Preparation time 2 hours (including chilling)

NATURAL PECTIN
ΦΥΣΙΚΗ ΠΗΚΤΙΝΗ
Fisiki piktini

- 11 lb (5 kg) under-ripe tart apples

Wash the apples and slice thinly, without peeling or coring. Put them into a large heavy pan and pour in water to cover. Cover the pan and bring to a boil, then reduce the heat, and simmer for 20–30 minutes, until softened. Line a large colander with a double thickness of cheesecloth (muslin) and place it in a large bowl. Tip the apple mixture into the colander and let drain for 24 hours without stirring or pressing, as this will make the juice cloudy. The next day, pour the strained juice into a pan, bring to a boil, and simmer until it has reduced by about half. Line a strainer with a double thickness of cheesecloth and strain the juice into a bowl. Let cool, then chill in the refrigerator until thickened. Pour into small, strong plastic bags, seal, and freeze. Alternatively, pour the pectin into sterilized small jars, cover, and heat-process them for 5 minutes. Either way, it keeps well up to a year. Add 1 cup (120 ml / 4 fl oz) pectin to every 5 cups (1.2 litres / 2 pints) low-pectin fruit juice to help it set. Pectin can be added to set jams, thus reducing the amount of sugar required. However, these jams must be consumed earlier than conventional jams as they become moldy quite quickly.

Makes 4 cups (1 litre / 1¾ pints)
Preparation time 24 hours (including draining)
Cooking time 30 minutes

- ° 4½ cups (500 g / 1 lb 2 oz) finely ground almonds
- ° 3½ cups (400 g / 14 oz) confectioners' (icing) sugar, plus extra for dusting
- ° 1 teaspoon vanilla extract or ¼ teaspoon almond extract
- ° 1 tablespoon freshly squeezed lemon juice
- ° 2 tablespoons rose water or 1 tablespoon apricot jam
- ° 2 egg whites, lightly beaten

MARZIPAN
ΠΑΣΤΑ ΑΜΥΓΔΑΛΟΥ
Pasta amigdalou

Combine the ground almonds, sugar, and vanilla or almond extract in a bowl. Sprinkle the mixture with the lemon juice and rose water, if using, or add the jam. Using a fork, gradually stir in the beaten egg whites, a little at a time, until the mixture is moist, then mix with your hand until all the egg white has been added. (Add as much egg white as necessary to produce a smooth, stiff paste.) Lightly dust a work surface with confectioners' sugar. Gather the mixture into a ball and knead it on the prepared work surface, but avoid over-kneading, as this will make the marzipan oily. Wrap in plastic wrap (cling film) and store in the refrigerator for up to 2 weeks. If it has dried out slightly, knead it with a little rose water until it becomes soft and pliable again. It also freezes well for several months.

Makes 2 lb (900 g)
Preparation time 15 minutes

- ° 3 tablespoons all-purpose (plain) flour
- ° 2 tablespoons cornstarch (cornflour)
- ° ½ cup (100 g / 3½ oz) superfine (caster) sugar
- ° 4 egg yolks
- ° 2 cups (450 ml / 16 fl oz) milk
- ° 2 tablespoons (25 g / 1 oz) butter, diced
- ° 1 teaspoon vanilla extract
- ° 1 cup (250 ml / 8 fl oz) whipped cream (optional)

PASTRY CREAM
ΚΡΕΜΑ ΖΑΧΑΡΟΠΛΑΣΤΙΚΗΣ
Krema zaxaroplastikis

Mix the flour, cornstarch and sugar in a heavy-bottomed nonstick pan. Lightly beat the egg yolks with 4 tablespoons of the milk, pour into the pan, and mix well. In another pan, bring the remaining milk to a boil and pour it gradually onto the egg and flour mixture, stirring vigorously. Stir the mixture over medium heat until it comes to a boil. Reduce the heat and continue to cook, stirring constantly, for about 15 minutes, or until the cream is thick and smooth. Remove from the heat and stir in the cubed butter and vanilla. If the cream is too stiff, gradually stir in a little milk until the desired consistency is reached. If the cream is too thin, add 2 teaspoons more cornstarch dissolved into 2 tablespoons milk, and continue cooking until it has thickened.
If the cream is lumpy, strain it through a fine sieve or process in a blender for 1 minute. Press a piece of plastic wrap (cling film) onto the surface to prevent it from forming a skin. When the cream is completely cold, fold in the whipped cream, if using. Pastry cream is good for filling for cakes and pastries. It keeps for up to 2 days in the refrigerator, but cannot be frozen.

Makes 2 cups (450 ml / 16 fl oz)
Preparation time 10 minutes
Cooking time 10 minutes

CHOCOLATE SAUCE
ΣΑΛΤΣΑ ΣΟΚΟΛΑΤΑΣ
Saltsa sokolatas

- 11 oz (300 g) semisweet (dark) chocolate, broken into pieces
- 1 cup (250 ml / 8 fl oz) whipping cream

Put the chocolate into a heavy pan and pour in the cream. Heat gently, stirring occasionally, until the chocolate has melted and the mixture is smooth. Remove from the heat and let cool until the mixture is lukewarm before using. If you like, flavor the sauce by stirring in vanilla or almond extract or a liqueur of your choice. The sauce can be poured over ice cream or used as a frosting (icing) for cakes and cookies (biscuits). If a thick consistency is required, let the sauce cool completely, then beat well until light and fluffy.

Makes about 1¾ cups (400 ml / 14 fl oz)
Preparation time 5 minutes
Cooking time 5 minutes

SPONGE COOKIES (BISCUITS)
ΜΠΙΣΚΟΤΑ ΠΑΝΤΕΣΠΑΝΙΟΥ
Biskota pantespaniou

- 1 cup (120 g / 4 oz) self-rising flour
- 4 eggs, separated
- 1 teaspoon vanilla extract
- ½ cup (100 g / 3½ oz) superfine (caster) sugar
- confectioners' (icing) sugar, for dusting

Sift the flour into a bowl. Whisk the egg whites in an electric mixer at high speed until soft peaks are formed. Gradually add the vanilla and the sugar, 1 tablespoon at a time, still whisking, until the meringue forms stiff peaks. Add the egg yolks 1 at a time. Stop beating and sift the flour onto the meringue mixture, then fold it in carefully, until it is thoroughly incorporated. Do not over-mix. Alternatively, beat the egg yolks with half the sugar for about 5 minutes, until thick and pale. Whisk the egg whites to a stiff meringue, gradually adding the remaining sugar. Fold the sifted flour into the beaten egg yolks, alternating with a few spoonfuls of meringue to loosen the batter. Fold in the remaining egg whites. Preheat the oven to 400°F (200°C / Gas Mark 6). Line a cookie sheet (baking tray) with waxed (greaseproof) paper. Spoon the mixture into a pastry (piping) bag fitted with a ½-inch (1-cm) plain tip (nozzle) and pipe lines or rounds onto the cookie sheet, leaving plenty of space in between to allow room for spreading. Generously dust the tops with confectioners' sugar. Bake for 8–10 minutes, or until lightly golden. Let cool and remove them carefully from the paper. They keep for 1 week in an airtight container, and for several months in the freezer. You can sandwich pairs of sponge cookies together with jam, or use to make layered cakes and tortes.

Makes 24 large or 40 small cookies
Preparation time 30 minutes
Cooking time 10 minutes

- 5 cups (1 kg / 2¼ lb) superfine (caster) sugar
- 2 tablespoons corn syrup or liquid glucose
- 2 teaspoons vanilla extract
- 3 oz (90 g) semisweet (plain) chocolate, cut into small pieces

CHOCOLATE FROSTING (ICING)
ΓΛΑΣΟ ΣΟΚΟΛΑΤΑΣ
Glaso sokolatas

First, make the vanilla fondant. Combine the sugar, vanilla extract, and 1 cup (250 ml / 8 fl oz) water in a heavy pan and stir over low heat until the sugar has dissolved. Cover the pan for 1 minute to let the steam dissolve any sugar crystals on the side of the pan. Increase the heat, bring to a boil, and simmer until the syrup reaches the soft-ball stage, or registers 234–240°F (112–115°C) on a candy (sugar) thermometer. Remove the pan from the heat and immediately set it into cold water to stop the cooking. Dampen a marble slab or cookie sheet (baking tray) with a wet towel and carefully pour the hot syrup onto it. Let cool for several minutes. Using a wet spatula, carefully scoop up the edges and fold them in toward the center. Repeat this several times. Continue working the mass in a figure of eight motion until it becomes opaque and too firm to work with the spatula. Dampen your hands and knead the fondant for about 10 minutes, until it is white and elastic. To make the frosting, put 8½ oz (240 g) fondant and the chocolate into a heatproof bowl, set it over a pan of gently simmering water, and stir constantly until it melts and forms a soft, glossy frosting. If it is too thick, stir in 2–3 tablespoons milk. Let cool and use to glaze cakes and cookies (biscuits). Store any leftovers in an airtight container.

Makes 1½ cups (325 ml / 11 fl oz)
Preparation time 30 minutes
Cooking time 5 minutes

- 1 cup (250 ml / 8 fl oz) whipping cream, chilled
- 2–4 tablespoons confectioners' (icing) sugar
- 1 teaspoon vanilla extract

WHIPPED CREAM
ΚΡΕΜΑ ΣΑΝΤΙΓΙ
Krema santigi

Beat the cream, sugar, and vanilla with an electric mixer until it is light and fluffy and almost tripled in volume. Do not over-mix, or the cream may curdle. To prevent curdling, keep the cream chilled until ready to use. If it does curdle, do not discard it. Mix it with hot milk, bring to a boil and thicken with 1 tablespoon cornstarch (cornflour) to make a rich and very tasty pastry cream, or heat with melted chocolate to make a chocolate sauce. Whipped cream can be stored in the refrigerator for 4–5 days and in the freezer for up to 6 months. Thaw in the refrigerator for 12 hours before using. Almond extract, grated citrus zest, or liqueurs may be substituted for the vanilla. To make a chocolate-flavored whipped cream, sift 2 tablespoons unsweetened cocoa powder with the confectioners' sugar before adding to the cream. Whipped cream may be lightened by folding in a small amount of stiffly whisked egg white.

Makes about 1 cup (250 ml / 8 fl oz)
Preparation time 5 minutes

SAUCES
ΣΑΛΤΣΕΣ
Saltses

If soup represents the ultimate prehistoric effort to make food more palatable, then sauce is its natural culmination. Although the French raised *la sauce* to an art form, some food historians credit ancient Greek cooks with the invention of basic white and brown sauces, also known as béchamel and gravy. As the ancient word for sauces, *perihimata* (literally "pour-ons"), reveals, just about anything that could be drizzled over food was considered a sauce, including olive oil, vinegar, honey, fruit syrup, melted fat, wine, melted cheese, and raw egg. These substances, alone or combined, were often flavored with herbs and imported spices. By the fifth century, cinnamon, ginger, and pepper from the East and silphium (a now-extinct plant much prized by the ancient Greeks) from North Africa were available to Greek chefs. Three famous sauces stand out in ancient Greek literature: *kandavlo*, a concoction of honey, milk, cheese, and oil; *mitotos*, a kind of garlic sauce of leeks, garlic, oil, cheese, honey, and, later, eggs; and a spicy sauce of Persian origin called *kariki*, for which Athenaeus lists no fewer than eighteen recipes. It was as universal as modern-day ketchup, so common that even now the Greek word for spices and condiments, *karikevmata*, retains the original spelling and meaning. However, Greeks have never had a real taste for elaborate or fancy sauces, preferring simple additions like a drizzle of olive oil here, or a pinch of oregano there. The most famous is *avgolemono*, the classic combination of beaten egg and lemon juice, which can go with just about anything.

The most recent addition to the list of traditional Greek sauces is tomato sauce. Although the tomato may have been known in the Aegean islands at an earlier date, the first record of it growing on the mainland was in the early 1800s. The prior of a Capuchin monastery at the site of the Lysicrates Monument in Plaka is thought to have been one of the first people to cultivate tomatoes in his kitchen garden. The prior is, perhaps, more famous for having prevented Lord Elgin from removing the monument. The monastery has now gone, but the beautiful fourth-century BC ruins still grace Lysicrates Square.

GENERAL INSTRUCTIONS

Greek sauces may be few and simple, but their role is important, for it is their flavor or color that give names to whole categories of dishes, such as *kokinista* dishes cooked with tomato sauce, *lemonata* dishes deglazed with lemon juice, *krasata* dishes deglazed with wine, *skordata* dishes with a garlic sauce, and *kaftera* dishes with a very hot, peppery sauce.

The most common, simplest, and easiest sauce in Greek cuisine for fried and roasted meat or poultry is one made by deglazing the pan: that is, adding some liquid, usually wine, lemon juice, or tomato juice, after the food has been cooked. To do this, sauté or roast the ingredients according to the recipe, remove them and keep them hot while you are preparing the sauce. Pour the deglazing liquid into the pan, adding enough to cover the base. Simmer until the liquid has reduced by about half. As the liquid simmers, scrape the base of the pan with a wooden spoon and stir to dissolve the residue and caramelized juices on the base. Choose the appropriate type of pan for whatever you are cooking. Too small or nonstick, and the juices will not caramelize; too large, and the juices spread out too much and will burn. To increase the quantity of sauce, add some reduced, good-quality stock and simmer to reduce to the desired consistency. To enrich the sauce, add a few tablespoons of heavy (double) cream or plain yogurt just before the end of cooking. When thickening a sauce by reducing it bear in mind that as it simmers, the water evaporates and the flavors intensify. Therefore, it is very important to use good ingredients. At the same time the salt becomes more concentrated, so avoid using very salty stocks and take care with commercial stocks.

Most Greek sauces can be prepared in advance and stored in small, tightly sealed jars in the refrigerator for a few days or the freezer for up to three months. Sterilized, preserved sauces can be stored in the cellar for up to one year. Pour a thin layer of olive oil onto the surface of preserved tomato sauce or tomato paste to prevent mould from forming and store in the refrigerator for up to one month. The simplest and healthiest sauces for dressing salads and almost any other kind of food are oil-lemon and oil-vinegar sauces.

BASIC TOMATO SAUCE
ΒΑΣΙΚΗ ΣΑΛΤΣΑ ΝΤΟΜΑΤΑΣ
Vasiki saltsa domatas

- 4 tablespoons olive oil
- 1 small onion, finely chopped
- 1–2 garlic cloves, finely chopped (optional)
- 2¼ lb (1 kg) fresh or canned tomatoes, peeled, seeded and puréed
- 1 tablespoon red wine vinegar
- 1 teaspoon sugar
- 2 tablespoons finely chopped fresh parsley
- salt and pepper

This is the main tomato sauce used in all vegetable and meat stews called *kokinista*, or "dishes in red."

Heat the olive oil in a heavy pan, add the onion and garlic, and cook over low heat, stirring occasionally, for about 5 minutes, until softened and translucent. Pour in the puréed tomatoes and vinegar, stir in the sugar and parsley, and season to taste with salt and pepper. Reduce the heat, cover, and simmer for about 20 minutes, or until the sauce is thick. Adjust the seasoning, if necessary, and serve the sauce with pasta, rice, fried potatoes, or fried vegetables.

Makes 2 cups (450 ml / 16 fl oz)
Preparation time 15 minutes
Cooking time 20 minutes

EASY MARINADE
ΕΥΚΟΛΗ ΜΑΡΙΝΑΤΑ
Efkoli marinata

- 1 part olive oil
- 2 parts red wine or wine vinegar
- a few garlic cloves, smashed
- bay leaves
- peppercorns
- spices or herbs, such as allspice berries or coriander seeds for pork or game, or oregano, marjoram, rosemary, or thyme for lamb

Combine all the ingredients in a bowl. Use as a basting sauce or to marinate meat, game, fish, poultry, or vegetables.

Preparation time 5 minutes

COOKED MARINADE
ΜΑΡΙΝΑΤΑ
Marinata

- 4 tablespoons olive oil
- 1 small carrot, sliced
- 1 small onion
- ½ small celery stalk, chopped
- 1 garlic clove, finely chopped
- 2 fresh parsley sprigs
- 5 black peppercorns
- 1 scallion (spring onion), chopped
- 1 bay leaf
- 1 clove
- 1½ cups (350 ml / 12 fl oz) dry white or red wine
- 4 tablespoons red wine vinegar

Heat the oil in a pan. Add the carrot, whole onion, celery, garlic, parsley, peppercorns, scallion, bay leaf, and clove, and cook, stirring constantly, for 5–10 minutes, until lightly browned. Pour in the wine and vinegar, cover, and simmer for 15 minutes. Remove from the heat and let cool. Remove and discard the whole onion, bay leaves, and cloves. Use to marinate meat or game.

Makes 2 cups (450 ml / 16 fl oz)
Preparation time 15 minutes
Cooking time 15 minutes

WHITE SAUCE
ΑΣΠΡΗ ΣΑΛΤΣΑ
Aspri saltsa

- 1 cup (250 ml / 8 fl oz) milk
- 1 tablespoon (15 g / ½ oz) butter
- 1 tablespoon all-purpose (plain) flour
- pinch of ground nutmeg
- salt and white pepper

FOR A THICK SAUCE

- 1 cup (250 ml / 8 fl oz) milk
- 2 tablespoons (25 g / 1 oz) butter
- 2 tablespoons all-purpose (plain) flour
- pinch of ground nutmeg
- salt and white pepper

Although it is better known as béchamel, most Greek cooks recognize this as the classic white sauce their grandmothers made. It was well known to ancient Greek and Roman cooks, who probably used olive oil instead of butter, and ground bulgur wheat or semolina as a thickener.

Pour the milk into a small pan and bring just to a boil, then remove from the heat. Melt the butter in a heavy nonstick pan, stir in the flour, and cook, stirring frequently, for 1 minute. Remove the pan from the heat and gradually pour in the hot milk, stirring constantly with a whisk until the mixture is smooth. If lumps form, strain the sauce into another pan. Return the sauce to medium heat and simmer, stirring constantly, for about 15 minutes, until thickened and smooth. Remove from the heat and season with nutmeg, salt, and white pepper. To enrich the sauce, add 1–2 egg yolks. For a velvety sauce, stir in 4 tablespoons heavy (double) cream.

Makes 1 cup (250 ml / 8 fl oz)
Preparation time 5 minutes
Cooking time 20 minutes

OIL-LEMON DRESSING
ΛΑΔΟΛΕΜΟΝΟ
Ladolemono

- 2 parts olive oil
- 1 part freshly squeezed lemon juice
- finely chopped fresh parsley or other fresh herb, such as basil, mint, dill, marjoram, oregano, thyme, or cilantro (coriander)
- salt and pepper

Put the ingredients into a screw-top jar, fasten the lid, and shake vigorously until thoroughly blended. Use on boiled greens, salads, broiled (grilled) fish and shellfish, and cold meats. When made with parsley, this sauce is the traditional Greek dressing for all broiled fish and shellfish. Plain and lightly flavored with the parsley, it is the perfect way to dress fish without smothering its light fragrance.

Preparation time 5 minutes

OIL-VINEGAR DRESSING
ΛΑΔΟΞΥΔΟ
Ladoxido

- 2 parts olive oil
- 1 part red wine vinegar
- pinch of dried oregano or mustard powder (optional)
- salt and pepper

Put the ingredients into a screw-top jar, fasten the lid, and shake vigorously until thoroughly blended. Use on any fresh vegetable salad. Flavor the dressing with oregano or mustard powder, depending on the occasion. You can add any other fresh or dried herb you like.

Preparation time 5 minutes

VINAIGRETTE DRESSING
ΣΑΛΤΣΑ ΒΙΝΕΓΚΡΕΤ
Saltsa vinegret

- ½ cup (120 ml / 4 fl oz) olive oil
- 4 tablespoons red wine vinegar
- ½ teaspoon salt
- 1 small garlic clove, finely chopped (optional)
- 1 teaspoon Dijon mustard
- ⅛ teaspoon pepper

Put the ingredients into a screw-top jar, fasten the lid, and shake vigorously until thoroughly blended. Use on salad greens (leaves) and on cold, cooked beans, lentils, and grains. Drizzle over warm broiled (grilled) or roasted vegetables. The dressing keeps in the refrigerator for 2 weeks.

Herb vinaigrette: Add your favorite herb or a mixture of fresh herbs, especially parsley, dill, marjoram, and cilantro (coriander).

Black olive vinaigrette: Whisk 2 teaspoons chopped capers, 4 table-spoons finely chopped pitted (stoned) Kalamata olives, 2 finely chopped drained, canned anchovy fillets, and 1 tablespoon chopped fresh mint with the basic ingredients.

Makes ¾ cup (175 ml / 6 fl oz)
Preparation time 10 minutes

ROAST GARLIC VINAIGRETTE
ΒΙΝΕΓΚΡΕΤ ΜΕ ΨΗΤΟ ΣΚΟΡΔΟ
Vinegret me psito skordo

- 10 garlic cloves
- ½ cup (120 ml / 4 fl oz) olive oil, plus extra for drizzling
- 4 tablespoons red wine vinegar
- ½ teaspoon dried thyme

Preheat the oven to 400°F (200°C / Gas Mark 6). Put the garlic in a bowl, drizzle with a little olive oil, and toss lightly to coat. Wrap the cloves tightly in aluminum foil and roast for 30 minutes, until very soft. Squeeze the pulp from the skins, combine with the remaining ingredients, and process in a food processor or blender.

Makes 1½ cups (350 ml / 12 fl oz)
Preparation time 40 minutes

GARLIC-VINEGAR SAUCE
ΣΚΟΡΔΟΣΤΟΥΜΠΙ
Skordostoubi

- 2–3 garlic cloves
- 5 tablespoons red wine vinegar

Mash the garlic in a bowl, add the vinegar, and mix until thoroughly blended. Use to marinate fresh or cooked vegetables.

Vefa's secret: Brush a salad bowl with a little of the sauce before you use it to give a light garlic fragrance to your salad.

Makes about ½ cup (120 ml / 4 fl oz)
Preparation time 5 minutes

- 1–2 eggs
- freshly squeezed juice of 1–2 lemons, strained
- hot soup or cooking liquid

EGG-LEMON SAUCE
ΣΑΛΤΣΑ ΑΥΓΟΛΕΜΟΝΟ
Saltsa avgolemono

Avgolemono is the most famous of Greek sauces. The exact quantities of egg and lemon juice depend on your own preferences.

Lightly beat the eggs in a bowl with the lemon juice. Gradually add a ladle of the hot soup or cooking liquid, whisking constantly. This prevents the eggs from curdling when they are added to the remaining hot liquid. Add the egg mixture to the soup or other cooked dish, stirring or shaking the pan to distribute the sauce evenly. Immediately remove from the heat. Set aside for several minutes before serving. The egg mixture will thicken the sauce to a lovely silken-smooth consistency.

Preparation time 5 minutes

- 3 egg yolks
- 4 tablespoons freshly squeezed lemon juice
- 1 teaspoon cornstarch (cornflour)
- 1 cup (250 ml / 8 fl oz) hot cooking liquid from the prepared dish
- 4 tablespoons heavy (double) cream (optional)

EGG-LEMON CREAM SAUCE
ΣΑΛΤΣΑ ΑΥΓΟΛΕΜΟΝΟ ΚΡΕΜΑ
Saltsa avgolemono krema

Beat the egg yolks with the lemon juice in a small, heavy pan. Put the cornstarch into a small bowl and stir in 1 tablespoon water to make a smooth paste, then pour it into the egg and lemon mixture. Gradually stir in the hot cooking liquid and heat gently, stirring constantly, until thick and creamy. Do not let the sauce boil or the egg yolks will curdle. Remove the pan from the heat and stir in the cream, if using. Pour the sauce over the prepared dish. This sauce is delicious spread over stuffed grape (vine) or cabbage leaves.

Makes 2 cups (450 ml / 16 fl oz)
Preparation time 10 minutes
Cooking time 10 minutes

- ½ cup (120 ml / 4 fl oz) olive oil
- 1 tablespoon Dijon mustard
- 2 tablespoons honey
- ½ teaspoon salt
- ¼ teaspoon pepper
- 4 tablespoons red wine vinegar

HONEY-MUSTARD SAUCE
ΣΑΛΤΣΑ ΜΟΥΣΤΑΡΔΑΣ ΜΕ ΜΕΛΙ
Saltsa moustardas me meli

Put the ingredients into a sealed container, fasten the lid, and shake vigorously until thoroughly blended and emulsified. Alternatively, process all the ingredients together in a blender or food processor. Use in fresh vegetable salads or drizzle over cold roasted or poached chicken or other meat.

Makes 1 cup (250 ml / 8 fl oz)
Preparation time 5 minutes

GREEK CHILI SAUCE
ΣΑΛΤΣΑ ΚΑΦΤΕΡΗ
Saltsa kafteri

- 3¼ lb (1.5 kg) ripe tomatoes, peeled and chopped
- 2 onions, grated
- ½ green bell pepper, seeded and very finely chopped
- ½ red bell pepper, seeded and very finely chopped
- 2 tablespoons sugar
- 1 teaspoon salt
- 1 tablespoon sweet paprika
- 1 teaspoon cayenne pepper
- 3 cloves
- 1 small cinnamon stick
- 1 teaspoon mustard powder
- 1 cup (250 ml / 8 fl oz) red wine vinegar

Put the tomatoes, onions, and bell peppers in a pan and cook over low heat, stirring occasionally, for 20–30 minutes. Remove the pan from the heat and process the mixture in a blender or pass through a food mill. Return to the pan, stir in the sugar, salt, paprika, cayenne, cloves, cinnamon, mustard, and vinegar, and simmer until thickened. Remove and discard the cloves and cinnamon stick and let the sauce cool completely. Store the sauce in a sealed container in the refrigerator. Serve with roasted meats or vegetables, pasta dishes, and as a dip for raw vegetables.

Makes about 3¾ cups (900 ml / 1½ pints)
Preparation time 1 hour

HONEY-WINE SAUCE OR MARINADE
ΟΙΝΟΜΕΛΟ
Inomelo

- 4 tablespoons thyme honey
- 4 tablespoons olive oil
- 4 tablespoons red wine vinegar
- 1 teaspoon dried thyme, oregano or rosemary
- ½ teaspoon chili flakes (optional)
- 1 garlic clove, crushed
- salt and pepper

Put the ingredients into a sealed container, fasten the lid, and shake vigorously until thoroughly blended. Use as a marinade or basting sauce for broiling (grilling) shellfish or vegetables.

Makes about 1 cup (250 ml / 8 fl oz)
Preparation time 5 minutes

MAYONNAISE
ΜΑΓΙΟΝΕΖΑ
Magioneza

- 2 egg yolks
- ½ teaspoon salt
- ½ teaspoon Dijon mustard
- 2 tablespoons freshly squeezed lemon juice
- white pepper
- 1 cup (250 ml / 8 fl oz) olive oil or corn oil

Process the egg yolks, salt, mustard, lemon juice, and white pepper in a blender or food processor until frothy. With the motor running, gradually add the oil through the lid or feeder tube, one drop at a time, until the sauce begins to emulsify. Add the remaining oil in a slow steady stream. Stop once or twice and scrape the mayonnaise down the sides of the blender with a spatula. When all the oil has been absorbed (after about 5 minutes), transfer the mayonnaise to a sealed container jar and store in the refrigerator until ready to use. If the mayonnaise curdles while you are adding the oil, switch off the machine. Beat another egg yolk in a bowl and, with the machine switched on, gradually add it to the curdled mayonnaise until smooth.

Makes about 1¼ cups (300 ml / ½ pint)
Preparation time 15 minutes

- 2 tablespoons olive oil or clarified butter
- 2 garlic cloves, finely chopped
- 1 lb 2 oz (500 g) small white mushrooms, thinly sliced
- ½ cup (120 ml / 4 fl oz) dry white wine
- 2 tablespoons finely chopped fresh parsley
- salt and pepper

MUSHROOM SAUCE
ΣΑΛΤΣΑ ΜΕ ΜΑΝΙΤΑΡΙΑ
Saltsa me manitaria

Heat the oil or butter in a pan, add the garlic, and cook over medium heat, stirring frequently, for a few minutes, until softened. Add the mushrooms, reduce the heat, and cook, stirring constantly, until the liquid evaporates. Pour in the wine, add the parsley, and season with salt and pepper. Simmer gently, uncovered, for about 20 minutes, until the mushrooms are tender and the liquid has almost completely evaporated. Remove the pan from the heat and serve the sauce hot or at room temperature with roast meat, poultry, game, or fish. For a richer sauce that can be served with pasta, stir in ½ cup (120 ml / 4 fl oz) heavy (double) cream just before the end of the cooking time and stir until heated through.

Serves 4
Preparation time 20 minutes
Cooking time 30 minutes

- 1 cup (250 ml / 8 fl oz) olive oil, plus extra for brushing
- 2¼ lb (1 kg) long red Florina peppers or other red bell peppers
- 4½ lb (2 kg) fresh ripe tomatoes, peeled, seeded and chopped
- 8 garlic cloves, finely chopped
- 2 tablespoons finely chopped fresh parsley
- ¼ teaspoon cayenne pepper
- salt and pepper

RED PEPPER SAUCE FROM FLORINA
ΣΑΛΤΣΑ ΜΕ ΚΟΚΚΙΝΕΣ ΠΙΠΕΡΙΕΣ
Saltsa me kokines piperies

Preheat the oven to 400°F (200°C / Gas Mark 6) and brush a roasting pan with oil. Add the peppers and roast, turning occasionally, for about 20 minutes, until the skins have charred. Remove from the oven and leave until cool enough to handle, then peel, seed, and chop the flesh into small pieces. Put the tomatoes, oil, garlic, and parsley in a large pan. Simmer gently, stirring occasionally, until most of the liquid has evaporated. Add the peppers and season with the cayenne pepper, salt, and pepper. Continue to simmer, stirring occasionally, for about 30–40 minutes, or until the sauce has been reduced to a very thick consistency. Remove from the heat and let cool. Ladle into sterilized containers, seal, cover with a layer of oil and store in the refrigerator for up to 6 months. Serve as a dip with sausages, burgers, meatballs, and broiled (grilled) or fried meat and fish. You can also use the sauce to prepare scrambled eggs and chicken paprika stew.

Makes 5 cups (1.2 litres / 2 pints)
Preparation time 20 minutes
Cooking time 40–60 minutes

SAUCE VELOUTÉ
ΣΑΛΤΣΑ ΒΕΛΟΥΤΕ
Saltsa veloute

- 2 tablespoons (25 g / 2 oz) butter
- 2 tablespoons all-purpose (plain) flour
- 2 cups (450 ml / 16 fl oz) meat, chicken or fish stock
- heavy (double) cream (optional)

Prepare this sauce according to the recipe for white sauce (see p 57), using stock instead of milk, and gently simmer over low heat until thickened. The thicker the sauce, the tastier it is. Occasionally skim off the skin that forms on top. If you like, you can stir a small quantity of heavy cream into the thickened sauce to make it richer.

Makes 2 cups (450 ml / 16 fl oz)
Preparation time 5 minutes
Cooking time 20–30 minutes

YOGURT-GARLIC SAUCE
ΓΙΑΟΥΡΤΙ ΣΚΟΡΔΑΤΟ
Giaourti skordato

- 1 cup (250 ml / 8 fl oz) strained plain or thick Greek yogurt
- 2 garlic cloves, crushed
- 2 tablespoons olive oil
- 1 tablespoon finely chopped fresh dill, plus extra to garnish (optional)
- salt and white pepper

Combine all the ingredients in a bowl and mix until thoroughly blended. Cover and chill in the refrigerator. Garnish with chopped dill, if you like. This is a delicious dip for raw or fried vegetables and shellfish.

Makes 1 cup (250 ml / 8 fl oz)
Preparation time 5 minutes

TAHINI SAUCE
ΣΑΛΤΣΑ ΤΑΧΙΝΙ
Saltsa tahini

- 1–2 garlic cloves, finely chopped
- ¼ teaspoon salt
- 5 tablespoons tahini
- 2–3 tablespoons freshly squeezed lemon juice
- salt and white pepper

Pound the garlic with the salt in a mortar and gradually blend in the tahini. Gradually add about 1½ cups (350 ml / 12 fl oz) water, a little at a time, working it into the sauce until the desired consistency is reached. Add as much lemon juice as you like and a pinch of white pepper. Alternatively, process the garlic, salt, tahini, half the water, the lemon juice, and pepper in a food processor until smooth, then add more water as required. Taste and add more salt if you like. Use as a dip, a dressing on salads, or as a sauce for broiled (grilled) and cooked vegetables. Covered with oil, tahini sauce keeps in an airtight container in the refrigerator for up to a month.

Makes 1½ cups (350 ml / 12 fl oz)
Preparation time 10 minutes

- 3 tablespoons olive oil
- 3–4 garlic cloves, thinly sliced
- 1 small fresh chile, quartered (optional)
- 1½ cups (350 ml / 12 fl oz) fresh tomato pulp or bottled strained tomatoes
- 1 teaspoon sugar
- 1 tablespoon red wine vinegar
- salt and pepper

TOMATO-GARLIC SAUCE
ΣΑΛΤΣΑ ΝΤΟΜΑΤΑΣ ΜΕ ΣΚΟΡΔΟ
Saltsa domatas me skordo

Heat the oil in a pan. Add the garlic and chile, if using, and cook for 1 minute. Remove with a slotted spoon and discard. Stir the tomatoes, sugar, and vinegar into the flavored oil and season with salt and pepper. Cover and simmer, stirring occasionally, for 30 minutes. Strain through a fine strainer.

Makes 1½ cups (350 ml / 12 fl oz)
Preparation time 35 minutes

- 5 tablespoons olive oil
- 1 onion, grated
- 1 garlic clove, finely chopped
- 1 lb 2 oz (500 g) ground (minced) meat
- 2¼ lb (1 kg) fresh or canned tomatoes, peeled and puréed
- 1 teaspoon sugar
- 1 tablespoon red wine vinegar
- 3 tablespoons finely chopped fresh parsley
- pinch of ground cinnamon or allspice (optional)
- salt and pepper

GROUND (MINCED) MEAT SAUCE
ΣΑΛΤΣΑ ΜΕ ΚΙΜΑ
Saltsa me kima

Heat the oil in a large pan. Add the onion and garlic and cook over low heat, stirring occasionally, for about 5 minutes, until softened and translucent. Add the ground meat, increase the heat to high, and cook, breaking up the meat with a fork, for about 15 minutes. Add the remaining ingredients, cover, and reduce the heat. Simmer, stirring occasionally, for about 1 hour, until the meat is tender and the sauce has reduced. This sauce can be served with pasta or rice or used for making moussaka, pastitsio, or other ground meat dishes.

Makes 3 cups (750 ml / 1¼ pints)
Preparation time 30 minutes
Cooking time 1 hour

MEZEDES

-

ΜΕΖΕΔΕΣ

-

Mezedes

One of the unique characteristics of Greek cuisine is its large variety of appetizers (starters) or *orektika*, also known as mezedes. Many believe the word to be Turkish, but in fact it has a long history going back to the ancient Persians, who called foods that were "awaiting their appetite" *maza*, which is also the ancient Greek word for barley bread. Whatever the origin, Greek mezedes are more than just tasters to whet the appetite or to precede the main meal. The variety, color, and flavors of Greek mezedes are such that people's appetite for the entrée (main course) is often diverted. Many a Greek meal begins and ends entirely with mezedes.

Since Homer, the Greeks have classified their diet into three distinct yet inseparable entities: *sitos-opson-poton*. *Sitos* were the staple foods, usually cereal-based, such as bread or gruel made from barley, wheat, or millet. *Poton* ("potion") was almost always wine (*inos*) or water, or both, as wine was rarely drunk without being mixed with water. The third part, *opson*, was by far the most important and is the most difficult to define. Originally, *opson* was any food eaten with *sitos*, such as vegetables, herbs, shellfish, or meat. Later, in the Classical period (the fifth century BC), the diminutive form—*opsarion*—came to mean "dainties" or "relish," particularly fish or shellfish delicacies. The modern Greek word for fish, *psari*, is derived from this distinction.

At the ancient Greek drinking get-togethers (*symposia*), balanced quantities of *opson* and *sitos* were always eaten together before the drinking of the *poton*. Although many scholars translate the word *opson* as mezedes or relish, in truth both *opson* and *sitos* constituted the meal, and the quantities and balance of these foods together was considered sufficient, but not excessive, in accordance with the Greek ideal of moderation in all things. Anyone who ate more than his share of opson was an *opsofagos*, or glutton. Following strict rules of etiquette, a limited number of diners reclined two or three to a couch, taking *sitos* (bread) with their left hands and *opson* with their right, with slaves bearing finger-bowls and towels. After the libation to the gods, the wine drinking began (watered down and in moderation to avoid drunkenness), accompanied by music, dancing flute-girls, poetry readings, and heady, serious discussion of the current political or philosophical topics. The Greek philosophers and poets were perhaps the first to discuss the role of food in their lives and the utopian society they envisioned. Plato's *Republic* and Aristophanes' comedies are typical examples. The Hellenistic Epicureans eulogized well-being and the pleasures of life, including food. Citizens of the Roman and Byzantine empires continued the symposium tradition, but eventually the strict rules of the early Christian Orthodox Church changed many of the older eating customs.

Today, like their ancestors, modern Greeks rarely drink without eating. Even a small glass of ouzo or wine is usually served with a few olives, sliced hard-boiled egg, bread, and sliced tomato. Few visitors to Greece can resist a tempting platter of mezedes served with a glass of anise-scented ouzo or the traditional pine-flavored retsina wine. Equally, just as at the ancient *symposia*, Greeks seldom eat or drink alone, sharing their food, drink, and ideas with at least one companion. Conversation is an important part of meze-eating, from watching the world go by and commenting on it, to story-telling, relating anecdotes, or debating political, religious or philosophical topics.

Today's popular *mezedopolia*, or mezedes cafes, offer as many as forty to fifty kinds of mezedes. The choices are almost endless, so deciding what to order can be difficult. Among aficionados, a certain protocol surrounds the ritual of drinking and eating of mezedes. Here are a few of the rules: mezedes time, with or without ouzo, can begin any time from late morning to early afternoon, spanning the hours between breakfast, which Greeks don't eat at all, and lunch, which they usually skip during the hot summer months. Another ouzo-mezedes period starts at dusk while watching the sunset, some time between 8:00 and 10:00 p.m. Greeks rarely even start thinking about dinner before 10:30 p.m. Thus, the ouzo-mezedes ritual often replaces lunch or dinner entirely. The rules are flexible, so long as enough time is allowed to enjoy both the food and drink. By nature, ouzo is an outdoor drink, so the setting is important—nibbling charcoal-grilled octopus by the seashore while people-watching, or looking at the fishermen repairing their nets on the quay, or sitting under a plane tree in a remote village square, sipping retsina with your skewered lamb *kokoretsi* or *bekri-mezedes* (wine-braised pork bites). The key component is a relaxing atmosphere, which fosters an Epicurean feeling of well-being.

The mezedes table is always small and the seating is informal. There is no need for fancy cutlery or table linen. Mezedes are piled high on a single communal platter with pieces of bread on the side. The food is picked up with your fingers, wooden toothpicks, or, if you must, tiny forks, and placed directly in the mouth. Individual plates are not necessary but there should be plenty of paper napkins on hand. The amounts usually depend on the number of people present but, in general, are moderate—two or three bites of each meze per person. The recipe quantities given here assume that several types of mezedes will be served, but variety and quality are more important than quantity. Ouzo or retsina is served by the *karafaki* (small pitcher or jug) or in small bottles accompanied by cold water and bowls of ice. Most Greeks drink ouzo neat or with ice or cold water which turns it milky-white. Above all, ouzo or wine should be sipped slowly and the food eaten at a leisurely pace to fully enjoy the truly Greek gastronomic experience of mezedes. This long-established way of enjoying food and drink creates a lifestyle that many Greeks wouldn't exchange for any other in the world, no matter where they go or how long they stay. Don't forget to say: "*Stin igia sas! Kali orexi!*" ("To your health! *Bon appétit!*")

SPRING (LENT)
ΑΝΟΙΞΗ (ΣΑΡΑΚΟΣΤΗ)
Anixi (Sarakosti)

Every vacation (holiday) period or feast day has its own traditional
mezedes, which reflect the season according to the ingredients available at the time. Spring is heralded by the Sarakosti, or Great Lenten
Fast, which precedes the Orthodox Easter, and during this time the
range of mezedes is determined by the rules of the fast, which prohibits
the consumption of eggs, dairy products, meat, and fish. Traditionally,
these products were used up during the three-week pre-Lenten Apokries
or Carnival period, which is similar to Mardi Gras. The most important
of the Lenten mezedes feature various shellfish and crustaceans including oysters, mussels, sea (king) scallops, grilled octopus, stuffed squid,
shrimp (prawns), and grilled or steamed langoustines, served with a trickle
of *ladolemono,* or olive oil and lemon juice dressing. Then there is the
famous *avgotaraho,* the cured fish roe of Missolonghi, and mezedes
made with fish roe paste such as taramosalata and *taramokeftedes.*
Other mezedes that might complete the platters of the *nistia* (fast) are
rice-stuffed grape (vine) leaves, pickled vegetables, and a variety of
olives. These are just a few of the dishes designed to enliven the austerity
of the diet of the weeks leading up to Easter. They bring spirit, color,
and flavor to a period otherwise characterized by self-restraint, religious
contrition, and detoxification of the body.

FRIED FAVA (BROAD) BEANS FROM CRETE
ΦΡΕΣΚΑ ΚΟΥΚΙΑ ΤΗΓΑΝΙΤΑ
Freska koukia tiganita

- 1 lb 2 oz (500 g) tender, very young fava (broad) beans in the pod
- 4–5 tablespoons all-purpose (plain) flour
- olive oil, for frying
- salt
- freshly squeezed lemon juice, to serve

Carefully snip off the tips of the fava bean pods, but leave them whole.
Wash them thoroughly. Bring 1¼ cups (300 ml / ½ pint) salted water
to a boil in a pan, add the beans, and cook for 2–3 minutes. Drain
well and pat dry with paper towels. Put the flour in a paper bag, add
the beans in batches, close the bag with one hand, and shake with
the other to coat the pods. Shake off any excess flour. Heat the oil in a
large, deep skillet or frying pan, add the beans, in batches if necessary,
and fry for about 10 minutes on each side, until lightly browned. Remove
with a slotted spoon and drain on paper towels. Serve sprinkled with
lemon juice. This is a wonderful appetizer or side dish to accompany
broiled (grilled) meat or fish.

Serves 4
Preparation time 20 minutes
Cooking time 30 minutes

- 2¾ cups (500 g / 1 lb 2 oz) dried lima (butter) beans, soaked for 24 hours in cold water to cover and drained
- 2 celery stalks with leaves
- 1 carrot
- 5 black peppercorns
- ⅔ cup (150 ml / ¼ pint) olive oil
- 1 large onion, grated
- 5–6 garlic cloves, thinly sliced
- 2¼ lb (1 kg) ripe tomatoes
- 1 teaspoon sugar
- salt and pepper
- ½ cup (25 g / 1 oz) finely chopped fresh parsley
- 2 pork sausages, cut into bite-size pieces (optional)
- 2 beefsteak (large) tomatoes, thinly sliced into rounds
- pinch of dried oregano

BAKED GIANT BEANS
ΓΙΓΑΝΤΕΣ ΠΛΑΚΙ
Gigantes plaki

Put the beans in a large pan, pour in water to cover, and add the celery, carrot, and peppercorns. Cover and bring to a boil, then reduce the heat, and simmer for about 1 hour, or until the beans are just tender. Drain and place them in an ovenproof dish. Preheat the oven to 350°F (180°C / Gas Mark 4). Meanwhile, heat half the olive oil in a pan. Add the onion and garlic and cook over low heat, stirring occasionally, for about 5 minutes, until softened and translucent. Push the tomatoes through a strainer into a bowl or process to a purée in a food processor, then stir into the pan together with the sugar, and season with salt and pepper. Remove from the heat and stir in the parsley and sausages, if using. Pour the sauce over the beans and arrange the sliced tomatoes on top. Season with salt and pepper, sprinkle with the oregano, and drizzle the remaining olive oil over the surface. Bake for about 1 hour, until the beans are tender and the sauce has reduced. It may be necessary to add some hot water during baking. Serve warm or at room temperature.

Serves 6
Preparation time 25 hours (including soaking)
Cooking time 1 hour

□ p 70

- 2 cups (400 g / 14 oz) dried fava (broad) beans or yellow split peas
- 4 cups (1 litre / 1¾ pints) vegetable stock
- ½ teaspoon paprika
- ½ teaspoon chili powder
- ¼ teaspoon baking soda (bicarbonate of soda)
- ¼ teaspoon salt
- ½ cup (15 g / ½ oz) finely chopped fresh dill
- 2 tomatoes, finely chopped
- 1 green bell pepper, seeded and finely chopped
- 1 small onion, grated
- 4 tablespoons dry bread crumbs
- all-purpose (plain) flour, for dusting
- vegetable oil, for deep-frying

FAVA (BROAD) BEAN CROQUETTES
ΚΕΦΤΕΔΕΣ ΜΕ ΦΑΒΑ
Keftedes me fava

Put the split peas into a pan, pour in the stock, and bring to a boil. Simmer for 45–60 minutes, until they are very soft and all the liquid has been absorbed. Remove the pan from the heat. Combine the cooked peas, paprika, chili powder, baking soda and salt in a bowl. Add the dill, tomatoes, bell pepper, onion, and bread crumbs and mix well. Form the mixture into bite-size balls and chill in the refrigerator for 30 minutes. Spread out the flour on a shallow plate and roll the balls in it to coat, shaking off any excess, then flatten slightly. Heat the oil in a deep-fryer to 350–375°F (180–190°C). Add the croquettes, in batches if necessary, and deep-fry for 5–10 minutes, until golden brown. Drain well and serve immediately.

Makes 20 croquettes
Preparation time 1½ hours (including chilling)
Cooking time 20 minutes

Baked giant beans, p 69

Rice-stuffed grape (vine) leaves, p 73

SPLIT PEA "CUSTARD"
ΦΑΒΑ
Fava

Bring a generous 4 cups (1 litre / 1¾ pints) water to a boil in a large pan. Add the split peas and bring back to a boil over medium heat, skimming off the scum that rises to the surface. Cover and simmer for about 35 minutes. Meanwhile, heat the olive oil in a small pan, add the grated onion, and cook over low heat, stirring occasionally, for a few minutes, until softened. Stir into the split peas together with the oregano and season with salt and pepper. Continue to simmer for 30 minutes more, or until the split peas have completely disintegrated. Remove the pan from the heat and vigorously beat the mixture with a wooden spoon until smooth, adding more water if necessary. Transfer to a wide, shallow dish or six individual bowls and sprinkle with parsley or dill and chopped scallions. Drizzle a little olive oil on top and sprinkle with lemon juice. As the mixture cools, it will set to a custard-like consistency. It is equally tasty served hot or cold.

Serves 6
Preparation time 10 minutes
Cooking time 1 hour

Note: Yellow split peas (*Lathyrus sativus*) are a popular legume (pulse) in Greece, known as *fava* when prepared in this way—no relation to the fava (broad) bean.

- 2½ cups (500 g / 1 lb 2 oz) green or yellow split peas
- ½ cup (120 ml / 4 fl oz) olive oil, plus extra for drizzling
- 1 small onion, grated
- pinch of dried oregano
- salt and pepper
- 3 tablespoons finely chopped fresh parsley or dill
- ½ cup (4) chopped scallions (spring onions)
- freshly squeezed lemon juice, for sprinkling

GARBANZO BEAN (CHICKPEA) FRITTERS
ΡΕΒΥΘΟΚΕΦΤΕΔΕΣ
Revithokeftedes

Drain the beans and grind to a coarse purée in a food processor. Scrape the purée into a bowl. Mix the tomato paste with 4 tablespoons water in another bowl, then stir into the beans. Add the onion, dill or mint, and olive oil, and season with salt and pepper. Mix in enough flour to make a medium-thick mixture that retains its shape. Cover and set aside for 1 hour. Heat the oil in a heavy skillet or frying pan, add large tablespoons of the mixture, a few at a time, and cook for 10 minutes, or until golden on both sides. Remove with a slotted spoon and drain well on paper towels. If you like, you can substitute ½ cup (120 ml / 4 fl oz) puréed fresh tomatoes for the tomato paste.

Serves 4
Preparation time 13 hours (including soaking and resting)
Cooking time 15 minutes

- 2¼ cups (1 lb 2 oz) dried garbanzo beans (chickpeas), soaked overnight in water to cover with 1 tablespoon salt
- 1 tablespoon tomato paste
- 1 large onion, grated
- 3 tablespoons finely chopped fresh dill or mint
- 2 tablespoons olive oil, plus extra for frying
- 2¼ cups (250 g / 9 oz) self-rising flour
- salt and pepper

- 2 tablespoons olive oil
- ¼ teaspoon crushed garlic
- 1 teaspoon mixed dried herbs, such as thyme, marjoram and rosemary
- 1 lb 2 oz (500 g) oyster mushrooms, cut into pieces
- salt and pepper

FOR THE VINAIGRETTE
- 2 tablespoons olive oil
- 1 tablespoon balsamic vinegar
- 2 tablespoons orange juice
- 1 tablespoon red wine vinegar
- 3–4 teaspoons honey

BROILED (GRILLED) MUSHROOMS WITH VINAIGRETTE
ΜΑΝΙΤΑΡΙΑ ΣΤΙ ΣΚΑΡΑ ΜΕ ΒΙΝΕΓΚΡΕΤ
Manitaria sti skara me vinegret

Combine the olive oil, garlic, and herbs in a bowl and brush the mushrooms with the mixture. Let marinate for 30 minutes. Meanwhile, put all the vinaigrette ingredients into a sealed jar, fasten the lid and shake until thoroughly blended. Preheat the broiler (grill). Broil (grill) the mushrooms for 5 minutes on each side. Transfer to a serving plate. Sprinkle with the vinaigrette and serve hot or at room temperature.

Serves 4
Preparation time 30 minutes (including marinating)
Cooking time 15 minutes

- 1 lb 2 oz (500 g) grape (vine) leaves, fresh or preserved in brine
- 2 cups (175 g / 6 oz) finely chopped scallions (spring onions)
- 2 large onions, chopped
- 2½ cups (500 g / 1 lb 2 oz) medium-grain rice
- ½ cup (25 g / 1 oz) chopped fresh parsley
- ½ cup (15 g / ½ oz) chopped fresh dill
- 2 cups (450 ml / 16 fl oz) olive oil
- 4 tablespoons pine nuts (optional)
- 4 tablespoons currants (optional)
- salt and pepper
- 2½ cups (600 ml / 1 pint) boiling water
- 5 tablespoons freshly squeezed lemon juice
- Tzatziki (p 152) or plain yogurt, to serve

RICE-STUFFED GRAPE (VINE) LEAVES
ΝΤΟΛΜΑΔΑΚΙΑ ΓΙΑΛΑΝΤΖΙ
Dolmadakia gialantzi

Rinse the grape leaves and trim off the stems, if necessary. Bring a pan of water to a boil, add the leaves, a few at a time, and blanch briefly, then drain, and let cool. Spread out some of the leaves to cover the base of a large, wide, heavy pan. Put the scallions and onions into a colander, sprinkle with a little salt, and rub with your fingers. Rinse with a little water and drain, then squeeze out as much liquid as possible. Combine the rice, onions, herbs, half the oil, the pine nuts, and currants, if using, in a bowl and season with salt and pepper. Lay a leaf out flat on the work surface, shiny side down. Put about 1 tablespoon of the rice mixture at the stem end in the middle, fold the sides over the filling, and loosely roll up into a neat parcel. Continue making grape leaf parcels until all the ingredients have been used. Arrange the stuffed leaves in the lined pan, side by side, seam side down. (You may have to make more than one layer.) Carefully pour the remaining oil, the boiling water, and lemon juice into the pan. Invert a heavy plate on the top of the parcels to prevent them from opening during cooking. Cover the pan and bring to a boil, then reduce the heat, and simmer for 35–40 minutes, until all the water has been absorbed. Remove from the heat, place a cotton towel or some paper towels between the pan and the lid to absorb the steam, and let cool. Transfer to a serving platter. Serve with Tzatziki or plain yogurt. They are just as good served cold the next day. *Dolmadakia* are one of the most famous mezedes in the Greek culinary repertoire. The parsley can be replaced with chopped fresh mint and the dill with chopped fennel fronds.

Serves 8
Preparation time 1 hour
Cooking time 35–40 minutes

☐ p 71

BROILED (GRILLED) OLIVES FROM CYPRUS
ΕΛΙΕΣ ΟΦΤΕΣ
Elies oftes

Soak large black olives in cold water for about 2 hours and drain.
Thread on wooden skewers and grill for 5 minutes on the barbecue.
Serve them hot sprinkled with ground coriander or dried oregano.

Preparation time 2 hours (including soaking)
Cooking time 5 minutes

FRIED EGGPLANTS (AUBERGINES)
AND ZUCCHINI (COURGETTES)
ΜΕΛΙΤΖΑΝΕΣ ΚΑΙ ΚΟΛΟΚΥΘΙΑ ΤΗΓΑΝΙΤΑ
Melitzanes ke kolokithia tiganita

- 2¼ lb (1 kg) eggplants (aubergines), cut into ¼-inch (5 mm) thick slices
- 2¼ lb (1 kg) zucchini (courgettes), cut into ¼-inch (5-mm) thick slices
- salt
- 1 teaspoon rapid-rise (fast-action) yeast
- 2 cups (225 g / 8 oz) all-purpose (plain) flour
- vegetable oil, for deep-frying
- Tzatziki (p 152) or Garlic sauce (p 153), to serve

Put the eggplant and zucchini slices into separate colanders, sprinkle
generously with salt, and let drain for about 2 hours. Meanwhile, make
the batter. Combine the yeast and flour and stir in enough warm water
to make a smooth, light batter as thick as heavy (double) cream. Set
the batter aside at room temperature for at least 30 minutes. Rinse the
eggplant slices well and squeeze out the excess water with your hands.
Rinse and drain the zucchini. Heat the oil in a deep-fryer to 350–375°F
(180–190°C). Dip the vegetable slices, one at a time, into the batter
and let the excess run off, then add them to the hot oil, and deep-fry
for a few minutes until golden brown. Remove with a slotted spoon and
drain on paper towels. Serve immediately with Tzatziki or Garlic sauce.

Serves 4
Preparation time 2½ hours (including salting and standing)
Cooking time 30 minutes

Note: The batter can also be made from all-purpose or self-rising flour
and club soda (soda water) or beer, omitting the yeast. Alternatively,
coat the zucchini in all-purpose flour, shake off the excess, and arrange,
side by side, on baking parchment until ready to fry. Deep-fry in hot
oil until golden brown. Remove with a slotted spoon and drain on paper
towels. For softer-textured eggplants, pat the slices dry and fry in hot oil,
without first dipping in batter or coating in flour. Drain well on paper
towels and serve hot.

- 2 tablespoons olive oil
- 2 garlic cloves, thinly sliced
- 1¼ cups (250 g / 9 oz) black olives
- 2 tablespoons red wine vinegar
- 1 teaspoon dried oregano
- 1 teaspoon dried thyme

MARINATED OLIVES
ΜΑΡΙΝΑΡΙΣΜΕΝΕΣ ΕΛΙΕΣ
Marinarismenes elies

Heat the oil in a skillet or frying pan. Add the garlic and cook over low heat, stirring frequently, for a few minutes. Remove with a slotted spoon and discard. Add the olives to the pan and stir in the hot oil for 1–2 minutes. Pour in the vinegar and sprinkle with the herbs. Stir and remove from the heat. Let the olives marinate for 12 hours before serving. These make a delicious appetizer served with ouzo, or can be used in salads or to accompany pasta dishes.

Serves 4
Preparation time 12 hours (including marinating)
Cooking time 5 minutes

- 2¼ lb (1 kg) cuttlefish, cleaned (see p 325)
- ⅔ cup (150 ml / ¼ pint) olive oil
- 2½ lb (1 kg) onions, thinly sliced
- 6 garlic cloves, finely chopped
- 3 tablespoons tomato paste
- 1 cup (250 ml / 8 fl oz) white wine
- 2 bay leaves
- 3 allspice berries
- 10 black peppercorns
- ½ teaspoon sugar

CUTTLEFISH IN WINE
ΣΟΥΠΙΕΣ ΚΡΑΣΑΤΕΣ
Soupies krasates

If the cuttlefish are small, leave them whole. Cut large cuttlefish cross-wise into rings. Rinse and drain well. Heat the oil in a heavy pan. Add the onions and garlic and cook over low heat, stirring occasionally, for about 5 minutes, until softened and translucent. Add the cuttlefish, partially cover, and cook until all the liquid has evaporated. Combine the tomato paste and wine, stir well, and pour the mixture over the cuttlefish. Add the bay leaves, allspice berries, peppercorns, and sugar, stir well, cover, and simmer over medium heat for about 1½ hours, until the cuttlefish is tender and the sauce has reduced and cooked down almost to the oil.

Serves 4
Preparation time 15 minutes
Cooking time 1¾ hours

Note: Squid or octopus can be used instead of cuttlefish. If using squid, follow the recipe above. If using octopus, it should first be blanched in a mixture of water and vinegar for a couple of minutes, then peel off the skin. Cut it into bite-size pieces and proceed as for the cuttlefish. As octopus requires longer to cook, it may be necessary to add more water. Simmer until the octopus is tender and the sauce has reduced.

☐ p 76

Cuttlefish in wine, p 75

ickled octopus, p 79

FISH ROE FRITTERS
ΤΑΡΑΜΟΚΕΦΤΕΔΕΣ
Taramokeftedes

Put the bread in a bowl, pour in water to cover, and let soak for 30 minutes. Squeeze out excess moisture with your hands. Crumble the bread into a large bowl, add the roe, garlic, onion, and herbs, and season with pepper. Knead gently to blend. Shape the mixture into 30 small balls, dust with flour, and gently flatten into patties. Heat the oil in a skillet or frying pan, add the fritters, and cook in batches, turning once, for 10–15 minutes, or until golden brown on both sides. Serve hot or at room temperature.

Makes 30 fritters
Preparation time 1¼ hours (including soaking)
Cooking time 30–45 minutes

- 1 lb 10 oz (750 g) day-old bread, crusts removed
- 7 oz (200 g) cured cod's roe
- 2–3 garlic cloves, finely chopped
- 1 large onion, grated
- 4 tablespoons finely chopped fresh mint
- 4 tablespoons finely chopped fresh parsley
- 1 teaspoon dried oregano (optional)
- pepper
- all-purpose (plain) flour, for dusting
- vegetable oil, for frying

BROILED (GRILLED) LANGOUSTINES
ΚΑΡΑΒΙΔΕΣ ΣΤΗ ΣΚΑΡΑ
Karavides sti skara

Preheat the broiler (grill). Rinse and drain the langoustines, then sprinkle them with salt. Place them belly down, cut in half lengthwise with a sharp knife and devein them. Beat together the butter, garlic, dill, and Tabasco in a bowl and season with a little salt and pepper. Using a small spatula, spread the cut surfaces of the langoustine halves with the flavored butter. Arrange on the broiler rack about 4 inches (10 cm) from the heat source and broil (grill) for 5–6 minutes. Serve immediately with lettuce leaves and lemon wedges. These are good served with sautéed vegetables such as zucchini (courgette) and carrot.

Serves 4
Preparation time 15 minutes
Cooking time 5 minutes

- 10 large langoustines, about 2¼ lb (1 kg) total weight
- 4 tablespoons (50 g / 2 oz) butter
- 1 small garlic clove, finely chopped
- 2 tablespoons finely chopped fresh dill
- 10 drops Tabasco sauce
- salt and pepper
- lettuce leaves and lemon wedges, to garnish

- 3¼ lb (1.5 kg) octopus, cleaned and cut into pieces
- 1 cup (250 ml / 8 fl oz) red wine vinegar
- olive oil, for drizzling
- dried oregano, to serve
- lemon wedges, to serve

FOR THE MARINADE
- ½ cup (120 ml / 4 fl oz) olive oil
- 1 cup (250 ml / 8 fl oz) white wine
- 1 teaspoon dried oregano
- 2 bay leaves
- 10 black peppercorns
- salt and pepper

GRILLED OCTOPUS FROM EVVOIA
ΧΤΑΠΟΔΙ ΣΤΑ ΚΑΡΒΟΥΝΑ
Oktapodi sta karvouna

For tender, melt-in-the mouth grilled octopus, boil it first. Put the octopus into a large pan, pour in the vinegar, add water to cover, and bring to a boil. Reduce the heat, cover and simmer for 1 hour, then drain and place into a bowl. Put all the marinade ingredients in a screw-top jar, fasten the lid and shake vigorously until thoroughly combined. Pour the mixture over the octopus and let marinate in the refrigerator, turning occasionally, for up to 24 hours. When ready to cook, drain the octopus and reserve the marinade. Grill the octopus on both sides on a barbecue over charcoal, basting frequently with the marinade, for about 15 minutes. Arrange the octopus on a platter, drizzle with a little olive oil, sprinkle with oregano and serve with lemon wedges. Serve immediately with ouzo and ice. This is the traditional summer meze served on the islands and in coastal eateries all over Greece, where you can see octopus hanging out in the sun to dry.

Serves 4
Preparation time 24¼ hours (including marinating)
Cooking time 1¼ hours

- 4½ lb (2 kg) fresh or frozen octopus
- 1 cup (250 ml / 8 fl oz) red wine vinegar
- 2 celery stalks, halved
- 2 small carrots, halved
- 1 onion, halved
- 10 black peppercorns
- salt
- pickled pimientos and chopped fresh parsley, to garnish

FOR THE MARINADE
- ½ cup (120 ml / 4 fl oz) olive oil
- 5 tablespoons red wine vinegar
- 10 black peppercorns
- salt

PICKLED OCTOPUS
ΧΤΑΠΟΔΙ ΞΥΔΑΤΟ
Htapodi xidato

Thaw (if frozen) and rinse the octopus, and peel off the translucent skin. Put it into a large pan, pour in the vinegar, and add water to cover. Bring to a boil, reduce the heat, cover, and simmer for about 1 hour. Drain well, rinse, and remove any remaining skin. Return to the pan, add the celery, carrots, onion, peppercorns, and a pinch of salt, and pour in water to cover. Bring to a boil, reduce the heat, cover, and simmer for about 1 hour, or until tender. Drain and transfer the octopus to a bowl. Put all the marinade ingredients into a screw-top jar, fasten the lid, and shake vigorously until thoroughly combined. Pour the mixture over the hot octopus. Let marinate in the refrigerator, turning frequently, for at least 24 hours. To serve, either cut the octopus into bite-size pieces or arrange whole on a platter with the tentacles spread out attractively, and spoon some of the marinade over it. Garnish with pimientos and parsley. This is a delicious, typical ouzo-meze.

Serves 6
Preparation time 24¼ hours (including marinating)
Cooking time 2 hours

🗔 p 77

MUSSEL FRITTERS
ΜΥΔΟΚΕΦΤΕΔΕΣ
Midokeftedes

Rinse and drain the mussels, then put them in a large pan with 4 tablespoons water, and cook over high heat, stirring constantly, for 5 minutes to release some of their liquid. Do not overcook them or they will shrink and toughen. Drain and let cool slightly, then grind in a food processor. Cook the unpeeled potatoes in salted boiling water for 20–30 minutes, until soft. Drain, peel, and mash with a fork. Combine the potatoes, mussels, onion, and dill and season with salt and pepper. Add enough bread crumbs to form a stiff mixture. Chill in the refrigerator for 1 hour. Heat the oil in a deep-fryer to 350–375°F (180-190°C). Shape the mixture into small patties, coat with flour, and deep-fry in batches for 5 minutes, or until golden brown. Serve hot sprinkled with lemon juice, or cold accompanied by Garlic sauce or Taramosalata.

Makes 30 fritters
Preparation time 1½ hours (including chilling)
Cooking time 30 minutes

- 1 lb 2 oz (500 g) shelled mussels
- 7 oz (200 g) potatoes
- 1 onion, grated
- 5 tablespoons finely chopped fresh dill
- salt and pepper
- 1⅓ cups (100 g / 3½ oz) dry bread crumbs
- all-purpose (plain) flour, for coating
- vegetable oil, for deep-frying
- freshly squeezed lemon juice, Garlic sauce (p 153), or Taramosalata (p 157), to serve

---

MUSSEL PILAF
ΜΥΔΟΠΙΛΑΦΟ
Midopilafo

Scrub the mussels under cold running water and pull off the "beards." Discard any with broken shells or that do not shut immediately when sharply tapped. Put them into a large pan, pour in ½ cup (120 ml / 4 fl oz) water, cover, and cook over high heat, shaking the pan occasionally, for 4–5 minutes, until the shells open. Immediately remove from the heat and drain, reserving the cooking liquid. Discard any mussels that remain shut. Strain the cooking liquid through a cheesecloth- (muslin-) lined strainer into a measuring cup and add enough water to make up to 3 cups (750 ml / 1½ pints). Pour into a pan and bring to a boil. Meanwhile, heat the oil in a large pan. Add the grated onion and scallions and cook over low heat, stirring occasionally, for 3–5 minutes, until softened and translucent. Add the rice and cook, stirring constantly, for 1–2 minutes, then pour in the hot cooking liquid. Season with salt, cover and simmer for about 20 minutes, until the rice is tender and all the liquid has been absorbed. Stir in the dill and mussels and season with pepper. Cover the pan with a cotton dish towel and put on the lid. Turn off the heat and leave the pan on the burner (hob) for 5 minutes to fluff up the rice. Serve sprinkled with lemon juice and cayenne pepper.

Serves 4
Preparation time 30 minutes
Cooking time 25 minutes

- 2¼ lb (1 kg) live mussels
- ½ cup (120 ml / 4 fl oz) olive oil
- 1 onion, grated
- ½ cup (4) finely chopped scallions (spring onions)
- 1¾ cups (350 g / 12 oz) long-grain rice
- salt and pepper
- ½ cup (15 g / ½ oz) finely chopped fresh dill
- freshly squeezed lemon juice and cayenne pepper, to serve

- 1 lb 10 oz (750 g) raw large shrimp (prawns)
- salt and white pepper
- Oil-lemon dressing (p 57)
- finely chopped fresh parsley, to garnish

STEAMED SHRIMP (PRAWNS) WITH OIL-LEMON DRESSING
ΓΑΡΙΔΕΣ ΑΧΝΙΣΤΕΣ ΛΑΔΟΛΕΜΟΝΟ
Garides ahnistes ladolemono

Peel the shrimp, leaving the heads and tail intact, and devein. Rinse and drain well. Pour ½ cup (120 ml / 4 fl oz) water into a large pan, season with salt and white pepper, and bring to a rapid boil. Put the shrimp into a steamer basket set over the pan, cover, and cook for 8–10 minutes. Transfer the shrimp to a platter and pour the oil-lemon dressing over them. Sprinkle with parsley and serve warm or at room temperature.

Serves 4
Preparation time 35 minutes
Cooking time 10 minutes

- 2¼ lb (1 kg) scallops in their shells
- ½ cup (100 g / 3½ oz) long-grain rice
- 4 tablespoons finely chopped fresh parsley
- 2 tablespoons finely chopped fresh dill
- 1 small onion, finely chopped
- 1 tablespoon tomato paste
- ½ cup (120 ml / 4 fl oz) olive oil
- salt and pepper

STUFFED SCALLOPS FROM LESVOS
ΚΤΕΝΙΑ ΓΕΜΙΣΤΑ
Ktenia gemista

Scrub the scallops under cold running water to remove any sand. Place them in a pan over low heat until they open. Remove the scallops from the pan and set aside. Strain the liquid released through a cheesecloth-(muslin-) lined strainer and reserve. Shuck the scallops, taking care not to separate the shells, and remove and discard the frilly "skirt" and black stomach sac. Blanch the shells in boiling water and set aside. Chop the scallop flesh and put it into a small pan, pour in the reserved liquid, and add the rice, parsley, dill, onion, and tomato paste. Simmer for 5 minutes, or until the vegetables are softened. Add the oil and remove the pan from the heat. Carefully stuff the reserved scallop shells two-thirds full with the rice mixture, close, and secure crosswise with kitchen string. Arrange the shells side by side in a large pan and pour in water to cover. Bring to a boil, reduce heat, and simmer for about 15 minutes. Remove with a slotted spoon and serve immediately.

Serves 6
Preparation time 30 minutes
Cooking time 20 minutes

FRIED SQUID
ΚΑΛΑΜΑΡΙΑ ΤΗΓΑΝΙΤΑ
Kalamaria tiganita

Rinse the squid under running water and drain. Leave finger-length squid whole, otherwise cut them into thick rings. Heat the oil in a deep-fryer to 400°F (200°C). Meanwhile, dip the squid into the batter and let the excess drain off, or coat with flour and shake off any excess. Deep-fry the squid or squid rings, a few at a time, in very hot oil for a few minutes until light golden brown. Remove with a slotted spoon and drain on paper towels. Arrange on a platter, sprinkle with salt, garnish with lemon wedges, and serve immediately with Tzatziki, Eggplant (Aubergine) dip or Taramosalata.

Serves 4
Preparation time 10 minutes
Cooking time 15 minutes

□ p 84

- 2¼ lb (1 kg) small squid, cleaned
- vegetable oil, for frying
- Batter for frying (p 47) or all-purpose (plain) flour, for coating
- salt
- lemon wedges, to garnish
- Tzatziki (p 152), Eggplant (Aubergine) dip (p 152), or Taramosalata (p 157), to serve

---

MARINATED SQUID
ΚΑΛΑΜΑΡΙΑ ΜΑΡΙΝΑΤΑ
Kalamaria marinata

Cut the squid into rings and simmer in a small amount of boiling water for about 20 minutes, or until tender. Drain and place in a bowl. Add the lemon juice, scallions, parsley, basil, bell pepper, vinegar, oil, and oregano. Cover and let marinate in the refrigerator for at least 12 hours. Serve the marinated squid on a bed of arugula and lettuce leaves.

Serves 4
Preparation time 12½ hours (including marinating)
Cooking time 20 minutes

- 1 lb 2 oz (500 g) squid, cleaned
- 2 tablespoons freshly squeezed lemon juice
- ½ cup (4) finely chopped scallions (spring onions)
- 1 tablespoon finely chopped fresh parsley
- 1 tablespoon finely chopped fresh basil
- ½ red bell pepper, seeded and finely chopped
- 4 tablespoons balsamic vinegar
- 3 tablespoons olive oil
- 1 teaspoon dried oregano
- 1 bunch of arugula (rocket) leaves
- Bibb or curly lettuce leaves
- salt and pepper

- 2¼ lb (1 kg) live snails
- ¾ cup (175 ml / 6 fl oz) olive oil
- 1 large onion, finely chopped
- 1 green bell pepper, seeded and finely chopped
- 1 cup (175 g / 6 oz) bulgur wheat
- 2 cups (450 ml / 16 fl oz) vegetable stock
- 2 tablespoons finely chopped fresh parsley
- 2 tablespoons finely chopped fresh mint
- 14 oz (400 g) canned tomatoes, finely chopped
- 1 tablespoon tomato paste
- salt and pepper

SNAILS WITH BULGUR WHEAT
ΣΑΛΙΓΚΑΡΙΑ ΜΕ ΠΛΙΓΟΥΡΙ
Saligaria me pligouri

Scrub the snails under cold running water to clean their shells. Remove and discard the hard membrane over the opening and place the snails in cold water. Discard any snails that do not poke their heads out of their shells. Drain, sprinkle with salt, and set aside for 5 minutes. Rinse again with cold water to remove any last traces of mucus. Put the snails into a large pan, pour in water to cover, and add salt. Bring to a boil, skimming off the scum that rises to the surface. Cook for 10 minutes, then drain, reserving the liquid, and rinse under cold running water. Allow the cooking liquid to settle, then remove 1 cup (250 ml / 8 fl oz) from the top and reserve. Heat the oil in a pan. Add the onion and bell pepper and cook over low heat, stirring occasionally for about 5 minutes, until softened. Add the bulgur wheat and cook, stirring frequently, for 2 minutes. Add the snails, stock, reserved snail-cooking liquid, parsley, mint, tomatoes, and tomato paste and season with salt and pepper. Simmer for 10 minutes, until the bulgur has absorbed all the liquid. Stir lightly, remove from heat, and serve hot.

Serves 6
Preparation time 30 minutes
Cooking time 30 minutes

Vefa's secret: Using a sharp knife, cut a small round piece from the curved top of each snail shell. This will enable the sauce to penetrate the flesh, making it tastier and easier to extract with a special snail fork.

- 2¼ lb (1 kg) large live snails
- 1 cup (250 ml / 8 fl oz) olive oil
- ½ cup (120 ml / 4 fl oz) red wine vinegar
- salt
- 1 tablespoon chopped fresh oregano (optional)
- 1 tablespoon chopped fresh thyme (optional)
- 1 tablespoon chopped fresh rosemary (optional)

BRAISED SNAILS FROM CRETE
ΧΟΧΛΙΟΙ ΜΠΟΥΡΜΠΟΥΡΙΣΤΟΙ
Hohlii bourbouristi

Plunge the snails into cold water and remove and discard the membrane that covers the opening. Discard any snails that do not poke their heads out of their shells. Put the snails in a colander and rinse well under cold running water to rid them of their mucus. Heat the oil in a heavy pan and add the snails, flat side down. Cook over high heat, stirring once or twice, for about 10 minutes. Pour the vinegar into the pan and stir well, scraping up any sediment from the base. Season with salt, add the herbs of your choice, and serve immediately. This is a wonderful meze served with Cretan *tsikoudia*, a type of raki.

Serves 6
Preparation time 30 minutes
Cooking time 10 minutes

Fried squid, p 82

heese-stuffed artichokes, p 86

SPRING (EASTER)
ΑΝΟΙΞΗ (ΠΑΣΧΑ)
Anixi (Paska)

In the heart of springtime comes Easter, the season when the lambs are small and tender and their organ meats (offal) are perfect for use in the various Easter mezedes such as *kokoretsi*, *gardoubes*, *tzigerosarmades*, or *bourekakia*, using finely chopped organ meats or fresh spring cheeses such as *anthotiri* or *mizithra*, similar to ricotta or cottage cheese, flavored with herbs such as fresh mint, oregano, thyme, dill, and parsley. These traditional mezedes introduce the Easter Feast, and are served with the first glasses of *tsipouro*, ouzo, or wine, while the lamb is still turning on the spit.

CHEESE-STUFFED ARTICHOKES
ΚΑΡΔΙΕΣ ΑΓΓΙΝΑΡΕΣ ΓΕΜΙΣΤΕΣ ΜΕ ΤΥΡΙΑ
Kardies aginaras gemistes me tiria

Using your fingers, open each artichoke slightly at the center and remove the chokes with a teaspoon. Trim any tough outer leaves with kitchen scissors, so the artichokes are about the same size. Drain on paper towels. Combine all the filling ingredients and stuff the artichoke centers, pushing in as much filling as possible. At this stage they can be frozen or kept in the refrigerator until required. Preheat the oven to 350°F (180°C / Gas Mark 4) and brush a cookie sheet (baking tray) with melted butter. Lightly brush the artichokes with melted butter and place on the prepared cookie sheet. Bake for about 20 minutes, until the tops are golden brown. Serve hot.

Makes 18 pieces
Preparation time 20 minutes
Cooking time 20 minutes

▢ p 85

- 18 canned small globe artichokes, drained and rinsed
- melted butter, for brushing

FOR THE FILLING
- 7 oz (200 g) anthotiro, ricotta or cream cheese
- 5 oz (150 g) kaseri, provolone or mozzarella cheese, crumbled or grated
- 3½ oz (100 g) kefalotiri or Parmesan cheese, grated
- 1 teaspoon mixed dried herbs, such as thyme, mint, parsley or marjoram
- ½ teaspoon paprika
- salt and pepper

- 1 lb 2 oz (500 g) anthotiro or ricotta cheese
- 1–2 eggs
- 4 tablespoons all-purpose (plain) flour, plus extra for coating
- 4 tablespoons finely chopped fresh mint
- 4 tablespoons finely chopped fresh parsley
- salt and pepper
- vegetable oil, for deep-frying

FRIED CHEESE BALLS FROM CRETE
ΜΠΑΛΑΚΙΑ ΜΕ ΑΝΘΟΤΥΡΟ
Balakia me anthotiro

Place the cheese in a bowl and mash with a fork. Add the eggs, flour, mint, and parsley, season with salt and pepper, and blend to a thick, pliable mixture. If it is soft and sticky, add more cheese. Cover with plastic wrap (cling film) and put the mixture in the refrigerator until required. Heat the oil in a deep-fryer to 350–375°F (180–190°C). Pinch off small pieces of the cheese mixture and roll between your palms to form balls the size of a small walnut. Coat with flour and fry in the hot oil, in batches if necessary, for 3–4 minutes, or until golden all over. Drain well and serve immediately.

Serves 6
Preparation time 30 minutes
Cooking time 15 minutes

□ p 88

- 4 tablespoons olive oil
- 1 small onion, thinly sliced
- 2 zucchini (courgettes), diced
- 4 tablespoons hot water
- 6 eggs
- 4 tablespoons milk
- salt and pepper
- 2 tablespoons finely chopped fresh mint
- 1–2 tablespoons grated kefalotiri or pecorino cheese

ZUCCHINI (COURGETTE) OMELET
ΣΦΟΥΓΓΑΤΟ ΜΕ ΚΟΛΟΚΥΘΙΑ
Sfougato me kolokithia

Sfougato is the Byzantine word for omelet, and the name refers to its sponge-like appearance. The word is still in use in various parts of Greece, and in some villages it is made in honor of Saint George.

Heat the oil in a heavy skillet or frying pan. Add the onion and cook over low heat, stirring occasionally, for about 5 minutes, until softened and translucent. Add the zucchini and cook for a few minutes more. Add the hot water, cover, and simmer for about 10 minutes, until the vegetables are tender. Beat the eggs with the milk in a bowl and season with salt and pepper. Add the eggs and the mint to the pan and cook over medium heat for about 10 minutes, until the eggs are set. Serve the *sfougato* immediately, sprinkled with the cheese.

Serves 4
Preparation time 20 minutes
Cooking time 10 minutes

Fried cheese balls from Crete, p 87

Easter omelet from Lesvos, p 91

EASTER OMELET
ΠΑΣΧΑΛΙΝΗ ΟΜΕΛΕΤΑ
Paskalini omeleta

- 1 spring lamb's pluck (heart, liver, spleen), about 1 lb (450 g), rinsed thoroughly
- 1 spring lamb's sweetbreads, soaked in several changes of cold water for 5 hours and drained
- ½ cup (120 ml / 4 fl oz) olive oil
- ½ cup (4) chopped scallions (spring onions)
- 5 tablespoons white wine
- 5 tablespoons finely chopped fresh dill
- 8–10 eggs, lightly beaten
- 2 tablespoons finely chopped fresh mint
- salt and pepper

Blanch the lamb's pluck and sweetbreads in boiling water for 5 minutes, then drain. Let cool, remove and discard any skin and fibers, and finely chop the meat. Heat the oil in a large, heavy skillet or frying pan over high heat. Add the scallions and cook, stirring frequently, for a few minutes, until softened. Add the meat, season with salt and pepper, and cook, stirring constantly, for 5 minutes more. Pour in the wine and when the alcohol has evaporated, cover the pan, and simmer for 30 minutes, or until the meat is tender and the liquid has reduced. Add the dill and eggs and stir lightly until just set (about 10 minutes). Remove the pan from the heat and serve the omelet immediately, sprinkled with the mint.

Serves 4
Preparation time 5¾ hours (including soaking)
Cooking time 10 minutes

OMELET WITH WILD ARTICHOKES
ΟΜΕΛΕΤΑ ΜΕ ΑΓΡΙΟΑΓΓΙΝΑΡΕΣ
Omeleta me agrioaginares

- 4 wild globe artichokes
- ½ cup (120 ml / 4 fl oz) olive oil
- 1 cup (7–8) finely chopped scallions (spring onions)
- ½ cup (120 ml / 4 fl oz) dry white wine
- 4 tablespoons finely chopped fresh dill
- 6 eggs
- 4 tablespoons milk
- 1 tablespoon finely chopped fresh mint
- salt and pepper

Trim the artichokes down to the tender hearts and bases by removing any tough outer leaves, and cut them into quarters. Heat the oil in a heavy, nonstick skillet or frying pan. Add the artichokes and cook over low heat for a few minutes. Add the scallions and cook, stirring occasionally, for 5 minutes more, until softened and translucent. Pour in the wine and when the alcohol has evaporated, add 4 tablespoons water. Cover and simmer for 10 minutes, until the artichokes are tender and the liquid has reduced. Stir in the dill. Meanwhile, lightly whisk the eggs in a bowl with the milk and season with salt and pepper. Pour the egg mixture into the skillet or frying pan, shake gently to mix, and cook over low heat for about 10 minutes, until the eggs have set. Serve immediately, sprinkled with chopped mint.

Serves 4
Preparation time 30 minutes
Cooking time 10 minutes

Note: This dish is traditional in Crete because wild artichokes grow everywhere in the Cretan countryside during Spring. It can also be made with cultivated artichokes. Wild artichokes are extremely spiny but they have no choke (the hairy, inedible interior). Unless the cultivated artichokes are very young, you will need to scoop out the choke with a teaspoon before cooking.

- 4 tablespoons olive oil
- 3 slices smoked ham or bacon, chopped
- 2 rustic sausages, chopped
- 1 lb 2 oz (500 g) fresh fava (broad) beans, cooked
- 2 tablespoons red wine vinegar
- 5 eggs, lightly beaten
- salt and pepper

OMELET WITH FAVA (BROAD) BEANS AND SAUSAGE FROM CYPRUS
ΚΑΡΔΑΜΙΞΙ
Kardamixi

Heat the oil in a skillet or frying pan. Add the ham and sausages and cook, stirring frequently, for 5–8 minutes, until lightly browned. Add the beans and cook, stirring constantly, for 5 minutes. Pour in the vinegar and, when it has evaporated, stir in the eggs and season with salt and pepper. Cook the omelet for 5 minutes, or until it is almost set and lightly browned on the underside. Flip it over with a spatula and cook the second side. When it is set, slide it onto a plate and serve immediately.

Serves 4
Preparation time 15 minutes
Cooking time 15 minutes

- 3 tablespoons (40 g / 1½ oz) butter, plus extra for greasing
- 1 small romaine lettuce, finely chopped
- 1 cup (7–8) finely chopped scallions (spring onions)
- 12 eggs, lightly beaten
- 5 oz (150 g) grated ladotiri or other hard, piquant cheese such as pecorino
- ½ cup (15 g / ½ oz) finely chopped fresh dill
- 2 tablespoons finely chopped fresh mint
- salt and pepper
- fresh mint leaves, to garnish

EASTER OMELET FROM LESVOS
ΠΑΣΧΑΛΙΝΟ ΣΦΟΥΓΓΑΤΟ
Paskalino sfougato

Preheat the oven to 400°F (200°C / Gas Mark 6) and grease an ovenproof dish with butter. Rub the lettuce leaves with a little salt to wilt them. Rinse well under cold running water and squeeze dry. Melt the butter in a pan. Add the lettuce and scallions and cook over low heat, stirring frequently for a few minutes, until the scallions have softened and the lettuce has wilted. Remove the pan from the heat and let cool slightly. Pour in the beaten eggs and add the cheese, dill, and mint, season with salt and pepper, and mix well. Pour the egg mixture into the prepared dish and bake for about 30 minutes, until the omelet is set. Serve hot, garnished with a few fresh mint leaves.

Serves 4
Preparation time 20 minutes
Cooking time 30 minutes

▢ p 89

CRAB-STUFFED ARTICHOKES
ΑΓΓΙΝΑΡΕΣ ΓΕΜΙΣΤΕΣ ΜΕ ΚΑΒΟΥΡΙ
Aginares gemistes me kavouri

- 12 fresh globe artichokes
- freshly squeezed juice of 1 lemon
- 3 tablespoons clarified butter, melted

FOR THE FILLING
- 12 oz (350 g) canned crab meat, drained
- 3 tablespoons olive oil
- ½ cup (4) finely chopped scallions (spring onions)
- ½ cup (50 g / 2 oz) finely chopped celery
- 1 garlic clove, finely chopped
- 4 tablespoon finely chopped green bell pepper
- 4 tablespoons finely chopped fresh parsley
- salt and pepper
- 1 cup (250 ml / 8 fl oz) thick White sauce (p 57)

Preheat the oven to 350°F (180°C / Gas Mark 4). Break off the artichoke stems and leaves and remove the chokes with a teaspoon, leaving only the hearts. (Alternatively, use prepared frozen artichoke hearts.) Bring a pan of salted water to a boil, add the lemon juice and artichoke hearts, and cook for about 10 minutes, until tender. Drain, brush with melted butter, and arrange in an ovenproof dish. Meanwhile, prepare the filling. Pick over and remove any pieces of shell from the crab meat. Heat the oil. Add the scallions, celery, garlic, and bell pepper and cook over low heat, stirring occasionally, for about 5 minutes, until softened. Stir in the crab meat and parsley and season with salt and pepper. Cook for 1-2 minutes, then remove from the heat. Stuff the artichoke cups with the mixture and spoon the white sauce over them. Bake for 30-35 minutes, until the tops are lightly browned. Serve while still warm.

Makes 12 pieces
Preparation time 25 minutes
Cooking time 55 minutes

SQUID WITH NETTLES FROM PONTUS
ΤΣΟΥΚΝΙΔΟΚΑΛΑΜΑΡΑ
Tsouknidokalamara

- 1 cup (250 ml / 8 fl oz) olive oil, plus extra for brushing
- 4 large squid, cleaned (see p 325)
- 1 lb 2 oz (500 g) nettles, wild greens, and spinach
- 1 onion, finely chopped
- 2 tablespoons capers
- 1 tablespoon finely chopped cilantro (coriander)
- 5 oz (150 g) anthotiro or ricotta cheese
- 2 tomatoes, thinly sliced
- 4 tablespoons freshly squeezed lemon juice
- salt and pepper

Preheat the oven to 350°F (180°C / Gas Mark 4) and brush an ovenproof dish with oil. Chop the squid tentacles and reserve the body sacs. Heat 5 tablespoons of the olive oil in a skillet or frying pan. Add the tentacles and stir-fry over high heat for 2-3 minutes, until light golden brown. Remove from the heat and set aside. Rinse and trim the greens and cook in boiling salted water for about 5 minutes, until tender. Drain well and squeeze out the excess liquid. Heat 5 tablespoons of the remaining oil in a pan. Add the onion and cook over low heat, stirring occasionally, for about 5 minutes, until softened and translucent. Stir in the greens and simmer for 5 minutes. Add the chopped squid, cilantro, capers, and cheese and season with salt and pepper. Stir well to mix and remove the pan from the heat. Stuff the squid sacs with the mixture about three-quarters full and secure the openings with wooden toothpicks. Put the stuffed squid in the prepared dish in a single layer and top with the sliced tomatoes. Drizzle over the remaining oil and bake for 20 minutes. Just before serving, sprinkle with the lemon juice. Serve hot or cold.

Serves 4
Preparation time 30 minutes
Cooking time 55 minutes

□ p 94

- 6 hard-boiled eggs
- 3–4 tablespoons Mayonnaise (p 60)
- ¼ teaspoon pepper
- 2 canned anchovies, drained and mashed, or 1 teaspoon anchovy paste
- 1 tablespoon freshly squeezed lemon juice
- 12 capers
- 12 small strips of red bell pepper or 12 canned anchovy fillets, drained
- 12 parsley leaves

TO SERVE
- arugula (rocket) leaves
- romaine lettuce leaves
- Oil-vinegar dressing made with balsamic vinegar (p 57)

EGGS STUFFED WITH ANCHOVIES
ΑΥΓΑ ΜΕ ΑΝΤΖΟΥΓΙΕΣ
Avga me antzougies

Peel the eggs and halve lengthwise. Remove the yolks without piercing the whites and mash them in a bowl. Reserve the whites. Add the mayonnaise, pepper, mashed anchovies or anchovy paste, and lemon juice to the mashed yolks. Mix until smooth and thoroughly blended. Spoon into the egg white halves and top with the capers, bell pepper and parsley. (If you like, you can spoon the mixture into a pastry (piping) bag fitted with a star tip (nozzle) and use this to fill the egg white halves. Wrap each caper in a strip of bell pepper or an anchovy fillet. Garnish each egg half with a parsley leaf and wrapped caper.) Dress the arugula and lettuce leaves with the oil-vinegar dressing and arrange the leaves on a serving platter. Place the egg halves on top and serve.

Serves 6
Preparation time 20 minutes

- 1 lb 2 oz (500 g) grape (vine) leaves, fresh or preserved in brine
- 1 lb 7 oz (650 g) lamb's liver
- 1 cup (250 ml / 8 fl oz) olive oil
- 1 cup (7–8) finely chopped scallions (spring onions)
- 1 small onion, grated
- 5 tablespoons medium-grain or risotto rice
- ½ cup (15 g / ½ oz) finely chopped fresh dill
- 2 tablespoons finely chopped fresh mint
- 2 eggs
- 5 tablespoons freshly squeezed lemon juice
- salt and pepper

STUFFED GRAPE (VINE) LEAVES FROM NORTHERN GREECE
ΣΑΡΜΑΔΑΚΙΑ
Sarmadakia

Rinse the grape leaves and trim off the stems, if necessary. Bring a pan of water to a boil, add the grape leaves, a few at a time, and blanch briefly, then drain, and let cool. Blanch the lamb's liver for about 5 minutes, or until half cooked, then remove from the pan, and finely chop. Pour half the oil into a small pan, add the scallions, grated onion, and ½ cup (120 ml / 4 fl oz) water, and bring to a boil. Reduce the heat and simmer until the liquid has reduced. Remove from the heat and stir in the chopped liver, rice, dill, and mint, and season with salt and pepper. Place 1–2 tablespoons of the filling at the base of each grape leaf and roll up, folding in the sides as you go. Place any unused or torn grape leaves over the base of a wide pan. Arrange the rolls on top, seam side down, in close-fitting rows. Pour the remaining oil and 1 cup (250 ml / 8 fl oz) water over them. Invert a plate on top of the rolls to prevent them from unraveling. Cover the pan and simmer for 30 minutes, or until only a little liquid remains. Beat the eggs with the lemon juice in a bowl, then beat in 2–3 tablespoons of the cooking juices. Remove the pan from the heat and pour the egg-lemon sauce over the rolls. Re-cover and let stand for a few minutes, then transfer to a platter. Serve hot.

Serves 6
Preparation time 1 hour
Cooking time 30 minutes

Note: Chicken livers can be substituted for the lamb's liver.

Squid with nettles from Pontus, p 92

Mixed lamb skewers, p 97

LAMB ROLLS
ΤΖΙΓΕΡΟΣΑΡΜΑΔΕΣ
Tzigerosarmades

Blanch the lamb's pluck and sweetbreads in boiling water for 5 minutes, then drain. Let cool, then remove and discard any skin and fibers, and coarsely chop the meat. Heat the oil in a pan, add the scallions, pour in 1 cup (250 ml / 8 fl oz) water, and simmer for 10 minutes, until most of the water evaporates. Stir in the meat and simmer for 10–20 minutes, or until almost all the liquid has evaporated. Remove the pan from the heat, add the dill, parsley, rice, and tomato juice or water, mix well, and set aside. Preheat the oven to 400°F (200°C / Gas Mark 6) and place a rack inside an ovenproof dish or roasting pan. Rinse the cauls in cold water mixed with the vinegar, then stretch them out on a cutting (chopping) board, and cut into 5-inch (12.5-cm) rounds or squares. Place 2 tablespoons of the filling on each piece and wrap tightly into rolls. Arrange the rolls on the prepared rack, folded side down, packed closely together. At this point they can be frozen. Bake for about 20 minutes, or until golden. Remove with a slotted spoon or a spatula and drain on paper towels. Transfer to a platter and serve immediately with tossed salad greens.

Serves 4
Preparation time 6 hours (including soaking)
Cooking time 20 minutes

- 1 spring lamb's pluck (heart, liver, and spleen)
- 1 spring lamb's sweetbreads, soaked in several changes of cold water for 5 hours and drained
- 3 tablespoons olive oil
- 1 cup (7–8) chopped scallions (spring onions)
- ½ cup (15 g / ½ oz) finely chopped fresh dill
- ½ cup (25 g / 1 oz) finely chopped fresh parsley
- ¼ cup (50 g / 2 oz) short-grain rice
- 4 tablespoons tomato juice or water
- 2–3 large lamb's cauls
- 2 tablespoons red wine vinegar
- tossed salad greens (leaves), to serve

BAKED MIXED MEAT BUNDLES
ΓΑΡΔΟΥΜΠΑΚΙΑ
Gardoubakia

Wash the organ meats (offal) very well and cut them into long narrow strips. Sprinkle with the oregano and season with salt and pepper. Wash the intestines thoroughly, turning them inside out (see p 167). Blanch briefly in boiling salted water and drain. Preheat the oven to 350°F (180°C / Gas Mark 4). Wrap a long piece of intestine around 3 strips of meat at a time to form small bundles, and set aside. Heat the oil in a pan. Add the scallions and cook over low heat, stirring occasionally, for 5 minutes, until softened and translucent. Stir in the dill, lemon juice, and stock, tomato juice, or water. Arrange the bundles in a shallow ovenproof dish and pour the sauce over them. Bake for about 1 hour. Serve hot.

Serves 4
Preparation time 1 hour
Cooking time 1 hour

Note: The meat strips can also be wrapped in lamb's caul before binding them with the intestine, and grilling over charcoal.

- 1 spring lamb's pluck (heart, liver, and spleen)
- 4 lamb's kidneys, cored
- pinch of dried oregano
- salt and pepper
- 2¼ lb (1 kg) spring lamb's intestines
- ½ cup (120 ml / 4 fl oz) olive oil
- ½ cup (4) chopped scallions (spring onions)
- 3 tablespoons finely chopped fresh dill
- 2 tablespoons freshly squeezed lemon juice
- 1 cup (250 ml / 8 fl oz) meat stock, tomato juice or water

- organ meats (offal) of
  2 spring lambs: 4 kidneys,
  2 livers, and 2 hearts
- 2 lamb's sweetbreads, soaked
  in several changes of cold water
  for 5 hours and drained
- pinch of dried oregano
- salt and pepper
- 3¼ lb (1.5 kg) spring
  lamb's intestines
- about 4 cups (about 1 litre / 1¾
  pints) red wine vinegar
- 3 large lamb's cauls, soaked
  in water to soften and cut into
  medium-size pieces
- olive oil, for brushing
- radishes and scallions (spring
  onions), to garnish
- lettuce leaves, to serve

MIXED LAMB SKEWERS
ΚΟΚΟΡΕΤΣΙ
Kokoretsi

Remove and discard any tubes, cores, and membranes from the kidneys, livers, hearts, and lungs and rinse well. Sprinkle with the oregano and salt and pepper and set aside. Wash the intestines carefully and thoroughly but do not cut into pieces. Place in a bowl, pour over vinegar to cover, and set aside for 30 minutes. Rinse with plenty of cold running water and drain. Thread the organ meats onto three long skewers and wrap the cauls around them. Secure them to the skewers by winding the intestines up and around, so that they cover the whole skewer. Brush with olive oil and chill in the refrigerator until ready to cook. (You can also wrap and freeze them. When ready to cook, thaw fully first.) Preheat the broiler (grill) or light the charcoal on a barbecue. Brush with oil and broil (grill) or, preferably, grill over charcoal, brushing frequently with oil and turning, for about 1 hour, or until browned all over and no pink juices flow when the meat is pricked with a fork. Make a bed of lettuce on a platter and top with the meat. Garnish with radishes and scallions and serve hot.

Serves 8–10
Preparation time 6 hours (including soaking)
Cooking time 1 hour

Note: You can also bake *kokoretsi* in a preheated oven at 400°F (200°C / Gas Mark 6) and then brown both sides under the broiler.

☐ p 95

- organ meats (offal) of 1 spring
  lamb: 1 heart, 1 liver, and
  2 kidneys
- 1 spring lamb's sweetbreads,
  soaked in several changes of cold
  water for 5 hours and drained
- 4 tablespoons olive oil
- 1 tablespoon freshly squeezed
  lemon juice
- 4 tablespoons white wine or water
- pinch of dried oregano
- salt and pepper
- lemon wedges, to garnish

FRIED MIXED LAMB
ΠΑΣΧΑΛΙΝΗ ΤΗΓΑΝΙΑ
Paskalini tigania

Rinse all the meat and cut into small pieces. Put it into a bowl with the oil, lemon juice, wine or water, and oregano and season with salt and pepper. Cover and let marinate, turning the pieces occasionally, for 3 hours. Transfer the mixture to a large heavy skillet or frying pan and cook gently for 10 minutes, or until the liquid has evaporated. Remove the lid and continue to cook for a further 5–10 minutes, stirring occasionally, until the meats are lightly browned all over. Remove from the heat and serve immediately, garnished with lemon wedges.

Serves 4
Preparation time 8½ hours (including soaking and marinating)
Cooking time 15–20 minutes

SUMMER
ΚΑΛΟΚΑΙΡΙ
Kalokeri

With the first heat of summer, Greek mezedes change, and are permeated with the flavors and scents of the Mediterranean. Now there is
a profusion of fish and shellfish, such as sardines, *marides* (whitebait),
anchovies, mullet, langoustines, lobster, octopus, and crab, together
with fresh summer vegetables like eggplants (aubergines) and zucchini
(courgettes), simply sliced, fried, and served with tangy yogurt tzatziki
or chopped up to make a variety of tasty vegetable fritters. This is
the season for ripe tomatoes and bell peppers, raw in salads, stuffed,
or made into sauces. With their bright flavors, these delicious seasonal
mezedes, served with ouzo or ice-cold retsina, perfectly evoke the
Greek summer.

BAKED EGGPLANTS (AUBERGINES) WITH CHEESE
ΜΕΛΙΤΖΑΝΕΣ ΜΕ ΤΥΡΙΑ ΣΤΟ ΦΟΥΡΝΟ
Melitzanes me tiria sto fourno

Halve the eggplants lengthwise and, using a sharp knife, make two
lengthwise slits in the flesh of each half, taking care not to pierce
the skin. Sprinkle with salt and set aside for 30 minutes. Meanwhile,
preheat the oven to 425°F (220°C / Gas Mark 7). Rinse the eggplant
halves and gently squeeze out the excess moisture. Put them in a single
layer, cut sides up, in an ovenproof dish. Brush with oil and bake for
30 minutes, until soft and lightly browned. Remove from the oven, brush
with a little more oil, and lightly press the flesh in the center of each with
the back of a spoon to make a hollow. Lay a slice of feta in each hollow
and cover with 3–4 tablespoons of the white sauce. Place a tomato
slice on top and sprinkle each eggplant half with 4 tablespoons of the
grated cheese. Return the dish to the oven and bake for 5–10 minutes
more, until the cheese has melted and is golden brown. Serve
immediately.

Serves 4
Preparation time 45 minutes (including salting)
Cooking time 40 minutes

- 2 long, thick eggplants (aubergines)
- salt
- olive oil, for brushing
- 4 slices feta cheese
- 4 slices tomato
- 1 cup (250 ml / 8 fl oz) thick White sauce (p 57)
- 1 cup (120 g / 4 oz) grated kefalograviera, regato or pecorino cheese

- 5 large eggplants (aubergines), thinly sliced lengthwise
- salt
- ½ cup (120 ml / 4 fl oz) olive oil
- all-purpose (plain) flour, for coating
- 2 eggs, lightly beaten with 2 tablespoons olive oil
- 1⅔ cups (120 g / 4 oz) dry bread crumbs
- vegetable oil, for frying

FOR THE FILLING
- 1 tablespoon (15 g / ½ oz) butter
- 1 tablespoon all-purpose (plain) flour
- 2¾ cups (300 g / 11 oz) crumbled mild feta cheese, or half feta and half ricotta
- ⅔ cup (150 ml / ¼ pint) hot milk
- 1 egg, lightly beaten
- 1¼ cups (150 g / 5 oz) grated Sifnos kefalograviera or other hard, full-flavored cheese, such as pecorino
- ¼ teaspoon grated nutmeg
- salt and pepper

CHEESE-STUFFED EGGPLANT (AUBERGINE) ROLLS FROM SIFNOS
ΜΠΟΥΡΕΚΑΚΙΑ ΜΕΛΙΤΖΑΝΑΣ
Bourekakia melitzanas

Layer the eggplant slices in a colander, sprinkling each layer with salt, and set aside for 30 minutes. Rinse under cold running water, gently squeeze out excess water, and pat dry with paper towels. Heat half the olive oil in a large, heavy skillet or frying pan, add the eggplant slices, in batches, and fry for a few minutes on each side, until softened and lightly browned. Add more oil to the pan as necessary. Drain the cooked eggplant slices on paper towels. To make the filling, melt the butter in a pan over low heat. Stir in the flour and cook, stirring constantly, for 3–5 minutes, until lightly browned. Remove the pan from the heat and add the feta and all the milk, whisking constantly. Return to low heat and cook, whisking constantly, until the sauce is thick and almost smooth. Remove from the heat and let cool slightly. Stir in the egg, grated cheese, and nutmeg, season with salt and pepper, and let cool completely. The filling should be very thick; if it isn't, add more grated cheese. Scoop 1–2 tablespoons of the cooled filling and shape into small cylinders. Place a cylinder on one end of an eggplant slice and roll up. Repeat until all the filling and eggplant slices have been used. Spread out the flour and bread crumbs in separate shallow dishes. Coat the eggplant rolls first with flour, then with the beaten egg mixture, and finally with bread crumbs. Chill in the refrigerator for 30 minutes, until the coating has set. Heat the vegetable oil in a deep-fryer to 350–375°F (180–190°C). Add the eggplant rolls, in batches if necessary, and fry for 10 minutes, until golden brown. Remove, drain on paper towels, and serve immediately.

Note: You can also cook the eggplants under the broiler (grill) or grill on a barbecue instead of frying them. Simply brush or spray the slices with a little olive oil and cook them for 3–4 minutes on each side. Breaded bourekakia will keep in the refrigerator for up to 12 hours and in the freezer for 1 month.

Makes 25 rolls
Preparation time 1½ hours (including salting and cooling)
Cooking time 10 minutes

EGGPLANT (AUBERGINE) FRITTERS
ΜΕΛΙΤΖΑΝΟΚΕΦΤΕΔΕΣ
Melitzanokeftedes

Preheat the broiler (grill). Spread out the eggplants on a cookie sheet (baking tray) and broil (grill), turning frequently, until the skin is blackened and charred and the flesh is soft. Remove from the broiler, halve the eggplants, and scoop out the flesh. Process to a purée in a food processor. This should produce about 2 cups (450 ml / 16 fl oz) purée. Scrape it into a large bowl, stir in the cheese, eggs, baking powder, parsley, onion, and garlic, and season with salt and pepper. Mix in enough fresh bread crumbs to form a soft, pliable mixture. Chill in the refrigerator for about 1 hour. Spread out the dry bread crumbs or flour on a shallow plate. Form the eggplant mixture into patties and gently roll in the bread crumbs or flour to coat. Pour the oil into a heavy skillet or frying pan to a depth of about ½ inch (5 mm) and heat. Add the patties, in batches, and cook until browned on both sides. Remove with a slotted spoon and drain on paper towels. Serve immediately with Tzatziki.

Serves 4
Preparation time 1½ hours (including chilling)
Cooking time 15–20 minutes

- 4½ lb (2 kg) eggplants (aubergines)
- 1 cup (120 g / 4 oz) mild kefalotiri, pecorino, or other hard cheese, grated
- 2 eggs, lightly beaten
- 1 teaspoon baking powder
- 4 tablespoons fresh parsley, finely chopped
- 1 small onion, very finely chopped
- 1 garlic clove, very finely chopped
- 1¾ cups (100 g / 3½ oz) fresh bread crumbs
- fine dry bread crumbs or all-purpose (plain) flour, for coating
- vegetable oil, for frying
- salt and pepper
- Tzatziki (p 152), to serve

BARLEY RUSKS WITH TOMATOES AND BELL PEPPERS FROM CRETE
ΝΤΑΚΟΣ ΜΕ ΝΤΟΜΑΤΑ ΚΑΙ ΠΙΠΕΡΙΕΣ
Dakos me domata ke piperies

Preheat the broiler (grill). Put the bell pepper halves on a cookie sheet (baking tray) in a single layer, skin sides up. Broil (grill) for 10 minutes until the skin is charred, then remove from the heat and let cool slightly. Peel off the skin and cut the flesh into strips. Put the bell pepper strips into a bowl, add the parsley, 1 tablespoon of the oil, and the vinegar. Season with salt and pepper, and mix well. Cover with plastic wrap (cling film) and chill in the refrigerator until required. Put the tomatoes, basil or mint, oregano and 1 tablespoon of the remaining oil into another bowl, season with salt and pepper, and mix well. Lightly moisten the rusks with water. Whisk the garlic with the remaining oil in a small bowl and brush the rusks with the mixture. Cover half the rusks with the bell pepper mixture and the other half with the herbed tomato mixture. Serve immediately.

Serves 6
Preparation time 30 minutes

- 1 yellow bell pepper, halved lengthwise and seeded
- 1 red bell pepper, halved lengthwise and seeded
- 1 green bell pepper, halved lengthwise and seeded
- 2 tablespoons finely chopped fresh parsley
- ½ cup (120 ml / 4 fl oz) olive oil
- 2 tablespoons balsamic vinegar
- salt and pepper
- 3 ripe tomatoes, seeded and finely chopped
- 5 tablespoons finely chopped fresh basil or mint
- ½ teaspoon dried oregano
- 3 large Cretan barley rusks, halved (p 537)
- 2 garlic cloves, crushed

- 3 Cretan barley rusks (p 537)
- 4 large, firm, ripe tomatoes, peeled, seeded, and diced
- 11 oz (300 g) Cretan sour mizithra or feta cheese, crumbled
- pinch of dried oregano
- salt and pepper
- ½ cup (120 ml / 4 fl oz) olive oil

CRETAN RUSK SALAD
ΝΤΑΚΟΣ
Dakos

Moisten all surfaces of the rusks with water and put them on a small platter. Spoon the tomatoes and the cheese on top of the rusks, sprinkle with the oregano, and season with salt and pepper. Drizzle the oil over the top. Alternatively, whisk the olive oil with 1 crushed garlic clove and 1 tablespoon balsamic vinegar. You could also sprinkle sliced pitted (stoned) black olives on the rusks with the other ingredients. This simple Cretan appetizer is often served with *tsikoudia*.

Serves 6
Preparation time 15 minutes

☐ p 102

- 1 lb 2 oz (500 g) long mild green or red peppers
- 1 long hot green chile pepper (optional)
- 3 tablespoons olive oil (optional)
- salt
- Oil-vinegar dressing (p 57)

BROILED (GRILLED) OR FRIED PEPPERS
ΠΙΠΕΡΙΕΣ ΨΗΤΕΣ Η ΤΗΓΑΝΙΤΕΣ
Piperies psites i tiganites

Make a slit in each pepper to release the steam while cooking. Grill over charcoal or fry in the oil, turning frequently, for about 10 minutes, until browned on all sides. Transfer the peppers to a deep plate, cover with plastic wrap (cling film), and let stand for a few minutes until cool enough to handle. While they are still hot, peel off the skins and sprinkle them with salt and oil-vinegar dressing to taste. If you fried the peppers, do not add dressing, but sprinkle with 2–3 tablespoons of the frying oil, salt, and vinegar to taste. The chile pepper will give the dish a slightly spicy flavor and you can use more of them, if you like. Peppers prepared this way taste better the second day and are especially delicious with ouzo or retsina.

Serves 4
Preparation time 10 minutes
Cooking time 10 minutes

☐ p 103

Cretan rusk salad, p 101

Broiled (grilled) or fried peppers, p 101

TOMATO FRITTERS FROM SANTORINI
ΝΤΟΜΑΤΟΚΕΦΤΕΔΕΣ
Domatokeftedes

Put the tomatoes into a colander, sprinkle with 1 teaspoon salt, and let drain for 1–2 hours. Sprinkle the onions with salt and rub lightly, then rinse well under cold running water. Squeeze out excess water. Combine the onions, tomatoes, mint or parsley, and oregano in a bowl, season with pepper, and stir in enough flour to make a stiff batter. Pour oil into a heavy skillet or frying pan to a depth of 1 inch (2.5 cm) and heat. Add tablespoons of the batter, in batches, and fry for 8–10 minutes, or until golden brown on both sides. Remove with a slotted spoon and drain on paper towels. Serve immediately.

Serves 4
Preparation time 2¼ hours (including salting)
Cooking time 30 minutes

- 2¼ lb (1 kg) ripe tomatoes, seeded and diced
- 1 lb 2 oz (500 g) onions, grated
- ½ cup (25 g / 1 oz) finely chopped fresh mint or parsley
- 1 teaspoon dried oregano
- salt and pepper
- 1½ cups (175 g / 6 oz) self-rising flour
- vegetable oil, for frying

GARLIC-STUFFED ZUCCHINI (COURGETTES)
ΚΟΛΟΚΥΘΑΚΙΑ ΜΕ ΣΚΟΡΔΟ
Kolokithakia me skordo

Trim the zucchini and, using a sharp knife, make 4 evenly spaced slits lengthwise along each one, making sure not to cut right through the ends. Preheat the oven to 350°F (180°C / Gas Mark 4). Combine the garlic, parsley, paprika, and half of the oil in a bowl and season with salt and pepper. Rub the garlic mixture into every slit in each zucchini, pressing with your thumb. Arrange the zucchini side by side in a single layer in an ovenproof dish and insert a slice of feta cheese into the uppermost slit. Pour ½ cup (120 ml / 4 fl oz) water and the remaining oil over the zucchini and dust with a little flour. Cover the dish with aluminum foil and bake for about 1½ hours, or until the zucchini are soft and the sauce has reduced. Serve hot or at room temperature. This is a delicious meze to serve with ouzo.

Serves 6
Preparation time 30 minutes
Cooking time 1½ hours

▢ p 106

- 12 small zucchini (courgettes), about 2¼ lb (1 kg) total weight
- 18 garlic cloves, thinly sliced
- 1 cup (50 g / 2 oz) chopped fresh parsley
- 1 teaspoon paprika
- ⅔ cup (150 ml / ¼ pint) olive oil
- salt and pepper
- 12 small, thin slices feta cheese
- ½ cup (120 ml / 4 fl oz) water
- 2–3 tablespoons all-purpose (plain) flour

- 20 zucchini (courgette) flowers
- 4 oz (120 g) feta cheese, crumbled
- scant 1 cup (100 g / 3½ oz) grated kefalograviera or pecorino cheese
- 2 tablespoons self-rising flour, plus extra for coating
- 2 eggs, lightly beaten
- 3 tablespoons finely chopped fresh mint
- pepper
- vegetable oil, for deep-frying

CHEESE-STUFFED ZUCCHINI (COURGETTE) FLOWERS FROM ANDROS
ΚΟΛΟΚΥΘΟΑΝΘΟΙ ΜΕ ΤΥΡΙ
Kolokithoanthi me tiri

Stuffed zucchini flowers are the most popular meze served in all the tavernas of Andros island and they have a lovely name. When you want to order this meze ask for *poulakia* ("little birds").

Wash the flowers in plenty of cold running water, trim the stems, and remove the pistils and stamens. Drain well. Beat the cheeses with the flour in a bowl and stir in the beaten eggs. Add the mint, season with pepper, and mix lightly. Place a heaping (heaped) tablespoon of the cheese mixture in the center of each flower and close by gently pressing the tips of the flower together. Heat the oil in a deep-fryer to 350–375°F (180–190°C). Meanwhile, coat the stuffed flowers with flour. Deep-fry the flowers for about 5 minutes, or until golden, then drain well. Serve this delicious meze with ouzo.

Serves 4
Preparation time 30 minutes
Cooking time 10 minutes

- 6 cups (1 kg / 2¼ lb) grated zucchini (courgette)
- 4 tablespoons olive oil
- ¼ cup (1 small) grated onion
- ¾ cup (80 g / 3 oz) all-purpose (plain) flour, plus extra for coating
- 1 teaspoon baking powder
- scant 1 cup (100 g / 3½ oz) grated kefalotiri, pecorino or regato cheese
- ½ cup (40 g / 1½ oz) fine dried bread crumbs
- 3 eggs, lightly beaten
- 4 tablespoons finely chopped fresh parsley, dill or mint
- salt and pepper
- vegetable oil, for deep-frying
- Tzatziki (p 152) or Garlic sauce (p 153), to serve

ZUCCHINI (COURGETTE) FRITTERS
ΚΟΛΟΚΥΘΟΚΕΦΤΕΔΕΣ
Kolokithokeftedes

Put the grated zucchini into a colander, sprinkle with ½ teaspoon salt, and let drain for about 1 hour. Gently press the zucchini between the palms of your hands to squeeze out the liquid. Heat the olive oil in a small skillet or frying pan. Add the onion and cook over low heat, stirring occasionally, for 3–5 minutes, until softened and translucent. Sift together the flour and baking powder into a small bowl. Combine the zucchini, onion, cheese, bread crumbs, flour mixture, eggs, and herbs in a bowl and season with salt and pepper. The mixture should be firm enough to hold its shape. If it is too soft, add more bread crumbs. Chill in the refrigerator for about 1 hour to firm up the mixture. Heat the vegetable oil in a deep-fryer to 350–375°F (180–190°C). Shape the mixture into patties and coat with flour, then deep-fry, in batches if necessary, for about 5 minutes, or until golden brown on both sides. Drain on paper towels and serve hot with Tzatziki or Garlic sauce.

Serves 4
Preparation time 2½ hours (including salting and chilling)
Cooking time 30 minutes

☐ p 107

Garlic-stuffed zucchini (courgettes), p 104

Zucchini (courgette) fritters, p 105

SCRAMBLED EGGS WITH RED PEPPER SAUCE
ΣΤΡΑΠΑΤΣΑΔΑ
Strapatsada

- 4 oz (120 g) feta cheese, crumbled
- 1 tablespoon finely chopped fresh parsley
- ½ cup (120 ml / 4 fl oz) Red pepper sauce (p 61)
- 8 eggs, lightly beaten
- 3–4 tablespoons clarified butter or olive oil
- salt and pepper

Stir the cheese, parsley, and red pepper sauce into the eggs. Melt the butter or heat the oil in a deep skillet or frying pan. Pour in the egg mixture and cook over medium-low heat, stirring occasionally, for 5–10 minutes, until just set, or until cooked to your taste. Transfer to a platter, season with salt and pepper, and serve immediately. As an alternative, replace the red pepper sauce with your own tomato sauce recipe with some chopped green bell pepper and a pinch of cayenne pepper or Tabasco for extra flavor.

Serves 4
Preparation time 10 minutes
Cooking time 10 minutes

CHEESE-STUFFED VEGETABLE ROLLS
ΡΟΛΑ ΛΑΧΑΝΙΚΩΝ ΜΕ ΤΥΡΙ
Rola lahanikon me tiri

- 2 long thin eggplants (aubergines), thinly sliced lengthwise
- 2 long thin zucchini (courgettes), thinly sliced lengthwise
- ½ cup (120 ml / 4 fl oz) olive oil
- 2 thick long green peppers, halved lengthwise and seeded
- 9 oz (250 g) feta cheese, cut into thin sticks (batons)

FOR THE SAUCE
- 2 tablespoons olive oil
- 2 garlic cloves, crushed
- 2 ripe tomatoes, chopped
- 2 tablespoons finely chopped fresh mint
- salt and pepper
- dried oregano, for sprinkling

Put the eggplants and zucchini in a colander, sprinkle with salt, and let drain for 1 hour. Rinse, squeeze out the excess liquid, and pat dry with paper towels. Preheat the broiler (grill). Heat half the oil in a large skillet or frying pan, add the eggplant and zucchini slices, in batches, and cook over medium heat for 3–4 minutes on each side, until lightly browned. Add more oil as necessary. Remove and set aside. Put the pepper halves on a cookie sheet (baking tray) and broil (grill) for about 10 minutes, until charred. Remove from the heat and when cool enough to handle, peel off the skin, and cut the flesh into strips. Place a cheese baton at one end of each vegetable slice and roll it up to enclose the cheese. Arrange the rolled vegetables, side by side and seam side down, in an ovenproof dish. Preheat the oven to 400°F (200°C / Gas Mark 6). To make the sauce, heat the oil in a pan. Add the garlic and cook over low heat, stirring frequently, for 2 minutes. Add the tomatoes and mint, season with salt and pepper, cover, and simmer for 15 minutes, until thickened. Put a teaspoon of the sauce on top of each vegetable roll, sprinkle with a little oregano, and bake for about 15 minutes. Serve hot or at room temperature.

Serves 8
Preparation time 1½ hours (including salting)
Cooking time 30 minutes

EASY CHEESE APPETIZER
ΤΥΡΟΜΕΖΕΣ
Tiromezes

- 4 square, thick slices feta cheese
- 1 large tomato, cut into 4 rounds
- 1 long green chile, thinly sliced
- pinch of dried oregano
- pepper
- olive oil, for drizzling

Preheat the broiler (grill). Put the cheese slices side by side in a shallow flameproof dish. Put a tomato slice on top of each feta square and top with the slices of chile. Sprinkle with oregano and pepper and drizzle with a little oil. Cook under the broiler for 6–8 minutes, until the tomato and chile are lightly browned. Serve immediately. This is delicious with a glass of ouzo.

Serves 4
Preparation time 5 minutes
Cooking time 8 minutes

FRIED TRIANGLES
ΜΠΟΥΡΕΚΑΚΙΑ ΤΗΓΑΝΙΤΑ
Bourekakia tiganita

- 1 lb 2 oz (500 g) ready-made phyllo dough (filo pastry)
- vegetable oil, for deep-frying

FOR THE CHEESE FILLING
- ½ cup (120 ml / 4 fl oz) milk
- 1 tablespoon cream of wheat or fine semolina
- 1 egg plus 1 egg yolk, lightly beaten
- 2 tablespoons olive oil
- 4 oz (120 g) feta cheese, crumbled
- scant 1 cup (100 g / 3½ oz) grated regato, pecorino, or other hard, full-flavored cheese
- salt and pepper

FOR THE MEAT FILLING
- 5 oz (150 g) ground (minced) beef
- 2 scallions (spring onions), finely chopped
- 1 small garlic clove, finely chopped
- 1 tablespoon finely chopped fresh dill
- 1 tablespoon finely chopped fresh parsley
- 1 tablespoon olive oil
- salt and pepper
- 2–3 tablespoons milk or water

To prepare the cheese filling, combine the milk and cream of wheat or semolina in a small pan. Simmer over medium heat, stirring constantly, for 2–3 minutes, until smooth and creamy. Remove from the heat, add all the remaining cheese filling ingredients, and mix well, then season with salt and pepper. The filling should be thick, not runny. If necessary, add more feta cheese. To prepare the meat filling, combine the beef, scallions, garlic, herbs, and olive oil in a small bowl and season with salt and pepper. Add enough milk or water to make a soft but not runny mixture. With a sharp knife, cut a 2-inch (5-cm) piece off the phyllo roll and cover the remaining roll to prevent it from drying out. Unroll the dough strips on a work surface. Put a teaspoon of cheese or meat filling in one corner of a strip and fold the other corner over the filling to form a triangle. Fold the triangle over and over on itself to the end of the strip, moistening the edge to seal and form a neat, small triangle. Repeat with the remaining phyllo and fillings. At this point, the triangles can be frozen, layered with wax (greaseproof) paper in an airtight container. Keep the cheese and meat triangles separate. When ready to cook, heat the vegetable oil in a deep-fryer to 350–375°F (180–190°C). Add the triangles to the hot oil, in batches if necessary, and cook for 5 minutes, or until golden brown. (It is not necessary to thaw them if frozen.) Drain and serve immediately.

Makes 50–60 triangles
Preparation time 1½ hours
Cooking time 15–30 minutes

ANCHOVY FRITTERS
ΓΑΥΡΟΚΕΦΤΕΔΕΣ
Gavrokeftedes

Pinch the head of a fish between your thumb and forefinger and pull it off—the guts should come away with it. Cut off the tail, pinch all along the top edge of the fish, and pull out the backbone—it should come away easily. Repeat with all the remaining fish. Rinse well, drain, and finely chop with a sharp knife. Tear the bread into small pieces, put it into a bowl, and add water to cover. Let soak for 20 minutes, then squeeze dry. Combine the fish, bread, onion, garlic, eggs, tomato, oregano, mint, olive oil, and vinegar in a bowl and season with salt and pepper. Gradually stir in enough flour to make a thick batter. Pour vegetable oil into a skillet or frying pan to the depth of about 1 inch (2.5 cm) and heat. Add spoonfuls of the batter, in batches, and cook over medium heat until golden brown on both sides. Drain on paper towels. Serve the fritters hot with Garlic sauce.

Serves 4
Preparation time 40 minutes
Cooking time 30 minutes

- 2¼ lb (1 kg) fresh anchovies
- 3 slices day-old bread, crusts removed
- 1 cup (1 large) grated onion
- 4 garlic cloves, very finely chopped
- 2 eggs, lightly beaten
- 1 large tomato, peeled and chopped
- 1 teaspoon dried oregano
- ½ cup (25 g / 1 oz) finely chopped fresh mint or 1 tablespoon dried mint
- 3 tablespoons olive oil
- 1 tablespoon red wine vinegar
- salt and pepper
- 2–3 tablespoons all-purpose (plain) flour
- vegetable oil, for frying
- Garlic sauce (p 153), to serve

PICKLED ANCHOVIES WITH GARLIC
ΓΑΥΡΑΚΙΑ ΣΤΟ ΞΥΔΙ
Gavrakia sto xidi

Pinch the head of a fish between your thumb and forefinger and pull it off—the guts should come away with it. Cut off the tail, pinch all along the top edge of the fish, and pull out the backbone—it should come away easily. Repeat with all the remaining fish. Rinse and drain well. Arrange the anchovies side by side on the base of a shallow, flat glass or other non-porous dish. Sprinkle with a little salt, garlic slices, and oregano or thyme. Make another layer, if necessary, until all the fish are used. Carefully pour in enough vinegar to cover the fish. Cover the dish with plastic wrap (cling film) and chill in the refrigerator for 24 hours. Drain off the vinegar and remove and discard the garlic. Pour in enough oil to cover the fish. They are now ready to serve, but can be stored in the refrigerator up to 15 days. This is a perfect meze for ouzo.

Serves 6
Preparation time 25 hours (including marinating)

- 2¼ lb (1 kg) fresh anchovies
- salt and pepper
- 4 garlic cloves, thinly sliced
- dried oregano or thyme, for sprinkling
- about 2¼ cups (500 ml / 18 fl oz) red wine vinegar
- about 2¼ cups (500 ml / 18 fl oz) olive oil

- 1 lb 2 oz (500 g) whitebait or other tiny fish
- 1 onion, thinly sliced
- salt and pepper
- all-purpose (plain) flour, to coat
- ½ cup (120 ml / 4 fl oz) olive oil

FRIED WHITEBAIT PIE FROM CHIOS
ΓΟΝΑΡΑΚΙ Η ΜΑΡΙΔΟΠΙΤΑ ΣΤΟ ΤΗΓΑΝΙ
Gonaraki i maridopita sto tigani

Rinse the fish, drain, and dry on paper towels. Put the onion in a colander, sprinkle with a little salt, and set aside for 30 minutes. Rinse and squeeze out excess liquid. Combine the fish and onion in a bowl, season with salt and pepper, add enough flour to coat, and toss well. Heat the oil in a heavy, nonstick skillet or frying pan and add the fish, spreading them out to cover the base of the pan and pressing them with a spatula so that they stick to each other. The layer of fish should be no thicker than 1 inch (2.5 cm), so you may need to cook in batches. Cook over medium heat for 8–10 minutes, until set, then turn over. (The easiest way to do this is to invert a plate over the pan and, holding the two together, turn the layer of fish onto the plate. Slide the fish back into the pan to cook the second side.) Cook for 8 minutes more, until lightly browned. Serve immediately. This is an excellent meze with ouzo.

Serves 4
Preparation time 45 minutes (including salting)
Cooking time 20 minutes

☐ p 112

- 2¼ lb (1 kg) fresh sardines, scaled (see p 114)
- ½ cup (120 ml / 4 fl oz) olive oil
- dried oregano (optional)
- 2 garlic cloves, finely chopped
- 4 tablespoons finely chopped fresh parsley
- salt and pepper
- Oil-lemon dressing (p 57)
- lemon slices and grilled tomatoes, to garnish

GRILLED SARDINES
ΣΑΡΔΕΛΕΣ ΨΗΤΕΣ
Sardeles psites

Cut off and discard the heads of the sardines. Slit the belly of each fish all the way down to the tail and pull out the guts. Rinse well. Open out the fish and place skin side up on a cutting (chopping) board. Press firmly along the backbone with the flat of your hand, then turn the fish over, pull away the backbone with your fingers, and cut it off at the tail end with kitchen scissors. Rinse the sardines again, drain, and line them up on a large tray. Combine half the oil, the oregano, garlic, and 1 tablespoon parsley in a bowl and season with salt and pepper. Drizzle the mixture over the fish. Brush a hinged wire rack with oil and place the fish in pairs (belly to belly) on it. Brush with oil, close the rack, and grill over charcoal for 4 minutes on each side. (You could also cook the sardines under the broiler (grill) in the kitchen.) Transfer to a platter, sprinkle with the remaining parsley, drizzle with oil-lemon dressing and garnish with lemon slices and grilled tomatoes. Excellent with *tsipouro* or ouzo.

Serves 4
Preparation time 30 minutes
Cooking time 10 minutes

Fried whitebait pie from Chios, p 111

sardines in oil and oregano, p 114

SARDINES IN OIL AND OREGANO
ΣΑΡΔΕΛΕΣ ΛΑΔΟΡΙΓΑΝΗ
Sardeles ladorigani

- 2¼ lb (1 kg) fresh sardines or anchovies
- ½ cup (120 ml / 4 fl oz) olive oil
- 5–6 garlic cloves, sliced
- 2 tablespoons red wine vinegar
- pinch of dried oregano
- salt and pepper

Scale the sardines by running one hand from tail to head while holding the fish by the tail under cold running water. Alternatively, put them in cold water to cover and rub with your fingers to remove the scales. Anchovies do not require scaling. Cut off and discard the heads of the sardines. To remove the guts, gently squeeze the belly of each fish, hold down the guts with a knife as they are exposed, and pull them out. To clean anchovies, pinch the head of a fish between your thumb and forefinger and pull it off—the guts should come away with it. Cut off the tail, pinch all along the top edge of the fish, and pull out the backbone—it should come away easily. Repeat with all the remaining anchovies. Rinse the fish, drain, and pat dry with paper towels. Heat the oil in a large heavy skillet or frying pan over high heat. Add the garlic and cook, stirring constantly, for about 1 minute. Put the fish in a single layer to cover the base of the skillet or frying pan, sprinkle with the vinegar and oregano, and season with salt and pepper. Cook over high heat for about 20 minutes, until the liquid has reduced. Serve hot or at room temperature. Alternatively, arrange the fish in a single layer with all the other ingredients in an ovenproof dish and bake in a preheated oven at 400°F (200°C / Gas Mark 6) for 20–30 minutes, or until the sardines are cooked and the liquid has reduced.

Serves 4
Preparation time 30 minutes
Cooking time 20–30 minutes

□ p 113

FRIED MUSSELS
ΜΥΔΙΑ ΤΗΓΑΝΙΤΑ
Midia tiganita

- vegetable oil, for deep-frying
- 2¼ lb (1 kg) large mussels, shucked (see p 324)
- Batter for frying (p 47) or all-purpose (plain) flour, for coating
- salt and pepper
- lemon wedges, to garnish
- Tzatziki (p 152), Eggplant (Aubergine) dip (p 152), or Taramosalata (p 157), to serve

Heat the oil in a deep-fryer to 390°F (200°C). Dip the mussels, one by one, in the batter or coat with flour, shaking off any excess. Carefully drop the mussels into the hot oil and deep-fry for a few minutes, until golden brown. Fry only a few mussels at a time to avoid lowering the temperature of the oil. Remove with a slotted spoon, drain, and arrange on a warm platter. Season with salt and pepper. Garnish with lemon wedges and serve immediately with Tzatziki, Eggplant (Aubergine) dip, or Taramosalata.

Serves 4
Preparation time 30 minutes
Cooking time 15 minutes

- 1 lb 2 oz (500 g) shrimp (prawns), peeled and deveined
- 4–5 scallions (spring onions) with long green leaves
- 2 tablespoons olive oil, plus extra for brushing
- 1 garlic clove, finely chopped
- 2 teaspoons all-purpose (plain) flour
- 4 tablespoons heavy (double) cream
- generous 1 cup (250 g / 9 oz) crab meat, flaked
- 2 tablespoons chopped fresh dill
- salt and pepper
- 9 sheets of phyllo dough (filo pastry)

FOR THE SAUCE
- 2 tablespoons freshly squeezed lemon juice
- 4 tablespoons olive oil
- 1 garlic clove, finely chopped
- 2 tablespoons finely chopped scallions (spring onions)
- 2 tablespoons finely chopped fresh dill
- 2 tablespoons finely chopped fresh parsley
- salt and pepper

SHELLFISH IN PHYLLO (FILO) PARCELS
ΔΕΜΑΤΑΚΙΑ ΜΕ ΘΑΛΑΣΣΙΝΑ
Dematakia me thalasina

Cut the shrimp into small pieces and set aside. Cut the leaves off from the scallions and discard any wilted ones. Finely chop the white part and blanch the green leaves in boiling water for 1–2 minutes, until pliable. Drain and set aside. Heat the oil in a pan. Add the chopped scallions and garlic and cook over low heat, stirring occasionally, for 3–5 minutes, until softened and translucent. Add the shrimp and cook, stirring frequently, for about 5 minutes, until they turn pink. Sprinkle with the flour and cook, stirring constantly, for 1 minute more. Stir in the cream and remove from the heat. Add the crab meat and dill and season with salt and pepper. Preheat the oven to 350°F (180°C / Gas Mark 4) and brush a cookie sheet (baking tray) with oil. Cut the phyllo sheets in half lengthwise. Brush the top half of each strip with oil and fold the bottom half over it. Brush again with oil, place a tablespoon of shrimp filling on the center bottom of each piece of dough and roll up. Twist the ends lightly and tie each parcel with the blanched scallion leaves. Put the parcels on the prepared cookie sheet, brush with oil, and sprinkle with a little water. Bake for 10–15 minutes, or until lightly browned. Meanwhile, prepare the sauce. Put all the ingredients in a blender and process until smooth and thick. Serve the shellfish parcels hot, accompanied by the herb sauce.

Makes 16–18 parcels
Preparation time 40 minutes
Cooking time 15 minutes

- 2¼ lb (1 kg) mussels
- 5 tablespoons olive oil
- 6 garlic gloves, thinly sliced
- ½ cup (120 ml / 4 fl oz) dry white wine
- 2 tablespoons finely chopped fresh oregano or marjoram or ½ teaspoon dried oregano
- salt and pepper
- 4 tablespoons heavy (double) cream

WINE-STEAMED MUSSELS FROM MYKONOS
ΜΥΔΙΑ ΑΧΝΙΣΤΑ ΣΕ ΚΡΑΣΙ
Midia ahnista se krasi

Scrub the mussels under cold running water and pull off the beards. Discard any with damaged shells or that do not shut immediately when sharply tapped. Drain the mussels well in a colander. Heat the oil in a large heavy pan. Add the garlic and cook over low heat, stirring frequently, for a few minutes, until lightly browned. Increase the heat to high, add the mussels, wine, and herbs, and season with salt and pepper. Cover and cook, shaking the pan occasionally, for 3–5 minutes, until the shells open. Remove from the heat and discard any that remain shut. Pour in the cream, shake to distribute evenly, and serve immediately with some of the pan juices. They are delicious with ouzo.

Serves 4
Preparation time 30 minutes
Cooking time 5 minutes

STUFFED MUSSELS
ΜΥΔΙΑ ΓΕΜΙΣΤΑ
Midia gemista

- ○ 4½ lb (2 kg) mussels
- ○ 2 tablespoons finely chopped fresh parsley
- ○ 4 garlic cloves, finely chopped
- ○ ¾ cup (40 g / 1½ oz) fresh bread crumbs
- ○ 5 tablespoons grated kefalotiri or pecorino cheese
- ○ 4 tablespoons olive oil
- ○ salt and pepper
- ○ lemon wedges, to garnish
- ○ buttered toast, to serve

Scrub the mussels under cold running water and pull off the beards. Discard any with damaged shells or that do not shut immediately when sharply tapped. Bring 2 cups (450 ml / 16 fl oz) water to a boil in a pan. Add the mussels and simmer for 8 minutes. Drain and discard any mussels that remain shut. Preheat the broiler (grill). Combine the parsley, garlic, bread crumbs, cheese, and half the oil in a bowl and season with salt and pepper. Discard the empty half shells. Put 1 tablespoon of the cheese mixture into each half shell and put the shells, filled side up, in a flameproof dish. Broil (grill) for 7–8 minutes, or until the topping is lightly browned. Drizzle the remaining oil over them and garnish with lemon wedges. Serve hot straight from the dish, accompanied by buttered toast.

Serves 4
Preparation time 30 minutes
Cooking time 10 minutes

▢ p 118

MUSSEL SAGANAKI WITH TOMATO FROM CHALKIDIKI
ΜΥΔΙΑ ΣΑΓΑΝΑΚΙ ΜΕ ΝΤΟΜΑΤΑ
Midia saganaki me domata

- ○ 1lb 2 oz (500 g) mussels, shucked (see p 324)
- ○ ¼ cup (60 ml / 2 fl oz) olive oil
- ○ ¼ cup (60 ml / 2 fl oz) water
- ○ 1 tablespoon tomato paste
- ○ 2 tablespoons finely chopped fresh or 1 teaspoon dried oregano
- ○ 1 red chile pepper, finely chopped
- ○ salt and pepper

Rinse the mussels, drain well, and pat dry with paper towels. Combine the oil, water, tomato paste, half the oregano, and the chile pepper in a pan, season with salt and pepper and bring to a boil. Lower the heat, cover, and simmer for 5 minutes. Increase the heat, add the mussels and cook for 5 minutes, or until just tender, shaking the pan 2 or 3 times. Remove from the heat, sprinkle with the remaining oregano, and serve immediately.

Serves 4
Preparation time 30 minutes
Cooking time 10 minutes

▢ p 119

- 1 octopus, about 3¼ lb (1.5 kg)
- ½ cup (120 ml / 4 fl oz) red wine vinegar
- 1 large onion, grated
- 2 garlic cloves, crushed
- ¼ cup (2–3) finely chopped scallions (spring onions)
- 5 oz (150 g) day-old bread, crusts removed, soaked in water and squeezed out
- 1 ripe tomato, peeled, seeded, and puréed
- 2 teaspoons dried oregano
- 3 tablespoons finely chopped fresh mint
- salt and pepper
- vegetable oil, for deep-frying
- all-purpose (plain) flour, for coating
- Garlic sauce (p 153) or Taramosalata (p 157), to serve

OCTOPUS CROQUETTES FROM KALYMNOS
ΟΧΤΑΠΟΔΟΚΕΦΤΕΔΕΣ
Ohtapokeftedes

Rinse and prepare the octopus for cooking (see p 325). Put it into a large pan, pour in the vinegar and enough water to cover, and cook for about 1 hour, until tender. Drain and let cool. Grind the octopus in a food processor or with two knives in a crisscross action. Transfer to a bowl, add the onion, garlic, scallions, soaked bread, tomato, oregano, and mint, season with salt and pepper, and knead lightly until the mixture is spongy and smooth. Cover and chill in the refrigerator for 1 hour. Heat the oil in a deep-fryer to 350–375°F (180–190°C). Shape the mixture into small balls and coat with flour, shaking off the excess. Deep-fry for about 5–10 minutes, or until golden brown. Serve hot accompanied by Garlic sauce or Taramosalata.

Serves 4
Preparation time 1½ hours (including chilling)
Cooking time 1¼ hours

- 1 cup (50 g / 2 oz) fresh bread crumbs
- ¼ teaspoon cayenne pepper
- 1 garlic clove, finely chopped
- 6 tablespoons melted butter
- salt
- 12 scallops on the half shell

BROILED (GRILLED) SCALLOPS
ΚΤΕΝΙΑ ΨΗΤΑ
Ktenia psita

Preheat the broiler (grill). Combine the bread crumbs, cayenne pepper, garlic, and melted butter in a bowl and season with salt. Arrange the scallops in a roasting pan just large enough to hold them in a single layer. Sprinkle each scallop with plenty of the bread crumb mixture and cook under the broiler for 2–3 minutes, or until the topping is browned and the scallop is just tender. Serve immediately. Alternatively, you can broil (grill) the scallops sprinkled with a mixture of melted butter, lemon juice, a few drops Tabasco sauce, crushed garlic, salt, and white pepper. Do not overcook or the scallops will become tough; 2–3 minutes to heat through is perfect.

Serves 4
Preparation time 10 minutes
Cooking time 3 minutes

Stuffed mussels, p 116

Mussel saganaki with tomato from Chalkidiki, p 116

BROILED SHRIMP (GRILLED PRAWNS)
ΓΑΡΙΔΕΣ ΣΤΗ ΣΚΑΡΑ
Garides stis skara

Peel and devein the shrimp, leaving the tails intact, then rinse, and drain. Put them into a bowl. Combine the lemon juice, oil, garlic, mustard, and parsley in a bowl, season with salt and pepper, pour the mixture over the shrimp, and toss well. Let marinate for at least 1 hour. Preheat the broiler (grill). Drain the shrimp and put them in the broiler pan. Broil (grill) for about 4 minutes on each side. Serve immediately.

Serves 4
Preparation time 1 hour 20 minutes (including marinating)
Cooking time 10 minutes

- 2¼ lb (1 kg) jumbo shrimp (king prawns)
- 2 tablespoons freshly squeezed lemon juice
- 4 tablespoons olive oil
- 1 small garlic clove, finely chopped
- 1 teaspoon Dijon mustard
- 1 tablespoon finely chopped fresh parsley
- salt and pepper

SHRIMP (PRAWN) AND EGGPLANT (AUBERGINE) ROLLS
ΜΠΟΥΡΕΚΑΚΙΑ ΜΕΛΙΤΖΑΝΑΣ ΜΕ ΓΑΡΙΔΕΣ
Bourekakia melitzanas me garides

Preheat the broiler (grill). Sprinkle the eggplant strips with a little salt and brush with a little olive oil. Broil (grill) for 2 minutes on each side, until lightly golden. Remove from the heat and set aside. Cut the shrimp in half and wrap a strip of eggplant around each piece. Beat the egg whites with the olive oil in a shallow dish. Spread out the bread crumbs and flour in separate shallow dishes. Season with salt and pepper. Coat the shrimp rolls first with the flour, then in the egg white mixture, and, finally, in the bread crumbs. Heat the vegetable oil in a deep-fryer to 350–375°F (180–190°C). Deep-fry the shrimp rolls for 10 minutes, or until golden. Serve immediately.

Makes 20 rolls
Preparation time 40 minutes
Cooking time 10 minutes

- 4 long eggplants (aubergines), cut lengthwise into thin strips
- 2 tablespoons olive oil, plus extra for brushing
- 10 jumbo shrimp (king prawns), peeled and deveined
- 2 egg whites
- dried bread crumbs, for coating
- all-purpose (plain) flour, for coating
- salt and pepper
- vegetable oil, for deep-frying

- 4 tablespoons olive oil
- 1 onion, finely chopped
- 7 oz (200 g) canned chopped or fresh tomatoes, peeled and diced
- ½ teaspoon sugar
- 5 tablespoons dry white wine
- 2 teaspoons dried oregano
- salt and pepper
- 16 jumbo shrimp (king prawns), peeled and deveined
- 3 tablespoons finely chopped fresh parsley or mint
- 3½ oz (100 g) feta cheese, diced

SHRIMP (PRAWN) SAGANAKI
ΓΑΡΙΔΕΣ ΣΑΓΑΝΑΚΙ
Garides saganaki

Heat the oil in a pan. Add the onion and cook over medium heat, stirring occasionally, for 4–5 minutes, until softened and translucent. Add the tomatoes, sugar, wine, and oregano and season with salt and pepper. Increase the heat to high and cook, uncovered, over high heat for 10 minutes, until thickened. Meanwhile, preheat the broiler (grill). Add the shrimp to the pan and cook for a few minutes more. Stir in the parsley or mint and transfer the mixture to a small flameproof dish. Sprinkle the cheese on top and broil (grill) for 5 minutes, until the cheese is melted and lightly browned. Serve immediately.

Serves 4
Preparation time 15 minutes
Cooking time 20 minutes

- 2¼ lb (1 kg) large squid
- 4 tablespoons olive oil, plus extra for brushing
- ½ cup (4) finely chopped scallions (spring onions)
- salt and pepper
- 4 tablespoons finely chopped fresh parsley
- 1 large red Florina or bell pepper, roasted and diced
- 5 oz (150 g) kefalograviera, regato or pecorino cheese, diced
- ¼ teaspoon cayenne pepper

FOR THE SAUCE
- 2 tablespoons freshly squeezed lemon juice
- 4 tablespoons olive oil
- 1 tablespoon finely chopped fresh parsley
- salt and pepper

GRILLED STUFFED SQUID
ΚΑΛΑΜΑΡΙΑ ΓΕΜΙΣΤΑ ΣΤΗ ΣΚΑΡΑ
Kalamaria gemista sti skara

Clean the squid (see p 325) and rinse. Set the body sacs aside and finely chop the tentacles and fins. Heat the oil in a pan. Add the scallions and cook over low heat, stirring occasionally, for 3–5 minutes, until softened. Add the chopped squid, season with salt and pepper, and cook, stirring constantly, until the pan juices have reduced. Remove from the heat, stir in the parsley, bell pepper, cheese, and cayenne pepper. Stuff the squid body sacs two-thirds full with the mixture and secure the opening with a wooden toothpick. Brush with olive oil and place on a hot, oiled, hinged wire barbecue basket. Grill on the barbecue, brushing occasionally with olive oil, for about 7 minutes on each side. To make the sauce, put all the ingredients into a screw-top jar, fasten the lid, and shake vigorously until thoroughly blended. Transfer the squid to a platter, slice, pour the sauce over them, and serve immediately.

Vefa's secret: Because squid shrink as they cook, steam the body sacs for 5 minutes first. That way you'll know exactly how much filling to add. In any case, do not overfill them or they will burst during cooking.

Serves 4
Preparation time 30 minutes
Cooking time 30 minutes

FALL (AUTUMN)
ΦΘΙΝΟΠΩΡΟ
Fthinoporo

The first cool days of fall (autumn) see another change in the range of mezedes, which now include seasonal ingredients such as legumes (pulses), chicken, salt fish, and all kinds of fritters made with pumpkin, garbanzo beans (chickpeas), fava (broad) beans, lentils, and potatoes. These dishes tantalize the palate and enliven the spirits during the cold days leading up to Christmas.

VEGETABLE FRITTERS
ΣΟΥΤΖΟΥΚΑΚΙΑ ΛΑΧΑΝΙΚΩΝ
Soutzoukakia lahanikon

Put the potatoes, carrots, and zucchini into a colander, toss with a little salt, and let drain for about 1 hour. Meanwhile, heat 2 tablespoons of the oil in a small pan. Add the onion and cook over low heat, stirring occasionally, for 3–5 minutes, until softened and translucent. Put the salted vegetables in a bowl, add the onion, parsley, mint, and egg, season with pepper, and stir in as much flour as necessary to make a stiff mixture that holds its shape. Dampen your hands and shape scoops of the mixture into patties. Heat the remaining oil in a large skillet or frying pan. Coat the patties with flour, shaking off the excess, and fry in the hot oil on both sides for 5–7 minutes, until golden brown. Drain on paper towels. Serve hot or at room temperature.

Makes 30 fritters
Preparation time 1½ hours (including salting)
Cooking time 5–7 minutes

- 2¼ cups (500 g / 1 lb 2 oz) grated potatoes
- 4 carrots, grated
- 4 zucchini (courgettes), grated
- ⅔ cup (150 ml / ¼ pint) olive oil
- ½ cup grated onion
- 4 tablespoons finely chopped fresh parsley
- 4 tablespoons finely chopped fresh mint
- 1 egg, lightly beaten
- salt and pepper
- about ½ cup (50 g / 2 oz) all-purpose (plain) flour, plus extra for coating

---

POTATO FRITTERS
ΠΑΤΑΤΟΚΕΦΤΕΔΕΣ
Patatokeftedes

Cook the potatoes in salted boiling water for 20–30 minutes, until soft. Drain, peel and purée in a food processor. Transfer the purée to a bowl, add the eggs, cheese, parsley, and onion, season with salt and pepper, and mix well. Cover with plastic wrap (cling film) and chill for 1–2 hours. Shape the potato mixture into patties with your hands and coat with bread crumbs or flour. Heat the oil in a deep-fryer to 350–375°F (180–190°C). Add the patties to the hot oil in batches, and cook for 5–10 minutes, until golden brown. Drain well and serve immediately.

Makes 20–25 fritters
Preparation time 2½ hours (including chilling)
Cooking time 30 minutes

- 2¼ lb (1 kg) potatoes, unpeeled
- 1 egg, plus 2 egg yolks, lightly beaten
- ¾ cup (80 g / 3 oz) grated kefalotiri, Parmesan or regato cheese
- 2 tablespoons finely chopped fresh parsley
- 2 tablespoons finely chopped onion
- salt and pepper
- fine bread crumbs or all-purpose (plain) flour, for coating
- vegetable oil, for deep-frying

- 15 long green peppers
- 9 oz (250 g) feta cheese, crumbled
- 2 tablespoons olive oil, plus extra for brushing
- pinch of dried oregano
- salt and pepper
- 1 hot green chile, finely chopped
- 1 tablespoon finely chopped fresh parsley
- 3–4 thick slices of bread, crusts removed, cut into large cubes

PEPPERS STUFFED WITH FETA
ΠΙΠΕΡΙΕΣ ΓΕΜΙΣΤΕΣ ΜΕ ΦΕΤΑ
Piperies gemistes me feta

Preheat the broiler (grill). Cut off tops of the peppers and remove the seeds, taking care not to pierce the sides. Combine the feta, olive oil, and oregano in a bowl, season with salt and pepper, and mash with a fork until smooth. Stir in the chile and parsley. Fill the peppers with the cheese mixture and insert a cube of bread to close the opening to prevent the cheese from leaking during cooking. Put the peppers into a flameproof dish or roasting pan, brush with a little olive oil, and cook under the broiler, turning so that all sides are cooked, for 15 minutes. The stuffed peppers can also be fried in a nonstick skillet or frying pan brushed with a little olive oil. Served hot or cold, this is a perfect meze with ouzo.

Makes 15 peppers
Preparation time 20 minutes
Cooking time 15 minutes

□ p 124

- 2¼ lb (1 kg) pumpkin or other yellow winter squash, peeled and grated
- 1⅔ cups (150 g / 5 oz) finely chopped spinach
- 3–4 fresh garlic stems, finely chopped, or 1 small garlic clove, finely chopped
- ½ cup (4) finely chopped scallions (spring onions)
- 5 tablespoons finely chopped fresh dill
- 5 tablespoons finely chopped fennel fronds
- 4 tablespoons finely chopped fresh mint
- salt and pepper
- 3 eggs, lightly beaten
- 2¼ cups (250 g / 9 oz) crumbled feta or other mild cheese
- pinch of ground cumin (optional)
- pinch of ground cinnamon (optional)
- scant 1½ cups (100 g / 3½ oz) dry bread crumbs
- all-purpose (plain) flour, for coating
- olive oil, for frying

PUMPKIN FRITTERS
ΚΕΦΤΕΔΕΣ ΜΕ ΚΙΤΡΙΝΟ ΚΟΛΟΚΥΘΙ
Keftedes me kitrino kolokithi

Put the grated pumpkin or squash into a colander, sprinkle with a little salt and let drain for 1–2 hours. Squeeze out the moisture with your hands. Combine the spinach, garlic, scallions, and herbs in a large bowl, sprinkle with salt and pepper, and knead the mixture lightly to bruise it. Add the drained pumpkin, eggs, cheese, and spices, if using, then gradually mix in the bread crumbs until the mixture is soft and pliable. Chill in the refrigerator for 30 minutes. Shape the pumpkin mixture into large round patties, coat them with flour, and flatten with the palms of your hands. Pour olive oil into a heavy skillet or frying pan to a depth of 1 inch (2.5 cm) and heat. Fry the patties in batches over medium heat for about 5 minutes, or until they are lightly browned on both sides. Remove with a spatula and drain on paper towels. These fritters are delicious served either hot or cold, accompanied by Tzatziki (p 152), Garlic sauce (p 153), or Eggplant (Aubergine) dip (p 152).

Makes 20–25 fritters
Preparation time 3 hours (including salting and chilling)
Cooking time 15 minutes

□ p 125

Peppers stuffed with feta, p 123

pumpkin fritters, p 123

FRITTERED GREENS BAKED WITH SAUCE
ΧΟΡΤΟΚΕΦΤΕΔΕΣ ΜΕ ΣΑΛΤΣΑ
Hortokeftedes me saltsa

Rinse the greens, drain well, and chop. Put them into a colander, sprinkle with a little salt, and rub with your fingers until wilted. Drain and squeeze out excess water. Put the greens, scallions, grated onion, dill, mint, oregano, eggs, feta, and oil in a bowl, season with salt and pepper, and mix in enough flour to make a thick batter. Stir in the baking powder. Pour oil into a large skillet or frying pan to a depth of about ¾ inch (1.5 cm) and heat. Add large spoonfuls of the batter and cook over medium heat on both sides until lightly browned. Remove with a spatula and drain the fritters on paper towels. Add the potatoes to the pan and cook on both sides until lightly browned. Remove with a spatula and drain on paper towels. Make a layer of all the potato rounds in the base of an ovenproof dish. Put the fritters on top. Put all the sauce ingredients in a small pan and simmer, stirring occasionally, for 15 minutes. Meanwhile, preheat the oven to 400°F (200°C / Gas Mark 6). Pour the sauce over the fritters and bake for 15–20 minutes. Serve immediately.

Makes 15–20 fritters
Preparation time 30 minutes
Cooking time 45 minutes

FOR THE FRITTERS
- 1½ lb (700 g) assorted leafy greens, such as spinach, mustard, endive, chard, fennel, amaranth, and arugula (rocket), trimmed
- 3 scallions (spring onions), finely chopped
- ¼ cup (1 small) grated onion
- 4 tablespoons finely chopped fresh dill
- 4 tablespoons finely chopped fresh mint
- 1 teaspoon dried oregano
- 2 eggs, lightly beaten
- 5 oz (150 g) feta cheese, crumbled
- 4 tablespoons olive oil, plus extra for frying
- salt and pepper
- about 1 cup (120 g / 4 oz) self-rising flour
- 1 teaspoon baking powder
- 2 large potatoes, sliced into ¼-inch (5-mm) rounds

FOR THE SAUCE
- 4 tablespoons olive oil
- 1½ cups (350 ml / 12 fl oz) tomato juice
- 4 tablespoons dry red wine
- 1 teaspoon sugar
- 1 small hot or mild chile, finely chopped

FRIED HALLOUMI CHEESE FROM CYPRUS
ΧΑΛΟΥΜΙ ΤΗΓΑΝΙΤΟ
Haloumi tiganito

Slice halloumi cheese into ½-inch (5-mm) thick pieces and fry in hot oil for 2–3 minutes on each side, until golden. Remove the fried cheese from the skillet or frying pan, drain well, and arrange on a plate. Sprinkle with freshly squeezed lemon juice and black pepper. Serve immediately.

Note: For a lighter version, broil (grill) the cheese and serve sprinkled with the lemon juice. If you cannot find halloumi cheese, use provolone.

Preparation time 5 minutes
Cooking time 5 minutes

📖 p 128

- 6 cups (700 g / 1½ lb) grated kaseri or Gouda cheese
- 2 tablespoons all-purpose (plain) flour
- 3 egg whites, lightly beaten
- ¼ teaspoon white pepper
- corn oil, for deep-frying

CHEESE CROQUETTES
ΚΡΟΚΕΤΕΣ ΤΥΡΙΟΥ
Kroketes tiriou

Combine the cheese, flour, beaten egg whites, and white pepper in a bowl. Chill in the refrigerator until the mixture is thick and pliable. If it is too soft and sticky, add more grated cheese until the mixture is firm enough to be shaped. Scoop up spoonfuls of the mixture and shape into little balls with your hands. At this stage the croquettes can be frozen or stored in the refrigerator until ready to use. Heat the corn oil in a deep-fryer to 350–375°F (180-190°C). Add the croquettes and cook, turning frequently, for about 15 minutes, until golden brown all over. Remove with a slotted spoon and drain on paper towels. Serve hot.

Makes 30 croquettes
Preparation time 40 minutes (including chilling)
Cooking time 15 minutes

Note: Cheese croquettes can be dipped in beaten egg white and rolled in fine dry bread crumbs before frying. This gives them a better shape.

- 2 eggs, lightly beaten
- 1 egg yolk, lightly beaten
- 4 tablespoons evaporated milk
- 1 lb 2 oz (500 g) feta cheese, crumbled
- ¼ teaspoon white pepper
- pinch of grated nutmeg
- 5 tablespoons melted butter
- 5 tablespoons olive oil, plus extra for brushing
- 1 lb 2 oz (500 g) ready-made phyllo dough (filo pastry)
- 1 egg yolk, beaten with 1 teaspoon water, for brushing
- sesame seeds, for sprinkling

BAKED CHEESE TRIANGLES
ΤΥΡΟΠΙΤΑΚΙΑ
Tiropitakia

Lightly mix together the eggs, egg yolk, milk, cheese, white pepper, and nutmeg in a bowl. If the mixture is thin and runny, add some more cheese. Combine the butter with the oil in a bowl. Lay the roll of phyllo on a cutting (chopping) board and cut off a piece 2½ inches (6 cm) wide. Keep the remaining roll tightly covered to prevent it from drying out. Unroll the cut strips and lay one on top of another, lightly brushing each one with the oil mixture. Put 1 teaspoon of the cheese filling in one corner and fold the other corner over it to form a triangle. Then fold the triangle over and over on itself to the end of the strip. Repeat the procedure with the remaining strips of phyllo. Preheat the oven to 400°F (200°C / Gas Mark 6) and brush a cookie sheet (baking tray) with oil. Arrange the triangles on the prepared cookie sheet. (At this stage you can wrap and freeze them. Remove from the freezer 10 minutes before baking.) Brush with the egg yolk mixture and sprinkle with sesame seeds. Bake for about 30 minutes, or until golden brown. Serve hot.

Makes 36–48 triangles
Preparation time 1 hour
Cooking time 30 minutes

☐ p 129

Fried halloumi cheese from Cyprus, p 126

Baked cheese triangles, p 127

STUFFED OMELETS WITH GARLIC CRUST
ΑΥΓΟΡΟΛΑ ΜΕ ΚΙΜΑ ΚΑΙ ΣΚΟΡΔΑΤΗ ΚΡΟΥΣΤΑ
Avgorola me kima ke skordati krousta

To make the filling, heat the oil in a pan. Add the onion and ground beef
and cook, stirring frequently and breaking up the meat with the spoon, for
8–10 minutes, until the onion is softened and the meat is lightly browned.
Season with salt and pepper, pour in 1 cup (250 ml / 8 fl oz) water,
partially cover, and simmer for 20–30 minutes, until the meat is tender
and the liquid has reduced. Remove the pan from the heat and let cool.
Stir in the cheese. Preheat the oven to 350°F (180°C / Gas Mark 4)
and brush an ovenproof dish with oil. Beat the eggs with 2 tablespoons
water in a bowl, season with salt and pepper, and stir in the cornmeal to
make a thin batter. Brush a small nonstick skillet or frying pan with oil and
heat. Add 2–3 tablespoons of the batter to the skillet and tilt the skillet to
spread, then cook for a minute or two, until the underside is set and lightly
browned. Flip the omelet over with a spatula and cook for 1 minute more,
or until the second side is lightly browned. Slide the omelet onto a plate
and keep warm. Cook more omelets in the same way, brushing the pan
with more oil, until all the egg mixture is used. Spoon 2–3 tablespoons
of the filling on top of each omelet and roll up, then put the rolled omelets
into the prepared dish in a single layer. Combine all the ingredients for
the sauce in a bowl and pour it over the rolls. Bake for about 20 minutes,
or until a golden crust forms on the surface of the omelets.

Makes 10 omelets
Preparation time 30 minutes (including cooling)
Cooking time 1 hour

FOR THE FILLING
- 5 tablespoons olive oil
- 1 onion, finely grated
- 1 lb 2 oz (500 g) ground (minced) beef
- salt and pepper
- scant 1 cup (100 g / 3 ½ oz) grated xeri (dried) mizithra, Parmesan, or salted ricotta cheese

FOR THE OMELETS
- olive oil, for brushing
- 6 eggs
- salt and pepper
- 5 tablespoons cornmeal

FOR THE SAUCE
- 2 cups (450 ml / 16 fl oz) strained plain or thick Greek yogurt
- 2 tablespoons red wine vinegar
- 2 garlic cloves, finely chopped
- 4 tablespoons water
- salt and white pepper

BAKED STUFFED ANCHOVIES
ΓΑΥΡΑΚΙΑ ΓΕΜΙΣΤΑ ΣΤΟ ΦΟΥΡΝΟ
Gavrakia gemista sto fourno

Preheat the oven to 400°F (200°C / Gas Mark 6) and brush a large
ovenproof dish with oil. Pinch the head of a fish between your thumb
and forefinger and pull it off—the guts should come away with it. Cut
off the tail, pinch all along the top edge of the fish, and pull out the
backbone—it should come away easily. Repeat with all the remaining
fish. Rinse them and pat dry with paper towels. Combine the cheese,
parsley, garlic, and olives in a bowl. Arrange the tomato slices in a
single layer in the prepared dish. Put 1 tablespoon of the cheese mixture
on each slice and top with one or two anchovies. Drizzle with olive
oil, sprinkle with oregano, season with salt and pepper, and bake for
30–35 minutes. Serve hot or cold.

Serves 4
Preparation time 20 minutes
Cooking time 35 minutes

- olive oil, for brushing and drizzling
- 1 lb 2 oz (500 g) anchovies
- 4 oz (120 g) feta cheese, crumbled
- ½ cup (25 g / 1 oz) finely chopped fresh parsley
- 3 garlic cloves, thinly sliced
- 5–6 Kalamata olives, pitted (stoned) and sliced
- 2–3 tomatoes, sliced crosswise
- pinch of dried oregano
- salt and pepper

- 3¼ lb (1.5 kg) anchovies
- salt and pepper
- pinch of dried oregano
- ½ cup (120 ml / 4 fl oz) olive oil
- 3 tablespoons freshly squeezed lemon juice

ANCHOVIES BAKED WITH OREGANO
ΓΑΥΡΑΚΙΑ ΣΤΟ ΦΟΥΡΝΟ ΡΙΓΑΝΑΤΑ
Gavrakia sto fourno riganata

Preheat the oven to 400°F (200°C / Gas Mark 6). Prepare the anchovies as described in the recipe for Baked stuffed anchovies (left). Repeat with all the remaining fish. Rinse the fish thoroughly and drain in a colander. Arrange them side by side in a single layer in an ovenproof dish. Season with salt and pepper, sprinkle with oregano, and drizzle with the olive oil and lemon juice. Bake for 40–45 minutes, or until the pan juices have reduced. Serve hot or at room temperature. This is an excellent meze to accompany a glass of ouzo.

Serves 6
Preparation time 30 minutes
Cooking time 45 minutes

- 2¼ lb (1 kg) salt cod
- 1¾ cups (100 g / 3½ oz) fresh bread crumbs
- 1 tablespoon olive oil
- 1 cup (250 ml / 8 fl oz) beer
- salt and pepper
- 2 tablespoons freshly squeezed lemon juice
- ½ cup (15 g / ½ oz) chopped fresh dill
- ½ cup (25 g / 1 oz) chopped fresh parsley
- ½ cup (4) finely chopped scallions (spring onions)
- 1 teaspoon dried oregano (optional)
- 1 cup (120 g / 4 oz) all-purpose (plain) flour
- vegetable oil, for frying
- Garlic sauce (p 153) and Beet (Beetroot) salad with garlic yogurt (p 184), to serve

SALT COD FRITTERS
ΚΕΦΤΕΔΕΣ ΜΠΑΚΑΛΙΑΡΟΥ
Keftedes bakaliarou

Remove the skin from the fish and cut the flesh into pieces. Put the pieces in a bowl, pour in water to cover, and let soak for 12–24 hours, changing the water three or four times (taste it to check whether enough salt has been removed). Drain the pieces of fish and remove the bones. Using a fork, flake the flesh into small pieces. Put the flaked fish into a bowl, stir in the bread crumbs, oil, and beer and season with salt, if necessary, and pepper. Add the lemon juice, herbs, and enough flour to make a loose mixture. Pour oil into a skillet or frying pan to a depth of about ½ inch (1 cm) and heat. Drop spoonfuls of the fish mixture into the hot oil and fry until browned on both sides. Remove with a slotted spoon and drain well on paper towels. Serve immediately with Garlic sauce and Beet (Beetroot) salad.

Makes 30–40 fritters
Preparation time 12½–24½ hours (including soaking)
Cooking time 20 minutes

FRIED SALT COD WITH GARLIC SAUCE
ΜΠΑΚΑΛΙΑΡΟΣ ΜΕ ΣΚΟΡΔΑΛΙΑ
Bakaliaros me skordalia

- ° 2¼ lb (1 kg) salt cod
- ° vegetable oil, for deep-frying
- ° Garlic sauce (p 153), to serve

FOR THE BATTER
- ° 1 cup (120 g / 4 oz) all-purpose (plain) flour
- ° 1 tablespoon olive oil
- ° 1 cup (250 ml / 8 fl oz) beer or club soda (soda water)
- ° salt and pepper
- ° 1 egg white, whisked to soft peaks

Remove the skin from the cod and cut the flesh into large pieces. Put the pieces in a bowl, pour in water to cover, and let soak for 12–24 hours, changing the water 3 or 4 times. Meanwhile, make the batter. Put the flour, olive oil, and beer or club soda into a food processor, season with salt and pepper, and process for 1 minute. Set aside for 1 hour. Drain the fish and pat dry with paper towels. Remove the bones and cut the fish into bite-size pieces. Heat the vegetable oil in a deep-fryer to 350–375°F (180–190°C). Fold the egg white into the batter. Dip the pieces of cod into the batter, one at a time, and deep-fry in the hot oil until golden brown. Serve hot, accompanied by Garlic sauce.

Makes 35–40 pieces
Preparation time 20¼ hours (including soaking and resting)
Cooking time 15–20 minutes

▢ p 134

TUNA SALAD
ΤΟΝΟΣΑΛΑΤΑ
Tonosalata

- ° 1 lb 2 oz (500 g) canned tuna, drained and flaked
- ° 1 long red pepper, broiled (grilled), peeled, seeded, and diced
- ° 2 hard-boiled eggs, chopped
- ° ¼ cup (40 g / 1½ oz) chopped dill pickles (pickled cucumbers) or cornichons
- ° 2 tablespoons capers
- ° ¼ cup (1–2) chopped scallions (spring onions)
- ° ¼ cup (25 g / 1 oz) chopped celery
- ° 4 tablespoons chopped fresh parsley
- ° 1 tablespoon finely chopped onion
- ° 2 tablespoons freshly squeezed lemon juice
- ° 1 teaspoon Dijon mustard
- ° 1 cup (250 ml / 8 fl oz) Mayonnaise (p 60)
- ° salt and pepper

Combine all the ingredients, except the mayonnaise, in a bowl and season with salt and pepper. Add the mayonnaise and toss lightly. If the mixture is stiff, add 2–3 tablespoons extra mayonnaise. Cover with plastic wrap (cling film) and chill in the refrigerator for at least 2 hours. Serve with crackers or use to fill bite-size choux puffs, crêpes, bouchées, tartlets, or scooped-out cherry tomatoes.

Serves 6
Preparation time 2½ hours (including chilling)

- 1 lb 2 oz (500 g) ground (minced) beef
- 2 eggs, lightly beaten
- ¼ cup (50 g / 2 oz) long-grain rice, cooked
- ½ teaspoon ground allspice
- ⅓ cup (2–3) finely chopped scallions (spring onions)
- 4 tablespoons finely chopped fresh parsley
- 4 tablespoons finely chopped fresh dill or mint
- 1¾ cups (200 g / 7 oz) crumbled feta cheese
- vegetable oil, for deep-frying
- ½ cup (50 g / 2 oz) all-purpose (plain) flour
- scant 1½ cups (100 g / 3½ oz) dry bread crumbs
- 2 eggs lightly beaten with 2 tablespoons olive oil
- salt and pepper

GROUND (MINCED) MEAT CROQUETTES FROM ASIA MINOR
ΚΕΦΤΕΔΕΣ ΠΟΛΙΤΙΚΟΙ
Keftedes politiki

To make the croquettes, combine all the ingredients, except the oil, flour and bread crumbs, in a bowl and season with salt and pepper. Knead until the mixture is soft and smooth, but holds its shape. If it is too stiff, moisten your hands with water while you are kneading to soften the mixture. Cover and chill in the refrigerator for 2 hours. Scoop portions of the mixture and roll into small oblong croquettes. Spread out the flour and bread crumbs in separate shallow dishes. Coat the croquettes first with flour, then with the beaten egg and olive oil mixture, and, finally, with the bread crumbs. Put the croquettes in a single layer on a platter and chill in the refrigerator for 30 minutes. Heat the vegetable oil in a deep-fryer to 350–375°F (180–190°C). Fry the croquettes in the hot oil for about 10 minutes, until cooked through and golden brown. Drain on paper towels and serve hot.

Makes 20–25 croquettes
Preparation time 3 hours (including chilling)
Cooking time 30 minutes

- 2 thick slices day-old bread, crusts removed
- ½ cup (120 ml / 4 fl oz) dry red wine
- 1 lb 2 oz (500 g) lean ground (minced) beef or veal
- 1 onion, finely chopped
- 2 garlic cloves, finely chopped
- 1 egg, lightly beaten
- 3 tablespoons chopped fresh parsley
- ½ teaspoon ground cumin
- salt and pepper
- all-purpose (plain) flour, for coating
- ½ cup (120 ml / 4 fl oz) olive oil
- rice, fried potatoes, or mashed potatoes, to serve

FOR THE SAUCE
- 2¼ lb (1 kg) tomatoes, peeled and chopped
- 1 tablespoon red wine vinegar
- 1 garlic clove, finely chopped
- 1 bay leaf
- ½ teaspoon sugar

MEAT ROLLS FROM SMYRNA
ΣΟΥΤΖΟΥΚΑΚΙΑ ΣΜΥΡΝΕΙΚΑ
Soutzoukakia smirneika

Tear the bread into small pieces, put it into a bowl, pour in the wine, and let soak until softened. Squeeze out and reserve any remaining wine. Combine the meat, soaked bread, onion, garlic, egg, parsley, and cumin in a bowl and season with salt and pepper. Mix until thoroughly blended and soft. If the mixture is stiff, add a little wine. Cover and chill for 1–2 hours. Moisten your hands, pinch off small portions of the meat mixture about the size of walnuts and shape into 20 oval rolls. Coat with flour, shaking off the excess. Heat the oil in a large skillet or frying pan. Add the meat rolls and cook for 20–30 minutes, or until golden all over. Remove with a slotted spoon and set aside. Strain the oil through a fine strainer into a clean pan. Add all the sauce ingredients and the reserved wine and simmer until the sauce has thickened. Drop in the meat rolls, stir to coat with the sauce, cover, and simmer for 15 minutes. Serve hot with rice or fried or mashed potatoes.

Makes 20 rolls
Preparation time 1½–2½ hours (including chilling)
Cooking time 45 minutes

Fried salt cod with garlic sauce, p 132

Peppers with sausages from Pelion, p 136

MEAT ROLLS WITH GARLIC
ΣΟΥΤΖΟΥΚΑΚΙΑ
Soutzoukakia

Combine all ingredients in a bowl and season with salt and pepper. Knead for 2 minutes until thoroughly blended. For light and fluffy meat rolls, the mixture must be soft. If it is stiff, moisten your hands with water and knead until the mixture is soft and light. Cover and chill for 1–2 hours. Light the barbecue or preheat the broiler (grill). Divide the meat mixture into 20 pieces and roll each into a sausage-shaped roll. Brush with olive oil. Cook over charcoal or under the broiler, turning frequently, for 10–15 minutes, or until browned all over. Serve hot sprinkled with lemon juice accompanied by Eggplant (Aubergine) dip, Tzatziki, or Red pepper sauce.

Makes 20 rolls
Preparation time 1¼ – 2¼ hours (including chilling)
Cooking time 20 minutes

- 1 lb 2 oz (500 g) ground (minced) beef or lamb
- 2 onions, grated
- 2–3 garlic cloves, finely chopped
- ½ cup (25 g / 1 oz) fresh bread crumbs
- 1 tablespoon red wine vinegar
- 4 tablespoons water
- 4 tablespoons olive oil, plus extra for brushing
- pinch of dried oregano
- salt and pepper

TO SERVE
- freshly squeezed lemon juice
- Eggplant (Aubergine) dip (p 152), Tzatziki (p 152), or Red pepper sauce (p 61)

PEPPERS WITH SAUSAGES FROM PELION
ΣΠΕΤΖΟΦΑΙ ΠΗΛΙΟΥ
Spetzofai piliou

The original recipe is made only with peppers (usually hot) and sausages, but nowadays, in most restaurants and homes in the city of Volos and Pelion villages, this lighter version of the dish is served.

Slice the eggplants into ½-inch (1-cm) thick rounds. Sprinkle with salt and let drain in a colander for 1 hour. Meanwhile, process the tomatoes to a purée in a food processor. Rinse the eggplant rounds and squeeze out excess water. Heat half the olive oil in a large skillet or frying pan. Add the eggplants and peppers and cook for 10–15 minutes, until lightly browned, then remove from the heat. Meanwhile, cook the sausages in a nonstick skillet or frying pan over medium heat until they have released their fat. Drain and discard the fat. Heat the remaining olive oil in the same pan and return the sausages to the pan with the tomatoes. Simmer for about 20 minutes, until the sauce has thickened. Meanwhile, preheat the oven to 350°F (180°C / Gas Mark 4). Remove the sausages with a slotted spoon and pile in the center of an ovenproof platter. Arrange the eggplants and peppers around the sausages and spoon the remaining sauce on top. Season with pepper, cover with aluminum foil, and bake for about 15 minutes. Serve hot.

Serves 6
Preparation time 1¼ hours (including salting)
Cooking time 35 minutes

- 3¼ lb (1.5 kg) eggplants (aubergines)
- 2¼ lb (1 kg) tomatoes, peeled and coarsely chopped
- ⅓ cup (80 ml / 3 fl oz) olive oil
- 1 lb 2 oz (500 g) long mild green peppers, seeded and sliced
- 1 lb 2 oz (500 g) spicy rustic sausages, thickly sliced
- salt and pepper

p 135

MEAT SKEWERS FROM ASIA MINOR
ΜΑΚΡΑΣΙΑΤΙΚΑ ΣΙΣ ΚΕΜΠΑΠ
Mikrasiatika siskebab

- 2¼ lb (1 kg) ground (minced) lamb
- 11 oz (300 g) ground (minced) beef
- 4 tablespoons onion juice (see note)
- 1 egg, lightly beaten
- 2 teaspoons finely chopped fresh parsley
- 1 tablespoon mixed ground coriander, curry powder, sweet paprika, and hot paprika
- salt and pepper
- olive oil, for brushing
- tomatoes and roasted hot green chile peppers, to serve

FOR THE YOGURT SAUCE
- ½ cup (120 ml / 4 fl oz) Mayonnaise (p 60)
- ½ cup (120 ml / 4 fl oz) strained plain or thick Greek yogurt
- 2 garlic cloves, crushed
- freshly squeezed lemon juice, to taste
- salt

Combine the meat, onion juice, egg, parsley, and spices in a bowl and season with salt and pepper. Knead to a soft, uniform mixture. Cover and chill in the refrigerator for 1 hour. Meanwhile, combine all the sauce ingredients in a bowl and season with salt. Cover and keep in the refrigerator until required. Light the barbecue or preheat the broiler (grill). Mold portions of the meat mixture around wooden skewers—they should be just a little thicker than your thumb. Moisten your hands and make them flatter and longer so that they cover about two-thirds of the length of the skewers. Brush them with olive oil and cook on the barbecue or under the broiler, brushing occasionally with olive oil, for 5 minutes on each side. Serve hot accompanied by tomatoes, roasted hot green chiles, and the yogurt sauce.

Serves 8
Preparation time 1¼ hours (including chilling)
Cooking time 10 minutes

Note: To make onion juice, finely grate a large onion into a strainer set over a bowl and let it drain.

STUFFED BULGUR CUPS FROM CYPRUS
ΚΟΥΠΕΣ ΚΥΠΡΟΥ
Koupes kiprou

- ½ teaspoon salt
- 2 cups (350 g / 12 oz) fine bulgur wheat
- ¼ cup (25 g / 1 oz) all-purpose (plain) flour
- vegetable oil, for deep-frying

FOR THE FILLING
- ½ cup (120 ml / 4 fl oz) olive oil
- 2 medium onions, grated
- 11 oz (300 g) ground (minced) pork
- salt and pepper
- ¼ cup (15 g / ½ oz) chopped fresh parsley

Pour 2½ cups (600 ml / 1 pint) water into a pan, add the salt, and bring to a boil. Put the bulgur wheat into a heatproof bowl, pour the salted water over it, cover, and set aside until it has absorbed the liquid. Meanwhile, prepare the filling. Heat the olive oil in a pan. Add the onions and cook over low heat, stirring occasionally, for about 5 minutes, until softened and translucent. Add the pork, season with salt and pepper, cover, and cook for 15 minutes. Toward the end of the cooking time, stir in the parsley. Remove the pan from the heat and set aside to cool. Add the flour to the bulgur wheat and knead until stiff enough to hold its shape. Take pieces of bulgur the size of a large walnut and roll into a ball in the palm of your hand. Moisten your index finger and carefully make a hole through the middle of the ball by turning it around the finger. Fill the opening with the cooled meat filling and close, pinching the bulgur into points on both sides. Heat the vegetable oil in a deep-fryer to 350–375°F (180–190°C). Deep-fry in batches for 5 minutes, or until golden. Drain and serve hot.

Makes 16–18 pieces
Preparation time 1 hour (including cooling)
Cooking time 20 minutes

WINTER
ΧΕΙΜΩΝΑΣ
Himonas

The mezedes of winter are influenced by the tradition of the annual pig slaughter, which was once customary in every Greek household. The tradition is now on the wane, although there are many areas of the countryside where it continues, and the occasion calls for a celebration. Immediately after the animal is slaughtered, the first piece of meat is cut off, roasted or fried, and offered to the man who performed the slaughter. The remaining meat and organ meats (offal) are turned into a variety of mezedes. Sausages (loukanika), chitterlings (tsigarides), smoked cured pork meats preserved in herbs and olive oil are among the winter delicacies eaten during the Twelve Days of Christmas and the rest of winter, accompanied by aromatic red wine.

KATAIFI PASTRY AND CHEESE ROLLS
ΚΑΤΑΙΦΙ ΜΕ ΤΥΡΙΑ
Kataifi me tiria

Grease an ovenproof dish with butter. Lightly beat two of the eggs in a bowl, season with pepper, and stir in the cheeses. Tease out the kataifi pastry and divide into 20–25 long sections. Keep the sections covered with a damp cloth to keep them moist. Take one section of kataifi and pat it gently between your palms. Place 1 tablespoon of the cheese mixture on it and fold it over the filling, shaping a ball. Continue until all the sections of kataifi are filled. Place them in the prepared dish, close together. Heat the 4 tablespoons butter and corn oil together and pour a teaspoon over each roll. At this point you can wrap and freeze the rolls or store them in the refrigerator for 24 hours. One hour before baking, lightly beat together the milk, cream, and remaining eggs. Pour the mixture over the rolls and let them stand for 1 hour, until they have absorbed the liquid. Preheat the oven to 350°F (180°C / Gas Mark 4). Bake the rolls for 35–40 minutes, or until golden brown. Serve immediately.

Makes 20–25 rolls
Preparation time 1½ hours (including standing)
Cooking time 35–40 minutes

Note: You can substitute 1 cup (175 g / 6 oz) finely chopped cured ham or bacon for 1 cup (120 g / 4 oz) of the cheese mixture.

▢ p 140

- 4 tablespoons (50 g / 2 oz) butter, plus extra for greasing
- 4 eggs
- pepper
- 7 oz (200 g) feta cheese, crumbled
- 1½ cups (175 g / 6 oz) grated kaseri or Gruyère cheese
- 11 oz (300 g) kataifi pastry
- 4 tablespoons corn oil
- ⅔ cup (150 ml / ¼ pint) milk
- ⅔ cup (150 ml / ¼ pint) heavy (double) cream

STUFFED LEEKS WITH EGG-LEMON SAUCE FROM PONTUS
ΨΑΡΟΣΑΡΜΑΔΑΚΙΑ
Prasosarmadakia

- 6–7 large thick leeks, white part only, 8–10 inches (20–25 cm) long
- ⅔ cup (150 ml / ¼ pint) olive oil
- 1 small leek, finely chopped
- 14 oz (400 g) ground (minced) pork
- ⅓ cup (65 g / 2½ oz) short-grain rice
- ¼ teaspoon ground cumin
- 4 tablespoons finely chopped fresh parsley
- 2 tablespoons finely chopped fresh mint
- salt and pepper
- 2 eggs
- 4 tablespoons freshly squeezed lemon juice

Remove and discard the outer layer of each thick leek. Blanch in boiling water for 5 minutes to soften, then drain. Carefully cut each leek lengthwise to the center, separate the layers, open, and flatten. Heat 5 tablespoons of the olive oil in a pan. Add the chopped leek and cook over low heat, stirring occasionally, for 3 minutes. Stir in the pork and cook, stirring occasionally and breaking up the meat, until it begins to brown. Stir in the rice, cumin, parsley, mint, and ½ cup (120 ml / 4 fl oz) water, season with salt and pepper, and simmer until the water is absorbed. Remove the pan from the heat and let cool. Place a tablespoon of the pork mixture at one end of each piece of leek and fold into triangles as for Baked cheese triangles (p 127). Arrange the *sarmadakia* side by side in a pan and pour the remaining oil over them. Place a plate slightly smaller than the width of the pan directly on top of the stuffed leeks. Pour in 2 cups (450 ml / 16 fl oz) boiling water, cover, and simmer for 1 hour. Beat the eggs with the lemon juice in a bowl, then beat in a ladleful of the hot pan juices. Pour the mixture over the stuffed leeks and shake the pan to distribute. Remove from the heat and serve hot.

Serves 4
Preparation time 1 hour (including cooling)
Cooking time 1½ hours

□ p 141

DRUNKEN PORK
ΜΠΕΚΡΗ ΜΕΖΕ
Bekri meze

- 1 lb 2 oz (500 g) boneless pork loin, cut into bite-size pieces
- 2 tablespoons Dijon mustard
- 4 tablespoons olive oil
- 2 garlic cloves, thinly sliced
- 1 cup (250 ml / 8 fl oz) dry red wine
- 1 cup (250 ml / 8 fl oz) tomato juice
- ½ teaspoon cayenne pepper
- ¼ teaspoon dried oregano
- ¼ teaspoon ground allspice
- salt and pepper
- Sour or Sweet trahana (p 280 or 281), to serve

Toss the pork in a bowl with the mustard until coated on all sides. Heat the oil in a heavy skillet or frying pan. Add the garlic and pork and cook over medium heat, stirring frequently, for about 10 minutes, until the meat is lightly browned. Stir in the wine, a little at a time, and cook over high heat until it has evaporated. Add the tomato juice, cayenne pepper, oregano, and allspice and season with salt and pepper. Simmer for about 10 minutes, until the meat is tender and the sauce has thickened. Serve immediately, with red wine and Sweet or Sour trahana.

Serves 6
Preparation time 10 minutes
Cooking time 25 minutes

□ p 143

Kataifi pastry and cheese rolls, p 138

Stuffed leeks with egg-lemon sauce from Pontus, p 139

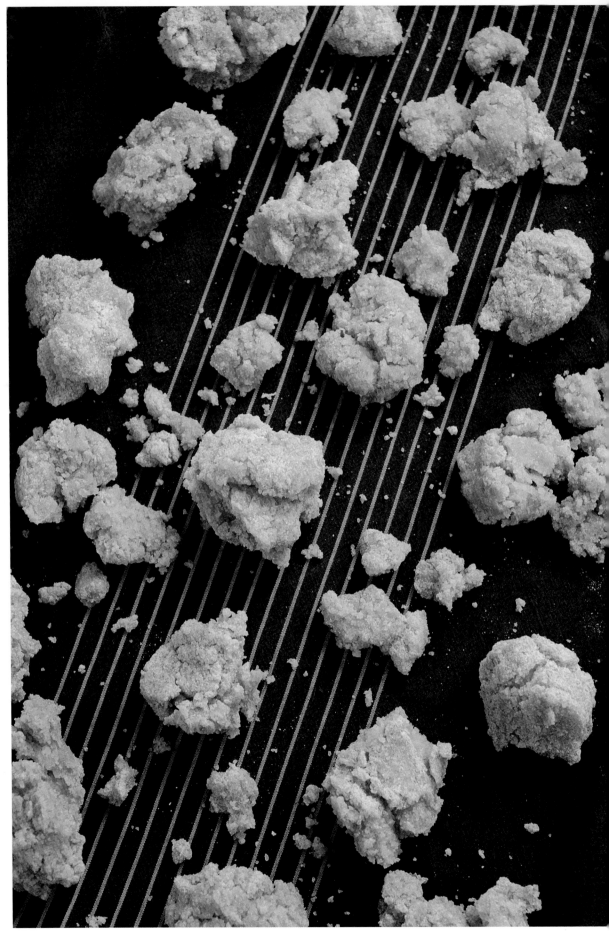

Trahana, pp 280-81

drunken pork (shown with trahana), p 139

SCRAMBLED EGGS WITH TOMATOES AND PRESERVED PORK FROM KALAMATA
ΚΑΓΙΑΝΑΣ ΜΕΣΣΗΝΙΑΣ
Kagianas mesinias

- 5 tablespoons olive oil
- 5 large ripe tomatoes, peeled, seeded, and coarsely chopped
- 9 oz (250 g) preserved pork or sausages, cut into bite-size pieces
- 8 eggs, lightly beaten
- salt and pepper

This dish is a specialty of Messinia, combining ripe tomatoes with fresh farm eggs and preserved pork, which is prepared and kept in pork fat all the year through. It is also prepared with pork sausages, which can be used as an alternative to the preserved pork.

Heat the oil in a large, heavy skillet or frying pan over high heat. Add the tomatoes and simmer uncovered, stirring occasionally, for about 15 minutes, until all the liquid has evaporated. Add the pork and cook, stirring constantly, for 8 minutes. Add the eggs and stir gently with a delicate movement. Remove from the heat when the eggs hold their shape; do not overcook. Season with salt and pepper and serve immediately.

Serves 6
Preparation time 20 minutes
Cooking time 30 minutes

BRAISED PORK WITH LEEKS FROM MACEDONIA
ΤΗΓΑΝΙΑ ΜΕ ΧΟΙΡΙΝΟ ΚΑΙ ΠΡΑΣΑ
Tigania me hirino ke prasa

- ½ cup (120 ml / 4 fl oz) olive oil
- 3¼ lb (1.5 kg) boneless pork shoulder, cubed
- 1 large onion, finely chopped
- 2 garlic cloves, thinly sliced
- 1 cup (250 ml / 8 fl oz) dry white wine
- 2 tablespoons finely chopped celery
- 5 large leeks (about 2¼ lb / 1 kg) white part only, cut into 1-inch (2.5-cm) pieces
- 10 black peppercorns
- salt and pepper
- 1 cup (250 ml / 8 fl oz) hot water
- lemon wedges, to serve

Heat the oil in a large, heavy pan. Add the pork and cook over high heat, stirring frequently, for about 10 minutes, until lightly browned on all sides. Add the onion and garlic and cook, stirring frequently, for 3–5 minutes, until softened and translucent. Pour in the wine and stir until the alcohol evaporates. Add the celery and leeks and cook for 2 minutes. Reduce the heat, stir in the peppercorns, season with salt and pepper, and add the hot water. Cover and simmer for about 1 hour, or until the meat and leeks are tender and the sauce has reduced. Serve garnished with lemon wedges.

Serves 6
Preparation time 20 minutes
Cooking time 1½ hours

- 2¼ lb (1 kg) potatoes
- salt and pepper
- pinch of grated nutmeg
- ½ cup (120 ml / 4 fl oz) olive oil, plus extra for frying
- 1 small onion, finely chopped
- 1 garlic clove, finely chopped
- 9 oz (250 g) ground (minced) beef
- 1 teaspoon dried oregano
- ½ cup (120 ml / 4 fl oz) hot water
- 2 tablespoons chopped fresh parsley

FOR THE COATING
- 1 cup (120 g / 4 oz) all-purpose (plain) flour
- 2 eggs, lightly beaten with 2 tablespoons olive oil
- 1¾ cups (100 g / 3½ oz) fresh bread crumbs

STUFFED POTATO RISSOLES
ΠΑΤΑΤΟΚΕΦΤΕΔΕΣ ΓΕΜΙΣΤΟΙ
Patatokeftedes gemisti

This traditional meze from Lesvos is served at engagement parties.

Cook the unpeeled potatoes in salted boiling water for 20–30 minutes until tender, then drain, and peel while still warm. Mash or purée with salt, pepper, and nutmeg and keep warm. To prepare the filling, heat the oil in a pan. Add the onion and garlic and cook over low heat, stirring occasionally, for 3–5 minutes, until softened. Add the meat and cook, stirring frequently and breaking it up with the spoon, for about 10 minutes, until it starts to brown. Add the oregano, season with salt and pepper, and pour in the hot water. Simmer for 25–30 minutes, until the meat is tender and the juices have reduced. Stir in the parsley, remove from the heat, and let cool. Place 2 tablespoons of warm mashed potato in the palm of your hand and flatten it. Put 1–2 teaspoons of the meat filling in the center and press closed to form rolls. Coat the rissoles with flour, shaking off any excess, dip in the beaten egg mixture, and roll in the bread crumbs. Heat olive oil in a skillet or frying pan. Add the rissoles and cook in batches, turning occasionally, for about 20 minutes, until golden brown. Drain on paper towels and serve hot.

Makes 20 rissoles
Preparation time 1 hour (including cooling)
Cooking time 40 minutes

□ p 146

- 1 lb 2 oz (500 g) boneless pork loin, cut into bite-size pieces
- 5 tablespoons olive oil
- 1 teaspoon dried oregano
- 4 tablespoons freshly squeezed lemon juice
- salt and pepper
- lemon wedges, to serve

FRIED PORK WITH OREGANO
ΧΟΙΡΙΝΗ ΤΗΓΑΝΙΑ ΡΙΓΑΝΑΤΗ
Hirini tigania riganati

Pat the pork pieces dry with paper towels. Heat the oil in a heavy skillet or frying pan, add the meat, and cook over medium heat, stirring frequently, for about 10 minutes, until lightly browned all over. Sprinkle with half the oregano, pour in the lemon juice and ½ cup (120 ml / 4 fl oz) water, and season with salt and pepper. Cover and simmer for 10 minutes, until the meat is tender and the liquid has reduced. Remove from the heat, sprinkle with the remaining oregano, and serve garnished with lemon wedges. This is an excellent meze to accompany a glass of *tsipouro* or red wine.

Serves 6
Preparation time 5 minutes
Cooking time 20 minutes

Stuffed potato rissoles, p 145

Dips, clockwise from top left: Garlic sauce, p 153, Taramosalata, p 157, Olive paste, p 153, Eggplant (Aubergine) dip, p 152, and Tzatziki, p 152

JELLIED PORK TERRINE
ΠΗΚΤΗ
Pikti

Put the meat into a pan, pour in water to cover, and add the onions, carrots, celery, parsley, garlic, bay leaves, peppercorns, and a pinch of salt. Cover the pan and bring to a boil over high heat, skimming off the scum that rises to the surface. Reduce the heat and simmer for 2–3 hours. Remove and reserve the meat and carrots with a slotted spoon. Remove the bones from the meat and return them to the stock. Continue to simmer for 30–40 minutes more. Meanwhile, cut the meat into small pieces, slice the carrots and put them into a bowl. Add the capers and pickles and set aside in the refrigerator. Stir the vinegar into the stock and simmer for 5 minutes more. Strain the stock through a cheesecloth- (muslin-) lined strainer into a bowl, let cool, then chill in the refrigerator. (It should measure about 6¼ cups / 1.5 litres / 2½ pints). Grease a 9 x 6 x 3-inch (23 x 15 x 8-cm) loaf pan with oil. Remove and discard the layer of fat that has formed on the surface of the stock. Pour the stock into a pan, heat gently, and stir in the dissolved gelatin. Remove from the heat and let cool to room temperature, then chill in the refrigerator until the mixture begins to set. Stir in the meat mixture and pour into the prepared loaf pan. Chill in the refrigerator until the mold sets. To remove from the pan, run a round-tipped knife around the sides of the pan to loosen, dip briefly in hot water, and unmold the *pikti* onto a platter. Chill until ready to serve.

Makes one 9-inch (23-cm) terrine
Preparation time 20 hours (including chilling and setting)
Cooking time 3–4 hours

- 4½ lb (2 kg) pork shoulder
- 3 small onions, halved
- 3 carrots, halved
- 1 small celery stalk
- 4 fresh parsley sprigs
- 4 garlic cloves
- 2 bay leaves
- 10 black peppercorns
- salt
- 3 tablespoons fine capers
- 4 tablespoons finely chopped dill pickles (pickled cucumbers)
- 5 tablespoons red wine vinegar
- vegetable oil, for greasing
- 1 tablespoon powdered gelatin dissolved in 4 tablespoons water

PORK SAUSAGES WITH CHILI SAUCE
ΛΟΥΚΑΝΙΚΑ ΜΕ ΚΑΦΤΕΡΗ ΣΑΛΤΣΑ
Loukanika me kafteri saltsa

Put the sausage into a heavy skillet or frying pan and stir over low heat for 5 minutes, until most of the fat has run out. Drain and discard the fat. Add the olive oil to the pan and stir for a few more minutes. Pour in the vinegar and, when it has evaporated, add the tomato juice and chili sauce. Cook uncovered, stirring constantly, until the sauce has thickened. Remove from the heat, season to taste with salt and pepper, and serve immediately. This is an excellent meze to serve with ouzo or red wine.

Serves 6
Preparation time 10 minutes
Cooking time 20–30 minutes

- 1 lb 2 oz (500 g) pork sausages, cut into bite-size pieces
- 2 tablespoons olive oil
- 2 tablespoons red wine vinegar
- ½ cup (120 ml / 4 fl oz) tomato juice
- 4 tablespoons Greek chili sauce (p 60)
- salt and pepper

- 11 oz (300 g) preserved pork or cooked pork (such as leg or shoulder)
- 2 hard-boiled eggs, chopped
- 2 tablespoons finely chopped dill pickles (pickled cucumbers)
- 2 tablespoons fine capers
- ½ cup (25 g / 1 oz) chopped fresh parsley
- 1 tablespoon powdered gelatin
- 1 cup (250 ml / 8 fl oz) Mayonnaise (p 60)
- 2 tablespoons freshly squeezed lemon juice
- salt and pepper
- lettuce leaves, to serve

PRESERVED PORK AND PARSLEY PÂTÉ
ΧΟΙΡΙΝΟ ΠΑΤΕ ΜΕ ΜΑΪΝΤΑΝΟ
Hirino paté me maintano

Flake the meat with a fork and put it into a bowl. Add the hard-boiled eggs, pickles, capers, and parsley. Pour 4 tablespoons water into a small heatproof bowl, sprinkle the gelatin over the surface, and set aside for 5 minutes to soften. Set the bowl over a pan of gently simmering water and heat until the gelatin is runny and clear. Remove from the heat and let cool slightly. Combine the mayonnaise, lemon juice, and gelatin in another bowl, season with salt and pepper, and gently stir into the meat mixture. Line a 3-cup (750-ml / 1¼-pint) mold with plastic wrap (cling film), spoon the mixture into it, and smooth the surface with the back of the spoon. Chill for 6 hours or overnight in the refrigerator. To serve, unmold onto a platter lined with lettuce leaves. Carefully remove the plastic wrap and serve.

Makes 1 large pâté
Preparation time 6¼ hours (including setting)

- scant 3 cups (500 g / 1 lb 2 oz) large dried white beans, such as lima (butter) beans, soaked overnight in cold water to cover and drained
- ½ cup (120 ml / 4 fl oz) olive oil
- 1 onion, finely chopped
- 9 oz (250 g) pastourma or pastrami, chopped
- 5 tablespoons dry white wine
- 2¼ lb (1 kg) ripe tomatoes, peeled, seeded, and finely chopped, or 14 oz canned tomatoes, drained and finely chopped
- ½ teaspoon sugar
- salt and pepper

GIANT BEANS WITH PASTRAMI FROM PONTUS
ΓΙΓΑΝΤΕΣ ΜΕ ΠΑΣΤΟΥΡΜΑ
Gigantes me pastourma

Cook the beans in boiling salted water for 30 minutes. Heat the oil in a large pan. Add the onion and cook over low heat, stirring occasionally, for about 5 minutes, until softened and translucent. Add the pastourma and continue cooking for 2 minutes. Drain the beans, add to the pan, and stir until heated through. Pour in the wine and, when the alcohol has evaporated, add the tomatoes and sugar. Season with salt and pepper. Cover and simmer for 1 hour, or until the beans are soft and the sauce has thickened. Serve hot or at room temperature.

Serves 6
Preparation time 12¼ hours (including soaking)
Cooking time 1¾ hours

FRIED LAMB'S LIVER WITH CORIANDER FROM CYPRUS
ΣΥΚΩΤΑΚΙΑ ΤΗΓΑΝΙΤΑ ΜΕ ΚΟΛΙΑΝΔΡΟ
Sikotakia tiganita me koliandro

- 5 tablespoons olive oil
- 1 lb 2 oz (500 g) lamb's liver, trimmed and cut into small pieces
- 4 tablespoons dry red wine
- 1 tablespoon ground coriander
- salt and pepper

Heat the olive oil in a heavy skillet or frying pan. Add the liver and cook briefly over medium heat, turning occasionally, until lightly browned on all sides but still pink in the middle. Pour in the wine, sprinkle with the coriander, salt, and pepper. Vigorously shake the pan several times, tossing the pieces of liver over the heat so they "jump up and down" and are completely covered with the coriander. Serve immediately. In Cyprus, this method of frying is called *antinahti*. Potatoes in their skins are also fried the same way and are called *antinahtes*.

Serves 4
Preparation time 5 minutes
Cooking time 10 minutes

BAKED MEAT AND SPINACH PATTIES FROM CYPRUS
ΠΡΟΠΕΤΕΣ ΚΥΠΡΟΥ
Propetes kiprou

- 1 lb 2 oz (500 g) spinach, coarse stalks removed
- 1 lb 2 oz (500 g) ground (minced) beef
- 1 cup (100 g / 3 ½ oz) grated kefalotiri or Parmesan cheese
- 1 garlic clove, finely chopped
- 1 large onion, grated
- 2 tablespoons dried bread crumbs
- 1 egg, lightly beaten
- salt and pepper
- all-purpose (plain) flour, for coating
- olive oil, for frying
- 7 oz (200 g) kaseri or Gouda cheese, thinly sliced
- Red pepper sauce (p 61), to serve

Chop the spinach and briefly blanch in boiling water, then drain well, and squeeze out excess liquid. Put it into a bowl, stir in the ground beef, kefalotiri or Parmesan, garlic, onion, bread crumbs, and egg, and season with salt and pepper. Knead the mixture until thoroughly blended. Chill the mixture for 1 hour, then shape into 25–30 round or oblong patties. Preheat the oven to 350°F (180°C / Gas Mark 4). Spread out the flour on a shallow plate and roll the patties in it to coat, shaking off any excess. Heat the oil in a skillet or frying pan, add the patties, in batches if necessary, and cook for about 5–10 minutes on each side, until golden brown. Using a slotted spoon, transfer the *propetes* to an ovenproof dish and place a small thin slice of kaseri or Gouda on top of each. Bake for about 15 minutes, or until the cheese melts and the ground beef is cooked through. Serve hot with Red pepper sauce.

Makes 25–30 patties
Preparation time 1½ hours (including chilling)
Cooking time 15 minutes

DIPS
ΝΤΙΠ
Dip

Among the favorites on any list of mezedes are those famous Greek salads that are usually called dips outside Greece. Although these dishes stand on their own as mezedes, they are usually served along with bread and other Greek mezedes such as meatballs, souvlaki, and fried eggplants (aubergines).

- 1 generous cup (250 g / 9 oz) dried garbanzo beans (chickpeas)
- 1 tablespoon salt
- 4 tablespoons tahini
- 1–2 garlic cloves, finely chopped
- salt and pepper
- 4 tablespoons olive oil
- 1–2 tablespoons freshly squeezed lemon juice
- finely chopped fresh parsley, to garnish
- pickled vegetables or pita bread, to serve

HUMMUS
ΧΟΥΜΟΥΣ
Humus

Put the garbanzo beans into a bowl, pour in water to cover, add 1 tablespoon salt, and let soak for 12 hours. Drain and rinse well. Put the beans into a pan, add water to cover, and cook for 1–2 hours, until very soft. Drain and push through a fine strainer into a bowl or process to a purée in a food processor. Beat the tahini with 1–2 tablespoons water. Combine the bean purée and garlic and season lightly with salt and pepper. Stirring constantly with a fork, gradually pour in the tahini mixture, then the olive oil, a little at a time, beating until smooth. Finally, add lemon juice to taste. Pour the hummus into a bowl and sprinkle with the parsley. Chill in the refrigerator for several hours before serving with pickled vegetables or pita bread.

Makes 2 cups (450 ml / 16 fl oz)
Preparation time 15–16 hours (including soaking and chilling)
Cooking time 1–2 hours

Vefa's secret: Adding salt instead of baking soda (bicarbonate of soda) to the soaking water for garbanzo beans softens them without causing them to darken, as baking soda does.

TZATZIKI
TZATZIKI
Tzatziki

- 3 cups (750 ml / 1¼ pints) plain yogurt
- 1 long, thin cucumber, peeled and finely chopped
- 3–4 garlic cloves, finely chopped
- ¼ teaspoon salt
- 3–4 tablespoons olive oil
- 3 tablespoons finely chopped fresh dill

Line a strainer with cheesecloth (muslin) or a double-thickness of paper towels and spoon the yogurt into it. Let drain over a bowl in the refrigerator for about 6 hours. Transfer the strained yogurt from the strainer to a bowl. Stir in the cucumber, garlic, salt, and oil. Cover and chill. Serve in a shallow bowl, sprinkled with the dill. This is excellent with bread, crackers, vegetable fritters, meatballs, or crudités.

Makes 2½ cups (600 ml / 1 pint)
Preparation time 7¼ hours (including draining and chilling)

☐ p 147

EGGPLANT (AUBERGINE) DIP
ΜΕΛΙΤΖΑΝΟΣΑΛΑΤΑ
Melitzanosalata

- 2¼ lb (1 kg) eggplants (aubergines)
- ¼ teaspoon salt, plus extra for sprinkling
- 2–3 garlic cloves, finely chopped
- ½ cup (120 ml / 4 fl oz) olive oil, plus extra for sprinkling
- about 4 tablespoons red wine vinegar
- 2 tablespoons chopped fresh parsley
- 1 mild green bell pepper, seeded and chopped
- 1 tomato, seeded and chopped

Preheat the broiler (grill) or light the barbecue. Broil or grill the eggplants, turning frequently, until the skins are charred and the flesh is softened. (Cooking over charcoal gives the salad a pleasant smoky flavor.) Remove from the heat and hold each eggplant briefly under cold running water until cool enough to handle, then peel immediately. Do not allow the unpeeled eggplants to cool completely or the flesh will turn black. When peeled, put them into a strainer and let cool completely. Chop the eggplant flesh and transfer to a bowl. Add the salt and garlic. Beating constantly with an electric mixer on medium speed, gradually add the oil, a few drops at a time, then in a slow, steady thin stream until all of it has been absorbed. Continue beating and gradually add vinegar to taste, a little at a time. Transfer to a serving dish, cover, and chill in the refrigerator. Garnish the eggplant salad with the parsley, chopped bell pepper, and tomato. Sprinkle with a little salt and olive oil and serve with crackers or crudités.

Makes 2 cups (450 ml / 16 fl oz)
Preparation time 2 hours (including chilling)
Cooking time 30 minutes

Note: You can substitute 2 tablespoons grated onion for the garlic and lemon juice for the vinegar. Alternatively, add ½ cup (120 ml / 4 fl oz) Mayonnaise (p 60) to the eggplant and garlic purée, plus a few drops of Tabasco sauce, if you like.

☐ p 147

- 5–6 garlic cloves, finely chopped
- ¾ teaspoon salt
- 2 potatoes, about 7 oz (200 g) total weight, cooked and peeled
- ¾ cup (50 g / 2 oz) day-old bread crumbs
- 4 tablespoons red wine vinegar
- 5 tablespoons water
- ½ cup (120 ml / 4 fl oz) olive oil

GARLIC SAUCE
ΣΚΟΡΔΑΛΙΑ ΜΕ ΨΩΜΙ
Skordalia me psomi

Process all the ingredients in a food processor at medium speed for 1–2 minutes, until smooth and thoroughly mixed. If the sauce is too thick, add some more water and process for 1–2 seconds more, or until the required consistency is reached.

Makes 2 cups (450 ml / 16 fl oz)
Preparation time 40 minutes

▢ p 147

- 2 oz (50 g) day-old bread, crusts removed
- 5 tablespoons water or fish stock
- 4–5 garlic cloves
- ½ teaspoon salt
- 2 small potatoes, cooked
- 4 tablespoons red wine vinegar
- ½ cup (120 ml / 4 fl oz) olive oil

POTATO-GARLIC SAUCE, ISLAND STYLE
ΑΛΙΑΔΑ, ΣΚΟΡΔΑΛΙΑ ΝΗΣΙΩΤΙΚΗ
Aliada, skordalia nisiotiki

Tear the bread into pieces, put it into a bowl, add the water or stock, and let soak. Meanwhile, crush the garlic cloves with the salt in a large mortar with a pestle. Gradually add the cooked potatoes, one at a time, blending well. Squeeze out the bread and gradually blend it into the mixture together with the vinegar. Beat in the oil, a little at a time, until it has all been absorbed and the mixture is thick and smooth. Serve the sauce with fried foods or boiled vegetables. This is the classic Greek sauce for boiled beets (beetroot).

Makes 2 cups (450 ml / 16 fl oz)
Preparation time 40 minutes

Note: The recipe can also be made in a food processor. Process all the ingredients together at medium speed for a few seconds. If the mixture is too stiff, add 1–2 tablespoons warm water and process for a few more minutes.

- ½ cup (50 g / 2 oz) cashew nuts
- 3½ cups (400 g / 14 oz) pitted (stoned) black olives, sliced
- 3 tablespoons olive oil (optional)
- 1–2 tablespoons red wine vinegar
- ½ teaspoon dried oregano
- 1 small garlic clove (optional)

OLIVE PASTE
ΠΑΣΤΑ ΕΛΙΑΣ
Pasta elias

Put the nuts into a food processor and grind to a smooth paste. Add the remaining ingredients and process for 1–2 minutes, until the mixture is well blended. Serve with crackers, spread on sandwiches, or use as a sauce for cooked pasta. This is a delicious meze with ouzo.

Makes 1 cup (250 ml / 8 fl oz)
Preparation time 30 minutes

▢ p 147

WALNUT-GARLIC SAUCE
ΣΚΟΡΔΑΛΙΑ ΜΕ ΚΑΡΥΔΙΑ
Skordalia me karidia

- 2 oz (50 g) bread, crusts removed
- 4 garlic cloves
- ½ teaspoon salt
- 1½ cups (175 g / 6 oz) finely ground walnuts
- 4 tablespoons red wine vinegar
- 5 tablespoons olive oil

Tear the bread into pieces, put it into a bowl, add 5 tablespoons water, and let soak. Meanwhile, crush the garlic with the salt in a mortar with a pestle. Add the ground walnuts, a little at a time, blending well. Gently squeeze out the bread and gradually work it into the mixture, alternating with small quantities of vinegar and olive oil. Beat well after each addition until the paste is smooth. If the mixture curdles, gradually blend in a small quantity of warm water. Cover and chill until ready to serve as a meze or to accompany fried fish or vegetable fritters.

Makes 2 cups (450 ml / 16 fl oz)
Preparation time 45 minutes (including chilling)

Vefa's secret: The sauce also can be made in a food processor or blender. Combine all the ingredients and process for a few seconds, until well blended. Add more garlic cloves if you like a fuller flavor.

PARSLEY AND BULGUR WHEAT SALAD
ΜΑΪΝΤΑΝΟΣΑΛΑΤΑ ΜΕ ΠΛΙΓΟΥΡΙ
Maintanosalata me pligouri

- ½ cup (80 g / 3 oz) medium bulgur wheat
- 1½ cups (80 g / 3 oz) finely chopped fresh parsley
- ¼ cup (15 g / ½ oz) finely chopped fresh mint
- 1 large tomato, peeled, seeded, and chopped
- ½ cup (4) finely chopped scallions (spring onions)
- ¼ cup (50 ml / 2 fl oz) freshly squeezed lemon juice
- 3 tablespoons olive oil
- ¼ teaspoon salt
- ½ teaspoon pepper
- lettuce leaves, to serve (optional)

Put the bulgur wheat into a bowl, pour in 1 cup (250 ml / 8 fl oz) water, and set aside for 30 minutes, then drain off any excess liquid. Transfer the drained bulgur wheat to another bowl and stir in the parsley, mint, tomatoes, scallions, and half the lemon juice. Set aside for another 30 minutes. Beat the oil with the remaining lemon juice, the salt, and pepper and pour the mixture over the salad. Serve on a bed of lettuce or in a shallow salad dish.

Makes 3 cups (500 g / 1 lb 2 oz)
Preparation time 1¼ hours (including soaking and standing)

- 2¼ lb (1 kg) eggplants (aubergines)
- 1 cup (120 g / 4 oz) pine nuts
- 2 garlic cloves, finely chopped
- ¼ teaspoon salt
- freshly ground white pepper
- 4 tablespoons olive oil
- 4 tablespoons red wine vinegar or freshly squeezed lemon juice
- finely chopped fresh parsley, to garnish

PINE NUT AND EGGPLANT (AUBERGINE) DIP
ΚΟΥΚΟΥΝΑΡΟΣΑΛΑΤΑ
Koukounarosalata

Light the barbecue or preheat the broiler (grill). Grill the eggplants over charcoal or broil (grill) under the broiler, turning frequently, for about 30 minutes, until the skins are charred and the pulp is soft. Unwrap, plunge into cold water, and peel immediately to prevent discoloration. Drain in a colander and cut crosswise into pieces. Pulse the pine nuts in a blender to form a smooth paste. Put the eggplants, garlic, salt, and pine nut paste into a food processor, season with white pepper, and process until thoroughly combined. With the motor running, gradually add the oil through the feeder tube, a drop at a time to begin with, then in a thin, steady stream. Gradually add the vinegar or lemon juice, a little at a time. Transfer the mixture to a bowl, cover with plastic wrap (cling film), and chill in refrigerator. Sprinkle with the parsley before serving. As an alternative, substitute 2 tablespoons finely grated onion for the garlic. For a spicier flavor, add several drops of Tabasco sauce.

Makes 3 cups (500 g / 1 lb 2 oz)
Preparation time 45 minutes (including chilling)
Cooking time 30 minutes

- 1 lb 2 oz (500 g) feta cheese
- 4 tablespoons olive oil, plus extra for frying (optional)
- 2 long hot green peppers
- ¼ teaspoon freshly ground pepper
- 1 tablespoon red wine vinegar
- crackers or breadsticks, to serve

SPICY FETA CHEESE DIP
ΚΤΥΠΗΤΗ ΜΕ ΠΙΠΕΡΙΑ Η ΤΥΡΟΚΑΦΤΕΡΗ
Ktipiti me piperia i tirokafteri

If the cheese is very salty and hard, soak it in cold water for 1 hour, then drain. Preheat the broiler (grill) or heat a little olive oil in a skillet or frying pan. Broil (grill) or fry the peppers, turning frequently, for 15–20 minutes, or until charred and blistered. Drain on paper towels and let stand until cool enough to handle, then peel and seed. Using a fork, mash the peppers and the feta together in a bowl, then gradually beat in the olive oil, 1 tablespoon at a time, until the mixture is smooth and thoroughly bended. (*Ktipiti* can also be prepared in a food processor.) Add ground pepper and vinegar to taste. If the mixture is too stiff, add some milk or cream to soften it. If hot peppers are not available, use mild ones and add 10–15 drops Tabasco sauce to give the spicy flavor. Serve with crackers or breadsticks.

Makes 2½ cups (600 ml / 1 pint)
Preparation time 1½ hours (including optional soaking)

RUSSIAN SALAD
ΡΩΣΙΚΗ ΣΑΛΑΤΑ
Rosiki salata

Put the beans into a pan, pour in water to cover, bring to a boil, and cook, for about 1 hour, until tender. Meanwhile, put the potato, carrot, and peas into another pan, add a little water, and cook for 10–15 minutes, until tender but still firm. Drain and let cool. Drain the beans and rinse well under cold running water, then let cool completely. Put the beans, cooked vegetables, capers, pickles, pimiento, and eggs into a bowl, season with salt and pepper, and mix well. Add the lemon juice and mayonnaise and toss lightly. Serve with crackers. This is delicious with meatballs or cod croquettes.

Makes 3 cups (500 g / 1 lb 2 oz)
Preparation time 12½ hours (including soaking)
Cooking time 1 hour

- ⅓ cup (50 g / 2 oz) small dried white beans, such as navy (haricot) beans, soaked overnight in cold water to cover and drained
- 1 potato, diced
- 1 large carrot, diced
- ¾ cup (80 g / 3 oz) shelled fresh or frozen peas
- 2 tablespoons capers
- 2 tablespoons chopped dill pickles (pickled cucumbers)
- 2 tablespoons chopped pimiento
- 2 hard-boiled eggs, chopped
- salt and pepper
- 1 tablespoon freshly squeezed lemon juice
- 1 cup (250 ml / 8 fl oz) Mayonnaise (p 60)
- crackers, to serve

CAPER DIP FROM SYROS
ΣΥΡΙΑΝΗ ΚΑΠΑΡΟΣΑΛΑΤΑ
Siriani kaparosalata

Cook the potatoes in boiling salted water for 25–30 minutes, or until tender. Drain and mash them with a potato masher, then gradually beat in the oil until smooth. Put the capers, onion, and vinegar into a blender and pulse to a paste. Stir the paste into the potato purée together with the mayonnaise. Season to taste with salt and pepper. Serve the salad cold, sprinkled with chopped parsley and accompanied by toasted garlic bread.

Makes 2 cups (450 ml / 16 fl oz)
Preparation time 30 minutes

Vefa's secret: Caper salad is also good with the addition of 1 tablespoon chopped dill pickles (pickled cucumbers). You can omit the mayonnaise if you like.

- 2 potatoes, peeled and quartered
- 5 tablespoons olive oil
- scant ¾ cup (120 g / 4 oz) capers, rinsed and drained
- 1 onion, grated
- 1–2 tablespoons red wine vinegar
- 2 tablespoons Mayonnaise (p 60)
- salt and pepper
- 2 tablespoons finely chopped fresh parsley, to garnish
- toasted garlic bread, to serve

- 6 thick slices of day-old bread, crusts removed
- 7 oz (200 g) cured cod's roe
- 2 tablespoons finely chopped onion
- 1¼ cups (300 ml / ½ pint) olive or corn oil
- 5 tablespoons freshly squeezed lemon juice
- 3 scallions (spring onions), thinly chopped, to garnish
- small Kalamata olives, to garnish
- crispbread, crackers, and ouzo, to serve

TARAMOSALATA
ΤΑΡΑΜΟΣΑΛΑΤΑ
Taramosalata

Tear the bread into pieces, put it into a bowl, pour in a little water, and let soak for 5 minutes, then gently squeeze out. Put the roe, onion, and a third of the oil in a food processor and process for a few seconds, until the roe is broken down and the mixture is blended. Add the soaked bread, a little at a time, processing after each addition until thoroughly blended. With the motor running, gradually add the remaining oil in a thin steady stream through the feeder tube until the mixture is smooth and combined. Add the lemon juice, a little at a time, and process for a few seconds until the paste is thickened and pale pink. If the taramosalata is too thick, add a little club soda (soda water) or water and beat until light and soft. Transfer to a serving dish, cover, and chill in the refrigerator. Garnish with the scallions and black olives. Serve with crispbread, crackers, and ouzo with ice.

Makes 2 cups (450 ml / 16 fl oz)
Preparation time 45 minutes (including chilling)

Note: You can substitute 7 oz (200 g) cooked, peeled potatoes for the bread and add ⅔ cup (65 g / 2 ½ oz) ground unsalted almonds, peanuts, or hazelnuts.

Vefa's secret: Both pink and white fish roe are available. The white is more expensive and delicate in flavor, but the pink gives the taramosalata its lovely color. Using half pink and half white fish roe is, perhaps, the ideal combination. Also, for a lighter texture, use half olive oil and half corn oil.

▢ p 147

- 1 medium slice day-old bread, crusts removed
- 4 tablespoons olive oil, plus extra for frying
- 2 oz (50 g) smoked herring roe
- 3 tablespoons freshly squeezed lemon juice

SMOKED HERRING ROE DIP FROM CYPRUS
ΡΕΓΓΟΣΑΛΑΤΑ
Regosalata

Tear the bread into pieces, put into a bowl, add 2–3 tablespoons cold water, and let soak. Meanwhile, heat a little olive oil in a skillet or frying pan. Add the roe and cook lightly on both sides for 5–8 minutes, until golden brown. Remove from the skillet and mash with a fork. Transfer to a food processor. Squeeze out the bread and add it to the roe with the 4 tablespoons oil and the lemon juice and process for a few seconds, until smooth and thoroughly blended.

Makes ¾ cup (175 ml / 6 fl oz)
Preparation time 15 minutes

SOUPS

-

ΣΟΥΠΕΣ

-

Soupes

Soup has been the comfort food of rich and poor alike almost since cooking began. It could have been sheer ingenuity, or perhaps just the threat of starvation, that first led to the addition of some old bones and leftovers to a pot of hot water with roots, herbs, and coarsely ground grain. Clay ovens and utensils, developed as far back as the fourth to fifth millennium BC, improved soup making and cookery in general. Analysis of residues from ancient cooking pots have established that meat, legumes (pulses), such as garbanzo beans (chickpeas), lentils, and fava (broad) beans, herbs, wild greens, barley, olive oil, and wine had been cooked in them—in other words, the same ingredients still used in modern Greek stews and soups.

The Greeks themselves consider *fasolada* (bean soup), not moussaka, to be their national dish. Lentils boiled with garlic, olive oil, and vinegar, a dish enjoyed by their ancestors, is the same *fakes soupa* that Greek mothers still ladle out for their families. Another soup of ancient lineage is the *magiritsa* or Easter soup made from the organ meats (offal) of the Paschal lamb. Any opportunity to taste an authentic *mageritsa* in the *agora* (central market) on Athinas Street in Athens, where it is found on the menu throughout the year, should not be missed. There is even a kind of "instant" soup made from *trahana*, a rough pasta often mentioned in medieval Byzantine sources. *Trahanosoupa* is prepared by simmering the dried pasta in water or broth, and served with lemon juice and grated cheese. Another classic soup with ancient origins is *avgolemono*, the delicious egg and lemon combination peculiar to Greek cuisine, which can refer to both soup and sauce. The addition of beaten egg and lemon to the plainest broth magically gives it a silky-smooth velvet texture. Many Greek cooks maintain that *avgolemono* can be used in just about any dish, unless it contains garlic or tomatoes.

Steaming hot meat soup is a staple dish in many Greek homes in winter, while fish soups are favorites in summer. Most Greek traditional soups are compound broths with the solid ingredients cut into small pieces and served with the liquid, and some of them are nourishing enough to make a meal in themselves. They can provide two courses from a single pot in the form of a broth and a meat or fish course. Soups are often served with toasted garlic bread, which in Greece is made with a mixture of olive oil, chopped garlic and oregano.

GENERAL INSTRUCTIONS

Making a soup is a relaxed process that is more or less rule-free. The basic method, whether it contains meat, vegetables, or fish, is the same. Simply simmer the ingredients in water or stock until they have yielded their flavors to the liquid. For meat soups, remove any scum that forms on the surface. After skimming, add the aromatic vegetables, cover, and simmer very gently. If you allow it to boil, the solid ingredients may disintegrate. A broth that is correctly set to simmer needs only to be left undisturbed. The proportion of vegetables to meat or fish can be varied according to your taste, but be careful not to overcook them unless you intend to purée them for a cream soup. To add extra flavor to the liquid, you can stud the onion with two or three whole cloves, or add a bay leaf, allspice berries, peppercorns, or thyme, depending on the other ingredients in the dish.

ARTICHOKE SOUP
ΣΟΥΠΑ ΜΕ ΑΓΓΙΝΑΡΕΣ
Soupa me aginares

- 6 globe artichokes
- 2 tablespoons freshly squeezed lemon juice
- 1 onion, sliced
- 2 leeks, white part only, sliced
- 2 tablespoons olive oil
- 3 cups (750 ml / 1¼ pints) chicken stock
- 1 potato, diced
- 6 fresh dill or parsley sprigs
- salt and pepper
- ½ cup (120 ml / 4 fl oz) strained plain or thick Greek yogurt

TO GARNISH
- 4 tablespoons plain yogurt
- 3 tablespoons finely chopped fresh dill or parsley

Trim the artichokes, removing the tough outer leaves and the hairy choke, leaving only the cup-shaped bases. Chop, and toss with half the lemon juice to prevent discoloration. Put them into a pan with the onion, leeks, and oil and cook over medium heat, stirring frequently, for about 8 minutes, until softened. Pour in the stock, add the potato, dill or parsley, and the remaining lemon juice, and season with salt and pepper. Bring to a boil, reduce the heat, cover, and simmer for about 20 minutes, or until the vegetables are tender. Remove from the heat and let cool slightly, then process to a purée in a blender or food processor. Pass the soup through a strainer into a bowl and let cool completely, then chill in the refrigerator for 3 hours. Shortly before serving, stir in the yogurt and taste and adjust the seasoning if necessary. Ladle into four soup bowls and serve cold, garnishing each with 1 tablespoon yogurt and a sprinkling of chopped dill or parsley.

Serves 4
Preparation time 3½ hours (including chilling)
Cooking time 30 minutes

BEAN SOUP
ΦΑΣΟΛΑΔΑ
Fasolada

Rinse the beans, put them into a large pan, and pour in cold water to cover. Bring to a boil, cover, and simmer for around 30 minutes, until almost tender. Drain and set aside. Meanwhile, heat the oil in a large heavy pan. Add the onion and cook over low heat, stirring occasionally, for about 5 minutes, until softened and translucent. Put the tomatoes and the tomato paste into a food processor and process to a purée, then stir into the pan. Add the carrots, celery, celery leaves, chile, if using, and bell pepper, if using, and pour in the hot water. Bring to a boil, add the drained beans, reduce the heat, cover, and simmer for 1–2 hours, until the beans are tender and the soup has thickened. Check frequently during cooking and add more hot water, if necessary. The cooking time and the amount of additional water depends on the quality, age, and condition of the beans. Serve hot, sprinkled with freshly ground black pepper and accompanied by olives, pickles, and smoked herring.

Serves 6
Preparation time 13 hours (including soaking)
Cooking time 1½–2½ hours

☐ p 164

- 2¾ cups (500 g / 1 lb 2 oz) small dried white beans, such as navy (haricot) beans, soaked overnight in cold water to cover and drained
- ½ cup (120 ml / 4 fl oz) olive oil
- 1 large onion, finely chopped
- 1 lb 2 oz (500 g) fresh or canned tomatoes, peeled and chopped
- 1 tablespoon tomato paste
- 2 carrots, sliced
- 1 small celery stalk, sliced, leaves reserved
- 1 small dried red chile, crushed (optional)
- 1 small green bell pepper, seeded and chopped (optional)
- 4 cups (1 litre / 1¾ pints) hot water
- pepper
- olives, pickles, and smoked herring, to serve

- scant 1½ cups (250 g / 9 oz) dried pinto or red kidney beans, soaked overnight in water to cover and drained
- scant 1½ cups (250 g / 9 oz) medium dried white beans, such as cannellini beans, soaked overnight in water to cover and drained
- 1 large onion, grated
- 2 large carrots, sliced
- 1 celery stalk, chopped, leaves reserved
- 1 small dried red chile, crushed (optional)
- 1 large green bell pepper, seeded and chopped
- 14 oz (400 g) canned chopped tomatoes or 2¼ lb (1kg) fresh ripe tomatoes, chopped
- 1 teaspoon sugar
- 1 tablespoon red wine vinegar
- 4 tablespoons finely chopped fresh parsley
- 4 cups (1 litre / 1¾ pints) hot water
- salt and pepper
- olives and pickled vegetables, to serve

MOUNT ATHOS MONASTERY BEAN SOUP
ΦΑΣΟΛΙΑ ΣΟΥΠΑ ΑΛΑΔΩΤΑ
Fasolia soupa aladota

If using red kidney beans, first rinse them and put them into a saucepan. Cover with water, bring to a boil and boil vigorously for 15 minutes. Drain, then rinse both kinds of beans and put them into a large pan. Pour in 8¾ cups (2 litres / 3½ pints) water and bring to a boil, then reduce the heat, and simmer for about 30 minutes. Drain and set aside. Meanwhile, put the onion in a large pan with ½ cup (120 ml / 4 fl oz) water and cook over medium heat, stirring constantly until all the liquid has evaporated. Add the carrot, celery, celery leaves, chile, if using, and bell pepper and cook, stirring constantly, until the vegetables have softened. Stir in the tomatoes, sugar, vinegar, parsley, drained beans, and hot water and season with salt and pepper. Cover and simmer the soup for 1½–2 hours, until the beans are tender and the soup has thickened. Check the soup frequently and add more hot water, if necessary. The cooking time and the amount of additional water required depends on the quality, age, and condition of the beans. Serve the soup hot with olives and pickled vegetables.

Serves 6
Preparation time 13 hours (including soaking)
Cooking time 2–2½ hours

- 2¾ cups (300 g / 11 oz) cooked peas
- 4 cups (1 litre / 1¾ pints) vegetable stock
- 2 tablespoons (25 g / 1 oz) butter
- 1 tablespoon all-purpose (plain) flour
- ½ cup (120 ml / 4 fl oz) strained plain or thick Greek yogurt
- salt and pepper
- croutons and finely chopped fresh dill, to garnish

CREAM OF PEA SOUP
ΣΟΥΠΑ ΚΡΕΜΑ ΜΕ ΑΡΑΚΑ
Soupa krema me araka

Put the peas in a blender, add a ladleful of the stock, and process until smooth. Melt the butter in a small pan, add the flour, and cook over low heat, stirring constantly, for 1 minute. Gradually stir in 1 cup (250 ml / 8 fl oz) of the remaining stock and cook over medium heat, stirring constantly, for 5 minutes. Stir in the puréed peas and remaining stock, reduce the heat, cover, and simmer for 5–10 minutes. Strain the soup into a clean pan, stir in the yogurt, season to taste with salt and pepper, and heat through. Serve immediately, garnished with croutons and finely chopped dill.

Serves 4
Preparation time 10 minutes
Cooking time 15 minutes

Bean soup, p 162

Traditional Easter soup from Corfu, p 167

MOUNT ATHOS MONASTERY LENTIL SOUP
ΦΑΚΕΣ ΣΟΥΠΑ ΑΛΑΔΩΤΕΣ
Fakes soupa aladotes

Rinse the lentils, then put them into a pan, pour in water to cover, and bring to a boil. Cook for 5 minutes, then drain, discarding the cooking liquid. This prevents the lentils from darkening during cooking. Process the tomatoes to a purée in a food processor. Put the onion and garlic in a large pan, add 6 tablespoons water, and cook until the water has evaporated and the onion and garlic have softened. Pour in 4 cups (1 litre / 1¾ pints) water, add the tomatoes, sugar and bay leaves, season with salt and pepper and bring to a boil. Add the lentils, reduce the heat, cover, and simmer for 30–60 minutes, or until the lentils are tender. Stir in the vinegar and oregano and cook for 5 minutes more. Remove the pan from the heat and remove and discard the bay leaves. Sprinkle the soup with freshly ground pepper and extra oregano and vinegar, if you like. Serve the soup hot or at room temperature, accompanied by olives and pickled vegetables.

Serves 4
Preparation time 15 minutes
Cooking time 30–60 minutes

- 2¼ cups (500 g / 1 lb 2 oz) green lentils
- 1 lb 2 oz (500 g) canned chopped tomatoes or fresh ripe tomatoes, peeled and chopped
- 1 small onion, grated
- 2 garlic cloves, sliced
- ½ teaspoon sugar
- 2 bay leaves
- salt and pepper
- 1 tablespoon red wine vinegar, plus extra to garnish
- 1 teaspoon dried oregano, plus extra to garnish
- olives and pickled vegetables, to serve

PASTA AND VEGETABLE SOUP
ΑΣΤΡΑΚΙ ΜΕ ΛΑΧΑΝΙΚΑ
Astraki me lahanika

Heat the oil in a large pan. Add the onion and leek and cook over low heat, stirring occasionally, for about 5 minutes, until softened and translucent. Pour in the vegetable stock, add the peas and bell peppers, increase the heat, and bring to a boil. Reduce the heat and simmer for 15 minutes. Add the pasta, paprika, and cayenne and season to taste with salt and pepper. Simmer for about 15 minutes more, until the vegetables and pasta are tender. Remove from the heat, stir in lemon juice to taste, and serve immediately, sprinkled with freshly ground pepper. The soup may also be served at room temperature. Greek cooks omit the olive oil during Lent and the soup is still delicious.

Serves 6
Preparation time 15 minutes
Cooking time 30 minutes

Note: If using garden peas or petit pois rather than Greek field peas, add them 5 minutes before the end of cooking.

- 5 tablespoons olive oil
- 1 large onion, finely chopped
- 1 small leek, white part only, finely chopped
- 5 cups (1.2 litres / 2 pints) vegetable stock
- ¾ cup (80 g / 3 oz) fresh or frozen peas
- ½ red bell pepper, seeded and finely chopped
- ½ yellow bell pepper, seeded and finely chopped
- scant 1 cup (100 g / 3½ oz) small pasta stars
- 1 teaspoon paprika
- ¼ teaspoon cayenne pepper
- salt and pepper
- freshly squeezed lemon juice, to taste

- 2 tablespoons (25 g / 1 oz) butter
- 4 scallions (spring onions), white part only, finely chopped
- 2 tablespoons finely chopped onion
- 1 tablespoon all-purpose (plain) flour
- 3 cups (750 ml / 1¼ pints) chicken or vegetable stock
- 1½ cups (350 g / 12 oz) puréed pumpkin or yellow winter squash
- ½ cup (120 ml / 4 fl oz) heavy (double) cream (optional)
- pinch of freshly grated nutmeg
- ½ teaspoon salt
- ¼ teaspoon freshly ground white pepper
- ½–⅔ cup (120-150 ml / 4-5 fl oz) plain yogurt, to garnish (optional)
- croutons or breadsticks, to serve

PUMPKIN OR WINTER SQUASH SOUP
ΣΟΥΠΑ ΜΕ ΚΙΤΡΙΝΟ ΚΟΛΟΚΥΘΙ
Soupa me kitrino kolokithi

Melt the butter in a pan. Add the scallions and onion and cook over low heat, stirring occasionally, for about 5 minutes, until softened and translucent. Sprinkle with the flour and cook, stirring constantly, for 1 minute. Gradually stir in the stock, stirring until thickened. Stir in the pumpkin or squash purée and simmer, stirring occasionally, for 10 minutes. Add the cream, if using, the nutmeg, salt, and white pepper and heat through, stirring constantly. If the soup is too thick, stir in a little more stock. Remove the pan from the heat and ladle the soup into bowls. If you did not use cream, add 2 tablespoons yogurt to each bowl. Serve immediately with croutons or breadsticks.

Serves 4
Preparation time 10 minutes
Cooking time 20 minutes

- 1 lb 2 oz (500 g) lamb's intestines
- 1 lamb's pluck (liver, heart, and spleen)
- red wine vinegar, for sprinkling
- ½ cup (120 ml / 4 fl oz) olive oil
- 1 cup (80 g / 3 oz) finely chopped scallions (spring onions)
- 1 onion, finely chopped
- 2 cups (450 ml / 16 fl oz) hot water
- ½ cup (25 g / 1 oz) finely chopped fresh parsley
- ½ cup (15 g / ½ oz) finely chopped fresh dill
- 3 tablespoons tomato paste
- salt and pepper

TRADITIONAL EASTER SOUP FROM CORFU
ΤΣΙΛΙΧΟΥΡΔΑ
Tsilihourda

Wash the intestines well. They are easier to clean if you cut them into 1–3 foot (30-60 cm) lengths and then, with the help of a knitting needle or thin skewer, turn the pieces inside out, and rinse them under cold running water. Put them into a bowl, sprinkle with a little vinegar, and set aside for 10 minutes, then rinse, and drain. Blanch them in salted water for 5 minutes, drain well, and chop finely. Blanch the lamb's pluck, drain well, and chop finely. Heat the oil in a large pan. Add the scallions and onion and cook over low heat, stirring occasionally, for about 5 minutes, until softened and translucent. Add all the chopped meat and cook, stirring constantly, for 5 minutes. Pour in the hot water, cover, and simmer for about 30 minutes, until the meat is almost tender. Add the herbs, stir in the tomato paste, season with salt and pepper, and simmer for 20 minutes more, until the meat is cooked and the liquid has thickened. Serve hot.

Serves 6
Preparation time 30 minutes
Cooking time 50 minutes

❑ p 165

TRAHANA SOUP
ΤΡΑΧΑΝΟΣΟΥΠΑ
Trahanosoupa

- 4 cups (1 litre / 1¾ pints) meat stock or water
- 3 tablespoons (40 g / 1½ oz) butter
- 3½ oz (100 g) Sour or Sweet trahana (p 280 or 281)
- 3½ oz (100 g) feta cheese, crumbled, plus extra to garnish
- salt and pepper
- finely chopped fresh parsley, to garnish
- freshly squeezed lemon juice, to serve (optional)

Trahana is a dried rustic pasta still made in August in many areas of Greece from milk and semolina flour. It is used to make this delicious winter soup.

Bring the stock or water to a boil in a large pan. Stir in the butter and the trahana and simmer for about 15 minutes, or until the trahana swells and the soup is thickened. Just before removing from the pan from heat, add the feta. Season with salt and pepper and serve hot, garnished with chopped parsley and extra crumbled feta. You can also serve the soup plain with freshly squeezed lemon juice.

Serves 4
Preparation time 5 minutes
Cooking time 15 minutes

CHICKEN AND VEGETABLE EGG-LEMON SOUP
ΣΟΥΠΑ ΜΕ ΛΑΧΑΝΙΚΑ ΑΥΓΟΛΕΜΟΝΟ
Soupa me lahanika avgolemono

- 3¼ lb (1.5 kg) chicken, poached, cooking liquid reserved
- 4 tablespoons (50 g / 2 oz) butter
- 1 large potato, diced
- 2 carrots, diced
- salt and pepper
- ½ cup (25 g / 1 oz) finely chopped fresh parsley
- 1 egg
- 4 tablespoons freshly squeezed lemon juice

Remove and discard the skin from the chicken. Cut the meat off the bones and finely chop the meat. Strain the reserved cooking liquid and pour 4 cups (1 litre / 1¾ pints) into a large pan. Add the butter, potato, and carrots, season with salt and pepper, and bring to a boil. Cook over medium heat for about 20 minutes, until the vegetables are tender. Add the chopped chicken and parsley and heat through. Whisk the egg and lemon juice together in a bowl, then gradually whisk in 4–5 tablespoons of the soup. Pour the egg-lemon mixture into the pan and stir gently or shake the pan to distribute it. Do not let the soup boil. Remove the pan from the heat and serve.

Serves 6
Preparation time 10 minutes
Cooking time 30 minutes

- 5 tablespoons olive oil
- 1 onion, coarsely chopped
- 4 cups (1 litre / 1¾ pints) chicken or vegetable stock
- salt and pepper
- 1½ cups (200 g / 7 oz) green (French) beans, cut into short lengths
- 4 artichoke hearts, cut into small pieces
- 2 zucchini (courgettes), diced
- ¾ cup (80 g / 3 oz) shelled fresh or frozen peas
- 10 white mushrooms, sliced
- 4 tablespoons chopped fresh parsley
- 2 tomatoes, peeled, seeded, and chopped
- 3½ oz (100 g) egg noodles (pasta)
- sesame bread sticks and feta cheese, to serve

SUMMER VEGETABLE SOUP
ΚΑΛΟΚΑΙΡΙΝΗ ΧΟΡΤΟΣΟΥΠΑ
Kalokerini hortosoupa

Heat the oil in a large pan. Add the onion and cook over high heat for 2–3 minutes, until softened and translucent. Pour in the stock and bring to a boil. Season with salt and pepper and add all the remaining ingredients except the noodles. Cover and simmer for about 15 minutes, until all the vegetables are almost tender. Add the noodles and cook for 8 minutes more, or until al dente. Serve the soup hot or at room temperature, sprinkled with freshly ground pepper and accompanied by sesame bread sticks and feta cheese.

Serves 4
Preparation time 30 minutes
Cooking time 1½ hours

p 170

- 5 tablespoons olive oil
- salt and pepper
- 11 oz (300 g) cabbage, coarsely chopped
- 2 potatoes, diced
- 2 small onions, coarsely chopped
- 2 carrots, diced
- 1 leek, white part only, thickly sliced
- 1 small fennel bulb, coarsely chopped
- 1 celery stalk, sliced
- 4 tablespoons chopped celery leaves
- 4 tablespoons freshly squeezed lemon juice
- croutons, to serve

WINTER VEGETABLE SOUP
ΧΕΙΜΩΝΙΑΤΙΚΗ ΧΟΡΤΟΣΟΥΠΑ
Himoniatiki hortosoupa

Pour 4 cups (1 litre / 1¾ pints) water into a large pan, add the olive oil, and bring to a boil. Season with salt and pepper and add all the remaining ingredients except the lemon juice. Cover and simmer for 30–40 minutes, or until the vegetables are tender and the soup has reduced. Stir in the lemon juice and remove from the heat. Ladle into bowls, sprinkle with freshly ground pepper, and serve with croutons.

Serves 4
Preparation time 30 minutes
Cooking time 30–40 minutes

Summer vegetable soup, p 169

Greek fisherman's soup, p 175

LENTEN VEGETABLE SOUP WITH TAHINI
ΣΟΥΠΑ ΜΕ ΛΑΧΑΝΙΚΑ ΑΛΑΔΩΤΗ
Soupa me lahanika aladoti

Put all the vegetables into a large pan, pour in 8¾ cups (2 litres / 3½ pints) water, and bring to a boil. Cook over medium heat for about 40 minutes, until the vegetables are softened and very tender. Strain the cooking liquid into a clean pan and process the vegetables to a purée in a food processor. Return the vegetables to the stock and bring to a boil. Meanwhile, beat the tahini with the lemon juice and 4 tablespoons water, then beat in 4–5 tablespoons of the hot soup. Pour this mixture into the soup, stirring vigorously. If the soup is too thick, add a little hot water. Combine the garnish ingredients and serve the soup in bowls, sprinkled with the garnish.

Serves 4
Preparation time 15 minutes
Cooking time 50 minutes

- 1 large carrot, coarsely chopped
- 1 potato, coarsely chopped
- 1 onion, coarsely chopped
- 1 zucchini (courgette), coarsely chopped
- 1 celery stalk, coarsely chopped
- 1 large tomato, peeled and coarsely chopped
- 2⅓ cups (200 g / 7 oz) coarsely chopped chard
- 1 red bell pepper, seeded and coarsely chopped
- 1 cup (250 ml / 8 fl oz) tahini
- 4 tablespoons freshly squeezed lemon juice
- salt and pepper

TO GARNISH
- 4 tablespoons finely chopped fresh parsley
- 4 tablespoons ground walnuts
- ¼ teaspoon cayenne pepper
- ¼ teaspoon ground coriander

WHITE BEAN SOUP FROM LEFKADA
ΑΣΠΡΗ ΦΑΣΟΛΑΔΑ
Aspri fasolada

This soup is known as white *fasolada*: bean soup without the usual tomatoes that make it red.

Rinse the beans, put them into a large pan, and pour in cold water to cover. Bring to a boil and cook for 30 minutes, until they begin to soften. Drain and discard the water. Return the beans to the pan, pour in the boiling water and half the oil, and add the carrots, celery, and onion. Cook over medium heat for about 1 hour, until the beans are tender and the liquid has reduced. Season with salt and pepper. Remove from the heat, add the remaining oil and the lemon juice, and serve hot or at room temperature.

Serves 6
Preparation time 12½ hours (including soaking)
Cooking time 1½ hours

- 2¾ cups (500 g / 1 lb 2 oz) small dried white beans, such as navy (haricot) beans, soaked overnight in cold water to cover and drained
- 4 cups (1 litre / 1¾ pints) boiling water
- ½ cup (120 ml / 4 fl oz) olive oil
- 2 carrots, thinly sliced
- 1 celery stalk, finely chopped
- 1 onion, grated
- 4 tablespoons freshly squeezed lemon juice
- salt and pepper

- 1 cup (175 g / 6 oz) wheat berries
- 2 cups (450 ml / 16 fl oz) tan (see method, right)
- 5 tablespoons olive oil
- 1 onion, thinly sliced
- 2 tablespoons finely chopped fresh mint
- salt and pepper

WHEAT BERRY SOUP WITH YOGURT FROM PONTUS
ΣΟΥΡΒΑΣ ΤΑΝΟΜΕΝΟΣ
Siourvas tanomenos

Tan is a thin low-fat yogurt made by mixing equal quantities of yogurt and ice water, adding a pinch of salt, and stirring vigorously. It is similar to buttermilk, low in fat and rich in lactic acid. A refreshing drink at any time of day, it is especially popular during the hot summer months. Its keeping qualities can be increased by simmering it, straining it through a cheesecloth (muslin) bag, and adding salt. It is called *bakitan* or *paskitan* in Pontic Greek and is used as an ingredient in many dishes of the Black Sea region.

Rinse the wheat berries well under cold running water and put them into a pan. Pour in 4 cups (1 litre / 1¾ pints) water, add a pinch of salt, and bring to a boil. Reduce the heat and simmer for about 1 hour, until tender. Remove the pan from the heat. Stir a ladle of the hot liquid into the tan, then stir the mixture into the soup. Heat the oil in a skillet or frying pan, add the onion, and cook, stirring occasionally, for about 8 minutes, until lightly golden. Stir the onion and mint into the soup. Serve the *siourvas* hot, sprinkled with freshly ground black pepper.

Serves 4
Preparation time 10 minutes
Cooking time 1 hour

- 4 tablespoons olive oil
- 1 lb 2 oz (500 g) oyster mushrooms, finely chopped
- 1 cup (7–8) finely chopped scallions (spring onions)
- 4 tablespoons finely chopped fresh dill
- 4 tablespoons finely chopped fresh parsley
- 4 cups (1 litre / 1¾ pints) hot vegetable stock or water
- salt and pepper
- scant ½ cup (80 g / 3 oz) long-grain rice
- 1 egg
- 4 tablespoons freshly squeezed lemon juice

EASTER SOUP FOR VEGETARIANS
ΜΑΓΕΙΡΙΤΣΑ ΧΟΡΤΟΦΑΓΩΝ
Magiritsa hortofagon

Heat the oil in a large pan. Add the mushrooms and cook, stirring occasionally, for a few minutes, until softened. Add the scallions and cook, stirring occasionally, for 3 minutes more. Add the dill and parsley, pour in the stock or water, season with salt and pepper, and bring to a boil. Add the rice, cover, and simmer for 20 minutes, until the rice and mushrooms are tender. Beat the egg in a bowl with the lemon juice, then beat in a ladle of the hot soup. Stir the egg-lemon mixture into the pan, then remove from the heat. Do not let the soup boil. Serve hot, sprinkled with freshly ground pepper.

Serves 4
Preparation time 20 minutes
Cooking time 30 minutes

MOUNT ATHOS FISH SOUP
ΑΓΙΟΡΕΙΤΙΚΗ ΣΟΥΠΑ ΡΟΦΟΥ
Agioritiki soupa rofou

Put the sliced onions into a pan, pour in 2 cups (450 ml / 16 fl oz) water, and simmer for 30 minutes. Meanwhile, prepare the fish. Cut off and reserve the head. Cut the fish into thick slices and arrange in an ovenproof dish. Preheat the oven to 350°F (180°C / Gas Mark 4). Drain the onion stock into a pitcher (jug) and discard the onions. Pour the onion stock over the fish. Arrange the garlic cloves around the fish, drizzle with half the oil, season with salt and pepper, and bake for about 25 minutes, or until the flesh flakes easily and the liquid has reduced. Meanwhile, prepare the soup. Cut out and discard the gills from the fish head, taking care with the gill spines if using grouper. Put the head in a large pan, pour in 8¾ cups (2 litres / 3½ pints) water, add the celery, whole onion, and carrots, and season with salt and pepper. Bring to a boil, then reduce the heat, and cook for 10–15 minutes. Remove the fish head and continue to simmer until the vegetables are soft (about 25 minutes). Strain the stock into a clean pan and reserve the fish head and vegetables. Carefully remove the flesh from the fish head and flake. Mash the vegetables, mix with the flaked fish, and stir into the reserved stock. Stir in the tomato paste, if using. Add the pasta and the remaining oil and simmer for 10 minutes, or until the pasta is tender. Serve the hot soup as the first course, sprinkled with half the chopped parsley and accompanied by lemon wedges. Serve the baked fish as the second course. Transfer it to a warm platter, pour the cooking juices over it, and sprinkle with the remaining parsley.

Serves 6
Preparation time 30 minutes
Cooking time 1½ hours

- 2¼ lb (1 kg) onions, sliced
- 1 grouper or other white fish, weighing about 6½ lb (3 kg), cleaned
- 8 garlic cloves
- ⅔ cup (150 ml / ¼ pint) olive oil
- salt and pepper
- 2–3 celery stalks with leaves
- 1 onion
- 2 large carrots
- 1 tablespoon tomato paste (optional)
- ¾ cup (80 g / 3 oz) orzo pasta
- 4 tablespoons finely chopped fresh parsley, to serve
- lemon wedges, to serve

- ½ cup (120 ml / 4 fl oz) olive oil
- 1 small onion, halved
- 1 small carrot, halved
- 2 celery stalks, halved
- 10 black peppercorns
- 3¼ lb (1.5 kg) white fish, such as cod, sea bass, or grouper, cleaned
- 5 tablespoons short-grain rice or 2 large potatoes, diced
- 1–2 eggs
- 5 tablespoons freshly squeezed lemon juice
- salt and pepper
- Mayonnaise (p 60), capers, pickles, and cooked greens, to serve

FISH SOUP WITH EGG-LEMON SAUCE
ΨΑΡΟΣΟΥΠΑ ΑΥΓΟΛΕΜΟΝΟ
Psarosoupa avgolemono

Pour 6¼ cups (1.5 litres / 2½ pints) water into a large pan and add the oil, onion, carrot, celery, peppercorns, and a pinch of salt. Bring to a boil, reduce the heat, cover, and simmer for 15 minutes. Meanwhile, rinse the fish and cut it in half if necessary. Remove the vegetables from the pan. Add the fish to the pan, bring back to a boil, reduce the heat, and simmer for 15–20 minutes, until the fish is just cooked (do not overcook it). Transfer the fish to a platter and let cool. Strain the stock into a clean pan and bring to a boil. Stir in the rice or potatoes, cover, and simmer for about 20 minutes. If using potatoes, remove them from the soup and mash them in a bowl with a fork. Stir some of the soup into the potatoes, then add the mixture to the pan. Lightly beat the eggs with the lemon juice in a bowl and beat in a ladleful of the hot soup, then stir the mixture into the soup. Remove the pan from the heat. Serve the hot soup, sprinkled with freshly ground pepper, as a first course, then serve the fish with mayonnaise, capers, pickles and a dish of cooked greens.

Serves 6
Preparation time 30 minutes
Cooking time 50 minutes

- 2¼ lb (1 kg) assorted small fish, scaled and cleaned
- 9 oz (250 g) onions, thinly sliced
- 9 oz (250 g) tomatoes, peeled and thinly sliced
- 2–3 tablespoons finely chopped fresh parsley
- 5 tablespoons olive oil
- salt and pepper

GREEK FISHERMAN'S SOUP
KAKABIA
Kakavia

This ancient soup is believed to be a forerunner of *bouillabaisse*. Traditional *kakavia* is made by Greek fishermen in a small pot or *kakavi* on the deck of their caique. The pot is lined with onions, then tomatoes and parsley. It is then covered with fish, and simple seasonings, olive oil and hot water are added. The soup is simmered until the vegetables and fish bones have disintegrated. It is eaten without being strained, accompanied by lots of bread and retsina.

Put the fish in a large pan and pour in water to cover. Bring to a boil, cover, and simmer for 20 minutes. Remove the fish and remove and discard any large bones. Strain the stock and return to the pan. Add the fish, onions, tomatoes, parsley, and oil and season with salt and pepper. Cover and simmer over low heat for 2–3 hours, or until the soup is rich and thickened. Serve hot, sprinkled with freshly ground pepper.

Serves 6
Preparation time 1 hour
Cooking time 3 hours

☐ p 171

SHRIMP (PRAWN) AND VEGETABLE BROTH
ΓΑΡΙΔΟΣΟΥΠΑ
Garidosoupa

Peel the shrimp, leaving the heads and tails intact. Devein, rinse, and drain well. Pour 1 cup (250 ml / 8 fl oz) water and the oil into a heavy pan, add the onion, chile, carrot, celery, garlic, and paprika, and season with salt, and pepper. Bring to a boil and cook over high heat for 5 minutes. Remove the vegetables with a slotted spoon, drain, and discard. Add the shrimp, cover the pan, and cook over high heat, stirring occasionally, for 7–8 minutes. Be careful not to overcook it or the shrimp will dry out. Remove the pan from the heat, and stir in the lemon juice. Serve the soup in deep plates sprinkled with the parsley or dill.

Serves 4
Preparation time 35 minutes
Cooking time 8 minutes

- 2 ¼ lb (1 kg) jumbo shrimp (king prawns)
- 4 tablespoons olive oil
- 1 small onion, halved
- 1 small chile, halved
- 1 small carrot, halved
- 1 celery stalk, cut into 3 pieces
- 1 garlic clove
- 1 teaspoon paprika
- salt and pepper
- 5 tablespoons freshly squeezed lemon juice
- 2 tablespoons finely chopped fresh parsley or dill

MUSSEL SOUP
ΣΟΥΠΑ ΜΕ ΜΥΔΙΑ
Soupa me midia

Scrub the mussels under cold running water and pull off the beards. Discard any with broken shells or that do not shut immediately when sharply tapped. Put them into a large pan, pour in ½ cup (120 ml / 4 fl oz) water, cover, and cook over high heat, shaking the pan occasionally, for 4–5 minutes, until the shells have opened. Remove the mussels with a slotted spoon and reserve ½ cup (120 ml / 4 fl oz) of the cooking liquid. Discard any mussels that remain shut. Mix the tomato paste with 2 tablespoons water in a bowl and stir into the puréed tomatoes. Heat the oil in a large pan. Add the garlic and cook over low heat for 2 minutes. Add the tomatoes, the reserved cooking liquid, the herbs, chile, sugar, and vinegar and season with salt and pepper. Simmer for 30 minutes. Meanwhile, remove the mussels from their shells. Add the mussels to the pan, stir, and heat through. Remove from the heat and serve the soup, sprinkled with freshly ground pepper and accompanied by toasted garlic bread.

Serves 4
Preparation time 20 minutes
Cooking time 30 minutes

- 3 ¼ lb (1.5 kg) mussels
- 1 tablespoon tomato paste
- 4 ripe tomatoes, peeled, seeded, and puréed
- 5 tablespoons olive oil
- 3 garlic cloves, finely chopped
- 4 tablespoons finely chopped fresh parsley
- 4 tablespoons finely chopped fresh basil
- 1 small dried red chile, crushed
- ½ teaspoon sugar
- 1 tablespoon balsamic vinegar
- salt and pepper
- toasted garlic bread, to serve

CLAM AND VEGETABLE SOUP
ΣΟΥΠΑ ΜΕ ΚΥΔΩΝΙΑ ΚΑΙ ΛΑΧΑΝΙΚΑ
Soupa me kidonia ke lahanika

- 3 tablespoons (40 g / 1½ oz) butter
- 2 scallions (spring onions), finely chopped
- 4 tablespoons chopped green bell pepper
- 4 tablespoons chopped celery
- 4 tablespoons chopped carrot
- 1 garlic clove, finely chopped
- 2 potatoes, diced
- 1 teaspoon salt
- ½ teaspoon black pepper, plus extra to serve
- 14 oz (400 g) shelled clams
- 4 tablespoons freshly squeezed lemon juice
- 2 tablespoons finely chopped fresh parsley

Melt the butter in a pan. Add the scallions, bell pepper, celery, carrot, and garlic and cook over medium heat, stirring frequently, for about 5 minutes, until the vegetables have softened. Add the potatoes, salt, and pepper, pour in 4 cups (1 litre / 1¾ pints) water, reduce the heat, cover, and simmer for about 30 minutes, until the potatoes are soft. Add the clams and cook for 5 minutes. If the soup is too thick, add a little hot water. Stir in the lemon juice, taste and adjust the seasoning, if necessary, and remove from the heat. Serve the soup immediately, sprinkled with freshly ground pepper and the parsley.

Serves 4
Preparation time 30 minutes
Cooking time 40 minutes

CHICKEN SOUP WITH EGG-LEMON SAUCE
ΚΟΤΟΣΟΥΠΑ ΑΥΓΟΛΕΜΟΝΟ
Kotosoupa avgolemono

- 1 small chicken, about 3¼ lb (1.5 kg)
- 4 tablespoons (50 g / 2 oz) butter or olive oil
- 1 small carrot, halved (optional)
- 1 small onion, halved (optional)
- salt and pepper
- ½ cup (100 g / 3½ oz) medium-grain rice
- 1–2 eggs
- 5 tablespoons freshly squeezed lemon juice

Remove and discard the skin from the chicken. Rinse the chicken well inside and out under cold running water, then put it into a large pan, and pour in water to cover. Bring to a boil over low heat, skimming off the scum that rises to the surface. Add the butter or oil, carrot, and onion, if using. Season with salt and pepper, cover, and simmer for about 40 minutes, or until the chicken is tender. Remove the chicken and vegetables, set aside, and keep warm. Strain the stock into a clean pan, bring back to a boil, add the rice, and stir well. Cover, reduce the heat, and simmer for about 20 minutes, until the rice is tender. Meanwhile, beat the eggs in a bowl with the lemon juice. Gradually beat in a ladleful of the hot soup, then stir the mixture into the soup. Remove the pan from the heat. Sprinkle with freshly ground black pepper and serve hot, accompanied by the chicken and vegetables. For a lighter version, omit the egg and prepare the soup using only the lemon juice.

Vefa's secret: By removing the skin before you cook the chicken, you remove most of the fat. However, when roasting a chicken, leave the skin on to prevent it from drying out, then discard the fat that drains out during cooking.

Serves 4
Preparation time 15 minutes
Cooking time 1 hour

LAMB MAGIRITSA
ΜΑΓΕΙΡΙΤΣΑ ΧΩΡΙΣ ΕΝΤΟΣΘΙΑ
Magiritsa horis entosthia

- 2¼ lb (1 kg) lamb shoulder on the bone, in large pieces
- 5 tablespoons olive oil
- 1 cup (7–8) finely chopped scallions (spring onions)
- 5 tablespoons finely chopped fresh dill
- 5 tablespoons finely chopped fresh parsley
- 5 tablespoons medium-grain rice, such as risotto rice
- salt and pepper
- 1 egg
- 5 tablespoons freshly squeezed lemon juice

Put the pieces of lamb into a large pan, pour in water to cover, and bring to a boil over low heat, skimming off the scum that rises to the surface. Simmer for about 1½ hours, or until the meat is tender and comes away from the bones. Remove the meat with a slotted spoon and let cool. Strain the stock into a bowl and let cool, then chill in the refrigerator for at least 8 hours or overnight. Remove the meat from the bones and discard both fat and bones. Finely chop or shred the pieces of meat and set aside. Remove and discard the solidified fat from the surface of the stock, pour the liquid into a measuring cup, and make up to 8¾ cups (2 litres / 3½ pints) with water. Pour it into a large pan and bring to a boil over high heat. Add the reserved meat, the oil, scallions, dill, parsley, and rice and season with salt and pepper. Reduce the heat, cover, and simmer for about 20 minutes, until the rice is tender. Meanwhile, lightly beat the egg in a bowl with the lemon juice and beat in a ladleful of the hot soup, then stir the mixture into the soup. Remove the pan from the heat and serve immediately.

Serves 4
Preparation time 10½ hours (including making and chilling the stock)
Cooking time 40 minutes

MEAT AND BULGUR WHEAT SOUP
ΚΡΕΑΤΟΣΟΥΠΑ ΜΕ ΠΛΙΓΟΥΡΙ
Kreatosoupa me pligouri

- 5 tablespoons olive oil
- 1 lb 2 oz (500 g) boneless pork or lamb, diced
- 2 onions, coarsely chopped
- ½ cup (120 ml / 4 fl oz) white wine
- 6¼ cups (1.5 litres / 2½ pints) meat stock
- generous 1 cup (200 g / 7 oz) bulgur wheat
- salt and pepper
- 4 tablespoons freshly squeezed lemon juice
- pinch of cayenne pepper

Heat the oil in a heavy pan. Add the meat and onions and cook over medium heat, stirring occasionally, for 8–10 minutes, until the meat is lightly browned. Pour in the wine and stir until the alcohol has evaporated, then pour in the stock. Reduce the heat, cover, and simmer for 15 minutes. Add the bulgur wheat, season with salt and pepper, and cook for 15 minutes more, until the meat and wheat are tender and the soup is quite thick. If you prefer a lighter soup, stir in a little hot water. Stir in the lemon juice and serve the soup sprinkled with a little cayenne pepper.

Serves 4
Preparation time 15 minutes
Cooking time 45 minutes

MEATBALL SOUP WITH EGG-LEMON SAUCE
ΓΙΟΥΒΑΡΛΑΚΙΑ ΑΥΓΟΛΕΜΟΝΟ
Giouvarlakia avgolemono

- 1 lb 2 oz (500 g) ground (minced) beef
- 1 small onion, finely chopped
- ¼ cup (50 g / 2 oz) short-grain rice
- 3 tablespoons finely chopped fresh parsley
- 2 tablespoons finely chopped fresh dill or mint
- 2 tablespoons olive oil
- salt and pepper
- all-purpose (plain) flour, for dusting
- 5 cups (1.2 litres / 2 pints) beef stock or water
- 4 tablespoons (50 g / 2 oz) butter
- 2 eggs
- 4 tablespoons freshly squeezed lemon juice

Combine the ground beef, onion, rice, herbs, and olive oil in a large bowl and season with salt and pepper. Knead briefly and shape into small balls. Spread out the flour on a shallow plate and roll the meatballs in it. Set aside. Pour the stock or water into a large pan, add the butter, season with salt and pepper, and bring to a boil. Add the meatballs, a few at a time to avoid lowering the temperature. Reduce the heat, cover, and simmer the *giouvarlakia* for about 30 minutes, until the meat and rice are cooked. Meanwhile, lightly beat the eggs with the lemon juice in a bowl. Beat in a ladleful of the hot cooking liquid, then gradually stir the mixture into the soup. Immediately remove the pan from the heat and serve the soup sprinkled with freshly ground pepper.

Serves 4
Preparation time 30 minutes
Cooking time 30 minutes

MEAT SOUP WITH TOMATOES
ΚΡΕΑΤΟΣΟΥΠΑ ΜΕ ΝΤΟΜΑΤΑ
Kreatosoupa me domata

- 2¼ lb (1 kg) stewing beef on the bone
- 1 large onion, halved and studded with 2 cloves
- 2 bay leaves
- 5 allspice berries
- 20 black peppercorns
- 4 tablespoons olive oil
- 1 small celery root (celeriac), quartered
- 3 carrots, thickly sliced
- 3 potatoes, cubed
- 2 ripe tomatoes, peeled, seeded, and chopped
- 1 cup (250 ml / 8 fl oz) tomato juice
- ½ teaspoon sugar
- 1 tablespoon red wine vinegar
- salt
- 1 dried red chile, crushed, to serve
- croutons, to serve

Put the meat into a large pan, pour in 8¾ cups (2 litres / 3¼ pints) water and add the onion, bay leaves, allspice berries, and peppercorns. Bring to a boil over medium heat, skimming off the scum that rises to the surface, then reduce the heat, cover, and simmer for about 1 hour, until the meat is tender. Remove the meat with a slotted spoon, drain well, and cut it off the bones. Strain the stock into a clean pan and add the oil, celery root, carrots, potatoes, tomatoes, tomato juice, sugar, and vinegar. Bring to a boil, cover, and simmer for 15 minutes. Return the meat to the pan, season with salt, and simmer for 15 minutes more, or until the vegetables are tender. Remove the pan from the heat. Serve in deep bowls, sprinkled with crushed chile and accompanied by croutons.

Serves 4
Preparation time 1 hour
Cooking time 1½ hours

SALADS

-

ΣΑΛΑΤΕΣ

-

Salates

It is inconceivable for a Greek to sit down to any meal without salad. From start to finish, one or more salads will grace the table and, unlike many countries where salad is eaten at the beginning or end of the meal, it will form an indispensable part of the meal. Raw or cooked, Greek salads tend to be simple, characteristic of the season, and designed to enhance the foods they accompany. They all feature simple, straightforward dressings, often top-quality olive oil beaten with freshly squeezed lemon juice or a fine wine vinegar, depending on personal preference and the type of vegetable. The secret is a minimum of handling and a good source of produce, ideally a good market or your own garden. An ordinary plate of freshly harvested greens or zucchini (courgettes) cooked and dressed with olive oil and lemon juice is a good partner for broiled (grilled) fish, while finely shredded cabbage or chopped lettuce leaves with onions and dill are thought to aid the digestion of meat. Heavy dressings with mayonnaise or cream sauces do not feature in the repertoire of traditional Greek salads, but have now become more popular. The combination salad, containing meat, fish or cheese, is also a relative newcomer to the Greek table. The serving quantities are based on serving the recipe as a side dish.

GENERAL INSTRUCTIONS

To make cooked salads, vegetables can be cooked or steamed and served dressed with oil-lemon or oil-vinegar sauce. They should never be overcooked, as this destroys their flavor and color as well as their nutritional value. Delicate greens are best boiled as briefly as possible, plunged into plenty of rapidly boiling water, and removed as soon as they are ready. Normally, cooked vegetable salads should be served warm immediately after they are ready. If they are prepared in advance, they can be reheated in the microwave or plunged for a few seconds into rapidly boiling water just before serving. Keep precooked vegetables well wrapped in the refrigerator. Pour the dressing over the salad, whether cooked or raw, a few minutes before serving, unless otherwise specified. If the leaves or vegetables are allowed to stand in the dressing for a long time, their color, flavor, and nutritional value are altered.

Almost all vegetables and greens can be eaten raw in salads and this makes them healthier and more nutritious. Marvelous fresh salads can be created not only with traditional salad vegetables, such as tomatoes, cucumbers, lettuce, and cabbage, but also with spinach, curly endive, cauliflower, and mushrooms. The ingredients should be as fresh as possible and rinsed and drained well before chopping. Chopping finely aids the digestion of greens. Use a sharp knife and cut them carefully to retain juiciness, freshness, and crispness. Leafy greens will keep for a surprisingly long time sealed inside plastic bags and stored in the refrigerator. Wash well and drain on paper towels first. Wilted fresh parsley, dill, mint, other herbs and leafy vegetables can be revived by putting them in a container of cold water. Careful but thorough tossing of the salad is necessary to coat the vegetables and leaves completely.

- 2¼ lb (1 kg) asparagus, trimmed

FOR THE DRESSING
- 4 tablespoons olive oil
- 2 tablespoons red wine vinegar
- 2 teaspoons Dijon or other mild mustard
- 1 garlic clove, finely chopped
- ¼ teaspoon sugar
- salt and pepper

ASPARAGUS WITH MUSTARD
ΣΠΑΡΑΓΓΙΑ ΜΕ ΜΟΥΣΤΑΡΔΑ
Sparagia me moustarda

Blanch the asparagus in a large pan of boiling water for 5–8 minutes, until tender, then drain carefully, and let cool. Put all the ingredients for the dressing in a screw-top jar, season with salt and pepper, fasten the lid, and shake vigorously. Pour the dressing over the cooked asparagus and let marinate for at least 2 hours before serving.

Serves 6
Preparation time 2¼ hours (including marinating)
Cooking time 5–8 minutes

- 1 lb 2 oz (500 g) curly endive
- 9 oz (250 g) wild asparagus (see note)
- 6 tablespoons olive oil
- 1 garlic clove, thinly sliced
- 2 slices toasted bread, crusts removed, diced
- 4 tablespoons coarsely chopped walnuts
- 2 tablespoons red wine vinegar
- 1 tablespoon balsamic vinegar
- salt and pepper

CURLY ENDIVE AND WILD ASPARAGUS SALAD
ΑΝΤΙΔΙΑ ΚΑΙ ΑΓΡΙΟΣΠΑΡΑΓΓΑ ΣΑΛΑΤΑ
Antidia ke agriosparaga salata

Pull off and discard the tough outer leaves of the curly endive, retaining the tender green leaves at the center. Rinse, but do not trim, the wild asparagus. If using cultivated asparagus, cut off and discard the woody ends of the spears. Cut the curly endive and asparagus into pieces. Heat 2 tablespoons of the olive oil in a skillet or frying pan. Add the garlic and cook over low heat, stirring frequently, for 1–2 minutes, then remove with a slotted spoon, and discard. Add the bread cubes, increase the heat to medium, and cook, stirring constantly, for a few minutes, until lightly browned. Set aside. Shortly before serving, arrange the curly endive and asparagus in layers on a platter with the croutons and walnuts sprinkled in between. Put both kinds of vinegar and the remaining olive oil into a screw-top jar, season with salt and pepper, fasten the lid, and shake vigorously until thoroughly blended. Pour the dressing over the salad and serve immediately.

Serves 4
Preparation time 15 minutes
Cooking time 5 minutes

Note: Use cultivated asparagus if wild is not available.

BEET (BEETROOT) SALAD WITH GARLIC YOGURT
ΠΑΤΖΑΡΙΑ ΜΕ ΓΙΑΟΥΡΤΙ ΣΚΟΡΔΑΤΟ
Patzaria me giaourti skordato

Put the beets into a pan, add boiling water to cover, and cook for about 30 minutes, or until tender. Rub or peel off the skin and cut into slices. Put the slices on a deep platter and pour half the vinegar and half the olive oil over them. Season with salt, cover, and let marinate at room temperature for 2–3 hours. Combine the yogurt, the remaining oil, the remaining vinegar, and the garlic in a bowl and season lightly with salt. Pour the mixture over the beet slices, cover, and chill in the refrigerator for 2 hours to let the flavors blend. Just before serving, sprinkle with the chopped walnuts.

Serves 6
Preparation time 5½ hours (including marinating and chilling)
Cooking time 30 minutes

□ p 186

- 2¼ lb (1 kg) tender young beets (beetroots), trimmed
- 4 tablespoons red wine vinegar
- 4 tablespoons olive oil
- salt
- 1 cup (250 ml / 8 fl oz) strained plain or thick Greek yogurt
- 3 garlic cloves, finely chopped
- ⅓ cup (40 g / 1½ oz) coarsely chopped walnuts

BLACK BEAN SALAD WITH RICE
ΡΥΖΟΣΑΛΑΤΑ ΜΕ ΦΑΣΟΛΙΑ
Rizosalata me fasolia

Put the beans into a large pan, pour in water to cover, bring to a boil, and boil vigorously for 15 minutes. Drain the beans, return to the pan, and pour in cold water to cover. Bring to a boil, reduce the heat, and simmer for about 1¼ hours, or until tender. Drain and let cool. Combine the beans, rice, scallions, olives, and mint in a bowl. Whisk all the dressing ingredients together in a bowl until thoroughly blended and season with salt and pepper. Pour the dressing over the salad and toss. Taste and adjust the seasoning, if necessary. Let the salad marinate in the refrigerator for 1–2 hours before serving.

Serves 6
Preparation time 15 hours (including soaking, cooling, and marinating)
Cooking time 1½ hours

- 1¾ cups (300 g / 11 oz) dried black beans, soaked for 12 hours in cold water to cover and drained
- 2⅔ cups (450 g / 1 lb) cooked long-grain rice
- ½ cup (4) finely chopped scallions (spring onions)
- 10 pimiento-stuffed green olives, sliced
- 2 tablespoons finely chopped fresh mint

FOR THE DRESSING
- 5 tablespoons olive oil
- 4 tablespoons red wine vinegar
- ¼ teaspoon crushed garlic
- 1 teaspoon Dijon mustard or 1 teaspoon mixed dried herbs, such as mint, cilantro (coriander), marjoram, and thyme
- salt and pepper

DRIED BEAN SALAD
ΦΑΣΟΛΙΑ ΣΑΛΑΤΑ
Fasolia salata

- generous 1⅓ cups (250 g / 9 oz) small dried white beans, such as navy (haricot) beans, soaked overnight in cold water to cover and drained
- 3 tablespoons red wine vinegar
- 1 small red onion or ½ mild Bermuda (sweet) onion, thinly sliced
- 3 scallions (spring onions), chopped
- 1 small mild green bell pepper, seeded and chopped
- 3 tablespoons finely chopped fresh parsley
- 3 tablespoons chopped dill pickles (pickled cucumbers)
- 2 tablespoons capers, rinsed and drained
- Oil-vinegar dressing (p 57)
- pitted (stoned) black olives, to garnish
- canned tuna in oil, to serve

Put the beans into a pan, pour in water to cover, and cook for 30 minutes, then drain, and rinse. Return the beans to the pan, pour in water to cover, and bring to a boil. Reduce the heat and simmer for about 1 hour, or until tender. (The cooking time depends on the size, age, and condition of the beans.) Drain, transfer to a bowl, pour the vinegar over them, and toss well. Add the onion, scallions, bell pepper, parsley, pickles, and capers, season, and mix lightly. Pour the oil-vinegar dressing over them and toss gently. Let marinate for several hours before serving. Transfer to a shallow dish, garnish with olives, and serve accompanied by drained canned tuna.

Serves 4
Preparation time 15–16 hours (including soaking and marinating)
Cooking time 1½ hours

Note: If you like, flake the tuna and mix into the salad. Cooked black-eyed peas (beans) can be served the same way.

GARBANZO (CHICKPEA) AND BORLOTTI BEAN SALAD
ΡΕΒΥΘΙΑ ΚΑΙ ΦΑΣΟΛΙΑ ΣΑΛΑΤΑ
Revithia ke fasolia salata

- scant ½ cup (100 g / 3½ oz) garbanzo beans (chickpeas)
- ¾ cup (100 g / 3½ oz) fresh or dried borlotti beans
- scant 1 cup (100 g / 3½ oz) shelled baby peas
- 1 small onion, thinly sliced
- romaine lettuce hearts, separated, to serve

FOR THE DRESSING
- 1 green bell pepper, seeded and finely chopped
- 1 garlic clove, finely chopped
- 2 tablespoons finely chopped fresh basil
- 5 tablespoons red wine vinegar
- 4 tablespoons olive oil
- salt and pepper

Soak the garbanzo beans and dried borlotti beans (if using) in cold water to cover overnight, then rinse and drain. Make the dressing. Put all the dressing ingredients into a screw-top jar, season with salt and pepper, fasten the lid, and shake vigorously until well blended. Set aside. Put the garbanzo and borlotti beans into a pan, pour in boiling water to cover, and cook for about 45 minutes, until softened. Meanwhile, cook the peas in a steamer set over a pan of boiling water for 7 minutes or until tender, then drain, and set aside. Drain the beans in a colander, rinse under cold running water, and drain again. Combine the beans, peas, and sliced onion in a serving bowl. Pour the dressing over them, mix well, and let marinate for at least 1 hour in the refrigerator. Serve the salad with whole romaine lettuce leaves.

Serves 4
Preparation time 10 hours (including soaking and marinating)
Cooking time 45 minutes

Beet (beetroot) salad with garlic yogurt, p 184

Arugula (rocket) salad with garbanzo beans (chickpeas), p 188

TRICOLOR BEAN SALAD
ΤΡΙΧΡΩΜΗ ΣΑΛΑΤΑ ΜΕ ΦΑΣΟΛΙΑ
Trihromi salata me fasolia

Put the black beans and black-eyed peas in a pan, pour in water to cover, bring to a boil, and boil vigorously for 15 minutes. Drain well and return to the pan. Add the white beans and pour in water to cover. Bring to a boil, reduce the heat, and simmer for 1¼ hours. Drain well, return to the pan, and pour in the vegetable stock. Cover and simmer for 15 minutes more, until tender. Drain well and tip into a bowl. Add the red kidney beans, mushrooms, scallions, and onion and toss gently to mix. Put all the ingredients for the dressing in a screw-top jar, fasten the lid, and shake vigorously until thoroughly blended. Pour the dressing over the salad, toss, and let marinate in the refrigerator for 2–3 hours before serving. Garnish the salad with thinly sliced tomato.

Serves 6
Preparation time 15–16 hours (including soaking and marinating)
Cooking time 1¾ hours

- ½ cup (100 g / 3½ oz) dried black beans, soaked overnight in cold water to cover and drained
- ½ cup (100 g / 3½ oz) dried black-eyed peas (beans), soaked overnight in cold water to cover and drained
- ½ cup (100 g / 3½ oz) small dried white beans, such as navy (haricot) beans, soaked overnight in cold water to cover and drained
- 6¼ cups (1.5 litres / 2½ pints) vegetable stock
- ¾ cup (100 g / 3½ oz) drained canned red kidney beans, rinsed
- 2–3 large mushrooms, sliced
- ½ cup (4) chopped scallions (spring onions)
- 1 onion, finely chopped
- thinly sliced tomato, to garnish

FOR THE DRESSING
- 5 tablespoons red wine vinegar
- 5 tablespoons finely chopped fresh parsley or basil
- 1 teaspoon Dijon mustard
- 1 small garlic clove, finely chopped
- 5 tablespoons olive oil

ARUGULA (ROCKET) SALAD WITH GARBANZO BEANS (CHICKPEAS)
ΡΟΚΑ ΣΑΛΑΤΑ ΜΕ ΡΕΒΥΘΙΑ
Roka salata me revithia

Cut the arugula or spinach leaves into large pieces with a pair of kitchen scissors and arrange on a large platter. Place the grated carrots, cucumber strips, and garbanzos on top. Put all the ingredients for the dressing in a screw-top jar, season with salt and pepper, fasten the lid, and shake until thoroughly blended. Pour the dressing over the salad just before serving.

Serves 4
Preparation time 15 minutes

☐ p 187

- 11 oz (300 g) arugula (rocket) or baby spinach leaves, coarse stalks removed
- 2 carrots, coarsely grated
- 1 small cucumber, cut into julienne strips
- generous 1 cup (200 g / 7 oz) cooked or drained canned garbanzo beans (chickpeas)

FOR THE DRESSING
- 4 tablespoons olive oil
- 2 tablespoons freshly squeezed lemon juice
- 1 tablespoon red wine vinegar
- 1 small garlic clove, finely chopped
- 10 drops Tabasco sauce
- salt and pepper

- ○ 2 cloves
- ○ 1 small onion
- ○ ⅔ cup (150 g / 5 oz) green lentils
- ○ 1 bay leaf
- ○ 2 teaspoons fresh thyme leaves or ½ teaspoon dried thyme
- ○ 2 small carrots, thinly sliced
- ○ 2 celery stalks, sliced
- ○ 3 scallions (spring onions), thinly sliced
- ○ generous 2¾ cups (200 g / 7 oz) sliced white mushrooms
- ○ 2 tablespoons freshly squeezed lemon juice
- ○ 1 small romaine lettuce, finely chopped, to serve
- ○ 1 tomato, cut into wedges, to serve
- ○ 1 tablespoon finely chopped fresh parsley, to serve

FOR THE DRESSING
- ○ 1 tablespoon Dijon mustard
- ○ 2 tablespoons freshly squeezed lemon juice
- ○ 1 teaspoon Tabasco sauce
- ○ 2 garlic cloves, finely chopped
- ○ ¼ teaspoon salt
- ○ 4 tablespoons olive oil
- ○ pepper

LENTIL AND MUSHROOM SALAD
ΦΑΚΕΣ ΚΑΙ ΜΑΝΙΤΑΡΙΑ ΣΑΛΑΤΑ
Fakes ke manitaria salata

Stick the cloves into the onion, put into a pan, and add the lentils, bay leaf, and thyme. Pour in 4 cups (1 litre / 1¾ pints) water and bring to a boil, then reduce the heat, and simmer for about 25 minutes, or until the lentils are soft but not disintegrating. Drain, remove and discard the onion and bay leaf, and put the lentils into a bowl. Add the carrots, celery, and scallions and mix well. Put the mushrooms into a pan and pour in the lemon juice and water to cover. Cook for 5 minutes, then drain, and mix them with the lentils. Put all the dressing ingredients into a screw-top jar, season with pepper, fasten the lid, and shake vigorously until thoroughly blended. Pour the dressing over the salad and let marinate in the refrigerator for at least 1 hour before serving. Serve the salad in the center of a platter surrounded by the finely chopped lettuce. Garnish with the tomato wedges and chopped parsley.

Serves 6
Preparation time 1½ hours (including marinating)
Cooking time 30 minutes

- ○ 2 heads Belgian endive, leaves separated
- ○ 8 oz (225 g) curly endive, chopped
- ○ 4 oz (120 g) radicchio, chopped
- ○ 1 onion, sliced into rings

FOR THE DRESSING
- ○ 1 tablespoon water
- ○ 2 tablespoons red wine vinegar
- ○ 2 teaspoons Dijon mustard
- ○ 3 tablespoons olive oil
- ○ salt and pepper

BELGIAN ENDIVE AND CURLY ENDIVE SALAD
ΑΝΤΙΔΙΑ ΣΑΛΑΤΑ
Antidia salata

Put all the dressing ingredients into a screw-top jar, season with salt and pepper, fasten the lid, and shake vigorously until thoroughly blended. Put the endive leaves in a bowl, sprinkle with 2 tablespoons of the dressing, and set aside. Put all the remaining salad greens in another bowl and lightly toss with the remaining dressing. Turn them onto the center of a large salad platter and arrange the Belgian endive leaves around the edges. Serve immediately.

Serves 6
Preparation time 10 minutes

CONSTANTINOPLE-STYLE SALAD
ΣΑΛΑΤΑ ΠΟΛΙΤΙΚΗ
Salata politiki

- 3¾ cups (350 g / 12 oz) shredded white cabbage
- 3 tablespoons chopped green bell pepper
- 3 tablespoons chopped red bell pepper
- 4 tablespoons chopped celery
- 1 large carrot, grated
- Oil-vinegar dressing (p 57)

Put the vegetables into a large salad bowl and toss well to mix. Cover the bowl with plastic wrap (cling film) and chill in the refrigerator for several hours, until ready to serve. Just before serving, pour the oil-vinegar dressing over the salad and toss well.

Serves 4
Preparation time 3½ hours (including chilling)

Note: Alternatively, add 1 cup (250 ml / 8 fl oz) strained plain or thick Greek yogurt to the tossed salad and mix well. Chill in the refrigerator for several hours before serving.

CUCUMBER AND TOMATO SALAD
ΑΓΓΟΥΡΟΝΤΟΜΑΤΑ
Agourodomata

- 2 large tomatoes
- 1 long cucumber, peeled and sliced
- 2 tablespoons finely chopped fresh parsley
- 1 small green mild chile (optional)
- 1 very small garlic clove, grated (optional)
- Oil-vinegar dressing (p 57)

Cut the tomatoes into 6–8 wedges. Put them into a bowl or on a salad platter and add the cucumber, parsley, chile, and garlic, if using. Pour the oil-vinegar dressing over the salad just before serving and toss lightly.

Serves 4
Preparation time 10 minutes

TOMATO AND ONION SALAD
ΝΤΟΜΑΤΟΣΑΛΑΤΑ ΜΕ ΚΡΕΜΜΥΔΙΑ
Domatosalata me kremidia

- 4 tomatoes
- 1 onion, sliced
- pinch of dried oregano
- Oil-vinegar dressing (p 57)
- salt and pepper

Cut the tomatoes into 6–8 wedges and put them into a bowl with the onion slices. Just before serving, pour the oil-vinegar dressing over the salad, taste and adjust the seasoning, if necessary, and serve.

Serves 4
Preparation time 5–10 minutes

☐ p 192

GRAPE AND LETTUCE SALAD FROM CORINTH
ΣΑΛΑΤΑ ΜΕ ΣΤΑΦΥΛΙΑ ΚΑΙ ΜΑΡΟΥΛΙ
Salata me stafilia ke marouli

- 7 oz (200 g) romaine lettuce leaves
- 7 oz (200 g) radicchio leaves
- 3½ oz (100 g) tiny seedless green grapes
- 1 oz (25 g) kefalotiri or Parmesan cheese shavings

FOR THE DRESSING
- ¼ cup (60 ml) olive oil
- 1 tablespoon red wine vinegar
- 1 tablespoon lemon juice
- salt and pepper
- 1 teaspoon Dijon mustard (optional)

Trim and separate the salad leaves, rinse and pat dry. Tear the leaves into bite-size pieces and combine in a large salad bowl. Arrange the grapes on the surface and sprinkle with the kefalotiri shavings. Just before serving, whisk together or shake the dressing ingredients until blended and pour over the salad. Toss and serve immediately.

Serves 4
Preparation time 15 minutes

p 193

CURLY ENDIVE AND SPINACH SALAD
ΑΝΤΙΔΙΑ ΜΕ ΣΠΑΝΑΚΙ
Antidia me spanaki

- 11 oz (300 g) curly endive
- 11 oz (300 g) baby spinach leaves
- 1 tablespoon (15 g / ½ oz) butter
- pinch of crushed garlic
- 2 slices of white bread, crusts removed, diced
- 4 tablespoons coarsely chopped walnuts
- 2 tablespoons grated kefalotiri or Parmesan cheese
- 3 tablespoons olive oil
- 2 tablespoons red wine vinegar
- salt and pepper

Preheat the oven to 350°F (180°C / Gas Mark 4). Discarding any tough outer leaves, cut the salad leaves into pieces. Melt the butter in a small skillet or frying pan. Add the garlic and cook for a few seconds, then stir in the cubes of bread, until well coated. Transfer to a cookie sheet (baking tray) and spread out. Bake for about 10 minutes, until golden brown and crisp. Set aside. When ready to serve, layer the curly endive and spinach in a glass salad bowl, sprinkling each layer with croutons and walnuts, then sprinkle the salad with the cheese. Whisk together the oil and vinegar in a small bowl and season with salt and pepper. Pour the dressing over the salad, toss well, and serve immediately.

Serves 4
Preparation time 20 minutes
Cooking time 15 minutes

SPINACH AND MUSHROOM SALAD
ΣΠΑΝΑΚΙ ΜΕ ΜΑΝΙΤΑΡΙΑ
Spanaki me manitaria

- 1⅔ cups (150 g / 5 oz) chopped baby spinach leaves
- 2 cups (150 g / 5 oz) sliced white mushrooms
- 2 tablespoons balsamic vinegar
- 3 tablespoons olive oil
- ½ teaspoon chili flakes
- 1 teaspoon toasted sesame seeds
- salt and pepper

Combine the spinach and mushrooms in a bowl. Put the vinegar, oil, chili flakes, and sesame seeds into a screw-top jar, season with salt and pepper, fasten the lid, and shake vigorously until thoroughly blended. Pour the dressing over the salad and toss just before serving.

Serves 4
Preparation time 15 minutes

Tomato and onion salad, p 190

Grape and lettuce salad from Corinth, p 191

GARDENER'S SALAD
ΣΑΛΑΤΑ ΤΟΥ ΚΗΠΟΥΡΟΥ
Salata tou kipourou

Finely chop the romaine leaves, reserving the heart. Cut the arugula and purslane or watercress into pieces. Arrange the greens on a serving platter. Cut the tomatoes into 8 wedges, without cutting all the way through, so that they open out like roses. Put the tomatoes on the bed of greens with the chiles, scallions, and olives. Sprinkle the capers over the top. Divide the lettuce heart into 4 parts and place beside the tomatoes. Put all the dressing ingredients into a screw-top jar, season with salt and pepper, fasten the lid, and shake vigorously until thoroughly blended. Pour the dressing over the salad just before serving.

Serves 4
Preparation time 30 minutes

p 196

- 1 small romaine lettuce
- 1 bunch of arugula (rocket), trimmed
- 1 bunch of purslane or watercress
- 2 small ripe tomatoes, peeled
- 4 pickled jalapeño chiles
- ½ cup (4) chopped scallions (spring onions)
- 8 Greek green olives
- 2 tablespoons capers, rinsed and drained

FOR THE DRESSING
- 4 tablespoons olive oil
- 3 tablespoons red wine vinegar
- 2 tablespoons chopped fresh or ½ teaspoon dried oregano or marjoram
- salt and pepper

GREEK VILLAGE SALAD
ΧΩΡΙΑΤΙΚΗ ΣΑΛΑΤΑ
Horiatiki salata

Cut each tomato into 6 wedges. Combine the tomatoes, cucumber, onion rings, olives, and feta in a large bowl. Sprinkle the salad with a little oregano and pour the oil-vinegar dressing to taste over it. Toss and serve garnished with the eggs, parsley, watercress, or arugula (if using).

Serves 4
Preparation time 15 minutes

p 197

- 2 large tomatoes
- 1 cucumber, peeled and sliced
- 1 red onion, thinly sliced into rings
- 10 Kalamata olives
- 4 oz (120 g) feta cheese, diced
- pinch of dried oregano
- Oil-vinegar dressing (p 57)
- 2 hard-boiled eggs, sliced or quartered (optional)
- chopped fresh parsley, watercress, or arugula (rocket), to garnish (optional)

ICEBERG SALAD
ΣΑΛΑΤΑ ΑΙΖΜΠΕΡΓΚ
Salata aisberg

Slice the iceberg into 6 wedges, without cutting all the way through the base, and open out the wedges. Place on a wide, shallow platter, arranging the wedges to resemble a star. Garnish with the grated carrots, celery slices, and pomegranate seeds. Put all the dressing ingredients into a screw-top jar, season with salt and pepper, fasten the lid, and shake vigorously until thoroughly blended. Drizzle the dressing over the salad and serve.

Serves 6
Preparation time 10 minutes

- 1 small iceberg lettuce
- 2 carrots, grated
- 2 celery stalks, thinly sliced
- 4 tablespoons pomegranate seeds

FOR THE DRESSING
- 2 tablespoons olive oil
- 2 tablespoons Mayonnaise (p 60)
- 3 tablespoons red wine vinegar
- 1 teaspoon mustard powder
- ¼ teaspoon sugar
- salt and pepper

LETTUCE AND DILL SALAD
ΜΑΡΟΥΛΟΣΑΛΑΤΑ ΜΕ ΑΝΙΘΟ
Maroulosalata me anitho

- 1 lb 2 oz (500 g) romaine or other long, firm lettuce
- ⅔ cup (5) finely chopped scallions (spring onions)
- 2 tablespoons finely chopped fresh dill
- Oil-vinegar dressing (p 57) or Oil-lemon dressing (p 57)

TO GARNISH
- radish flowers (optional, see p 198)
- tender lettuce leaves
- fresh dill sprigs

Stack several lettuce leaves together and roll up loosely like a cigar. Using a sharp knife, cut crosswise into strips about ⅛ inch (3 mm) wide. Put the lettuce, scallions, and dill into a salad bowl, cover the salad, and chill in the refrigerator for up to 3 hours, if not serving immediately. Just before serving, pour the dressing over the salad and toss gently. Garnish with radish rosettes, whole tender lettuce leaves, and fresh dill sprigs.

Serves 4
Preparation time 10 minutes

MARINATED VEGETABLES
ΛΑΧΑΝΙΚΑ ΜΑΡΙΝΑΤΑ
Lahanika marinata

- 5 oz (150 g) green (French) beans, trimmed
- 1 large carrot, sliced into rounds
- 1 large red bell pepper, seeded and cut into julienne strips
- 7 oz (200 g) small cauliflower florets
- 2 small zucchini (courgettes), sliced
- 6 large mushrooms, sliced

FOR THE MARINADE
- ½ cup (120 ml / 4 fl oz) olive oil
- 5 tablespoons red wine vinegar
- 2 garlic cloves, finely chopped
- 3 tablespoons finely chopped fresh parsley, dill, or mint

Whisk together all the marinade ingredients in a bowl and set aside. Cut the beans into thirds. Bring a small pan of salted water to a boil, add the beans and carrot, and blanch for 10 minutes, or until tender, then drain. Put them into a bowl and add the bell pepper, cauliflower, zucchini, and mushrooms. Pour in the marinade and toss well. Cover with plastic wrap (cling film) and let marinate in the refrigerator for at least 24 hours before serving.

Serves 4
Preparation time 24¼ hours (including marinating)
Cooking time 10 minutes

FESTIVE WINTER SALAD
ΧΕΙΜΩΝΙΑΤΙΚΗ ΓΙΟΡΤΙΝΗ ΣΑΛΑΤΑ
Himoniatiki giortini salata

- 2 cups (250 g / 9 oz) grated white cabbage
- 2 cups (300 g / 11 oz) grated carrots
- 2 cups (250 g / 9 oz) grated radicchio
- 1 large daikon (mooli), thinly sliced
- 4 oz (120 g) canned pimientos, drained
- 2 heads Belgian endive, separated into leaves
- Oil-lemon dressing (p 57)

Arrange the grated cabbage, carrots, and radicchio in concentric circles on a large round platter. Roll the slices of the daikon into cones, secure with wooden toothpicks, and let soak in cold water for 2–3 hours. Remove the toothpicks from the cones and arrange them in the shape of a daisy at the center of the salad. Cut the pimientos into small pieces and place one inside each cone. Surround the salad with Belgian endive leaves pointing outward like rays. Just before serving, sprinkle the salad with the oil-lemon dressing.

Serves 6
Preparation time 2½–3½ hours (including soaking)

Gardener's salad, p 194

Greek village salad, p 194

MIXED VEGETABLE SALAD
ΣΑΛΑΤΑ ΛΑΧΑΝΙΚΩΝ
Salata lahanikon

Cut the arugula into pieces with kitchen scissors and arrange on the base of a glass salad bowl. Put the tomatoes on top and sprinkle with the crumbled feta. Separate the purslane or watercress into sprigs and arrange on top of the feta. Top with the cucumber rounds. Garnish with radishes. Cover with plastic wrap (cling film) and keep in the refrigerator until required. Just before serving, put all the dressing ingredients into a screw-top jar, season with salt and pepper, fasten the lid, and shake vigorously until thoroughly blended. Pour the dressing over the salad and serve.

Serves 4
Preparation time 1½ hours

Note: If you like, you can cut the radishes into flowers. The easiest way to do this is to cut off the root and then, using a small sharp knife, cut out thin wedges from the center outward to about two-thirds down. Put the radish in a bowl of ice water for 30 minutes to "bloom."

- 1 bunch of arugula (rocket), trimmed
- 2 tomatoes, cut into bite-size pieces
- 5 oz (150 g) feta cheese, crumbled
- 1 bunch of purslane or watercress
- 1 large cucumber, cut into rounds
- 6–8 radishes, to garnish (see note)

FOR THE DRESSING
- 3 tablespoons olive oil
- 2 tablespoons red wine vinegar
- 1 teaspoon Dijon mustard
- ½ teaspoon honey
- salt and pepper

BROILED (GRILLED) VEGETABLE SALAD
ΣΑΛΑΤΑ ΜΕ ΨΗΤΑ ΛΑΧΑΝΙΚΑ
Salata me psita lahanika

First make the sesame sauce. Pound the garlic with the salt in a mortar and gradually blend in the tahini. Gradually add about 1 cup (250 ml / 8 fl oz) water, a little at a time, working it into the sauce until the desired consistency is reached. Add as much lemon juice as you like and a pinch of white pepper. Alternatively, process the garlic, salt, tahini, half the water, the lemon juice, and pepper in a food processor until smooth, then add more water as required. Set aside. Preheat the broiler (grill) and brush a cookie sheet (baking tray) with oil. Put all the vegetables into a large shallow bowl. Combine the 5 tablespoons oil with the garlic, vinegar, herbs, salt, and pepper in a screw-top jar, fasten the lid, and shake vigorously until thoroughly blended. Pour the mixture over the vegetables and toss to coat evenly. Drain and arrange vegetables on the prepared cookie sheet. Broil (grill) for about 5 minutes, then turn the vegetables over with tongs, and broil for 5 minutes more, or until the vegetables are tender. Arrange the spinach and arugula leaves on a large platter and top with the broiled vegetables. Drizzle with the sesame sauce and serve immediately.

Serves 6
Preparation time 45 minutes
Cooking time 10 minutes

- 5 tablespoons olive oil, plus extra for brushing
- 1 large onion, sliced
- 2 zucchini (courgettes), sliced
- 1 red bell pepper, seeded and quartered
- 1 yellow bell pepper, seeded and quartered
- 2 long eggplants (aubergines), sliced crosswise
- 1 large potato, thinly sliced
- 1 garlic clove, finely chopped
- 4 tablespoons balsamic vinegar
- 1 teaspoon mixed dried thyme, rosemary, and oregano
- ½ teaspoon salt
- ¼ teaspoon pepper
- 3½ oz (100 g) baby spinach leaves
- 3½ oz (100 g) arugula (rocket) leaves

FOR THE SESAME SAUCE
- 1–2 garlic cloves, finely chopped
- ¼ teaspoon salt
- 4 tablespoons tahini
- 2–3 tablespoons freshly squeezed lemon juice
- freshly ground white pepper

- 1 cup (150 g / 5 oz) grated carrots
- 1 cup (120 g / 4 oz) finely chopped white cabbage
- 1 cucumber, diced
- ½ yellow bell pepper, seeded and cut into julienne strips
- ½ red bell pepper, seeded and cut into julienne strips
- ½ green bell pepper, seeded and cut into julienne strips
- ½ cup (100 g / 3 ½ oz) diced celery root (celeriac) or daikon (mooli)
- 4 tablespoons finely chopped fresh dill
- red bell pepper or tomato flower, to garnish (optional)

FOR THE DRESSING
- 2 tablespoons red wine vinegar
- 1 tablespoon freshly squeezed lemon juice
- 5 tablespoons olive oil
- 15 drops of Tabasco sauce
- pinch of grated garlic
- ½ teaspoon mustard powder
- salt and pepper

MULTICOLOR SALAD
ΠΟΛΥΧΡΩΜΗ ΣΑΛΑΤΑ
Polihromi salata

Store the prepared vegetables separately in the refrigerator until ready to serve. Put all the dressing ingredients into a screw-top jar, season with salt and pepper, fasten the lid, and shake vigorously until thoroughly blended. Put the vegetables into a salad bowl, pour the dressing over them, and toss well. If you like, garnish with a flower cut out from a red bell pepper or a tomato.

Serves 6
Preparation time 35 minutes

- 4 potatoes, about 1 lb 2 oz (500 g) total weight
- 1 small onion, sliced in rings
- ⅓ cup (2 – 3) chopped scallions (spring onions)
- 2 tablespoons chopped fresh parsley, mint, or dill
- 1 carrot, cooked and sliced

FOR THE DRESSING
- 5 tablespoons olive oil
- 4 tablespoons freshly squeezed lemon juice or vinegar
- ½ teaspoon mustard powder (optional)
- salt and pepper

POTATO SALAD
ΠΑΤΑΤΟΣΑΛΑΤΑ
Patatosalata

Cook the potatoes, unpeeled, for 25 – 30 minutes, or until tender. Drain, peel, and cut into thick slices. Put them into a salad bowl and add the onion, scallions, herbs, and carrot. Put all the dressing ingredients into a screw-top jar, season with salt and pepper, fasten the lid, and shake vigorously until thoroughly blended. Pour the dressing over the salad and toss. Cover with plastic wrap (cling film) and let marinate for 1 hour before serving.

Serves 4
Preparation time 1¼ hours (including marinating)
Cooking time 30 minutes

BROILED (GRILLED) ZUCCHINI (COURGETTE), HALLOUMI, AND LETTUCE SALAD

ΨΗΤΑ ΚΟΛΟΚΥΘΙΑ ΜΕ ΧΑΛΟΥΜΙ

Psita kolokithia me haloumi

Preheat the broiler (grill). Put all the dressing ingredients into a screw-top jar, season with salt and pepper, fasten the lid, and set aside. Halve the zucchini lengthwise, season with salt and pepper, and brush with olive oil. Broil (grill) for about 8 minutes, turning once, until tender and lightly browned. Remove from the broiler and cut them diagonally into bite-size pieces. Put them into a bowl. Shake the jar of dressing vigorously until thoroughly combined, then pour it over the zucchini. Just before serving, tear the lettuce and radicchio into pieces and place them on a deep salad platter. Pour the dressed zucchini over them. Put the cheese on a sheet of aluminum foil and broil until lightly browned. Sprinkle the pieces of cheese over the salad, garnish with mint leaves, and serve immediately.

Serves 4
Preparation time 10 minutes
Cooking time 10 minutes

❑ p 202

- 9 oz (250 g) small zucchini (courgettes)
- salt and pepper
- olive oil, for brushing
- 9 oz (250 g) romaine lettuce hearts
- 9 oz (250 g) radicchio hearts
- 5 oz (150 g) halloumi or Provolone cheese, diced
- fresh mint leaves, to garnish

FOR THE DRESSING

- 3 tablespoons olive oil
- 2 tablespoons balsamic vinegar
- 1 teaspoon honey
- 1 teaspoon Dijon mustard
- salt and pepper

HOT POTATO SALAD WITH SMOKED TROUT

ΖΕΣΤΗ ΠΑΤΑΤΟΣΑΛΑΤΑ ΜΕ ΚΑΠΝΙΣΤΗ ΠΕΣΤΡΟΦΑ

Zesti patatosalata me kapnisti pestrofa

Preheat the oven to 350°F (180°C/Gas Mark 4) and brush an ovenproof dish with oil. Combine the mayonnaise, mustard, lemon juice, potatoes, onion, and celery in a bowl. Spread one third of the potato mixture in the base of the prepared dish. Sprinkle with half the flaked trout. Spread half the remaining potato mixture on top and sprinkle with the remaining flaked trout. Cover with the remaining potato mixture. Toss the bread crumbs with the 2 tablespoons oil in a small bowl and sprinkle over the top. Bake for 15 minutes and serve hot.

Serves 4
Preparation time 15 minutes
Cooking time 15 minutes

Note: You can also serve the salad without baking it. It is equally delicious.

- 3 tablespoons olive oil, plus extra for brushing
- ½ cup (120 ml/4 fl oz) Mayonnaise (p 60)
- 2 teaspoons Dijon mustard
- 2 tablespoons freshly squeezed lemon juice
- 12 oz (350 g) cooked potatoes, diced
- 2 tablespoons grated onion
- ⅓ cup (½ stalk) finely chopped celery
- 9 oz (250 g) smoked trout fillet, skinned and flaked
- ¾ cup (50 g/2 oz) dry bread crumbs

- 1 lb 2 oz (500 g) small octopuses, cleaned
- 1 lb 2 oz (500 g) potatoes
- 1 large ripe avocado
- 2 tablespoons freshly squeezed lemon or lime juice
- 1 bunch arugula (rocket), trimmed
- 2 scallions (spring onions), thinly sliced
- toasted garlic bread or croutons, to serve

FOR THE MARINADE
- 2 tablespoons olive oil
- 4 tablespoons freshly squeezed lemon or lime juice
- 1 red chile, finely chopped
- 1 garlic clove, finely chopped

FOR THE TOMATO DRESSING
- 4 small tomatoes, peeled and cubed
- 4 tablespoons finely chopped fresh parsley
- 1 small onion, finely chopped
- 2 tablespoons red wine vinegar
- 3 tablespoons olive oil
- 1 tablespoon balsamic vinegar
- pepper

POTATO SALAD WITH OCTOPUS
ΠΑΤΑΤΟΣΑΛΑΤΑ ΜΕ ΧΤΑΠΟΔΙ
Patatosalata me htapodi

Rinse the octopuses, cut in half (unless they are very small), and put into a bowl. Put all the ingredients for the marinade in a screw-top jar, fasten the lid, and shake vigorously until thoroughly blended. Pour the mixture over the octopuses and let marinate in the refrigerator for at least 2 hours. Cook the potatoes in salted boiling water for 15–20 minutes, until tender. (You could also cook them in the microwave if you like.) Drain and let cool, then cut into bite-size pieces. Combine all the dressing ingredients in a bowl and season with pepper. Preheat the broiler (grill). Meanwhile, peel the avocado, cut it in half lengthwise, and remove the pit (stone). Dice the flesh and toss with the lemon or lime juice in a bowl to prevent discoloration. Drain the octopuses and broil (grill), turning once or twice, for about 5 minutes, until the tentacles are twisted. Arrange the arugula leaves on a platter. Spoon the potatoes over them and sprinkle with the avocado and scallions. Arrange the octopuses on top and sprinkle the salad with the dressing. Serve immediately, accompanied by toasted garlic bread or croutons.

Serves 6
Preparation time 2 hours (including marinating)
Cooking time 20–25 minutes

☐ p 203

Broiled (grilled) zucchini (courgette), halloumi, and lettuce salad, p 200

Potato salad with octopus, p 201

VEGETABLES

-

ΛΑΧΑΝΙΚΑ

-

Lahanika

The very essence of Greek cuisine lies in its skillfully prepared and deftly seasoned vegetable dishes. Although vegetables were not highly valued in ancient Greece (compared with foods like bread, fish, or meat), ordinary people have depended on them for centuries. Socrates lists vegetables as one of the essential parts of the citizens' diet in Plato's *Republic,* and asparagus, chard, beet (beetroot), kale, cabbage, capers, cardoons, chervil, onions, lettuce, and radish are all mentioned in classical Greek texts. Wild greens, such as nettles, arugula (rocket), mustard leaves, wild spinach, and dandelion, have been collected since antiquity, along with a wide range of herbs including dill, wild fennel leaves and seeds, carrot seeds, celery, cilantro (coriander) leaves and seeds, hyssop, mint, and rosemary, thyme and oregano. Most of these are still in use in the Greek kitchen. In fact, judicious use of herbs and spices is one of the chief characteristics of traditional Greek cooking.

Eventually, as varieties were improved and new ones were introduced, vegetables became more important to the cuisine of the Greek world. During the development of the Orthodox Christian religion, many dishes based solely on vegetables and herbs came into being. These dishes are called *ladera,* referring to the use of olive oil in their preparation. *Ladera* are typically served on Wednesdays, Fridays, and other holy days of religious abstention. While the Western Church has mostly abandoned the age-old institution of religious fasting, the Orthodox fast, which excludes all meat, fish, eggs, and dairy products for periods of up to seven weeks during Lent, is still actively practiced by millions of Orthodox Christians. Healthy and filling substitutes for meat dishes, Greek *ladera* are surprisingly tasty and satisfying alternatives for anyone's diet—no wonder many Greeks prefer them to meat dishes.

GENERAL INSTRUCTIONS

Use good extra-virgin olive oil; the flavor and richness that olive oil gives to a dish cannot be achieved with any other oil. If you have not cooked Greek vegetable dishes before, measure the oil carefully. Too little and the dish will be tasteless; too much and it will be unappetizingly rich and heavy. Greeks believe that the correct amount of oil in a dish is essential to make it taste right. Most of the recipes also call for chopped or grated onion. Before you cook it, grate it into a colander, sprinkle with a little salt, rinse with a little water, and squeeze out the extra moisture. This reduces some of the pungency and makes the dish lighter. Do not brown the onion when sautéing it; just cook it gently in hot oil until it is soft and translucent.

Fresh Greek field peas are very different from the small garden peas or petits pois used in other countries. Greek peas are larger, have tougher skins, do not taste as sweet, and take much longer to cook. The recipe timings given here are for Greek peas. Fresh or frozen petits pois can be substituted, but they should be added 5 minutes before the end of the cooking time. Eggplants (aubergines) and courgettes (zucchini) are often salted and left to drain prior to cooking. This draws out moisture from the vegetables and prevents them from absorbing too much oil. In all the recipes, fresh tomatoes can be replaced by canned tomatoes or tomato paste diluted with water. Two tablespoons tomato paste diluted with 1 cup (250 ml / 8 fl oz) water is equivalent to 1 cup (250 ml / 8 fl oz) tomato juice or puréed fresh tomatoes. Fresh tomatoes should only be used if they are ripe and in season. Although you can find most vegetables in the supermarket at any time of year, no vegetable ever tastes as good as when it is in season locally. Follow the seasons, use vegetables when their flavor and texture are at their peak, and, ideally, purchase them from a good market, or grow them yourself. Do not store vegetables for too long, or they will deteriorate in flavor and texture, and their nutritional value often diminishes as well.

Do not overcook the vegetables in *ladera* dishes. They are meant to be gently simmered with a minimum of water and olive oil until the pan juices have reduced and cooked down "almost to the oil," as Greek cooks say. When cooking *ladera*, add salt and pepper toward the end when the dish is almost ready. Do not add all the liquid specified in the recipe at the beginning of cooking, but add boiling water during cooking, as necessary. *Ladera* and other dishes prepared with olive oil are traditionally served lukewarm or at room temperature, the point at which the aromatic elements of the dish are at their peak.

- 2¼ lb (1 kg) young fava (broad) beans in their pods, trimmed
- 5 globe artichokes
- 3 tablespoons freshly squeezed lemon juice
- ½ cup (120 ml / 4 fl oz) olive oil
- 1 cup (7–8) finely chopped scallions (spring onions)
- ½ cup (15 g / ½ oz) finely chopped fresh dill
- salt and pepper
- lemon wedges, to garnish
- feta cheese, to serve

ARTICHOKES AND FAVA (BROAD) BEANS
ΑΓΓΙΝΑΡΕΣ ΜΕ ΚΟΥΚΙΑ
Aginares ke koukia

Cut the tender fava bean pods in half and shell the larger beans. Break off the stems of the artichokes, cut the bases flat, and pull off any small base leaves. Remove any tough outer leaves and scoop out the hairy choke from the center, leaving only the cup-shaped heart. As you prepare each artichoke, put it into a bowl of water with 1 tablespoon of the lemon juice to prevent discoloration. Heat the oil in a pan over medium heat. Add the scallions and cook over low heat, stirring occasionally, for about 5 minutes, until softened. Add the beans, drained artichokes, and dill, season with salt and pepper, and pour in 1 cup (250 ml / 8 fl oz) water. Cover and simmer for about 30 minutes, or until the beans and artichokes are tender and the sauce has reduced. Remove from the heat and sprinkle the vegetables with the remaining lemon juice, gently shaking the pan to distribute it evenly. Serve hot or at room temperature, garnished with lemon wedges and accompanied by feta cheese. Follow the same procedure to cook plain fava beans.

Serves 4
Preparation time 1 hour
Cooking time 30 minutes

❑ p 208

Artichokes and fava (broad) beans, p 207

Fricassee of oyster mushrooms, p 216

CONSTANTINOPLE-STYLE ARTICHOKES
ΑΓΓΙΝΑΡΕΣ ΠΟΛΙΤΙΚΕΣ
Aginares politikes

Break off the artichoke stems, trim the bases, and remove the tough dark green leaves and the chokes, leaving the tender cup-shaped bases. As you prepare each artichoke, put it into a bowl of water mixed with 2 tablespoons of the lemon juice and the flour to prevent discoloration. Heat the oil in a large wide pan over high heat. Add the onion, scallions, and carrots and cook, stirring occasionally, for 3–4 minutes, until softened. Drain the artichokes and add to the pan together with the potatoes, peas, if using, and dill. Season with salt and pepper and pour in 1 cup (250 ml / 8 fl oz) hot water. Cover and simmer for about 30 minutes, or until the artichokes and potatoes are tender and the sauce has reduced. If necessary, add more hot water during cooking. Beat the egg with the remaining lemon juice in a bowl and whisk in a ladle of the cooking juices, then pour the mixture over the artichokes. Shake the pan to distribute the sauce evenly. Remove the pan from the heat. Arrange the artichoke hearts on a platter, fill with the chopped vegetables and peas, and surround with the potato quarters.

Serves 4
Preparation time 30 minutes
Cooking time 30 minutes

Note: You can also dress the dish with plain lemon juice, in which case you can add ½ teaspoon cornstarch (cornflour) to thicken the sauce.

- 8 globe artichokes
- 6 tablespoons freshly squeezed lemon juice
- 2 tablespoons all-purpose (plain) flour
- ½ cup (120 ml / 4 fl oz) olive oil
- 1 onion, grated
- 4 scallions (spring onions), chopped
- 2 carrots, sliced
- 2 large potatoes, cut into quarters
- 1 cup (120 g / 4 oz) peas (optional)
- 4 tablespoons finely chopped fresh dill
- salt and pepper
- 1 egg

BRAISED RED BEANS
ΜΠΑΡΜΠΟΥΝΟΦΑΣΟΥΛΑ
Barbounofasoula

Heat the oil in a large pan. Add the onion and cook over low heat, stirring frequently, for about 5 minutes, until softened and translucent. Add all the other ingredients and simmer for 1–2 hours, until they are softened and the liquid has reduced to a thick sauce. Add a little hot water during cooking, if the dish seems dry. Serve hot or at room temperature, accompanied by feta cheese or olives.

Serves 4
Preparation time 30 minutes
Cooking time 1–2 hours

Note: The shelled fresh beans will take around 1 hour to cook. Soaked, dried beans need 2 hours.

- ½ cup (120 ml / 4 fl oz) olive oil
- 1 onion, grated
- 2¼ lb (1 kg) fresh cranberry or borlotti beans, or dried cranberry or borlotti beans, soaked overnight in water to cover and drained
- 1 lb 2 oz (500 g) fresh or canned tomatoes, puréed
- 1 tablespoon tomato paste (optional)
- ½ teaspoon sugar
- ½ cup (25 g / 1 oz) finely chopped fresh parsley
- 1 small, long green chile, sliced
- 2 cups (450 ml / 16 fl oz) hot water
- salt and pepper
- feta cheese or olives, to serve

FAVA (BROAD) BEANS WITH PEAS
ΑΡΑΚΑΣ ΜΕ ΚΟΥΚΙΑ
Arakas me koukia

- 2¼ lb (1 kg) young fava (broad) beans in their pods, trimmed
- 5 tablespoons olive oil
- 1 cup (7–8) finely chopped scallions (spring onions)
- 4½ cups (500 g / 1 lb 2 oz) shelled peas
- ½ cup (15 g / ½ oz) finely chopped fresh dill
- salt and pepper
- 1 cup (250 ml / 8 fl oz) hot water
- 2 tablespoons freshly squeezed lemon juice

Rinse the fava bean pods, cut in half and shell any tough, older beans. Heat the oil over high heat. Add the scallions and cook, stirring frequently, for 2–3 minutes, until softened. Add the beans, peas, and dill, season with salt and pepper, and pour in the hot water. Reduce the heat, cover, and simmer for up to 1 hour, or until the vegetables are tender and the sauce has reduced. Remove from the heat and pour in the lemon juice, shaking the pan to distribute it evenly. Serve hot or at room temperature.

Serves 6
Preparation time 40 minutes
Cooking time 1 hour

Note: Adjust the cooking time to suit the age and quality of the beans and peas (Greek peas take longer to cook than garden peas). You can substitute a chopped tomato for the lemon juice if you like.

STUFFED CELERY ROOT (CELERIAC)
ΣΕΛΙΝΟΡΙΖΕΣ ΓΕΜΙΣΤΕΣ
Selinorizes gemistes

- 1 lb 2 oz (500 g) celery leaves or chard leaves
- 2 large celery roots (celeriacs), about 1½ lb (700 g) total weight, peeled and thickly sliced
- ½ cup (120 ml / 4 fl oz) olive oil
- ½ cup (4) finely chopped scallions (spring onions)
- 1 cup (250 ml / 8 fl oz) tomato juice
- 2 ripe tomatoes, finely chopped
- 2 large potatoes, scooped into small balls
- salt and pepper
- 2 tablespoons freshly squeezed lemon juice
- lemon slices and fresh parsley sprigs, to garnish

The recipe is from the Messinia region of the Peloponnese, where it is served as a main dish.

Discard any hard stems and wilted leaves from the celery leaves and chop the fresh and tender ones. Blanch briefly in boiling water, then drain, and set aside. Blanch the celery root in boiling water, drain, and let stand until cool enough to handle. Press the center of each slice with the back of a spoon to make a depression. Heat the oil in a pan. Add the scallions and cook over low heat, stirring occasionally, for 5 minutes, until softened. Pour in the tomato juice, add the tomatoes, celery leaves, celery root, and potato balls and season with salt and pepper. Cover and simmer, without stirring, for about 45 minutes, or until the vegetables are tender and the sauce has reduced. It may be necessary to add a little hot water during cooking. Add the lemon juice and shake the pan to distribute it evenly, then remove from the heat. To serve, arrange the celery root rounds on a platter. Using a slotted spoon, fill the centers with the cooked vegetables. Pour the sauce on top and garnish with lemon slices and parsley sprigs. Serve hot.

Serves 4
Preparation time 30 minutes
Cooking time 45 minutes

BAKED EGGPLANTS (AUBERGINES)
ΚΑΠΑΚΩΤΗ
Kapakoti

Peel the eggplants and cut them lengthwise into 4–6 slices, depending on their size. Sprinkle with salt and let drain in a colander for 1 hour. Rinse thoroughly and squeeze gently to remove the excess liquid. Heat half the oil in a skillet or frying pan. Add the eggplant slices, in batches if necessary, and cook, turning occasionally, for 8–10 minutes, until lightly browned on both sides. Remove from the pan and drain on paper towels. Heat the remaining oil in a pan. Add the onion or garlic and cook over low heat, stirring occasionally, for 4–5 minutes, until softened. Add the tomatoes, season with salt and pepper, and cook for about 15 minutes, until the sauce thickens lightly. Meanwhile, preheat the oven to 300°F (150°C / Gas Mark 2). Layer the eggplant slices in an ovenproof dish, sprinkle with the sliced chile, and pour the sauce over them. Cover with aluminum foil and bake for about 2 hours, or until the eggplants are very tender and the sauce has reduced. Serve at room temperature, sprinkled with the parsley.

Serves 4
Preparation time 1½ hours (including salting)
Cooking time 2½ hours

- 4½ lb (2 kg) eggplants (aubergines)
- 5 tablespoons olive oil
- 1 large onion, sliced, or 6 garlic cloves, sliced
- 1 lb 2 oz (500 g) fresh or canned tomatoes, chopped
- salt and pepper
- 1 long green chile, sliced (optional)
- 2 tablespoons finely chopped fresh parsley

EGGPLANT (AUBERGINE) AND RICE DOLMADES FROM PONTUS
ΝΤΟΛΜΑΔΕΣ ΦΟΥΡΝΟΥ ΜΕ ΜΕΛΙΤΖΑΝΕΣ
Dolmades fournou me melitzanes

Sprinkle the eggplants with salt and let drain in a colander for 30 minutes. Rinse, drain well, and squeeze out the excess water. Heat half the oil in a pan. Add the eggplants, scallions, onion, and garlic and cook over low heat for 5 minutes, until softened. Add the lemon juice, pour in ½ cup (120 ml / 4 fl oz) water, and simmer for 10 minutes. Add the rice and herbs, season with salt and pepper, and cook, stirring constantly, for 5 minutes. Remove from the heat and let cool. Preheat the oven to 350°F (180°C / Gas Mark 4) and brush an ovenproof dish with oil, blanch the grape leaves in boiling water for 2–3 minutes, then drain. Place 1 teaspoon of the filling on the dull side of each leaf, turn in the sides, and roll up. Arrange the stuffed grape leaves, seam side down, in the prepared dish. Combine the tomatoes with the remaining oil in a bowl, season with salt and pepper, and ladle the mixture over the grape leaf rolls. Bake for 1 hour, or until the rice is tender, adding water if necessary. Serve hot or at room temperature.

Serves 4
Preparation time 1½ hours (including salting and cooling)
Cooking time 1½ hours

- 3 eggplants (aubergines), 2¼ lb (1 kg) total weight, peeled and diced
- ¾ cup (175 ml / 6 fl oz) olive oil, plus extra for brushing
- 1 cup (7–8) finely chopped scallions (spring onions)
- 1 small onion, grated
- 2 garlic cloves, finely chopped
- 2 tablespoons freshly squeezed lemon juice
- generous 1 cup (225 g / 8 oz) medium-grain rice
- 1 teaspoon dried oregano
- 4 tablespoons finely chopped fresh mint
- 2 tablespoons finely chopped fresh dill
- salt and pepper
- 2¼ lb (1 kg) ripe tomatoes, peeled, seeded, and finely chopped or 14 oz (400 g) chopped canned tomatoes
- 1 lb 2 oz (500 g) grape (vine) leaves

EGGPLANT (AUBERGINE) ROLLS WITH CHEESE
ΡΟΛΑ ΜΕΛΙΤΖΑΝΑΣ ΜΕ ΑΝΘΟΤΥΡΟ
Rola melitzanas me anthotiro

- 4 x 9-oz (250-g) round eggplants (aubergines), very thinly sliced lengthwise
- ½ cup (120 ml / 4 fl oz) olive oil
- 11 oz (300 g) anthotiro or ricotta cheese
- 1 cup (120 g / 4 oz) grated kefalograviera or pecorino cheese
- 4 tablespoons coarsely chopped sun-dried tomatoes
- 4 tablespoons finely chopped fresh basil or mint
- salt and freshly ground white pepper

FOR THE TOMATO SAUCE
- 3 tablespoons olive oil
- 1 garlic clove, sliced
- 1 small chile, quartered (optional)
- 1 lb 2 oz (500 g) ripe tomatoes, peeled, seeded, and puréed
- 1 teaspoon sugar
- 1 tablespoon red wine vinegar
- salt and pepper

Sprinkle the eggplant slices with salt and let drain in a colander for 1 hour. Meanwhile, make the tomato sauce. Put all the ingredients into a pan, season with salt and pepper and cook over medium heat for 15–20 minutes, until thickened. Remove from the heat and set aside. Rinse the eggplant slices under cold running water, squeeze out the excess liquid, and pat dry with paper towels. Heat 5 tablespoons of the oil in a skillet or frying pan, add the eggplant slices, and cook for about 8 minutes, turning once, until lightly browned. Remove from the skillet and drain on paper towels. Combine the anthotiro, half the kefalograviera, the sun-dried tomatoes, the remaining oil, and the basil or mint in a bowl and season with salt and white pepper. Put 1 tablespoon of the mixture at the end of each eggplant slice and roll into cylinders. Pour half the tomato sauce into a rectangular ovenproof dish, arrange the rolls on top, seam side down, pour the remaining sauce over them, and sprinkle with the remaining cheese. (At this stage the dish may be frozen.) Bake for 35–40 minutes. Serve hot or at room temperature.

Serves 4
Preparation time 1½ hours (including salting)
Cooking time 1 hour

CONSTANTINOPLE-STYLE STUFFED EGGPLANTS (AUBERGINES)
ΜΕΛΙΤΖΑΝΕΣ ΠΟΛΙΤΙΚΕΣ
Melitzanes politikes

- 6 long thin eggplants (aubergines), 3¼ lb (1.5 kg) total weight
- 1¾ cups (250 g / 9 oz) grated carrots
- ½ cup (25 g / 1 oz) chopped fresh parsley
- ½ cup (50 g / 2 oz) finely chopped celery
- 4 garlic cloves, finely chopped
- 1 cup (250 ml / 8 fl oz) olive oil
- fried potatoes and green olives, to serve

FOR THE SAUCE
- 2¼ lb (1 kg) ripe tomatoes, peeled, seeded, and grated
- 1 tablespoon tomato paste
- 1 teaspoon sugar
- 1 tablespoon red wine vinegar
- 1 cinnamon stick
- salt and pepper

Peel the eggplants and, using a sharp knife, make 3 lengthwise slits in the flesh from top to the bottom of each one without cutting all the way through. Sprinkle with salt and let drain for 1 hour. Meanwhile, combine the carrots, parsley, celery, and garlic in a bowl. Rinse the eggplants under cold running water and gently squeeze out any excess water. Fill the slits with the carrot mixture and press lightly to close. Heat the olive oil a large heavy pan. Add the eggplants and cook over medium heat, turning carefully, for 8–10 minutes, until golden on all sides. Remove with a slotted spoon and drain on paper towels. Drain off all but 2–3 tablespoons of the oil and reheat. Stir in all the ingredients for the sauce, season with salt and pepper and bring to a boil. Return the eggplants to the pan, cover, and simmer for about 30 minutes, until the eggplants are tender and the sauce has thickened. Remove and discard the cinnamon stick before serving with fried potatoes and green olives.

Serves 6
Preparation time 1½ hours (including salting)
Cooking time 40 minutes

EGGPLANT (AUBERGINE) AND PEPPER CASSEROLE
ΜΕΛΙΤΖΑΝΕΣ ΚΑΙ ΠΙΠΕΡΙΕΣ ΜΕ ΤΥΡΙ
Melitzanes ke piperies me tiri

- 4½ lb (2 kg) eggplants (aubergines), peeled and thickly sliced
- ⅔ cup (150 ml / ¼ pint) olive oil
- 2¼ lb (1 kg) long green peppers, seeded and cut into wide strips
- 3 garlic cloves, thinly sliced
- 2¼ lb (1 kg) fresh ripe tomatoes, puréed
- ½ teaspoon sugar
- 1 tablespoon red wine vinegar
- 4 tablespoons finely chopped fresh parsley
- 1 lb 2 oz (500 g) feta cheese, thinly sliced
- pinch of oregano
- salt and pepper

Sprinkle the eggplant slices with salt and let drain in a colander for 2 hours. Rinse well, drain, and squeeze out the excess water with your hands. Heat ½ cup (120 ml / 4 fl oz) of the olive oil in a skillet or frying pan. Add the eggplant slices and bell pepper strips and cook, turning occasionally, for about 10 minutes, until lightly browned. Remove from the skillet and drain on paper towels. (Alternatively, brush with olive oil and broil (grill) for about 8 minutes, turning once, until lightly browned. This will require less oil.) Heat the remaining oil in a pan. Add the garlic and cook over low heat, stirring frequently, for 3–4 minutes, until lightly browned. Add the tomatoes, sugar, vinegar, and parsley, season with salt and pepper, and simmer for about 15 minutes, until the sauce has thickened slightly. Meanwhile, preheat the oven to 350°F (180°C / Gas Mark 4). Layer the eggplants and bell peppers in an ovenproof dish and pour half the sauce over them. Cover with the sliced cheese, drizzle with the remaining sauce, and sprinkle with the oregano. Bake for 20–30 minutes, or until the sauce has reduced and the top is lightly browned. Serve immediately.

Serves 6
Preparation time 2½ hours (including salting)
Cooking time 1–1¼ hours

Vefa's secret: Peeling the peppers is easier if you put them in a plastic bag to cool after roasting or broiling (grilling).

SAUTÉED FENNEL WITH GARLIC
ΦΙΝΟΚΙΟ ΣΩΤΕ ΜΕ ΣΚΟΡΔΟ
Finokio sauté me skordo

- 5 tablespoons olive oil
- 8 small fennel bulbs, halved
- 6 garlic cloves, peeled
- ½ cup (120 ml / 4 fl oz) water or tomato juice
- salt and pepper
- 4 tablespoons finely chopped fennel fronds
- 2 tablespoons freshly squeezed lemon juice

Heat the oil in a large heavy skillet or frying pan. Add the fennel and garlic and cook, turning frequently, for 10–15 minutes, until lightly browned on all sides. Add the water or tomato juice, season with salt and pepper, cover, and simmer for 15 minutes, until the fennel is tender and the sauce has reduced. Stir in the fennel fronds and lemon juice, gently shaking the pan to distribute them evenly. Serve immediately.

Serves 4
Prepare time 20 minutes
Cooking time 25–30 minutes

- 5 tablespoons olive oil
- 1 cup (7–8) thinly sliced scallions (spring onions)
- 2–3 garlic cloves, thinly sliced
- 1 red bell pepper, seeded and cut into julienne strips
- 1 green bell pepper, seeded and cut into julienne strips
- 2¼ lb (1 kg) tomatoes, peeled and puréed
- 1 cup (250 ml / 8 fl oz) dry white wine
- 1 teaspoon dried thyme
- salt and pepper
- 4 small fennel bulbs, thinly sliced crosswise
- 1 cup (50 g / 2 oz) coarse white bread crumbs

FENNEL BAKED WITH BELL PEPPERS AND ONIONS
ΦΙΝΟΚΙΟ ΣΤΟ ΦΟΥΡΝΟ ΜΕ ΠΙΠΕΡΙΕΣ ΚΑΙ ΚΡΕΜΜΥΔΙΑ
Finokio sto fourno me piperies ke kremidia

Heat the oil in a large pan. Add the scallions, garlic, and bell peppers and cook over low heat, stirring occasionally, for 5–8 minutes, until softened. Stir in the tomatoes and simmer for 5 minutes more. Pour in the wine, add the thyme, season with salt and pepper, and bring to a boil. Add the fennel, cover, and simmer for 7–8 minutes, until tender. Meanwhile, preheat the oven to 350°F (180°C / Gas Mark 4). Using a slotted spoon, transfer the vegetables to a small deep ovenproof dish, spreading them out evenly. Pour the sauce over them and sprinkle with the bread crumbs. Bake for 45–50 minutes. Serve hot or at room temperature.

Serves 4
Preparation time 20 minutes
Cooking time 1–1¼ hours

- 2¼ lb (1 kg) slender leeks, trimmed and cut into 2-inch (5-cm) pieces
- 1 lb 2 oz (500 g) celery root (celeriac), peeled and cut into 2-inch (5-cm) pieces
- salt and pepper
- ½ cup (120 ml / 4 fl oz) olive oil
- 2 eggs
- 4 tablespoons freshly squeezed lemon juice

LEEKS AND CELERY ROOT (CELERIAC) WITH EGG-LEMON SAUCE
ΠΡΑΣΟΣΕΛΙΝΟ ΑΥΓΟΛΕΜΟΝΟ
Prasoselino avgolemono

Blanch the leeks and celery root in separate pans of boiling water for about 5 minutes, then drain, and set aside. Heat the oil in a heavy pan over high heat. Add the leeks and cook, stirring constantly, for 5 minutes. Pour in ½ cup (120 ml / 4 fl oz) water, cover, and simmer for 10 minutes. Add the celery root, season with salt and pepper, and simmer, stirring frequently, for 15 minutes more, until the vegetables are tender but still firm and the sauce has reduced. If necessary, add a little more water during cooking. Lightly beat the eggs with the lemon juice in a bowl and whisk in a ladleful of the hot pan juices, then pour the egg-lemon mixture over the vegetables, shaking the pan gently to distribute it evenly. Sprinkle with pepper and serve immediately. This dish is an excellent accompaniment for broiled (grilled) or roasted meats.

Serves 4
Preparation time 15 minutes
Cooking time 45 minutes

LEEKS WITH RICE
ΠΡΑΣΟΡΥΖΟ
Prasorizo

Blanch the leeks in boiling water for 5 minutes, then drain in a colander. Heat the oil in a heavy pan. Add the onion and cook over low heat, stirring occasionally, for 4–5 minutes, until softened. Add the leeks and tomato juice or water and season with salt. Cover and simmer for 30 minutes, adding more water if necessary. Stir in the rice, celery, parsley, and bell pepper, cover, and simmer for 30 minutes more, until the leeks and rice are tender and all the liquid has been absorbed. Remove from the heat and sprinkle with the lemon juice and pepper, shaking the pan to distribute them evenly. Serve garnished with lemon wedges and accompanied by feta cheese or olives.

Serves 4
Preparation time 15 minutes
Cooking time 1 hour

- 3¼ lb (1.5 kg) slender leeks, cut into 1-inch (2.5-cm) pieces
- ½ cup (120 ml / 4 fl oz) olive oil
- 1 onion, grated
- 1 cup (250 ml / 8 fl oz) tomato juice or water
- ½ cup (80 g / 3 oz) medium-grain rice
- 2 celery stalks, sliced
- 3 tablespoons finely chopped fresh parsley
- 1 small green bell pepper, seeded and chopped
- 2 tablespoons freshly squeezed lemon juice
- salt and pepper
- lemon wedges, to garnish
- feta cheese or olives, to serve

FRICASSEE OF OYSTER MUSHROOMS
ΦΡΙΚΑΣΕ ΜΕ ΜΑΝΙΤΑΡΙΑ ΠΛΕΥΡΩΤΟΥΣ
Frikase me manitaria plevrotous

Briefly blanch the scallions in boiling water, then drain. Heat the oil in a large pan. Add the mushrooms and cook over low heat, stirring occasionally, for 8–10 minutes, until softened. Add the scallions, lettuce, dill, and parsley, season with salt and pepper, and pour in the hot water. Bring to a boil, cover, and simmer for 30 minutes, until the vegetables are tender but still firm and the liquid has reduced to a thick sauce. Beat the egg with the lemon juice in a bowl and whisk in a ladleful of the pan juices, then pour the egg-lemon mixture into the pan, shaking it gently to distribute it evenly. Serve hot.

Serves 4
Preparation time 15 minutes
Cooking time 40 minutes

Vefa's secret: This vegetarian dish will also appeal to carnivores. To make it for vegans, omit the egg and finish the dish only with lemon juice. Without egg-lemon sauce, it is also good served at room temperature.

☐ p 209

- 1 lb 2 oz (500 g) scallions (spring onions), cut into short lengths
- 5 tablespoons olive oil
- 1 lb 2 oz (500 g) oyster mushrooms, cut into large pieces
- 9 oz (250 g) romaine lettuce, cut into pieces
- 4 tablespoons finely chopped fresh dill
- ½ cup (25 g / 1 oz) finely chopped fresh parsley
- salt and pepper
- ½ cup (120 ml / 4 fl oz) hot water
- 1 egg
- 4 tablespoons freshly squeezed lemon juice

- 4 tablespoons olive oil
- 4 tablespoons (50 g / 2 oz) butter
- 1 large onion, grated
- 3 garlic cloves, finely chopped
- 9 oz (250 g) oyster mushrooms, cut in strips
- 9 oz (250 g) white button mushrooms, sliced
- 4 tablespoons dry white wine
- 3 cups (750 ml / 1¼ pints) chicken stock
- ¼ teaspoon grated nutmeg
- salt and pepper
- 14 oz (400 g) orzo or other tiny pasta
- 1½ cups (175 g / 6 oz) grated kefalograviera or pecorino cheese

BAKED MUSHROOM CASSEROLE
ΓΙΟΥΒΕΤΣΙ ΜΕ ΜΑΝΙΤΑΡΙΑ
Giouvetsi me manitaria

Heat half the oil with half the butter in a large pan. Add the onion and garlic and cook over low heat, stirring occasionally, for 4–5 minutes, until softened. Add both kinds of mushrooms and cook, stirring constantly, until their liquid has evaporated. Pour in the wine, increase the heat to high, and cook, stirring constantly, for a few minutes. Pour in the stock, add the nutmeg, and season with salt and pepper. Reduce the heat and simmer for 20 minutes. Meanwhile, preheat the oven to 350°F (180°C / Gas Mark 4). Heat the remaining oil with the remaining butter in a skillet or frying pan. Add the pasta and cook, stirring frequently, until it starts to brown. Transfer the pasta to an earthenware dish with a lid. Add the mushrooms with their cooking liquid, cover, and bake for 1¼ hours. Remove the dish from the oven and remove the lid. Sprinkle with the grated cheese, return the dish to the oven, and bake, uncovered, for 15 minutes more, until the cheese has melted and the top is lightly browned. Serve hot.

Serves 6
Preparation time 20 minutes
Cooking time 2 hours

- 1 lb 2 oz (500 g) fresh okra
- 2 tablespoons red wine vinegar or freshly squeezed lemon juice
- ½ cup (120 ml / 4 fl oz) olive oil
- 1 onion, grated
- 1 lb 2 oz (500 g) fresh or canned tomatoes, puréed
- 5 tablespoons finely chopped fresh parsley
- ½ teaspoon sugar
- 3 lemon slices, skin removed
- 1 ripe tomato, sliced
- salt and pepper

BRAISED OKRA
ΜΠΑΜΙΕΣ ΓΙΑΧΝΙ
Bamies giahni

Cut the stems off the okra, taking care not to pierce the pods. Dip the cut ends into salt and let drain in a colander for 30 minutes. Rinse well in water mixed with 1 tablespoon of the lemon juice or red wine vinegar. Heat the oil in a wide shallow pan. Add the onion and cook over low heat, stirring occasionally, for 4–5 minutes, until softened. Add the tomatoes, parsley, sugar, and lemon slices and season with pepper. Cover and simmer for 10 minutes. Add the okra and stir gently to coat with the sauce, place the tomato slices on top, and season it with a little salt and pepper. Cover and bring to a boil over medium heat. Reduce the heat and simmer for about 15 minutes, adding a little water if the dish seems dry. Okra is delicate, so take care not to overcook it. Remove from the heat and carefully spoon onto individual plates. This is equally delicious served hot or at room temperature.

Serves 4
Preparation time 30–40 minutes (including salting)
Cooking time 30 minutes

Note: Do not stir while cooking okra; shake the pan gently to prevent sticking. You can use frozen okra, in which case thaw and rinse first with 1 tablespoon lemon juice or vinegar. There is no need to salt it.

OKRA WITH TRAHANA
ΜΠΑΜΙΕΣ ΜΕ ΞΥΝΟΧΟΝΤΡΟ
Bamies me xinohondro

Cut the stems off the okra, taking care not to pierce the pods. Dip the cut ends into salt and let drain in a colander for 30 minutes. Rinse well in water mixed with 1 tablespoon of the lemon juice or red wine vinegar. Heat half the oil in a large pan. Add the onion, scallions, and garlic and cook over low heat, stirring occasionally, for 5 minutes, until softened. Pour in the wine and simmer until it has evaporated. Add the tomatoes, fennel, parsley, remaining lemon juice, and chile, if using, cover, and simmer for 15 minutes. Meanwhile, heat the remaining oil in a skillet or frying pan. Add the okra and cook over low heat, stirring occasionally, for 5 minutes, then stir it into the sauce. Cover and simmer for 5 minutes more. Add the trahana and season with salt and pepper, shaking the pan to distribute the ingredients evenly. Cover and simmer for 15 minutes, adding a little hot water, if necessary. Serve the dish hot or at room temperature.

Serves 6
Preparation time 50 minutes (including salting)
Cooking time 30 minutes

Note: Although the method of cooking this dish appears simple, it needs careful attention to be properly prepared. Do not overcook the trahana or the okra. The trahana should not be mushy and the okra should retain its shape. You can also use frozen okra, in which case thaw and rinse first with 1 tablespoon lemon juice or vinegar. There is no need to salt it.

- 1 lb 10 oz (750 g) fresh okra
- 3 tablespoons freshly squeezed lemon juice or red wine vinegar
- ¾ cup (175 ml / 6 fl oz) olive oil
- 1 onion, finely chopped
- ½ cup (4) finely chopped scallions (spring onions)
- 2 garlic cloves, thinly sliced
- 4 tablespoons red wine
- 3 large ripe tomatoes, peeled, seeded, and chopped or 14 oz (400 g) chopped canned tomatoes
- ½ cup (15 g / ½ oz) chopped fresh fennel
- ½ cup (25 g / 1 oz) finely chopped fresh parsley
- 1 chile, finely chopped (optional)
- 5 oz (150 g) Sour trahana (p 280)
- salt and pepper

BAKED ONIONS FROM NAOUSA
ΚΡΕΜΜΥΔΙΑ ΣΤΟ ΦΟΥΡΝΟ ΟΡΦΑΝΑ
Kremidia sto fourno orfana

Plunge the onions into a pan of boiling water, turn off the heat, and let soak for 1–2 hours. This helps the skins to slip off more easily. Drain and peel. Preheat the oven to 350°F (180°C / Gas Mark 4). Heat the oil in a large pan. Add the onions and the garlic and cook over low heat, stirring occasionally, for 5–8 minutes, until they start to soften. Add all the remaining ingredients, season with salt and pepper, and mix well. Pour the mixture into an ovenproof dish, cover with aluminum foil, and bake for about 2 hours, until the onions are tender and the sauce has reduced. Serve hot.

Serves 6
Preparation time 1¼–2¼ hours (including soaking)
Cooking time 2¼ hours

- 4½ lb (2 kg) small pearl (pickling) onions or shallots
- ½ cup (120 ml / 4 fl oz) olive oil
- 6 garlic cloves
- 2¼ lb (1 kg) ripe tomatoes, finely chopped
- 1 cup (250 ml / 8 fl oz) dry red wine
- 2 tablespoons red wine vinegar
- 3 bay leaves
- 20 black peppercorns
- 10 allspice berries
- salt and pepper

ONIONS IN VINEGAR SAUCE
ΚΡΕΜΜΥΔΑΚΙΑ ΣΤΟ ΞΥΔΙ
Kremidakia sto xidi

- 1 lb 2 oz (500 g) small pearl (pickling) onions or shallots
- 5 tablespoons olive oil
- ½ cup (120 ml / 4 fl oz) sherry vinegar or red wine vinegar
- 1 cup (250 ml / 8 fl oz) hot water
- 1 garlic clove, chopped
- 1 red chile, chopped
- 1 fresh thyme sprig
- 1 bay leaf
- 1 teaspoon black peppercorns
- 1 teaspoon salt
- 1 tablespoon sugar

Plunge the onions into a pan of boiling water, turn off the heat, and let soak for 1–2 hours. This helps the skins slip off more easily. Drain and peel. Heat the oil in a large wide pan. Add the onions and cook over low heat, stirring occasionally, for about 10 minutes, until golden all over. Pour in the vinegar and hot water, add the garlic, chile, herbs, peppercorns, salt, and sugar, cover, and simmer for about 30 minutes, until the onions are tender. Remove from the heat and let cool completely. This dish is an excellent accompaniment to meat or game.

Serves 4
Preparation time 1¼–2¼ hours (including soaking)
Cooking time 40 minutes

BELL PEPPERS STUFFED WITH CHEESE
ΠΙΠΕΡΙΕΣ ΜΕ ΤΥΡΙΑ ΣΤΟ ΦΟΥΡΝΟ
Piperies me tiria sto fourno

- 6 small red bell peppers
- 4 tablespoons olive oil, plus extra for brushing
- 2 egg yolks
- ½ cup (120 ml / 4 fl oz) thick White sauce (p 57)
- 2 tablespoons (25 g / 1 oz) butter
- 14 oz (400 g) tomatoes, crushed
- salt and pepper
- 3½ oz (100 g) feta cheese, crumbled
- ¾ cup (80 g / 3 oz) grated kefalograviera, regato or pecorino cheese
- ¾ cup (80 g / 3 oz) grated kaseri or mozzarella cheese
- 3 oz (80 g) Metsovone or any lightly smoked semi-hard cheese, grated
- generous ½ cup (100 g / 3½ oz) chopped cured ham
- 1 tablespoon dried oregano

Cut the tops off the bell peppers just below the stems and reserve. Remove and discard the seeds, rinse the bell peppers, and pat dry with paper towels. Heat the oil in a skillet or frying pan. Add the bell peppers and their "caps" and cook, turning frequently, for about 5 minutes. Remove from the heat and drain on paper towels. Beat the egg yolks into the white sauce, one at a time, then set aside. Melt the butter in a pan, add the tomatoes, season with salt and pepper, and simmer for about 15 minutes, until thickened. Meanwhile, preheat the oven to 350°F (180°C / Gas Mark 4) and brush an ovenproof dish with oil. Combine half the tomato sauce, the four types of cheese, and the ham in a bowl. Stuff the bell peppers three-quarters full with the mixture, spoon 2 tablespoons of the white sauce on top of the filling in each bell pepper, replace the caps, and arrange side by side in the prepared dish. Pour the remaining tomato sauce over the stuffed bell peppers and bake for 30 minutes. Transfer to a platter and spoon the sauce around the bell peppers. Serve hot.

Serves 6
Preparation time 30 minutes
Cooking time 30 minutes

POTATO AND BELL PEPPER CASSEROLE
ΠΑΤΑΤΕΣ ΚΑΙ ΠΙΠΕΡΙΕΣ ΣΤΟ ΦΟΥΡΝΟ
Patates ke piperies sto fourno

Preheat the oven to 350°F (180°C / Gas Mark 4) and grease a 10 x 12-inch (25 x 30-cm) ovenproof dish with butter. Melt the 3 tablespoons butter in a pan. Add the onion and cook over low heat, stirring occasionally, for 4–5 minutes, until softened. Stir in the flour and cook, stirring constantly, for 1 minute. Add the milk all at once and cook, stirring vigorously, until the sauce thickens. Remove from the heat and let cool slightly, then stir in the cheese and parsley, and season to taste with salt and white pepper. Season the potato slices with salt and spread out half of them on the base of the prepared dish. Spread half the sauce on top and arrange the strips of bell pepper over it. Layer the remaining potatoes over the bell peppers and cover with the rest of the sauce. Bake for 1¼ hours, until the potatoes are tender and the topping is golden. If it browns too quickly, cover with aluminum foil. Serve hot, garnished with a rosemary or parsley sprig.

Serves 4
Preparation time 30 minutes
Cooking time 1¼ hours

Vefa's secret: If you want to speed up the baking time, parboil the potatoes first.

- 3 tablespoons (40 g / 1½ oz) butter, plus extra for greasing
- 1 onion, grated
- 3 tablespoons all-purpose (plain) flour
- 2 cups (450 ml / 16 fl oz) milk
- 1 cup (120 g / 4 oz) grated regato or pecorino cheese
- 2 tablespoons finely chopped fresh parsley
- salt and white pepper
- 2¼ lb (1 kg) potatoes, thinly sliced
- 1 lb 2 oz (500 g) red bell peppers, roasted, peeled, seeded, and cut into thick strips
- 1 fresh rosemary or parsley sprig, to garnish

CRACKED POTATOES TOSSED WITH CORIANDER FROM CYPRUS
ΠΑΤΑΤΕΣ ΑΝΤΙΝΑΧΤΕΣ
Patates antinahtes

Hit each unpeeled potato lightly with a wooden meat mallet so that it cracks slightly. Pour enough olive oil into a large heavy pan to cover the potatoes and heat. Add the potatoes in batches, and fry until golden on all sides. Drain off the oil. Return the pan to the heat and add the wine, coriander, and lemon juice. Cover the pan and, holding it with both hands, shake it vigorously over the heat several times, tossing the potatoes so that they "jump" around in it and become coated in coriander. Continue doing this until all the liquid has evaporated and the potatoes are covered all over with the coriander. Drain the potatoes on paper towels, season with salt and pepper, and serve hot with meat or game.

Serves 4
Preparation time 20 minutes
Cooking time 45 minutes

☐ p 222

- 15 small new potatoes
- olive oil, for frying
- 5 tablespoons dry red wine
- 1 tablespoon coarsely ground coriander seeds
- 2 tablespoons freshly squeezed lemon juice
- salt and pepper

BRAISED POTATOES
ΠΑΤΑΤΕΣ ΓΙΑΧΝΙ
Patates giahni

- 3¼ lb (1.5 kg) potatoes, cut into wedges
- 1 tablespoon freshly squeezed lemon juice
- ½ cup (120 ml / 4 fl oz) olive oil
- 1 onion, grated
- 1 garlic clove, thinly sliced
- 2¼ lb (1 kg) fresh or canned tomatoes, puréed
- 1 teaspoon sugar
- 1 bay leaf
- 5 allspice berries
- 1 cup (250 ml / 8 fl oz) beef stock or water
- 4 tablespoons finely chopped fresh parsley
- salt and pepper
- black olives or feta cheese, to serve

Put the potato wedges into a bowl, add the lemon juice, and toss. Heat the oil in a large pan over high heat. Add the onion and garlic and cook, stirring frequently, for 3–4 minutes, until softened. Add the potatoes, tomatoes, sugar, bay leaf, allspice berries, beef stock or water, and parsley and stir well. Cover and simmer, shaking the pan occasionally, for 45 minutes, until the potatoes are tender and the sauce has reduced. Do not stir during cooking or the potatoes will crumble. Season with salt and pepper, remove from the heat and discard the bay leaf and allspice berries. Serve the dish hot or at room temperature, accompanied by black olives or feta cheese.

Serves 4
Preparation time 30 minutes
Cooking time 45 minutes

FRIED POTATOES, GREEK-STYLE
ΠΑΤΑΤΕΣ ΤΗΓΑΝΙΤΕΣ
Patates tiganites

- 4½ lb (2 kg) potatoes, cut into ⅛-inch (3-mm) thick rounds
- olive oil, for deep-frying
- salt or ½ cup (50 g / 2 oz) grated kefalotiri, pecorino, or Parmesan cheese

If you are not going to cook the potato slices immediately, put them in a bowl of cold water to avoid discoloration. When you are ready to cook, drain well and pat dry. Heat the oil in a deep-fryer to 350–375°F (180–190°C). Add the potato slices to the hot oil, in batches if necessary, and deep-fry until crisp and golden brown. Remove and drain on paper towels. Sprinkle with a little salt or grated hard cheese, preferably kefalotiri, and serve immediately. These make an excellent accompaniment for souvlaki, fried meatballs, and broiled (grilled) or roasted meats.

Serves 6
Preparation time 15 minutes
Cooking time 15 minutes

Cracked potatoes tossed with coriander from Cyprus, p 220

spinach with rice, p 225

POTATOES ROASTED WITH LEMON OR TOMATO
ΠΑΤΑΤΕΣ ΦΟΥΡΝΟΥ ΛΕΜΟΝΑΤΕΣ Η ΜΕ ΝΤΟΜΑΤΑ
Patates fournou lemonates i me domata

- 4½ lb (2 kg) potatoes, cut into wedges
- 5 tablespoons freshly squeezed lemon juice or 1 lb 2 oz (500 g) tomatoes, peeled and puréed
- pinch of dried oregano
- 1 garlic clove, finely chopped (optional)
- salt and pepper
- 5 tablespoons olive oil
- 5 tablespoons (65 g/2½ oz) butter

Put the potato wedges into a bowl. For lemon-roasted potatoes, add the lemon juice, oregano, and garlic, season with salt and pepper, and toss well, then let stand for 1 hour. Meanwhile, preheat the oven to 350°F (180°C/Gas Mark 4). Transfer the potato mixture to an ovenproof dish, drizzle with the oil, and dot with butter. Cover the dish with aluminum foil and roast for 1 hour. Remove the aluminum foil and continue roasting, basting occasionally with the pan juices, for 30 minutes more, until the potatoes are tender and lightly browned. If necessary, add some water during cooking. For tomato-roasted potatoes, mix the potatoes with the puréed tomatoes, oregano, and garlic and season with salt and pepper. Transfer the potato mixture to an ovenproof dish, drizzle with the oil, and dot with butter. Cover the dish with aluminum foil and roast for 1 hour. Remove the aluminum foil and continue roasting for 40 minutes more, until the potatoes are tender and the sauce has reduced. Serve hot. These make an excellent accompaniment for roast meat or poultry.

Serves 6
Preparation time 1¼ hours (including standing)
Cooking time 1½–1¾ hours

BAKED POTATOES WITH MUSHROOMS AND YOGURT
ΠΑΤΑΤΕΣ ΨΗΤΕΣ ΜΕ ΜΑΝΙΤΑΡΙΑ ΚΑΙ ΓΙΑΟΥΡΤΙ
Patates psites me manitaria ke giaourti

- 6 large potatoes, about 9 oz (250 g) each
- 4 tablespoons olive oil
- 3⅔ cups (250 g/9 oz) sliced small white button mushrooms
- 2 garlic cloves, finely chopped
- 2 tablespoons finely chopped fresh parsley
- salt and pepper
- ¾ cup (80 g/3 oz) grated kefalotiri, regato or pecorino cheese
- 1 cup (250 ml/8 fl oz) strained yogurt or thick Greek yogurt
- 3 scallions (spring onions), white parts only, finely chopped

Preheat the oven to 400°F (200°C/Gas Mark 6). Wrap each potato in aluminum foil and bake for 1½ hours, or until tender. Heat the oil in a skillet or frying pan. Add the mushrooms and garlic and cook over low heat, stirring occasionally, for 5 minutes, until softened. Add the parsley, season with salt and pepper, and remove from the heat. Make 2 parallel cuts on the flat side of each potato and pull open carefully with your fingers. Sprinkle the openings with the mushroom mixture and the cheese. Put 2 tablespoons yogurt on top of each and sprinkle with chopped scallions. Serve immediately.

Serves 6
Preparation time 20 minutes
Cooking time 1½ hours

SPINACH WITH RICE
ΣΠΑΝΑΚΟΡΥΖΟ
Spanakorizo

- ⚬ 3¼ lb (1.5 kg) spinach, coarse stalks removed
- ⚬ ½ cup (120 ml / 4 fl oz) olive oil
- ⚬ 1 small onion, finely chopped
- ⚬ ½ cup (4) chopped scallions (spring onions)
- ⚬ 1 cup (250 ml / 8 fl oz) tomato juice or hot water
- ⚬ 4 tablespoons finely chopped fresh dill
- ⚬ salt and pepper
- ⚬ scant ½ cup (80 g / 3 oz) medium-grain rice
- ⚬ lemon wedges, to garnish
- ⚬ black olives or feta cheese, to serve

Roughly chop spinach leaves and rinse well, then put them into a pan, and cook over medium heat, stirring frequently, for a few minutes, until wilted. Drain and set aside. Heat the oil in a large heavy pan. Add the onion and scallions and cook over low heat, stirring occasionally, for 5 minutes, until softened and translucent. Pour in the tomato juice or water, add the spinach and dill, season with salt and pepper, and stir well. Using a wooden spoon, spread the spinach mixture evenly over the base of the pan and make hollows at random with the back of the spoon. Spoon small amounts of rice into the hollows and cover them with the spinach mixture. Cover and simmer over low heat for 15–20 minutes, until the rice swells and most of the liquid has been absorbed. Do not overcook, and do not stir during cooking. Turn off the heat and place a thick layer of paper towels between the pan and the lid to absorb the steam for 10–15 minutes. Take off the lid, sprinkle with pepper, and serve the spanakorizo garnished with lemon wedges and accompanied by black olives or feta cheese. It is still delicious served at room temperature the next day.

Serves 4
Preparation time 30 minutes (including standing)
Cooking time 30 minutes

☐ p 223

STUFFED ZUCCHINI (COURGETTE) FLOWERS
ΚΟΛΟΚΥΘΟΛΟΥΛΟΥΔΑ ΓΕΜΙΣΤΑ
Kolokitholoulouda gemista

- ⚬ ½ cup (120 ml / 4 fl oz) olive oil
- ⚬ 1 cup (7–8) finely chopped scallions (spring onions)
- ⚬ 2 tablespoons grated onion
- ⚬ 2 small zucchini (courgettes), grated
- ⚬ 1 lb 2 oz (500 g) tomatoes, finely chopped
- ⚬ 2 tablespoons freshly squeezed lemon juice
- ⚬ ½ cup (15 g / ½ oz) finely chopped fresh dill or (25 g / 1 oz) fresh mint
- ⚬ ½ cup (25 g / 1 oz) finely chopped fresh parsley
- ⚬ scant 1 cup (175 g / 6 oz) short-grain rice, such as risotto rice
- ⚬ salt and pepper
- ⚬ 25 zucchini (courgette) flowers
- ⚬ 1 tablespoon tomato paste

Heat half the oil in a pan. Add the scallions, onion, and zucchini and cook over low heat, stirring occasionally, for 5 minutes, until softened. Add the tomatoes and lemon juice and cook for 5 minutes more. Add the herbs and rice, season with salt and pepper, mix well, and remove from the heat. Remove the stamens from the zucchini flowers. Put 1 tablespoon of the filling in each flower and carefully fold in the top edges. Arrange them side by side on the base of a large pan in one or two layers. Stir the tomato paste with 1 cup (250 ml / 8 fl oz) water in a bowl and pour the mixture over the stuffed flowers together with the remaining oil. Sprinkle with pepper, cover, and simmer for 20 minutes, until most of the sauce has reduced and the rice is tender. The flowers are equally tasty served hot or at room temperature.

Serves 4
Preparation time 20 minutes
Cooking time 30 minutes

BRAISED BABY ZUCCHINI (COURGETTES) WITH AMARANTH
ΚΟΛΟΚΥΘΙΑ ΜΕ ΒΛΗΤΑ ΓΙΑΧΝΙ
Kolokithia me vlita giahni

Separate the flowers from the zucchini and remove the stamens. Slice the zucchini into small rounds. Coarsely chop the amaranth leaves. Heat the oil in a pan. Add the onion and garlic and cook over low heat, stirring occasionally, for 5 minutes, until softened and translucent. Add the zucchini and cook, stirring frequently, for 5–6 minutes. Add the tomatoes, cover, and simmer for 7–8 minutes, until they have released some of their liquid. Add the amaranth, zucchini flowers, and celery, season with salt and pepper, and cook over low heat until the amaranth has wilted. Stir gently, cover, and simmer, adding a little water if necessary, for about 15 minutes, or until the vegetables are tender and the pan juices have reduced. Do not stir during cooking, just shake the pan with a circular motion to distribute the juices without disturbing the vegetables. Serve hot or at room temperature, sprinkled with lemon juice, if using.

Serves 4
Preparation time 20 minutes
Cooking time 30 minutes

Note: Spinach can be substituted for the amaranth. Do not overcook it. The greens and zucchini should keep some bite to retain their flavor.

- 1 lb 2 oz (500 g) small zucchini (courgettes), preferably with their flowers
- 2¼ lb (1 kg) amaranth leaves, coarse stalks removed
- ¾ cup (175 ml / 6 fl oz) olive oil
- 1 onion, sliced
- 2–3 garlic cloves, sliced
- 2¼ lb (1 kg) ripe tomatoes, peeled, seeded, and finely chopped
- 2–3 tender celery stalks, chopped
- salt and pepper
- 2 tablespoons freshly squeezed lemon juice (optional)

ZUCCHINI (COURGETTE) FLOWERS STUFFED WITH BULGUR WHEAT
ΚΟΛΟΚΥΘΟΑΝΘΟΙ ΜΕ ΠΛΙΓΟΥΡΙ
Kolokithoanthi me pligouri

Put the bulgur wheat into a bowl, pour in 1½ cups (350 ml / 12 fl oz) water, and let stand for about 30 minutes, until almost all the water has been absorbed. Heat half the oil in a pan. Add the onion and cook over low heat, stirring occasionally, for 5 minutes, until softened and translucent. Drain the bulgur and add it to the pan together with the herbs, season with salt and pepper, stir, and remove from the heat. Remove the stamens from the zucchini flowers. Put 1 tablespoon of the filling in each flower and carefully fold in the top edges. Arrange them side by side on the base of a small pan in one or two layers and sprinkle with the remaining oil and the hot water or tomato juice. Combine the paprika and cayenne pepper and sprinkle the mixture over the stuffed flowers. Cover and simmer, adding more water if necessary, for about 20 minutes, until the sauce has reduced.

Serves 4
Preparation time 50 minutes (including standing)
Cooking time 25 minutes

- ⅔ cup (120 g / 4 oz) bulgur wheat
- ½ cup (120 ml / 4 fl oz) olive oil
- 1 large onion, grated
- 3 tablespoons finely chopped fresh parsley
- 3 tablespoons finely chopped fresh mint
- salt and pepper
- 20 zucchini (courgette) flowers
- ½ cup (120 ml / 4 fl oz) hot water or tomato juice
- 1 teaspoon paprika
- ½ teaspoon cayenne pepper

ZUCCHINI (COURGETTES) STUFFED WITH RICE
ΚΟΛΟΚΥΘΙΑ ΓΕΜΙΣΤΑ ΜΕ ΡΥΖΙ
Kolokithia gemista me rizi

- 8 thick zucchini (courgettes), 2¾ lb (1.2 kg) total weight, trimmed
- ¾ cup (175 ml / 6 fl oz) olive oil
- 1 onion, grated
- 4 oz (120 g) feta cheese, crumbled
- ¼ cup (50 g / 2 oz) short-grain rice, such as risotto rice
- 1 egg, lightly beaten
- 3 tablespoons finely chopped fresh parsley
- salt and pepper
- 9 oz (250 g) fresh or canned tomatoes, puréed
- ½ teaspoon sugar

Blanch the zucchini in boiling water for 5 minutes, then drain in a colander, and let cool. Using an apple corer or vegetable peeler, carefully hollow out the centers to leave a thin even layer of flesh next to the skin. Do not pierce the skin. Finely chop half the flesh (you will not need the rest) and sprinkle with a little salt, then let drain in a colander for 1 hour. Rub the zucchini flesh between your palms and squeeze out excess liquid, then set aside. Heat 4 tablespoons of the oil in a pan. Add the onion and cook over a low heat, stirring occasionally, for about 5 minutes, until softened. Add the chopped zucchini flesh, increase the heat to medium, and cook, stirring frequently, until all the liquid has evaporated. Remove from the heat and let cool. Stir in the feta, rice, egg, and parsley and season with salt and pepper. Fill the zucchini shells with the rice and zucchini mixture and arrange them in a single layer, side by side, in a large shallow pan. Combine the puréed tomatoes, sugar, and the remaining oil in a bowl, pour the mixture over the zucchini, and season with pepper. Cover and simmer over medium heat, adding a little hot water if necessary, for about 1 hour, or until the zucchini are tender and the sauce has reduced. Serve the dish hot, sprinkled with pepper.

Serves 4
Preparation time 1½ hours (including salting and cooling)
Cooking time 1¼ hours

BAKED MIXED VEGETABLES
ΜΠΡΙΑΜΙ
Briami

- 2 eggplants (aubergines)
- 2 zucchini (courgettes)
- 9 oz (250 g) fresh green (French) beans
- 2 potatoes
- 2 small carrots
- 1 green bell pepper, seeded
- 1 red bell pepper, seeded
- 2 large ripe tomatoes, chopped
- 1 large onion, chopped
- 6 large mushrooms, thickly sliced
- ⅔ cup (150 ml / ¼ pint) olive oil
- 1½ cups (350 ml / 12 fl oz) tomato juice
- 1 long green chile, thinly sliced
- 2–3 garlic cloves, finely chopped
- ½ cup (25 g / 1 oz) finely chopped fresh parsley
- salt and pepper

Cut the eggplants and zucchini into bite-size pieces, sprinkle them with salt and let drain in separate colanders for about 1 hour. Rinse and squeeze out the excess water. Preheat the oven to 350°F (180°C / Gas Mark 4). Cut the green beans, potatoes, carrots, and bell peppers into bite-size pieces, add the tomatoes, onion, and mushrooms, and put them in a large ovenproof dish with the eggplants and zucchini. Pour the olive oil and tomato juice over the vegetables. Add the chile, garlic, and parsley, season with salt and pepper, and mix lightly. Bake, stirring twice, for about 2 hours, until the vegetables are lightly browned and the cooking liquid has reduced. Cover the dish with aluminum foil if the vegetables brown too quickly. Serve hot or at room temperature.

Serves 6
Preparation time 1¾ hours (including salting)
Cooking time 2 hours

VEGETABLE AND GARBANZO BEAN (CHICKPEA) CASSEROLE
ΤΑΒΑΣ ΜΕ ΛΑΧΑΝΙΚΑ ΚΑΙ ΡΕΒΥΘΙΑ
Tavas me lahanika ke revithia

Sprinkle the eggplant slices with salt and let drain in a colander for 1 hour. Rinse under cold running water, squeeze out excess liquid, and pat dry with paper towels. Heat ½ cup (120 ml / 4 fl oz) of the oil in a skillet or frying pan. Add the eggplant slices and cook, turning occasionally, for 8–10 minutes, until lightly golden. Remove with a slotted spoon and drain on paper towels. Add the zucchini and mushrooms to the skillet and cook, stirring and turning occasionally, for 7–8 minutes, then remove with a slotted spoon, and drain on paper towels. Preheat the oven to 350°F (180°C / Gas Mark 4). Heat 2 tablespoons of the remaining the oil in a pan. Add the onion and garlic and cook over low heat, stirring occasionally, for 5 minutes, until softened. Add the bell peppers and cook, stirring frequently, for 5 minutes more, until softened. Stir in the garbanzo beans and thyme, season with salt and pepper, and remove from the heat. Line the base of an ovenproof dish with the eggplants and zucchini and spoon the bean mixture evenly on top. Cover the garbanzos with the mushrooms and sliced tomatoes, drizzle with the remaining oil, and bake for 50–60 minutes. Sprinkle with the grated cheese and bake for 15 minutes more. This dish is equally good served hot or at room temperature.

Serves 4
Preparation time 1½ hours (including salting)
Cooking time 1½–1¾ hours

- 2 long eggplants (aubergines), sliced
- ¾ cup (175 ml / 6 fl oz) olive oil
- 4 zucchini (courgettes), sliced
- 4 large portobello mushrooms, sliced
- 1 onion, grated
- 1 garlic clove, finely chopped
- 1 red bell pepper, seeded and finely chopped
- 1 green bell pepper, seeded and finely chopped
- generous 1 cup (200 g / 7 oz) canned, drained garbanzo beans (chickpeas)
- 2 teaspoons dried thyme
- salt and pepper
- 4 tomatoes, thinly sliced
- ¼ cup (25 g / 1 oz) grated kefalotiri or Parmesan cheese

- 3 large tomatoes
- 1 green bell pepper
- 1 red bell pepper
- 1 yellow bell pepper
- 2 small round zucchini (courgettes)
- 1 large round eggplant (aubergine)
- ¾ cup (175 ml / 6 fl oz) olive oil
- 1 large onion, grated
- 2¼ cups (450 g / 1 lb) medium-grain rice
- ½ cup (25 g / 1 oz) finely chopped fresh mint
- 3 tablespoons tomato paste
- 1 tablespoon tomato ketchup
- ¼ teaspoon ground allspice
- 2 large potatoes, cut into wedges
- 1 cup (250 ml / 8 fl oz) tomato juice
- salt and pepper

STUFFED VEGETABLES
ΛΑΧΑΝΙΚΑ ΓΕΜΙΣΤΑ
Lahanika gemista

Slice off and reserve the tops of the tomatoes, bell peppers, and zucchini. Scoop out the pulp from the tomatoes and zucchini with a spoon and seed the bell peppers without piercing the skin. Sprinkle the interior of the vegetable "shells" with a little salt and set aside. Cut the eggplant in half lengthwise and scoop out most of the flesh to form 2 shells. Blanch the eggplant and zucchini shells in boiling water for 5 minutes, then drain. Arrange all the vegetable shells in a large ovenproof dish. Finely chop the scooped-out flesh from the tomatoes, eggplant, and zucchini. Heat half the oil in a pan over high heat. Add the onion and cook, stirring frequently, for 3–4 minutes, until softened. Add the tomato, eggplant, and zucchini flesh and cook over high heat, stirring frequently, for 10 minutes. Remove from the heat, stir in the rice, mint, tomato paste, tomato ketchup, and allspice, and season with salt and pepper. Preheat the oven to 350°F (180°C / Gas Mark 4). Fill the vegetable shells three-quarters full with the mixture and replace the tops on the tomatoes, bell peppers, and zucchini. (If there is any filling left over, use it to stuff zucchini flowers.) Put the potato wedges between the stuffed vegetables, pour the tomato juice on top, and sprinkle with a little salt and pepper. Spoon the remaining olive oil over the potatoes and the stuffed vegetables. Bake for about 2 hours, or until lightly browned. If the tops begin to brown too quickly, cover loosely with a piece of aluminum foil. It may be necessary to add some water during baking to prevent sticking. Serve hot or at room temperature.

Serves 6
Preparation time 45 minutes
Cooking time 2¼ hours

☐ p 230

Stuffed vegetables, p 229

Mixed spring vegetable stew, p 232

FRIED SUMMER VEGETABLES IN TOMATO SAUCE
ΤΗΓΑΝΙΤΑ ΛΑΧΑΝΙΚΑ ΜΕ ΝΤΟΜΑΤΑ
Tiganita lahanika me domata

Sprinkle the eggplant slices with salt and let drain in a colander for 1 hour. Lightly sprinkle the zucchini slices with salt and let drain in a colander for 30 minutes. Meanwhile heat 4 tablespoons of the oil in a large wide pan. Add the onion or garlic and cook over low heat, stirring occasionally, for 3–5 minutes, until softened. Add the tomatoes, sugar, vinegar, and parsley, season with salt and pepper, cover, and simmer for about 15 minutes, until thickened. Remove from the heat and set aside. Rinse the eggplants and squeeze out the excess moisture. Heat the remaining olive oil in a large skillet or frying pan. Add the eggplant, potatoes, and bell peppers in batches and cook, turning occasionally, for 8–10 minutes, until golden. Remove with a slotted spoon and drain well on paper towels. Lightly dust the zucchini slices with flour, add to the skillet, and cook, turning occasionally, for 10 minutes, until golden brown. Layer the fried vegetables in a wide pan and pour the tomato sauce over them. Heat gently, shaking the pan to distribute the sauce evenly. Served hot or at room temperature, this is a favorite summer dish.

Serves 6
Preparation time 1½ hours (including salting)
Cooking time 30 minutes

- 1 lb 2 oz (500 g) eggplants (aubergines), sliced
- 1 lb 2 oz (500 g) zucchini (courgettes), sliced
- ¾ cup (175 ml / 6 fl oz) olive oil
- 1 small onion, grated or 2 garlic cloves, thinly sliced
- 2¼ lb (1 kg) ripe tomatoes, peeled, seeded, and finely chopped or 14 oz (400 g) canned chopped tomatoes
- 1 teaspoon sugar
- 1 tablespoon red wine vinegar
- 4 tablespoons finely chopped fresh parsley
- salt and pepper
- 1 lb 2 oz (500 g) potatoes, sliced
- 1 lb 2 oz (500 g) green bell peppers, seeded and quartered
- all-purpose (plain) flour, for dusting

MIXED SPRING VEGETABLE STEW
ΑΝΟΙΞΙΑΤΙΚΟ ΤΟΥΡΛΟΥ
Anixiatiko tourlou

Cut off the artichoke stems, trim the bases, and remove all the thick green leaves and the chokes, leaving only the cup-shaped hearts. Rub with the lemon halves to prevent discoloration and place in a bowl of water mixed with the flour and lemon juice. Heat the oil in a large pan. Add the onion and cook over low heat, stirring occasionally, for 5 minutes, until softened. Add the tomatoes, sugar, vinegar, and parsley or dill and season with salt and pepper. Add the beans, drained artichoke hearts, potatoes, and peas, cover, and simmer for about 40 minutes, until the vegetables are tender and the sauce has reduced. Serve the *tourlou* hot or at room temperature. This recipe can be easily adapted to suit whatever vegetables you have on hand.

Serves 4
Preparation time 1 hour
Cooking time 45 minutes

☐ p 231

- 4 globe artichokes
- 1 lemon, halved
- 1 tablespoon all-purpose (plain) flour
- 1 tablespoon freshly squeezed lemon juice
- ⅔ cup (150 ml / ¼ pint) olive oil
- 1 onion, grated
- 2¼ lb (1 kg) ripe tomatoes, peeled, seeded, and finely chopped or 14 oz (400 g) canned chopped tomatoes
- 1 teaspoon sugar
- 1 tablespoon red wine vinegar
- ½ cup (25 g / 1 oz) finely chopped fresh parsley or (15 g / ½ oz) dill
- salt and pepper
- 1 lb 2 oz (500 g) young fava (broad) beans in their pods, trimmed and halved
- 2¼ lb (1 kg) potatoes, quartered
- 2¼ lb (1 kg) fresh peas, shelled

BAKED VEGETABLE CASSEROLE
ΛΑΧΑΝΙΚΑ ΣΤΟ ΦΟΥΡΝΟ
Lahanika sto fourno

- 9 oz (250 g) spinach, coarse stalks removed
- 2 large round eggplants (aubergines), sliced
- 5 tablespoons olive oil
- 3⅔ cups (250 g / 9 oz) sliced mushrooms
- 7 oz (200 g) anthotiro or ricotta cheese, crumbled
- ¼ teaspoon grated nutmeg
- 1 tablespoon finely chopped fresh basil
- 1 cup (250 ml / 8 fl oz) tomato juice
- 1 cup (250 ml / 8 fl oz) plain yogurt
- 2 eggs
- 4 tablespoons grated kefalotiri or Parmesan cheese
- 2 tablespoons finely chopped fresh parsley

Preheat the broiler (grill). Rinse the spinach leaves and cut into thick strips, then cook them in just the water clinging to the leaves for 5 minutes. Drain and squeeze out the excess liquid with your hands. Brush the eggplant slices with some of the olive oil and broil (grill) for 5 minutes on each side to soften. Place half of them in the base of a 12-inch (30-cm) tart pan or quiche dish. Preheat the oven to 350°F (180°C / Gas Mark 4). Heat the remaining oil in a pan. Add the mushrooms and cook over low heat, stirring occasionally, for 5–7 minutes, until most of their liquid has evaporated. Combine the spinach, crumbled cheese, nutmeg, and basil in a bowl, spread the mixture over the eggplants, and pour half the tomato juice on top. Sprinkle the mushrooms over the spinach mixture and place the remaining eggplant slices on top of them. Pour the remaining tomato juice over them. Beat the yogurt with the eggs in a bowl and pour the mixture over the vegetables. Sprinkle with grated cheese and parsley and bake for 30 minutes, or until the top is golden brown. Serve hot or at room temperature.

Serves 4
Preparation time 30 minutes
Cooking time 50 minutes

VEGETABLE-STUFFED CHARD FROM CYPRUS
ΝΤΟΛΜΑΔΕΣ ΜΕ ΛΑΧΑΝΙΚΑ
Dolmades me lahanika

- 2¼ lb (1 kg) chard, stalks removed
- ¾ cup (175 ml / 6 fl oz) olive oil
- 1 large onion, grated
- 1 leek, white part only, finely chopped
- 1 small zucchini (courgette), grated
- 1 carrot, grated
- ½ cup (50 g / 2 oz) finely chopped cabbage
- 2 artichoke hearts, finely chopped
- 4 tablespoons finely chopped fresh parsley
- 4 tablespoons finely chopped fresh mint
- 1 tablespoon finely chopped celery
- 1 cup (225 g / 8 oz) short-grain rice
- salt and pepper
- 2 large ripe tomatoes, peeled, seeded, and puréed, or 1¾ cups (400 ml / 14 fl oz) tomato juice
- 2 tablespoons freshly squeezed lemon juice
- 1 teaspoon sugar

Rinse and briefly blanch the chard leaves in boiling water, then drain well. Heat half the oil in a pan. Add the onion and leek and cook over low heat, stirring occasionally, for 5 minutes, until softened. Add the zucchini, carrot, cabbage, and artichoke hearts and cook over medium heat for 5–10 minutes more, until softened. Remove from the heat, stir in the herbs, celery, and rice, and season with salt and pepper. Cut the chard leaves into the desired size and lay out on the work surface. Put 1 tablespoon of the rice mixture on the bottom end of each leaf, turn in the edges, and roll up into a parcel. Line a large pan with the remaining leaves and arrange the rolls in the pan. Combine the puréed tomatoes, lemon juice, the remaining olive oil, the sugar, and 1 cup (250 ml / 8 fl oz) water in a bowl, season with salt and pepper, and pour the mixture over the rolls. Invert a heavy plate over them to hold them in place during cooking. Cover the pan and simmer, adding a little hot water if necessary, for about 20 minutes, until nearly all the liquid has been absorbed and the rice is tender. Serve hot or at room temperature.

Serves 6
Preparation time 45 minutes
Cooking time 40 minutes

VEGETABLE MOUSSAKA
ΜΟΥΣΑΚΑΣ ΜΕ ΛΑΧΑΝΙΚΑ
Mousakas me lahanika

Sprinkle the eggplant and zucchini slices with salt and let drain in separate colanders for 1 hour. Rinse under cold running water and squeeze out the excess liquid. Heat ½ cup (120 ml / 4 fl oz) of the oil in a large skillet or frying pan. Add the eggplants and zucchini and cook, turning frequently, for 5–8 minutes, until just beginning to color. Remove with a slotted spoon and drain on paper towels. Heat the remaining oil in a large pan. Add the onion and cook over low heat, stirring occasionally, for 5 minutes, until softened. Add the bell pepper and cook for 5–8 minutes more, until softened. Add the tomatoes, parsley, and dill, season with salt and pepper, and simmer for 10 minutes, until thickened. Meanwhile, preheat the oven to 350°F (180°C / Gas Mark 4). To make the white sauce, melt the butter in a small pan. Stir in the flour and cook, stirring constantly, for 1 minute. Remove from the heat and add the milk, all at once, then return to the heat, and simmer, stirring constantly, until thickened and smooth. Remove from the heat, stir in the egg yolks, and season with salt, nutmeg and white pepper. Put the eggplant slices on the base of a rectangular ovenproof dish and cover with the zucchini slices. Combine all the cheeses in a bowl and sprinkle them evenly over the zucchini. Pour the tomato sauce on top and cover with the white sauce. Bake for about 1 hour, or until the top is golden brown. This is equally good hot or at room temperature.

Serves 6
Preparation time 1½ hours (including salting)
Cooking time 1¾ hours

- 3¼ lb (1.5 kg) eggplants (aubergines), sliced
- 2¼ lb (1 kg) zucchini (courgettes), sliced
- ¾ cup (175 ml / 6 fl oz) olive oil
- 1 onion, finely chopped
- 1 green bell pepper, seeded and very coarsely chopped
- 2¼ lb (1 kg) tomatoes, peeled, seeded, and finely chopped
- 5 tablespoons finely chopped fresh parsley
- 5 tablespoons finely chopped fresh dill
- 1¼ cups (150 g / 5 oz) crumbled feta cheese
- 1 cup (100 g / 3½ oz) grated regato or pecorino cheese
- 1 cup (100 g / 3½ oz) grated kefalotiri or Parmesan cheese
- salt and pepper

FOR THE WHITE SAUCE
- 2 tablespoons (25 g / 1 oz) butter
- 3 tablespoons all-purpose (plain) flour
- 3 cups (750 ml / 1¼ pints) hot milk
- 3 egg yolks
- pinch of grated nutmeg
- salt and freshly ground white pepper

VEGETABLE RAGOUT
ΛΑΧΑΝΙΚΑ ΓΙΑΧΝΙ
Lahanika giahni

Heat the oil in a large pan. Add the onion, scallions, garlic, mushrooms, leeks, and bell pepper and cook over low heat, stirring occasionally, for about 8 minutes, until softened. Add the potatoes and cook, stirring frequently, for another 2 minutes. Combine the tomato paste with the hot water in a bowl and pour it into the pan. Add the chopped tomato, season to taste with salt and pepper, cover, and simmer for 15 minutes, until the potatoes are half cooked. Add the herbs, re-cover the pan, and simmer for 15 minutes more, until the vegetables are tender but still firm and the sauce has thickened. Serve hot.

Serves 6
Preparation time 30 minutes
Cooking time 45 minutes

- ⅔ cup (150 ml / ¼ pint) olive oil
- 1 onion, grated
- ½ cup (4) finely chopped scallions (spring onions)
- 3 garlic cloves, finely chopped
- 1 lb 2 oz (500 g) oyster mushrooms, trimmed
- 2¼ lb (1 kg) leeks, white and tender green part, sliced
- 1 red bell pepper, seeded and sliced
- 2¼ lb (1 kg) potatoes, cut into bite-size cubes
- 1 tablespoon tomato paste
- 2 cups (450 ml / 16 fl oz) hot water
- 1 large ripe tomato, peeled, seeded, and finely chopped
- salt and pepper
- 5 tablespoons finely chopped fresh parsley
- 1 teaspoon dried oregano or thyme

- 1¾ lb (800 g) large eggplants (aubergines), thickly sliced
- olive or vegetable oil, for frying
- 1 lb 5 oz (600 g) zucchini (courgettes), thickly sliced
- 1 lb 5 oz (600 g) potatoes, sliced
- 4 tablespoons olive oil, plus extra for brushing and drizzling
- 1 onion, grated
- 2 garlic cloves, thinly sliced
- 1 lb 5 oz (600 g) ground (minced) beef
- 1 lb 2 oz (500 g) tomatoes, peeled and puréed or 14 oz (400 g) canned tomatoes, puréed
- 1 tablespoon tomato paste
- 1 teaspoon sugar
- salt and pepper
- 4 tablespoons finely chopped fresh parsley
- 2 egg whites
- 3 tablespoons fine dry bread crumbs
- 1 cup (100 g / 3½ oz) grated regato or pecorino cheese
- 2 tomatoes, thinly sliced

BAKED VEGETABLES WITH GROUND (MINCED) BEEF
ΛΑΧΑΝΙΚΑ ΜΕ ΚΙΜΑ ΣΤΟ ΦΟΥΡΝΟ
Lahanika me kima sto fourno

Sprinkle the eggplants and zucchini with a little salt and let drain in separate colanders for 1 hour. Squeeze out the excess liquid, rinse under cold running water, and pat dry. Heat the oil for frying in a skillet or frying pan. Add the potatoes and cook over medium heat, stirring frequently, for about 8 minutes, then remove with a slotted spoon, and drain on paper towels. Add the eggplants to the skillet and fry over medium heat, stirring frequently, for about 8 minutes, then remove with a slotted spoon, and drain on paper towels. Add the zucchini to the skillet and cook over medium heat, stirring frequently, for about 8 minutes, then remove with a slotted spoon, and drain on paper towels. Heat the 4 tablespoons olive oil in large pan. Add the onion and garlic and cook over low heat, stirring occasionally, for 5 minutes, until softened. Add the ground beef and cook, stirring and breaking up the meat with a spoon, for 8–10 minutes, until all traces of pink have disappeared. Stir in the puréed tomatoes, tomato paste, and sugar, season with salt and pepper, cover, and simmer for about 30 minutes, until thickened. Stir in the parsley and remove from the heat. Lightly whisk the egg whites in a bowl and fold into the meat mixture.

Preheat the oven to 400°F (200°C / Gas Mark 6), brush a deep 8 x 12-inch (20 x 30-cm) ovenproof dish with oil and sprinkle with one-third of the bread crumbs. Line the base with the eggplant slices and sprinkle them with half the remaining bread crumbs and one-third of the grated cheese. Spread half the meat mixture evenly on top and cover with the potato slices. Sprinkle with the remaining bread crumbs and half the remaining grated cheese. Spread the remaining meat mixture in the dish, cover with the zucchini slices, and sprinkle with the remaining cheese. Top with the sliced tomatoes, season with salt and pepper, and drizzle with a little olive oil. Bake for about 50 minutes, until the cheese is lightly browned. Serve hot.

Serves 10
Preparation time 1½ hours (including salting)
Cooking time 1½ hours

Vefa's secret: To avoid cooking the egg whites when you add them to the hot meat sauce, temper them first by gradually stirring in 2–3 tablespoons of the meat sauce, then add the mixture to the pan.

LEGUMES (PULSES) AND RICE

-

ΟΣΠΡΙΑ ΚΑΙ ΡΥΖΙ

-

Ospria ke rizi

Legumes (pulses) are the dried mature seeds of a variety of leguminous plants including lima (butter) beans, peas, fava (broad) beans, lentils, and garbanzo beans (chickpeas). Some, including peas and fava beans, are eaten fresh in spring and early summer when the pods are still juicy, but the pods toughen as the seeds within them mature, so they are also dried for future use. An excellent source of protein and other nutrients, legumes, together with wheat or barley, have been staples of the human diet since the prehistoric era. Wild legumes were gathered for food as far back as the eighth millennium BC. Neolithic farmers, taking advantage of the efficient reproductive system of leguminous plants, learned to cultivate them as they had done cereals (grains). As well as their high nutritional value, another benefit of dried legumes is that they can be stored for long periods and reconstituted with water: a real advantage when supplies of fresh food were low. Traditionally an important and inexpensive source of nutrition to people throughout the Mediterranean, legumes continue to play an essential role in the cuisine of the region. Of the wide variety of legumes familiar to modern cooks, only some were known before the end of the fifteenth century, including lentils, fava beans, garbanzo beans and split peas. Green beans, navy (haricot) beans, borlotti or cranberry beans, kidney beans and black beans were all introduced to Europe after the discovery of the New World.

GENERAL INSTRUCTIONS

Legumes (pulses) have always provided an important source of nutrition to people who fast for long periods during the year. Cooked plainly, with or without olive oil, and flavored with aromatic vegetables and fresh tomatoes, they featured in the most popular dishes of Lent. When combined with meat they are best cooked separately to retain their distinctive flavor. Many legumes are sold with the skins removed and therefore cook quickly, but they can easily lose their shape, resulting in a mushy purée. The simplest way to cook legumes is to simmer them gently in water with herbs and aromatic vegetables until tender. Apart from lentils, which require no soaking at all, most legumes should be soaked before use. First rinse them under cold running water, put them into a bowl, and pour in cold water to cover. Let them soak overnight so that they reabsorb moisture and swell. If you soak them in hot water, they will need less time to swell. Drain and discard the soaking water and cook the legumes in fresh water. Legumes become harder with age as they continue to dry out. Stored in a cool, dark, dry place, they will keep almost indefinitely, but it is best not to use any that are more than a year old, as the longer they are stored, the more difficult it is to cook them until tender.

Most beans, lentils, and garbanzo beans (chickpeas) should be boiled vigorously in plenty of water and then drained before further cooking according to the recipe. This makes the dishes more easily digestible and prevents lentils from discoloring. Some beans, notably red kidney beans, contain a toxin that must be destroyed by pre-boiling them vigorously for 15 minutes before draining and adding fresh water.

- ○ 14 oz (400 g) dried giant white beans or lima (butter) beans, soaked for 24 hours in cold water to cover and drained
- ○ 3½ cups (200 g / 7 oz) fresh bread crumbs
- ○ ½ cup (25 g / 1 oz) finely chopped fresh parsley
- ○ ½ cup (120 ml / 4 fl oz) plain yogurt
- ○ 1 tablespoon Dijon mustard
- ○ 1 tablespoon freshly squeezed lemon juice
- ○ ⅓ cup (2–3) finely chopped scallions (spring onions)
- ○ 2 egg whites, lightly beaten
- ○ ⅔ cup (40 g / 1½ oz) fine dried bread crumbs
- ○ olive oil, for frying
- ○ Garlic yogurt or Tzatziki (p 152), to serve

BEAN FRITTERS (CROQUETTES)
ΦΑΣΟΥΛΟΚΕΦΤΕΔΕΣ
Fasoulokeftedes

Pop the beans out of their skins, put them into a pan, and pour in water to cover. Bring to a boil, then reduce the heat, and simmer for about 1 hour, or until very tender. Drain and process to a purée in a food processor. Scrape the purée into a bowl, add the fresh bread crumbs, parsley, yogurt, mustard, lemon juice, scallions, and egg whites, and knead until thoroughly mixed. Form the mixture into 18 balls, coat them in the dry bread crumbs, and flatten lightly with your hands. Heat the oil in a nonstick, heavy skillet or frying pan. Add the patties, in batches if necessary, and cook over medium heat for 3 minutes on each side, until golden brown. Drain on paper towels and serve hot accompanied by Garlic yogurt or Tzatziki.

Serves 6
Preparation time 24¼ hours (including soaking)
Cooking time 1¼ hours

- ○ scant 1½ cups (250 g / 9 oz) dried medium white beans, such as cannellini beans, soaked overnight in cold water to cover and drained
- ○ ¾ cup (175 ml / 6 fl oz) olive oil
- ○ 1 large onion, thinly sliced
- ○ 2¼ lb (1 kg) Savoy cabbage, cored and cut in chunks
- ○ 1 cup (250 ml / 8 fl oz) hot water
- ○ scant ½ cup (80 g / 3 oz) long-grain rice
- ○ 1 tablespoon tomato paste
- ○ 1 small chile, chopped
- ○ salt and pepper
- ○ 1 tablespoon red wine vinegar
- ○ 1 teaspoon sugar
- ○ ½ teaspoon sweet paprika

BEANS WITH CABBAGE FROM PONTUS
ΦΑΣΟΥΛΟΓΟΥΛΙΑ
Fasoulogoulia

Put the beans into a pan, pour in water to cover, and bring to a boil. Reduce the heat and simmer for 1 hour, then drain. Heat half the oil in a large pan. Add half the onion and cook over low heat, stirring occasionally, for about 5 minutes, until softened and translucent. Add the cabbage and cook, stirring constantly, for a few minutes, until wilted. Pour in the hot water, cover, and simmer for 30 minutes. Add the beans, rice, tomato paste, and chile. Season with salt and pepper, cover, and simmer for 30 minutes, until the rice is tender and the liquid has reduced. Meanwhile, heat the remaining oil in a small skillet or frying pan. Add the remaining onion and cook over low heat, stirring occasionally, for 5 minutes, until softened. Sprinkle with the vinegar, sugar, and paprika and cook, stirring frequently, for 20–30 minutes, until the liquid has evaporated and the onion has caramelized. Spoon the beans and rice onto a serving dish, spread the caramelized onions on top, and serve immediately.

Serves 4
Preparation time 12½ hours (including soaking)
Cooking time 2 hours

□ p 240

Beans with cabbage from Pontus, p 239

bean, spinach, and sausage casserole, p 242

BEAN, SPINACH, AND SAUSAGE CASSEROLE
ΓΙΓΑΝΤΕΣ ΜΕ ΣΠΑΝΑΚΙ ΚΑΙ ΛΑΧΑΝΙΚΑ ΣΤΟ ΦΟΥΡΝΟ
Gigantes me spanaki ke lahanika sto fourno

Put the beans into a pan, pour in water to cover, and bring to a boil. Reduce the heat and simmer for about 30 minutes, then drain, and tip into an ovenproof dish. Preheat the oven to 350°F (180°C / Gas Mark 4). Meanwhile, heat half the oil in a skillet or frying pan. Add the sausage, onion, and garlic and cook over low heat for 5 minutes, until the onion has softened. Stir in the tomatoes and parsley, season with salt and pepper, and simmer for 5 minutes. Pour the mixture over the beans, stir well, and bake, adding a little hot water if necessary, for about 50 minutes, until the beans are soft. Meanwhile, roughly chop the spinach, and cook over low heat for 2–3 minutes, until wilted. Drain well. Heat the remaining olive oil in a skillet or frying pan, add the spinach, and cook over low heat for about 5 minutes. Remove the beans from the oven and dot with the spinach. Bake for 5 minutes more. Serve hot.

Serves 4
Preparation time 24½ hours (including soaking)
Cooking time 1¼ hours

□ p 241

- 11 oz (300 g) dried giant white beans or lima (butter) beans, soaked for 24 hours in cold water to cover and drained
- ½ cup (120 ml / 4 fl oz) olive oil
- 9 oz (250 g) pork sausages, cut into bite-size pieces
- 1 onion, grated
- 2 garlic cloves, finely chopped
- 1 lb 2 oz (500 g) ripe tomatoes, peeled and finely chopped or 14 oz (400 g) canned chopped tomatoes
- 4 tablespoons finely chopped fresh parsley
- salt and pepper
- 1 lb 2 oz (500 g) fresh spinach, rinsed and coarse stalks removed

DRIED RED BEAN STEW
ΚΟΚΚΙΝΑ ΞΕΡΑ ΦΑΣΟΛΙΑ ΓΙΑΧΝΙ
Kokina xera fasolia giahni

Put the beans into a pan, pour in water to cover, and bring to a boil. Boil vigorously for 15 minutes. Drain, return the beans to the pan, pour in water to cover, and bring to a boil, then reduce the heat and simmer for 15 minutes. Meanwhile, heat the oil in a large pan. Add the onion and cook over low heat, stirring occasionally, for 5 minutes, until softened. Drain the beans and add to the pan together with the tomatoes, tomato paste, thyme, marjoram, parsley, chile, and hot water. Simmer gently for 1–2 hours, until the beans are soft and the sauce has thickened. Add a little hot water if the dish seems dry. Season to taste with salt and pepper and add more crushed chile for a spicier flavor if you like. Serve hot or at room temperature, accompanied by feta cheese or black olives.

Serves 6
Preparation time 12¼ hours (including soaking)
Cooking time 1½–2½ hours

□ p 244

- 2¾ cups (500 g / 1 lb 2 oz) dried red kidney beans, soaked overnight in water to cover and drained
- ¾ cup (175 ml / 6 fl oz) olive oil
- 1 onion, grated
- 1 lb 2 oz (500 g) fresh or canned tomatoes, puréed
- 1 tablespoon tomato paste (optional)
- ½ teaspoon dried thyme
- ½ teaspoon dried marjoram
- ½ cup (25 g / 1 oz) finely chopped fresh parsley
- 1 small dried chile, crushed
- 1 cup (250 ml / 8 fl oz) hot water
- salt and pepper
- feta cheese or black olives, to serve

- ½ cup (120 ml / 4 fl oz) olive oil
- 1 large onion, finely chopped
- 2 carrots, finely chopped
- ⅔ cup (120 g / 4 oz) dried black-eyed peas (black-eye beans), soaked overnight in cold water to cover and drained
- 2 tomatoes, peeled, seeded, and finely chopped
- 1 teaspoon dried marjoram
- 1 teaspoon chili flakes
- 2 bay leaves
- 2 cups (450 ml / 16 fl oz) water
- salt and pepper
- 1 cup (120 g / 4 oz) fresh or frozen peas
- ⅔ cup (150 ml / ¼ pint) plain yogurt, to garnish

BLACK-EYED PEA (BLACK-EYE BEAN) AND GREEN PEA STEW
ΜΑΥΡΟΜΑΤΙΚΑ ΦΑΣΟΛΙΑ ΓΙΑΧΝΙ ΜΕ ΑΡΑΚΑ
Mavromatika fasolia giahni me araka

Heat the oil in a pan. Add the onion and carrots and cook over low heat, stirring occasionally, for 5 minutes, until softened. Add the black-eyed peas, tomatoes, marjoram, chili flakes, and bay leaves, stir in 2 cups (450 ml / 16 fl oz) water, cover, and simmer for about 50 minutes, until the beans are tender. Season with salt and pepper, add the green peas, and pour in a little hot water if the dish seems dry. Re-cover the pan and simmer for 15 minutes more. Remove and discard the bay leaves and divide the stew among individual warm plates. Garnish each plate with 1–2 tablespoons yogurt.

Serves 4
Preparation time 12¼ hours (including soaking)
Cooking time 1¼ hours

Note: If using garden peas, add them 5 minutes before the end of the cooking time.

- 2¾ cups (500 g / 1 lb 2 oz) dried black-eyed peas (black-eye beans), soaked overnight in cold water to cover and drained
- 9 oz (250 g) tender fennel stalks and leaves, sliced
- ⅔ cup (150 ml / ¼ pint) olive oil
- 1 onion, grated
- 3 ripe tomatoes, peeled, seeded, and finely chopped
- 1 teaspoon dried oregano
- 1 bay leaf
- salt and pepper
- 4 tablespoons finely chopped fresh parsley

BLACK-EYED PEAS (BLACK-EYE BEANS) WITH FENNEL
ΜΑΥΡΟΜΑΤΙΚΑ ΦΑΣΟΛΙΑ ΜΕ ΜΑΡΑΘΟ
Mavromatika fasolia me maratho

Put the black-eyed peas into a pan, pour in water to cover, and bring to a boil. Reduce the heat and simmer for about 1 hour, or until they begin to soften. Drain well. Blanch the fennel in a pan of boiling water for 5 minutes, then drain. Heat the oil in a large pan. Add the onion and cook over low heat, stirring occasionally, for about 5 minutes, until softened and translucent. Stir in the black-eyed peas and tomatoes and simmer for 20 minutes. Add the fennel, oregano, and bay leaf, season with salt and pepper, and simmer for 10 minutes more, or until the black-eyed peas are cooked and the sauce has thickened. Sprinkle with the parsley and remove from the heat. This dish is equally good served hot or at room temperature.

Serves 6
Preparation time 12½ hours (including soaking)
Cooking time 1¾ hours

Note: If fennel stalks and leaves are not available, use 1 fennel bulb cut into julienne strips and a few chopped celery leaves.

Dried red bean stew, p 242

Garbanzo bean (chickpea) and eggplant (aubergine) casserole from Serres, p 247

FAVA (BROAD) BEAN PURÉE
ΚΟΥΚΙΑ ΦΑΒΑ
Koukia fava

- 5⅔ cups (1 kg / 2¼ lb) dried fava (broad) beans
- 1 teaspoon baking soda (bicarbonate of soda)
- 5 tablespoons olive oil
- 1 large onion, finely chopped
- 2 bay leaves
- 5 allspice berries
- salt and pepper
- olive oil, freshly squeezed lemon juice, and dried oregano, to serve

Parboil the fava beans for 5 minutes, then drain, and pinch out and discard the black spots (if necessary). Put them into a bowl, pour in water to cover, and let soak for 12 hours. Drain and peel off the skins. Sprinkle the beans with the baking soda in a dish and set aside for 30 minutes. Rinse under cold running water and drain well. Heat the oil in a pan. Add the onion and cook over low heat, stirring occasionally, for 5 minutes, until softened and translucent. Add the beans, bay leaves, and allspice berries, season with salt and pepper, and pour in hot water to cover. Bring to a boil, reduce the heat, cover, and simmer for 1–1½ hours, until the beans are very soft and disintegrating. Remove the bay leaves and allspice berries, drain and mash the beans. Serve hot or at room temperature, drizzled with olive oil and lemon juice, and sprinkled with oregano. Sometimes the bean purée is served with caramelized onions. To do this, heat a little olive oil in a skillet or frying pan and cook sliced onions, sprinkled with a little sugar, over medium heat for 20–30 minutes, or until they turn golden, and then scatter over the bean purée.

Serves 6
Preparation time 12¾ hours (including soaking and standing)
Cooking time 1–1½ hours

FAVA (BROAD) BEANS WITH OREGANO
ΚΟΥΚΙΑ ΓΙΑΧΝΙ ΜΕ ΡΙΓΑΝΗ
Koukia giahni me rigani

- generous 2¾ cups (500 g / 1 lb 2 oz) dried fava (broad) beans
- ½ cup (120 ml / 4 fl oz) olive oil
- 1 large onion, finely chopped
- 2 tablespoons freshly squeezed lemon juice
- 2 tablespoons finely chopped fresh or 1 teaspoon dried oregano, plus extra to serve
- 1 small dried red chile, crushed
- 2 teaspoons paprika, plus extra to serve
- salt and pepper
- 1 cup (250 ml / 8 fl oz) hot water
- 3 tablespoons finely chopped scallions (spring onions)

Remove the black spots from the beans (if necessary) and put them into a bowl. Add water to cover and let soak for 12 hours. Drain and peel, then put the beans into a pan, and pour in water to cover. Bring to a boil, reduce the heat, and simmer for 15 minutes. Drain well. Heat the oil in a pan. Add the onion and cook over low heat, stirring occasionally, for 5 minutes, until softened. Add the lemon juice, oregano, chile, paprika, and beans, season with salt and pepper, and pour in the hot water. Cover and simmer, adding more hot water if necessary, for 1–1¼ hours, until the beans are tender and the sauce has reduced. Serve sprinkled with extra paprika, the chopped scallions and a pinch of oregano.

Serves 4
Preparation time 12¼ hours (including soaking)
Cooking time 1½ hours

- 1⅓ cups (300 g / 11 oz) dried garbanzo beans (chickpeas), soaked for 12 hours in cold water to cover with 1 tablespoon salt
- ¾ cup (175 ml / 6 fl oz) olive oil, plus extra for drizzling
- 1 large onion, sliced
- 4 garlic cloves, thinly sliced
- 14 oz (400 g) canned chopped tomatoes
- ½ teaspoon ground allspice
- 1 teaspoon paprika
- ½ teaspoon dried oregano, plus extra for sprinkling
- salt and pepper
- 4 large eggplants (aubergines), cut in ¼-inch (5-mm) thick slices
- 3 large tomatoes, thinly sliced

GARBANZO BEAN (CHICKPEA) AND EGGPLANT (AUBERGINE) CASSEROLE FROM SERRES
ΡΕΒΥΘΙΑ ΜΕ ΜΕΛΙΤΖΑΝΕΣ
Revithia me melitzanes

Drain and rinse the garbanzo beans and put them into a large pan with water to cover. Bring to a boil, skimming off the scum that rises to the surface, cover, and simmer for 30 minutes. Heat 4 tablespoons of the oil in a small skillet or frying pan. Add the onion and garlic and cook over low heat, stirring occasionally, for 5 minutes, until softened. Add the contents of the skillet to the garbanzo beans with the canned tomatoes, allspice, paprika, and oregano. Season with salt and pepper and simmer for 1 hour more, until the garbanzo beans are tender. Meanwhile, sprinkle the eggplant slices with salt and let drain in a colander for 1 hour. Rinse, drain, and squeeze out the excess moisture. Preheat the oven to 350°F (180°C / Gas Mark 4). Heat the remaining oil in a skillet or frying pan. Add the eggplant slices and cook, turning frequently, for about 8 minutes. Remove with a slotted spoon and drain. Arrange half the eggplant slices on the base of an ovenproof dish. Spread the garbanzo bean mixture over them and cover with the remaining eggplant slices. Top with the tomato slices, sprinkle with oregano, season with salt and pepper, and drizzle with a little olive oil. Bake for about 50 minutes. Serve hot or at room temperature.

Serves 4
Preparation time 13½ hours (including soaking)
Cooking time 50 minutes

□ p 245

- scant ½ cup (100 g / 3½ oz) dried garbanzo beans (chickpeas), soaked for 12 hours in cold water to cover with 1 tablespoon salt
- 5 tablespoons olive oil
- ½ teaspoon cumin seeds
- 2 small onions, thinly sliced
- 2 garlic cloves, finely chopped
- 1 teaspoon paprika
- ½ teaspoon cayenne pepper
- salt and pepper
- 1 cup (250 ml / 8 fl oz) hot water
- 1 lb 2 oz (500 g) yellow winter squash, peeled and cut into bite-size pieces
- 2 tablespoons chopped fresh cilantro (coriander)

GARBANZO BEANS (CHICKPEAS) WITH YELLOW WINTER SQUASH
ΠΕΒΥΘΙΑ ΜΕ ΚΙΤΡΙΝΗ ΚΟΛΟΚΥΘΑ
Revithia me kitrini kolokitha

Drain the garbanzo beans and rinse well. Heat the oil in a pan. Add the cumin seeds and stir over medium heat for 1 minute. Add the onions and garlic and cook, stirring constantly, for 3–5 minutes, until softened. Add the garbanzo beans, paprika, and cayenne, season with salt and pepper, and pour in the hot water. Cover and simmer for 15 minutes. Add the squash and half the cilantro and cook for about 15 minutes, or until the vegetables are tender and the sauce has reduced. Remove from the heat and serve immediately, sprinkled with the remaining cilantro.

Serves 4
Preparation time 12¼ hours (including soaking)
Cooking time 40 minutes

GARBANZO BEANS (CHICKPEAS) WITH SPINACH
ΡΕΒΥΘΙΑ ΜΕ ΣΠΑΝΑΚΙ
Revithia me spanaki

Drain the garbanzo beans and rinse well. Heat half the oil in a pan. Add the onions and cook over low heat, stirring occasionally, for 5 minutes, until softened and translucent. Add the garbanzo beans and tomato juice and bring to a boil, then reduce the heat, and simmer for 30–40 minutes. Mix the spinach with the dill and put half in the base of a large pan. Spoon the garbanzo beans on top, cover with the remaining spinach, season with salt and pepper, and pour in the remaining oil. Cover and bring to a boil, then reduce the heat and simmer for 30–35 minutes, until the garbanzo beans are tender but not mushy and the sauce has reduced. Serve sprinkled with the lemon juice.

Serves 4
Preparation time 12¼ hours
Cooking time 1¼ hours

☐ p 250

- generous 1 cup (250 g / 9 oz) dried garbanzo beans (chickpeas), soaked for 12 hours in cold water to cover with 1 tablespoon salt
- ⅔ cup (150 ml / ¼ pint) olive oil
- 2 large onions, thinly sliced
- 1 cup (250 ml / 8 fl oz) tomato juice
- 2¼ lb (1 kg) spinach, coarse stalks removed, torn into pieces
- ½ cup (15 g / ½ oz) finely chopped fresh dill
- salt and pepper
- 4 tablespoons freshly squeezed lemon juice

PHYLLO (FILO) WITH GARBANZO BEANS (CHICKPEAS) FROM ASIA MINOR
ΣΙΝΙ ΜΑΝΤΙ ΜΕ ΡΕΒΥΘΙΑ
Sini manti me revithia

Preheat the oven to 350°F (180°C / Gas Mark 4). Roll up the phyllo sheets and cut into ½-inch (1-cm) strips. (Alternatively, use a pasta machine to make the phyllo strips.) Unroll the phyllo strips and arrange roughly on the base of a large ovenproof dish. Sprinkle with half the oil and bake for 25 minutes, until well browned. Meanwhile, heat the remaining oil in a pan. Add the onion and cook over low heat, stirring occasionally, for 5 minutes, until softened. Drain and rinse the garbanzo beans, stir them into the onion and pour in water to cover. Bring to a boil, reduce the heat, and simmer for about 1 hour, until tender. Season to taste with salt and pepper. Ladle the garbanzo bean mixture into a measuring cup and add water, if necessary, to make up 5 cups (1.25 litres / 2¼ pints). Spoon the garbanzo beans and the liquid over the top of the phyllo noodles, return to the hot oven, and bake for about 40 minutes, until all the liquid has been absorbed and the phyllo has swelled. Serve hot, sprinkled with fresh lemon juice.

Serves 6
Preparation time 12¾ hours (including soaking)
Cooking time 1¾ hours

- 10 sheets of Homemade phyllo dough (filo pastry), p 46, slightly dried
- ¾ cup (175 ml / 6 fl oz) olive oil
- 1 large onion, finely chopped
- 1⅓ cups (300 g / 11 oz) dried garbanzo beans (chickpeas), soaked for 12 hours in cold water to cover with 1 tablespoon salt
- salt and pepper
- 4 tablespoons freshly squeezed lemon juice

OVERNIGHT-BAKED GARBANZO BEANS (CHICKPEAS) FROM SIFNOS
ΡΕΒΥΘΙΑ ΣΤΟ ΦΟΥΡΝΟ
Revithia sto fourno

- 2¼ cups (500 g / 1 lb 2 oz) dried garbanzo beans (chickpeas), soaked for 12 hours in cold water to cover with 1 tablespoon salt
- 1 tablespoon all-purpose (plain) flour
- 2 large onions, sliced
- 1 teaspoon black peppercorns
- 2 garlic cloves, finely chopped (optional)
- ⅔ cup (150 ml / ¼ pint) olive oil
- salt
- freshly squeezed lemon juice, to serve

Drain and rinse the garbanzo beans (chickpeas) and put them into an ovenproof casserole dish. Sprinkle with the flour and stir. Put the onions into a bowl, pour in water to cover, and let soak for 1 hour, then drain. Preheat the oven to 300°F (150°C / Gas Mark 2). Stir the onions into the garbanzo beans together with the peppercorns, garlic, if using, and oil, and season with salt. Pour in water to cover. Cover the casserole dish tightly. (If you like, you can seal the edges with a stiff paste made from flour and water.) Bake overnight. Serve hot or at room temperature, sprinkled with fresh lemon juice.

Serves 6
Preparation time 13¼ hours (including soaking)
Cooking time 8–10 hours

LENTILS WITH RICE AND ONIONS FROM CYPRUS
ΦΑΚΕΣ ΜΟΥΤΖΕΝΤΡΑ
Fakes moutzentra

- 1⅓ cups (300 g / 11 oz) green lentils
- 4 cups (1 litre / 1¾ pints) boiling water
- ½ cup (100 g / 3½ oz) long-grain rice
- 2 tablespoons freshly squeezed lemon juice
- salt and pepper
- ½ cup (120 ml / 4 fl oz) olive oil
- 3 onions, sliced
- olives and Taramosalata (p 157), to serve

Put the lentils into a pan, pour in water to cover, bring to a boil, and cook for 5 minutes over high heat. Drain well, return to the pan, and pour in the boiling water, then cover and cook for 10 minutes. Add the rice and lemon juice, season with salt and pepper, re-cover the pan, and simmer for 20 minutes more, until the lentils and rice are tender and all the liquid has been absorbed. Meanwhile, heat the oil in a skillet or frying pan. Add the onions and cook over low heat, stirring occasionally, for 8–10 minutes, until lightly browned. Stir the onions into the lentil and rice mixture. Serve hot, accompanied by olives and Taramosalata.

Serves 4
Preparation time 10 minutes
Cooking time 35 minutes

☐ p 251

Garbanzo beans (chickpeas) with spinach, p 248

MOUNT ATHOS LENTILS WITH OCTOPUS AND RICE
ΦΑΚΕΣ ΜΕ ΧΤΑΠΟΔΙ ΚΑΙ ΡΥΖΙ
Fakes me htapodi ke rizi

- 1 fresh or frozen octopus, about 2¼ lb (1 kg), cleaned (see p 325)
- ½ cup (120 ml / 4 fl oz) red wine vinegar
- generous 1 cup (250 g / 9 oz) green lentils
- 4 scallions (spring onions), chopped
- 2 tomatoes, peeled, seeded, and chopped
- 1 red bell or long Florina pepper, seeded and diced
- 1 yellow bell pepper, seeded and diced
- ½ cup (100 g / 3½ oz) medium-grain rice, such as risotto rice
- salt and pepper
- ½ cup (120 ml / 4 fl oz) olive oil

Put the octopus into a pan, pour in water to cover, add the vinegar, and cook for 1 hour. Meanwhile, put the lentils into another pan, pour in water to cover, bring to a boil, then simmer for 5 minutes. Drain well, return to the pan, pour in 3 cups (750 ml / 1¼ pints) water, and add the scallions. Bring to a boil, reduce the heat, and simmer for 15 minutes. Drain the octopus and let cool, then remove and discard the black membranes, and cut it into large pieces. Preheat the oven to 350°F (180°C / Gas Mark 4). Transfer the lentils with their cooking liquid to an ovenproof dish. Add the octopus, tomatoes, bell peppers, and rice, season with salt and pepper, pour in the oil, and stir lightly. Bake for 40 minutes, until the rice is tender and has absorbed all the liquid. Serve hot or at room temperature.

Serves 6
Preparation time 30 minutes
Cooking time 1¾ hours

Vefa's secret: If using fresh octopus, freezing it for 2–3 days before cooking will help tenderize it.

LENTILS WITH LAMB AND ONIONS
ΦΑΚΕΣ ΜΕ ΑΡΝΙ
Fakes me arni

- ½ cup (120 ml / 4 fl oz) olive oil
- 1 lb 2 oz (500 g) boneless lamb, diced
- 1 onion, grated
- 2 garlic cloves, thinly sliced
- 1 teaspoon chopped fresh rosemary
- 1 teaspoon dried thyme
- 1 bay leaf
- 14 oz (400 g) canned chopped tomatoes, puréed
- 1 celery stalk, chopped
- ½ teaspoon cayenne pepper
- 1 lb 2 oz (500 g) pearl (pickling) onions or shallots
- salt and pepper
- 1⅓ cups (300 g / 11 oz) green lentils

Heat the oil in a large, heavy pan. Add the lamb and cook over medium heat for 8–10 minutes, until browned all over. Add the grated onion, the garlic, rosemary, thyme, and bay leaf and cook, stirring frequently, for 5 minutes. Add the tomatoes, celery, cayenne pepper, and pearl onions. Season with salt and pepper, cover, and simmer, adding a little water if necessary, for 1¼ hours, or until the meat and onions are tender. Meanwhile, put the lentils into a pan, pour in water to cover, and cook for 5 minutes. Drain well. Add the lentils to the lamb, pour in ½ cup (120 ml / 4 fl oz) hot water and cook for 15–20 minutes more, until the lentils are soft and the liquid has reduced. Serve hot.

Serves 4
Preparation time 20 minutes
Cooking time 1¾ hours

- 2 tablespoons olive oil
- 1 onion, finely chopped
- 2 cups (450 ml / 16 fl oz) meat stock
- ½ cup (100 g / 3½ oz) dried green peas
- 14 oz (400 g) potatoes, quartered
- 4 tablespoons finely chopped fresh dill
- 2 tablespoons (25 g / 1 oz) butter
- 2 tablespoons freshly squeezed lemon juice
- salt and pepper
- cayenne pepper

DRIED PEA AND POTATO PURÉE
ΠΟΥΡΕΣ ΜΕ ΑΡΑΚΑ ΚΑΙ ΠΑΤΑΤΕΣ
Poures me araka ke patates

Heat the oil in a nonstick pan. Add the onion and cook over low heat, stirring occasionally, for 5 minutes, until softened and translucent. Pour in the stock and bring to a boil, then add the peas, potatoes, and dill. Cover and simmer, adding more water if necessary, for about 40 minutes, or until the vegetables are tender. Remove from the heat and let cool slightly. Process the mixture to a smooth purée in a food processor, then return to the pan. Add the butter and lemon juice, season with salt and pepper, and stir over low heat until heated through. Divide among individual bowls, sprinkle with a pinch of cayenne pepper, and serve hot or at room temperature. This is an excellent side dish for roast chicken or red meat.

Serves 4
Preparation time 20 minutes
Cooking time 40 minutes

- ¾ cup (130 g / 4½ oz) dried small white beans, such as navy (haricot) beans, soaked for 12 hours in cold water to cover
- ¾ cup (130 g / 4½ oz) dried red kidney beans, soaked separately for 12 hours in cold water to cover
- 4 cups (1 litre / 1¾ pints) vegetable stock
- ½ cup (120 ml / 4 fl oz) olive oil
- 1 onion, grated
- 2 garlic cloves, finely chopped
- 2 leeks, white part only, chopped
- 4 tablespoons white wine
- 4 tablespoons finely chopped fresh dill
- 4 tablespoons finely chopped fresh parsley
- salt and pepper
- 6 large red or green bell peppers

FOR THE SAUCE
- 4 tablespoons olive oil
- 1½ cups (375 ml / 13 fl oz) tomato juice
- ½ teaspoon sugar
- 1 tablespoon red wine vinegar
- salt and pepper

BELL PEPPERS STUFFED WITH BEANS
ΠΙΠΕΡΙΕΣ ΓΕΜΙΣΤΕΣ ΜΕ ΦΑΣΟΛΙΑ
Piperies gemistes me fasolia

Drain and rinse the beans, then put the kidney beans into a pan, pour in water to cover, and bring to a boil. Boil vigorously for 15 minutes, then drain. Put the white beans and kidney beans into a pan, pour in the vegetable stock, and bring to a boil. Reduce the heat and simmer for about 1 hour, until tender. Drain well. Heat 4 tablespoons of the oil in a large pan. Add the onion, garlic, and leeks and cook over low heat, stirring occasionally, for 5 minutes, until softened. Pour in the wine, cover, and simmer for 15 minutes, until the leeks are half cooked. Stir in the beans, add the dill and parsley, season with salt and pepper, and remove from the heat. Meanwhile, slice the tops off the bell peppers and reserve. Remove and discard the seeds. Heat the remaining oil in a skillet or frying pan. Add the bell peppers and their tops and cook over medium heat, turning frequently, for about 8 minutes. Remove from the skillet and drain on paper towels. Preheat the oven to 350°F (180°C / Gas Mark 4). Fill the bell peppers with the bean mixture and arrange in a large ovenproof dish in a single layer. To make the sauce, heat the oil in a pan, then add the tomato juice, sugar, and vinegar. Season with salt and pepper and simmer for about 10 minutes. Add 2 tablespoons of the sauce to each bell pepper and pour the remaining sauce around them. Cover with aluminum foil and bake for 40–45 minutes. Serve hot.

Serves 6
Preparation time 13 hours (including soaking)
Cooking time 40–45 minutes

RICE
PYZI
Rizi

Native to the Far East, rice (*Oriza sativa*) first came to the attention
of the ancient Greeks on one of Alexander the Great's expeditions.
However, it was not valued as a food by the ancient Greeks and
Romans, but rather as a medicinal ingredient of "therapeutic" desserts
or cakes designed to treat digestive disorders. Rice with clarified butter
was said to have been a favorite dish of the Prophet Muhammad and
this might have inspired Arab traders to take rice to the coast of north
Africa, Spain, and Sicily, and across the Sahara to West Africa. By
the fifteenth century it was flourishing on the plains of Italy. Rice
remained a luxury in Greece, although limited crops were grown in
the river deltas of northern and central Greece before World War II.
Since 1950, however, its importance has steadily increased to the point
where Greece is now an exporter of rice. The chief rice-growing areas
are Missolonghi and Lamia in central Greece, Thessaloniki, and Serres
in Macedonia. Almost all types of rice are represented, including short-
grain soup rice, medium-grain rice, and long-grain varieties for pilafs.

GENERAL INSTRUCTIONS

Greeks mainly use rice in combination with other ingredients as a
stuffing. Inside a variety of edible wrappings, such as tomatoes, leaves,
or bell peppers, rice stuffings transform this basic grain from an accompaniment into a dish in its own right. Stuffed dishes are an important
part of Greek cuisine, and there are countless variations. Rice is also
served plain or cooked as a pilaf with a rich tomato sauce to accompany meat and shellfish dishes. To achieve the fluffy, separate grains
characteristic of pilaf, first sauté the rice in a little fat or oil, then simmer
undisturbed and tightly covered in a measured quantity of water or
other liquid. (Consult the package instructions for the precise amount
of liquid.) The fat prevents the grains from sticking together. Any whole
or cracked grain can be cooked in the same way, and bulgur wheat,
a popular grain in Greek cooking, is often used to replace rice. Rice
will absorb twice its own volume of liquid, but when cooking other
grains, measure the volume of the grains in a measuring cup, add the
same volume of liquid at the beginning of cooking, and the same amount
again midway through cooking. You may even need to add more later
if the liquid has all been absorbed, but the grains are not yet tender.

To steam rice, first soak it in cold water for about 1 hour, then drain.
Bring the water in the pan to a boil, put the rice into the steamer and set
it over the water. Cover and steam for 25–30 minutes, or until tender.
Certain other grains also need to be soaked in water before cooking.
Wild rice should be soaked in boiling water to cover for 1 hour and then
drained. Cook it in three times its volume of boiling water for about 45
minutes, until the water has been absorbed and the grains are tender.

- ½ cup (25 g / 1 oz) dried porcini mushrooms
- 3 cups (750 ml / 1¼ pints) boiling water
- 5 tablespoons olive oil, plus extra for brushing
- 5 garlic cloves, thinly sliced
- 5 scallions (spring onions), finely chopped
- 1½ cups (325 g / 11½ oz) long-grain rice
- 1½ teaspoons salt
- 2¾ cups (200 g / 7 oz) sliced white mushrooms
- 1 red or yellow bell pepper, seeded and finely chopped
- ½ cup (25 g / 1 oz) finely chopped fresh parsley or dill
- pepper

MUSHROOM PILAF
ΠΙΛΑΦΙ ΜΕ ΜΑΝΙΤΑΡΙΑ
Pilafi me manitaria

Put the porcini mushrooms in a bowl, pour in the boiling water, and let soak for 1 hour. Meanwhile, brush a 5-cup (1.25-litre / 2¼-pint) mold with oil and set aside. Remove the mushrooms from the water one at a time, shake off the excess water, and chop finely. Let the water settle, then remove and reserve 2 cups (450 ml / 16 fl oz) from the top. Heat half the oil in a pan. Add the porcini mushrooms, half the garlic, and half the scallions and cook over low heat, stirring occasionally, for 5 minutes, until softened. Add the rice and stir well until the grains are thoroughly coated in oil. Add the salt, the reserved mushroom soaking liquid, and 1 cup (250 ml / 8 fl oz) boiling water. Cover and simmer for 20 minutes, until all the liquid has been absorbed. Meanwhile, heat the remaining oil in another pan. Add the remaining onions and remaining garlic and cook over low heat, stirring occasionally, for 5 minutes, until softened. Add the white mushrooms and bell pepper and cook, stirring frequently, for about 15 minutes, until softened. Add the cooked rice and the parsley or dill and season with pepper. Stir lightly for 1 minute to mix. Spoon the rice mixture into the prepared mold, packing it down firmly, then turn out onto a platter. Serve immediately.

Serves 4
Preparation time 1½ hours (including soaking)
Cooking time 50 minutes

- ½ cup (100 g / 3½ oz) wild rice
- 4 tablespoons (50 g / 2 oz) butter
- 1 onion, finely chopped
- 1 small carrot, diced
- generous 1 cup (225 g / 8 oz) long-grain rice
- 2 cups (450 ml / 16 fl oz) hot beef or chicken stock
- 1 teaspoon salt
- ½ cup (50 g / 2 oz) roasted cashew nuts, coarsely chopped
- 4 tablespoons finely chopped fresh parsley

CASHEW PILAF
ΠΙΛΑΦΙ ΜΕ ΚΑΣΙΟΥΣ
Pilafi me kasious

Parboil the wild rice for 10 minutes, then drain. Melt the butter in a large pan. Add the onion and carrot and cook over low heat, stirring occasionally, for 5 minutes, until softened. Add both kinds of rice and stir for 1 minute, until the grains are thoroughly coated in oil. Pour in the hot stock, add the salt, cover, and simmer for 20–25 minutes, until the rice is tender and the liquid has been absorbed. Stir in the cashew nuts and parsley. Serve immediately.

Serves 4
Preparation time 15 minutes
Cooking time 35–40 minutes

RICE WITH LENTILS AND VEGETABLES
ΡΥΖΙ ΜΕ ΦΑΚΕΣ ΚΑΙ ΛΑΧΑΝΙΚΑ
Rizi me fakes ke lahanika

- ° 1 eggplant (aubergine), diced
- ° 4 tablespoons olive oil
- ° 2 garlic cloves, thinly sliced
- ° 1 lb 2 oz (500 g) ripe tomatoes, chopped
- ° 4 tablespoons chopped fresh basil leaves
- ° scant ½ cup (100 g / 3 ½ oz) green lentils
- ° 3 tablespoons (40 g / 1 ½ oz) butter
- ° 1 onion, finely chopped
- ° 2 cups (450 ml / 16 fl oz) vegetable stock
- ° ½ cup (100 g / 3 ½ oz) long-grain rice
- ° 2 cups (300 g / 11 oz) mixed diced vegetables, such as potato, carrot, zucchini (courgette), artichoke hearts, and peas

Put the eggplant into a colander, sprinkle with salt, and let drain for 30 minutes. Rinse and squeeze out the excess moisture. Heat the oil in a small pan. Add the garlic and cook over low heat, stirring frequently, for 1–2 minutes, then remove with a slotted spoon. Add the eggplant and cook, stirring frequently, for 5–6 minutes, until softened. Add the tomatoes and basil and simmer for 15 minutes, until thickened. Meanwhile, parboil the lentils for 5 minutes in boiling water and drain. Melt the butter in a large pan. Add the onion and cook over low heat, stirring occasionally, for 5 minutes, until softened. Pour in the vegetable stock and bring to a boil. Add the rice, lentils, and mixed vegetables, cover, and simmer for about 20 minutes, until the vegetables and rice are tender. Stir in the eggplant and tomato sauce and cook for 5 minutes more. Serve hot or at room temperature.

Serves 4
Preparation time 45 minutes (including salting)
Cooking time 1 hour

SPICED RICE WITH TOMATOES AND BELL PEPPERS
ΠΙΚΑΝΤΙΚΟ ΝΤΟΜΑΤΟΡΥΖΟ
Pikadiko domatorizo

- ° 6 tablespoons (80 g / 3 oz) butter
- ° 1 small onion, finely chopped
- ° 3 garlic cloves, finely chopped
- ° 1½ cups (325 g / 11½ oz) long-grain rice
- ° 1½ teaspoons salt
- ° 1 teaspoon sugar
- ° ¼ teaspoon white pepper
- ° ¼ teaspoon ground cumin
- ° ½ teaspoon cayenne pepper
- ° ½ teaspoon ground coriander
- ° 2¼ lb (1 kg) ripe tomatoes, peeled and chopped, or 1¾ lb (800 g) canned chopped tomatoes
- ° 1 tablespoon tomato paste
- ° 1 cup (250 ml / 8 fl oz) vegetable stock
- ° 1 red bell pepper, seeded and finely chopped
- ° olives, to serve

Melt the butter in a large pan. Add the onion and garlic and cook over low heat, stirring occasionally, for 5 minutes, until softened. Stir in the rice and cook, stirring constantly, for 2 minutes, until the grains are thoroughly coated in butter. Add the salt, sugar, spices, tomatoes, tomato paste, and stock. Mix well, cover, increase the heat to high, and bring to a boil. Reduce the heat and simmer for 20 minutes. Stir in the bell pepper and simmer for 5 minutes more. Serve hot or at room temperature, accompanied by olives.

Serves 4
Preparation time 30 minutes
Cooking time 35 minutes

▢ p 258

- 5 tablespoons olive oil
- 1 onion, finely chopped
- 1 leek, white part only, finely chopped
- 2 celery stalks, thinly sliced
- 2¾ cups (200 g / 7 oz) sliced small white mushrooms
- 2 carrots, cut into julienne strips
- 14 oz (400 g) canned chopped tomatoes, drained
- 1 teaspoon sugar
- 2 tablespoons finely chopped fresh basil
- ¼ teaspoon cayenne pepper
- salt
- 1½ cups (325 g / 11½ oz) medium-grain rice

RICE WITH VEGETABLE SAUCE
ΡΥΖΙ ΜΕ ΣΑΛΤΣΑ ΛΑΧΑΝΙΚΩΝ
Rizi me saltsa lahanikon

Heat the oil in a pan. Add the onion and leek and cook over low heat, stirring occasionally, for 5 minutes, until softened. Add the celery, mushrooms, and carrots, increase the heat to medium, and cook, stirring occasionally, for 10 minutes, until softened. Add the tomatoes, sugar, basil, and cayenne pepper and season with salt. Increase the heat to high and bring to a boil, stirring constantly. Reduce the heat, cover, and simmer for 30 minutes, or until thickened. Meanwhile, bring 3 cups (750 ml / 1¼ pints) water to a boil in a pan. Stir in salt, add the rice, cover, and cook until all the water has been absorbed and the rice is fluffy. Serve the rice in deep plates, topped with the vegetable sauce.

Serves 4
Preparation time 30 minutes
Cooking time 45 minutes

- 6 tablespoons (80 g / 3 oz) butter
- 2¼ cups (450 g / 1 lb) long-grain rice
- 5 cups (1.2 litres / 2 pints) vegetable or meat stock
- salt and pepper
- 10 saffron threads, crushed
- finely chopped fresh parsley and grated kefalotiri or Parmesan cheese, to garnish

SAFFRON PILAF
ΠΙΛΑΦΙ ΜΕ ΣΑΦΡΑΝΙ
Pilafi me safrani

Melt the butter in a pan over high heat. When it begins to brown, add the rice, and cook, stirring constantly, until it turns opaque. Pour in 4 cups (1 litre / 1¾ pints) of the stock, add a pinch of salt, and bring to a boil. Reduce the heat, cover, and simmer for about 20 minutes, or until the rice has absorbed all the liquid and small holes appear on the surface. Stir the saffron into the remaining stock, add it to the rice, and stir gently. Place a clean dish towel over the top of the pan, replace the lid, and remove from the heat. Let the pilaf rest for 5–8 minutes. Serve, sprinkled with finely chopped parsley and grated cheese. This is an excellent accompaniment to roast or braised meat or fish.

Serves 6
Preparation time 20 minutes (including resting)
Cooking time 20 minutes

☐ p 259

Spiced rice with tomatoes and bell peppers, p 256

saffron pilaf, p 257

TOMATO PILAF
NTOMATOPYZO
Domatorizo

Heat the oil in a pan over high heat. Add the garlic and cook, stirring frequently, for 1–2 minutes. Add the tomatoes, cover, reduce the heat, and simmer for 30 minutes, or until thickened. Stir in the parsley, sugar, vinegar, stock, paprika, and cayenne pepper, season with salt and pepper, increase the heat, and bring to a boil. Add the rice, reduce the heat, cover, and simmer for about 20 minutes, until the rice is just tender but the liquid has not all been absorbed. Remove from the heat, place a paper towel between the lid and the pan, and let rest until the rice has swollen. Serve hot or at room temperature, accompanied by olives.

Serves 4
Preparation time 30 minutes (including resting)
Cooking time 1 hour

- 5 tablespoons olive oil
- 5 garlic clove, thinly sliced
- 2¼ lb (1 kg) fresh or canned tomatoes, puréed
- 3 tablespoons finely chopped fresh parsley
- 1 teaspoon sugar
- 1 tablespoon red wine vinegar
- 1½ cups (350 ml / 12 fl oz) vegetable stock or water
- 1 teaspoon paprika
- ¼ teaspoon cayenne pepper
- salt and pepper
- black olives, to serve

RICE WITH SHELLFISH AND TOMATO SAUCE
PYZI ME ΘΑΛΑΣΣΙΝΑ ΚΑΙ ΣΑΛΤΣΑ ΝΤΟΜΑΤΑΣ
Rizi me thalasina ke saltsa domatas

Peel and devein the shrimp, leaving the heads intact. Bring 3 cups (750 ml / 1¼ pints) water to a boil in pan. Stir in the paprika, add the shrimp and mussels, and cook for 5 minutes. Using a slotted spoon, transfer to a bowl. Remove and discard the heads and cut the shrimp into pieces. Strain the cooking liquid through a cheesecloth- (muslin-) lined strainer into a bowl, measure, and make up to 3 cups (750 ml / 1¼ pints) with water. Pour into a pan and bring to a boil. Add the rice and simmer for about 20 minutes, until all the liquid has been absorbed and the rice is fluffy. Meanwhile, prepare the sauce. Cook the onion, leeks, garlic, and bell peppers in a pan with 1 tablespoon water until softened. Add the tomatoes, sugar, vinegar, dill, and cayenne pepper. Simmer until slightly thickened. Remove from the heat, add the cooked shrimp and mussels, and season with salt and pepper. Spoon the rice onto a platter and pour the shellfish and tomato mixture on top.

Serves 6
Preparation time 20 minutes
Cooking time 45 minutes

▢ p 262

- 1 lb 2 oz (500 g) raw shrimp (prawns)
- 1 tablespoon paprika
- 1 lb 2 oz (500 g) raw shelled mussels
- 2 cups (400 g / 14 oz) basmati rice

FOR THE SAUCE
- 1 large onion, sliced
- 2 leeks, white part only, finely chopped
- 3 garlic cloves, finely chopped
- ½ green bell pepper, seeded and cut into julienne strips
- ½ red bell pepper, seeded and cut into julienne strips
- 4 ripe tomatoes, peeled, seeded, and chopped
- 1 teaspoon sugar
- 1 tablespoon red wine vinegar
- 4 tablespoons finely chopped fresh dill or parsley
- ½ teaspoon cayenne pepper
- salt and pepper

FOR THE MEAT SAUCE

- 7 tablespoons olive oil
- 1 onion, grated
- ½ cup (4) chopped scallions (spring onions)
- 14 oz (400 g) ground (minced) beef
- 2¼ lb (1 kg) ripe tomatoes, peeled, seeded, and chopped
- 1 teaspoon sugar
- 2½ teaspoons red wine vinegar
- salt and pepper
- 1½ cups (100 g / 3½ oz) thinly sliced white mushrooms
- 4 tablespoons finely chopped fresh parsley

FOR THE RICE

- 3 cups (750 ml / 1¼ pints) chicken stock or water
- 1½ teaspoons salt
- 1½ cups (325 g / 11½ oz) long-grain rice

RICE WITH GROUND (MINCED) MEAT AND MUSHROOM SAUCE
ΡΥΖΙ ΜΕ ΣΑΛΤΣΑ ΚΙΜΑ ΚΑΙ ΜΑΝΙΤΑΡΙΑ
Rizi me saltsa kima ke manitaria

First, prepare the sauce. Heat 4 tablespoons of the oil in a pan over medium heat. Add the onion and scallions and cook, stirring occasionally, for 3–5 minutes, until softened. Add the ground beef and cook, stirring frequently and breaking up the meat with a spoon, for 8–10 minutes, until lightly browned. Add the tomatoes, sugar, and vinegar, season with salt and pepper, cover, and simmer for about 50 minutes. Meanwhile, heat the remaining oil in a skillet or frying pan. Add the mushrooms and cook, stirring occasionally, for 5 minutes. Add the mushrooms along with the parsley to the meat. To prepare the rice, bring the stock or water to a boil in a pan. Stir in the salt, add the rice, and bring back to a boil. Turn off the heat and leave the rice to rest on the stove for 10 minutes. Serve the rice topped with the meat sauce.

Serves 4
Preparation time 15 minutes
Cooking time 1 hour

- ⅔ cup (80 g / 3 oz) raisins or golden raisins
- 1 teaspoon salt
- 1½ cups (325 g / 11½ oz) long-grain rice
- scant 1 cup (175 g / 6 oz) sugar
- ¾ cup (80 g / 3 oz) slivered almonds, toasted
- 5 tablespoons clarified butter
- 7 oz (200 g) angel-hair or vermicelli pasta, lightly crushed
- olive oil, for brushing
- ground cinnamon, to sprinkle
- walnut halves, to decorate
- honey, for drizzling

BRIDE'S PILAF
ΤΟ ΠΙΛΑΦΙ ΤΗΣ ΝΥΦΗΣ
To pilafi tis nifis

Bride's pilaf is an old recipe from the village of Tripolis on the shore of the Black Sea. It was served by the bride as a sweet treat to her friends when they visited with gifts and candy (sweets) before the wedding.

Place the raisins in a bowl, pour in water to cover, and let soak for 15 minutes, then drain. Bring 4 cups (1 litre / 1¾ pints) water to a boil in a large pan. Stir in the salt and rice, cover, and simmer for 15 minutes. Stir in the sugar and simmer for 5 minutes more, until the rice has absorbed all the water and is fluffy. Remove from the heat and stir in the raisins and almonds. Melt the butter in a pan. Add the pasta and cook stirring constantly, until golden. Stir into the rice, cover the pan with a dish towel, place the lid on top, and set aside to rest for 10 minutes. Brush a 5-cup (1.25-litre / 2¼-pint) mold with oil, and fill it with the rice, packing it down firmly. Turn it out onto a platter. Sprinkle with the cinnamon and decorate with the walnuts. Serve in bowls, drizzled with honey. Alternatively, the pilaf can be packed into individual molds, and served on small plates.

Serves 6
Preparation time 35 minutes (including soaking and resting)
Cooking time 30 minutes

Rice with shellfish and tomato sauce, p 260

Chicken pilaf wrapped in phyllo (filo), p 265

ANGEL-HAIR PILAF
ΠΙΛΑΦΙ ΦΙΔΑΤΟ
Pilafi fidato

Combine the chicken, onion, coriander, paprika, and allspice in a bowl. Cover and let marinate in the refrigerator for 1 hour. Meanwhile, heat half the oil in a pan. Add the pasta, almonds, and golden raisins and cook over low heat, stirring frequently, for a few minutes, until the pasta is lightly browned. Remove from the heat. Heat the remaining oil in another pan. Add the chicken and onion mixture and cook over low heat, stirring constantly, for 3–4 minutes. Add the hot stock, season with salt and pepper, and bring to a boil. Add the rice, cover, and simmer for about 20 minutes, until the rice is cooked and all the liquid has been absorbed. Gently stir in the pasta mixture and serve immediately.

Serves 4
Preparation time 1 hour 15 minutes (including marinating)
Cooking time 30 minutes

- 2 small skinless, boneless chicken breast portions, finely chopped
- 1 onion, grated
- ½ teaspoon ground coriander
- ½ teaspoon hot paprika
- ½ teaspoon ground allspice
- ½ cup (120 ml / 4 fl oz) olive oil
- 5 oz (150 g) angel-hair pasta, broken into small pieces
- 3 tablespoons blanched and coarsely chopped almonds
- 2 tablespoons golden raisins
- 3¼ cups (850 ml / 1½ pints) hot chicken stock
- salt and pepper
- 1½ cups (325 g / 11½ oz) long-grain rice

CRETAN WEDDING PILAF
ΓΑΜΟΠΙΛΑΦΟ ΧΑΝΙΩΝ
Gamopilafo hanion

Bring a large pan of water to a boil. Stir in a pinch of salt, add the meat and chicken pieces, and simmer, skimming off any scum that rises to the surface, for about 2 hours, until all the meat is tender. (If the chicken is cooked before the goat or lamb, remove it from the pan and set aside while the rest of the meat finishes cooking.) Transfer all the meat to a platter with a slotted spoon, season with salt and pepper, and keep warm. Measure the cooking liquid and make up to 6¼ cups (1.5 litres / 2½ pints) with water. Return to the pan and bring back to a boil. Add the rice and cook over medium heat, stirring constantly, for 15 minutes. Be careful not to overcook the rice—about 1 cup (250 ml / 8 fl oz) of the cooking liquid should remain in the pan. Stir in the lemon juice and remove from the heat. Place a dish towel between the pan and the lid and let stand for 10 minutes. Melt the clarified butter in a large skillet or frying pan, pour it over the rice, and stir gently. Transfer the rice to a warm platter, place the meat around it, and serve immediately.

Serves 8
Preparation time 15 minutes
Cooking time 2½ hours

Note: This recipe has been substantially reduced for household use. When made for a typical Cretan wedding, which can include up to 1,500 guests, the stock is made in huge cauldrons. Cooking the stock and stirring the rice is always a job for the men. The female friends and relatives of the bride prepare the other dishes.

- 3¼ lb (1.5 kg) young goat (kid) or lamb, cut into portions
- 1 chicken, cut into portions
- salt and pepper
- 2¼ cups (450 g / 1 lb) medium-grain rice
- 4 tablespoons freshly squeezed lemon juice
- 1 cup (225 g / 8 oz) clarified butter

- 1 small chicken, about 2¼ lb (1 kg), skinned
- 10 black peppercorns
- 1 small carrot
- 1 small onion
- 1½ cups (325 g / 11½ oz) long-grain rice
- ⅔ cup (150 ml / ¼ pint) melted butter, plus extra for brushing
- 1 onion, finely chopped
- scant 1 cup (100 g / 3½ oz) blanched almonds, slivered
- ½ cup (50 g / 2 oz) pine nuts
- 2 tablespoons currants
- salt and pepper
- 6 sheets of phyllo dough (filo pastry), ready-made or see p 46

CHICKEN PILAF WRAPPED IN PHYLLO (FILO)
ΠΙΛΑΦΙ ΤΥΛΙΧΤΟ
Pilafi tilihto

Put the chicken into a large pan, pour water to cover, add the peppercorns, carrot, and onion, and season with salt. Bring to a boil, then reduce the heat, and simmer for about 1 hour, or until tender. Remove with a slotted spoon and let cool, then remove the bones, and shred the flesh. Strain the stock, measure and make up to 5 cups (1.2 litres / 2 pints) with water. Reserve 2 cups (450 ml / 16 fl oz) and bring the remaining stock to a boil in a pan. Add the rice, cover, and cook for 10 minutes, until almost tender. Drain the rice and spread it out on a clean dish towel to drain until completely dry. Heat half the melted butter in a large pan. Add the onion, almonds, and pine nuts and cook over low heat, stirring occasionally, for about 5 minutes, until the onions are softened. Increase the heat to medium, add the rice, and cook, stirring constantly, for 1 minute, until the grains are thoroughly coated with butter. Stir in the chicken, currants, and reserved stock and season with salt and pepper. Simmer for 10 minutes, then remove from the heat. Preheat the oven to 400°F (200°C / Gas Mark 6) and brush an oval ovenproof dish, 9 x 14 inches (23 x 35 cm), with melted butter. Line the base of the prepared dish with the sheets of phyllo, letting it hang over the sides, and brush with melted butter. Spread the rice mixture into the dish, gather the overhanging phyllo, and fold it over the filling to form a *boureki,* or large pie. Brush with the remaining melted butter and bake for about 20 minutes, until the phyllo is golden. Let cool for 5 minutes before transferring to a platter. Serve immediately.

Serves 6
Preparation time 20 minutes
Cooking time 2 hours

☐ p 263

PASTA

-

ZYMAPIKA

-

Zimarika

Pasta spans continents, countries, languages, and cultures, but it is very difficult to explain its nature and origins definitively. It seems that no one person actually "invented" pasta or noodles, nor is it true that the Venetian traveler Marco Polo brought them back from China. In fact, pasta is as old—or maybe older—than bread itself, and has been part of Greek cooking for centuries. Whatever its history and derivation, the wide variety of pasta, in countless shapes and with names of untraceable origin, testifies to its long-standing place in Greek cuisine. It is the product of the ingenuity of domestic cooks who have tried to find ways of nourishing their families with the most basic ingredients available made as tasty and filling as possible. Greeks consume about 21 pounds (9.5 kg) of commercially produced pasta per person each year, but to find Greek pasta, or makaronia, at its best, seek out the homemade products made in small stores (shops) and local cooperatives.

Pasta dishes are served as entrées (main courses), often in hearty one-dish meals, rather than as first courses as they are in Italy. Greek pasta is traditionally cooked in the sauce rather than in water, but now the method of part-cooking the pasta in water before adding it to the sauce is also very common. Baked pasta dishes are one example of this. The pasta used is called orzo, probably a short form of the ancient Greek word for rice, oriza. Because rice was so expensive, clever cooks came up with a substitute by rolling tiny pieces of dough to resemble it. In Greece, this pasta is usually known as kritharaki, or little barley grains, which it also resembles. Baked pasta dishes are sometimes made with hilopites, a kind of square egg noodle (pasta). In the days before pasta machines, hilopites were made by winding a thin sheet of phyllo dough (filo pastry) several times around a thin wooden rolling rod, and then quickly splitting the layers of dough lengthwise so that the strips fell neatly into a pile. They were then easily cut crosswise into small squares.

Pasta dishes are still served at memorial services as a reminder of the ancient Isles of the Blessed or makaron nisoi, the peaceful resting place of ancient heroes and demi gods. Modern Greek makaronia dishes, such as makarones from Samothraki and pasha makarouna, are served on the last day of Carnival or Cheese-Fare Sunday, the day before the start of Lent, when dishes made with pasta and cheese are customary. Typical varieties of pasta include makaroni kofto, or "cut macaroni," known elsewhere as elbow macaroni, and the handmade herisia makaronia that is still made on the island of Chios. Short pieces of dough are rolled around twigs or reeds, which are then removed before cooking, a simple but effective method for making the hole in the macaroni. There is also the simple trahana, a kind of dried, shredded free-form pasta made from flour and sheep's milk in nearly every rural Greek home in August. The dough is rubbed through a coarse strainer and the crumbs are left to dry on tables or beds covered with cotton sheets. The trahana is then stored in sacks in a dry cellar. This is probably one of the oldest forms of pasta and although it is unsophisticated, it has filled hungry stomachs for centuries.

Probably the most interesting and complex Greek pasta comes from the area formerly known as Pontus on the southern coast of the Black Sea. Pontic women have always been adept at making many kinds of phyllo (filo) and pasta, which they dried and kept ready for use when required. When needed, they are cooked in boiling water or stock and served with dairy products such as yogurt and butter. The *manti* of Asia Minor are tiny pieces of pasta filled with meat or other fillings, often shaped like little boats. The dough is cut and folded in various shapes—the smaller they are, the more skilled the cook—to create a dish for special occasions. *Manti* are thought to have originated in central Asia and are related to *mantou*, a range of ravioli-type pasta or dumplings found from Iran to China, Korea, and Japan in the Far East. These dishes are typical of the cuisine of the Pontic Greeks, from where they spread through Asia Minor.

GENERAL INSTRUCTIONS

Homemade dough for filled pasta can be rolled to a thickness of ⅛ inch (3 mm), a little thicker than the sheets for layered pasta. It should be as moist and flexible as possible so that it can be easily molded around the stuffing. Use fresh pasta sheets immediately, as they tend to dry out quickly. Allow a margin of 2 inches (5 cm) between the mounds of filling when preparing ravioli, and dampen the edges well. Do not overfill, and be careful to avoid leaving traces of filling between the edges you need to seal. To prevent them sticking together, place the filled pasta shapes spaced well apart on a floured dish towel until ready to use. Homemade pasta is usually cooked immediately after making it. Many well-known shapes can be made at home and many are best suited to particular recipes; a baked dish of layered pasta is best made with lasagne, for example, while ziti is the perfect choice for pastitsio, and long strands of pasta can be coiled to make "nests" for cooked meat or shellfish.

The basic way to cook fresh or dried pasta is to boil it in salted water and then mix it with a sauce in a serving dish. Fresh pasta cooks in around 2–5 minutes, while dried pasta requires 5–12 minutes. The precise time depends on the thickness and dryness of the pasta, and the quality of the ingredients. To prevent the pasta from sticking, use plenty of salted water, about 4¼ quarts (4 litres / 7 pints) for every 1 lb 2 oz (500 g) pasta, add 2 tablespoons olive oil, and make sure that the water is boiling rapidly before adding it to the pan. This helps to keep the pasta separated. Stir gently at the beginning and keep the water at a steady boil throughout the cooking time. Test the pasta after the first 5 minutes of cooking. Carefully lift out a few strands and pinch it or taste it to check if it is al dente: in other words, just tender but retaining some bite. Repeat at 1-minute intervals until the pasta is ready, then drain immediately and transfer to a warm bowl or individual plates. Add cheese and sauce, toss, and serve immediately. The sauce can be very simple, such as a light coating of olive oil or butter, or a more complicated meat or shellfish sauce. Homemade fresh noodles are usually simply served with butter and sprinkled with grated cheese.

HOMEMADE EGG NOODLES (PASTA)
ΧΥΛΟΠΙΤΕΣ
Hilopites

- 4½ cups (500 g / 1 lb 2 oz) strong white bread flour, plus extra for dusting
- 1 tablespoon salt
- 3 cups (500 g / 1 lb 2 oz) fine semolina
- 10 eggs, lightly beaten
- ½–1 cup (120–250 ml / 4–8 fl oz) milk

Sift together the flour, salt, and semolina into a large bowl. Add the eggs and, kneading constantly, gradually pour in enough milk to form a smooth, elastic dough. Cover and let stand for 1 hour. Divide the dough into pieces and roll out on a lightly floured work surface as thinly as possible. Transfer to a cotton tablecloth and let dry for a few minutes. Wrap a dough sheet around the rolling pin and make a lengthwise slit with a sharp knife to create a stack of long strips. Remove the rolling pin. Cut the strips lengthwise into ½-inch (1-cm) strips and then crosswise into ½-inch (1-cm) squares. Repeat with the remaining dough sheets. Spread out the pasta squares on the tablecloth and let dry in a cool, well-ventilated place for 5–6 days. Store them in a cotton bag in a cool dark place or store them in the refrigerator.

Makes about 3 lb (1.25 kg)
Preparation time 5½–6½ days (including standing and drying)

CHEESE-FILLED PASTA
ΛΑΤΖΑΝΙΑ ΑΣΤΥΠΑΛΑΙΑΣ
Latzania astipaleas

- 4½ cups (500 g / 1 lb 2 oz) all-purpose (plain) flour, plus extra for dusting
- 1 teaspoon salt
- 2 eggs, lightly beaten
- 2–3 tablespoons water
- melted butter, to serve

FOR THE FILLING
- 11 oz (300 g) anthotiro or ricotta cheese
- ¼ teaspoon ground allspice or grated nutmeg
- ½ teaspoon saffron threads, crumbled
- pepper

This dish is served on the island of Astypalaia on the last day of Carnival (Cheese-Fare Sunday), the day before the beginning of Lent and the final day on which dairy products can be consumed before Easter.

To make the dough, sift together the flour and salt into a bowl. Mix in the eggs and knead, adding enough water to make a firm, elastic dough. Let rest for 1 hour. Meanwhile, prepare the filling. Combine all the filling ingredients in a bowl and season with pepper. Divide the dough into 6–8 pieces and roll out on a lightly floured work surface into very thin sheets. Cut into strips 2½ x 3 inches (6 x 8 cm). Place a teaspoon of filling in the center of each strip, roll up from the long side, and twist the ends together, sealing them with your fingers. They will resemble tiny Christmas crackers. Arrange the *latzania* on a floured dish towel and let dry for up to 12 hours. Cook in plenty of salted boiling water for about 8–10 minutes, or until tender. Remove with a slotted spoon and serve hot, drizzled with sizzling melted butter.

Serves 10–12
Preparation time 14 hours (including resting and drying)
Cooking time 10 minutes

▢ p 272

- 1 tablespoon salt
- 1 lb 2 oz (500 g) floumaria or ready-made long egg noodles (pasta)
- 2¼ cups (250 g / 9 oz) dried mizithra or pecorino cheese
- 2¼ cups (250 g / 9 oz) coarsely grated kefalotiri, regato, or Parmesan cheese
- ½ cup (25 g / 1 oz) finely chopped fresh mint
- 3 tablespoons butter, melted, for serving

FOR THE FLOUMARIA
- 2¼ cups (250 g / 9 oz) strong white bread flour
- 1½ cups (250 g / 9 oz) fine semolina
- ½ tablespoon salt
- 5 eggs, lightly beaten
- ½ cup (120 ml / 4 fl oz) milk
- cornstarch (cornflour), for dusting

CHEESE-FARE SUNDAY NOODLES (PASTA) FROM SAMOTHRAKI
ΜΑΚΑΡΟΝΕΣ ΣΑΜΟΘΡΑΚΗΣ
Makarones samothrakis

These traditional homemade noodles, known as *floumaria*, are served on Cheese-Fare Sunday on the island of Samothraki.

If making *floumaria*, sift together the flour, semolina, and salt into a bowl, stir in the eggs, and gradually add enough milk to make a firm, smooth dough. Cover and let rest for 1 hour. Divide the dough into balls about the size of a tangerine. Lightly dust a work surface with cornstarch and roll out each piece into a sheet about ⅛ inch (3 mm) thick. Cut into long strips about 3 inches (8 cm) wide. Sprinkle with cornstarch to prevent them from sticking. Cut each wide strip crosswise into short, narrow strips about ½ inch (1 cm) wide and spread out on dish towels to dry for 3–4 days. Store in cotton bags in a cool dark place for up to 4–6 months.

Bring 8¼ cups (2 litres / 3½ pints) water to a boil in a large pan, add the salt, the noodles, and cook for 8 minutes, or until al dente. Sprinkle a large platter with several tablespoons of each kind of cheese and some chopped mint. Spread a layer of noodles on top and sprinkle with more cheese and mint. Continue making layers in this way, ending with a layer of cheese and mint. Heat the butter in a pan until it begins to brown, then gradually drizzle spoonfuls of it over the noodles. Cover for several minutes, then serve.

Serves 4
Preparation time 20 minutes
Cooking time 8 minutes

- 5 oz (150 g) long egg noodles (pasta), such as tagliatelle
- 6 eggs
- 9 oz (250 g) feta cheese, crumbled
- ⅓ cup (80 g / 3 oz) clarified butter, melted
- pepper

FETA OMELET WITH EGG NOODLES (PASTA)
ΟΜΕΛΕΤΑ ΜΕ ΦΕΤΑ ΚΑΙ ΧΥΛΟΠΙΤΕΣ
Omeleta me feta ke hilopites

Cook the noodles in salted boiling water for 10 minutes or until just tender, then drain and tip into a bowl. Lightly beat the eggs in another bowl and stir in the crumbled feta. Fold the cheese mixture into the noodles. Heat half the butter in a large deep skillet or frying pan, add the noodles, and cook until crisp. Invert onto a large plate. Add the remaining butter to the skillet and heat. Slide the noodle omelet into the skillet and cook the second side until crisp. Remove from the heat, season with pepper, cut into wedges, and serve immediately.

Serves 4
Preparation time 15 minutes
Cooking time 10 minutes

▢ p 273

Cheese-filled pasta, p 270

frittata omelet with egg noodles (pasta), p 271

FLOUR DUMPLINGS FROM KARYSTOS
ΚΟΥΡΚΟΥΜΠΙΝΕΣ ΡΟΥΚΛΙΩΤΙΚΕΣ
Kourkoubines roukliotikes

These traditional fresh dumplings are served in the region of Karystos in southern Evvoia on Cheese-Fare Sunday and other special occasions, with tomato sauce from the *kokinista* dishes. The resemblance of *kourkoubines* to Italian gnocchi may be because Evvoia was ruled by the Venetians from 1204 until the second half of the fifteenth century.

Dust a large baking pan with flour and set aside. Pour the milk into a large pan, add 1 teaspoon salt, and bring to a boil. Simmer for 5 minutes, then remove from the heat, and let cool. Pour the milk and the oil into a large bowl, then gradually add the flour, kneading to make a soft and elastic dough. Pinch off small portions of dough and roll into ½-inch (1-cm) thick ropes, then, using a sharp knife cut into ½-inch (1-cm) lengths. Flatten slightly and make a depression in the middle with your index finger, or quickly roll the pieces of dough across a fine grater with your index finger to form a shell-shaped dumpling. Put the dumplings into the prepared pan and cover with a damp cloth. Bring a large deep pan of water to a boil over high heat, add a pinch of salt, add the dumplings, and cook for 20 minutes. Meanwhile, sprinkle a dish with half the grated cheese. Using a slotted spoon, transfer the cooked dumplings to the dish. Heat the butter in a small pan and pour it over the dumplings. Sprinkle with the remaining cheese and serve with pieces of *saganaki* (fried kefalotiri or halloumi cheese) in the center.

Serves 10
Preparation time 1 hour
Cooking time 30 minutes

- 4½ cups (500 g / 1 lb 2 oz) all-purpose (plain) flour, plus extra for dusting
- 1 cup (250 ml / 8 fl oz) milk, preferably goat's milk
- salt
- 1 tablespoon olive oil
- 4 tablespoons melted butter
- 1 cup (120 g / 4 oz) grated kefalotiri, regato or Parmesan cheese

- 4½ cups (500 g / 1 lb 2 oz) all-purpose (plain) flour, plus extra for dusting
- salt and pepper
- 4 tablespoons olive oil
- olive oil, for frying

FRIED AND BOILED NOODLES (PASTA)
ΜΑΓΙΡΙ
Magiri

This dish comes from Crete, and the locals say *"magiri ki os t'ahiri,"* meaning that they can digest a plate of *magiri* in the time it takes them to feed the animals and come back, ready for another helping.

Sift the flour and 1 teaspoon salt into a bowl and make a well in the center. Pour in 1⅓ cups (325 ml / 11 fl oz) water and the oil and mix to a firm dough. Knead until smooth and elastic. Divide the dough into 10, cover, and let rest for 30 minutes. Roll it out on a lightly floured work surface into very thin sheets and wrap them around the rolling pin. Using a sharp knife, cut the dough along the length of the rolling pin into long wide strips. Keeping them stacked, cut lengthwise into ½-inch (1-cm) strips, then crosswise into ½-inch (1-cm) squares. Dust with flour to prevent them from sticking together. Spread the pasta out on dish towels in the refrigerator to dry slightly. Pour oil into a large skillet or frying pan to a depth of about 1 inch (2.5 cm) and heat. Add half the pieces and cook until crisp and golden brown. Meanwhile, bring 4 cups (1 litre / 1 ¾ pints) water to a boil in a pan, stir in 1 teaspoon salt, add the remaining pasta, and cook until they float. Stir in the fried noodles together with most of their cooking oil. Mix well, then taste, and season with salt and pepper. Serve immediately in deep plates with some of the cooking liquid while the fried *magiri* are still crisp.

Serves 6
Preparation time 1½ hours (including resting)
Cooking time 15 minutes

- 3 tablespoons tahini
- 1 onion, grated
- 14 oz (400 g) canned chopped tomatoes
- 1 tablespoon balsamic vinegar
- 1 tablespoon tomato paste
- 8 allspice berries
- 1 bay leaf
- pinch of ground cinnamon
- 4 tablespoons finely chopped fresh mint
- salt and pepper
- 2 tablespoons olive oil
- 14 oz (400 g) spaghetti
- ¾ cup (80 g / 3 oz) ground walnuts
- 4 tablespoons sesame seeds, lightly roasted
- 10 Kalamata olives, pitted (stoned)

LENTEN SPAGHETTI WITH TAHINI
ΝΗΣΤΙΣΙΜΟ ΣΠΑΓΚΕΤΙ ΜΕ ΤΑΧΙΝΙ
Nistisimo spageti me tahini

Put the tahini in a pan, add the onion, and cook over medium heat, stirring constantly, for 4–5 minutes, until softened. Add the tomatoes, vinegar, tomato paste, allspice berries, bay leaf, cinnamon, and mint and season with salt and pepper. Simmer for about 15 minutes, until thickened. Meanwhile, bring a large of pan of water to a boil, stir in salt and the oil, add the pasta, and cook for 8–10 minutes, or until al dente. Drain, transfer to a shallow dish, and pour the sauce over it. Sprinkle with walnuts and sesame seeds, garnish with the olives, and serve hot or at room temperature.

Serves 4
Preparation time 10 minutes
Cooking time 20 minutes

LENTEN SPAGHETTI FROM CORFU
ΜΑΚΑΡΟΝΙΑ ΑΛΑΔΩΤΑ
Makaronia aladota

Put the roe into a bowl, pour in tepid water to cover, and let soak for 1 hour, then drain well. Heat ½ cup (120 ml / 4 fl oz) of the oil in a pan. Add the onions and garlic and cook over low heat, stirring occasionally, for 5 minutes, until softened and translucent. Increase the heat to medium, add the roe, and cook, stirring constantly, for 1–2 minutes. Pour in the tomato juice and vinegar, add the bay leaf, allspice berries, and sugar. Season with pepper and cook for 15 minutes, until the sauce has thickened. Meanwhile, bring a large pan of water to a boil, stir in salt and the remaining olive oil, add the spaghetti, and cook for 8–10 minutes, or until al dente. Meanwhile, combine the bread crumbs and walnuts in a bowl. Drain the pasta and spread about one third of it on a serving platter. Sprinkle with one third of the bread crumb mixture and top with one third of the sauce. Repeat the layers twice more. Serve hot, sprinkled with chopped parsley.

Serves 4
Preparation time 1 hour 20 minutes (including soaking)
Cooking time 25 minutes

- 3½ oz (100 g) cured cod's roe
- ⅔ cup (150 ml / ¼ pint) olive oil
- 2 onions, finely chopped
- 3 garlic cloves, thinly sliced
- 2 cups (450 ml / 16 fl oz) tomato juice
- 1 tablespoon red wine vinegar
- 1 bay leaf
- 6 allspice berries
- 1 teaspoon sugar
- salt and pepper
- 1 lb 2 oz (500 g) thick spaghetti or bucatini
- 4 tablespoons dry bread crumbs
- 1 cup (120 g / 4 oz) walnuts, crushed
- 3 tablespoons finely chopped fresh parsley

CHEESE PASTITSIO
ΠΑΣΤΙΤΣΙΟ ΜΕ ΤΥΡΙΑ
Pastitsio me tiria

Bring a large pan of water to a boil, stir in salt and the oil, add the pasta, and cook for 8–10 minutes, or until al dente. Drain, tip into a bowl, and let cool slightly. Preheat the oven to 350°F (180°C / Gas Mark 4). Brush a 10 x 14-inch (25 x 35-cm) ovenproof dish with butter and sprinkle with the bread crumbs. Add the melted butter, crumbled feta, grated kaseri or Gruyère, allspice, and mint to the pasta and season with pepper and salt, if necessary. Lightly whisk the egg whites in another bowl, then fold into the pasta mixture, and set aside. When the white sauce is cool, stir in the egg yolks, cream, nutmeg, and grated kefalotiri, regato, or Parmesan cheese. Spread half the pasta mixture over the base of the prepared dish and pour half the white sauce evenly over it. Cover with the remaining pasta mixture and pour the remaining white sauce evenly over the top. Smooth the surface and bake for about 40 minutes, or until the top is golden brown. Let stand for 10 minutes before serving.

Serves 6
Preparation time 40 minutes (including standing)
Cooking time 50 minutes

- salt and pepper
- 2 tablespoons olive oil
- 14 oz (400 g) wide pasta tubes such as ziti, large macaroni, or penne
- 4 tablespoons melted butter, plus extra for brushing
- 2 tablespoons fine bread crumbs
- 9 oz (250 g) feta cheese, crumbled
- generous 2 cups (250 g / 9 oz) grated kaseri or Gruyère cheese
- ½ teaspoon ground allspice
- 2 tablespoons finely chopped fresh mint (optional)
- 2 eggs, separated
- 3 cups (750 ml / 1¼ pints) light White sauce (p 57)
- ½ cup (120 ml / 4 fl oz) heavy (double) cream
- pinch of grated nutmeg
- ¾ cup (80 g / 3 oz) grated kefalotiri, regato, or Parmesan cheese

- 2 eggplants (aubergines), diced
- 2 zucchini (courgettes), cut in half lengthwise and sliced
- ½ cup (120 ml / 4 fl oz) olive oil
- 1 onion, grated
- 2 garlic cloves, finely chopped
- 12 oz (350 g) orzo pasta
- 1 celery stalk, thinly sliced
- 2 carrots, thinly sliced
- salt and pepper
- 2¼ lb (1 kg) tomatoes, peeled, seeded, and chopped
- 2 cups (450 ml / 16 fl oz) hot water
- ½ cup (50 g / 2 oz) grated kefalotiri or Parmesan cheese

ORZO WITH VEGETABLES
ΓΙΟΥΒΕΤΣΙ ΜΕ ΛΑΧΑΝΙΚΑ
Giouvetsi me lahanika

Sprinkle the eggplants and zucchini with salt and let drain in separate colanders for 1 hour. Rinse and squeeze out the excess water. Preheat the oven to 350°F (180°C / Gas Mark 4). Heat half the olive oil in a large pan over high heat. Add the onion and garlic and cook, stirring frequently, for 3–4 minutes, until softened. Add the eggplants and zucchini, reduce the heat to medium, and cook, stirring occasionally, for about 8 minutes, until lightly browned. Heat the remaining oil in another pan. Add the pasta and cook over medium heat, stirring constantly, for 2–3 minutes. Transfer to an ovenproof dish, add the zucchini, eggplants, celery, and carrots, and season with salt and pepper. Add the tomatoes and pour in the hot water. Bake, adding more hot water if necessary, for 1 hour, until the pasta is tender. Serve hot, sprinkled with the grated cheese.

Serves 4
Preparation time 1½ hours (including salting)
Cooking time 1 hour

Note: For a better texture, you can also fry the eggplants and zucchini in hot oil, drain on paper towels, and add to the dish 15 minutes before the end of the cooking time.

☐ p 278

- 1 cup (120 g / 4 oz) polenta or fine cornmeal
- 1½ teaspoons salt
- 3 tablespoons olive oil
- 6 tablespoons clarified butter
- 1 onion, finely chopped
- ½ cup (50 g / 2 oz) grated kefalotiri or Parmesan cheese

POLENTA FROM ASIA MINOR
ΚΑΤΣΑΜΑΚΙ Η ΜΑΛΑΚΙ
Katsamaki i malaki

Put the polenta and salt into a pan, pour in 4 cups water and the oil, and mix well. Cook over medium heat, stirring constantly with a wooden spoon, until it thickens and begins to come away from the side of the pan. Remove from the heat. Melt the butter in a small skillet or frying pan. Add the onion and cook over low heat, stirring occasionally, for 10 minutes, until softened and golden. Dip a tablespoon in the onion-butter mixture to grease it, then scoop out a heaping (heaped) spoonful of the polenta with a circular motion, and arrange the little mounds on a platter. Pour the onion-butter sauce over them, sprinkle with the grated cheese, and serve immediately.

Serves 4
Preparation time 10 minutes
Cooking time 30 minutes

Orzo with vegetables, p 277

Halloumi ravioli from Cyprus, p 280

HALLOUMI RAVIOLI FROM CYPRUS
ΡΑΒΙΟΛΕΣ ΜΕ ΧΑΛΟΥΜΙ
Ravioles me haloumi

Sift together the flour and salt into a bowl. Add the egg, oil, and 2–3 tablespoons water and knead, gradually adding as much water as necessary to form a firm dough. Gather into a ball, cover with a damp dish towel, and let rest for 30 minutes. Meanwhile, prepare the filling. Combine the cheese and mint in a bowl. Add enough beaten egg to make a stiff mixture. Roll pieces of the mixture into short rods, then cut off 1-inch (2.5-cm) pieces. Divide the dough into 6 pieces and keep them covered with a damp dish towel until required. Roll out a piece on a lightly work surface into a thin sheet. Put pieces of the cheese mixture in rows spaced 2 inches (5 cm) apart on the surface. Using a pastry brush, dampen the spaces around the filling. Roll out a second sheet of dough to the same size as the first, place it over the filling, and press with your fingers to expel the air and seal. Cut the ravioli into rounds or squares and transfer to a floured cloth. Make more ravioli with the remaining dough and filling in the same way. (You can store it uncooked in the refrigerator for 1 week and in the freezer for up to 3 months.) Bring the chicken stock to a boil in a large pan. Add the ravioli, bring back to a boil, and cook for about 8 minutes, or until al dente. Using a slotted spoon, transfer the ravioli to a platter, drizzle with the hot melted butter, and sprinkle with grated cheese. Serve immediately.

Serves 4
Preparation time 1 hour (including resting)
Cooking time 10 minutes

□ p 279

- 2 cups (225 g / 8 oz) strong white bread flour, plus extra for dusting
- ¼ teaspoon salt
- 1 egg
- 2 tablespoons olive oil
- 6¼ cups (1.5 litres / 2½ pints) chicken stock
- 5 tablespoons melted clarified butter
- grated halloumi or provolone cheese, for sprinkling

FOR THE FILLING
- 2¼ cups (250 g / 9 oz) grated halloumi or provolone cheese
- 2 tablespoons chopped fresh mint or 1 teaspoon dried mint
- 2 eggs, lightly beaten

SOUR TRAHANA
ΤΡΑΧΑΝΑΣ ΞΥΝΟΣ
Trahanas xinos

Pour the milk in a large ceramic bowl, add the yogurt and salt, and mix well with a wooden spoon. Place a thick dish towel on top, cover with a thick blanket, and let stand in a warm place, stirring occasionally with a wooden spoon, for 18 hours. Gradually stir in the semolina or bulgur wheat mixture to form a thick dough. Break the dough into rough walnut-sized pieces and put them on a thick cotton cloth in a single layer. Let stand in a dark, well-ventilated place for 2–6 hours, or until dry and crumbly. Rub through a coarse strainer, then spread out on a thick cotton cloth, and leave in a cool place for 4–5 days, until completely dry. Store in a cotton bag hanging in a cool place or in the refrigerator.

Makes 3¼ lb (1.5 kg)
Preparation time 6 days (including standing and drying)

- 3¼ cups (800 ml / 1½ pints) sheep's milk
- ½ cup (120 ml / 4 fl oz) plain yogurt
- 1 tablespoon salt
- 8¾ cups (1.5 kg / 3¼ lb) coarse semolina, or half semolina and half bulgur wheat

SWEET TRAHANA
ΓΛΥΚΟΣ ΤΡΑΧΑΝΑΣ
Glikos trahanas

- 3¼ cups (800 ml / 1½ pints) milk
- 1 tablespoon salt
- 8¾ cups (1.5 kg / 3¼ lb) semolina, or half semolina and half bulgur wheat

Bring the milk to a boil in a pan, stirring constantly. Add the salt, reduce the heat, and gradually add the semolina or semolina and bulgur wheat mixture, stirring constantly with a wooden spoon for 10–15 minutes, until very thick. Remove from the heat, cover with a thick cotton towel, and let cool. Break the dough into small, rough pieces and put them on a thick cotton cloth in a single layer. Let stand in a dark, well-ventilated place for about 2 hours, until dry and crumbly. Rub the pieces through a coarse strainer, then spread out on a thick cotton cloth, and leave in a cool place for 4–5 days, until completely dry. Store in a cotton bag hanging in a cool place or in the refrigerator.

Makes 3¼ lb (1.5 kg)
Preparation time 5½ days (including cooling and drying)

🖿 p 282

TAGLIATELLE WITH CREAMED SQUASH
ΤΑΛΙΑΤΕΛΕΣ ΜΕ ΚΡΕΜΑ ΚΟΛΟΚΥΘΙ
Taliateles me krema kolokithi

- 4 tablespoons clarified butter, melted
- 2 leeks, thinly sliced
- 2¼ lb (1 kg) yellow winter squash, peeled, seeded, and diced
- salt and pepper
- 1½ cups (350 ml / 12 fl oz) milk
- pinch of grated nutmeg
- 2 tablespoons olive oil
- 1 lb 2 oz (500 g) tagliatelle pasta
- 4 tablespoons toasted pine nuts

Heat the butter in a pan. Add the leeks and cook over medium-low heat, stirring occasionally, for 5 minutes, until softened. Add the squash, season with salt and pepper, and simmer for 10 minutes. Stir in the milk and when it comes to a boil, reduce the heat, and cook for 10 minutes more, or until the squash is tender. Remove from the heat, add the nutmeg, and let cool slightly. Put the mixture into a food processor and process until smooth. Meanwhile, bring a large pan of water to a boil, stir in salt and the oil, add the tagliatelle, and cook for 8–10 minutes, until al dente. Drain, divide the tagliatelle among bowls, and top with the creamed squash and pine nuts. Sprinkle with plenty of pepper and serve.

Serves 4
Preparation time 15 minutes
Cooking time 30 minutes

Sweet trahana, p 281

stuffed pasta from Asia Minor, p 287

THE PASHA'S MACARONI DISH FROM KOS
ΠΑΣΑ ΜΑΚΑΡΟΥΝΑ
Pasha makarouna

Pasha makarouna, a rich pasta dish that resembles pastitsio, has its roots in the era of Turkish rule in Greece. It is prepared for weddings, engagement parties, and other special occasions. The name says it all, for it is expensive and time-consuming to make, a splendid dish fit for a *pasha*, a high-ranking Turkish official.

Lightly beat the eggs with 2 tablespoons of the oil and the butter in a bowl. Sift together the flour and salt into another bowl, then gradually mix the flour mixture into the egg mixture and knead to form a smooth, firm dough. Divide it into 10 pieces, cover with plastic wrap (cling film), and let rest for several hours. Ideally, prepare the dough the night before it is required. Roll out the dough on a lightly floured work surface into very thin sheets or use a pasta machine. Cut into wide strips, roughly 2 x 6 inches (5 x 15 cm), and place on dish towels. When all the pasta strips have been prepared, bring a large pan of water to a boil. Stir in salt and the remaining oil, add the pasta, a few pieces at a time, and cook for 5–7 minutes. Using a slotted spoon, transfer them to a bowl of cold water, then lift them out, and put on dish towels to dry.

To prepare the filling, melt the butter in a pan. Add the onion and cook over low heat, stirring occasionally, for 5 minutes, until softened. Add the ground beef, allspice, and cinnamon, season with salt and pepper, and cook, stirring frequently and breaking up the meat with a spoon, for 8–10 minutes, until the meat is lightly browned. Simmer gently until the pan juices have been evaporated. Meanwhile, preheat the oven to 350°F (180°C / Gas Mark 4) and brush a 10 x 14-inch (25 x 35-cm) ovenproof dish with oil. Cover the base of the prepared dish with a layer of pasta strips and sprinkle with about 4 tablespoons of the grated cheese. Make another layer of pasta sheets, sprinkle with cheese, and cover with some of the meat mixture. Continue layering the pasta sheets, cheese, and meat until you have 12–14 layers, ending with a layer of grated cheese. Cut into squares with a sharp knife, brush the top with the melted clarified butter, and bake for 1 hour, until lightly golden. Remove from the oven, carefully pour in the stock, return to the oven, and bake for 15–20 minutes more. There should be some cooking juices left in the base of the dish. Let rest for 10–15 minutes before serving.

Serves 8
Preparation time 5 hours (including resting)
Cooking time 1½ hours

- 4 eggs
- 4 tablespoons olive oil, plus extra for brushing
- 1 tablespoon melted butter
- 3½ cups (400 g / 14 oz) all-purpose (plain) flour
- 1 teaspoon salt
- 4 cups (450 g / 1 lb) grated dried mizithra, Parmesan, or other hard cheese
- 4 tablespoons melted clarified butter
- 3 cups (750 ml / 1¼ pints) beef stock

FOR THE FILLING
- ½ cup (120 g / 4 oz) butter
- 1 large onion, grated
- 2¼ lb (1 kg) ground (minced) beef
- ¼ teaspoon ground allspice
- pinch of ground cinnamon
- salt and pepper

- 2¼ lb (1 kg) squid, cleaned (see p 325)
- 7 tablespoons olive oil
- 6 garlic cloves, thinly sliced
- 5 tablespoons dry white wine
- 2 teaspoons fresh thyme leaves
- 1 small radicchio
- ½ cup (4) finely chopped scallions (spring onions)
- salt and pepper
- 1 lb 2 oz (500 g) farfalle pasta

PASTA WITH GARLIC SQUID
ΜΑΚΑΡΟΝΙΑ ΜΕ ΣΚΟΡΔΑΤΑ ΚΑΛΑΜΑΡΙΑ
Makaronia me skordata kalamaria

Cut the body sacs of the squid into ¾-inch (1.5-cm) rings. Leave the tentacles whole. Heat 5 tablespoons of the oil in a pan. Add the garlic and cook over low heat, stirring frequently, for about 2 minutes. Increase the heat to high, add the squid, and fry for 1 minute. Pour in the wine, add the thyme, cover, and simmer for about 50 minutes, or until the squid is tender and the sauce has thickened. Reserve 6 radicchio leaves for the garnish and finely shred the remainder. Add the scallions and shredded radicchio to the pan, season with salt and pepper, and cook over medium heat until the radicchio and scallions are tender. Meanwhile, bring a large pan of water to a boil, stir in salt and the remaining oil, add the pasta, and cook for 8–10 minutes, or until al dente. Drain the pasta and toss with the squid sauce. Spoon the mixture into the reserved radicchio leaves and serve sprinkled with pepper.

Serves 6
Preparation time 20 minutes
Cooking time 1 hour

- 2¼ lb (1 kg) boneless pork shoulder
- 1 small onion, halved
- 10 black peppercorns
- 10 allspice berries
- 1 cup (175 g / 6 oz) bulgur wheat
- ½ cup (120 ml / 4 fl oz) olive oil or melted clarified butter, plus extra for brushing
- salt and pepper
- 4–5 sheets of homemade or commercial phyllo dough (filo pastry)

STUFFED PASTA POUCHES
ΜΑΝΤΟΥΔΙΑ
Mantoudia

Put the meat, onion, peppercorns, allspice berries, and a pinch of salt into a pan, pour in 6¼ cups (1.5 litres / 2½ pints) water, and bring to a boil. Reduce the heat and simmer for about 1 hour, or until tender. Remove the meat with a slotted spoon and chop finely. Reserve the stock. Bring 2 cups (450 ml / 16 fl oz) of the reserved stock to a boil in a pan, stir in the bulgur wheat and oil or clarified butter, season with salt and pepper, and simmer for 10 minutes. Remove from the heat and stir in the chopped meat. Cover and set aside for about 1 hour, until the stock has been absorbed. Preheat the oven to 350°F (180°C / Gas Mark 4) and brush 2 cookie sheets (baking trays) with oil or butter. Spread the phyllo dough on a work surface and cut into 3-inch (7.5-cm) squares. Place a teaspoon of meat filling in the center of each square, moisten the edges and press them together to form small pouches. Put the *mantoudia* on the prepared baking trays, brush with oil or melted butter, and bake for about 30 minutes, until golden. Remove from the oven, pour the reserved stock over the *mantoudia*, and bake for 30 minutes more, or until all the stock has been absorbed. Serve hot.

Serves 10
Preparation time 2½ hours (including standing)
Cooking time 1 hour

STUFFED PASTA BAKED IN TOMATO SAUCE FROM LIMNOS
ΒΑΛΑΝΕΣ ΓΕΜΙΣΤΕΣ
Valanes gemistes

To make the dough, sift together the flour, semolina, and salt into a bowl and make a well in the center. Add the egg and milk and gradually mix with the dry ingredients, kneading until the dough is firm and no longer sticky. Gather into a ball, cover with a damp dish towel, and let rest for 1 hour. Meanwhile, prepare the filling. Heat the oil in a pan. Add the beef, pork, onion, and garlic and cook over low heat, stirring frequently and breaking up the ground meat with a spoon, for 8–10 minutes, until the meat is lightly browned. Pour in the wine, add the tomatoes, and season with salt and pepper. Simmer for about 20 minutes, or until thickened. Remove from the heat and let cool slightly, then stir in the egg and cheese. To make the sauce, heat the oil in a pan. Add the garlic and cook over a low heat, stirring frequently, for 1–2 minutes. Pour in 1 cup (250 ml / 8 fl oz) water, add the tomatoes and tomato paste, cover, and bring to a boil. Add the herbs and season with salt and pepper. Re-cover the pan, reduce the heat, and simmer for 15–20 minutes. Meanwhile, preheat the oven to 350°F (180°C / Gas Mark 4), grease an ovenproof dish with butter, and pour in the milk. Divide the dough into 3 pieces and roll out each piece to a thick sheet on a work surface dusted with cornstarch. Cut each sheet into 4-inch (10-cm) squares. Put 2–3 tablespoons of the filling in the center of each square, moisten the edges, and pinch them together to form pouches. Put the pouches into the prepared dish, side by side, and pour the sauce over them. Cover with aluminum foil and bake for 1 hour. Remove the foil and sprinkle the top of the dish with the cheese. Bake for 10 minutes more, or until the cheese has melted and become golden. Serve hot.

Serves 4
Preparation time 1½ hours (including resting)
Cooking time 2¼ hours

FOR THE DOUGH
- 2¼ cups (250 g / 9 oz) all-purpose (plain) flour
- 2½ tablespoons fine semolina
- ¼ teaspoon salt
- 1 egg, lightly beaten
- ½ cup (120 ml / 4 fl oz) milk
- 2–3 tablespoons cornstarch (cornflour)

FOR THE FILLING
- 4 tablespoons olive oil
- 4 oz (120 g) ground (minced) beef
- 4 oz (120 g) ground (minced) pork
- 1 small onion, grated
- 1 garlic clove, finely chopped
- 4 tablespoons dry white wine
- ½ cup (130 g / 4½ oz) canned chopped tomatoes
- salt and pepper
- 1 egg, lightly beaten
- ½ cup (50 g / 2 oz) grated Gruyère cheese

FOR THE SAUCE
- 5 tablespoons olive oil
- 1 garlic clove, thinly sliced
- 7 oz (200 g) canned chopped tomatoes
- 1½ teaspoons tomato paste
- 2 tablespoons finely chopped fresh parsley
- 2 tablespoons finely chopped fresh basil
- salt and pepper

TO FINISH
- butter, for greasing
- 4 tablespoons milk
- ½ cup (50 g / 2 oz) grated kefalograviera, regato or pecorino cheese

- 4½ cups (500 g / 1 lb 2 oz) all-purpose (plain) flour
- 1 teaspoon salt
- 2 eggs, lightly beaten
- 1 cup (250 g / 8 oz) butter
- 8¾ cups (2 litres / 3½ pints) beef stock
- 1 cup (250 ml / 8 fl oz) sheep's milk yogurt
- 1 garlic clove, crushed

FOR THE FILLING
- 1 lb 2 oz (500 g) ground (minced) beef
- 1 large onion, grated
- 2 tablespoons finely chopped fresh parsley (optional)
- salt and pepper

STUFFED PASTA FROM ASIA MINOR
MANTI
Manti

The *manti* of Asia Minor is a dish consisting of tiny pieces of pasta dough filled with meat or other fillings. The dough is cut and folded in various shapes—the smaller they are, the more skilled the cook—and is often made for celebrations.

To make the dough, sift together the flour and salt into a bowl, make a well in the center, and add the beaten eggs. Gradually mix in the dry ingredients, adding a little water at a time—no more than ½ cup (120 ml / 4 fl oz)—to make a smooth, firm dough that comes away from your fingers. Shape it into a ball, cover with plastic wrap (cling film), and let rest for 30 minutes. Meanwhile, make the filling. Combine the ground meat, onion, and parsley, in a bowl and season with salt and pepper. Using a pasta machine, roll out strips of dough very thinly. Alternatively, roll out by hand on a lightly floured work surface. Cut the strips into 1-inch (2.5-cm) squares. Place a small piece of filling, about the size of a hazelnut, in the center of each square. Moisten the edges with water and fold the opposite corners of the squares over the filling and press to seal them. Melt half the butter in a heavy skillet or frying pan and fry the *manti*, until golden. Bring the stock to a boil in a pan, add the *manti*, and cook for 15 minutes, until tender. Meanwhile, melt the remaining butter in a small pan. Drain the *manti*, transfer to a deep platter, and pour the melted butter over them. Whisk together the yogurt and garlic in a bowl. Serve the pasta immediately with the garlic yogurt. Alternatively, you could place the *manti* in a greased ovenproof dish, pour the melted butter over the top, and bake in an oven preheated to 350°F (180°C / Gas Mark 4), until lightly browned. Pour the stock over them and cover with aluminum foil. Reduce the heat to 300°F (150°C / Gas Mark 2) and bake, adding more stock if necessary, until tender.

Serves 6
Preparation time 1½ hours
Cooking time 15 minutes

□ p 283

RIGATONI WITH MEATBALLS AND EGGPLANTS (AUBERGINES)
ΡΙΓΚΑΤΟΝΙ ΜΕ ΚΕΦΤΕΔΑΚΙΑ
Rigatoni me keftedakia

Place the eggplant cubes in a colander, sprinkle with salt, and let drain for 1 hour. Combine the ground meat, 2 tablespoons of the olive oil, the garlic, herbs, egg, and bread crumbs in a bowl and season with salt and pepper. Knead to a light and pliable mixture, occasionally moistening your hands with water. Shape the mixture into small round balls. Heat 6 tablespoons of the remaining olive oil in a skillet or frying pan. Add the meatballs and cook over medium heat until lightly browned all over. Remove with a slotted spoon and drain on paper towels. Strain the oil, return it to the skillet, and reheat. Add the tomatoes, sugar, and vinegar and cook over medium heat for 10–15 minutes, until thickened. Rinse the eggplants and squeeze out the excess liquid. Heat the vegetable oil in a deep-fryer to 350–375°F (180–190°C / Gas Mark 4–5). Add the eggplant cubes and deep-fry until golden brown. Alternatively, heat the oil in a skillet or frying pan and shallow fry for 8–10 minutes until golden brown. Drain on paper towels. Add the eggplants and meatballs to the sauce and cook, stirring constantly, for a few minutes to heat through. Meanwhile, bring a large pan of water to a boil, stir in salt and the remaining olive oil, add the pasta, and cook for 8–10 minutes, or until al dente. Drain and tip onto a shallow platter, spoon the meatball sauce on top, and sprinkle with the grated cheese. Serve immediately.

Serves 4
Preparation time 1½ hours (including salting)
Cooking time 1 hour

- 2 large eggplants (aubergines), cut into small cubes
- 7 oz (200 g) ground (minced) beef
- 7 oz (200 g) ground (minced) pork
- ⅔ cup (150 ml / ¼ pint) olive oil
- 2 garlic cloves, finely chopped
- 2 tablespoons finely chopped fresh basil
- 1 tablespoon finely chopped fresh marjoram or mint
- 1 egg, lightly beaten
- 1 tablespoon dried bread crumbs
- salt and pepper
- 2¼ lb (1 kg) tomatoes, peeled, seeded, and puréed
- ½ teaspoon sugar
- 1 tablespoon red wine vinegar
- vegetable oil, for deep-frying
- 11 oz (300 g) rigatoni pasta
- ½ cup (50 g / 2 oz) grated mild kefalotiri or Parmesan cheese

PASTA WITH MEAT SAUCE
ΜΑΚΑΡΟΝΙΑ ΜΕ ΚΙΜΑ
Makaronia me kima

Heat 5 tablespoons of the oil in a large pan. Add the onion and garlic and cook over low heat, stirring occasionally, for 5 minutes, until softened. Add the ground beef and cook, stirring frequently and breaking it up with a spoon, for about 15 minutes. Add the allspice, tomatoes, vinegar, sugar, and parsley, season with salt and pepper, cover, and simmer for about 1 hour. Meanwhile, bring a large pan of water to a boil, stir in salt and the remaining oil, add the pasta, and cook for 8–10 minutes, or until al dente. Drain and serve immediately, topped with the hot meat sauce and sprinkled with grated cheese.

Serves 4
Preparation time 15 minutes
Cooking time 1¼ hours

- 7 tablespoons olive oil
- 1 onion, grated
- 2 garlic cloves, finely chopped
- 1 lb 2 oz (500 g) ground (minced) beef
- ¼ teaspoon ground allspice or 5 allspice berries
- 2 cups (450 ml / 16 fl oz) puréed peeled fresh or canned tomatoes
- 1 tablespoon red wine vinegar
- 1 teaspoon sugar
- 3 tablespoons finely chopped fresh parsley
- salt and pepper
- 1 lb 2 oz (500 g) spaghetti or other long pasta
- grated dried mizithra, kefalotiri, or Parmesan cheese, for sprinkling

- 1 lb 5 oz (600 g) country sausages, thickly sliced
- 14 oz (400 g) canned chopped tomatoes
- 1 tablespoon tomato paste
- ½ teaspoon sugar
- 6 tablespoons olive oil
- 1 lb 5 oz (600 g) mixed bell peppers, seeded and cut in strips
- 1 large onion, sliced
- 1 lb 2 oz (500 g) ready-made egg noodles (pasta) or Homemade egg noodles (pasta), p 270
- ½ cup (50 g /2 oz) grated mild kefalotiri or regato, or Parmesan cheese

SAUSAGES WITH BELL PEPPERS AND EGG NOODLES (PASTA)
ΛΟΥΚΑΝΙΚΑ ΜΕ ΠΙΠΕΡΙΕΣ ΚΑΙ ΧΥΛΟΠΙΤΕΣ
Loukanika me piperies ke hilopites

Cook the sausages over medium-low heat in a nonstick skillet or frying pan, turning occasionally, for 8–10 minutes, until they are lightly browned and have released their fat. Remove and drain on paper towels. Drain off and discard the fat and reheat the skillet. Add the tomatoes, tomato paste, and sugar. Cover and simmer for 15 minutes, until thickened. Heat 4 tablespoons of the oil in another skillet or frying pan. Stir in the bell peppers and onion, cover, and cook over low heat, stirring occasionally, for about 15 minutes, until light golden brown. Meanwhile, bring 3 cups (750 ml / 1¼ pints) water to a boil in a large pan, stir in salt and the remaining oil, add the noodles, and cook for 8–10 minutes, or until the noodles are al dente. Transfer the noodles to a platter and cover first with the bell peppers, and then the sausages and sauce. Sprinkle with the grated cheese and serve immediately.

Serves 4
Preparation time 10 minutes
Cooking time 30 minutes

- 7 tablespoons olive oil
- 1 onion, finely chopped
- 2 garlic cloves, crushed
- 1 fresh red chile, seeded and finely chopped
- 6 canned anchovy fillets in oil, drained and chopped
- 14 oz (400 g) canned chopped tomatoes
- 2 ripe tomatoes, peeled, seeded, and chopped
- 2 tablespoons pitted (stoned) and chopped Kalamata olives
- 1 tablespoon capers
- 1 tablespoon finely chopped fresh or 1 teaspoon dried oregano
- 12 oz (350 g) spaghetti or linguine
- salt and pepper
- grated kefalotiri or Parmesan cheese, for sprinkling

SPAGHETTI WITH ANCHOVY SAUCE
ΣΠΑΓΚΕΤΙ ΜΕ ΣΑΛΤΣΑ ΑΝΤΖΟΥΓΙΑΣ
Spageti me saltsa antzougias

Heat 5 tablespoons of the oil in a large pan. Add the onion, garlic, and chile and cook over low heat, stirring occasionally, for 5 minutes, until softened. Add the anchovies and stir for 1 minute. Add the canned and fresh tomatoes, olives, capers, and oregano. Cover and simmer for 5–10 minutes, until thickened. Meanwhile, bring a large pan of water to a boil, stir in salt and the remaining oil, add the pasta, and cook for 8–10 minutes, or until al dente. Drain the pasta, add it to the pan of sauce, and stir gently. Serve immediately on warm plates, sprinkled with pepper and grated cheese.

Serves 4
Preparation time 10 minutes
Cooking time 15 minutes

FISH

-

ΨΑΡΙ

-

Psari

Fish has been an essential part of Greek cuisine since the start of Hellenic civilization, and Greek art and literature are rich in references to the importance of fish and shellfish in everyday life. The National Archaeological Museum of Athens has a magnificent 1500 BC fresco of a young fisherman holding his catch of fish, and there are many vase paintings depicting fish being caught, transported, sold, and prepared for cooking. Aristotle also recorded the habits, habitats, life cycles, and diseases of Aegean marine life in his *History of Animals*. At about the same time, special terracotta plates for serving fish became popular in southern Italy and Athens. They were decorated with illustrations of fish and other sea creatures around the edges and had wells in the center to hold the dipping sauce.

In ancient Greece, fresh fish was as popular as it was expensive, and the fish merchants were the cleverest tradesmen in the Athenian *agora*, or market. Keeping fish fresh without refrigeration or even ice in the hot weather must have been a tremendous challenge. In an early version of consumer rights protection, regulations were introduced that forbade wetting the fish with cold water. In *The Deipnosophists*, Athenaeus preserved for posterity sixty-two fragments from Europe's oldest cook-book, *The Life of Luxury*, by Sicilian poet-gourmand Archestratos in the fourth century BC. These extracts, written in verse, record fascinating details about Greek cuisine and gastronomy in antiquity. Archestratos appears to have confined his advice almost exclusively to fish, although there are several references to bread, wine, and desserts. He recommends which fish are best, where and when to procure them, and even gives cooking tips. His instructions for tuna are to slice it and bake it, sprinkle it lightly with salt, and brush it with oil, while for conger eel he recommends boiling it in salt water, then sprinkling it with green herbs.

The presence of luxury fish on ancient Greek tables served to demonstrate the status and wealth of the host, much as caviar does today. However, good-quality fresh fish are becoming increasingly scarce and more expensive in modern Greece as a result of over-fishing and pollution of the Aegean and the eastern Mediterranean. Although imports of frozen fish and shellfish have increased, Greeks still consider their local waters the source of the finest fish. While this may seem biased, the high concentration of salts and minerals in certain areas of the Mediterranean Sea might explain why its fish are considered tastier. In Greece, good fresh fish are available at large supermarkets, local fish stores, and the weekly *laiki* (farmers' market), as well as the fish stalls of the central market in Athens. There are also large markets near Piraeus at the *icthyoscala* (the harbor where the fishing vessels unload their catch) and in Rafina where the ferryboats leave for Evvoia. In northern Greece, try the covered market in Thessaloniki and the port of Kavala. You can also buy directly from the fishermen's *caique*, but be sure to get there at the crack of dawn for the pick of the catch. Many local tavernas will clean and broil (grill) your fish for you, particularly if you are a regular customer.

Greek recipes for fresh fish almost always leave the head intact—most Greek cooks wouldn't dream of cooking a fish without its head. The cheeks and other parts of the head are also savored as delicacies. However, the fish must be absolutely fresh, and it is at its best simply broiled (grilled) or poached and served with *ladolemono*—oil-lemon dressing with chopped fresh parsley or other herbs such as oregano. Smelt, pilchard, and other small fry are delicious floured and fried whole in hot olive oil, while baking with tomatoes, herbs, and wine lends a new dimension to humble fish like anchovies and sardines. There are also several recipes in which the fish is baked and left to marinate in the tangy vinegar sauce known as *savore*. Many fish can also be braised in tomato sauce, either on the stove top (hob) or in the oven.

GENERAL INSTRUCTIONS

With fish, the relationship between price and quality is not always directly proportional. As a rule, fish that are in season and therefore available in large quantities are less expensive. Since fish is more perishable than meat or poultry, you must be sure that it is absolutely fresh. When you buy whole fish, look for red gills, bright eyes, and shiny scales. The flesh should be soft but springy. Fresh fish has a clean, pleasant smell of seawater. If you buy fish fillets or steaks, look for translucent rather than milky flesh. Fillets with dried edges and traces of discoloration will be stale.

Whole fish should be scaled and cleaned before cooking, and you can ask your fish store (fishmonger) to do this for you. To clean the fish yourself, slit the belly with a sharp knife from the head to the bottom fin and remove all the innards. You can trim off the fins, but leave the head and tail intact. Rinse well under cold running water to remove any traces of blood, and pat dry with paper towels. Sprinkle it with a little freshly squeezed lemon juice and store it, covered, in the refrigerator. Fish and shellfish will stay fresh for no more than a day.

Like meat, fish and shellfish can be broiled (grilled), baked, stewed, fried, and poached. As the flesh of fish is more delicate than meat, it requires relatively brief cooking. The cooking time will depend on its size and the level of heat. Larger fish need a longer time and lower temperatures; smaller fish need less time and higher temperatures. There is nothing less appetizing than an overcooked, dried-out fish. Grilling over charcoal is a good way to cook most fish, and it can be first be marinated or brushed with lemon juice, olive oil, and herbs. In general, strong-flavored herbs should be avoided, but rosemary or oregano, for example, are good with oily fish such as mackerel, bonito, or tuna. Slash the fish lengthwise along the backbone on both sides before you marinate so that the flavors penetrate the flesh. Serve it dressed with plain oil-lemon sauce and finely chopped fresh parsley. Small fish, such as anchovies, sardines, and smelts, are best suited to deep-frying. They should be dredged in flour or rolled in bread crumbs and cooked briefly in very hot oil. The coating protects it from drying out by sealing in the juices. Large fish are also delicious poached or steamed in a court-bouillon or vegetable stock, which gives a special aroma to the fish. Fish and shellfish suitable for poaching are sole, trout, cod, grouper, salmon, lobster, shrimp (prawns), mussels, and crab. The poaching liquid should be kept below a simmer; the surface should tremble but never bubble. When poaching large fish, start it in cold liquid so that the flesh cooks evenly. Finally, any fish can be cooked in the oven, and oily fish are ideal for baking with onions, plenty of parsley, and olive oil. As a general rule, all fish baked in the oven should be covered with vegetables, aluminum foil, or liquid to protect their flesh from direct heat. To test whether a fish is cooked, place the tip of a knife on the thickest part of the back, just behind the gills. The flesh should separate from the bone easily. It will also have changed color from translucent to opaque.

Salt cod should be soaked in cold water for at least 48 hours in three or four changes of water to restore its plumpness, tenderness, and white color. You can shorten the soaking time by cutting the fish into pieces and removing the skin before you put it into the water. After soaking, cut the fish into serving portions and remove the skin. The fish is now ready to be poached, fried, baked, or stewed.

BAKED ANCHOVIES
ΓΑΥΡΟΣ ΣΤΟ ΦΟΥΡΝΟ
Gavros sto fourno

Pinch the head of an anchovy between your thumb and forefinger and pull it off—the guts should come away with it. Pinch all along the top edge of the fish and pull out the backbone—it should come away easily. Repeat with the remaining anchovies. If using other small fish, scale them by running one hand from tail to head, holding the fish by the tail under cold running water. Alternatively, put them into cold water to cover and rub them to remove the scales. Cut off and discard the heads. To remove the guts, gently squeeze the belly, hold down the guts with a knife as they are exposed, and pull them out. Rinse the fish thoroughly and drain well. Preheat the oven to 400°F (200°C / Gas Mark 6). Heat the oil in a pan. Add the onions and garlic and cook over low heat for 5 minutes, until softened. Remove from the heat, add the parsley, and season with salt and pepper. Combine the tomato paste and wine in a bowl and add to the pan. Place the fish in two rows in an ovenproof dish with some of the sauce and the lemon slices in between. Pour the remaining sauce over the fish and top with the tomato slices. Season with salt and pepper and drizzle with a little olive oil. Bake for 1 hour, or until the sauce has reduced. Serve hot or at room temperature.

Serves 4
Preparation time 40 minutes
Cooking time 1 hour

☐ p 296

- 3¼ lb (1.5 kg) anchovies, sardines, or other small fish
- ⅔ cup (150 ml / ¼ pint) olive oil, plus extra for drizzling
- 4 large onions, sliced
- 6 garlic cloves, thinly sliced
- 2 cups (120 g / 4 oz) chopped fresh parsley
- salt and pepper
- 2 tablespoons tomato paste
- 4 tablespoons dry white wine
- 3 thin lemon slices, rind removed
- 2 large ripe tomatoes, thinly sliced

- 4 tablespoons olive oil, plus extra for brushing
- 1 bonito or tuna, about 3¼ lb (1.5 kg), cleaned
- 2 tablespoons freshly squeezed lemon juice
- 2 garlic cloves, finely chopped
- pinch of dried oregano
- salt and pepper
- Cooked beet (beetroot) salad with garlic yogurt (p 184), or cooked greens, to serve

BONITO BAKED IN A PARCEL
ΠΑΛΑΜΙΔΑ ΣΤΟ ΛΑΔΟΧΑΡΤΟ
Palamida sto ladoharto

Preheat the oven to 425°F (220°C / Gas Mark 7) and brush a large roasting pan with oil. Cut out three layers of wax (greaseproof) paper or aluminum foil large enough to enclose the fish completely and place the fish on top. Put the oil, lemon juice, garlic, and oregano into a screw-top jar, season with pepper, fasten the lid, and shake vigorously until thoroughly combined. Rub the fish inside and out with the mixture. Wrap the fish in the wax paper or foil, securing the ends with kitchen string. Place in the roasting pan and brush the paper or foil with a little oil. Bake for 10 minutes, then reduce the temperature to 375°F (190°C / Gas Mark 5), and bake for 35–40 minutes more, or until the fish is tender. Serve the fish hot with Cooked beet (beetroot) salad or cooked greens.

Serves 4
Preparation time 15 minutes
Cooking time 45 minutes

- 1 bonito or tuna, about 2¼ lb (1 kg), scaled, cleaned and cut into slices
- salt and pepper
- 1 lb 2 oz (500 g) young fava (broad) beans
- 4–5 scallions (spring onions), finely chopped
- ½ cup (15 g / ½ oz) chopped fresh dill or fennel fronds
- ½ cup (120 ml / 4 fl oz) olive oil
- 4 tablespoons freshly squeezed lemon juice

BONITO BAKED WITH FAVA (BROAD) BEANS
ΠΑΛΑΜΙΔΑ ΣΤΟ ΦΟΥΡΝΟ ΜΕ ΦΡΕΣΚΑ ΚΟΥΚΙΑ
Palamida sto fourno me freska koukia

Wash the slices of fish well to remove any trace of blood, sprinkle with salt and pepper, and let stand for 30 minutes. Meanwhile, preheat the oven to 350°F (180°C / Gas Mark 4). Trim the tips of the fava bean pods. If some are tough, shell the beans and discard the pods. Combine the fava beans with half the scallions and half the dill or fennel fronds and spread them out in a roasting pan or ovenproof dish. Season with salt and pepper and drizzle with half the oil. Place the fish slices on top, sprinkle with the remaining scallions and remaining herbs, and drizzle with the rest of the oil. Bake for 15–20 minutes, then remove from the oven, carefully stir the beans, and turn over the fish slices. Return to the oven and bake for 15–20 minutes more. Remove from the oven, drizzle with lemon juice, and serve hot or at room temperature.

Serves 4
Preparation time 40 minutes (including standing)
Cooking time 30–40 minutes

Note: You can substitute thickly sliced eel for the bonito or tuna, and dried fava beans for the fresh ones. If using dried beans, soak them overnight in cold water to cover and shell them before cooking, and simmer until tender before proceeding.

Baked anchovies, p 294

Gilt-head sea bream baked in parcels, p 298

297

GILT-HEAD SEA BREAM BAKED IN PARCELS
ΤΣΙΠΟΥΡΕΣ ΣΤΗ ΛΑΔΟΚΟΛΑ

Tsipoures sti ladokola

Remove any pin bones from the fish with tweezers, season with salt and pepper, brush with oil, and chill for 30 minutes. Meanwhile, cook the potatoes in salted boiling water for 10 minutes. Heat 2½ tablespoons of the oil in a pan. Add the fennel, carrot, celery, and zucchini and cook over high heat, stirring frequently, for 5 minutes. Pour in half the wine and let the alcohol evaporate, then cover and simmer for 10 minutes, or until the vegetables are almost tender. Add the dill, season with salt and pepper, and remove from the heat. Heat 2½ tablespoons of the remaining oil in a nonstick skillet or frying pan. Cook the fish fillets, skin side down, in batches for a few minutes until lightly browned. Preheat the oven to 400°F (200°C / Gas Mark 6). Cut 4 pieces of wax (greaseproof) paper into 12 x 16-inch (30 x 40-cm) rectangles. Make a bed of potato slices in the center of each rectangle. Spread one quarter of the vegetables on top of the potatoes and top with the fish, skin side down. Place a tomato slice and a rosemary sprig on each fish. Sprinkle 1 tablespoon each of olive oil and wine over each, and season with salt and pepper. Fold the sides over the fish and twist the edges to seal. Place in a roasting pan and bake for 15 minutes. Serve in the parcels.

Serves 4
Preparation time 45 minutes (including chilling)
Cooking time 45 minutes

☐ p 297

- ○ 2 gilt-head sea bream or porgy, about 1 lb 10 oz (750 g) each, scaled, cleaned and filleted
- ○ salt and pepper
- ○ generous ½ cup (135 ml / 4½ fl oz) olive oil, plus extra for brushing
- ○ 2 potatoes, sliced into rounds
- ○ 1 small fennel bulb, sliced
- ○ 1 carrot, sliced
- ○ 1 celery stalk with leaves, chopped
- ○ 1 zucchini (courgette), sliced
- ○ 1 cup (250 ml / 8 fl oz) dry white wine
- ○ 2 tablespoons finely chopped fresh dill
- ○ 1 large tomato, sliced into rounds
- ○ 4 fresh rosemary sprigs

BROILED (GRILLED) GILT-HEAD SEA BREAM
ΤΣΙΠΟΥΡΑ ΨΗΤΗ

Tsipoura psiti

Preheat the broiler (grill) or light the barbecue and brush a hinged wire rack with oil. Rinse the fish thoroughly under cold running water, drain well and season with salt and pepper. If the fish are thick, make a slash on each side along the spine. Rub inside and out with the olive oil. Place the fish in the prepared rack, close securely, and cook under the broiler or grill over charcoal, brushing occasionally with a little oil, for about 10 minutes on each side. Transfer the fish to a warm platter or individual plates and pour the oil-lemon dressing over them. Garnish with finely chopped fresh parsley and serve with steamed vegetables.

Serves 4
Preparation time 15 minutes
Cooking time 20 minutes

☐ p 300

- ○ ½ cup (120 ml / 4 fl oz) olive oil, plus extra for brushing
- ○ 4 gilt-head sea bream or porgy, 11 oz (300 g) each, scaled and cleaned
- ○ salt and pepper
- ○ Oil-lemon dressing (p 57) and steamed vegetables, to serve
- ○ finely chopped fresh parsley, to garnish

- 4 red bream, porgy or other white fish fillets, about 6 oz (175 g) each
- all-purpose (plain) flour, for coating
- 2 tablespoons olive oil
- baby spinach or lettuce leaves, to serve
- lemon slices, to garnish

FOR THE SAUCE
- generous 1 cup (130 g / 4½ oz) Kalamata olives, pitted (stoned) and finely chopped
- 4 tablespoons olive oil
- 2 tablespoons freshly squeezed lemon juice
- 1 garlic clove, finely chopped
- 1 small dried red chile, crushed
- salt and pepper

RED BREAM WITH OIL-LEMON SAUCE AND OLIVES
ΛΙΘΡΙΝΙ ΜΕ ΛΑΔΟΛΕΜΟΝΟ ΚΑΙ ΕΛΙΕΣ
Lithrini me ladolemono ke elies

To make the sauce, put all the ingredients into a screw-top jar, season with salt and pepper, fasten the lid, and shake vigorously until thoroughly blended. Remove any pin bones from the fish fillets with tweezers. Season with salt and pepper and coat with flour, shaking off any excess. Heat the oil in a heavy, nonstick skillet or frying pan. Add 2 of the fillets and cook for 4 minutes on each side, until golden. Remove with a slotted spatula (fish slice) and keep warm while you cook the remaining fillets in the same way. Meanwhile, toss the spinach or lettuce with some of the sauce and divide it among individual plates. Place a fish fillet on each bed of spinach or lettuce, drizzle with the remaining sauce, and serve immediately, garnished with lemon slices.

Serves 4
Preparation time 20 minutes
Cooking time 20 minutes

- 2¼ lb (1 kg) cod or other white fish fillets, skinned and cut into small pieces
- 1¼ cups (80 g / 3 oz) bread crumbs made from day-old bread
- 1 large onion, grated
- 4 garlic cloves, finely chopped
- 2 eggs, lightly beaten
- 1 large tomato, peeled, seeded, and grated
- 1 teaspoon dried oregano
- 4 tablespoons finely chopped fresh mint, basil or parsley
- 1 teaspoon Worcestershire sauce
- 2 tablespoons olive oil
- salt and pepper
- all-purpose (plain) flour
- 2–4 tablespoons olive or corn oil, for frying
- Garlic sauce (p 153), to serve

COD CROQUETTES
ΚΡΟΚΕΤΕΣ ΜΠΑΚΑΛΙΑΡΟΥ
Kroketes bakaliarou

Combine the fish, bread crumbs, onion, garlic, eggs, tomato, oregano, mint, Worcestershire sauce, and 2 tablespoons olive oil in a bowl and season with salt and pepper. Gradually mix in enough flour to make a soft, thick consistency. Heat the olive or corn oil in a skillet or frying pan. Drop spoonfuls of the fish mixture into the pan and cook over medium heat for 5–8 minutes on each side, turning once, until golden brown on both sides. Serve with Garlic sauce.

Serves 4
Preparation time 30 minutes
Cooking time 30 minutes

Broiled (grilled) gilt-head sea bream, p 298

Braised salt cod with onions, p 302

BRAISED SALT COD WITH ONIONS
ΜΠΑΚΑΛΙΑΡΟΣ ΠΑΣΤΟΣ ΓΙΑΧΝΙ
Bakaliaros pastos giahni

- 2¼ lb (1 kg) salt cod
- all-purpose (plain) flour, for coating
- ⅔ cup (150 ml / ¼ pint) olive oil
- 2¼ lb (1 kg) onions, thinly sliced
- 2–3 garlic cloves
- 2¼ lb (1 kg) tomatoes, peeled, seeded, and puréed
- 1 tablespoon red wine vinegar
- pinch of cayenne pepper
- pepper

Skin the fish and cut the flesh into 3-inch (7.5-cm) pieces. Rinse off any loose salt under cold running water, then put into a bowl, pour in water to cover, and let soak in the refrigerator, changing the water several times, for 20–24 hours. Drain the fish and remove and discard the bones. Pat dry and coat the fish with flour. Heat the oil in a heavy pan. Add the fish and cook over high heat for 5 minutes, or until lightly browned on both sides. Remove with a slotted spoon and set aside. Add the onions and garlic to the pan, lower the heat, and cook, stirring occasionally, for 5 minutes, until softened. Stir in the tomatoes, vinegar, and cayenne and season with pepper. Simmer for 40 minutes, until thickened. Return the fish to the pan and simmer for 15 minutes more, until the pan juices have reduced. It is equally good served hot or cold.

Serves 4
Preparation time 20¼–24¼ hours (including soaking)
Cooking time 1 hour

Note: Half the onions can be replaced with seeded, thinly sliced green bell peppers.

🖵 p 301

SALT COD BAKED WITH GREENS
ΜΠΑΚΑΛΙΑΡΟΣ ΜΕ ΧΟΡΤΑ
Bakaliaros me horta

- 2¼ lb (1 kg) salt cod, soaked in several changes of cold water for 48 hours and drained
- 1 lb 2 oz (500 g) spinach, coarse stalks removed
- 1 lb 2 oz (500 g) assorted greens, such as chard, amaranth, or fennel, coarse stalks removed
- 1 cup (250 ml / 8 fl oz) olive oil
- ½ cup (4) finely chopped scallions (spring onions)
- 4 tablespoons finely chopped fresh dill
- 6 garlic cloves, thinly sliced
- 14 oz (400 g) canned chopped tomatoes
- salt and pepper

Skin the cod and rinse under cold running water. Put it into a pan, pour in water to cover, and cook for 10 minutes. Drain well, remove the bones, and cut into serving pieces. Blanch the spinach and greens in a pan of boiling water for 2 minutes, drain well, and chop. Heat half the oil in a skillet or frying pan. Add the scallions and cook over low heat, stirring occasionally, for 5 minutes, until softened. Combine the onions, spinach, and greens in a bowl, add the dill, and spread the mixture over the base of an ovenproof dish. Put the pieces of cod on top. Preheat the oven to 350°F (180°C / Gas Mark 4). Heat the remaining oil in a small pan. Add the garlic and cook over low heat, stirring frequently, for 1–2 minutes. Add the tomatoes and season with salt and pepper. Simmer for 10 minutes, until the sauce starts to thicken, then remove from the heat, and spoon it over the cod and greens. Bake for 1 hour, until the sauce is thick and glossy. Serve immediately.

Serves 4
Preparation time 48½ hours (including soaking)
Cooking time 1 hour

- 2¼ lb (1 kg) salt cod
- 5–6 potatoes, quartered
- 5 garlic cloves, thinly sliced
- 1 large onion, grated
- 1 cup (250 ml / 8 fl oz) olive oil
- 1 teaspoon dried oregano
- salt and pepper
- 5 tablespoons freshly squeezed lemon juice
- finely chopped fresh parsley, to garnish

SALT COD LEFKADA-STYLE
ΜΠΑΚΑΛΙΑΡΟΣ ΓΙΑΧΝΙ ΛΕΥΚΑΔΑΣ
Bakaliaros giahni lefkadas

Remove and discard the skin from the cod and cut the flesh into serving pieces. Put them into a bowl, pour in water to cover, and let soak in the refrigerator, changing the water 3–4 times, for 20–24 hours. Drain and put into a large flameproof casserole with the potatoes, garlic, onion, half the oil, and the oregano, and pour in water to cover. Season with pepper and, if necessary, a pinch of salt. Cover and simmer for 30 minutes, or until the cod and potatoes are tender and the pan juices have reduced. Beat the remaining oil with the lemon juice and pour it over the fish, shaking the pan to distribute the sauce evenly. Bring back to a boil, remove from the heat, season with pepper, and sprinkle with parsley. Serve immediately.

Serves 4
Preparation time 20¼–24¼ hours (including soaking)
Cooking time 30 minutes

- 2¼ lb (1 kg) salt cod
- 1 large potato, boiled
- 4 tablespoons red wine vinegar
- 3 garlic cloves, finely chopped
- 1 cup (250 ml / 8 fl oz) olive oil
- all-purpose (plain) flour, for dusting
- 1 tablespoon tomato paste
- ½ teaspoon sugar
- salt and pepper

SALT COD SANTORINI-STYLE
ΜΠΡΑΝΤΑΔΑ ΜΠΑΚΑΛΙΑΡΟΥ
Bradada bakaliarou

Divide the cod into serving pieces, remove and discard the skin, and put into a bowl. Pour in water to cover and let soak in the refrigerator, changing the water 3–4 times, for 20–24 hours. Put the potato, vinegar, and garlic into a food processor and process to a purée. With the motor running, gradually add 5 tablespoons of the olive oil through the feeder tube, until smooth. Drain the cod and remove as many bones as possible. Pat the pieces dry with paper towels and coat with flour, shaking off any excess. Heat 5 tablespoons of the remaining oil in a skillet or frying pan. Add the pieces of cod and cook for about 8 minutes, until golden on both sides. Remove with a slotted spoon and drain on paper towels. Preheat the oven to 350°F (180°C / Gas Mark 4). Mix the tomato paste with 1 cup (250 ml / 8 fl oz) water in a bowl. Heat the remaining oil, stir in the tomato paste mixture, add the sugar, and season with pepper and salt, if necessary. Simmer the tomato sauce for 8 minutes, then gradually stir in the garlic sauce, and cook, stirring constantly, until smooth and creamy. Put the fried cod in a shallow ovenproof dish and pour the garlic-tomato sauce over. Bake for 10–15 minutes. Serve immediately.

Serves 6
Preparation time 20–24 hours (including soaking)
Cooking time 30 minutes

SALT COD WITH CURRANTS
ΜΠΑΚΑΛΙΑΡΟΣ ΜΕ ΣΤΑΦΙΔΕΣ
Bakaliaros me stafides

- 3¼ lb (1.5 kg) salt cod
- 1 lb 2 oz (500 g) potatoes, peeled and cubed
- 11 oz (300 g) onions, thinly sliced
- 14 oz (400 g) can tomato juice
- 2 cloves garlic, finely chopped
- 2 tablespoons finely chopped fresh parsley
- 4 tablespoons dry white wine
- 1 cup (160 g / 5½ oz) currants
- salt and pepper
- 1 cup (250 ml / 8 fl oz) olive oil

Rinse the salt cod and remove the skin. Cut into serving pieces and place in a bowl of cold water to cover. Soak the fish for 20–24 hours, changing the water 3 or 4 times. Preheat the oven to 350°F (180°C / Gas Mark 4). Drain the fish in a colander, pressing out any excess water, and remove and discard the bones. Put the potatoes and other ingredients, except the oil, in a roasting pan, and mix well. Put the fish pieces on top and pour the oil over them. Bake in the oven for about 1 hour, or until the potatoes and fish are tender and the liquid has reduced. Serve hot.

Serves 6
Preparation time 20 hours (including soaking)
Cooking time 1 hour

FISH STEW FROM CORFU
ΜΠΟΥΡΔΕΤΟ
Bourdeto

- 3¼ lb (1.5 kg) mixed fish, such as scorpion fish, snapper, and perch, scaled and cleaned
- freshly squeezed juice of 1 lemon
- sea salt and pepper
- 1 lb 2 oz (500 g) onions, finely chopped
- 3–4 garlic cloves, finely chopped
- 2 bay leaves
- 1 teaspoon dried thyme
- 1 teaspoon dried rosemary
- 1 cup (250 ml / 8 fl oz) dry white wine
- 1–2 teaspoons cayenne pepper
- 2 tablespoons tomato paste mixed with 4 tablespoons freshly squeezed lemon juice (optional)
- ¾ cup (175 ml / 6 fl oz) olive oil

This is a Corfiot specialty, and the name is a corruption of the Venetian *brodetto* (soup). More stew than soup, it relies on simple, fine-quality ingredients. The more varied the fish is, the more delicious the dish. The Corfiots like to add plenty of paprika or cayenne pepper as well as several grindings of black pepper.

Sprinkle the fish with lemon juice and sea salt and set aside for 1 hour. Drain and place in a shallow, wide pan. Add the onions, garlic, bay leaves, thyme, rosemary, and wine. Sprinkle with plenty of cayenne and black pepper. Add the tomato paste mixture, if using, and the oil. Bring to a boil, cover, and simmer for 40 minutes, until the cooking liquid has reduced and the fish flakes easily. Serve immediately.

Serves 6
Preparation time 1¼ hours (including marinating)
Cooking time 40 minutes

□ p 306

FISH ROLLED IN GRAPE (VINE) LEAVES
ΨΑΡΙ ΣΕ ΚΛΗΜΑΤΟΦΥΛΛΑ
Psari se klimatofila

- 1 lb 2 oz (500 g) young grape (vine) leaves
- ½ cup (120 ml / 4 fl oz) olive oil
- 1 leek, white part only, finely chopped
- ½ cup (4) finely chopped scallions (spring onions)
- 1 onion, grated
- 1 large carrot, grated
- 4 tablespoons finely chopped fresh dill
- 4 tablespoons finely chopped fresh parsley
- salt and pepper
- 2¼ lb (1 kg) monkfish or grouper fillets, skinned and cut into 1¼ x 2½-inch (3 x 6-cm) pieces
- 1 cup (250 ml / 8 fl oz) boiling water
- 2 egg whites
- 4 tablespoons freshly squeezed lemon juice

Rinse the grape leaves and trim off the stems, if necessary. Blanch them a few at a time, then drain and let cool. Line the base of a wide pan with the coarse or broken grape leaves. Heat half the oil in a small pan. Add the leek, scallions, grated onion, and carrot and cook over low heat, stirring occasionally, for 5–8 minutes, until softened. Stir in the herbs and season with salt and pepper. Spread out a grape leaf, place a piece of fish and 2 tablespoons of the vegetable mixture at the stem end, season with pepper, and roll up. Prepare more rolls in the same way. Place them, seam side down, on the base of the pan. Pour in the remaining olive oil and invert a plate over the stuffed grape leaves to prevent them from unraveling. Pour in the boiling water and simmer for 35 minutes, or until the grape leaves are tender and the pan juices have reduced. Beat the egg whites with the lemon juice in a bowl, then stir in several spoonfuls of the hot pan juices. Pour the egg and lemon mixture over the rolls and shake the pan to distribute evenly. Serve immediately.

Serves 4
Preparation time 50 minutes
Cooking time 35 minutes

GROUPER WITH OKRA FROM CRETE
ΡΟΦΟΣ ΝΕ ΜΠΑΜΙΕΣ ΣΤΟ ΦΟΥΡΝΟ
Rofos me bamies sto fourno

- 1 lb 2 oz (500 g) fresh okra
- 1 tablespoon red wine vinegar or freshly squeezed lemon juice
- 1 grouper or other firm-fleshed white fish such as sea bass or bream, 3¼ lb (1.5 kg), scaled and cleaned
- salt and pepper
- 1 teaspoon dried thyme
- 1 teaspoon dried oregano
- ⅔ cup (150 ml / ¼ pint) olive oil, plus extra for brushing
- 1 lb 2 oz (500 g) potatoes, thickly sliced
- 1 onion, finely chopped
- ½ cup (5) finely chopped scallions (spring onions)
- 3 garlic cloves, thinly sliced
- 2¼ lb (1 kg) tomatoes, peeled, seeded, and finely chopped or 14 oz (400 g) canned chopped tomatoes
- ½ cup (120 ml / 4 fl oz) dry white wine

Cut the stems off the okra without piercing the pods. Dip the cut ends into salt and let drain in a colander for 30 minutes. Rinse well in water mixed with the vinegar or lemon juice. Rinse the fish and pat dry. Season with salt and pepper, sprinkle with half the thyme and oregano, and set aside for 30 minutes. Preheat the oven to 350°F (180°C / Gas Mark 4) and brush a roasting pan with oil. Arrange the potatoes in the middle of the pan in slightly overlapping concentric circles. Season with salt and pepper and drizzle with a little oil. Make 2–3 slashes on each side of the fish and place on top of the potatoes. Combine the okra, onion, scallions, and garlic in a bowl and sprinkle the mixture around the fish, then sprinkle with the remaining thyme and oregano. Spoon the tomatoes over the fish and okra and pour in the wine and remaining oil. Cover with aluminum foil and bake for 30–45 minutes. Remove the foil and bake for 10–15 minutes more, or until tender. Serve hot.

Serves 4
Preparation time 1 hour (including salting and marinating)
Cooking time 1 hour

▢ p 307

Fish stew from Corfu, p 304

grouper with okra from Crete, p 305

FISH-STUFFED LETTUCE LEAVES

ΜΑΡΟΥΛΟΝΤΟΛΜΑΔΕΣ ΨΑΡΙΟΥ

Maroulodolmades psariou

Put the bulgur wheat into a bowl, pour in the tomato juice, and let soak for 1 hour. Pour the wine and 1 cup (250 ml / 8 fl oz) water into a wide, nonstick pan and bring to a boil. Add the salmon and cod and cook for 5 minutes. Remove from the heat, lift out the fish, and strain and reserve the cooking liquid. Let the fish cool slightly, then skin, and chop. Return the cooking liquid to the pan, add the leeks and zucchini, and simmer until the vegetables are tender and most of the liquid has evaporated. Add half the oil, the lemon zest, onion, and parsley, season with salt and pepper, and cook for 5 minutes. Remove the pan from the heat. Drain the bulgur, add it to the pan, together with the fish, and mix gently. Steam the lettuce leaves for 1–2 minutes until softened, and pat dry. Place 1–2 leaves on the base of a wide, shallow pan and cut the rest into 2–3 pieces, depending on their size. Place 2 tablespoons of filling at the base of each piece of leaf and roll up, folding in the sides as you go. Arrange them in the pan, seam side down, in tight-fitting rows. Sprinkle with the sugar and lemon juice and pour in the remaining oil and the hot water. Invert a plate over the lettuce rolls to prevent them from unraveling, cover, and simmer for about 20 minutes, until tender. Transfer the rolls to a platter and make the sauce: Pass the cooking liquid through a fine strainer and mix with the yogurt to make a smooth, creamy sauce. Pour the sauce over the rolls and serve immediately.

Serves 4
Preparation time 1 hour
Cooking time 20 minutes

- ½ cup (80 g / 3 oz) bulgur wheat
- 1 cup (250 ml / 8 fl oz) tomato juice
- ½ cup (120 ml / 4 fl oz) dry white wine
- 11 oz (300 g) salmon fillet
- 1 lb 2 oz (500 g) cod fillet
- 2 leeks, white and tender green parts, finely chopped
- 2 zucchini (courgettes), grated
- ⅔ cup (150 ml / ¼ pint) olive oil
- 1 teaspoon grated lemon zest
- 1 onion, grated
- 5 tablespoons finely chopped fresh parsley
- salt and pepper
- 20–30 large romaine lettuce leaves
- ½ teaspoon sugar
- 3 tablespoons freshly squeezed lemon juice
- 1 cup (250 ml / 8 fl oz) hot water
- 2 tablespoons strained plain or thick Greek yogurt

MARINATED MACKEREL

ΣΚΟΥΜΠΡΙΑ ΜΑΡΙΝΑΤΑ

Skoubria marinata

Rinse the fish and pat dry. Season with salt and pepper and coat with flour, shaking off any excess. Pour oil into a skillet or frying pan to a depth of ¾ inch (1.5 cm) and heat. Add the mackerel and cook for 5–7 minutes on each side, or until the flesh flakes easily. Remove from the skillet and keep warm. Transfer 2 tablespoons of the oil to a pan and heat. Stir in the 2 tablespoons flour and cook, stirring constantly, for a few minutes, until lightly browned. Stir in the garlic, vinegar, tomatoes, sugar, bay leaf, and rosemary, season with salt and pepper, and simmer for about 15 minutes, until thickened. Pour the sauce over the fried fish, sprinkle with parsley or mint, and serve hot or at room temperature.

Serves 4
Preparation time 15 minutes
Cooking time 30 minutes

- 4 mackerel, about 2¼ lb (1 kg), scaled and cleaned
- salt and pepper
- 2 tablespoons all-purpose (plain) flour, plus extra for coating
- olive oil, for frying
- 2 garlic cloves, finely chopped
- 3 tablespoons red wine vinegar
- 2¼ lb (1 kg) tomatoes, pulped and strained
- ½ teaspoon sugar
- 1 bay leaf
- ½ teaspoon dried rosemary
- finely chopped fresh parsley or mint, to garnish

MACKEREL WITH CAPERS FROM SYROS
ΣΚΟΥΜΠΡΙΑ ΜΕ ΚΑΠΑΡΗ
Skoubria me kapari

- 4 large mackerel, about 2½ lb (1.2 kg), scaled and cleaned
- salt and pepper
- all-purpose (plain) flour, for coating
- ¾ cup (150 ml / ¼ pint) olive oil
- 1 cup (150 g / 5 oz) capers in brine
- 1 onion, finely chopped
- 1–2 garlic cloves, thinly sliced
- 1 lb 2 oz (500 g) tomatoes, peeled and puréed or 14 oz (400 g) canned tomatoes, puréed
- pinch of cayenne pepper
- ½ teaspoon sugar

Rinse the fish and pat dry with paper towels. Season with salt and pepper and coat with flour, shaking off the excess. Heat half the oil in a skillet or frying pan. Add the mackerel and cook for a few minutes on each side until lightly browned. Transfer to an ovenproof dish. Rinse the capers, and soak them in cold water for 10 minutes. Drain and pat dry with paper towels. Preheat the oven to 350°F (180°C / Gas Mark 4). Reserve 2 tablespoons of the oil and heat the remainder in a pan over medium heat. Add the onion and garlic and cook, stirring occasionally, for 4–5 minutes, until softened. Add the tomatoes, cayenne, sugar, and ½ cup (120 ml / 4 fl oz) water, season with pepper, and bring to a boil. Add half the capers and simmer for 10 minutes. Pour the sauce over the fish and bake for 30–40 minutes, or until the sauce has reduced. Meanwhile, heat the reserved oil in a small skillet. Add the remaining capers and cook, stirring frequently, for about 5 minutes. Sprinkle the fried capers over the fish and serve immediately.

Serves 4
Preparation time 30 minutes (including soaking)
Cooking time 30–40 minutes

MACKEREL BAKED WITH EGGPLANTS (AUBERGINES) FROM PONTUS
ΚΟΛΙΟΣ ΜΕ ΜΕΛΙΤΖΑΝΕΣ ΣΤΟ ΦΟΥΡΝΟ
Kolios me melitzanes sto fourno

- 3¼ lb (1.5 kg) eggplants (aubergines), diced
- ½ cup (120 ml / 4 fl oz) olive oil, plus extra for brushing
- 1 onion, finely chopped
- 3 garlic cloves, thinly sliced
- 2¼ lb (1 kg) tomatoes, peeled, seeded, and finely chopped or 14 oz (400 g) canned chopped tomatoes
- ½ teaspoon sugar
- 1 tablespoon red wine vinegar
- salt and pepper
- ½ cup (25 g / 1 oz) finely chopped fresh parsley
- 2 tablespoons finely chopped fresh basil
- 4 mackerel, about 2¼ lb (1 kg), scaled and cleaned

Sprinkle the eggplants with salt and let drain in a colander for 1 hour. Rinse and squeeze out the excess liquid. Heat half the oil in a skillet or frying pan. Add the eggplants and cook over medium heat, stirring frequently, for 5–8 minutes, until lightly browned. Remove with a slotted spoon and set aside. Heat the remaining oil in a pan. Add the onion and garlic and cook over low heat, stirring occasionally, for 5 minutes, until softened. Add the tomatoes, sugar, and vinegar, season with salt and pepper, and simmer for 15–20 minutes, until thickened. Meanwhile, preheat the oven to 350°F (180°C / Gas Mark 4). Remove the sauce from the heat and stir in the parsley and basil. Rinse the fish under cold running water and pat dry with paper towels. Season with salt and pepper, brush with a little olive oil, and place them in an ovenproof dish. Surround them with the eggplants, pour the sauce over the top, and bake, turning the fish once, for 30–40 minutes, or until the sauce has reduced and the fish flakes easily. Serve hot or at room temperature.

Serves 4
Preparation time 1¼ hours (including salting)
Cooking time 1½ hours

MONKFISH WITH POTATOES AND EGG-LEMON SAUCE
ΠΕΣΚΑΝΔΡΙΤΣΑ ΜΕ ΠΑΤΑΤΕΣ ΑΥΓΟΛΕΜΟΝΟ
Peskandritsa me patates avgolemono

- 5 tablespoons olive oil
- 20 black peppercorns
- 1 large onion, finely chopped
- 2¼ lb (1 kg) monkfish tails or grouper, scaled and cleaned
- 2¼ lb (1 kg) potatoes, cut into pieces
- 2 large carrots, thickly sliced
- 1 egg
- 5 tablespoons freshly squeezed lemon juice
- salt and pepper

Pour 1 cup (250 ml / 8 fl oz) water into a large pan, add the oil, peppercorns, and a pinch of salt, and bring to a boil. Add the onion, fish, potatoes, and carrots, cover, and simmer for 25 minutes, or until tender. Lightly beat the egg with the lemon juice in a small bowl and beat in a ladleful of the hot cooking liquid, then stir the mixture into the pan. Serve hot in soup plates with the hot broth, sprinkled with pepper.

Serves 4
Preparation time 35 minutes
Cooking time 30 minutes

MARINATED RED MULLET FROM CORFU
ΜΠΑΡΜΠΟΥΝΙΑ ΣΑΒΟΡΟ ΚΕΡΚΥΡΑΣ
Barbounia savoro kerkiras

- 3¼ lb (1.5 kg) small red mullet or snapper, scaled and cleaned
- salt and pepper
- 2 tablespoons all-purpose (plain) flour
- vegetable oil, for frying
- 1 cup (250 ml / 8 fl oz) tomato juice
- 3 cups (750 ml / 1¼ pints) olive oil
- 1 cup (250 ml / 8 fl oz) red wine vinegar
- 15 garlic cloves
- 1 tablespoon dried rosemary

This is a very old recipe that predates refrigerators by hundreds of years, as it keeps well in a cool place.

Rinse the fish under cold running water and pat dry with paper towels. Season with salt and pepper. Put the flour into a plastic bag, add the fish, a few at a time, and shake to coat. Transfer the fish to a colander and shake to remove excess flour. Heat the vegetable oil in a skillet or frying pan. Add the fish and cook for around 5 minutes on each side, or until cooked through. Remove from the skillet and let cool. Pour the tomato juice, olive oil, and vinegar into a pan, add the garlic and rosemary, season with salt, and simmer for 10–15 minutes, until the garlic has softened. Pour a little of the hot marinade into an earthenware bowl and make a layer of the fish, side by side. Pour in some more of the marinade and make a second layer of fish. Continue making layers in the same way until all the fish has been used. Pour in the remaining marinade to cover the fish. Let marinate in the refrigerator for at least 3–4 days. Covered with oil and stored in a cool place, fish prepared in this way will keep for several days, and the flavor continues to improve.

Serves 6
Preparation time 3–4 days (including marinating)
Cooking time 30 minutes

▢ p 312

- 2½ lb (1.2 kg) small red mullet or snapper, scaled and cleaned
- salt and pepper
- 1 cup (120 g / 4 oz) all-purpose (plain) flour
- olive oil, for frying

TO SERVE (OPTIONAL)
- lettuce leaves
- lemon slices
- radishes

FRIED RED MULLET
ΜΠΑΡΜΠΟΥΝΙΑ ΤΗΓΑΝΙΤΑ
Barbounia tiganita

Rinse the fish under cold running water and pat dry with paper towels. Season with salt and pepper. Put the flour into a plastic bag, add the fish, a few at a time, and shake to coat. Transfer the fish to a colander and shake to remove excess flour. Heat the oil in a skillet or frying pan. Add the fish and cook for 5–7 minutes on each side. Line a platter with lettuce leaves, top with the fish, garnish with lemon slices and radishes (if using), and serve immediately.

Serves 4
Preparation time 30 minutes
Cooking time 15 minutes

- 4 red mullet or snapper, 2¼ lb (1 kg) total weight, scaled and cleaned
- salt and pepper
- ½ cup (120 ml / 4 fl oz) olive oil, plus extra for brushing
- 5 garlic cloves, finely chopped
- ½ cup (25 g / 1 oz) finely chopped fresh parsley
- 5 oz (150 g) grape (vine) leaves, blanched
- 4 tablespoons freshly squeezed lemon juice
- 1 lemon, thinly sliced

RED MULLET BAKED IN GRAPE (VINE) LEAVES
ΜΠΑΡΜΠΟΥΝΙΑ ΤΥΛΙΧΤΑ ΣΕ ΚΛΗΜΑΤΟΦΥΛΛΑ
Barbounia tilihta se klimatofila

Rinse the fish under cold running water and pat dry with paper towels. Season with salt and pepper, brush with a little oil, and chill in the refrigerator for 30 minutes. Preheat the oven to 350°F (180°C / Gas Mark 4) and brush an ovenproof dish with oil. Combine the garlic and parsley in a bowl, season with salt and pepper, and divide the mixture among the cavities of the fish. Wrap each fish in 1 or 2 grape leaves, depending on its size, leaving the heads and tails uncovered. Put the fish into the prepared dish, pour the oil and lemon juice over them, and place a slice of lemon on each. Bake for about 20 minutes, or until the fish flakes easily, and serve immediately.

Serves 4
Preparation time 45 minutes (including chilling)
Cooking time 20 minutes

▢ p 313

Marinated red mullet from Corfu, p 310

red mullet baked in grape (vine) leaves, p 311

PERCH STIFADO
ΠΕΡΚΑ ΣΤΙΦΑΔΟ
Perka stifado

- 2¼ lb (1 kg) small pearl (pickling) onions or shallots, fresh or frozen
- ½ cup (120 ml / 4 fl oz) olive oil, plus extra for brushing
- 5 garlic cloves
- 5 tablespoons red wine
- 14 oz (400 g) canned chopped tomatoes
- 1 tablespoon tomato ketchup
- 2 bay leaves
- 6 allspice berries
- salt and pepper
- 2¼ lb (1 kg) perch fillets

Blanch the onions or shallots for 1 minute. Drain, let cool slightly, and peel off the skins. Heat the oil in a pan. Add the onions and garlic and cook over low heat, stirring occasionally, for about 8 minutes, until lightly browned. Pour in the wine, add the tomatoes, tomato ketchup, bay leaves, and allspice berries, season with salt and pepper, and bring to a boil. Cover and simmer, adding a little water if necessary, for about 1 hour, or until the onions are tender and the sauce has begun to thicken. Meanwhile preheat the oven to 350°F (180°C / Gas Mark 4) and brush an ovenproof dish with oil. Rinse the fish fillets, cut into serving portions, and place in the prepared dish. Spoon the onions and sauce over them, cover with aluminum foil, and bake for 15 minutes. Remove the foil and bake for 15 minutes more. Serve hot.

Serves 4
Preparation time 20 minutes
Cooking time 1½ hours

Vefa's secret: The sweet-and-sour flavor of tomato ketchup intensifies the flavor of fresh tomatoes. Tuna fillets make a good substitute for perch.

PERCH WITH EGGPLANTS (AUBERGINES)
ΠΕΡΚΑ ΜΕ ΜΕΛΙΤΖΑΝΕΣ
Perka me melitzanes

- 3 large eggplants (aubergines), 2 lb (900 g), cut into bite-size pieces
- 1 lb 2 oz (500 g) potatoes, sliced
- salt and pepper
- olive oil, for brushing
- 2 perch fillets, 1 lb 2 oz (500 g) each, or 4 smaller ones

FOR THE SAUCE
- 5 tablespoons olive oil
- 1 onion, grated
- 2 garlic cloves, thinly sliced
- 14 oz (400 g) fresh or canned tomatoes, finely chopped
- 1 tablespoon tomato ketchup
- 4 tablespoons finely chopped fresh basil or parsley
- salt and pepper

Preheat the broiler (grill). Season the eggplants and potatoes with a little salt and pepper, brush with oil, and spread out on a cookie sheet (baking tray). Broil (grill), turning frequently, for 8–10 minutes, until lightly golden on all sides. Preheat the oven to 350°F (180°C / Gas Mark 4). Meanwhile, make the sauce. Heat the oil in a pan. Add the onion and garlic and cook over low heat for 5 minutes, until softened. Add the tomatoes, tomato ketchup, and basil, season with salt and pepper, and simmer for 10 minutes, until slightly thickened. Spread several tablespoons of sauce over the base of an ovenproof dish. Put the potatoes and eggplants on top, pour the remaining sauce over them (reserving a few tablespoons), cover with aluminum foil, and bake for 45 minutes. Remove the dish from the oven, season the fish fillets with salt and pepper, and place them between the potatoes and eggplants. Spoon a few tablespoons of sauce over them and return to the oven. Bake, uncovered, for 20–30 minutes more, or until the fish is cooked, adding a little water if needed. Serve hot or at room temperature.

Serves 4
Preparation time 30 minutes
Cooking time 2 hours

- 5 tablespoons olive oil, plus extra for brushing
- 2 scallions (spring onions), finely chopped
- 1 small onion, grated
- 1 lb 2 oz (500 g) spinach, coarse stalks removed
- salt and pepper
- 2 tablespoons finely chopped fresh parsley
- 1 sea bass, about 2½ lb (1.2 kg), scaled and cleaned
- 4 tablespoons dry white wine

STUFFED SEA BASS
ΛΑΥΡΑΚΙ ΓΕΜΙΣΤΟ
Lavraki gemisto

Heat half the oil in a pan. Add the scallions and grated onion and cook over low heat, stirring occasionally, for 5 minutes, until softened. Meanwhile, chop the spinach. Add it to the pan, season with salt and pepper, increase the heat to medium, and cook, stirring constantly, for about 5 minutes, until wilted. Remove the pan from the heat and stir in the parsley. Preheat the oven to 400°F (200°C / Gas Mark 6). To remove the backbone of the fish, insert a sharp knife into the opening between the flesh and bones of the fish just below the gill cover. Release the top fillet from the skeleton by sliding the knife all the way down to the tail. Cut the backbone with scissors, leaving the two halves of the fish connected and the head and tail intact. Carefully detach the backbone from the second fillet and discard. Remove any pin bones with tweezers. Rinse the fish under cold running water to remove all traces of blood and pat dry with paper towels. Season the fish inside and out with salt and pepper, brush with oil, and put it on the base of an ovenproof dish. Fill the cavity with the spinach mixture and sprinkle the fish with the wine. Cover with aluminum foil and bake for 25–35 minutes, or until the flesh flakes easily. Remove from the oven and serve immediately.

Serves 4
Preparation time 25 minutes
Cooking time 45 minutes

- ½ cup (120 ml / 4 fl oz) olive oil, plus extra for brushing
- 2 small onions, thinly sliced into rings
- 4 sea bass fillets, about 9 oz (250 g) each
- salt and pepper
- 2 garlic cloves, sliced
- 2 tablespoons finely chopped fresh parsley
- 2 teaspoons fresh thyme
- 3 tomatoes, sliced
- 2 tablespoons tomato paste
- 1 large green, red, or yellow bell pepper, seeded and cut into strips
- 5 black Kalamata olives, pitted (stoned)
- 5 green olives, pitted (stoned)
- 4 tablespoons dry white wine

BAKED SEA BASS WITH OLIVES
ΛΑΥΡΑΚΙ ΜΕ ΕΛΙΕΣ
Lavraki me elies

Preheat the oven to 425°F (220°C / Gas Mark 7) and brush a large ovenproof dish with oil. Lightly rub the onion rings with salt until softened, rinse, and squeeze out excess water with your hands. Rinse the fish fillets under cold running water and pat dry with paper towels. Season with salt and pepper and brush with oil. Combine the onions, garlic, parsley, thyme, 2 of the sliced tomatoes, tomato paste, and bell pepper strips with a pinch each of salt and pepper in a bowl. Spread half the mixture on the base of the dish and lay the fish fillets over the top. Sprinkle the remaining vegetable mixture on top of the fish and sprinkle with the olives. Top with the remaining tomato slices and pour the wine and oil over them. Bake, basting 3–4 times with the pan juices, for 30–35 minutes. Serve hot.

Serves 4
Preparation time 40 minutes
Cooking time 30–35 minutes

RED SNAPPER, SPETSES-STYLE
ΣΥΝΑΓΡΙΔΑ ΑΛΑ ΣΠΕΤΣΙΩΤΑ
Sinagrida ala spetsiota

Rinse the fish thoroughly to remove all traces of blood and pat dry with paper towels. Make 3–4 parallel slashes on both sides of the fish with a sharp knife to ensure even cooking. Put the fish into an ovenproof dish and rub it all over with lemon juice, salt, and pepper. Pour half the oil over the fish, sprinkle with the flour, and set aside for 1 hour. Preheat the oven to 350°F (180°C / Gas Mark 4). Heat the remaining oil in a pan over high heat. Add the onion and garlic and cook, stirring frequently, for 3–4 minutes, until softened. Add the tomato juice, wine, and chopped parsley, and simmer for about 15 minutes, or until thickened. Pour the sauce over the fish and bake, occasionally basting with the pan juices, for about 1 hour.

Serves 6
Preparation time 1½ hours (including marinating)
Cooking time 1 hour

- 3¼ lb (1.5 kg) red snapper or other white fish, scaled and cleaned
- 4 tablespoons freshly squeezed lemon juice
- salt and pepper
- ½ cup (120 ml / 4 fl oz) olive oil
- 2 tablespoons all-purpose (plain) flour
- 1 onion, sliced
- 4 garlic cloves, thinly sliced
- 1 cup (250 ml / 8 fl oz) tomato juice
- ½ cup (120 ml / 4 fl oz) dry white wine
- 4 tablespoons finely chopped fresh parsley

RED SNAPPER STIFADO
ΦΑΓΚΡΙ ΣΤΙΦΑΔΟ
Fagri stifado

Rinse the fish under cold running water to remove all traces of blood and pat dry with paper towels. Cut into thick pieces, cover with plastic wrap (cling film), and chill in the refrigerator until required. If using fresh onions or shallots, blanch them for 1 minute, drain and let cool, and remove skins. If using frozen, thaw them in a colander, rinse with cold water, and drain well. Heat the oil over high heat in a wide pan. Add the onions and garlic and cook, stirring occasionally, for 3–5 minutes, until softened. Pour in the wine, add the tomatoes, bay leaves, and allspice berries, and season with salt and pepper. Cover and simmer for about 1 hour, or until tender. Add the fish and simmer for 20–30 minutes longer, until the fish is cooked through and the sauce has reduced. Serve hot.

Serves 4
Preparation time 1 hour
Cooking time 1½ hours

- 3¼ lb (1.5 kg) red snapper, scaled and cleaned
- 2¼ lb (1 kg) small pearl (pickling) onions or shallots, fresh or frozen
- ½ cup (120 ml / 4 fl oz) olive oil
- 6 garlic cloves
- ½ cup (120 ml / 4 fl oz) dry white wine
- 2 large tomatoes, peeled, seeded, and puréed
- 2 bay leaves
- 6 allspice berries
- salt and pepper

- ½ cup (120 ml / 4 fl oz) olive oil, plus extra for brushing
- 8 sole fillets, 3¼ lb (1.5 kg) total weight, skinned
- salt and pepper
- ½ teaspoon ground nutmeg
- 1 onion, grated
- 2 garlic cloves, finely chopped
- 3 scallions (spring onions), thinly sliced
- ½ cup (25 g / 1 oz) finely chopped fresh mint
- ½ cup (25 g / 1 oz) finely chopped fresh parsley
- 1 lb 2 oz (500 g) sorrel leaves or spinach, coarse stalks removed
- 2 small tomatoes, sliced

SOLE FILLET ROLLS STUFFED WITH HERBS
ΡΟΛΑ ΓΛΩΣΣΑΣ ΜΕ ΜΥΡΩΔΙΚΑ
Rola glosas me mirodika

Preheat the oven to 400°F (200°C / Gas Mark 6) and brush an ovenproof dish with oil. Season the fish fillets with salt and pepper and sprinkle with the nutmeg. Heat 2 tablespoons of the oil in a pan. Add the onion, garlic, and scallions and cook over low heat, stirring occasionally, for 5 minutes, until softened. Stir in the mint and parsley, season with salt and pepper, and remove from the heat. Briefly blanch the sorrel or spinach in boiling water and drain. Spread 1–2 tablespoons of the onion and herb mixture over each fish fillet and roll it up. Mix the remaining onion and herb mixture with the sorrel and spread out over the base of the prepared dish. Put the sole rolls on top. Place a tomato slice on top of each roll. Season with a little salt and pepper and drizzle the remaining oil all over the fish. Bake for 20 minutes, or until the vegetables and fish are tender. Serve hot.

Serves 4
Preparation time 30 minutes
Cooking time 20 minutes

- 4 swordfish steaks, 7 oz (200 g) each
- 4 tablespoons olive oil, plus extra for brushing
- salt and pepper
- 4 small tomatoes, peeled and thinly sliced
- ¼ cup (1–2) finely chopped scallions (spring onions)
- 4 tablespoons finely chopped fresh parsley
- 1 small green chile, thinly sliced
- 2 tablespoons freshly squeezed lemon juice
- lemon wedges, to garnish

BAKED SWORDFISH
ΞΙΦΙΑΣ ΣΤΟ ΦΟΥΡΝΟ
Xifias sto fourno

Preheat the oven to 400°F (200°C / Gas Mark 6). Brush the fish steaks with oil and season with salt and pepper. Cut 4 large pieces of aluminum foil or baking parchment, put a fish steak in the center of each, and divide the sliced tomatoes among them. Combine the scallions, parsley, and chile in a bowl and sprinkle the mixture over the tomatoes. Drizzle each portion with 1 tablespoon of the oil and ½ tablespoon of the lemon juice. Fold over the foil or paper to enclose the fish, place the parcels on a cookie sheet (baking tray), and bake for 15–20 minutes. Serve immediately, garnished with lemon wedges.

Serves 4
Preparation time 15 minutes
Cooking time 20 minutes

Note: Sautéed green (French) beans go well with this dish. Steam them first, then drain and sauté in hot melted butter. Season with salt and pepper and add chopped fresh parsley and lemon juice before serving.

SWORDFISH SOUVLAKI

ΞΙΦΙΑΣ ΣΟΥΒΛΑΚΙ
Xifias souvlaki

Preheat the broiler (grill) or light the barbecue. Rinse the fish, pat dry with paper towels, and cut into bite-size pieces. Thread the fish onto the skewers, alternating with pieces of onion, bell pepper, and tomato. If you like, put 1–2 small pieces of chile on each skewer. Season with salt and pepper and brush all over with oil. Cook under the broiler or grill over charcoal for about 8 minutes on each side. Check regularly to avoid overcooking. Remove from the heat and put the skewers on a platter. Put the lemon juice and extra olive oil in a screw-top jar, fasten the lid, shake vigorously until thoroughly combined, and pour the dressing over the skewers. Serve immediately with broiled vegetables.

Serves 4
Preparation time 40 minutes
Cooking time 15–20 minutes

- 2¼ lb (1 kg) swordfish, monkfish, or grouper fillets, skinned
- 1 large onion, cut into 1-inch (2.5-cm) dice
- 1 large green bell pepper, seeded and cut into 1-inch (2.5-cm) squares
- 2 large tomatoes, cut into 1-inch (2.5-cm) dice or 6–8 cherry tomatoes, halved
- 1–2 chiles (optional), cut into pieces
- salt and pepper
- 5 tablespoons olive oil, plus extra for brushing
- 4 tablespoons freshly squeezed lemon juice
- broiled (grilled) vegetables, to serve

SWORDFISH WITH VEGETABLES

ΞΙΦΙΑΣ ΜΕ ΛΑΧΑΝΙΚΑ
Xifias me lahanika

Preheat the broiler (grill). Heat 3 tablespoons of the oil in a heavy pan. Add the celery, onion, garlic, and bell pepper and cook over low heat, stirring occasionally, for 5–7 minutes, until softened. Add the tomatoes, herbs, sugar, cayenne, and half the lemon juice, season with salt and pepper, and cook, stirring constantly, for 10–15 minutes, or until the vegetables are tender and glossy. Remove the vegetables from the heat and keep warm. Meanwhile, brush the swordfish fillets with the remaining oil and remaining lemon juice, season lightly with salt and pepper, and broil (grill) for 4–6 minutes on each side. Alternatively, fry the fish on both sides in a nonstick skillet or frying pan. Serve hot, topping each fillet with 3–4 tablespoons of the vegetables.

Serves 4
Preparation time 20 minutes
Cooking time 30 minutes

- 5 tablespoons olive oil
- 5 tablespoons chopped celery
- 1 onion, chopped
- 1 garlic clove, finely chopped
- 4 tablespoons seeded and chopped red bell pepper
- 5 oz (150 g) tomatoes, chopped
- ¼ teaspoon dried oregano
- ½ teaspoon dried rosemary or 2 tablespoons chopped fresh cilantro (coriander) or basil
- ¼ teaspoon dried thyme
- ¼ teaspoon sugar
- ¼ teaspoon cayenne pepper
- 2 tablespoons freshly squeezed lemon juice
- salt and pepper
- 4 swordfish fillets

- 4 trout, 11 oz (300 g) each, scaled and cleaned
- salt and pepper
- 1 cup (15 g / ½ oz) finely chopped fresh dill
- 16 lemon slices
- 4 garlic cloves, thinly sliced
- ⅔ cup (150 ml / ¼ pint) olive oil, plus extra for drizzling
- 1 lb 2 oz (500 g) scallions (spring onions), white and tender green parts, cut into ¾-inch (1.5-cm) lengths
- 1 lb 2 oz (500 g) tomatoes, peeled, seeded, and finely chopped, or 14 oz (400 g) canned chopped tomatoes

BAKED TROUT WITH SCALLIONS (SPRING ONIONS) FROM MACEDONIA
ΠΕΣΤΡΟΦΕΣ ΜΕ ΦΡΕΣΚΑ ΚΡΕΜΜΥΔΑΚΙΑ ΣΤΟ ΦΟΥΡΝΟ
Pestrofes me freska kremidakia sto fourno

Preheat the oven to 350°F (180°C / Gas Mark 4). Rinse the fish under cold running water and pat dry with paper towels. Season with salt and pepper and place in an ovenproof dish just large enough to hold them. Divide half the dill and half the lemon slices among the cavities and add 2 or 3 garlic slices per fish. Heat the oil in a pan. Add the scallions and remaining garlic and cook over low heat, stirring occasionally, for 5 minutes, until softened. Add the tomatoes, season with salt and pepper, and simmer for about 10 minutes, until the sauce begins to thicken. Stir in the remaining dill and remove from the heat. Spoon the sauce between and around the fish. Place 3 lemon slices on top of each fish and drizzle a little oil over them. Bake for 20–30 minutes, or until the flesh flakes easily. Serve immediately.

Serves 4
Preparation time 20 minutes
Cooking time 30 minutes

Vefa's secret: Instead of using lemon slices, you could try putting 2 thin slices of tomato on top of each fish. The juices released during cooking will give more flavor to the fish and will prevent it from drying out.

- 3¼ lb (1.5 kg) tuna steaks or other large fish steaks
- 2 tablespoons red wine vinegar
- ½ cup (120 ml / 4 fl oz) olive oil
- 2¼ lb (1 kg) onions, sliced
- 10 garlic cloves, thinly sliced
- 1 lb 2 oz (500 g) tomatoes, peeled, seeded, and chopped
- salt and pepper
- 2 cups (120 g / 4 oz) finely chopped fresh parsley
- 2 large ripe tomatoes, sliced

TUNA BAKED WITH ONIONS
ΤΟΝΟΣ ΠΛΑΚΙ ΣΤΟ ΦΟΥΡΝΟ
Tonos plaki sto fourno

Rinse the fish under cold running water and pat dry with paper towels. Season with salt and sprinkle with the vinegar. Put the fish steaks side by side in an ovenproof dish. Heat half the oil in a large pan. Add the onions and garlic and cook over low heat, stirring occasionally, for 5 minutes, until softened. Preheat the oven to 400°F (200°C / Gas Mark 6). Add the chopped tomatoes to the pan, season with salt and pepper, and simmer for 10–15 minutes, until slightly thickened. Stir in the parsley, remove the pan from the heat, and spread the sauce over the fish steaks. Season with salt and pepper and drizzle with the remaining oil. Bake for 30–40 minutes, or until the pan juices have reduced. If you like your tuna pink in the middle, cook it a little less. Serve hot or at room temperature.

Serves 6
Preparation time 30 minutes
Cooking time 30–40 minutes

SHELLFISH (SEAFOOD)

-

ΘΑΛΑΣΣΙΝΑ

-

Thalasina

Most Greek shellfish (seafood) dishes are served as mezedes or first courses, but some of these recipes can also be served as entrées (main courses). There are three groups of shellfish: crustaceans (shrimp (prawns), lobster, crab), mollusks (clams, scallops, mussels), and cephalopods (octopus, squid, cuttlefish). Cephalopods are less popular outside the Mediterranean but they have remained favorites in Greek shellfish cookery and are especially appreciated during the Lenten fast, served with sauce and cooked with pasta, greens, rice, or olives. Whether baked, broiled (grilled), fried, or poached, shellfish from the waters of the Aegean has a unique flavor, and is considered by many be the most exquisite and delicate available anywhere.

Shellfish such as lobster, shrimp (prawns), crab, and mussels is even more delicate and perishable than fish, and can be sold alive, raw, cooked, or frozen. Oysters, clams, and cockles can be delicious raw, but they must be alive and you must be confident that they come from unpolluted sources. Take particular care when cooking shellfish dishes, as they become tough when not cooked correctly. Cook them briefly with very little wine or water, or steam them in the liquid they release as they are heated. Strain and reserve the liquid to use when preparing the sauce, or to cook any other ingredients in the recipe. Return the shellfish to the pan 5 minutes before the dish is ready, just to have enough time to be heated through.

SHRIMP (PRAWNS)
ΓΑΡΙΔΕΣ
Garides

Many, but not all, shrimp are bluish-gray when raw, even when frozen, and turn deep pink when cooked. For maximum flavor, they can be steamed, simmered, fried, or broiled (grilled) whole in their shells. Sometimes they need to be peeled and have the heads or tails removed before cooking. To do this, twist off the head and gently pull off the legs with the shell still attached. To remove the tail, gently pull it off by holding the fan at the end of the tail. Head, tails, and shells can be simmered to make a shellfish stock to add flavor to the dish. It is advisable to remove the black line—the intestine—that runs along the back of shrimp. This is called deveining. Make a cut along the back of each shrimp and lift out the vein with a pointed wooden skewer or knife.

CRAYFISH AND LANGOUSTINES
ΚΑΡΑΒΙΔΕΣ
Karavides

Crayfish are small, freshwater crustaceans. Langoustines, also known as scampi or Norway lobster, live in the sea and have long, thin pincers. Their shells are tougher than those of shrimp (prawns) and are pink when raw, turning redder as they cook. Most of the meat is in the tail. If very large, they should be blanched before cooking. Devein as described above before eating or using in a recipe. Slit the underside with a pair of scissors before cooking or broiling (grilling) to make it easier to remove the shell. In general, crayfish are more common than langoustines in America, and langoustines are more common in Europe. Either can be used in these recipes.

LOBSTER
ΑΣΤΑΚΟΣ
Astakos

When choosing a lobster, make sure it feels heavy for its size, and that it is alive, or was alive until very recently. Lightweight lobsters may have been starved, or may have recently shed their shell and not yet grown into their new one. True lobsters come from the cold northern waters of the Atlantic Ocean. They have large edible claws, one usually larger than the other, whereas spiny or rock lobsters from warmer waters do not. Most of their edible meat is in the tail. The American lobster is generally regarded as one of the finest flavored. These lobsters are dark green when raw but turn deep orange-pink when cooked. Female lobsters are preferred as they are larger and tastier and often contain a pink roe, called coral, which is excellent in sauces or lobster salad. The soft gray-green liver, or tomalley, is also edible. White spots on the shells are a sign of age.

To prepare for cooking, tie the claws securely, bend the tail toward the head, and tie in place. It is recommended to put the live lobster into the freezer for 2 hours before cooking, or to insert a sharp knife at the back of the head and cut swiftly right through before cooking. Plunge the lobster head first into a large pan of boiling water, bring back to a boil, cover, and cook for 30 minutes for a 2¼-lb (1-kg) lobster, until it turns orange. Increase the cooking time by 10 minutes for every additional 1 lb 2 oz (500 g). If you like, you can add shellfish seasoning or aromatics, such as celery, carrot, onions, paprika, cayenne pepper, and bay leaf to the cooking liquid. Remove the lobster from the pan, place it belly down on a board, making sure its legs are not trapped underneath it, and put a heavy weight on top to straighten it. When cool, cut it in half lengthwise through the shell with a sharp knife. Remove the coral (if there is one) and retain the tomalley for a salad, sauce, or garnish. Remove and discard the black vein and the stomach sac. Carefully remove the meat from the claws and legs. If you want to retain the whole claws for a garnish, use a special lobster pick to avoid breaking the meat. Serve the prepared lobster in the half shell.

CRAB
ΚΑΒΟΥΡΑΣ
Kavouras

There are many varieties of edible crabs, including blue crab, king crab, Dungeness crab, brown crab, and stone crab (claws only). Crabs are usually available live or cooked, and cooked crab meat is sold fresh, frozen, pasteurized and packed into containers, or canned. Live crabs are usually steamed, boiled, or broiled (grilled). To remove the meat, break off the claws and legs and crack the underside open. Split apart, then remove and discard the gills (or "dead man's fingers"). Scoop out the brown meat with a teaspoon and the white meat with a crab pick. Pick over the meat to remove any pieces of shell. Crack open the legs and claws with lobster crackers, nutcrackers, or the back of a heavy knife and remove the meat. Remove and discard the long piece of cartilage from the claw meat.

CLAMS
ΚΥΔΩΝΙΑ
Kidonia

Soft-shell clams are those with soft, easily broken shells. They are never eaten raw and should be soaked in salted water for 2 hours before steaming or frying. Clams are sold live, cooked, canned, or frozen. Live clams should have a pleasant seawater smell and can be stored in the refrigerator covered with a damp towel for at least 2–3 hours. Those that are alive will open slightly. Discard any that remain shut. Rinse in several changes of water and, if gritty, scrub with a stiff brush. To open them, insert a small knife between the shells opposite the hinge. Those that are alive will immediately snap shut; discard any that don't. Run the tip of the knife along the edge to the hinge and twist the blade to the upright position to open. Clams also open easily when briefly steamed or microwaved. Carefully remove the meat, discarding the sac with its sandy contents. Rinse the flesh briefly and cook according to the recipe.

SCALLOPS
KTENIA
Ktenia

Most scallops are sold already shucked, and most fish stores (fishmongers) will shuck them for you. Fresh scallop meat should be firm, shiny pale beige or cream-colored, and moist. You can use the small, darker bay (queen) or large white sea (king) scallops. Beware of very white scallops, as this is an indication that they may have been soaked to increase their weight. If you want to shuck live scallops, hold the scallop in a cloth in one hand, flat shell uppermost. Insert the blade of a short knife between the shells and run it across the roof of the flat shell to sever the internal muscle. Remove the top shell. Remove and discard the "skirt" and black stomach sac. Run the knife blade underneath the scallop to detach it from the bottom shell and cut off the ligament. Retain the orange coral, or roe, as it is an excellent addition to sauces and delicious spread on crackers. Scallop shells make a perfect serving dish for the cooked meat, but should be boiled vigorously before use to remove any toxins. Pan-fry or steam scallops for no longer than 6–8 minutes, depending on the size. Overcooking toughens them.

MUSSELS
ΜΥΔΙΑ
Midia

Like clams, mussels are sold live and as they are cooked only briefly, they must be absolutely fresh. Their shells are usually closed, so check for movement by tapping the shells and discarding any that do not close, and avoid those that are broken. Also discard any that feel unusually heavy, as they may be full of sand. Scrub the shells under cold running water and scrape off any barnacles with a knife or a stiff brush. Then place in a pan of clean, salted water for several hours to expel any sand or grit they contain. Pull off the "beards." You can shuck mussels in a similar way to clams (see above), inserting the knife on the straighter side of the shell. Alternatively, open by steaming in a pan with a small quantity of wine and aromatic herbs. Remove from the heat as soon as they open and discard any that remain shut. Farmed mussels are also sometimes available shucked and packed in seawater. Empty them into a colander placed in a bowl, pour in cold water to cover, and let soak for 30 minutes, occasionally rubbing gently with your fingers to release any sand and impurities. Drain and repeat once or twice until the water runs clear. Mussels become tough if overcooked; 5 minutes should be enough to keep them soft and juicy. To serve with pasta or rice, use the mussel-cooking liquid to prepare the sauce and add the mussels to the cooked dish just before you remove it from the heat.

OYSTERS
ΣΤΡΕΙΔΙΑ
Stridia

Most oysters, even native wild ones, are fattened in sheltered beds. They should be stored, cleaned, and shucked in a manner similar to that for clams and mussels. To be appreciated fully, European and Portuguese or Pacific oysters should be eaten raw, with their juices, from the half shell. They should always be prized open with an oyster knife, as opening them with heat tends to toughen their flesh. Avoid overcooking; stew, broil (grill), or fry for no more than 4–5 minutes, until their edges curl.

OCTOPUS
ΧΤΑΠΟΔΙ
Htapodi

Meaty octopus—all flesh, no bones, and little waste—is very popular in Greece and is widely available cleaned, fresh, or frozen, and ready to cook. If purchased fresh, it needs to be tenderized. You can do this by beating it with a meat bat or against a hard surface—40 times, according to Greek fishermen—or simply by placing it in the freezer for a few days. To clean it, turn the body inside out and pull out the entrails, including the ink sac. Remove and discard the cartilage-like strips on the sides of the body and the stomach sac. Rinse well, turn the octopus the right way out, and pinch out the beak from the center of the tentacles. Octopus is usually skinned by peeling off the grayish membrane before or after cooking, but the skin and suckers are both edible. To pre-cook, put it into a pan, pour in water to cover, add ½ cup (120 ml / 4 fl oz) red wine vinegar, and simmer until it starts to soften. Shrinkage is considerable, so try to buy larger specimens of about 2¼ lb–3¼ lb (1–1.5 kg). For broiling (grilling), however, choose baby octopus, one for each serving. If they are less than 4 inches (10 cm) long, they do not need tenderizing.

SQUID AND CUTTLEFISH
ΚΑΛΑΜΑΡΙ ΚΑΙ ΣΟΥΠΙΑ
Kalamari ke soupia

Squid are popular the world over, probably because they are quick and to easy prepare in a variety of ways. Long and slender, they range in size from finger-length for frying to larger ones for stuffing. The cuttlefish is related to squid, but has a rounder and fleshier body. Fresh and frozen squid and cuttlefish are widely available. Only the tentacles and the fleshy body sac are eaten. To clean, pull off the heads; the innards, including the ink sac, will come away with them. (If you want to reserve the ink sac, cut it away from the intestines and place in a bowl of cold water.) Using a sharp knife, cut off the tentacles from just above the eyes. Squeeze out the beak and discard, together with the rest of the head. Pull out the translucent quill from the body sac of the squid, or the hard white cuttlebone from the cuttlefish. Rinse thoroughly under running water and peel off the translucent membrane. Drain well before cooking. At this point, squid and cuttlefish can be cut into rings for frying, into squares for cooking, or left whole for stuffing. Do not separate the tentacles. It is best to simmer large squid and cuttlefish in a small quantity of water until all the juices evaporate to tenderize them before further cooking. This step reduces shrinkage and toughening. Small squid or cuttlefish can be sweated without water to tenderize them.

CRAYFISH WITH WILD CHARD

ΚΑΡΑΒΙΔΕΣ ΜΕ ΑΓΡΙΟΣΕΣΚΟΥΛΑ

Karavides me agrioseskoula

- 20 crayfish or langoustines
- 2¼ lb (1 kg) wild chard, tough stalks removed
- salt and pepper
- ½ cup (25 g / 1 oz) finely chopped fresh mint
- ½ cup (100 g / 3½ oz) long-grain rice
- 10 garlic cloves, thinly sliced, or 10 scallions (spring onions), white and tender green parts, chopped
- ½ cup (120 ml / 4 fl oz) olive oil

Peel the shellfish, keeping the heads intact, and devein. Crush the shells in a mortar with pestle or in a food processor. Put the crushed shells into a pan, pour in 1 cup (250 ml / 8 fl oz) water, bring to a boil, and simmer for 5 minutes. Strain the stock into a bowl and set aside. Cut the chard leaves into thick strips, sprinkle with salt and pepper, and wring them with your hands to squeeze out excess liquid and wilt them. Rinse well under cold running water. Combine the chard, mint, rice, and garlic or scallions in a bowl and spread the mixture over the base of a wide pan. Place the crayfish on top and pour in the reserved stock and the oil. Season with salt and pepper, cover, and simmer for about 20 minutes, or until the liquid has reduced. Serve hot or at room temperature.

Serves 4
Preparation time 30 minutes
Cooking time 20 minutes

Note: If you can't find wild chard, use spinach.

CRAYFISH STEW

ΚΑΡΑΒΙΔΕΣ ΚΟΚΚΙΝΙΣΤΕΣ

Karavides kokinistes

- 3¼ lb (1.5 kg) crayfish or langoustines
- ½ cup (120 ml / 4 fl oz) olive oil
- 1 onion, grated
- 2¼ lb (1 kg) ripe tomatoes, peeled, seeded, and puréed, or 14 oz (400 g) canned tomatoes, puréed
- 1 tablespoon Greek chili sauce (p 60)
- 2 bay leaves
- 5–6 allspice berries
- salt and pepper
- rice or tagliatelle, to serve

Using a pair of scissors, slit the undersides of the shellfish lengthwise without removing the shells. Heat the oil in a large pan. Add the onion and cook over low heat, stirring occasionally, for 5 minutes, until softened. Add the tomatoes, chili sauce, bay leaves, and allspice berries, season with salt and pepper, and simmer until the sauce has reduced. Add the shellfish and toss until thoroughly coated with the sauce. Simmer for 10 minutes, or until the shellfish are cooked through and the sauce is thick and glossy. Serve with rice or tagliatelle.

Serves 4
Preparation time 15 minutes
Cooking time 45 minutes

☐ p 328

- 6–8 cuttlefish, 2¼ lb (1 kg) total weight, cleaned (see p 325)
- 1 large onion, finely chopped
- ¾ cup (175 ml / 6 fl oz) olive oil
- 3 garlic cloves, finely chopped
- 4 tablespoons freshly squeezed lemon juice
- 3–4 tablespoons short-grain rice or dried bread crumbs
- 4 tablespoons pine nuts
- 4 tablespoons finely chopped fresh dill
- 4 tablespoons finely chopped fresh parsley
- salt and pepper
- 1¾ lb (800 g) canned artichoke hearts, drained and rinsed
- ½ cup (120 ml / 4 fl oz) dry white wine
- 1 tablespoon all-purpose (plain) flour

CUTTLEFISH AND ARTICHOKE HEARTS
ΣΟΥΠΙΕΣ ΚΑΙ ΑΓΓΙΝΑΡΕΣ
Soupies ke aginares

Finely chop the tentacles and set aside. Sweat the cuttlefish body sacs in a pan over high heat with 1–2 tablespoons water, stirring constantly, for 5 minutes, until most of the liquid has evaporated. Prick them with a wooden skewer. Heat half the oil in a pan. Add the onion and garlic and cook over low heat, stirring occasionally, for 5 minutes, until softened. Add the tentacles, 2–3 tablespoons water, and 1 tablespoon of the lemon juice, and simmer for a few minutes until most of the liquid has evaporated. Remove the pan from the heat, stir in the rice or bread crumbs, pine nuts, dill, and parsley, and season with salt and pepper. Stuff the cuttlefish body sacs with the mixture and put them into a wide pan. Pour in the remaining oil and cook the cuttlefish on all sides, until lightly browned. Put the artichoke hearts into the pan around the cuttlefish. Pour in the wine and 5 tablespoons water, cover, and simmer for about 30 minutes, or until the stuffed cuttlefish are tender. Combine the flour and remaining lemon juice in a bowl and stir in 2–3 tablespoons of the cooking liquid, then add the mixture to the pan. Simmer, shaking the pan occasionally, for 5 minutes more, until the sauce thickens. Serve hot.

Serves 4
Preparation time 1 hour
Cooking time 50 minutes

- 2¼ lb (1 kg) cuttlefish, cleaned (see p 325)
- 1 cup (250 ml / 8 fl oz) olive oil
- 2¼ lb (1 kg) onions, thinly sliced
- 6 garlic cloves
- 3 tablespoons tomato paste
- 1 cup (250 ml / 8 fl oz) white wine
- 2 bay leaves
- 3 allspice berries
- 10 black peppercorns
- ½ teaspoon sugar
- salt and pepper
- rice pilaf, to serve

CUTTLEFISH IN WINE
ΣΟΥΠΙΕΣ ΚΡΑΣΑΤΕΣ
Soupies krasates

If the cuttlefish are very small, leave them whole. If large, cut the body sacs and tentacles into rings. Place in a colander, drain, and pat dry with paper towels. Heat the oil in a large heavy pan. Add the onions and garlic and cook over low heat, stirring occasionally, for 5 minutes, until softened. Add the cuttlefish and cook for a few minutes, stirring occasionally, until all the liquid has evaporated. Combine the tomato paste and wine in a bowl and pour the mixture over the cuttlefish. Add the bay leaves, allspice berries, peppercorns, and sugar, season with salt and pepper, and stir well. Cover and simmer over medium heat for 1¼ hours, or until the cuttlefish are tender and the sauce has thickened. Remove from the heat, discard the bay leaves and allspice berries, and serve hot, accompanied by rice pilaf.

Serves 4
Preparation time 30 minutes
Cooking time 1½ hours

Crayfish stew, p 326

Cuttlefish with mixed greens and rice, p 330

CUTTLEFISH WITH MIXED GREENS AND RICE
ΣΟΥΠΙΕΣ ΜΕ ΧΟΡΤΑ ΚΑΙ ΡΥΖΙ
Soupies me horta ke rizi

Cut the cuttlefish body sacs into bite-size pieces, but leave the tentacles whole. Put the cuttlefish into a colander and rinse under cold running water, then drain and pat dry. Put 2 tablespoons water into a large pan and bring to a boil. Add the greens and cook for 5 minutes, then drain, squeezing out as much liquid as possible. Heat the oil in another large pan. Add the onion and scallions and cook over low heat, stirring occasionally, for 5 minutes, until softened and translucent. Add the cuttlefish, increase the heat to high, and cook, stirring constantly, until their liquid has evaporated. Add the brandy and cook until the alcohol has evaporated. Pour in the hot water, cover, and simmer for 30 minutes, or until the cuttlefish are tender. Add the greens, dill, and rice, season with salt and pepper, and simmer for 20 minutes more, until the rice and greens are tender. Mix the lemon juice with a little hot cooking liquid in a bowl, then add to the pan, shaking it to distribute the mixture evenly. Cook for 1 minute more. Serve hot or at room temperature.

Serves 6
Preparation time 1 hour
Cooking time 1 hour

☐ p 329

- 2¼ lb (1 kg) cuttlefish, cleaned (see p 325)
- 2¼ lb (1 kg) mixed greens, such as amaranth, nettles, sorrel and spinach, coarse stalks removed
- ½ cup (120 ml / 4 fl oz) olive oil
- 1 onion, finely chopped
- ½ cup (4) finely chopped scallions (spring onions)
- 4 tablespoons brandy
- 1 cup (250 ml / 8 fl oz) hot water
- ½ cup (15 g / ½ oz) finely chopped fresh dill
- ½ cup (100 g / 3½ oz) long-grain rice
- salt and pepper
- 4 tablespoons freshly squeezed lemon juice

LOBSTER WITH OIL-LEMON DRESSING
ΑΣΤΑΚΟΣ ΒΡΑΣΤΟΣ ΛΑΔΟΛΕΜΟΝΟ
Astakos vrastos ladolemono

Bring a large pan of water to a boil, add the onion, carrot, celery, salt and peppercorns or shellfish seasoning, and simmer for 10 minutes. Add the lemon juice and bring back to a boil. Boil the prepared lobster for 25 minutes or until the flesh is just opaque and firm, remove, and drain, then weigh it down to cool as described on p 323. Turn it over and, using kitchen scissors, cut each side along the entire length. Pull away the bony membrane that protects the underside. Carefully remove the flesh, devein, and slice. Arrange the slices on a platter. Cut out the meat from the head, the red coral, and the dark green tomalley or liver. Crack the claws and legs and remove the meat. Put it on the platter with the rest of the lobster meat, drizzle with the oil-lemon dressing, and sprinkle with parsley. Serve immediately with cooked asparagus or broccoli.

Serves 4
Preparation time 30 minutes
Cooking time 20 minutes

- 1 onion
- 1 carrot
- 1 celery stalk
- 2 teaspoons salt
- 10 black peppercorns or 1 teaspoon shellfish seasoning
- 4 tablespoons freshly squeezed lemon juice
- 1 large live lobster or two smaller ones, 3¼ lb (1.5 kg), prepared for cooking (see p 323)
- Oil-lemon dressing (p 57)
- finely chopped fresh parsley, to garnish
- cooked asparagus or broccoli, to serve

- 2¼ lb (1 kg) langoustines or crayfish
- ½ cup (120 ml / 4 fl oz) olive oil
- 1 large onion, finely chopped
- ½ cup (120 ml / 4 fl oz) dry white wine
- 3 cups (750 ml / 1¼ pints) boiling water
- salt and pepper
- 14 oz (400 g) canned chopped tomatoes
- 1 teaspoon sugar
- 1 tablespoon red wine vinegar
- ½ teaspoon cayenne pepper
- 4 tablespoons (50 g / 2 oz) butter
- 12 oz (350 g) orzo pasta
- 3 tablespoons butter, melted
- 1 tablespoon paprika

LANGOUSTINE CASSEROLE WITH ORZO
ΓΙΟΥΒΕΤΣΙ ΜΕ ΚΑΡΑΒΙΔΕΣ
Giouvetsi me karavides

Rinse the langoustines, cut off their antennae and side claws, and drain well. Heat the oil in a large pan. Add the onion and cook over a low heat, stirring occasionally, for 5 minutes, until softened. Add the langoustines, increase the heat to medium, and cook, stirring constantly, for 2–3 minutes. Pour in the wine and boiling water, season with salt and pepper, and cook for 8 minutes. Meanwhile, preheat the oven to 350°F (180°C / Gas Mark 4). Remove the langoustines with a slotted spoon, drain well, and set aside. Add the tomatoes, sugar, vinegar, and cayenne to the pan and bring to a boil. Meanwhile, heat the butter in a skillet or frying pan. Add the orzo and cook over high heat, stirring constantly, for a few minutes. Transfer the orzo to a wide deep oven-proof dish, pour the tomato mixture over it, and bake for about 1 hour, or until the orzo is soft and has absorbed almost all the liquid. If the orzo has not softened, add a little water and bake for few more minutes. Place the langoustines on top of the orzo, brush with the melted butter, sprinkle with the paprika, and bake for 5 minutes more, until heated through. Serve immediately.

Serves 4
Preparation time 10 minutes
Cooking time 1 hour

Vefa's secret: Sautéing the orzo before baking gives it a nice crust and prevents it from becoming mushy. Peeling langoustines is easy if you slit their shells lengthwise along the top and undersides with a pair of scissors. You can do this before or after cooking.

- 2 cooked lobster tails, about 1¾ lb (800 g)
- 2 tablespoons capers
- ¾ cup (80 g / 3 oz) cooked peas
- 4 small canned artichoke hearts, drained and quartered
- 1 hard-boiled egg, chopped
- 4 tablespoons finely chopped dill pickles (pickled cucumbers)
- 1 large carrot, cooked and diced
- 2 tablespoons finely chopped fresh parsley
- salt and pepper
- 2 tablespoons freshly squeezed lemon juice
- 1½ cups (350 ml / 12 fl oz) Mayonnaise (p 60)
- lettuce hearts, to garnish

LOBSTER SALAD
ΑΣΤΑΚΟΣΑΛΑΤΑ
Astakosalata

Cut the lobster tails in half lengthwise and remove the black vein with the tip of a knife. Remove the meat and cut it into small pieces. Reserve the half shells. Combine the pieces of lobster, capers, peas, artichoke hearts, egg, dill pickles, carrot, and parsley in a bowl and season with salt and pepper. Sprinkle with the lemon juice, add the mayonnaise, and toss lightly. Cover and keep in the refrigerator until ready to serve. Gently scrub the lobster half shells. Spoon the salad into the half shells, mounding it up, and surround with lettuce hearts.

Serves 4
Preparation time 45 minutes
Cooking time 20 minutes

OCTOPUS STIFADO
ΧΤΑΠΟΔΙ ΣΤΙΦΑΔΟ
Htapodi stifado

Put the octopus into a large saucepan, add ½ cup (120 ml / 4 fl oz) of the red wine vinegar, pour in water to cover, and cook for about 45 minutes, until half tender. Drain well and cut into bite-size pieces. Put the onions or shallots into a bowl, pour in boiling water to cover, and let stand for a few minutes, then drain, and peel off the skins. Heat the oil in a pan. Add the onions or shallots and garlic and cook over low heat, stirring occasionally, for 5–8 minutes, until softened. Pour in the remaining red wine vinegar, add the peppercorns, allspice berries, bay leaves, tomatoes, sugar, and balsamic vinegar, season with salt and pepper, and stir. Cover, and simmer for about 50 minutes. Add the octopus and continue cooking for 50 minutes more, or until the onions or shallots and octopus are tender. If the sauce needs further thickening, strain it into another pan and simmer to thicken. Serve hot or at room temperature.

Serves 4
Preparation time 1½ hours
Cooking time 2¼ hours

- 1 octopus, about 4½ lb (2 kg), cleaned and skinned (see p 325)
- ¾ cup (175 ml / 6 fl oz) red wine vinegar
- 3¼ lb (1.5 kg) small pearl (pickling) onions or shallots
- ⅔ cup (150 ml / ¼ pint) olive oil
- 10 garlic cloves
- 1 tablespoon black peppercorns
- 10 allspice berries
- 2 bay leaves
- 14 oz (400 g) canned or fresh tomatoes, peeled and puréed
- 1 teaspoon sugar
- 2 tablespoons balsamic vinegar
- salt and pepper

OCTOPUS WITH ARTICHOKES
ΧΤΑΠΟΔΙ ΜΕ ΑΓΓΙΝΑΡΕΣ
Htapodi me aginares

Pour the wine and 4 cups (1 litre / 1¾ pints) water into a large pan, add the garlic, and bring to a boil. Add the octopus, cover, and simmer for about 1 hour, until soft. Meanwhile, remove the tough leaves and chokes from the artichokes, leaving only the hearts (see p 207). Cut in half and put them into a bowl of water mixed with 2 tablespoons of the lemon juice and the flour to prevent discoloration. Drain the octopus and reserve 1 cup (250 ml / 8 fl oz) of the cooking liquid. Let cool, then cut into bite-size pieces. Heat the oil in a pan. Add the onions and cook over low heat, stirring occasionally, for 5 minutes, until softened. Drain the artichokes and add to the pan, together with the carrots, reserved cooking liquid, and hot water, and season with salt and pepper. Cover and simmer for 20 minutes. Add the octopus and dill, taste and adjust the seasoning, if necessary, and cook for 15 minutes more, or until the artichokes are tender and the liquid has reduced. Add the remaining lemon juice. Serve hot or at room temperature.

Serves 4
Preparation time 1 hour
Cooking time 35 minutes

- 1 cup (250 ml / 8 fl oz) dry white wine
- 2 garlic cloves
- 1 octopus, about 3¼ lb (1.5 kg), cleaned (see p 325)
- 8 globe artichokes
- 6 tablespoons freshly squeezed lemon juice
- 1 tablespoon all-purpose (plain) flour
- ½ cup (120 ml / 4 fl oz) olive oil
- 2 onions, sliced
- 1 large carrot, sliced
- ½ cup (120 ml / 4 fl oz) hot water
- salt and pepper
- 4 tablespoons finely chopped fresh dill

OCTOPUS BAKED WITH POTATOES
ΧΤΑΠΟΔΙ ΣΤΟ ΦΟΥΡΝΟ ΜΕ ΠΑΤΑΤΕΣ
Htapodi sto fourno me patates

- 1 octopus, about 5½ lb (2.5 kg), cleaned (see p 325) and cut into serving pieces
- 4½ lb (2 kg) potatoes, cut into wedges
- ¾ cup (175 ml / 6 fl oz) olive oil
- 3–4 garlic cloves, thinly sliced
- 2 large tomatoes, peeled, seeded, and chopped
- 2 tablespoons dried oregano
- salt and pepper
- 4 tablespoons freshly squeezed lemon juice
- lemon wedges, to garnish

Preheat the oven to 350°F (180°C / Gas Mark 4). Put the pieces of octopus into a roasting pan and surround with the potato wedges. Heat the oil in a skillet or frying pan. Add the garlic and cook over medium heat, stirring constantly, for 1–2 minutes. Add the tomatoes and oregano, season with salt and pepper, and cook, stirring constantly, for 1 minute. Remove the pan from the heat and spoon the mixture over the octopus and potatoes. Sprinkle with the lemon juice and bake, adding as much water as necessary to prevent it drying out, for about 2 hours, or until the octopus and potatoes are tender and the sauce has reduced. Serve hot, garnished with lemon wedges.

Serves 6
Preparation time 30 minutes
Cooking time 2 hours

▢ p 334

OCTOPUS WITH BEANS
ΧΤΑΠΟΔΙ ΜΕ ΦΑΣΟΛΙΑ
Htapodi me fasolia

- 1 teaspoon dried oregano
- 1 teaspoon dried rosemary
- 1 tablespoon chopped fresh basil
- ½ cup (120 ml / 4 fl oz) olive oil
- 1¾ cups (300 g / 11 oz) medium dried white beans, such as cannellini
- 4 cups (1 litre / 1¾ pints) vegetable stock
- 3¼ lb (1.5 kg) octopus, cleaned (see p 325)
- 4 tablespoons red wine vinegar
- 1 bay leaf
- 20 black peppercorns
- 1 large onion, finely chopped
- 3 ripe tomatoes, peeled, seeded, and finely chopped
- salt and pepper

Put the herbs into a screw-top jar, pour in the oil, and let stand for 12 hours. Put the beans into a bowl, pour in water to cover, and let soak for 12 hours. Drain the beans, put them into a pan, pour in the vegetable stock, and cook for 1 hour, until half tender. Meanwhile, skin and rinse the octopus and put it into a large pan. Add the vinegar, bay leaf, and peppercorns and cook for 1 hour, until half cooked. Remove and drain. Heat the herb-flavored oil in another pan. Add the onion and cook over low heat, stirring occasionally, for 5 minutes, until softened. Add the drained beans, tomatoes, and octopus, season with salt and pepper, and simmer, adding water if necessary, until the beans and octopus are tender and the sauce has thickened. Serve hot or at room temperature.

Serves 4
Preparation time 13 hours (including soaking)
Cooking time 2 hours

Octopus baked with potatoes, p 333

Octopus with eggplants (aubergines), p 336

OCTOPUS WITH EGGPLANTS (AUBERGINES)
ΧΤΑΠΟΔΙ ΜΕ ΜΕΛΙΤΖΑΝΕΣ
Htapodi me melitzanes

- 3¼ lb (1.5 kg) octopus, cleaned (see p 325)
- 4 tablespoons red wine vinegar
- 1 bay leaf
- 20 black peppercorns
- 4½ lb (2 kg) eggplants (aubergines), cut into bite-size pieces
- 1 cup (250 ml / 8 fl oz) olive oil
- 1 onion, grated
- 1 garlic clove, thinly sliced
- 3 large ripe tomatoes, peeled, seeded, and finely chopped
- 1 teaspoon sugar
- 2 tablespoons balsamic vinegar
- salt and pepper
- 4 tablespoons finely chopped fresh parsley

Put the octopus into a large pan, add the vinegar, bay leaf, and peppercorns, and pour in water to cover. Cook for about 45 minutes. Meanwhile, sprinkle the eggplants with salt and let drain in a colander for 30 minutes. Heat half the oil in a pan. Add the onion and garlic and cook over low heat, stirring occasionally, for 5 minutes, until softened. Add the tomatoes, sugar, and balsamic vinegar, season with salt and pepper, and cook for 5 minutes. Drain the octopus, cut into bite-size pieces, and add to the sauce. Cover and simmer for about 35 minutes, or until the octopus is tender and the sauce has thickened. Meanwhile, rinse the eggplants, drain, and squeeze out the excess moisture. Heat the remaining oil in a skillet or frying pan. Add the eggplants and cook over medium heat, stirring frequently, for 8–10 minutes, until lightly golden, then remove, and drain on paper towels. Add the eggplants and parsley to the sauce and simmer for 10 minutes more. Serve hot or at room temperature.

Serves 4
Preparation time 1 hour
Cooking time 1 hour

□ p 335

OCTOPUS WITH FENNEL AND OLIVES
ΧΤΑΠΟΔΙ ΜΕ ΜΑΡΑΘΟ ΚΑΙ ΕΛΙΕΣ
Htapodi me maratho ke elies

- 1 octopus, 3¼ lb (1.5 kg), cleaned (see p 325)
- ½ cup (120 ml / 4 fl oz) red wine vinegar
- ½ cup (120 ml / 4 fl oz) olive oil
- 1 cup (7–8) chopped scallions (spring onions)
- 1 cup (250 ml / 8 fl oz) red wine
- 10 pitted (stoned) and halved green olives
- 2 fennel bulbs, sliced
- ½ cup (15 g / ½ oz) finely chopped fennel fronds or fresh dill
- salt and pepper

Put the octopus into a large pan, pour in the vinegar and water to cover, and cook for about 40 minutes. Drain and cut into bite-size pieces. Heat the oil in a pan. Add the scallions and cook over low heat, stirring occasionally, for 5 minutes, until softened. Add the octopus and cook, stirring constantly, for 1–2 minutes. Pour in the wine and cook for 1–2 minutes more, until the alcohol has evaporated. Add the olives, fennel, and fennel fronds, cover, and simmer for about 1 hour, until the octopus and vegetables are tender. Season with pepper (and salt, depending on how salty the olives are) and simmer for 10 minutes more. Serve hot or at room temperature.

Serves 4
Preparation time 1 hour
Cooking time 1¼ hours

OCTOPUS WITH FRESH OREGANO
ΧΤΑΠΟΔΙ ΜΕ ΦΡΕΣΚΙΑ ΡΙΓΑΝΗ
Htapodi me freskia rigani

- 3¼ lb (1.5 kg) octopus, cleaned (see p 325) and cut into bite-size pieces
- ½ cup (120 ml / 4 fl oz) olive oil
- 2 onions, grated
- 1 cup (250 ml / 8 fl oz) dry white wine
- 1 tablespoon tomato paste
- 1 cup (50 g / 2 oz) fresh oregano leaves
- 1½ cups (40 g / 1½ oz) fennel fronds or fresh dill, finely chopped
- 2¼ lb (1 kg) potatoes, thickly sliced
- salt and pepper

Put the octopus into a pan with 4 tablespoons water, cover, and cook over low heat for 15 minutes, or until most of the liquid has evaporated. Add the oil and onions and cook, stirring occasionally, for 5 minutes, until softened. Pour in the wine and stir, scraping the base of the pan. Mix the tomato paste with 1 cup (250 ml / 8 fl oz) water in a bowl and add to the pan. Bring to a boil, cover, and simmer for 30 minutes, or until the octopus is half cooked. Blanch the oregano for 1 minute, then drain, and add to the pan, together with the fennel and potatoes. Pour in enough water to half-cover the potatoes and cook, stirring occasionally, for 30 minutes, or until the octopus and potatoes are tender and the liquid has reduced.

Serves 4
Preparation time 30 minutes
Cooking time 1½ hours

OCTOPUS WITH LENTILS AND GREENS
ΧΤΑΠΟΔΙ ΜΕ ΦΑΚΕΣ ΚΑΙ ΧΟΡΤΑ
Htapodi me fakes ke horta

- 4½ lb (2 kg) octopus, cleaned (see p 325)
- 2 tablespoons red wine vinegar
- ½ cup (120 ml / 4 fl oz) dry white wine
- scant 1 cup (200 g / 7 oz) green lentils
- 2 onions, sliced
- 1 lb 2 oz (500 g) greens, such as spinach and chard, coarse stalks removed and leaves coarsely torn
- 4 tomatoes, peeled, seeded, and chopped
- 1 red bell pepper, seeded and chopped
- ½ cup (4) finely chopped scallions (spring onions)
- 2 garlic cloves, thinly sliced
- 1 bay leaf
- ⅔ cup (150 ml / ¼ pint) olive oil
- salt and pepper
- 1 teaspoon dried oregano

Put the octopus into a pan, pour in water to cover, add the vinegar and wine, and cook for about 1 hour, until tender. Meanwhile, put the lentils and onions into another pan, pour in 2 cups (450 ml / 16 fl oz) water, and cook for 30 minutes, then remove from the heat. Do not drain. Preheat the oven to 400°F (200°C / Gas Mark 6). Drain the octopus, cut it into pieces and spread out on the base of an ovenproof dish. Add the lentils with their cooking liquid, together with the greens. Add the tomatoes, bell pepper, scallions, garlic, and bay leaf. Drizzle with the oil, season with salt and pepper, and sprinkle with the oregano. Cover the dish with aluminum foil and bake for about 45 minutes, or until the sauce has thickened. Serve hot or at room temperature.

Serves 6
Preparation time 1½ hours
Cooking time 45 minutes

SPICY SCALLOPS WITH BELL PEPPER SAUCE
ΚΤΕΝΙΑ ΜΕ ΣΑΛΤΣΑ ΠΙΠΕΡΙΑΣ
Ktenia me saltsa piperias

Put the bell peppers in a steamer over a pan of boiling water, cover, and cook for about 8 minutes, until softened. Remove from the heat, peel, and put the flesh into a food processor. Season with salt and pepper, add the Tabasco and garlic, and pulse 3–4 times, until smooth. Heat half the oil in a pan. Pour in the bell pepper sauce and bring to a boil over high heat, stirring constantly. Remove from the heat and stir in the yogurt, then cover the pan to keep warm. Heat the remaining oil in a nonstick, heavy pan. Add the scallops and scallions and cook the scallops for 2–2½ minutes on each side. Sprinkle with chopped parsley and serve immediately with the bell pepper sauce, accompanied by pasta or rice.

Serves 4
Preparation time 20 minutes
Cooking time 5 minutes

- 2 red bell peppers, seeded and quartered
- salt and pepper
- 10 drops Tabasco sauce
- 1 garlic clove, finely chopped
- 5 tablespoons olive oil
- 4 tablespoons strained plain or thick Greek yogurt
- 1 lb 2 oz (500 g) scallops, shucked
- 4 scallions (spring onions), thinly sliced
- finely chopped fresh parsley, to garnish
- pasta or rice, to serve

SHRIMP (PRAWNS) WITH TOMATO SAUCE AND SPINACH
ΓΑΡΙΔΕΣ ΜΕ ΝΤΟΜΑΤΑ ΚΑΙ ΣΠΑΝΑΚΙ
Garides me domata ke spanaki

Cut any large spinach leaves in half. Heat 4 tablespoons of the oil in a small pan. Add the garlic and cook over low heat, stirring frequently, until just beginning to brown. Add the spinach and nutmeg, season with salt and pepper, and cook, stirring occasionally, for about 5 minutes, until the spinach has wilted. Remove the pan from the heat, cover, and set aside. Heat the remaining oil in a skillet or frying pan. Add the shrimp and cook over high heat, stirring frequently, for 2 minutes. Pour in the ouzo and cook for 2 minutes more, then pour in the wine, and cook for another 2 minutes, until the alcohol has evaporated. Transfer the shrimp to a plate with a slotted spoon. Add the tomatoes and sugar to the pan and boil over high heat for 5 minutes. Slide the shrimp back into the pan and sprinkle with the oregano. Shake the pan to distribute the sauce evenly, then remove from the heat. Divide the spinach among individual warmed plates, place 3 shrimp on each, and pour the sauce over them. Serve immediately.

Serves 4
Preparation time 30 minutes
Cooking time 20 minutes

- 1 lb 2 oz (500 g) spinach, coarse stalks removed
- ¾ cup (175 ml / 6 fl oz) olive oil
- 2 garlic cloves, finely chopped
- pinch of grated nutmeg
- salt and pepper
- 12 jumbo shrimp (king prawns), peeled and deveined with heads and tails left intact (see p 322)
- 4 tablespoons ouzo
- 4 tablespoons dry white wine
- 1 lb 2 oz (500 g) tomatoes, peeled, seeded, and chopped
- 1 teaspoon sugar
- ½ teaspoon dried oregano

- 2¼ lb (1 kg) shrimp (prawns)
- ½ cup (120 ml / 4 fl oz) olive oil
- 2 onions, sliced
- 4 garlic cloves, thinly sliced
- 1 large leek, white part only, finely chopped
- 14 oz (400 g) canned chopped tomatoes
- 1 tablespoon tomato paste
- 2 celery stalks, sliced
- 1 yellow bell pepper, seeded and cut into julienne strips
- 1 Florina or other red bell pepper, seeded and cut into julienne strips
- 1 green bell pepper, seeded and cut into julienne strips
- salt and pepper
- ½ cup (120 ml / 4 fl oz) hot water
- ½ cup (25 g / 1 oz) finely chopped fresh parsley

SHRIMP (PRAWN) CASSEROLE WITH VEGETABLES FROM THESSALONIKI
ΓΑΡΙΔΕΣ ΠΛΑΚΙ
Garides plaki

Peel the shrimp, leaving the heads intact, and devein (see p 322). Heat the oil in a pan. Add the onions, garlic, and leek and cook over low heat, stirring occasionally, for 5 minutes, until softened. Add the tomatoes, tomato paste, celery, and bell peppers, season with salt and pepper, and pour in the hot water. Bring to a boil, cover, and simmer for about 30 minutes, until the vegetables are tender and the liquid has cooked down to the oil. Lay the shrimp on top, sprinkle with the parsley, season with salt and pepper, and cook for 8 minutes more. Serve hot.

Serves 4
Preparation time 30 minutes
Cooking time 40 minutes

Note: The word plaki usually refers to fish baked in the oven. Here the shrimp are combined with the usual vegetables, but cooked on the stove top (hob) instead.

☐ p 340

- 4 long, thin eggplants (aubergines)
- ½ cup (120 ml / 4 fl oz) olive oil
- 20 jumbo shrimp (king prawns), peeled and deveined with heads and tails intact (see p 322)
- 2 garlic cloves, thinly sliced
- 9 oz (250 g) canned or fresh tomatoes, puréed
- 1 tablespoon tomato paste
- ½ teaspoon sugar
- 1 tablespoon balsamic vinegar
- ½ teaspoon dried thyme
- ½ teaspoon dried marjoram
- 2 tablespoons finely chopped fresh parsley
- salt and pepper

SHRIMP (PRAWN) AND EGGPLANT (AUBERGINE) ROLLS BAKED IN TOMATO SAUCE
ΡΟΛΑ ΓΑΡΙΔΑΣ ΜΕ ΜΕΛΙΤΖΑΝΕΣ
Rola garidas me melitzanes

Cut the eggplants lengthwise into 5 thin slices. Sprinkle with salt and let drain in a colander for 1 hour. Rinse the eggplant slices under cold running water and gently squeeze out the excess water with your hands. Reserve 2 tablespoons of the oil and heat the remainder in a skillet or frying pan. Add the eggplant slices, in batches if necessary, and cook for about 4 minutes on each side, until lightly browned. Remove from the pan and drain on paper towels. Roll a slice of eggplant around each shrimp and put the rolls in a single layer, seam side down, in an ovenproof dish. Heat the reserved oil in a pan. Add the garlic and cook, stirring frequently, for 1–2 minutes. Add the tomatoes, tomato paste, sugar, vinegar, and herbs, season with salt and pepper, and simmer for 15–20 minutes, or until thickened. Meanwhile, preheat the oven to 400°F (200°C / Gas Mark 6). Ladle the sauce over the shrimp and eggplant rolls and bake for 10–15 minutes.

Serves 4
Preparation time 1¼ hours (including salting)
Cooking time 30–40 minutes

Shrimp (prawn) casserole with vegetables from Thessaloniki, p 339

broiled (grilled) shrimp (prawns) in honey-wine marinade, p 342

BROILED (GRILLED) SHRIMP (PRAWNS) IN HONEY-WINE MARINADE
ΓΑΡΙΔΕΣ ΨΗΤΕΣ ΜΕ ΟΙΝΟΜΕΛΟ
Garides psites me inomelo

Put all the marinade ingredients in a screw-top jar, fasten the lid, and shake vigorously until thoroughly blended. Put the shrimp and mushrooms into a large bowl, pour the marinade over them, cover, and let marinate in the refrigerator, stirring occasionally, for 6 hours. Preheat the broiler (grill). Drain the shrimp and mushrooms, reserving the marinade, and thread them alternately onto skewers. Broil (grill), basting with the marinade, for about 4 minutes on each side. Serve immediately, with cocktail sauce if you like.

Serves 4
Preparation time 6¼ hours (including marinating)
Cooking time 10 minutes

▢ p 341

- ○ 16 jumbo shrimp (king prawns), peeled and deveined with tails intact (see p 322)
- ○ 16 medium white mushrooms
- ○ cocktail sauce, to serve (optional)

FOR THE HONEY-WINE MARINADE
- ○ 2 tablespoons honey
- ○ 4 tablespoons olive oil
- ○ 4 tablespoons red wine vinegar
- ○ 1 teaspoon dried thyme or rosemary
- ○ 1 garlic clove, finely chopped
- ○ salt and pepper

BAKED SHRIMP (PRAWN) CASSEROLE
ΓΑΡΙΔΕΣ ΓΙΟΥΒΕΤΣΙ
Garides giouvetsi

Put the shrimp into a pan, add 4 tablespoons water, bring to a boil, and cook for 5 minutes. Drain, reserving the cooking liquid. Melt the butter or heat the oil in a pan. Add the onion and cook over low heat, stirring occasionally, for 5 minutes, until softened. Add the carrot and bell pepper and cook, stirring occasionally, for 5 minutes more. Pour in the tomatoes and reserved cooking liquid, season with salt and pepper, and simmer for 15–20 minutes, until thickened. Meanwhile, preheat the oven to 400°F (200°C/ Gas Mark 6) and brush an ovenproof dish with oil. Remove the sauce from the heat and stir in the feta and parsley. Spoon the shrimp over the base of the prepared dish and pour the sauce over them. Sprinkle with the diced cheese and a little cayenne, if using, and dot the top with butter or drizzle with oil. Bake for about 30 minutes, until the top is lightly browned.

Serves 6
Preparation time 45 minutes
Cooking time 30 minutes

- ○ 3¼ lb (1.5 kg) shrimp (prawns), peeled and deveined (see p 322)
- ○ 4 tablespoons (60 g / 2¼ oz) butter, plus extra for dotting, or 4 tablespoons olive oil, plus extra for brushing and drizzling
- ○ 1 large onion, chopped
- ○ 1 carrot, sliced
- ○ 1 green bell pepper, seeded and cut into julienne strips
- ○ 2¼ lb (1 kg) fresh tomatoes or 14 oz (400 g) canned tomatoes, puréed
- ○ salt and pepper
- ○ 9 oz (250 g) feta cheese, crumbled
- ○ 4 tablespoons finely chopped fresh parsley
- ○ 5 oz (150 g) kaseri or Gruyère cheese, diced
- ○ pinch of cayenne pepper (optional)

- 1 lb 2 oz (500 g) squid, cleaned and cut into rings (see p 325)
- 1 lb 2 oz (500 g) leeks, white and tender green parts, sliced crosswise
- ⅔ cup (150 ml / ¼ pint) olive oil
- 2 garlic cloves, sliced
- 2 tomatoes, peeled, seeded, and chopped
- 1 tablespoon tomato paste
- 1 teaspoon sugar
- 1 teaspoon red wine vinegar
- 1 small green chile, finely chopped
- 4 tablespoons chopped celery
- 9 oz (250 g) potatoes, cut into bite-size pieces
- salt and pepper
- 4 tablespoons finely chopped fresh parsley

SQUID BRAISED WITH VEGETABLES
ΚΑΛΑΜΑΡΙΑ ΜΕ ΠΡΑΣΑ ΚΑΙ ΠΑΤΑΤΕΣ
Kalamaria me prasa ke patates

Put the squid rings into a pan, cover with water, cover and cook over medium heat for about 1 hour, until the juices have evaporated. Meanwhile, blanch the leeks for 3–4 minutes in boiling water and drain. Heat the oil in a heavy pan. Add the squid rings and garlic and cook over medium-high heat, stirring frequently, for 2–3 minutes. Stir in the tomatoes, tomato paste, sugar, vinegar, chile, celery, leeks, and potatoes, season with salt and pepper, and pour in ½ cup (120 ml / 4 fl oz) water. Bring to a boil, lower the heat, partially cover, and simmer for about 30 minutes, until the squid, leeks, and potatoes are tender and the sauce has reduced. Serve immediately, sprinkled with the parsley.

Serves 4
Preparation time 20 minutes
Cooking time 1½ hours

Note: You can omit the potatoes and replace them with an additional 8 oz (225 g) leeks, if you like.

- 2¼ lb (1 kg) eggplants (aubergines), cut in bite-size cubes
- 1½ lb (700 g) squid, cleaned and cut into bite-size pieces (see p 325)
- 7 tablespoons olive oil
- 2 large onions, sliced
- 3 garlic cloves, thinly sliced
- 5 tablespoons white wine
- 10 black peppercorns
- 5 allspice berries
- salt and pepper
- 1 lb 2 oz (500 g) green bell peppers, seeded and cut into thick rings
- 1 red or green chile, chopped
- rice pilaf, to serve

SQUID WITH BELL PEPPERS AND EGGPLANTS (AUBERGINES)
ΚΑΛΑΜΑΡΙΑ ΜΕ ΠΙΠΕΡΙΕΣ ΚΑΙ ΜΕΛΙΤΖΑΝΕΣ
Kalamaria me piperies ke melitzanes

Sprinkle the eggplant cubes with salt and let drain in a colander for 1 hour. Meanwhile, put the squid into a pan, cover with water and cook over low heat until most of the liquid has evaporated. Rinse the eggplants and squeeze out the excess moisture. Heat 5 tablespoons of the oil in a heavy pan. Add the onions and garlic and cook over low heat, stirring occasionally, for 5 minutes, until softened. Add the squid and cook, stirring constantly, for 1 minute. Pour in the wine, add the peppercorns and allspice berries, and season with salt and pepper. Cover and simmer for about 1 hour, until the squid is tender. Meanwhile, heat the remaining oil in a skillet or frying pan. Add the eggplant cubes, bell pepper rings, and chile and cook over medium heat, stirring frequently, for about 8 minutes, until softened and golden. Stir into the squid and simmer until the sauce has reduced. Serve hot or at room temperature, accompanied by rice pilaf.

Serves 4
Preparation time 1¼ hours (including salting)
Cooking time 1¼ hours

SQUID PASTITSIO
ΠΑΣΤΙΤΣΙΟ ΜΕ ΚΑΛΑΜΑΡΙΑ
Pastitsio me kalamaria

Put the squid or cuttlefish into a pan and cook over medium heat, stirring constantly, until most of the liquid has evaporated. Put the mushrooms into the food processor and process until finely chopped. Heat 2 tablespoons of the oil in a skillet or frying pan. Add the mushrooms and cook over medium heat, stirring frequently, for 5 minutes, until lightly browned. Remove from the heat. Reserve 2 tablespoons of the oil and heat the remaining oil in a pan. Add the onion and garlic and cook over low heat, stirring occasionally, for 5 minutes, until softened. Add the squid or cuttlefish and mushrooms, stir in the tomatoes, tomato paste, tomato ketchup, bay leaf, and allspice and season lightly with salt and pepper. Cover and simmer for 25–30 minutes, until the sauce has thickened and the squid or cuttlefish are tender. Remove from the heat, add the parsley, and adjust the seasoning, if necessary. Mix the cornstarch to a paste with 2 tablespoons water in a bowl. Pour the cream into a small pan, stir in the cornstarch paste, bring to a boil and cook until slightly thickened. Stir in the nutmeg and season lightly with salt and pepper.

Bring a large pan of water to a boil, stir in salt and the reserved oil, add the pasta, and cook for 8–10 minutes, or until al dente. Meanwhile, preheat the oven to 400°F (200°C / Gas Mark 6) and brush a 10 x 14-inch (25 x 35-cm) ovenproof dish with oil. Drain the pasta and toss with the cream mixture and the cheese. Line the base of the prepared dish with half the phyllo sheets, brushing well with melted butter. Spoon half the pasta mixture on top of the phyllo and spread the sauce over it. Spoon in the remaining pasta mixture and cover with the remaining phyllo sheets, brushing with melted butter. Cut through the phyllo layer with a sharp knife into 6 pieces and sprinkle the surface with a little water. Bake the pastitsio for 40–50 minutes. Let stand for 8 minutes before serving.

Serves 6
Preparation time 1 hour
Cooking time 40–50 minutes

- 1 lb 2 oz (500 g) squid or cuttlefish, cleaned and finely chopped (see p 325)
- 2 lb (900 g) fresh white mushrooms, or 1 lb 5 oz (600 g) canned sliced mushrooms, drained
- 7 tablespoons olive oil, plus extra for brushing
- 1 onion, grated
- 2 garlic cloves, finely chopped
- 1 lb 5 oz (600 g) tomatoes, peeled and puréed
- 1 tablespoon tomato paste
- 2 tablespoons tomato ketchup
- 1 bay leaf
- pinch of ground allspice
- salt and pepper
- 5 tablespoons finely chopped fresh parsley
- 1 teaspoon cornstarch (cornflour)
- 1 cup (250 ml / 8 fl oz) heavy (double) cream
- pinch of ground nutmeg
- 11 oz (300 g) wide macaroni or ziti pasta
- 1¼ cups (150 g / 5 oz) grated Parmesan or regato cheese
- 6 sheets phyllo dough (filo pastry)
- 5 tablespoons (70 g / 2¾ oz) butter, melted

- 4 large green or red bell peppers
- ½ cup (120 ml / 4 fl oz) olive oil
- 1 red bell pepper, seeded and finely chopped
- 4 scallions (spring onions), finely chopped
- 3 garlic cloves, thinly sliced
- ⅔ cup (150 g / 5 oz) risotto or medium-grain rice
- 4 cups (1 litre / 1¾ pints) hot vegetable stock
- 1 lb 2 oz (500 g) squid, cleaned and cut into small pieces (see p 325)
- ½ cup (120 ml / 4 fl oz) dry white wine
- 1 tomato, peeled, seeded, and chopped
- 2 tablespoons finely chopped fresh dill
- 5 tablespoons pine nuts
- salt and pepper

BELL PEPPERS STUFFED WITH SQUID AND RICE

ΠΙΠΕΡΙΕΣ ΓΕΜΙΣΤΕΣ ΜΕ ΚΑΛΑΜΑΡΙΑ ΡΥΖΟΤΟ

Piperies gemistes me kalamaria rizoto

Preheat the oven to 300°F (150°C / Gas Mark 2). Slice the tops off the large bell peppers and carefully remove the seeds. Brush with a little of the oil, put into an ovenproof dish, and roast for about 35 minutes, until they begin to soften. Heat half of the remaining oil in a pan. Add the chopped bell pepper, scallions, and garlic and cook over high heat, stirring frequently, for about 5 minutes. Add the rice and cook, stirring constantly, for 2–3 minutes, until it becomes translucent. Add the stock, ½ cup (120 ml / 4 fl oz) at a time, and cook, stirring frequently, for about 20 minutes, until the rice is tender and creamy. Meanwhile, turn the oven up to 350°F (180°C / Gas Mark 4). Heat the remaining oil in a nonstick pan. Add the squid and cook over low heat until the juices have evaporated. Increase the heat to high, pour in the wine, and cook for a few minutes until the alcohol has evaporated. Add the squid, tomato, dill, and pine nuts to the risotto, season with salt and pepper, and mix gently with a fork. Fill the prepared bell peppers with the squid risotto and bake for about 35 minutes. Serve hot or at room temperature.

Serves 4
Preparation time 1 hour
Cooking time 35 minutes

STUFFED SQUID
ΚΑΛΑΜΑΡΙΑ ΓΕΜΙΣΤΑ
Kalamaria gemista

Pierce the body sacs of the squid in several places with a skewer, slice off the tip at the pointed end of each body sac, and chop the tentacles. Heat half the oil in a pan. Add the onion and squid tentacles and cook over medium heat, stirring frequently, for 5 minutes. Remove from the heat, stir in the rice, dill, currants, and pine nuts, and season with salt and pepper. Stuff the body sacs with the rice mixture, filling them about half-full. Secure the openings with wooden toothpicks. (To "pre-shrink" the body sacs before stuffing, sweat them in a nonstick pan over medium heat for 5 minutes, then stuff them two-thirds full.) Heat the remaining oil in a large pan. Add the squid, pour in the wine, lemon juice, and 1 cup (250 ml / 8 fl oz) water, cover, and simmer for 45 minutes, until the squid are tender.

Serves 4
Preparation time 30 minutes
Cooking time 50 minutes

Note: Small cuttlefish can be substituted for the squid. You can also add 3–4 chopped tomatoes, half to the filling and the rest to the sauce.

- 3¼ lb (1.5 kg) small squid, cleaned (see p 325)
- ½ cup (120 ml / 4 fl oz) olive oil
- 1 onion, grated
- ¼ cup (50 g / 2 oz) long-grain rice
- ½ cup (15 g / ½ oz) finely chopped fresh dill
- 2 tablespoons currants
- 2 tablespoons pine nuts
- salt and pepper
- ½ cup (120 ml / 4 fl oz) white wine
- 1 tablespoon freshly squeezed lemon juice

SPAGHETTI WITH SHELLFISH
ΣΠΑΓΚΕΤΙ ΜΕ ΘΑΛΑΣΣΙΝΑ
Spageti me thalasina

Pour the wine and ½ cup (120 ml / 4 fl oz) water into a large pan and bring to a boil. Add the shrimp and cook for 1 minute, then remove with a slotted spoon. Add the mussels to the pan and cook for 1 minute, then remove with a slotted spoon. Add the clams to the pan and cook for 1 minute, then remove with a slotted spoon. Reserve the cooking liquid. Heat ½ cup (120 ml / 4 fl oz) of the oil in a pan. Add the onion and garlic and cook over low heat, stirring occasionally, for 5 minutes, until softened. Add the squid and cook, stirring frequently, until the liquid has almost evaporated. Add the tomatoes, tomato paste, sugar, and reserved cooking liquid, stir well, and simmer for about 20 minutes, until the squid is tender and the sauce has thickened. Add the shrimp, mussels, clams, parsley or basil, and mint, season with salt and pepper, and simmer briskly for 5 minutes. Remove the pan from the heat. Meanwhile, bring a large pan of water to a boil, stir in salt and the remaining olive oil, add the spaghetti, and cook for 8–10 minutes, or until al dente. Drain and toss with the sauce, then serve immediately.

Serves 4
Preparation time 30 minutes
Cooking time 40 minutes

- ½ cup (120 ml / 4 fl oz) dry white wine
- 1 lb 2 oz (500 g) shrimp (prawns), peeled and deveined (see p 322)
- 9 oz (250 g) shelled mussels
- 8 small clams, scrubbed (see pp 323–4)
- ⅔ cup (150 ml / ¼ pint) olive oil
- 1 onion, sliced into rings
- 2–3 garlic cloves, finely chopped
- 9 oz (250 g) squid, cleaned and cut into rings (see p 325)
- 14 oz (400 g) canned chopped tomatoes
- 1 tablespoon tomato paste
- ½ teaspoon sugar
- 1 tablespoon finely chopped fresh parsley or basil
- 1 tablespoon finely chopped fresh mint
- salt and pepper
- 11 oz (300 g) spaghetti

- 6 jumbo shrimp (king prawns)
- 1 lb 2 oz (500 g) clams, scrubbed (see pp 323–4)
- ½ cup (120 ml / 4 fl oz) olive oil
- 1 large onion, finely chopped
- 5 garlic cloves, thinly sliced
- 1 hot chile, finely chopped
- 2¼ lb (1 kg) tomatoes, peeled, seeded, and chopped
- 2 bay leaves
- 1 fresh thyme sprig
- 1 fresh rosemary sprig
- 14 oz (400 g) squid, cleaned (see p 325) and cut into rings
- 4 tablespoons dry white wine
- 1 tablespoon freshly squeezed lemon juice
- 12 scallops, shucked
- salt and pepper
- rice pilaf, to serve

SPICY SHELLFISH STEW
ΘΑΛΑΣΣΙΝΑ ΜΕ ΠΙΚΑΝΤΙΚΗ ΣΑΛΤΣΑ
Thalasina me pikadiki saltsa

Peel the shrimp, leaving the heads and tails intact, and devein (see p 322). Put the clams into a large pan, add a little water, cover, and bring to a boil. Cook over medium heat for 4–5 minutes, until the shells open. Drain and discard any that remain shut. Heat the oil in a large pan. Add the onion, garlic, and chile and cook over low heat, stirring occasionally, for 5 minutes, until softened. Add the tomatoes, cover, and simmer for 10 minutes. Add the bay leaves, thyme, rosemary, and squid, cover, and simmer for 15 minutes more. Pour in the wine and lemon juice, add the shrimp and scallops, and season with salt and pepper. Cook for 8–10 minutes, then add the clams, stir gently once or twice, and remove from the heat. Serve hot, accompanied by rice pilaf.

Serves 6
Preparation time 20 minutes
Cooking time 40 minutes

- 1 small octopus, about 1 lb 2 oz (500 g), cleaned (see p 325)
- 4 squid or cuttlefish, cleaned
- 1 lb 2 oz (500 g) jumbo shrimp (king prawns), peeled and deveined (see p 322)
- olive oil, for brushing
- 1 lb 2 oz (500 g) live mussels, scrubbed (see p 324)
- ½ cup (120 ml / 4 fl oz) white wine

FOR THE GARLIC SAUCE
- 3 garlic cloves, finely chopped
- 1 tablespoon fresh oregano
- ½ cup (120 ml / 4 fl oz) olive oil
- 3 tablespoons freshly squeezed lemon juice

FOR THE LEMON-CAPER SAUCE
- 1 tablespoon capers
- 1 tablespoon finely chopped scallions (spring onions)
- 1 tablespoon finely chopped fresh mint
- 1 cup (250 ml / 8 fl oz) Mayonnaise (p 60)
- 1 tablespoon freshly squeezed lemon juice
- pepper

GRILLED SHELLFISH
ΘΑΛΑΣΣΙΝΑ ΣΤΑ ΚΑΡΒΟΥΝΑ
Thalasina sta karvouna

Several hours in advance, brush the octopus, squid or cuttlefish, and shrimp with oil. Cover and chill in the refrigerator until ready to cook. Meanwhile, make the sauces. Combine all the ingredients for the garlic sauce, cover, and chill in the refrigerator. Mash the capers with a fork, combine with the rest of the lemon-caper sauce ingredients, cover, and chill in the refrigerator. Light the barbecue. Put the octopus, squid or cuttlefish, and shrimp in separate, oiled hinged barbecue racks and close securely. Put the mussels into a flameproof dish, sprinkle with the wine, and cover. Grill the squid or cuttlefish and octopus for 8–10 minutes on each side. Meanwhile, put the dish of mussels on the barbecue grill and cook for 6–8 minutes, until they open. Discard any that remain closed. Cook the shrimp for 2–3 minutes on each side. Be careful not to overcook any of the shellfish. Serve the shellfish hot accompanied by the sauces.

Serves 4
Preparation time 2 hours (including chilling)
Cooking time 20 minutes

Note: You can also cook the shellfish under the broiler (grill), brushing with olive oil when you turn them over to cook the second side.

FISHERMAN'S PILAF
ΠΙΛΑΦΙ ΤΟΥ ΨΑΡΑ
Pilafi tou psara

Pour ½ cup (120 ml / 4 fl oz) water into a pan and bring to a boil. Add the shrimp and cook for 5 minutes, then remove with a slotted spoon and let cool. Add the mussels and scallops to the pan and cook for 5 minutes. Meanwhile, peel and devein the shrimp (see p 322). Remove the mussels and scallops from the pan with a slotted spoon and set aside. Add the clams to the pan and cook for 4–5 minutes, until they open. Remove with a slotted spoon and discard any that remain shut. Reserve the cooking liquid. Heat the oil in a large, heavy pan. Add the onion and garlic and cook over low heat, stirring occasionally, for 5 minutes, until softened. Add the bell pepper and cook, stirring frequently, for 5 minutes more, until softened. Add the tomatoes, tomato ketchup, parsley, and cayenne. Season with salt and pepper, increase the heat to medium, and simmer for about 20 minutes, until the sauce is very thick. Measure the reserved cooking liquid, make it up to 2 cups (450 ml / 16 fl oz) with water, and pour it into the pan. Bring to a boil, stir in the rice, reduce the heat to low, cover, and simmer for about 20 minutes, until almost all the liquid has been absorbed and the rice is tender. Add the shellfish, stir gently, and simmer for 3 minutes more. If using the pine nuts, melt the butter in a skillet or frying pan, add the pine nuts and cook over low heat, stirring frequently, for 1–2 minutes, until lightly browned. Garnish the pilaf with the pine nuts, if using. Serve immediately. You can also serve the pilaf at room temperature.

Serves 6
Preparation time 30 minutes
Cooking time 1¼ hours

Note: You can also spoon the pilaf into a greased fluted cake pan, press it down well, and turn out onto a large platter, then scatter with pine nuts.

- 8 oz (225 g) shrimp (prawns)
- 8 oz (225 g) shelled mussels
- 8 oz (225 g) shucked scallops
- 8 oz (225 g) clams, scrubbed
- ½ cup (120 ml / 4 fl oz) olive oil
- 1 large onion, thinly sliced
- 2 garlic cloves, sliced
- 1 green bell pepper, seeded and cut into small strips
- 1 lb 5 oz (600 g) tomatoes, peeled and chopped
- 2 tablespoons tomato ketchup
- 3 tablespoons chopped fresh parsley
- pinch of cayenne pepper
- salt and pepper
- 1½ cups (275 g / 10 oz) long-grain rice
- 2 tablespoons (25 g / 1 oz) butter (optional)
- 4 tablespoons pine nuts (optional)

- 1 lb 2 oz (500 g) shrimp (prawns)
- 1 teaspoon paprika
- 7 oz (200 g) shelled mussels
- ½ cup (120 ml / 4 fl oz) olive oil
- 3 large onions, sliced
- 6 garlic cloves, thinly sliced
- ⅔ red bell pepper, seeded and finely chopped
- ¼ red chile, finely chopped
- 14 oz (400 g) canned chopped tomatoes
- 2 tablespoons tomato paste
- 4 tablespoons tomato ketchup
- 2 tablespoons mixed peppercorns
- 10 allspice berries
- 2 bay leaves
- 2¼ lb (1 kg) Pickled octopus (p 77), cut into 1-inch (2.5-cm) pieces
- 4 tablespoons balsamic vinegar
- 7 oz (200 g) shucked scallops (optional)
- salt and pepper
- cooked rice, to serve

SHELLFISH STIFADO
ΘΑΛΑΣΣΙΝΑ ΣΤΙΦΑΔΟ
Thalasina stifado

Peel the shrimp, leaving the heads and tails intact, and devein. Put them into a pan with ½ cup (120 ml / 4 fl oz) water and the paprika. Bring to a boil and cook for 4 minutes, then remove with a slotted spoon. Reserve the cooking liquid. Remove and discard the heads and tails, cut the shrimp into pieces, and set aside. Put the mussels into a pan and cook over high heat for 5 minutes to release some of their juices. Do not overcook, or they will become tough. Drain and reserve the liquid. Heat the oil in a pan. Add the onions and garlic and cook over low heat, stirring occasionally, for 5 minutes, until softened. Add the bell pepper, chile, tomatoes, tomato paste, tomato ketchup, peppercorns, allspice berries, bay leaves, reserved shrimp cooking liquid, and reserved mussel liquid. Stir well to mix, and simmer for 30 minutes, or until thickened. Add the octopus and vinegar, reduce the heat, and simmer for 20 minutes, until the sauce thickens again. Add the scallops (if using), mussels and shrimp, season with salt and pepper, and simmer for 5–7 minutes more. Serve with cooked rice.

Serves 6
Preparation time 40 minutes
Cooking time 1¼ hours

- 1 red bell pepper, seeded and cut into 2-inch (5-cm) squares
- 1 green bell pepper, seeded and cut into 2-inch (5-cm) squares
- 1 yellow bell pepper, seeded and cut into 2-inch (5-cm) squares
- 16 crayfish or shrimp (prawns), peeled and deveined (see p 322)
- 16 scallops, shucked
- 2 tablespoons olive oil
- 1½ cups (350 g / 12 oz) cooked long-grain rice, to serve
- salt and pepper

FOR THE DILL SAUCE
- 4 tablespoons Mayonnaise (p 60)
- ½ cup (120 ml / 4 fl oz) strained plain or thick Greek yogurt
- 4 tablespoons finely chopped fresh dill
- 1 tablespoon freshly squeezed lemon juice

SHELLFISH SOUVLAKI WITH DILL SAUCE
ΣΟΥΒΛΑΚΙ ΜΕ ΘΑΛΑΣΣΙΝΑ ΚΑΙ ΣΑΛΤΣΑ ΑΝΙΘΟ
Souvlaki me thalasina ke saltsa anitho

To make the dill sauce, put all the ingredients into a bowl and beat with a fork until thoroughly blended. Cover and place in the refrigerator for at least 2 hours to let the flavors mingle. Light the barbecue or preheat the broiler (grill). Blanch the bell peppers in boiling water for 1–2 minutes, then remove with a slotted spoon, and immediately refresh in ice water. Drain well. Thread the bell peppers in pairs onto 8 wooden skewers between the crayfish or shrimp and the scallops, allowing 2 crayfish or shrimp and 2 scallops per skewer. Place the skewers on a rack and brush with the oil. Grill over charcoal or cook under the broiler for 2–3 minutes on each side, until the scallops become opaque. Be careful not to overcook or the shellfish will dry out. Divide the rice among individual warmed plates and place 2 skewers on each. Serve immediately, seasoned with salt and pepper and topped with 2–3 tablespoons of the dill sauce.

Serves 4
Preparation time 2½ hours (including standing)
Cooking time 5 minutes

POULTRY

-

ΠΟΥΛΕΡΙΚΑ

-

Poulerika

In Greece, the classic way of cooking poultry is in a pot on the top of the stove, stewed or braised with pasta, rice, or a vegetable such as okra, peas, or potatoes. Favorite sauces contain tomatoes, lemon juice, or wine and are flavored with bay leaves, garlic, oregano, thyme, allspice, and pepper. No matter what is to be cooked with it, the chicken, whether whole or cut into pieces, is always browned first in oil or some other fat. The pan used must be just wide enough to hold the chicken pieces side by side so that the moisture they release evaporates quickly and the meat browns instead of steaming. Too much space between the pieces will allow the fat to burn. Butter gives the chicken a rich flavor, but olive oil is a healthier choice than butter and also produces good results, adding its unique flavor and special aroma.

Oven-roasted chicken is even easier, requiring only an occasional basting. A favorite Sunday dish is pot-roasted lemon chicken, seasoned with oregano or thyme and surrounded by sliced potatoes. Another method is to thread the meat on a spit that turns it as it cooks, combining the direct heat from a broiler (grill) with the even warmth of an oven. This is the most common cooking method for meat in Greece. Whatever the source of the heat, broiling (grilling) requires more care than oven-roasting. Adjust the heat control on conventional broilers, or the height of the barbecue grill when cooking over charcoal, to increase or decrease the heat as necessary and thus prevent the meat from burning or drying out. As a general rule, broil (grill) poultry under or over medium heat, positioning it at least 3 inches (7.5 cm) from the heat source.

Most of the chicken's fat is located in and under the skin, so removing the skin before you stew or braise chicken will make the dish lighter. Marinating chicken beforehand in an oil-based marinade will help keep it succulent, and another trick to keep the flesh moist is to brine it before cooking. To do this, fill a large bowl or pail with enough water to cover the bird. Add salt, allowing 4 tablespoons for every 4 cups (1 litre / 1¾ pints) water, and stir to dissolve. Let the bird soak in a cool place. Soak a chicken for 1 hour per 1 lb 2 oz (500 g), but for no longer than 8 hours in total. You can also soak turkey in brine in the same way. If you intend to roast or broil (grill) the chicken, pat the skin dry with paper towels and let stand, uncovered, in the refrigerator for the same amount of time it was soaked. This results in both moist flesh and crisp skin when the chicken is cooked. Do not remove the skin when you plan to roast or broil the chicken, as the fat underneath it melts during cooking, basting the flesh and keeping it tender. Chicken breast portions are particularly difficult to keep moist and are best used for kabobs (kebabs) and brochettes. Thread cubes of chicken breast onto skewers with vegetables such as red bell pepper, tomato, onions, and mushrooms. Brush them frequently with olive oil or a marinade while they are broiling (grilling) so that they do not burn before the meat is cooked. Another good technique with chicken breast pieces is to cut a slit along the thick edge of each piece to form a pocket, then stuff it with a piece of chilled butter and some herbs, coat it with bread crumbs, and fry it.

To test whether the chicken is cooked, pierce the thickest part of the piece (or the thigh if it is a whole chicken) with a sharp knife; if the juices run clear, it is ready. If there are any traces of pink, it should be cooked for a little longer.

- ⅔ cup (150 ml / ¼ pint) olive oil
- 2¼ lb (1 kg) skinless, boneless chicken breast cut into 1½-inch (4-cm) cubes
- 1 onion, grated
- 2 garlic cloves, thinly sliced
- 1 tablespoon tomato paste
- 2 tomatoes, peeled, seeded, and finely chopped
- salt and pepper
- 2 tablespoons finely chopped fresh parsley
- ⅓ cup (50 g / 2 oz) capers
- scant 1 cup (100g / 3½ oz) green olives, pitted (stoned) and sliced
- 11 oz (300 g) ready-made egg noodles (pasta) such as tagliatelle, or Homemade egg noodles (pasta), p 270
- ⅓ cup (40 g / 1½ oz) grated dry mizithra or Parmesan cheese

CHICKEN WITH CAPERS, OLIVES, AND EGG NOODLES (PASTA)
ΚΟΤΟΠΟΥΛΟ ΜΕ ΚΑΠΑΡΗ, ΕΛΙΕΣ, ΚΑΙ ΧΥΛΟΠΙΤΕΣ
Kotopoulo me kapari, elies, ke hilopites

Heat ½ cup (120 ml / 4 fl oz) of the oil in a heavy pan. Add the chicken and cook over medium heat, stirring occasionally, for 5–8 minutes, until lightly browned all over. Remove with a slotted spoon and drain any excess oil back into the pan. Add the onion and garlic to the pan, reduce the heat, and cook, stirring occasionally, for 5 minutes, until softened. Add the tomato paste and cook, stirring constantly, for 2–3 minutes, then add the tomatoes and chicken, and season with salt and pepper. Cover and simmer for 15–20 minutes, until the chicken is tender, adding a little water if it seems dry. Rinse the capers and olives well under running water, then drain, and pat dry. Set the capers aside. Add the olives to the pan, stir gently and simmer for 5 minutes, then add the parsley. Meanwhile, cook the noodles in salted boiling water to cover according to the directions on the package. Drain well and tip onto a warmed deep platter. Heat the remaining oil in a small heavy skillet or frying pan. Add the capers and cook, stirring frequently, for a few minutes, then remove, and drain on paper towels. Spoon the chicken and sauce over the noodles and sprinkle with the fried capers and grated cheese. Serve immediately.

Serves 4
Preparation time 20 minutes
Cooking time 40 minutes

CHICKEN WITH FRESH OREGANO
ΚΟΤΟΠΟΥΛΟ ΜΕ ΦΡΕΣΚΙΑ ΡΙΓΑΝΗ
Kotopoulo me freskia rigani

Rub the chicken with the lemon and season with salt and pepper. Heat the oil in a heavy pan. Add the chicken pieces and cook over medium heat, turning occasionally, for 8–10 minutes, until lightly browned all over. Pour the wine over them and cook for a few minutes until the alcohol has evaporated. Add the oregano and lemon juice, cover, and simmer, for about 45 minutes, or until the chicken is tender. Remove from the heat and serve with fried or mashed potatoes.

Serves 4
Preparation time 10 minutes
Cooking time 1 hour

- 1 chicken, about 3¼ lb (1.5 kg), cut into serving pieces
- 1 lemon, cut in wedges
- salt and pepper
- 5 tablespoons olive oil
- 1 cup (250 ml / 8 fl oz) white wine
- 3 tablespoons fresh oregano, chopped
- 2 tablespoons freshly squeezed lemon juice
- fried or mashed potatoes, to serve

CHICKEN WITH SCALLIONS (SPRING ONIONS) AND FENNEL
ΚΟΤΟΠΟΥΛΟ ΜΕ ΚΡΕΜΜΥΔΑΚΙΑ ΚΑΙ ΜΑΡΑΘΟ
Kotopoulo me kremidakia ke maratho

Heat the oil in a large heavy pan. Add the chicken and cook over medium heat, turning occasionally, for 8–10 minutes, until lightly browned all over. Pour in the lemon juice and 1 cup (250 ml / 8 fl oz) water, cover, and simmer for 15 minutes. Add the potato, scallions, and fennel, season with salt and pepper, and simmer for 20–30 minutes more, or until the chicken and vegetables are tender and the sauce has thickened. If using egg-lemon sauce, beat a few tablespoons of the hot pan juices into the egg-lemon mixture, pour it over the chicken, and shake the pan to distribute it evenly. Serve immediately.

Serves 4
Preparation time 15 minutes
Cooking time 40 minutes

- 5 tablespoons olive oil
- 1 chicken, about 3¼ lb (1.5 kg), cut into serving pieces
- 2 tablespoons freshly squeezed lemon juice
- 1 potato, grated
- 1 lb 2 oz (500 g) scallions (spring onions), chopped
- 1 lb 2 oz (500 g) fennel fronds or fresh dill, coarsely chopped
- salt and pepper
- Egg-lemon sauce (p 59, optional)

- ¾ cup (175 ml / 6 fl oz) olive oil
- 1 chicken, about 3¼ lb (1.5 kg), cut into serving pieces
- 5 tablespoons freshly squeezed lemon juice
- 4½ lb (2 kg) potatoes, cut into pieces
- pinch of dried oregano
- salt and pepper

CHICKEN WITH LEMON SAUCE AND POTATOES
ΚΟΤΟΠΟΥΛΟ ΛΕΜΟΝΑΤΟ ΜΕ ΠΑΤΑΤΕΣ
Kotopoulo lemonato me patates

Heat the oil in a large pan over high heat. Add the chicken pieces and cook, turning occasionally, for 8–10 minutes, until lightly browned on all sides. Pour in the lemon juice, add the potatoes and oregano, and season with salt and pepper. Add enough hot water to cover the potatoes, reduce the heat, cover, and simmer for about 1 hour, or until the chicken and potatoes are tender and the sauce has reduced. Serve immediately. Alternatively, fry the chicken in 4 tablespoons oil and brown the potatoes in the remainder. Add them to the casserole 20 minutes before the end of the cooking time.

Serves 4
Preparation time 15 minutes
Cooking time 1¼ hours

□ p 356

- 1 chicken, about 3¼ lb (1.5 kg), quartered
- salt and pepper
- 5 tablespoons olive oil
- 3 garlic cloves, thinly sliced
- 1 tablespoon finely chopped fresh thyme, marjoram, or oregano
- 5 tablespoons dry white wine
- 1¾ lb (800 g) tomatoes, peeled and finely chopped or 14 oz (400 g) canned chopped tomatoes
- 1¼ cups (150 g / 5 oz) Kalamata olives, pitted (stoned) and halved
- spaghetti, to serve

CHICKEN WITH OLIVES
ΚΟΤΟΠΟΥΛΟ ΜΕ ΕΛΙΕΣ
Kotopoulo me elies

Season the chicken with salt and pepper. Heat the oil in a pan. Add the chicken and cook over medium heat, turning occasionally, for 8–10 minutes, until lightly browned all over. Add the garlic and thyme and cook, stirring constantly, for 5 minutes. Pour in the wine and simmer until the alcohol has evaporated. Add the tomatoes, cover, and simmer for 30 minutes. Add the olives, re-cover the pan, and simmer for 30 minutes more, until the chicken is tender and the sauce has thickened. Transfer the chicken to a platter and pour the sauce over it. Serve immediately with spaghetti.

Serves 4
Preparation time 15 minutes
Cooking time 1¼ hours

□ p 357

Chicken with lemon sauce and potatoes, p 355

Chicken with olives, p 355

CHICKEN STIFADO
ΚΟΤΟΠΟΥΛΟ ΣΤΙΦΑΔΟ ΣΤΟ ΦΟΥΡΝΟ
Kotopoulo stifado sto fourno

- 3¼ lb (1.5 kg) small pearl (pickling) onions or shallots
- ¾ cup (175 ml / 6 fl oz) olive oil
- 1 chicken, about 3¼ lb (1.5 kg), cut into serving pieces
- 1 cup (250 ml / 8 fl oz) dry red wine
- 1 teaspoon sugar
- 1 tablespoon tomato paste
- 6 garlic cloves
- ½ teaspoon dried rosemary
- 10 black peppercorns
- ½ teaspoon ground mace
- 1 bay leaf
- salt and pepper
- rice pilaf, to serve

Blanch the onions for 2–3 minutes in boiling water, then drain, let cool slightly, and peel. Heat half the oil in a large heavy skillet or frying pan. Add the chicken and cook over medium heat, turning occasionally, for 8–10 minutes, until lightly browned all over. Using a slotted spoon, transfer the chicken to an ovenproof dish. Pour the wine into the skillet and cook, scraping up the sediment from the base of the skillet with a wooden spoon, for 3–4 minutes, then add to the chicken. Preheat the oven to 400°F (200°C / Gas Mark 6). Meanwhile, heat the remaining oil in a heavy pan. Add the onions, cover, and cook over low heat for 5–10 minutes, until lightly browned. Uncover, sprinkle with the sugar, and stir until caramelized. Transfer the onions to the ovenproof dish. Combine the tomato paste with 1 cup (250 ml / 8 fl oz) water in a bowl and pour the mixture over the chicken, then add the garlic, rosemary, peppercorns, mace, and bay leaf, and season with salt and pepper. Cover and bake for 1–1½ hours. Serve hot, with rice pilaf.

Serves 4
Preparation time 30 minutes
Cooking time 1–1½ hours

CHICKEN WITH PICKLED LEMON FROM CORFU
ΚΟΤΟΠΟΥΛΟ ΜΕ ΛΕΜΟΝΟΦΛΟΥΔΕΣ
Kotopoulo me lemonofloudes

- 1 chicken, about 3¼ lb (1.5 kg), cut into serving pieces
- ⅓ cup (40 g / 1½ oz) all-purpose (plain) flour
- ½ cup (120 ml / 4 fl oz) olive oil
- 1 onion, grated
- 1 garlic clove, finely chopped
- thinly sliced rind of 1 pickled lemon
- ⅔ cup (65 g / 2½ oz) green olives, pitted (stoned), chopped, soaked in water for 3 hours, and drained
- salt and pepper
- 2 tablespoons freshly squeezed lemon juice
- mashed potatoes or rice pilaf, to serve

To make the pickled lemon, cut 4 lemons into quarters. With a sharp knife, remove the flesh and as much of the white pith as possible. Soak the lemon rind in water to cover for 12 hours, then drain. Arrange in layers in a bowl, sprinkling each layer with a handful of coarse sea salt. Let stand for at least 1 week. Before using, rinse well in plenty of cold running water. To make the dish, coat the chicken pieces with the flour. Heat the oil in a large pan. Add the chicken and cook over medium heat, turning occasionally, for 8–10 minutes, until lightly browned all over. Add the onion and garlic and cook, stirring occasionally, for 2–3 minutes. Add the pickled lemon, olives, and ½ cup (120 ml / 4 fl oz) water and season with salt and pepper. Bring to a boil, cover, and simmer for about 30 minutes, or until the chicken is cooked through and the liquid has reduced. Add the lemon juice and shake the pan to distribute it evenly. Serve hot on a bed of mashed potatoes or rice pilaf.

Serves 4
Preparation time 7–8 days (including making the pickled lemon)
Cooking time 45 minutes

🖻 p 360

CHICKEN WITH SAUERKRAUT AND GARBANZO BEANS (CHICKPEAS)
ΚΟΤΟΠΟΥΛΟ ΜΕ ΛΑΧΑΝΟ ΤΟΥΡΣΙ ΚΑΙ ΡΕΒΥΘΙΑ
Kotopoulo me lahano toursi ke revithia

- ⅔ cup (150 g / 5 oz) garbanzo beans (chickpeas), soaked for 12 hours in cold water to cover with 1 tablespoon salt
- 1 chicken, about 3¼ lb (1.5 kg), cut into serving pieces and skinned
- salt and pepper
- ½ cup (120 ml / 4 fl oz) olive oil
- 1 lb 2 oz (500 g) sauerkraut, finely chopped
- 2 leeks, white parts only, chopped
- 1 tablespoon sweet paprika
- ½–1 teaspoon chili flakes, according to taste
- about 1 cup (120 g / 4 oz) all-purpose (plain) flour

Drain and rinse the garbanzo beans under cold running water. Put the beans into a pan, pour in water to cover, and cook for 20 minutes, skimming off the scum that rises to the surface. Drain well, reserving 2 cups (450 ml / 16 fl oz) of the cooking liquid. Preheat the oven to 325 °F (160 °C / Gas Mark 3). Season the chicken with salt and pepper and put the pieces into a deep ovenproof dish. Heat the oil in a pan. Add the sauerkraut and leeks and cook over low heat, stirring occasionally, for 5 minutes, until softened. Stir in the paprika and chili flakes and cook for 1 minute more. Sprinkle the garbanzo beans, sauerkraut, and leeks around the chicken, pour in the reserved cooking liquid, and season with a little salt, if necessary, and pepper. Combine the flour with 2–3 table-spoons water to make a thick paste and use the paste to seal the edges of the pan. Bake for 3–4 hours, or until the chicken and garbanzo beans are meltingly tender. Remove from the oven and let rest for 10 minutes before serving.

Serves 6
Preparation time 12 hours (including soaking)
Cooking time 3½–4½ hours

CHICKEN SOUVLAKI
ΣΟΥΒΛΑΚΙ ΚΟΤΟΠΟΥΛΟ
Souvlaki kotopoulo

- 1¾ lb (800 g) skinless, boneless chicken breast portions, cut into 1-inch (2.5-cm) cubes
- pinch of dried oregano, plus extra for sprinkling
- 2–3 tablespoons olive oil
- 2 onions, quartered (optional)
- 2 green bell peppers, seeded and cut into 1-inch (2.5-cm) squares (optional)
- 1–2 tablespoons freshly squeezed lemon juice
- salt and pepper
- Pita bread for souvlaki (p 514) and Tzatziki (p 152), to serve

Put the chicken into a large bowl, add the oregano and oil, season with pepper, and toss well. Cover and let marinate in the refrigerator, turning occasionally, for 6 hours or overnight. Preheat the broiler (grill) or light the barbecue. Drain and thread the meat onto skewers, alternating with the onions and bell peppers, if using. Drain the oil into a screw-top jar, add the lemon juice, fasten the lid, and shake vigorously until thoroughly combined. Brush the souvlaki with the mixture. Grill the skewers over charcoal or cook under the broiler, turning twice and brushing frequently with the oil-lemon marinade, for 10–15 minutes, or until the chicken is cooked through. Do not overcook, as chicken is lean and tends to dry out. Season with salt, sprinkle with oregano, and serve immediately with Pita bread and Tzatziki.

Serves 4
Preparation time 6¼ hours (including marinating)
Cooking time 10–15 minutes

☐ p 361

Chicken with pickled lemon from Corfu, p 358

Chicken souvlaki, p 359

CHICKEN WITH TRAHANA
ΚΟΤΟΠΟΥΛΟ ΤΡΑΧΑΝΑ
Kotopoulo me trahana

Heat the oil in a large, heavy pan. Add the chicken and cook over medium heat, turning occasionally, for 8–10 minutes, until lightly browned all over. Add the onions and garlic and cook for 2 minutes more, until softened. Add the tomato juice, tomato, allspice berries, cinnamon stick, if using, and 1 cup (250 ml / 8 fl oz) hot water, and season with salt and pepper. Cover and simmer for about 45 minutes, or until the chicken is cooked through. Transfer the chicken pieces to a platter with a slotted spoon and keep warm. Measure the cooking liquid and make up to 2 cups (450 ml / 16 fl oz) with water, then pour into a pan, and bring to a boil. Stir in the trahana, cover, and simmer for 5–8 minutes, or until the trahana has softened and absorbed all the liquid. Return the chicken pieces to the pan and heat gently. Serve immediately.

Serves 4
Preparation time 30 minutes
Cooking time 1¼ hours

Note: Ready-made trahana is precooked. If using, stir it into the sauce, bring to a boil, cover, and turn off the heat. It will be ready to serve in 10 minutes. If using homemade trahana, be careful not to overcook it or it will turn to mush.

□ p 364

- ½ cup (120 ml / 4 fl oz) olive oil
- 1 chicken, about 3¼ lb (1.5 kg), cut into serving pieces
- 2 onions, finely chopped
- 2 garlic cloves, thinly sliced
- 1 cup (250 ml / 8 fl oz) tomato juice
- 1 tomato, peeled, seeded, and chopped
- 4–5 allspice berries
- 1 cinnamon stick (optional)
- salt and pepper
- 8 oz (225 g) Sour or Sweet trahana (p 280 or 281), or ready-made trahana

---

CHICKEN WITH YOGURT
ΚΟΤΟΠΟΥΛΟ ΓΙΑΟΥΡΤΑΒΑ
Kotopoulo giaourtava

Preheat the oven to 350°F (180°C / Gas Mark 4). Heat the oil in a skillet or frying pan. Add the chicken and cook over medium heat, stirring occasionally, for 6–8 minutes, until lightly golden. Reduce the heat, add the scallions, and cook, stirring occasionally, for 4–5 minutes, until softened. Remove from the heat and let cool slightly. Stir in both types of cheese and the mint and season with salt and pepper. Beat the yogurt with the eggs in a bowl and stir into the chicken mixture. Transfer to an ovenproof dish or divide among 4 individual ramekins and bake for about 30 minutes, or until the top is golden. Serve hot.

Serves 4
Preparation time 20 minutes
Cooking time 30 minutes

- 5 tablespoons olive oil
- 1¾ lb (800 g) skinless, boneless chicken breast, cut into thin strips
- ½ cup (4) finely chopped scallions (spring onions)
- 1¾ cups (200 g / 7 oz) grated Gruyère cheese
- scant 1 cup (100 g / 3½ oz) grated kefalotiri or Parmesan cheese
- 2 tablespoons finely chopped fresh mint
- salt and pepper
- 2¼ cups (500 ml / 18 fl oz) strained plain or thick Greek yogurt
- 3 eggs, lightly beaten

- 4 large onions, sliced
- ½ cup (120 ml / 4 fl oz) olive oil
- 1 large chicken, about 3¼ lb (1.5 kg), cut into serving pieces
- ⅓ cup (80 g / 3 oz) currants
- 1 small cinnamon stick
- salt
- 20 black peppercorns
- ⅔ cup (150 ml / ¼ pint) hot chicken stock
- ⅓ cup (50 g / 2 oz) long-grain rice

BRAISED CHICKEN FROM KASTORIA
ΚΟΤΟΠΟΥΛΟ ΚΑΠΑΜΑ
Kotopoulo kapama

Steam the onions over boiling water for 10 minutes and drain well. Heat the oil in a large pan. Add the chicken pieces and cook over medium heat, turning occasionally, for 8–10 minutes, until lightly browned all over. Transfer to a platter with a slotted spoon. Add the onions to the pan and cook over medium heat, stirring constantly, for 5 minutes, until softened. Add the currants, cinnamon stick, and peppercorns, return the chicken to the pan, season with salt, and pour in half the stock. Cover and simmer for 30 minutes. Remove and discard the cinnamon stick. Add the rice and remaining stock to the pan and simmer for 20 minutes more, until the rice has absorbed the liquid and is fluffy. Serve immediately.

Serves 4
Preparation time 30 minutes
Cooking time 1 hour

- 2 small chickens, 2¼ lb (1 kg) each
- 2 small oranges
- broiled (grilled) vegetables and fried potatoes, to serve

FOR THE MARINADE
- 4 tablespoons freshly squeezed orange juice
- 4 tablespoons brandy
- 4 tablespoons honey
- 1 teaspoon dried oregano
- 1 teaspoon dried thyme
- 1 dried bay leaf, crumbled
- salt and pepper

CHARCOAL-GRILLED CHICKEN
ΚΟΤΟΠΟΥΛΟ ΣΤΑ ΚΑΡΒΟΥΝΑ
Kotopoulo sta karvouna

Combine all the ingredients for the marinade in a bowl and season with salt and pepper. Brush the marinade all over the chickens, inside and out. Cover and let marinate in the refrigerator, brushing occasionally with the juices, for 12 hours. Light the barbecue. Drain the chickens and reserve the marinade. Rub the skin of the oranges to release the aroma, place them in the cavities of the chickens, and tie the legs with trussing thread. Thread the chickens onto a long skewer or barbecue rotisserie spit and secure. Fit the spit to the barbecue about 12 inches (30 cm) from the charcoal and grill, rotating constantly, for 1 hour, or until cooked through. Brush all over several times with the marinade. When the chickens are cooked, remove the oranges and cut them into pieces to serve with the chicken. Serve hot with broiled vegetables and fried potatoes.

Serves 4
Preparation time 12¼ hours (including marinating)
Cooking time 1 hour

☐ p 365

Chicken with trahana, p 362

Charcoal-grilled chicken, p 363

CHICKEN MEATBALLS WITH CILANTRO (CORIANDER)

ΚΕΦΤΕΔΑΚΙΑ ΚΟΤΟΠΟΥΛΟΥ ΜΕ ΚΟΛΙΑΝΔΡΟ

Keftedakia kotopoulou me koliandro

Tear the bread into small pieces, put it into a bowl, pour in water to cover, and let soak. Meanwhile, combine the chicken, onion, scallions, cilantro, chili sauce, cumin, if using, and 2 tablespoons oil in a bowl and season with salt and pepper. Lightly squeeze out the bread, add to the chicken mixture with the egg, and knead until blended, soft, and pliable. Chill in the refrigerator for 30 minutes. Meanwhile, make the yogurt sauce. Combine the yogurt, oil, garlic, cilantro, and lemon juice in a bowl, season with salt, and chill in the refrigerator for 15 minutes. Dampen your hands and form the mixture into small balls. Heat the oil in a deep-fryer to 350–375°F (180–190°C). Roll the meatballs in flour to coat, shaking off any excess, and cook in batches in the hot oil for about 5 minutes, or until browned on all sides. Remove and drain on paper towels. Serve hot, accompanied by the yogurt sauce sprinkled with cayenne pepper.

Serves 4
Preparation time 40 minutes (including chilling)
Cooking time 15 minutes

- 2 oz (50 g) day-old bread, crusts removed
- 1 lb 2 oz (500 g) ground (minced) chicken
- 1 small onion, finely grated
- ¼ cup (4) finely chopped scallions (spring onions)
- 3 tablespoons finely chopped fresh cilantro (coriander)
- 2 tablespoons Greek chili sauce (p 60)
- ¼ teaspoon ground cumin (optional)
- 2 tablespoons olive oil
- salt and pepper
- 1 egg, lightly beaten
- olive oil, for frying
- all-purpose (plain) flour, for coating

FOR THE YOGURT SAUCE

- 1 cup (250 ml / 8 fl oz) plain yogurt
- 1 tablespoon olive oil
- 1 garlic clove, finely chopped
- 1 tablespoon finely chopped fresh cilantro (coriander)
- 1 tablespoon freshly squeezed lemon juice
- salt
- pinch of cayenne pepper

CHICKEN ROLL FROM SERRES
ΚΟΤΟΠΟΥΛΟ ΝΤΟΛΜΑ
Kotopoulo dolma

- 1 chicken, about 3¼ lb (1.5 kg)
- 5 slices pancetta, chopped
- 1¼ cups (150 g / 5 oz) grated kefalotiri or Parmesan cheese
- 3¼ lb (1.5 kg) small, round potatoes
- ½ cup (120 ml / 4 fl oz) olive oil
- ½ cup (120 ml / 4 fl oz) dry white wine
- 1 tablespoon Dijon mustard
- salt
- ½ teaspoon paprika

Preheat the oven to 350°F (180°C / Gas Mark 4). Carefully remove and reserve the chicken skin. Remove the meat from the bones and chop into small pieces. Trim and wash the chicken skin, spread out on a work surface, and place alternate layers of chopped chicken, pancetta, and cheese on top. Roll up and secure with kitchen string or trussing thread. Place the chicken roll in a roasting pan and surround with the potatoes. Put the oil, wine, and mustard into a screw-top jar, fasten the lid, and shake vigorously until thoroughly blended, then pour the mixture over the chicken and potatoes. Season with salt and sprinkle with the paprika. Bake, basting occasionally, for 1½ hours, or until the potatoes are tender and the chicken roll is golden brown. Remove from the oven and let stand for 10 minutes before slicing. Serve hot.

Serves 6
Preparation time 30 minutes
Cooking time 1½ hours

CHICKEN CASSEROLE WITH ORZO
ΓΙΟΥΒΕΤΣΙ ΜΕ ΚΟΤΟΠΟΥΛΟ
Giouvetsi me kotopoulo

- 2 eggplants (aubergines), cut into bite-size pieces
- 1 cup (250 ml / 8 fl oz) olive oil
- 1 zucchini (courgette), sliced
- 1 lb 10 oz (750 g) skinless, boneless chicken, cut into bite-size pieces
- 1 large onion, sliced
- 2 garlic cloves, finely chopped
- 4 large tomatoes, peeled, seeded, and coarsely chopped
- 1 red bell pepper, seeded and cut into julienne strips
- 1 yellow bell pepper, seeded and cut into julienne strips
- salt and pepper
- 11 oz (300 g) orzo pasta
- 2 cups (450 ml / 16 fl oz) hot chicken stock or water
- ½ cup (50 g / 2 oz) grated mild kefalograviera or Cheddar cheese (optional)

Sprinkle the eggplant pieces with salt and let drain in a colander for 1 hour. Rinse, squeeze out the excess water, and pat dry with paper towels. Heat 5 tablespoons of the oil in a skillet or frying pan. Add the pieces of eggplant and cook over medium heat, stirring frequently, for 6–8 minutes, until lightly browned. Remove with a slotted spoon and set aside. Add the zucchini slices to the skillet and cook, stirring frequently, for 6–8 minutes, until lightly browned. Remove with a slotted spoon and set aside. Heat half the remaining oil in a large pan. Add the chicken and cook over medium heat, stirring frequently, for 6–8 minutes, until lightly browned on all sides. Add the onion and garlic and cook, stirring frequently, for 4–5 minutes, until softened. Add the tomatoes, bell peppers, eggplants, and zucchini, season with salt and pepper, cover, and simmer for 20–25 minutes, or until the vegetables are half cooked. Heat the remaining oil in a small skillet. Add the orzo and cook over high heat, stirring constantly, for a few minutes, then stir it into the pan. Pour in the hot stock or water, cover, and simmer for 8–10 minutes, or until the orzo is tender. If you like, you can empty the pan into a flameproof dish, sprinkle with grated cheese, and broil (grill) for 7–8 minutes, until the cheese has melted and is lightly browned. Serve immediately.

Serves 4
Preparation time 1¼ hours (including salting)
Cooking time 1½ hours

CHICKEN STEW WITH TOMATO SAUCE
ΚΟΤΟΠΟΥΛΟ ΚΟΚΚΙΝΙΣΤΟ
Kotopoulo kokinisto

This recipe is the basis for a whole range of Greek chicken dishes. By combining it with vegetables, legumes (pulses), rice, or pasta, you can create a variety of wonderful recipes.

Heat the oil in a large pan. Add the chicken and cook over medium heat, turning frequently, for 8–10 minutes, until lightly browned all over. Remove with a slotted spoon and set aside. Add the onion to the pan and cook over low heat, stirring occasionally, for 5 minutes, until softened. Return the chicken to the pan, pour in the tomatoes, add the vinegar and sugar, and season with salt and pepper. Cover and simmer for about 1 hour, or until the chicken is cooked through and the sauce is thick and glossy. Serve the dish hot with puréed or fried potatoes, rice, pasta, or broiled vegetables.

Serves 4
Preparation time 30 minutes
Cooking time 1 hour

- 5 tablespoons olive oil
- 1 chicken, 3¼ lb (1.5 kg), cut into serving pieces
- 1 small onion, grated
- 1 lb 2 oz (500 g) fresh tomatoes, peeled and puréed, or 14 oz (400 g) canned tomatoes, puréed
- 1 tablespoon red wine vinegar
- 1 teaspoon sugar
- salt and pepper
- puréed or fried potatoes, rice, pasta, or broiled (grilled) vegetables, to serve

---

CHICKEN STEW WITH GARBANZO BEANS (CHICKPEAS)
ΚΟΤΟΠΟΥΛΟ ΚΟΚΚΙΝΙΣΤΟ ΜΕ ΡΕΒΥΘΙΑ
Kotopoulo kokinisto me revithia

Put the garbanzo beans into a bowl, pour in water to cover, stir in 1 tablespoon salt, and let soak overnight. Drain and rinse the beans and put them into a pan. Add the vegetable stock, bring to a boil, and cook for 30 minutes, then remove from the heat. Meanwhile, heat the oil in a large pan. Add the chicken and cook over medium heat, turning frequently, for 8–10 minutes, until golden brown all over. Add the onion, leek, carrot, garlic, and bell peppers and cook, stirring frequently, for 5 minutes, until softened. Stir in the tomatoes or tomato juice, chicken stock, sugar, oregano, basil or parsley, and chili flakes. Add the garbanzo beans together with their cooking liquid and taste and adjust the seasoning, if necessary. Simmer for 35–40 minutes, until the chicken and beans are tender. Serve hot, sprinkled with basil or parsley.

Serves 4
Preparation time 12½ hours (including soaking)
Cooking time 35–40 minutes

p 370

- 1⅓ cups (300 g / 11 oz) garbanzo beans (chickpeas)
- 2 cups (450 ml / 16 fl oz) vegetable stock
- 5 tablespoons olive oil
- 1 chicken, about 3¼ lb (1.5 kg), cut into serving pieces
- 1 large onion, grated
- 1 small leek, white part only, finely chopped
- 1 large carrot, diced
- 2 garlic cloves, finely chopped
- 1 red bell pepper, seeded and cut into ½-inch (1-cm) squares
- 1 yellow bell pepper, seeded and cut into ½-inch (1-cm) squares
- 14 oz (400 g) canned tomatoes, puréed, or 1½ cups (350 ml / 12 fl oz) tomato juice
- 1 cup (250 ml / 8 fl oz) chicken stock
- 1 teaspoon sugar
- ½ teaspoon dried oregano
- 2 tablespoons finely chopped fresh basil or parsley, plus extra for sprinkling
- 1 teaspoon chili flakes
- salt and pepper

- 1 quantity Chicken stew with tomato sauce (p 368)
- 1 lb 2 oz (500 g) okra
- 2 tablespoons red wine vinegar
- 4 lemon slices, rind removed
- 1 tomato, sliced
- salt and pepper
- 2 tablespoons olive oil
- ½ cup (120 ml / 4 fl oz) olive oil

CHICKEN STEW WITH OKRA
ΚΟΤΟΠΟΥΛΟ ΜΕ ΜΠΑΜΙΕΣ
Kotopoulo me bamies

Prepare the chicken according to the recipe (left), but omit the salt. Meanwhile, cut the stems off the okra, taking care not to pierce the pods. Dip the cut ends into salt, place in a colander, sprinkle with the vinegar, and set aside for 30 minutes. Rinse under cold running water and drain well. When the chicken is almost cooked and the sauce is thick, add the okra and lemon slices, shaking the pan to distribute them evenly. Put the tomato slices on top, season with salt and pepper, and sprinkle with the oil. Cover and simmer for about 15 minutes, or until the okra is tender but firm. Alternatively, you can cook the stew in the oven. Preheat the oven to 350°F (180°C / Gas Mark 4). Cover with aluminum foil and bake for about 45 minutes, or until the chicken is tender. Stir in the okra halfway through the cooking time, and add a little extra water if necessary. Serve immediately, seasoned with pepper.

Serves 4
Preparation time 40 minutes
Cooking time 1¼ hours

□ p 371

- ⅔ cup (150 ml / ¼ pint) olive oil
- 1 cockerel or chicken, 2¼ lb (1 kg), cut into serving pieces
- 1 large onion, grated
- 2 tablespoons tomato paste
- 2¼ lb (1 kg) tomatoes, peeled, seeded, and finely chopped
- 1 tablespoon red wine vinegar
- 1 teaspoon sugar
- 2 bay leaves
- 8 allspice berries
- salt and pepper
- 10 black peppercorns
- 14 oz (400 g) ziti or other tube-shaped pasta
- grated kefalotiri or Parmesan cheese, to serve

COCKEREL STEW WITH PASTA FROM CORFU
ΠΑΣΤΙΤΣΑΔΑ ΜΕ ΚΟΚΟΡΑ
Pastitsada me kokora

Heat ½ cup (120 ml / 4 fl oz) of the oil in a large pan. Add the cockerel or chicken pieces, a few at a time, and cook over medium heat, turning occasionally, for 8–10 minutes, until golden brown all over. Transfer to a platter. Add the onion and cook over low heat, stirring occasionally, for 5 minutes, until softened. Combine the tomato paste with 4 tablespoons water and add to the pan, together with the tomatoes, vinegar, sugar, bay leaves, allspice berries, and peppercorns. Season with salt and pepper. Bring to a boil, scraping up any sediment from the base of the pan with a wooden spoon. Return the cockerel or chicken to the pan, reduce the heat, cover, and simmer, adding a little water if necessary, for about 40 minutes–1 hour (depending on the age of the bird), or until the meat is tender and the sauce has thickened. Meanwhile, bring a large pan of water to a boil, stir in salt and the remaining olive oil, add the pasta, and cook for 8–10 minutes, or until al dente. Drain, tip onto a deep platter, and pour the sauce and meat on top. Serve immediately, accompanied by grated cheese.

Serves 4
Preparation time 30 minutes
Cooking time 1½ hours

Chicken stew with garbanzo beans (chickpeas), p 368

COCKEREL COOKED IN WINE FROM LAKONIA
ΚΟΚΟΡΑΣ ΚΡΑΣΑΤΟΣ
Kokoras krasatos

The town of Sparti in Lakonia has an interesting old tradition known as *pistrofia* ("return") associated with this dish. One week after her wedding, the bride would return with her new husband to her parents' home for the first time. On the way, the couple would stop by the village spring and the bride would throw in a coin and make a wish. She would then draw a pitcher (jug) of water from the spring to take to her family home. Meanwhile, her mother and grandmother cooked a special family meal of cockerel in wine sauce in honor of the newlyweds. It was believed that if the couple ate cockerel, their first child would be a boy. During the preparation of the dish, wine was ceremonially poured into the pot, accompanied by wishes for good fortune and many male children for the couple. Cockerel was usually an old, tough but flavorful bird that required long slow cooking. Such birds are not often available today, although large older birds can be obtained from specialist butchers. Chicken can also be used successfully in this recipe.

Rub the pieces of cockerel or chicken with salt and lemon juice and set aside for 30 minutes. Rinse under cold running water and place in a large bowl. Add all the marinade ingredients, turn to coat, and let marinate in the refrigerator overnight. Drain the bird, reserving the marinade. Heat the oil in a large pan. Add the onions and cook over low heat, stirring occasionally, for about 8 minutes, until lightly browned. Remove with a slotted spoon and set aside. Add the pieces of cockerel or chicken and cook, turning occasionally, for 8–10 minutes, until lightly browned all over. Add the marinade to the pan and add half the red wine. Bring to a boil and cook for 5 minutes. Combine the tomato paste with 4 tablespoons water in a bowl, then add to the pan. Cover and simmer for 20 minutes. Add the onions, re-cover, and simmer, adding the remaining wine if necessary, for 20 minutes to 1 hour more (depending on the age of bird), until the meat and onions are tender. Using a slotted spoon, transfer the meat and onions to a platter and keep warm. Bring the cooking juices to a boil and simmer until reduced to a thick sauce. Serve with white rice or fried potatoes.

Serves 4
Preparation time 12½ hours (including marinating)
Cooking time 45 minutes–1½ hours

- 1 cockerel or chicken, 3¼ lb (1.5 kg), cut into serving pieces
- salt
- freshly squeezed juice of 1 lemon
- ½ cup (120 ml / 4 fl oz) olive oil
- 1 lb 2 oz (500 g) small pearl (pickling) onions or shallots
- 2 cups (450 ml / 16 fl oz) red wine
- 2 tablespoons tomato paste
- white rice or fried potatoes, to serve

FOR THE MARINADE
- ½ cup (120 ml / 4 fl oz) red wine
- ½ cup (120 ml / 4 fl oz) sweet white wine
- 2 bay leaves
- 4 tablespoons olive oil
- 7 allspice berries
- 10 black peppercorns
- 1 strip of thinly pared orange zest

- 1 cockerel or chicken, about 3¼ lb (1.5 kg)
- 1 lemon, halved
- salt and pepper
- ½ cup (120 ml / 4 fl oz) olive oil
- 1 large onion, grated
- ½ cup (4) finely chopped scallions (spring onions)
- 9 oz (250 g) ground (minced) beef
- scant ½ cup (80 g / 3 oz) medium-grain rice
- 3 tablespoons finely chopped fresh mint
- 1 tablespoon currants (optional)
- ¼ teaspoon ground allspice
- pinch of ground cinnamon (optional)
- ½ cup (120 ml / 4 fl oz) hot water
- 2½ lb (1.2 kg) potatoes, cut into wedges
- 1 tablespoon tomato paste

STUFFED COCKEREL FROM SAMOS
ΚΟΚΟΡΑΣ ΓΕΜΙΣΤΟΣ
Kokoras gemistos

Preheat the oven to 325°F (160°C / Gas Mark 3). Rub the inside and outside of the cockerel or chicken with lemon and set aside for 30 minutes. Rinse the bird, pat dry, and season with salt and pepper. Heat 2 tablespoons of the oil in a pan. Add the onion, scallions, and beef and cook over medium heat, breaking up the meat with a spoon, for 8–10 minutes, until lightly browned. Add the rice, mint, currants, allspice, cinnamon, if using, and hot water, and season with salt and pepper. Remove from the heat and let cool. Fill the bird's cavity with the mixture and put it into a roasting pan, then put the potatoes around it. Combine the tomato paste with 1 cup (250 ml / 8 fl oz) water and pour the mixture over the potatoes, season with salt and pepper, and drizzle with the remaining olive oil. Cover and bake for 40 minutes to 1 hour. Remove the cover and bake for around 1 hour more, increasing the heat if necessary, until the bird and potatoes are golden (the time will depend on the age of the bird). Transfer to a hot platter and serve.

Serves 4
Preparation time 1 hour
Cooking time 2 hours

- ½ cup (120 ml / 4 fl oz) olive oil
- 1 lb 2 oz (500 g) shallots, blanched and peeled (see p 358)
- 4 garlic cloves, thinly sliced
- 1 large capon, rooster or chicken, about 5½ lb (2.5 kg)
- salt and pepper
- 1½ cups (350 ml / 12 fl oz) dry white wine
- 1 dried bay leaf, crumbled
- 1 teaspoon dried thyme
- 1 teaspoon dried mixed herbs, such as mint, marjoram, or rosemary
- 1 tablespoon all-purpose (plain) flour

ROAST CAPON WITH WINE AND SHALLOTS
ΚΑΠΟΝΙ ΚΡΑΣΑΤΟΣ ΜΕ ΚΡΕΜΜΥΔΙΑ
Kaponi krasatos me kremidia

Preheat the oven to 350°F (180°C / Gas Mark 4). Heat the oil in a large pan. Add the shallots and garlic and cook over medium heat, stirring occasionally, for 5 minutes, until softened. Rub the bird with salt and pepper and put it into a roasting pan with a lid. Put the shallots around it and strain the cooking oil over them. Pour in the wine and ½ cup (120 ml / 4 fl oz) water, sprinkle with the herbs, cover, and bake for 1–1½ hours, or until the meat and shallots are almost tender (chicken will take less time than capon or rooster). Drain off the pan juices into a small bowl and skim off 2–3 tablespoons fat from the surface. Make the remaining juices up to 1 cup (250 ml / 8 fl oz) with water, if necessary. Heat the fat in a pan, stir in the flour, and cook, stirring constantly, for 1–2 minutes, until slightly browned. Add the reserved juices gradually and stir over medium heat until slightly thickened. Pour the sauce over the bird, return to the oven, uncovered, and cook, basting occasionally, for 20–30 minutes more, until it is well browned. Remove from the oven, transfer to a platter, and surround with the shallots. Serve immediately.

Serves 6
Preparation time 30 minutes
Cooking time 1½–2 hours

CHICKEN PASTITSIO
ΠΑΣΤΙΤΣΙΟ ΜΕ ΚΟΤΟΠΟΥΛΟ
Pastitsio me kotopoulo

Heat 5 tablespoons of the oil in a pan. Add the garlic and onion and cook, stirring occasionally, for 3 minutes. Add the chicken and cook, stirring frequently, for 10 minutes. Add the allspice, coriander, basil, tomatoes, vinegar, and sugar and season with salt and pepper. Simmer for 20 minutes, or until the chicken is tender and the sauce has thickened. Remove from the heat. Preheat the oven to 350°F (180°C / Gas Mark 4), grease a 10 x 14-inch (25 x 35-cm) ovenproof dish with butter, and sprinkle with the bread crumbs. Break the pasta in half, bring a large pan of water to a boil, stir in salt and the remaining oil, add the pasta, and cook for 8–10 minutes, or until al dente. Drain, let cool slightly, and stir in the graviera or Gruyère cheese. Spread half the pasta over the base of the prepared dish, add the chicken mixture, and top with the remaining pasta. Combine the white sauce with the nutmeg and beaten eggs, season with salt and white pepper, and spread it over the pasta. Sprinkle with kefalotiri or Parmesan cheese and bake for 40–50 minutes, or until the top is golden. Let stand for 10 minutes before serving.

Serves 6
Preparation time 1 hour
Cooking time 40–50 minutes

Note: You can replace the fresh chicken with leftover roast or boiled chicken. Make the tomato sauce the same way but add the chopped chicken 5–10 minutes before the end.

- 7 tablespoons olive oil
- 3 garlic cloves, finely chopped
- 1 onion, grated
- 14 oz (400 g) skinless, boneless chicken, very finely chopped
- ¼ teaspoon ground allspice
- ½ teaspoon ground coriander
- 4 tablespoons finely chopped fresh basil
- 14 oz (400 g) tomatoes, peeled, seeded, and finely chopped
- 1 teaspoon red wine vinegar
- 1 teaspoon sugar
- salt and pepper
- butter, for greasing
- 3¼ cups (225 g / 8 oz) fine bread crumbs
- 14 oz (400 g) long, hollow pasta such as bucatini or ziti
- 3 cups (350 g / 12 oz) grated graviera or Gruyère cheese
- 3 cups (750 ml / 1¼ pints) White sauce (p 57)
- ¼ teaspoon grated nutmeg
- 2 eggs, beaten
- freshly ground white pepper
- 2 tablespoons grated kefalotiri or Parmesan cheese

- 1 large cabbage, about
  3¼ lb (1.5 kg)
- 1 small chicken, about 2¼ lb
  (1 kg), skinned
- 10 black peppercorns
- 1 large onion, chopped
- scant ½ cup (80 g / 3 oz)
  medium-grain rice
- ½ cup (25 g / 1 oz) chopped
  fresh parsley
- 1 cup (250 ml / 8 fl oz) puréed
  fresh tomatoes
- ½ teaspoon cayenne pepper
- ⅔ cup (150 ml / ¼ pint) olive oil
- salt and pepper
- ⅔ cup (150 ml / ¼ pint)
  tomato juice
- 1 tablespoon paprika
- ½ cup (120 ml / 4 fl oz) hot water
- 4 tablespoons freshly squeezed
  lemon juice

CABBAGE ROLLS WITH CHICKEN
ΛΑΧΑΝΟΝΤΟΛΜΑΔΕΣ ΜΕ ΚΟΤΟΠΟΥΛΟ
Lahanodolmades me kotopoulo

Using a sharp knife, cut around the core of the cabbage and remove it. Blanch the cabbage in a large pan of boiling water, with the cut side down, for 3–4 minutes, or until the leaves are pliable. Drain, let cool, and then separate the leaves. If the center is still tough, blanch again in boiling water. Remove and discard tough leaves and cut the larger leaves into 2 or 3 long pieces. Put the chicken into a pan, pour in water to cover, add the peppercorns, and season with salt. Bring to a boil and simmer for about 40 minutes, or until cooked through. Drain and let cool. Cut the meat off the bones and shred, then mix with the onion, rice, parsley, tomatoes, cayenne, and half the oil in a bowl and season with salt and pepper. Line the base of a wide shallow nonstick pan with 2–3 cabbage leaves. Place a tablespoon of the chicken mixture on the base of each cabbage leaf, turn in the sides, and roll up. Arrange the rolls in the pan, side by side and seam side down. Make more than one layer if necessary. Add the remaining oil, the tomato juice, paprika, and hot water. Invert a heavy plate on top of the cabbage rolls. Simmer, adding more hot water if necessary, for about 35 minutes, until the cabbage rolls are tender, and the sauce has reduced. Remove from the heat, sprinkle with the lemon juice, and shake the pan to distribute it evenly. Serve hot.

Serves 6
Preparation time 1¼ hours
Cooking time 35 minutes

PORK

-

XOIPINO

-

Hirino

Pork can be stored, frozen, and cooked in exactly the same ways as other meats, using all the classic methods. Fresh pork must be cooked thoroughly and is therefore usually broiled (grilled) for longer than beef or lamb. Because of this, it must be well protected from drying out. Small lean cuts should be brushed well with olive oil before broiling (grilling) to keep them moist. Pork should be broiled at a lower temperature to prevent the flesh from burning before the meat is cooked through. Large cuts may need barding (or covering with strips of lard or pork fat) to be successfully roasted in the oven.

Roast pork at a relatively low temperature. Put it into a preheated oven at 400°F (200°C / Gas Mark 6) and roast for 10 minutes, then reduce the oven temperature to 325°F (160°C / Gas Mark 3) to cook the meat through. If you remove the barding before the pork is cooked through, you should baste it regularly to build up a glaze on the surface. To broil (grill) perfect pork chops, always let the chops come to room temperature first. Trim off excess fat, leaving a ½-inch (1-cm) margin along the outer edge. A thin membrane that shrinks when it is heated lies between the fat and the lean meat. To prevent the chop from curling up, slit the membrane by cutting right through the fat to the lean meat at 2-inch (5-cm) intervals. Brush the chops on both sides with olive oil, season with salt and pepper, and sprinkle with any dried herb, such as oregano, thyme, marjoram, or rosemary. Let the chops stand at room temperature for about 1 hour to allow the flavors of the herbs to penetrate the meat. Put the chops on a preheated broiler (grill) pan and sear the meat at medium heat for 1 minute on each side. Reduce the heat and cook, turning once more during the cooking time. Cook 1-inch (2.5-cm) thick chops for 5 minutes more on each side; thicker chops may need up to twice as long. Remove from the heat and transfer to a platter. Let rest for a few minutes in a warm place before serving.

Pork is the most suitable meat for souvlaki or broiled (grilled) kabobs (kebabs). Cut the meat into 1-inch (2.5-cm) cubes, trimming off the visible fat. Cut an equal number of slightly smaller squares of raw vegetables such as onion, tomatoes, and bell peppers. You can also include small white mushrooms. Marinate the pieces in olive oil, a little wine, and some herbs for at least 2–3 hours (preferably overnight) in the refrigerator. Thread the meat, alternating with the vegetables, onto long skewers. Broil (grill) at medium heat, turning frequently, for 15 minutes. The vegetables provide moisture and help to trap the natural juices of the meat. Ground (minced) pork mixtures wrapped in caul and all kinds of pork sausages are also good broiled. Prick the skin of each sausage in two or three places with a skewer before putting under the broiler (grill) or into a skillet or frying pan. This allows the fat to run out during cooking and also lets the steam escape.

As fresh or salt pork is generally cooked during the Greek winter, it is usually poached, braised, or stewed with winter vegetables such as cabbage, leeks, celery root (celeriac), stewing onions, and carrots. It is often cooked with dried beans, lentils, and peas, which are also available during the winter months. Although fresh pork and all kinds of vegetables are now available at any time of year, most Greeks still follow the seasons in their cooking. Popular combinations include pork with sauerkraut and pork with lima (butter) beans.

To test whether pork is cooked, pierce the thickest part of the meat with a sharp knife or metal skewer; if the juices run clear without any trace of pink, the pork is ready.

SPIT-ROASTED PORK KABOBS (KEBABS)
ΚΟΝΤΟΣΟΥΒΛΙ
Kodosouvli

- 4½ lb (2 kg) boneless pork loin or leg, cut into large serving portions
- pinch of dried oregano
- salt and pepper
- 4–5 tablespoons olive oil
- 3–4 tablespoons freshly squeezed lemon juice
- 2–3 large green bell peppers, seeded and halved
- 2–3 large firm tomatoes, halved
- 1 large onion, halved and separated into layers
- chopped fresh oregano, to garnish

FOR THE MUSTARD SAUCE
- 2 tablespoons Dijon mustard
- 4 tablespoons olive oil
- 2 tablespoons freshly squeezed lemon juice
- 1 teaspoon honey
- salt and pepper

Put the meat into a large bowl and season with oregano, salt, and pepper. Put the oil and lemon juice into a screw-top jar, fasten the lid, and shake vigorously until thoroughly combined. Pour the mixture into the bowl, toss well to coat the meat, cover, and let marinate in the refrigerator, turning occasionally, for 6 hours or overnight. Drain the meat, reserving the marinade. Thread the meat onto a barbecue rotisserie spit, alternating with bell peppers, tomatoes, and onions. Grill slowly over charcoal, rotating constantly and basting the meat occasionally with the marinade, for 1–2 hours, or until cooked through. Meanwhile, make the mustard sauce. Put all the ingredients into a screw-top jar, season with salt and pepper, fasten the lid, and shake vigorously until thoroughly blended. Serve the pork sprinkled with fresh oregano and accompanied by the mustard sauce.

Serves 6
Preparation time 6 hours (including marinating)
Cooking time 1–2 hours

Note: If you don't have a rotisserie spit, you can cook the kodosouvli on a regular barbecue, turning the skewers frequently and making sure not to position the meat too close to the charcoal.

⬜ p 380

Spit-roasted pork kabobs (kebabs), p 379

Pork chops in wine, p 382

PORK SOUVLAKI
ΣΟΥΒΛΑΚΙ ΧΟΙΡΙΝΟ
Souvlaki hirino

Put the meat, oregano, and 2–3 tablespoons of the oil into a large bowl, season with pepper, and toss well. Cover and let marinate in the refrigerator, turning occasionally, for 6 hours or overnight. Preheat the broiler (grill) or light the barbecue. Thread the meat onto the skewers, alternating with the onions, bell peppers, and tomatoes, if using. Put the remaining oil and the lemon juice into a screw-top jar, fasten the lid, and shake vigorously until thoroughly blended, then brush the souvlaki with the mixture. Cook them under the broiler or grill over charcoal, turning twice and brushing occasionally with the oil-lemon marinade, for about 15 minutes, or until cooked through. Do not overcook, as the meat tends to dry out quickly. Season with salt, sprinkle with fresh oregano, and serve immediately with Pita bread, Tzatziki, Fried potatoes Greek-style, and a fresh vegetable salad.

Serves 4
Preparation time 6 hours (including marinating)
Cooking time 15–20 minutes

- 3¼ lb (1.5 kg) boneless leg of pork, cut into 1-inch (2.5-cm) cubes
- pinch of dried oregano
- 5 tablespoons olive oil
- 2 onions, quartered (optional)
- 2 green bell peppers, seeded and cut into 1-inch (2.5-cm) squares (optional)
- 2 firm tomatoes, cut into 1-inch (2.5-cm) squares or 8 whole cherry tomatoes (optional)
- 1–2 tablespoons freshly squeezed lemon juice
- salt and pepper
- chopped fresh oregano, to garnish

TO SERVE
- Pita bread for souvlaki (p 514)
- Tzatziki (p 152)
- Fried potatoes Greek-style (p 221)
- vegetable salad

PORK CHOPS IN WINE
ΜΠΡΙΖΟΛΕΣ ΧΟΙΡΙΝΕΣ ΚΡΑΣΑΤΕΣ
Brizoles hirines krasates

Season the chops with salt and pepper. Heat the oil in a skillet or frying pan large enough to hold the chops in a single layer. Add the chops and cook over medium heat for 2–3 minutes on each side, until lightly browned. Pour in half the wine and cook for a few minutes until the alcohol has evaporated, then pour in 5 tablespoons water, cover, and simmer for about 20 minutes, or until cooked through. Increase the heat and let the chops sizzle. Pour in the remaining wine and cook for 1–2 minutes, until the alcohol has evaporated. Serve immediately on warm plates with 1–2 tablespoons of the wine sauce, garnished with lemon wedges, and accompanied by fried potatoes and greens.

Serves 4
Preparation time 5 minutes
Cooking time 35 minutes

Note: You can also add pitted (stoned) green or black Greek olives. Blanch 10 olives to remove the salt, rinse in cold water, and drain. Add to the chops when the alcohol has evaporated, cover, and simmer for 5 minutes.

▢ p 381

- 4 large pork loin chops, ¾-inch (1.5-cm) thick
- salt and pepper
- 4 tablespoons olive oil
- ⅔ cup (150 ml / ¼ pint) dry white or red wine
- 4 lemon wedges
- fried potatoes and greens, to serve

- 3¼ lb (1.5 kg) boneless pork shoulder, trimmed and cut into 1½-inch (4-cm) cubes
- 2 tablespoons coarsely ground coriander
- 1½ cups (350 ml / 12 fl oz) dry red wine
- salt and pepper
- ½ cup (120 ml / 4 fl oz) olive oil
- 1 cup (250 ml / 8 fl oz) hot meat stock or water
- plain yogurt, to serve

FOR THE BULGUR PILAF
- 2 tablespoons olive oil
- 1 onion, grated
- 2 large tomatoes, peeled, seeded, and puréed
- salt and pepper
- 1 cup (175 g / 6 oz) bulgur wheat

CORIANDER PORK WITH BULGUR PILAF FROM CYPRUS
ΑΦΕΛΙΑ ΜΕ ΠΛΙΓΟΥΡΙ
Afelia me pligouri

Put the pork into a bowl, add the coriander, pour in the wine, and toss well to coat. Cover and let marinate in the refrigerator for at least 12 hours. Drain the meat, reserving the marinade. Season the pork with salt and pepper. Heat the oil in a large pan. Add the pork and cook over medium heat, stirring frequently, for 8–10 minutes, until lightly browned all over. Pour in the stock or water and the reserved marinade. Reduce the heat, cover, and simmer, adding more water if necessary, for 1–1¼ hours, or until the meat is tender. Remove and reserve 1 cup (250 ml / 8 fl oz) of the cooking liquid. Continue to cook the pork until the sauce is thick. Meanwhile, prepare the bulgur pilaf. Heat the oil in another pan. Add the onion and cook over low heat, stirring occasionally, for 5 minutes, until softened. Add the tomatoes and cook, stirring occasionally, for 10 minutes. Add the reserved cooking liquid and 1 cup (250 ml / 8 fl oz) water and season with salt and pepper. Bring to a boil and add the bulgur wheat, then turn off the heat. Stir well, cover, and let the bulgur absorb all the liquid. Separate the grains with a fork and serve with the meat, accompanied by plain yogurt.

Serves 4
Preparation time 12¼ hours (including marinating)
Cooking time 1½ hours

- 1½ cups (300 g / 11 oz) medium-grain rice
- 5 tablespoons olive oil
- 1½ lb (700 g) boneless pork, cubed
- 1 large onion, finely chopped
- 2 garlic cloves, thinly sliced
- 2 carrots, finely chopped
- 3 tablespoons raisins or currants
- 1 apple, quartered
- salt and pepper
- 4 tablespoons finely chopped fresh parsley
- 4 tablespoons finely chopped fresh dill

PORK AND RICE FROM PONTUS
ΠΛΟΦ
Plof

Put the rice into a bowl, pour in water to cover, add a pinch of salt, and let soak for 1 hour. Heat the oil in a pan. Add the meat and cook over medium heat, stirring frequently, for 8–10 minutes, until browned all over. Add the onion, garlic, and carrots and cook, stirring occasionally, for 4–5 minutes, until softened. Drain the rice and stir it into the pan with the raisins or currants. Cook, stirring constantly, for 5 minutes. Pour in 4 cups (1 litre / 1¾ pints) water, add the apple, season with salt and pepper, and bring to a boil. Reduce the heat, cover, and simmer for about 30 minutes, until the meat is tender and the rice has absorbed almost all the liquid. Stir in the parsley and dill, remove the pan from the heat, cover with a cotton dish towel, and let stand for about 10 minutes, until the rice has absorbed the steam and swollen. Remove and discard the apple and serve.

Serves 4
Preparation time 1¼ hours (including soaking)
Cooking time 35 minutes

PORK WITH COLOCASIA FROM CYPRUS
ΧΟΙΡΙΝΟ ΜΕ ΚΟΛΟΚΑΣΙ
Hirino me colocasia

Colocasia is an edible tuber that resembles sweet potato, although they are not related. It tastes sweet and needs more water than soil in order to grow. It was known to the ancient Greeks and is still grown and cooked today on the islands of Crete, Andros, Ikaria, and Cyprus.

Scrub, peel, and wipe the colocasia, celery root or sweet potato with a cloth. Do not rinse, or it will become too slippery to handle. Using a spoon, dig out small uneven pieces. Heat the oil in a large pan. Add the meat and cook over medium heat, turning frequently, for 8–10 minutes, until lightly browned. Using a slotted spoon, transfer to another pan. Add the colocasia to the hot oil and cook, stirring occasionally, for 5 minutes, then transfer to the pan with the meat. Add the onion to the hot oil, reduce the heat, and cook, stirring occasionally, for 5 minutes, then transfer the onion and oil to the pan with the meat and colocasia. Stir the tomato paste into the stock or water and add to the pan with the celery, tomatoes, and cayenne. Cover and simmer, adding more water if necessary, for 1½ hours, or until the meat and colocasia are tender and the sauce has thickened. Season with salt. Serve hot.

Serves 4
Preparation time 30 minutes
Cooking time 1¾ hours

- 2¼ lb (1 kg) colocasia, celery root (celeriac), or sweet potato
- ⅔ cup (150 ml / ¼ pint) olive oil
- 3¼ lb (1.5 kg) pork shoulder, cut into serving pieces
- 1 large onion, finely chopped
- 1 tablespoon tomato paste
- 1 cup (250 ml / 8 fl oz) chicken stock or water
- 1 celery stalk, sliced
- 4 tomatoes, peeled, seeded, and chopped or 14 oz (400 g) canned chopped tomatoes
- pinch of cayenne pepper
- salt

PORK WITH PEPPERS FROM FLORINA
ΧΟΙΡΙΝΟ ΜΕ ΠΙΠΕΡΙΕΣ
Hirino me piperies

Heat half the oil in a wide, shallow pan. Add the meat and cook over medium heat, turning occasionally, for 8–10 minutes, until lightly browned. Add the onions, garlic, vinegar, tomatoes, allspice berries, bay leaves, and cayenne, if using, and season with salt and pepper. Stir well, reduce the heat, cover, and simmer for about 1 hour, or until the meat is tender. Meanwhile, heat the remaining oil in a skillet or frying pan. Add the peppers and cook over low heat, turning occasionally, for 8 minutes, or until softened. Remove from the skillet and drain on paper towels. When they are cool enough to handle, peel off the skins and put the flesh into the pan, around and between the pieces of meat. Do not stir. Simmer for 15 minutes, or until the liquid has reduced. Serve hot.

Serves 4
Preparation time 15 minutes
Cooking time 1¼ hours

☐ p 386

- 1 cup (250 ml / 8 fl oz) olive oil
- 2¼ lb (1 kg) boneless pork shoulder, cut into serving pieces
- 4 onions, coarsely chopped
- 3 garlic cloves, halved
- 2 tablespoons red wine vinegar
- 14 oz (400 g) canned chopped tomatoes
- 6 allspice berries
- 2 bay leaves
- ½ teaspoon cayenne pepper (optional)
- salt and pepper
- 2¼ lb (1 kg) long Florina or red bell peppers, halved and seeded

- 3¼ lb (1.5 kg) pork shoulder
- 20 black peppercorns
- 1 small onion studded with 3 cloves
- ½ cup (120 ml / 4 fl oz) olive oil
- 3¼ lb (1.5 kg) sauerkraut, soaked (if salty), well rinsed, and chopped
- 2 tablespoons tomato paste
- 1 teaspoon hot paprika
- 1 teaspoon cayenne pepper
- ½ cup (80 g / 3 oz) bulgur wheat
- 2 tablespoons (25 g / 1 oz) butter
- salt and pepper

PORK WITH SAUERKRAUT AND BULGUR WHEAT FROM DRAMA
ΧΟΙΡΙΝΟ ΜΕ ΛΑΧΑΝΟ ΤΟΥΡΣΙ ΚΑΙ ΠΛΙΓΟΥΡΙ
Hirino me lahano toursi ke pligouri

Put the meat into a pan, pour in water to cover, add the peppercorns and clove-studded onion, and bring to a boil. Reduce the heat and simmer for 30 minutes. Drain, reserving 2 cups (450 ml / 16 fl oz) of the cooking liquid. Cut the meat into small pieces and discard the bones. Heat the oil in a pan. Add the sauerkraut and cook over low heat, stirring occasionally, for 5 minutes. Stir the tomato paste into the reserved cooking liquid and add to the pan, together with the paprika and cayenne. Season with salt, if necessary. Cover and simmer for 20 minutes. Meanwhile, preheat the oven to 350°F (180°C / Gas Mark 4). Drain the sauerkraut, reserving the cooking liquid, and layer it in an ovenproof dish with the pieces of pork and the bulgur wheat to create 3 layers. Pour the reserved cooking liquid over the top and dot with the butter. Season with pepper, cover with aluminum foil, and bake for 30 minutes. Remove the foil and bake for 30 minutes more, or until the sauerkraut and bulgur wheat are tender. Serve hot.

Serves 4
Preparation time 30 minutes
Cooking time 1½ hours

- ½ cup (120 ml / 4 fl oz) olive oil
- 1¾ lb (800 g) boneless pork, cut into serving pieces
- 1 onion, grated
- 1 large leek, white and tender green part, finely chopped
- 1 cup (250 ml / 8 fl oz) hot water
- salt and pepper
- 2¼ lb (1 kg) mixed wild greens, such as chard, sorrel, dandelion, amaranth
- ½ cup (25 g / 1 oz) finely chopped fennel leaves
- 4 tablespoons freshly squeezed lemon juice
- lemon wedges, to garnish

PORK WITH WILD GREENS
ΧΟΙΡΙΝΟ ΜΕ ΑΓΡΙΑ ΧΟΡΤΑ
Hirino me agria horta

Heat the oil in a large pan. Add the meat and cook over medium heat, turning occasionally, for 8–10 minutes, until lightly browned all over. Using a slotted spoon, transfer to a plate. Add the onion and leek to the pan, reduce the heat, and cook, stirring occasionally, for 5 minutes, until softened. Return the meat to the pan, pour in the hot water, and season with salt and pepper. Cover and simmer for about 1 hour, or until the meat is tender. Meanwhile, blanch the wild greens for a couple of minutes in boiling water, then drain, and add them to the pan with the fennel. Simmer for 20–30 minutes more, or until the greens are tender and the liquid has reduced. Sprinkle with the lemon juice and remove from the heat. Serve hot, garnished with lemon wedges.

Serves 4
Preparation time 20 minutes
Cooking time 1¾ hours

☐ p 387

Pork with peppers from Florina, p 384

ork with wild greens, p 385

PORK SKEWERS WITH YOGURT AND TOMATO SAUCE

ΣΟΥΒΛΑΚΙΑ ΜΕ ΓΙΑΟΥΡΤΙ ΚΑΙ ΣΑΛΤΣΑ ΝΤΟΜΑΤΑΣ

Souvlakia me giaourti ke saltsa domatas

Thread the cubes of pork onto 8 wooden skewers, put them on a platter, sprinkle with oregano, season with pepper, and brush with olive oil. Cover and leave in the refrigerator until required. To make the sauce, melt the butter in a pan. Add the garlic and cook over low heat, stirring frequently, for 1–2 minutes. Add the tomatoes, sugar, and cayenne, season with pepper, and simmer for 5–10 minutes, or until thickened. Remove from the heat and let cool, then chill in the refrigerator. An hour before serving, preheat the broiler (grill) or light the barbecue. Brush both sides of the pita breads with the melted butter and broil (grill) them for a couple of minutes under the broiler, or grill over charcoal. Keep warm. Cook the kabobs (kebabs) under the broiler or grill over charcoal for 10–15 minutes, or until cooked through, brushing with oil and turning frequently. Meanwhile, heat the beef stock and the tomato sauce in separate pans. Cut the pita breads into pieces and divide among individual soup plates. Spoon 5–6 tablespoons hot beef stock into each plate and spread 2–3 tablespoons yogurt on top. Slide the meat off 2 skewers onto each plate and spoon 3–4 tablespoons tomato sauce over the meat. Sprinkle with pepper and cayenne. Serve immediately.

Serves 4
Preparation time 30 minutes
Cooking time 30 minutes

□ p 390

- 2¼ lb (1 kg) boneless pork, cubed
- pinch of dried oregano
- pepper
- olive oil, for brushing
- 8 Pita breads for souvlaki (p 514)
- 5 tablespoons (70 g / 2¾ oz) butter, melted
- 1½ cups (350 ml / 12 fl oz) beef stock
- 2¼ cups (500 ml / 18 fl oz) strained plain or thick Greek yogurt
- pinch of cayenne pepper

FOR THE TOMATO SAUCE
- 3 tablespoons (40 g / 1½ oz) butter
- 1 garlic clove, finely chopped
- 1½ cups (350 ml / 12 fl oz) puréed fresh tomatoes
- 1 teaspoon sugar
- pinch of cayenne pepper
- pepper

- 3 tablespoons olive oil
- 4½ lb (2 kg) boned and rolled pork shoulder
- salt and pepper
- ½ cup (120 ml / 4 fl oz) dry white wine
- roast potatoes and sautéed vegetables, to serve

FOR THE STUFFING
- 2 tablespoons clarified butter
- 1 onion, grated
- ½ cup (50 g / 2 oz) pistachio or cashew nuts, coarsely chopped
- 1 cup (50 g / 2 oz) fresh bread crumbs
- 1 large tart apple, peeled, cored, and cubed
- 1 celery stalk, finely chopped
- 2 tablespoons finely chopped fresh parsley
- 2 tablespoons freshly squeezed lemon juice
- salt and pepper

STUFFED ROAST PORK
ΣΠΑΛΑ ΧΟΙΡΙΝΗ ΓΕΜΙΣΤΗ
Spala hirini gemisti

Preheat the oven to 425°F (220°C/ Gas Mark 7) and brush a roasting pan with oil. To make the stuffing, melt the butter in a small pan. Add the onion and nuts and cook over low heat, stirring occasionally, for 5 minutes, until the onion is softened and the nuts are lightly browned. Add the bread crumbs, apple, celery, and parsley and cook, stirring constantly, for 5–10 minutes, until the apple is soft. Add the lemon juice, season with salt and pepper, and remove from the heat. Untie the pork and unroll on a work surface. Spread the stuffing evenly over it, then roll, and tie securely with kitchen string. Rub the pork roll all over with salt and pepper, brush with oil, and place in the prepared roasting pan. Roast for about 30 minutes, or until the skin starts to brown. Reduce the oven temperature to 350°F (180°C / Gas Mark 4) and roast for 1½–2 hours more, or until the juices run clear when the meat is pierced with a skewer or sharp knife. Transfer the pork to a platter and keep warm. Add the wine to the roasting pan and stir over medium heat, scraping up any sediment from the base of the pan with a wooden spoon. Transfer to a pan and let settle for a few minutes until the fat floats up to the surface. Skim off and discard as much fat as you can. Simmer the sauce until slightly reduced and remove from the heat. Serve the meat hot, accompanied by the sauce, roast potatoes, and sautéed vegetables.

Serves 6
Preparation time 20 minutes
Cooking time 2½–3 hours

- 4½ lb (2 kg) leeks, white and tender green parts, cut into 2-inch (5-cm) lengths
- ⅔ cup (150 ml / ¼ pint) olive oil
- 2¼ lb (1 kg) boneless pork, cut into serving pieces
- 1 onion, grated
- 2 cups (450 ml / 16 fl oz) puréed fresh or canned tomatoes or meat stock
- 1 celery stalk, finely chopped
- salt and pepper

PORK STEW WITH LEEKS FROM MACEDONIA
ΧΟΙΡΙΝΟ ΜΕ ΠΡΑΣΑ
Hirino me prasa

Parboil the leeks in lightly salted water for about 10 minutes, then drain, and set aside. Heat the oil in a heavy pan over high heat. Add the pieces of pork and cook, turning occasionally, for 6–8 minutes, until browned all over. Add the onion, reduce the heat, and cook, stirring occasionally, for 5 minutes, until softened. Add the tomatoes or stock and celery, season with salt and pepper, cover, and simmer for about 1 hour. Add the leeks and simmer, adding more water if necessary, for 30 minutes more, until the meat and leeks are tender and the sauce has reduced. Serve immediately, seasoned with pepper.

Serves 4
Preparation time 30 minutes
Cooking time 1½ hours

Pork skewers with yogurt and tomato sauce, p 388

Pork with beans from Florina, p 393

STUFFED CABBAGE FROM MACEDONIA
ΛΑΧΑΝΟ ΓΕΜΙΣΤΟ
Lahano gemisto

Bring a large pan of salted water to a boil. Add the cabbage and blanch for 5 minutes, then drain. Line a round dish with a piece of cheesecloth (muslin) large enough to cover the cabbage and set the cabbage on top. Combine the ground pork, sausage or bacon, rice, onion, garlic, and oil in a bowl and season with salt and pepper. Gently separate out the cabbage leaves without breaking them. Remove the cabbage heart and fill the space with one third of the meat mixture. Spoon the remaining mixture between the leaves and lift up to enclose the stuffing. Wrap the cabbage in the cheesecloth and tie with kitchen string, then put it into a pan just large enough to hold it. Pour the hot stock and melted butter on top. Cover and simmer for 1½ hours, or until it is tender. Lift out of the pan, transfer to a shallow platter, and remove the cheesecloth. Divide it into 6 pieces, pour some of the pan juices on top, and serve with lemon wedges. If using the egg-lemon sauce, beat a ladleful of the hot pan juices into it, then stir into the liquid in the pan. Remove from the heat and pour over the cabbage. Serve immediately.

Serves 6
Preparation time 40 minutes
Cooking time 1½ hours

- 1 cabbage, about 3¼ lb (1.5 kg), cored and coarse outer leaves removed
- 14 oz (400 g) ground (minced) pork
- 3½ oz (100 g) smoked sausage or bacon, finely chopped
- ½ cup (100 g / 3½ oz) medium-grain rice
- 1 onion, finely chopped
- 1 garlic clove, finely chopped
- 5 tablespoons olive oil
- salt and pepper
- 1½ cups (350 ml / 12 fl oz) hot meat stock
- 5 tablespoons (70 g / 2¾ oz) butter, melted
- lemon wedges, to garnish
- Egg-lemon sauce (p 59, optional)

CURED PORK FROM THRACE
ΠΑΣΙΟΡΤΗ
Pasiorti

Pasiorti is a traditional cured pork dish that is stored in a sealed clay jar and eaten in February, when the Christmas pig has been used up.

Put the pork into a large pan, cover with water and bring to a boil. Simmer, skimming off the scum, for 1½ hours, or until nearly tender. Add the salt and cook for 30 minutes more. Remove the meat, strain the liquid into a bowl, let cool, and chill for at least 2 hours. Remove and reserve the fat from the surface (discard the liquid). Measure the fat and make up to 3 cups (500 g / 1 lb 2 oz) with butter, lard or back fat, if necessary. Melt the fat in a large pan. Add the leeks and cook over low heat, stirring occasionally, for 5 minutes, until softened. Add the oregano, pepper, and paprika. Add the pork and cook for 10 minutes, then let cool completely. Spoon the mixture into a dish with a lid, cover, and seal the edges with stiff flour-and-water dough. Store in the refrigerator. Once opened, cover the pork with oil and eat within a few days.

Makes 11 lb (5 kg)
Preparation time 3½ hours (including chilling and cooling)
Cooking time 2½ hours

- 11 lb (5 kg) pork belly, cut into medium-size pieces
- 2 tablespoons salt
- butter, lard or pork back fat, if necessary
- 3–4 leeks, finely chopped
- 1 tablespoon dried oregano
- 1 tablespoon pepper
- 1 tablespoon mild paprika

PORK WITH BEANS FROM FLORINA
ΧΟΙΡΙΝΟ ΜΕ ΦΑΣΟΛΙΑ
Hirino me fasolia

- 4½ lb (2 kg) boned and rolled pork loin
- 4–6 garlic cloves, sliced
- 4 tablespoons olive oil
- 4 tablespoons freshly squeezed lemon juice
- salt and pepper
- 1 lb 2 oz (500 g) dried lima (butter) beans, soaked overnight in cold water to cover and drained
- 1 bay leaf
- 1 onion, studded with 3 cloves
- 2 fresh parsley sprigs
- 1 carrot
- ½ teaspoon black peppercorns
- 4 tablespoons clarified butter
- 1 large onion, finely chopped
- 2 tablespoons finely chopped fresh parsley

Preheat the oven to 325°F (160°C / Gas Mark 3). Make small cuts all over the pork and insert the garlic slices. Put the pork into a deep ovenproof dish just large enough to hold it. Rub the meat with the oil, lemon juice, salt, and pepper. Pour in 1 cup (250 ml / 8 fl oz) water, cover with aluminum foil, and roast, occasionally basting with the cooking juices, for about 3 hours. Meanwhile, put the beans into a large pan, pour in water to cover, and add the bay leaf, the onion, parsley, carrot, and peppercorns. Bring to a boil, skim off any scum, cover, and cook for 1–1½ hours, until the beans are soft. Remove the pork from the dish, reserving the juices, and keep warm. Melt the butter in a large pan. Add the chopped onion and cook over low heat, stirring occasionally, for 5 minutes, until softened. Strain the reserved cooking juices into the pan, cover, and simmer for 10 minutes, or until the onion is tender. Drain the beans, discarding the flavorings, and mix with the onion. Simmer for a few minutes more until the beans are glazed. Slice the pork and serve hot with the beans, sprinkled with the chopped parsley.

Serves 6
Preparation time 12½ hours (including soaking)
Cooking time 3¼ hours

□ p 391

PORK WITH WHEAT BERRIES
ΒΑΣΙΛΗΣ
Vasilis

- 12 oz (350 g) pork tongue
- 5 tablespoons olive oil
- 1 onion, finely chopped
- scant 1 cup (200 g / 7 oz) garbanzo beans (chickpeas), soaked overnight in water to cover with 1 tablespoon salt and drained
- 12 oz (350 g) salt pork with fat, soaked overnight in cold water to cover and drained, or thick-cut unsmoked bacon
- 4 oz (120 g) wheat berries, soaked overnight in water to cover and drained
- 1 fresh rosemary sprig
- 2 bay leaves
- 20 black peppercorns
- freshly squeezed lemon juice, for sprinkling
- salt and pepper

This is a traditional New Year's dish from the island of Serifos in the Cyclades. The grain and legumes (pulses), fertility symbols, were eaten to ensure a fruitful year ahead, while the tongue was thought to offer protection against malicious gossip and slander.

Blanch the tongue in boiling water for 5 minutes and drain, then cut it into small pieces. Heat the oil in a pan. Add the onion and tongue and cook over low heat, stirring occasionally, for 5 minutes, until the onion has softened. Meanwhile, rinse the garbanzo beans in cold water. Add the pork, garbanzo beans, wheat berries, rosemary, bay leaves, and peppercorns to the pan, pour in 4 cups (1 litre / 1¾ pints) water and bring to a boil. Cover and simmer for 1½ hours. Taste and adjust the seasoning, if necessary, and serve hot, sprinkled with lemon juice.

Serves 4
Preparation time 12 hours (including soaking)
Cooking time 1½ hours

BEEF, VEAL, AND GROUND (MINCED) MEAT

-

ΒΟΔΙΝΟ, ΜΟΣΧΑΡΙ, ΚΑΙ ΚΙΜΑΣ

-

Vodino, moshari, ke kimas

Greeks have always been fond of meat, although it has not always been widely available. Greece's arid, mountainous terrain has little pasture suitable for grazing cattle, and the land is better suited to raising goats and sheep to provide milk for cheese, wool, and, less often, meat. Oxen and bullocks were far more valuable as work animals. Pigs, domesticated from wild boar in Asia Minor, were kept in pens in forested areas and allowed to forage for acorns. Hens were kept mainly for egg production and were put into the pot only after they had outlived their productive lives. Game has always been a valued but sporadic source of nourishment.

However, the ingenuity of Greek cooks through the ages has more than compensated for any deficiencies in supply. Homer's heroes may have preferred their meat spit-roasted, but by the Classical period Greeks had already developed a number of ways of cooking meat, including in meatballs, salt pork stewed with herbs and vinegar, or whole game birds baked in flaky pastry. Most visitors to modern Greece will be familiar with souvlaki and gyros, famous street foods that have changed little in 3,000 years. Simple broiled (grilled) dishes like souvlaki do not really represent the variety and true excellence of good Greek cooking, however. Its essence is in its *magirefto* ("cooked") dishes, which the Greeks consider in a class of their own. To them, broiling (grilling) or frying foods just before serving is not even considered cooking, but is called *tis oras*, or "of the moment." Cooked dishes, on the other hand, are delicious combinations of meat, sauce, and vegetables, simmered for hours with olive oil, herbs, and spices or layered in a casserole and baked in the oven. For thousands of years, these dishes have been cooked in clay vessels like today's *giouvetsi*, and ancient dishes of this type have been discovered all over Greece.

Greek cooks have always been ingenious in making a little meat go a long way. In particular, they have a way with ground (minced) meat, whether on its own or kneaded with onions, spices, or herbs. Every family has treasured recipes for meatballs, either fried as *keftedes*, broiled (grilled) as *soutzoukakia*, or poached as *giouvarlakia*. Combined with vegetables, rice, or pasta, some ground meat dishes have become classics of Greek cuisine. Moussaka, pastitsio, *dolmadakia* (stuffed grape (vine) leaves), and *gemista* (stuffed tomatoes and bell peppers) have become popular all around the world. Stuffings may simply consist of meat trimmings, flavorings such as garlic, onions, parsley, or other fresh herbs, and rice. Sometimes eggs, tomatoes, and vegetables such as spinach, leeks, or wild greens, are also included. Ground meat mixtures can be wrapped individually in caul, phyllo (filo) sheets, or large leaves, such as grape, cabbage, or chard. They also can be used to stuff the cavities of poultry, game birds, suckling pigs, or lambs, as well as layering between vegetables or pasta or filling hollowed-out vegetables, such as tomatoes, bell peppers, zucchini (courgettes), eggplants (aubergines), and onions. A topping of sauce or cream (usually tomato sauce or white sauce) prevents the upper layer of vegetables or meat from drying out, provides a pleasant contrast in texture, and *anthotiro* or *kefalotiri* cheese are often added for extra flavor.

Although every kind of meat is now available throughout the year, many Greeks still eat meat in its traditional season. Pork is still best in winter, the traditional time for the slaughter, lamb and young goat (or kid) in spring and summer, and game in the fall (autumn). Beef, veal, and poultry are eaten at any time of year. Just as in ancient times, roasted, broiled (grilled), or boiled meat is still an important part of many festive occasions in Greece. The sight of rows of lambs and kids being spit-roasted in the streets and squares at Easter is truly impressive, and no wedding, baptism, or name-day celebration would be complete without at least one meat dish, often lamb or kid roasted in the oven with potatoes.

GENERAL INSTRUCTIONS

In Greece, meat is usually served well done. Aged beef is eaten only occasionally, and milk-fed veal is much more popular, but many of the recipes can be adapted for both beef and veal. Many Greeks are horrified by rare meat and prefer the melt-in-the-mouth tenderness of well-cooked beef or veal. They have many ways of cooking it: roasted in the oven or on the spit, grilled over charcoal or cooked under the broiler (grill), fried with a little fat or oil, braised or stewed or baked in wine, stock, lemon juice, or tomato juice. Large cuts of beef or veal will keep for 3–5 days, during which time the flavor will continue to improve slightly. Ground (minced) meat spoils faster than larger cuts, so it is best eaten on the day of purchase. It can be stored in the refrigerator for 24 hours and in the freezer for no longer than 4 months. Pre-cooked ground meat can be safely stored in the refrigerator for 2–3 days before use. Meat can be kept for longer in the freezer, wrapped tightly, sealed, and frozen promptly. It is best not to freeze it for more than one month. The safest way to thaw meat is in the refrigerator. Steaks and chops take about one day, but larger cuts may need as many as 3–4 days.

Knowing what part of the animal a cut of meat has come from is important for cooking it successfully, because each part has different qualities that suit different cooking methods. Meat consists of muscle tissue, and well-protected muscles that are rarely used, such as the loin, fillet and rump, have a smooth texture with few fibers. These are the most tender, but also the most expensive cuts. They need only brief cooking at high heat to bring out their flavor while preserving the natural juices, and the dry heat methods—roasting, broiling (grilling), and frying—are the most suitable. These cuts are often marinated beforehand in olive oil and lemon juice and seasoned with herbs such as oregano, thyme, or rosemary.

The most developed muscles are in the legs, chest, flank, neck, and tail, and these parts require long cooking at low temperature, with the addition of liquid, and therefore braising and poaching are the best ways to make the most of these cuts. Some parts, such as the shoulder, are neither as tough as the legs and neck, nor as tender as the back. They can be roasted, fried, or broiled (grilled), and can also be braised or pot-roasted, which are popular cooking methods in Greece. Meat cooked in this way should be browned first. To do this, wipe each piece with paper towels and heat the oil in a heavy pan until it is almost smoking. Add the meat, but do not crowd the pan, as this lowers the temperature and the meat will steam rather than brown. Brown the meat on all sides, turning occasionally, then simmer slowly. The amount of water or other liquid required will depend on the size of the pan and the quality of the ingredients. Add less than the recipe specifies, and a little more during cooking if necessary. Always add hot water to avoid lowering the temperature as the dish cooks. When cooking meat and vegetable stews, part-cook the meat first before adding the vegetables at a later stage (the timing will depend on the freshness and type of vegetables). Meat should be cooked on the bone for extra flavor, unless otherwise specified.

Aside from the baked and stuffed dishes mentioned above, a simple and effective way of cooking ground (minced) meat is to broil (grill) it on skewers. The meat will be more succulent if it is chopped by hand, rather than ground. Chop the meat finely and knead the mixture until the ingredients are evenly blended. Let it rest in the refrigerator for about 30 minutes to make it firmer. Take a portion of the mixture with dampened hands and mold it around the skewer, shaping it into a "sausage" 4–4½ inches (10–11 cm) long. Choose square or flat skewers, as the meat may slip on round ones, and brush them with oil to make it easier to slide the meat off for serving. Make sure that the broiler (grill) is thoroughly preheated. The broiling (grilling) time will range from 8 to 15 minutes, depending on the size.

BEEF STEW WITH PASTA FROM CORFU
ΠΑΣΤΙΤΣΑΔΑ ΚΕΡΚΥΡΑΙΚΗ
Pastitsada kerkiraiki

Heat ½ cup (120 ml / 4 fl oz) of the oil in a heavy pan over high heat. Add the meat and cook, stirring frequently, for about 8 minutes, until browned all over. Add the onion, reduce the heat, and cook, stirring occasionally, for 5 minutes, until softened. Add the tomatoes, tomato paste, vinegar, sugar, cinnamon stick, cloves, and basil and season with salt and pepper. Cover and simmer, adding water if necessary, for 1¼–1½ hours, or until the meat is tender and the sauce has reduced. Meanwhile, bring a large pan of water to a boil, stir in salt and the remaining oil, add the pasta, and cook for 8–10 minutes, or until al dente. Drain well and tip onto a deep platter. Add the meat and pour the sauce on top. Sprinkle with grated cheese, season with pepper, and serve immediately.

Serves 6
Preparation time 30 minutes
Cooking time 1½ hours

- ⅔ cup (150 ml / ¼ pint) olive oil
- 3¼ lb (1.5 kg) lean stewing beef or veal, cut into serving pieces
- 1 large onion, grated
- 2¼ lb (1 kg) tomatoes, peeled, seeded, and chopped
- 2 tablespoons tomato paste
- 1 tablespoon red wine vinegar
- 1 teaspoon sugar
- 1 small cinnamon stick
- 2 cloves
- 1 tablespoon chopped fresh basil
- salt and pepper
- 1 lb 2 oz (500 g) thick tube-shaped pasta, such as macaroni or ziti
- grated dried mizithra, kefalotiri, or Parmesan cheese, to garnish

- ½ cup (120 ml / 4 fl oz) olive oil
- 2¼ lb (1 kg) boneless lean stewing beef, cubed
- 1 onion, grated
- 2 cups (450 ml / 16 fl oz) puréed peeled fresh or canned tomatoes
- 1 tablespoon red wine vinegar (optional)
- 1 teaspoon sugar
- 2–3 allspice berries
- 5–6 black peppercorns
- 4½ lb (2 kg) eggplants (aubergines)
- pinch of grated nutmeg
- 1 cup (250 ml / 8 fl oz) light White sauce (p 57)
- salt and pepper
- 11 oz (300 g) Gruyère cheese, grated
- 2 tablespoons finely chopped fresh parsley

CONSTANTINOPLE BEEF STEW WITH EGGPLANT (AUBERGINE) PURÉE
ΠΟΛΙΤΙΚΟ ΜΟΣΧΑΡΙ ΜΕ ΠΟΥΡΕ ΜΕΛΙΤΖΑΝΑΣ
Politiko moshari me poure melitzanas

Heat the oil in a pan. Add the meat and cook over high heat, stirring frequently, for about 8 minutes, until browned all over. Add the onion, reduce the heat, and cook, stirring occasionally, for 5 minutes, until softened. Add the tomatoes, vinegar, if using, sugar, allspice berries, and peppercorns and season with salt. Cover and simmer, adding water if necessary, for about 1½ hours, until the meat is tender and the sauce has reduced. Meanwhile, make the eggplant purée. Preheat the broiler (grill). Broil (grill) the eggplants, turning frequently, until the skins are charred and the flesh has softened. Remove from the heat and refresh under cold running water. Halve, scoop out the flesh with a spoon, and process to a purée in the food processor. Stir the purée and nutmeg into the white sauce, season with salt and pepper, and cook over medium heat, stirring constantly, for 5–6 minutes. Reduce the heat, add the cheese, and stir until melted and smooth. Serve hot topped with the beef and tomato sauce, sprinkled with the finely chopped parsley.

Serves 4
Preparation time 30 minutes
Cooking time 1¾ hours

- ½ cup (120 ml / 4 fl oz) olive oil
- 3¼ lb (1.5 kg) stewing veal or beef, cut into serving pieces
- 1 onion, finely chopped
- 2 cups (450 ml / 16 fl oz) puréed peeled fresh or canned tomatoes
- 4 tablespoons finely chopped fresh parsley (optional)
- 1 tablespoon red wine vinegar
- 1 teaspoon sugar
- salt and pepper
- Fried potatoes Greek-style (p 221), mashed potatoes, pasta, or rice, to serve

VEAL STEW WITH TOMATOES
ΜΟΣΧΑΡΙ ΚΟΚΚΙΝΙΣΤΟ
Moshari kokinisto

This dish is the base for a variety of entrées (main courses) called *kokinista*, which literally means "red stew." They can be varied by adding vegetables, pasta, or rice. Peas or potatoes are particularly good additions. Parsley can be replaced by any fresh or dried herbs, or spices such as cumin, allspice berries, cinnamon, and cloves.

Heat the oil in a heavy pan. Add the meat and cook over medium heat, turning occasionally, for about 8 minutes, until browned all over. Add the onion and cook, stirring occasionally, for 2–3 minutes, until softened. Add the tomatoes, parsley, if using, vinegar, and sugar, season with salt and pepper, and stir well. Reduce the heat, cover, and simmer, adding a little water if needed, for 1½ hours, until the meat is tender and the sauce is thick. Serve hot with potatoes, pasta, or rice.

Serves 6
Preparation time 20 minutes
Cooking time 1½ hours

▢ p 400

Veal stew with tomatoes, p 399

Veal stifado, p 402

BEEF WITH GREEN ALMONDS
ΚΡΕΑΣ ΜΕ ΤΡΥΦΕΡΑ ΑΜΥΓΔΑΛΑ
Kreas me trifera amigdala

Heat the oil in a large pan. Add the meat and cook over medium heat, turning occasionally, for 8–10 minutes, until lightly browned all over. Add the onion, reduce the heat, and cook for 5 minutes, until softened. Pour in the wine, add the tomatoes and sugar, and season with salt and plenty of pepper. Bring to a boil, cover, and simmer for 45 minutes, or until the meat is half cooked. Wash the almonds and score them on both sides with a sharp knife. Add them to the pan, re-cover, and simmer for 1 hour more, or until the meat is tender and the liquid has reduced. Stir in the lemon juice and cook for 1–2 minutes more. Serve hot.

Serves 4
Preparation time 30 minutes
Cooking time 1¾ hours

Note: Green almonds are picked in spring and early summer before they have dried out. Cretans love to nibble their tender, slightly sour skin and sweet milky flesh with *tsikoudia*. Unfortunately, there is no substitute.

- ⅔ cup (150 ml / ¼ pint) olive oil
- 2¼ lb (1 kg) stewing beef, cut into serving pieces
- 1 onion, grated
- 4 tablespoons dry white wine
- 1 lb 2 oz (500 g) tomatoes, peeled, seeded, and finely chopped or 14 oz (400 g) canned chopped tomatoes
- 1 teaspoon sugar
- salt and pepper
- 1 lb 2 oz (500 g) fresh green almonds (see note)
- 1 tablespoon freshly squeezed lemon juice

VEAL STIFADO
ΜΟΣΧΑΡΙ ΣΤΙΦΑΔΟ
Moshari stifado

Combine all the marinade ingredients in a bowl. Add the meat, turning to coat, cover, and let marinate in the refrigerator, turning occasionally, for 1–2 days. Remove the meat from the marinade and strain the liquid into a bowl, reserving the flavorings. Blanch the onions in boiling water for 1 minute, drain, and peel. Heat the oil in a large heavy pan. Add the onions in batches, and cook over medium heat for 8–10 minutes, until lightly browned. Remove each batch with a slotted spoon. Add the meat to the pan and cook, turning occasionally, for about 8 minutes, until lightly browned all over. Pour in the reserved marinade and season with salt and pepper. Add 2 of the bay leaves, 6 of the peppercorns, and 6 of the allspice berries. Add the tomatoes, cover, and bring to a boil, then reduce the heat and simmer for about 30 minutes. Add the onions and 3 of the reserved garlic cloves. Re-cover the pan and simmer for 1½ hours, until the meat and onions are tender and the sauce is very thick. If the sauce has not reduced enough, strain it and boil rapidly until thickened. Pour it back over the meat and serve hot.

Serve 6
Preparation time 24–48 hours (including marinating)
Cooking time 2½ hours

⬚ p 401

- 2¼ lb (1 kg) stewing veal or beef, cut into serving pieces
- 4½ lb (2 kg) small pearl (pickling) onions or shallots
- 1 cup (250 ml / 8 fl oz) olive oil
- salt and pepper
- 3 cups (750 ml / 1¼ pints) puréed peeled fresh or canned tomatoes

FOR THE MARINADE
- ½ cup (120 ml / 4 fl oz) olive oil
- 1 cup (250 ml / 8 fl oz) dry red wine
- 2 tablespoons red wine vinegar
- 3 bay leaves
- 20 black peppercorns
- 10 allspice berries
- 4 garlic cloves

- 3¼ lb (1.5 kg) boned and rolled veal shoulder
- 4 tablespoons dry white wine
- 1 tablespoon cornstarch (cornflour)
- 1 tablespoon Dijon mustard
- 1 cup (250 ml / 8 fl oz) meat stock
- 4 tablespoons heavy (double) cream

FOR THE STUFFING
- 4 tablespoons melted butter
- 3 slices of bacon, finely chopped
- 1 onion, grated
- 1 small garlic clove, finely chopped
- 1¾ cups (100 g / 3½ oz) bread crumbs
- ½ teaspoon dried thyme
- ½ teaspoon dried marjoram
- ½ teaspoon dried fennel fronds or fennel seeds
- ½ cup (50 g / 2 oz) pistachio nuts, coarsely chopped
- 1 egg, lightly beaten
- salt and pepper

HERB-STUFFED VEAL SHOULDER
ΣΠΑΛΑ ΜΟΣΧΑΡΙΣΙΑ ΓΕΜΙΣΤΗ
Spala mosharisia gemisti

Preheat the oven to 400°F (200°C / Gas Mark 6). To make the stuffing, melt the butter in a skillet or frying pan. Add the bacon, onion, and garlic and cook over low heat, stirring occasionally, for 5 minutes, until the onion has softened. Add the bread crumbs and cook, stirring constantly, for 2–3 minutes, then remove from the heat, and let cool slightly. Stir in the thyme, marjoram, fennel, nuts, and egg and season with salt and pepper. Unroll the meat, lay it out flat, and spread the stuffing evenly over the boned side, then roll up again, and tie with kitchen string. Season with salt and pepper and place in a roasting pan. Roast for 20 minutes, then reduce the oven temperature to 350°F (180°C / Gas Mark 4), cover with aluminum foil, and roast, adding a little water if necessary, for 1½ hours more, or until the meat is tender. Transfer the meat to a platter. Pour the wine into the roasting pan and cook over medium heat, scraping up the sediment from the base and sides of the pan with a with a wooden spoon, for 2–3 minutes. Pour the mixture into a clean pan. Combine the cornstarch, mustard, and 4 tablespoons of the stock in a bowl and add to the pan, pour in the remaining stock, and simmer, stirring constantly, until thickened. Stir in the cream and heat through for 1–2 minutes, then remove from heat. Remove and discard the string, cut the meat into slices, and serve immediately with the sauce.

Serves 6
Preparation time 1 hour
Cooking time 2 hours

□ p 404

Herb-stuffed veal shoulder, p 403

VEAL ROLL STUFFED WITH SPINACH
ΜΟΣΧΑΡΙ ΡΟΛΟ ΜΕ ΣΠΑΝΑΚΙ
Moshari rolo me spanaki

Blanch the spinach for 1 minute in boiling water, then drain well, and gently squeeze out the excess liquid with your hands. Melt 4 tablespoons (50 g / 2 oz) of the butter in a pan. Add the onion and spinach and cook over high heat, stirring constantly, for 5 minutes. Season with salt and pepper and remove from the heat. Unroll the meat, lay it out flat on a work surface, and spread the spinach mixture over it. Beat the eggs in a bowl and stir in the milk and cheese. Melt 3 tablespoons (40 g / 1½ oz) of the remaining butter in a large skillet or frying pan. Pour in the egg mixture and cook, shaking the skillet gently and stirring with the back of a fork until the mixture starts to set. Tilt the skillet and lift the side of the omelet to let the uncooked egg run underneath, then cook for 1–2 minutes more, until just set. Turn the omelet over on top of the spinach filling. Season lightly with salt and pepper. Roll up the meat tightly from the long edge and tie securely with kitchen string. Melt the remaining butter in a large pan. Add the rolled veal and cook over medium heat, turning frequently, for about 10 minutes, until lightly browned all over. Pour in the wine, cover, and simmer, occasionally adding a little water, for about 2 hours, until the meat is tender and the sauce has thickened. Lift out the veal, remove and discard the string, and cut into slices. If more sauce is required, stir the cornstarch into the stock, add to the pan, and bring to a boil, stirring constantly, until thickened. Put the sliced veal on a platter and serve with buttered vegetables or fried potatoes, and the sauce (if using).

Serves 6
Preparation time 30 minutes
Cooking time 2½ hours

- 1 lb 2 oz (500 g) spinach, coarse stalks removed, chopped
- generous ⅔ cup (160 g / 5½ oz) butter
- 2 tablespoons grated onion
- salt and pepper
- 3¼ lb (1.5 kg) boned and rolled breast of veal
- 3 eggs
- 2 tablespoons milk
- 2 tablespoons grated Parmesan cheese
- ½ cup (120 ml / 4 fl oz) white wine
- 1 teaspoon cornstarch (cornflour) (optional)
- 1 cup (250 ml / 8 fl oz) meat stock (optional)
- buttered vegetables or fried potatoes, to serve

- 1 lb 2 oz (500 g) prunes, pitted (stoned)
- 2 cups (450 ml / 16 fl oz) Mavrodaphne or other sweet red wine
- 3¼ lb (1.5 kg) boneless stewing veal, cut into 1½-inch (4-cm) cubes
- 1 fresh rosemary sprig
- 2 garlic cloves, halved
- ½ cup (120 ml / 4 fl oz) olive oil
- salt and pepper
- ¾ cup (80 g / 3 oz) blanched almonds
- ½ teaspoon chopped fresh rosemary
- mashed potatoes and carrots or Saffron pilaf (p 257), to serve

VEAL WITH PRUNES AND ALMONDS
ΜΟΣΧΑΡΙ ΜΕ ΔΑΜΑΣΚΗΝΑ ΚΑΙ ΑΜΥΓΔΑΛΑ
Moshari me damaskina ke amigdala

Put the prunes into a bowl, pour in ½ cup (120 ml / 4 fl oz) of the wine, and let soak for 6 hours. Put the veal into a bowl, pour in the remaining wine, add the rosemary sprig and garlic, and let marinate in the refrigerator overnight. Drain the meat and pat dry. Reserve the wine but discard the rosemary sprig and garlic. Heat the oil in a heavy pan. Add the meat and cook over medium heat, stirring frequently, for 8–10 minutes, until browned all over. Add the reserved wine, season with salt and pepper, cover, and simmer for 45 minutes, until the meat is half cooked. Meanwhile, preheat the oven to 350°F (180°C / Gas Mark 4). Put the almonds into a nonstick skillet or frying pan and cook over medium heat, stirring constantly, for 1–2 minutes, or until lightly golden, then remove from the heat. Be careful not to burn them. Transfer the meat and its cooking liquid to an ovenproof dish and add the almonds, chopped rosemary, and the prunes with their wine. Cover with aluminum foil and bake for about 45 minutes, or until the meat is meltingly tender. Serve accompanied by mashed potatoes and carrots or Saffron pilaf.

Serves 4
Preparation time 12 hours (including marinating and soaking)
Cooking time 1¾ hours

□ p 405

VEAL STEW WITH QUINCE
ΜΟΣΧΑΡΙ ΜΕ ΚΥΔΩΝΙΑ
Moshari me kidonia

- ⅔ cup (150 g / 5 oz) butter
- 3¼ lb (1.5 kg) stewing veal, cut into serving pieces
- 1 onion, grated
- 1 cup (250 ml / 8 fl oz) meat stock
- 1½ cups (350 ml / 12 fl oz) puréed peeled fresh or canned tomatoes
- 5 allspice berries
- 2 tablespoons sugar
- salt and pepper
- 3¼ lb (1.5 kg) quinces
- 2 tablespoons freshly squeezed lemon juice
- pinch of grated nutmeg

Melt half the butter in a heavy pan. Add the meat and cook over medium heat, turning occasionally, for about 8 minutes, until lightly browned all over. Add the onion and cook for 6–7 minutes, until beginning to brown. Pour in half the stock, add the tomatoes, allspice berries, and half the sugar, and season with salt and pepper. Reduce the heat, cover, and simmer for 1½ hours, or until the meat is tender and the sauce has reduced. Meanwhile, peel and core the quinces, cut them into pieces, and sprinkle with the lemon juice. Melt the remaining butter in a skillet or frying pan. Add the quinces and cook over medium heat, stirring occasionally, for 5 minutes, until lightly browned. Sprinkle with the remaining sugar and cook, stirring constantly, for 1–2 minutes, until caramelized. Pour in the remaining stock and transfer the mixture to the pan with the meat. Stir lightly, cover, and simmer, without stirring, until the quinces are tender but still firm and the sauce is thick and glossy. Sprinkle with the nutmeg, season with pepper, and serve.

Serves 6
Preparation time 30 minutes
Cooking time 2 hours

◻ p 410

VEAL TONGUE IN WINE SAUCE
ΓΛΩΣΣΑ ΜΟΣΧΑΡΙΣΙΑ ΚΡΑΣΑΤΗ
Glosa mosharisia krasati

- 1 veal tongue, about 1¾ lb (800 g), washed and trimmed
- 4 tablespoons freshly squeezed lemon juice
- salt and pepper
- 5 tablespoons (65 g / 2½ oz) clarified butter
- 7¼ cups (500 g / 1 lb 2 oz) sliced mushrooms
- 4 tablespoons brandy
- ½ cup (120 ml / 4 fl oz) dry white wine
- pinch of dried oregano
- pinch of dried thyme

Rub the tongue with a little salt and half the lemon juice, rinse well, put it into a pan with water to cover. Bring to a boil, drain, and discard the water. Transfer to a clean pan and cover with hot water. Season with salt and pepper, cover, and simmer for 2 hours, or until tender. Remove from the heat and let cool in the cooking liquid, then peel off the skin and slice. Melt half the butter in a large, heavy shallow pan. Add the tongue slices and cook, turning once, for 8–10 minutes, until lightly browned. Meanwhile, melt the remaining butter in a skillet or frying pan. Add the mushrooms and cook over high heat for 7–8 minutes. Transfer the mushrooms to the pan with the tongue and increase the heat. Once it is very hot, turn off the heat, add the brandy, and carefully flambée for a few minutes, until the alcohol has evaporated. Shake the pan gently, pour in the wine and remaining lemon juice, add the dried herbs, and season. Boil briskly for a few minutes, then serve immediately.

Serves 4
Preparation time 2½ hours (including cooling)
Cooking time 2¼ hours

- 1¼ cups (80 g / 3 oz) dried bread crumbs
- 1 cup (250 ml / 8 fl oz) milk
- 9 oz (250 g) ground (minced) pork
- 1½ lb (700 g) ground (minced) beef
- 1 large onion, grated
- 4 tablespoons finely chopped fresh parsley
- 1 tablespoon finely chopped fresh oregano
- 1 teaspoon paprika
- 1 egg, lightly beaten
- 1 tablespoon finely chopped fresh mint or 1 teaspoon dried mint
- salt and pepper
- olive oil, for brushing

FOR THE FILLING
- 4 oz (120 g) feta cheese
- ½ cup (150 g / 5 oz) tomato paste
- ½ teaspoon cayenne pepper
- 2 tablespoons finely chopped fresh mint

STUFFED MEATBALLS FROM ASIA MINOR
ΜΠΑΡΟΥΤΟΚΕΦΤΕΔΕΣ
Baroutokeftedes

Put the bread crumbs into a large bowl, pour in the milk, and let soak for 15 minutes, until the liquid has been absorbed. Add the ground pork, ground beef, onion, parsley, oregano, paprika, egg, and mint, season with salt and pepper, and knead until smooth and thoroughly combined. Cover with plastic wrap and chill for 30 minutes. Divide the mixture into 12 pieces, shape them into large oval patties, and flatten slightly. Crumble the feta cheese and combine with the ingredients for the filling in a bowl. Put 2 tablespoons of the filling in the center of 6 patties and cover them with the remaining 6 patties, pressing the edges firmly together to enclose the filling. Brush the patties with oil and fry in a nonstick pan for 5–8 minutes on each side, or until golden and cooked through. Alternatively, cook under a preheated broiler (grill) for 5–6 minutes on each side. Serve immediately.

Serves 6
Preparation time 1 hour
Cooking time 20 minutes

- 1 cup (250 ml / 8 fl oz) olive oil
- 4 large potatoes, sliced
- 1 lb 2 oz (500 g) ground (minced) beef
- ½ teaspoon sweet paprika
- ½ teaspoon dried thyme
- 3 tablespoons finely chopped fresh mint or ½ teaspoon dried mint
- 2 eggs, beaten
- ½ cup (25 g / 1 oz) fine dried bread crumbs
- 1 onion, grated
- salt and pepper
- flour, for coating
- 2 large onions, sliced
- 1 cup (250 ml / 8 fl oz) beef stock
- 2 teaspoons hot paprika
- grated kefalotiri or Parmesan cheese, for sprinkling

BAKED MEATBALLS WITH POTATOES AND ONIONS FROM KOZANI
ΤΑΒΑΣ ΜΕ ΚΕΦΤΕΔΕΣ ΚΑΙ ΚΡΕΜΜΥΔΙΑ
Tavas me keftedes ke kremidia

Heat half the oil in a heavy skillet or frying pan. Add the potatoes and cook over medium heat, turning occasionally, for 5–7 minutes, until golden. Remove with a slotted spoon and drain. Combine the ground beef, 3 tablespoons of the oil, the sweet paprika, herbs, eggs, bread crumbs, and grated onion into a bowl, season with salt and pepper, and knead with dampened hands until thoroughly combined. Shape into small balls and coat lightly with flour. Reheat the oil in the skillet, add the meatballs, and cook over medium heat for 7–8 minutes, until golden all over. Heat the remaining oil in a heavy pan. Add the sliced onions and cook over low heat, for 5 minutes, until softened. Add the stock and hot paprika, season with salt and pepper, and bring to a boil. Cover and simmer for 20 minutes, until tender. Preheat the oven to 400°F (200°C / Gas Mark 6). Spread the potato slices in an ovenproof dish, put the meatballs on top, and spoon the onion mixture over them. Bake for 30 minutes, until the potatoes are tender and lightly browned. Serve immediately, sprinkled with grated cheese.

Serves 4
Preparation time 1 hour
Cooking time 30 minutes

Veal stew with quince, p 408

Meatballs with yogurt from Thrace, p 412

411

MEATBALLS WITH YOGURT FROM THRACE
ΠΑΠΟΥΔΑ ΘΡΑΚΙΩΤΙΚΗ ΜΕ ΚΕΦΤΕΔΕΣ
Papouda thrakiotiki me keftedes

Preheat the oven to 350°F (180°C / Gas Mark 4) and brush a large ovenproof dish with oil. Bring a pan of salted water to a boil, add the sliced onions, and cook for 10 minutes. Meanwhile, tear the bread into pieces, put it into a bowl with the wine, and let soak for 5 minutes. Drain the onions and set aside. Squeeze out the bread and combine it with the ground beef, parsley, chopped onion, oil, vinegar, and egg. Season with salt and pepper, and knead until thoroughly blended. Shape the mixture into large round patties. Spread the cooked onions in the base of the prepared dish, put the meatballs on top, and dot with the butter. Add 2–3 tablespoons water and bake for 30 minutes. Meanwhile, prepare the sauce. Lightly beat the egg yolks in a bowl, then beat in the yogurt and vinegar until smooth and thoroughly combined. Remove the dish from the oven, spoon the sauce over the patties, and bake for 20 minutes longer, or until crisp and golden. Serve immediately.

Serves 4
Preparation time 30 minutes
Cooking time 1 hour

p 411

- 4 tablespoons olive oil, plus extra for brushing
- 2¼ lb (1 kg) onions, sliced
- 2 slices day-old bread, crusts removed
- 4 tablespoons red wine
- 1 lb 2 oz (500 g) ground (minced) beef
- 4 tablespoons finely chopped fresh parsley
- 1 small onion, finely chopped
- 2 tablespoons red wine vinegar
- 1 egg, lightly beaten
- salt and pepper
- 4 tablespoons (50 g / 2 oz) butter, cut into pieces

FOR THE SAUCE
- 2 egg yolks
- 1 cup (250 ml / 8 fl oz) strained plain or thick Greek yogurt
- 2 tablespoons red wine vinegar

MEAT-STUFFED QUINCES
ΚΥΔΩΝΙΑ ΓΕΜΙΣΤΑ ΜΕ ΚΙΜΑ
Kidonia gemista me kima

Blanch the quinces for 3 minutes, then drain. Cut in half and scoop out most of the flesh with a spoon, leaving about ⅛ inch (3 mm) attached to the skin. Cut off a slice from the base so that they will stand flat. Brush with melted butter and sprinkle with a little sugar. Heat the remaining butter in a pan. Add the onion and pine nuts and cook over low heat, stirring occasionally, for 5 minutes, until softened. Add the ground meat, rice, cinnamon, and ½ cup (120 ml / 4 fl oz) water and season with salt and pepper. Simmer for about 30 minutes. Remove from the heat and let cool slightly, then stir in 1 egg white. Fill the quince halves with the meat mixture. Preheat the oven to 350°F (180°C / Gas Mark 4) and brush an ovenproof dish with melted butter. Beat the yogurt with the remaining eggs and spread the mixture over the tops of the stuffed quinces. Put them in the prepared dish and pour in ½ cup (120 ml / 4 fl oz) water. Sprinkle with the grated cheese and bake for 1½ hours, or until golden. Serve immediately with a fresh vegetable salad.

Serves 6
Preparation time 1 hour
Cooking time 1½ hours

- 3 large quinces, about 2¼ lb (1 kg)
- ½ cup (120 g / 4 oz) butter, melted, plus extra for brushing
- 1 teaspoon sugar
- 1 onion, finely chopped
- ⅓ cup (40 g / 1½ oz) pine nuts
- 1 lb 2 oz (500 g) ground (minced) lamb, or 9 oz (250 g) ground (minced) beef mixed with 9 oz (250 g) ground (minced) lamb or pork
- 3 tablespoons medium-grain rice
- pinch of ground cinnamon
- salt and pepper
- 2 eggs, separated
- 1 cup (250 ml / 8 fl oz) plain yogurt
- 1 cup (120 g / 4 oz) grated kefalotiri or Parmesan cheese
- fresh vegetable salad, to serve

MEAT-STUFFED APPLES
ΜΗΛΑ ΓΕΜΙΣΤΑ ΜΕ ΚΙΜΑ
Mila gemista me kima

- 12 very small or 6 large firm eating apples
- 1 tablespoon sugar
- ½ cup (120 ml / 4 fl oz) olive oil, plus extra for drizzling
- 1 onion, grated
- 11 oz (300 g) ground (minced) beef
- 2 tablespoons finely chopped fresh parsley
- 2 tablespoons finely chopped fresh mint
- pinch of ground cinnamon
- 2 cups (450 ml / 16 fl oz) beef stock
- salt and white pepper
- 2 tablespoons long-grain rice
- ¼ cup (25 g / 1 oz) pine nuts
- 2 tablespoons currants
- pinch of grated nutmeg
- 1½ cups (350 ml / 12 fl oz) White sauce (p 57)

Slice a horizontal piece off the top of each apple and discard. Carefully remove the flesh from inside, leaving ¼ inch (5 mm) attached to the skin. Blanch the apples for 3 minutes, taking care not to overcook them. Drain and sprinkle the insides with the sugar. Heat the oil in a pan. Add the onion and ground beef and cook over medium heat, stirring and breaking up the meat with the spoon, for 6–8 minutes, until lightly browned. Add the parsley, mint, cinnamon, and half the stock. Season with salt and white pepper, cover, and simmer for 20 minutes. Preheat the oven to 400°F (200°C / Gas Mark 6). Remove the pan from the heat and stir in the rice, pine nuts, and currants. Stuff the apples with the meat mixture and put them into an ovenproof dish, cut ends up. Stir the nutmeg into the white sauce and spread 1–2 tablespoons of it over the surface of each apple. Pour the remaining stock into the pan used to make the stuffing and cook, scraping up the sediment from the base with a wooden spoon, then pour it around the stuffed apples. Drizzle with oil and season with salt and pepper. Bake for 1 hour. Serve immediately.

Serves 6
Preparation time 1 hour
Cooking time 1 hour

▢ p 414

MEAT-STUFFED ZUCCHINI (COURGETTES) WITH EGG-LEMON SAUCE
ΚΟΛΟΚΥΘΙΑ ΜΕ ΚΙΜΑ ΑΥΓΟΛΕΜΟΝΟ
Kolokithia me kima avgolemono

- 10 zucchini (courgettes), 4½ lb (2 kg) total weight, trimmed
- 5 tablespoons olive oil
- 1 onion, grated
- 1 lb 2 oz (500 g) ground (minced) beef
- ½ cup (100 g / 3½ oz) medium-grain rice
- ½ cup (25 g / 1 oz) finely chopped fresh parsley, or ¼ cup (15 g / ½ oz) finely chopped dill
- salt and pepper
- 4 tablespoons (50 g / 2 oz) butter, melted
- 2 eggs
- 5 tablespoons freshly squeezed lemon juice

Using a vegetable peeler or apple corer, scoop out most of the flesh lengthwise from inside the zucchini, leaving a thin layer next to the skin. Heat the oil in a pan. Add the onion and cook over low heat, stirring occasionally, for 5 minutes, until softened. Remove from the heat, mix with the beef, rice, and parsley or dill in a bowl, and season with salt and pepper. Loosely stuff the zucchini shells with the meat mixture, leaving a gap at the top. Put them in a wide shallow pan and pour in 1½ cups (350 ml / 12 fl oz) water and the melted butter. Cover and simmer for about 1 hour, or until the meat and rice are tender and the sauce has reduced. Do not overcook. Beat the eggs with the lemon juice in a bowl, beat in 2–3 tablespoons of the hot pan juices, add the mixture to the pan and shake to distribute it evenly. Serve warm.

Serves 5
Preparation time 30 minutes
Cooking time 1 hour

Meat-stuffed apples, p 413

eat-stuffed eggplants (aubergines), p 417

MEAT-STUFFED TOMATOES AND BELL PEPPERS

ΝΤΟΜΑΤΟΠΙΠΕΡΙΕΣ ΜΕ ΚΙΜΑ

Domatopiperies me kima

Slice off the stem ends of the bell peppers and remove the seeds with a teaspoon, reserving the lids. Slice off the stem ends of the tomatoes and carefully scoop out most of the flesh, leaving a thin layer next to the skin and reserving the lids. Sprinkle the tomatoes with salt, turn upside down, and let drain. Put the tomato flesh into a blender or food processor and process to a purée, then mix with the sugar, tomato juice, and tomato paste. Heat half the oil in a large pan. Add the onion and ground beef and cook over high heat, stirring frequently and breaking up the meat with the spoon, for 10–15 minutes, until the meat is lightly browned. Stir in the tomato mixture and season with salt and pepper. Cook over medium heat for about 10 minutes, or until slightly thickened. Remove from the heat and stir in the rice, parsley, and mint, if using. Strain the mixture through a colander into a bowl and reserve the cooking liquid. Preheat the oven to 350°F (180°C / Gas Mark 4). Stuff the bell peppers and tomatoes two-thirds full with the meat and rice mixture. Arrange the stuffed vegetables in a shallow ovenproof dish and set the reserved lids on top. Put the potato slices between the stuffed vegetables, spoon the reserved cooking liquid over them, and season lightly with salt and pepper. Drizzle the remaining oil over the stuffed vegetables and dot the potatoes with the butter. Bake, adding a little water if necessary, for about 1½ hours, or until all the vegetables are tender and the tops are brown. Serve immediately.

Serves 4
Preparation time 1 hour
Cooking time 1½ hours

- 4 large green bell peppers
- 4 large firm, ripe tomatoes
- ½ teaspoon sugar
- 1 cup (250 ml / 8 fl oz) tomato juice
- 2 tablespoons tomato paste
- ⅔ cup (150 ml / ¼ pint) olive oil
- 1 onion, finely chopped
- 1 lb 2 oz (500 g) lean ground (minced) beef
- salt and pepper
- scant ½ cup (80 g / 3 oz) medium-grain rice
- 5 tablespoons finely chopped fresh parsley
- 2 tablespoons finely chopped fresh mint (optional)
- 3 large potatoes, each sliced lengthwise into 8 pieces
- 3 tablespoons (40 g / 1½ oz) butter, cut into pieces

- 4 eggplants (aubergines), 2¼ lb (1 kg), halved lengthwise
- 1 cup (250 ml / 8 fl oz) olive oil
- 3 scallions (spring onions), finely chopped
- 1 onion, grated
- 1 lb 2 oz (500 g) ground (minced) beef
- 1 lb 2 oz (500 g) peeled, seeded, and chopped fresh or canned tomatoes
- ½ cup (25 g / 1 oz) finely chopped fresh parsley
- salt and pepper
- 1 egg white
- 2 egg yolks, lightly beaten
- 1 cup (120 g / 4 oz) grated kefalotiri or Parmesan cheese
- 1½ cups (350 ml / 12 fl oz) thick White sauce (p 57)
- 2 tomatoes, thinly sliced
- ½ cup (120 ml / 4 fl oz) hot water

MEAT-STUFFED EGGPLANTS (AUBERGINES)
ΜΕΛΙΤΖΑΝΕΣ ΠΑΠΟΥΤΣΑΚΙΑ
Melitzanes papoutsakia

Make 2 or 3 slashes in the flesh of each eggplant half with a knife, taking care not to cut through the outer skin. Sprinkle liberally with salt and let drain in a colander for 1–2 hours. Rinse under cold running water and squeeze out any excess moisture. Heat half the oil in a skillet or frying pan. Add the eggplants and cook over medium heat, turning occasionally, for 6–8 minutes, until lightly browned, then remove from the skillet, and drain on paper towels. Put them into an ovenproof earthenware dish, side by side and flesh side up. Heat the remaining oil in a pan. Add the scallions and onion and cook over low heat, stirring occasionally, for 5 minutes, until softened. Stir in the ground beef and cook, stirring and breaking up the meat with the spoon, for about 10 minutes, until lightly browned. Add the tomatoes and parsley, season with salt and pepper, and mix well. Reduce the heat, cover, and simmer for 10 minutes, until the sauce has reduced. Remove from the heat and let cool. Preheat the oven to 350°F (180°C / Gas Mark 4). Lightly beat the egg white and stir it into the meat mixture. With the back of a large spoon, press a cavity in the center of each eggplant half and divide the filling evenly into each eggplant "shell," heaping it up. Fold the egg yolks and half the grated cheese into the white sauce and spread the sauce evenly over the stuffed eggplants. Garnish with half the tomato slices, sprinkle with the remaining cheese, and season with pepper. Pour the hot water into the dish and bake for about 1 hour, or until the tops are golden brown. Serve immediately.

Serves 4
Preparation time 2–3 hours (including salting and cooling)
Cooking time 1 hour

☐ p 415

MEAT-STUFFED GRAPE (VINE) LEAVES
ΝΤΟΛΜΑΔΑΚΙΑ ΜΕ ΚΙΜΑ
Dolmadakia me kima

Cut the stems off the grape leaves. Blanch them in batches for 3 minutes, drain, and let cool. Combine the ground meat, onion, herbs, rice, and half the oil in a bowl and season with salt and pepper. Knead until the mixture is thoroughly combined. Line the base of a large deep pan with a layer of grape leaves. Lay the remaining grape leaves, shiny side down, on a flat surface. Place a tablespoon of the filling in the center of each, fold in the sides, and roll up into neat parcels. Pack the parcels closely together in layers, seam side down, in the prepared pan. Pour in the remaining oil and dot with the butter. Invert a plate just large enough to fit the pan on top of the parcels to keep them from unraveling. Set the pan over medium heat, carefully pour in the boiling water, and cover. Simmer for 40 minutes, or until the rice has absorbed half the liquid and the parcels are tender. Lightly beat the eggs with the lemon juice, then beat in 1 cup (250 ml / 8 fl oz) of the pan juices. Pour the mixture over the rolls and gently shake the pan to distribute it. Let stand for 15 minutes. Sprinkle with pepper and serve immediately.

Serves 6
Preparation time 1 hour (including cooling)
Cooking time 50 minutes

- 1 lb 2 oz (500 g) fresh or canned grape (vine) leaves, rinsed
- 1 lb 2 oz (500 g) ground (minced) beef
- 1 lb 2 oz (500 g) ground (minced) pork
- 1 large onion, grated
- 5 tablespoons finely chopped fresh parsley
- 5 tablespoons finely chopped fresh dill or mint
- ½ cup (100 g / 3½ oz) medium-grain rice
- ⅔ cup (150 ml / ¼ pint) olive oil
- salt and pepper
- 4 tablespoons (50 g / 2 oz) butter, cut into pieces
- 1 cup (250 ml / 8 fl oz) boiling water
- 2 eggs
- 5 tablespoons freshly squeezed lemon juice

MEAT AND POTATO PIE
ΠΙΤΑ ΜΕ ΚΙΜΑ ΚΑΙ ΠΑΤΑΤΕΣ
Pita me kima ke patates

Heat the oil in a heavy pan. Add the onion and garlic and cook over low heat for 5 minutes, until softened. Increase the heat, add the beef and cook, breaking up the meat with the spoon, for about 5 minutes, until lightly browned. Stir in the tomato paste, thyme, and allspice, season with salt and pepper, and cook for 2 minutes, then remove from the heat. Preheat the oven to 350°F (180°C / Gas Mark 4) and brush a 10-inch (25-cm) round ovenproof dish with oil. Cover the base of the dish with half the potato slices. Season with salt and pepper and sprinkle with one third of the grated cheese. Spread the meat mixture on top, smoothing it evenly. Sprinkle with half of the remaining cheese and cover with the remaining potato slices. Pour in the stock, cover with aluminum foil, and bake, adding a little water if necessary, for 1 hour 20 minutes, or until the potatoes are tender. Remove from the oven, brush with melted butter, and sprinkle with the remaining cheese. Bake for 10 minutes more, until golden. Rest for 5 minutes before slicing. Serve hot.

Serves 4
Preparation time 30 minutes
Cooking time 1½ hours

- 4 tablespoons olive oil, plus extra for brushing
- 1 large onion, finely chopped
- 1 garlic clove, finely chopped
- 1 lb 2 oz (500 g) ground (minced) beef
- 1 tablespoon tomato paste
- ½ teaspoon dried thyme
- ¼ teaspoon ground allspice
- salt and pepper
- 2¼ lb (1 kg) potatoes, thinly sliced
- 2¾ cups (300 g / 11 oz) grated kefalograviera or other semi-hard cheese such as Cheddar
- 1 cup (250 ml / 8 fl oz) beef stock
- 4 tablespoons melted butter

- 4½ lb (2 kg) eggplants (aubergines), cut into ½-inch (1-cm) slices
- ½ cup (120 ml / 4 fl oz) olive oil
- 1 onion, grated
- 2 garlic cloves, sliced
- 1 lb 2 oz (500 g) lean ground (minced) beef
- 2 cups (450 ml / 16 fl oz) peeled fresh or canned tomatoes, puréed
- ¼ teaspoon ground allspice
- ½ teaspoon sugar
- salt and pepper
- 1 egg white, lightly beaten
- 5 tablespoons finely chopped fresh parsley
- butter, for greasing
- 5 tablespoons fine dried bread crumbs
- scant 1 cup (100 g / 3½ oz) grated kefalotiri, Parmesan, or regato cheese
- 5 tablespoons heavy (double) cream
- 3 egg yolks, lightly beaten
- 3 cups (750 ml / 1¼ pints) light White sauce (p 57)

MOUSSAKA
ΜΟΥΣΑΚΑΣ
Mousakas

Sprinkle the eggplant slices with salt and let drain in a colander for 1 hour. Rinse, squeeze out the excess water and pat dry. Heat half the oil in a skillet or frying pan. Add the eggplants and cook over medium heat, turning occasionally, for 6–8 minutes, until lightly browned on both sides. Remove with a slotted spoon and drain on paper towels. Heat the remaining oil in a heavy pan. Add the onion and garlic and cook over low heat, stirring occasionally, for 5 minutes, until softened. Increase the heat to medium, add the ground beef, and cook, stirring and breaking up the meat with the spoon, for 10 minutes, until lightly browned. Add the tomatoes, allspice, and sugar and season with salt and pepper. Reduce the heat and simmer for 15–20 minutes, or until all the liquid has evaporated. Remove from the heat and let cool, then fold in the egg white and parsley. Preheat the oven to 400°F (200°C / Gas Mark 6) and grease a deep ovenproof dish, 10 x 14 inches (25 x 35 cm), with butter and sprinkle with 2 tablespoons of the bread crumbs. Cover the base of the dish with half the prepared eggplant slices, overlapping them slightly. Spread half the meat mixture on top and sprinkle with half the grated cheese and 2 tablespoons of the remaining bread crumbs. Cover with the remaining eggplant slices, spread the remaining meat mixture on top, and sprinkle with the remaining cheese and remaining bread crumbs. (At this point, the dish may be covered and frozen. Thaw before baking.) Stir the cream and egg yolks into the white sauce and spread it evenly over the surface of the dish. Bake for about 50 minutes, or until the top is golden brown. Remove from the oven and let stand for 15 minutes before serving.

Serves 6
Preparation time 2 hours (including salting, cooling, and standing)
Cooking time 50 minutes

Note: You can replace half or all the eggplants with sliced potatoes or zucchini (courgettes). If using potatoes, line the base of the dish with them to absorb the juices.

☐ p 420

Moussaka, p.419

astitsio, p 422

PASTITSIO
ΠΑΣΤΙΤΣΙΟ
Pastitsio

Heat ½ cup (120 ml / 4 fl oz) of the oil in a large pan. Add the onion and cook over low heat, stirring occasionally, for 5 minutes, until softened. Increase the heat to medium, add the ground beef, and cook, stirring and breaking up the meat with the spoon, for 10–15 minutes, until lightly browned. Stir in the tomatoes, tomato paste, cinnamon (if using), sugar, and parsley and season with salt and pepper. Reduce the heat and simmer for 15–20 minutes, or until the liquid has reduced. Remove from the heat and let cool for 5 minutes. Fold in the egg white and ½ cup (50 g / 2 oz) of the kefalograviera or Cheddar cheese. Taste and adjust the seasoning if necessary. Bring a large pan of water to a boil, stir in salt and the remaining oil, add the pasta, and cook for 8–10 minutes, or until al dente. Drain and toss with the melted butter, then let cool. Preheat the oven to 350°F (180°C / Gas Mark 4), brush a 10 x 14-inch (25 x 35-cm) ovenproof dish with melted butter and sprinkle with the bread crumbs. Stir the Gruyère cheese into the cooled pasta. Fold the egg yolks and the remaining kefalograviera or Cheddar into the white sauce, season with salt and pepper, and stir in the nutmeg. Line the base of the prepared dish with half the pasta mixture and spread the meat mixture on top. Cover with the remaining pasta and pour the white sauce over it. Bake for about 1 hour, or until the top is golden brown. Let the dish stand for 15 minutes before cutting into serving pieces. Serve hot.

Serves 4
Preparation time 1½ hours (including cooling)
Cooking time 1 hour

□ p 421

- ⅔ cup (150 ml / ¼ pint) olive oil
- 1 onion, grated
- 1 lb 2 oz (500 g) ground (minced) beef
- 1 cup (250 ml / 8 fl oz) puréed peeled fresh or canned tomatoes
- 1 tablespoon tomato paste
- pinch of ground cinnamon (optional)
- ½ teaspoon sugar
- 3 tablespoons finely chopped fresh parsley
- salt and pepper
- 1 egg white, lightly beaten
- scant 1 cup (100 g / 3½ oz) grated kefalograviera or other semi-hard cheese such as Cheddar
- 11 oz (300 g) thick tube-shaped pasta, such as macaroni or ziti
- 4 tablespoons melted butter, plus extra for brushing
- 2 tablespoons fine bread crumbs
- 2 cups (225 g / 8 oz) grated Gruyère cheese
- 3 egg yolks, lightly beaten
- 3 cups (750 ml / 1¼ pints) light White sauce (p 57)
- pinch of grated nutmeg

- 4 tablespoons olive oil, plus extra for brushing
- 2¼ lb (1 kg) large eggplants (aubergines), thinly sliced lengthwise
- scant 1 cup (100 g / 3½ oz) grated regato or Parmesan cheese
- 2 eggs, lightly beaten
- 2 cups (450 ml / 16 fl oz) thick White sauce (p 57)
- 9 oz (250 g) thick tube-shaped pasta, such as macaroni or ziti
- 2 cups (225 g / 8 oz) grated Gruyère or other semi-hard cheese such as Cheddar

FOR THE MEAT SAUCE
- 2 tablespoons olive oil
- 2 garlic cloves, thinly sliced
- 1 lb 2 oz (500 g) ground (minced) beef
- 2 cups (450 ml / 16 fl oz) peeled puréed tomatoes or tomato juice
- 1 teaspoon sugar
- 2 teaspoons red wine vinegar
- 4 tablespoons finely chopped fresh parsley
- salt and pepper

EGGPLANT (AUBERGINE) PASTITSIO
ΜΑΚΑΡΟΝΙΑ ΜΕ ΜΕΛΙΤΖΑΝΕΣ ΠΑΣΤΙΤΣΙΟ
Makaronia me melitzanes pastitsio

Preheat the broiler (grill) and brush a 12-inch (30-cm) ovenproof dish with oil. Spread out the eggplant slices on a cookie sheet (baking tray), sprinkle with salt, brush with olive oil, and broil (grill) for 5 minutes on each side, or until lightly golden. Line the base of the prepared dish with the eggplant slices. To make the meat sauce, heat the oil in a pan. Add the garlic and ground beef and cook over medium heat, stirring and breaking up the meat with a spoon, for about 10 minutes, or until lightly browned. Add the tomatoes or tomato juice, sugar, vinegar, and parsley and season with salt and pepper. Reduce the heat, cover, and simmer for about 15 minutes, until it has thickened. Stir the regato or Parmesan cheese and the eggs into the white sauce while it is still hot. Preheat the oven to 350°F (180°C / Gas Mark 4). Bring a large pan of water to a boil, stir in salt and half the oil, add the pasta, and cook for 8–10 minutes, or until al dente. Drain and stir in the Gruyère cheese and remaining oil. Spread half the macaroni mixture over the eggplant slices and pour half the white sauce on top. Spoon the meat mixture evenly over the sauce and cover with the remaining macaroni. Spread the remaining white sauce on top and bake for about 40 minutes, or until the top is golden. Let the pastitsio stand for 10 minutes before turning out onto a platter. Serve immediately.

Serves 6
Preparation time 1 hour (including cooling)
Cooking time 40 minutes

LAMB

-

APNI

-

Arni

Lamb is many Greeks' favorite meat, and they cook it in many different ways. Most lamb comes from young animals (less than one year old), and milk-fed lamb, also known as spring lamb, is less than two months old. Traditionally, the whole lamb is either cooked in the oven with potatoes flavored with oregano, or roasted on a spit. While Greeks like to braise or stew other meats, they particularly like to broil (grill), fry, and roast lamb. The meat is well flavored and tender, so that any part of the animal can be roasted. Leg is the classic oven-roast, but a whole breast, rolled and stuffed, is also a good choice and is enough to serve quite a large party. Tender cuts, such as leg slices and loin chops, are perfect for broiling (grilling) or frying, even when prepared simply with a marinade of olive oil and herbs or coated with egg and bread crumbs. They are best when served slightly rare; the dry heat of the broiler (grill) creates a delicious contrast between the crisp brown exterior and pink juicy interior. Cubes of lamb are also suitable for broiling on skewers, while breast, neck, and shoulder are perfect for braising with all kinds of vegetables, legumes (pulses), and grains. The rules for broiling, frying, roasting, or braising lamb are much the same as for the other meats, and it is usually cooked on the bone. As lamb is more tender than beef, it needs less cooking at a carefully controlled temperature so that the meat will cook without losing its natural juices.

Whatever the method of cooking, trim off as much fat as possible, as some lamb fat has a pungent flavor that can easily penetrate the lean meat. This is especially important with older animals. If the meat has been affected by the flavor of the fat, you can improve it by serving it with a sharp sauce or by marinating for a few hours before cooking. Lamb is not hung for as long as beef: 3 to 4 days at a controlled temperature and humidity level are enough to improve the texture and flavor of the meat. Fresh, good-quality lamb can be kept in the refrigerator for up to 4 days. Ground (minced) lamb should not be kept for more than 24 hours and ideally should be eaten on the day of purchase. Lamb can be stored successfully in the freezer, but some enzymes continue to be active and these will affect the color, flavor, and texture of the meat over time. Greeks love to cook lamb organ meats (offal), including sweetbreads, hearts, lungs, livers, kidneys, spleens, and intestines, and use them to prepare delicious mezedes. As organ meats are all highly perishable, they should be bought absolutely fresh and should come from a spring lamb. Heart, lungs, kidneys, and liver should be bright and glossy. Sweetbreads should have a pale pinkish-white color. They are best eaten on the day of purchase. It is best not to store raw organ meats in the refrigerator or in the freezer, but if you clean and blanch them first, they can be kept for 1 day in the refrigerator, or for 1 month in the freezer.

- 6 lb 10 oz (3 kg) leg of lamb or young goat (kid)
- salt and pepper
- 1 lb 2 oz (500 g) chard, coarse stalks removed, cut into 2-inch (5-cm) strips
- 1 lb 2 oz (500 g) spinach, coarse stalks removed, cut into 2-inch (5-cm) strips
- ½ cup (120 ml / 4 fl oz) olive oil
- 1 onion, chopped
- ½ cup (25 g / 1 oz) finely chopped tender fennel tips
- ½ cup (25 g / 1 oz) finely chopped fresh parsley
- ½ cup (25 g / 1 oz) finely chopped fresh mint
- 9 oz (250 g) feta cheese, crumbled
- ½ cup (100 g / 3 ½ oz) medium-grain rice
- 4 tablespoons freshly squeezed lemon juice

LAMB WITH AROMATIC GREENS
ΑΡΝΙ ΜΕ ΜΥΡΩΔΙΚΑ ΧΟΡΤΑ
Arni me mirodika horta

Preheat the oven to 350°F (180°C / Gas Mark 4). Season the meat with salt and pepper and place in a large ovenproof dish. Cover and roast for 1½ hours. Meanwhile, rinse the chard and spinach in cold water and put them into a large pan with just the water clinging to the leaves after rinsing. Cover and cook over low heat, stirring occasionally, for 5 minutes, until wilted. Heat the oil in a pan. Add the onion and cook over low heat, stirring occasionally, for 5 minutes, until softened. Add the chard, spinach, fennel, parsley, mint, feta, and rice, season with salt and pepper, and mix well. Spread the vegetable mixture around the meat, sprinkle with the lemon juice, and roast, turning once or twice, for 45 minutes more, or until the meat is golden brown and the vegetables and rice are tender. Serve immediately.

Serves 6
Preparation time 30 minutes
Cooking time 2¼ hours

Note: Other wild greens can be used in this dish, such as wild garlic or dandelion.

- ¾ cup (175 ml / 6 fl oz) olive oil
- 4½ lb (2 kg) stewing lamb, trimmed of fat and cut into serving pieces
- 1 onion, grated
- salt and pepper
- 2¾ lb (1.25 kg) canned artichoke hearts, drained and rinsed, or 3¼ lb (1.5 kg) small zucchini (courgettes), cut into 3–4 pieces
- ½ cup (15 g / ½ oz) finely chopped fresh dill
- 2 eggs
- 5 tablespoons freshly squeezed lemon juice

LAMB WITH ARTICHOKES OR ZUCCHINI (COURGETTES)
ΑΡΝΙ ΜΕ ΑΓΓΙΝΑΡΕΣ Η ΚΟΛΟΚΥΘΙΑ ΑΥΓΟΛΕΜΟΝΟ
Arni me aginares i kolokithia avgolemono

Heat the oil in a large pan. Add the meat and cook over medium heat, turning occasionally, for 8–10 minutes, until lightly browned all over. Add the onion, reduce the heat, and cook, stirring occasionally, for 5 minutes, until softened. Add ½ cup (120 ml / 4 fl oz) water, season with salt and pepper, cover, and simmer for 1¼ hours. Add the artichoke hearts or zucchini and dill to the pan, re-cover, and simmer for 15–20 minutes more, or until the vegetables are tender but still firm. Beat the eggs with the lemon juice in a bowl, then gradually beat in 3–4 tablespoons of the hot pan juices. Pour the mixture into the pan and swirl to distribute the sauce evenly. Remove from the heat and let stand for 5 minutes before serving.

Serves 6
Preparation time 15 minutes
Cooking time 1¾ hours

LAMB WITH BULGUR WHEAT
ΑΡΝΑΚΙ ΜΕ ΠΛΙΓΟΥΡΙ
Arnaki me pligouri

Put the bulgur wheat into a bowl, pour in 1 cup (250 ml / 8 fl oz) water, and set aside until it has absorbed all the water. Meanwhile, heat the oil in a large pan. Add the meat and cook over medium heat, stirring frequently, for about 8 minutes, until lightly browned all over. Add the chopped onion, garlic, rosemary, and thyme, season with salt and pepper, and cook, stirring frequently, for 5 minutes. Pour in the tomato juice, add the onions, cover, and simmer, adding a little water if necessary, for 1½ hours, until the lamb and onions are tender. Add the bulgur wheat and simmer for 5–10 minutes more, then remove from the heat, and serve immediately.

Serves 4
Preparation time 20 minutes
Cooking time 2 hours

- 1 cup (175 g / 6 oz) coarse bulgur wheat
- 5 tablespoons olive oil
- 1½ lb (700 g) boneless stewing lamb, trimmed and cut into large cubes
- 1 onion, finely chopped
- 1 garlic clove, finely chopped
- ½ teaspoon dried rosemary
- ½ teaspoon dried thyme
- salt and pepper
- 1 cup (250 ml / 8 fl oz) tomato juice
- 1 lb 2 oz (500 g) pearl (pickling) onions or shallots, blanched
- ½ teaspoon cayenne pepper

LAMB WITH LEEKS AND CELERY ROOT (CELERIAC) FROM THESSALY
ΑΡΝΙ ΠΡΑΣΟΣΕΛΙΝΟ
Arni prasoselino

Blanch the leeks and celery root in boiling water for 5 minutes and drain well. Heat the oil in a large pan. Add the meat and cook over medium heat, turning occasionally, for 8–10 minutes, until lightly browned all over. Pour in the stock or water, cover, and simmer for 30 minutes. Add the leeks and simmer for 10 minutes more, then add the celery root, and mix gently. Cover and simmer, adding a little more water or stock if necessary, for 30–40 minutes more, or until the meat and vegetables are tender and the sauce has reduced. Lightly beat the eggs in a bowl with the lemon juice, then beat in 3–4 tablespoons of the hot pan juices. Pour the mixture into the pan and swirl to distribute it evenly. Do not stir. Season with pepper and serve immediately.

Serves 4
Preparation time 40 minutes
Cooking time 1¼ hours

- 3¼ lb (1.5 kg) leeks, cut into 1½-inch (4-cm) pieces
- 1 lb 2 oz (500 g) celery root (celeriac), cut into quarters
- ½ cup (120 ml / 4 fl oz) olive oil
- 2¼ lb (1 kg) boneless stewing lamb, trimmed and cut into serving pieces
- ½ cup (120 ml / 4 fl oz) meat stock or water
- 2 eggs
- 5 tablespoons freshly squeezed lemon juice
- pepper

- 4½ lb (2 kg) eggplants (aubergines), sliced lengthwise into ¼-inch (5-mm) thick strips
- 1 cup (250 ml / 8 fl oz) olive oil
- 3¼ lb (1.5 kg) boneless stewing lamb, trimmed and cut into cubes
- 1 onion, finely chopped
- 2¼ lb (1 kg) peeled fresh or canned tomatoes, puréed
- 1 teaspoon sugar
- ½ cup (25 g / 1 oz) finely chopped fresh parsley
- salt and pepper
- 1 red bell pepper, seeded and cut into small squares
- 1 green bell pepper, seeded and cut into small squares

LAMB STEW WITH EGGPLANTS (AUBERGINES)
ΑΡΝΙ ΚΟΚΚΙΝΙΣΤΟ ΜΕ ΜΕΛΙΤΖΑΝΕΣ
Arni kokinisto me melitzanes

Sprinkle the eggplants with salt and let drain in a colander for 1 hour. Rinse and squeeze out the excess moisture. Heat half the oil in a skillet or frying pan. Add the eggplants and cook over medium heat, turning occasionally, for 8 minutes, until lightly browned. Remove and drain. Heat the remaining oil in a large pan. Add the meat and cook over medium heat, stirring frequently, for about 8 minutes, until golden brown. Add the onion and cook, stirring constantly, for 1 minute. Add the puréed tomatoes, sugar, and parsley and season with salt and pepper. Cover and simmer for 1½ hours, or until the meat is tender and the sauce is thick. Preheat the oven to 400°F (200°C / Gas Mark 6). Lay two eggplant strips in the shape of cross, place a cube of meat in the center, and fold the ends of eggplant over it to make a parcel. Put a piece of red and green bell pepper on top and secure with a wooden toothpick. Repeat with the rest of the meat and eggplant. Arrange the parcels close together in a shallow ovenproof dish and pour the sauce over them. Season with salt and pepper and bake for 15–20 minutes.

Serves 6
Preparation time 1½ hours (including salting)
Cooking time 2 hours

□ p 430

- 5½ lb (2.5 kg) leg of lamb
- 5 tablespoons freshly squeezed lemon juice
- pinch of dried oregano
- salt and pepper
- 5 tablespoons olive oil
- 4½ lb (2 kg) potatoes, quartered
- 5 tablespoons (65 g / 2½ oz) butter

ROAST LAMB WITH POTATOES
ΑΡΝΙ ΣΤΟ ΦΟΥΡΝΟ ΜΕ ΠΑΤΑΤΕΣ
Arni sto fourno me patates

Preheat the oven to 300°F (150°C / Gas Mark 2). Put the meat into a roasting pan. Rub half the lemon juice all over it, sprinkle all over with oregano, and season with salt and pepper. Pour over the olive oil and roast, basting and turning occasionally, for about 2 hours. Add a little water during cooking if it gets dry. Put the potatoes around the meat, season with salt and pepper, sprinkle with oregano, dot with butter, and sprinkle with the remaining lemon juice. Add ½ cup (120 ml / 4 fl oz) water, increase the oven temperature to 350°F (180°C / Gas Mark 4), and roast for 1½ hours more, or until the meat and potatoes are tender and golden brown. Serve hot.

Serves 6
Preparation time 30 minutes
Cooking time 3½ hours

Lamb stew with eggplants (aubergines), p 429

lamb baked with orzo, p 432

LAMB BAKED WITH ORZO
ΑΡΝΙ ΓΙΟΥΒΕΤΣΙ ΜΕ ΚΡΙΘΑΡΑΚΙ
Arni giouvetsi me kritharaki

Heat the oil in a large pan. Add the meat and cook over medium heat, turning occasionally, for 8–10 minutes, until lightly browned all over. Add the puréed tomatoes, garlic, and sugar, season with salt and pepper, cover, and simmer for 1 hour. Meanwhile, melt the butter in a nonstick skillet or frying pan. Add the orzo and cook over high heat, stirring constantly, for 5 minutes, until lightly golden. Transfer the orzo to a large ovenproof dish or divide among 6 individual dishes. (In Greece, a special clay pot called a *giouvetsi* is used for this dish.) Preheat the oven to 350°F (180°C / Gas Mark 4). Put the pieces of lamb on top of the orzo and pour the tomato sauce over them. Carefully add the water and cover the dish with aluminum foil. Bake for 1½ hours. Remove from the oven and put the tomato slices on top of the lamb, sprinkle with the cheese, and season with pepper. Return to the oven and bake, adding a little more water if necessary, for 30 minutes more, until the liquid has almost all been absorbed and the pasta is al dente. Serve immediately with extra grated cheese.

Serves 6
Preparation time 30 minutes
Cooking time 2¼ hours

Note: Veal, beef, pork, chicken, or even shellfish can be substituted for the lamb, adjusting the cooking times as necessary.

▢ p 431

- ½ cup (120 ml / 4 fl oz) olive oil
- 3¼ lb (1.5 kg) stewing lamb, trimmed and cut into serving pieces
- 3 cups (750 ml / 1¼ pints) puréed peeled fresh tomatoes or puréed canned tomatoes
- 4 garlic cloves, sliced
- ½ teaspoon sugar
- 4 tablespoons (50 g / 2 oz) butter
- 1 lb 2 oz (500 g) orzo pasta
- 3 cups (750 ml / 1¼ pints) hot water
- 1 tomato, thinly sliced
- ½ cup (50 g / 2 oz) grated kefalotiri or Parmesan cheese, plus extra to garnish
- salt and pepper

LAMB WITH SPINACH FROM THESSALY
ΑΡΝΙ ΜΕ ΣΠΑΝΑΚΙ
Arni me spanaki

Heat the oil in a large pan. Add the meat and cook over high heat, turning occasionally, for about 8 minutes, until lightly browned all over. Add the onion and cook, stirring frequently, for 3–4 minutes, until softened. Add the tomatoes, vinegar, and sugar, season with salt and pepper, cover, and simmer, adding a little water if necessary, for 1¼ hours, until the meat is tender and the sauce has reduced. Meanwhile, blanch the spinach for 1–2 minutes, drain, and add to the pan together with the parsley. Do not stir, just shake the pan to distribute it evenly, then cover, and cook for about 5–10 minutes, being careful not to overcook. Serve immediately.

Serves 4
Preparation time 30 minutes
Cooking time 1½ hours

- ⅔ cup (150 ml / ¼ pint) olive oil
- 2¼ lb (1 kg) boneless stewing lamb, trimmed and cut into serving pieces
- 1 onion, grated
- 2¼ lb (1 kg) tomatoes, peeled and chopped, or 14 oz (400 g) canned chopped tomatoes
- 1 tablespoon red wine vinegar (optional)
- 1 teaspoon sugar
- salt and pepper
- 1¾ lb (800 g) spinach, coarse stalks removed, rinsed and coarsely chopped
- ½ cup (25 g / 1 oz) finely chopped fresh parsley or dill

- 2¼ lb (1 kg) fresh red beans, shelled, or 2¼ cups (500 g / 1 lb 2 oz) dried red kidney or pinto beans, soaked overnight in cold water to cover and drained
- ½ cup (120 ml / 4 fl oz) olive oil
- 3¼ lb (1.5 kg) boneless lamb shoulder, trimmed and cut into serving pieces
- 1 onion, grated
- 1¾ cups (400 ml / 14 fl oz) tomato juice
- 1 tablespoon tomato paste
- 1 teaspoon sugar
- 1 tablespoon red wine vinegar
- ½ cup (25 g / 1 oz) finely chopped fresh parsley
- 1 small chile, chopped
- salt and pepper

LAMB IN TOMATO SAUCE WITH RED BEANS
ΑΡΝΙ ΚΟΚΚΙΝΙΣΤΟ ΜΕ ΚΟΚΚΙΝΑ ΦΑΣΟΛΙΑ
Arni kokinisto me kokina fasolia

If using fresh beans, rinse them under cold running water and drain. If using dried beans, put them into a pan, pour in water to cover, and bring to a boil. Boil vigorously for 15 minutes, then drain and discard the water, pour in fresh water to cover, bring to a boil and simmer for 15–30 minutes, or until half cooked. Drain and discard the water. Heat the oil in a large pan. Add the meat and cook over high heat, turning occasionally, for 8–10 minutes, until lightly browned all over. Add the onion, reduce the heat, and cook, stirring occasionally, for 5 minutes, until softened. Pour in the tomato juice and add the tomato paste, sugar, vinegar, parsley, chile, and beans. Mix well, season with salt and pepper, and pour in 2 cups (450 ml / 16 fl oz) water. Cover and simmer over low heat, adding a little more water if necessary, for 1–2 hours, until the meat and beans are tender and the liquid has reduced. Serve hot or at room temperature.

Serves 6
Preparation time 30 minutes
Cooking time 1½–2½ hours

- 3–4 garlic cloves, thinly sliced
- salt and pepper
- pinch of dried oregano (optional)
- 1 leg of lamb, about 6 lb 10 oz (3 kg)
- 2 tablespoons freshly squeezed lemon juice
- olive oil, for brushing
- Lemon-roasted potatoes (p 224) and mustard, to serve

LEG OF LAMB IN PAPER
ΜΠΟΥΤΙ ΑΡΝΙΣΙΟ ΣΤΟ ΛΑΔΟΧΑΡΤΟ
Bouti arnisio sto ladoharto

Preheat the oven to 350°F (180°C / Gas Mark 4). Season the slices of garlic with salt and pepper and sprinkle with oregano, pressing it on with your fingers. Using a sharp knife, make 20–25 incisions in the surface of the meat and insert the seasoned garlic. Rub the meat with the lemon juice and brush with oil. Cut a piece of baking parchment large enough to hold the meat and brush with oil. Wrap it around the leg of lamb and secure with kitchen string. Put the lamb into a roasting pan and brush the outside of the parcel with a little oil. Roast for 2½ hours. Unwrap, cut into slices, and serve hot with Lemon-roasted potatoes and mustard.

Serves 6
Preparation time 20 minutes
Cooking time 2½ hours

□ p 434

Leg of lamb in paper, p 433

stuffed lamb roll in grape (vine) leaves, p 436

STUFFED LAMB ROLL IN GRAPE (VINE) LEAVES

ΑΡΝΙ ΡΟΛΟ ΣΕ ΚΛΗΜΑΤΟΦΥΛΛΑ

Arni rolo se klimatofila

Preheat the oven to 350°F (180°C / Gas Mark 4). Unroll the meat, lay it out flat on a work surface, and season with salt and pepper. Rinse the spinach in cold water and cook over low heat in just the water clinging to the leaves after rinsing, for 4–5 minutes, until wilted. Drain well. Heat half the oil in a pan. Add the spinach and cook, stirring frequently, for 4–5 minutes. Spread it out on top of the meat. Combine the cheese and mint in a bowl and sprinkle the mixture down the middle of the meat. Roll up and tie securely with kitchen string. Brush a piece of wax (greaseproof) paper large enough to enclose the meat with some of the remaining oil and line it with 2–3 layers of grape leaves. Drizzle with oil, season with a little salt and pepper, and place the meat roll on top. Wrap the paper around it and secure with kitchen string. Put the parcel into an ovenproof dish just large enough to hold it, pour in ½ cup (120 ml / 4 fl oz) water, and bake for 3 hours. Remove from the oven and open the parcel while it is still in the dish. Remove the meat and let rest for 10 minutes before slicing. Meanwhile, pour the wine and the cooking juices into a small pan and cook over medium heat for 5 minutes. Mix the cornstarch to a paste with 2 tablespoons water in a bowl, add to the pan, and cook, stirring constantly, until thickened. Season with salt and pepper and pour the sauce over the sliced meat. Serve immediately with buttered seasonal vegetables.

Serves 6
Preparation time 30 minutes
Cooking time 3¼ hours

Note: Lamb is cooked this way in many parts of Greece, and each region uses its own local cheese in the stuffing—graviera in Crete, ladotiri in Lesvos, kalathaki in Limnos, kefalograviera in Epirus, and formaela in Sterea Ellada.

☐ p 435

- 1 boned and rolled leg of lamb, about 4½ lb (2 kg)
- salt and pepper
- 1 lb 2 oz (500 g) spinach, coarse stalks removed, cut into thick strips
- ½ cup (120 ml / 4 fl oz) olive oil
- 1¾ cups (200 g / 7 oz) coarsely grated halloumi or mozzarella cheese
- 2 tablespoons finely chopped fresh mint
- 5 oz (150 g) grape (vine) leaves, blanched
- 5 tablespoons dry white wine
- 1 tablespoon cornstarch (cornflour)
- buttered seasonal vegetables, to serve

STUFFED LEGS OF SPRING LAMB
ΑΡΝΙΣΙΑ ΜΠΟΥΤΑΚΙΑ ΡΟΛΑ
Arnisia boutakia rola

- 2 boned and rolled legs of spring lamb, about 2¼ lb (1 kg) each
- 2 tablespoons olive oil
- 2 garlic cloves, finely chopped
- 1 tablespoon paprika
- 1 cup (250 ml / 8 fl oz) dry white wine
- 1 cup (250 ml / 8 fl oz) vegetable stock
- salt and pepper
- rice pilaf, to serve

FOR THE STUFFING
- 5 tablespoons olive oil
- 2 garlic cloves, finely chopped
- 3 small leeks, white and tender green parts, finely chopped
- 5 scallions (spring onions), finely chopped
- 1 cup (120 g / 4 oz) sun-dried tomatoes, finely chopped
- 1 cup (50 g / 2 oz) finely chopped fresh parsley
- 1 teaspoon paprika
- 2 egg whites, lightly beaten
- salt and pepper

Untie the legs of lamb and lay them out flat on a work surface. Combine the 2 tablespoons oil, garlic, paprika, and a sprinkling of pepper in a bowl and rub the mixture all over the meat. Let marinate in the refrigerator for 1 hour. Meanwhile, preheat the oven to 425°F (220°C / Gas Mark 7). To prepare the stuffing, heat half the oil in a pan. Add the garlic, leeks, and scallions and cook over low heat, stirring occasionally, for 5 minutes, until softened. Remove from the heat, stir in the sun-dried tomatoes, parsley, paprika, and egg whites, and season with salt and pepper. Divide the filling between the legs of lamb, spreading it evenly. Roll up each leg and secure with kitchen string. Place the rolled legs in a roasting pan, pour in the wine, stock, and remaining oil, and roast for 20 minutes. Reduce the oven temperature to 350°F (180°C / Gas Mark 4) and roast, basting occasionally with the cooking juices, for 1 hour more, or until the meat is tender and browned. Remove from the oven and let rest for 15 minutes, then cut into slices with a sharp carving knife. Pour the pan juices over the meat and serve immediately, accompanied by rice pilaf.

Serves 8
Preparation time 1¼ hours (including marinating)
Cooking time 1½ hours

POT ROAST LAMB WITH LEMON
ΑΡΝΙ ΛΕΜΟΝΑΤΟ ΚΑΤΣΑΡΟΛΑΣ
Arni lemonato katsarolas

- 5 tablespoons olive oil
- 3¼ lb (1.5 kg) leg of lamb, trimmed and cut into serving pieces
- 5 tablespoons freshly squeezed lemon juice
- ½ cup (120 ml / 4 fl oz) hot water
- salt and pepper
- 1 teaspoon dried oregano, or other dried herb of your choice
- sautéed vegetables, to serve
- 2¼ lb (1 kg) potatoes, quartered (optional)

Heat the oil in a large heavy pan. Add the meat and cook over high heat, turning occasionally, for 8 – 10 minutes, until lightly browned all over. Pour in the lemon juice and water, season with salt and pepper, and sprinkle with the oregano. Bring to a boil, reduce the heat, cover, and simmer, adding a little more water if necessary, for about 1½ hours, or until the meat is tender and the sauce has thickened. Serve with sautéed vegetables. Alternatively, when the meat is nearly cooked, add quartered potatoes, pour in enough hot water to cover, and simmer for 20 minutes more, or until the meat and potatoes are tender and the sauce has thickened.

Serves 6
Preparation time 15 minutes
Cooking time 1½ hours

Note: Any other meat—pork, chicken, game, veal, or beef—can be cooked in this way. This recipe is the basis of a variety of wonderful meat dishes known as *lemonata*.

ROAST LAMB WITH RICE AND YOGURT
ΑΡΝΙ ΣΤΟ ΦΟΥΡΝΟ ΜΕ ΓΙΑΟΥΡΤΙ
Arni sto fourno me giaourti

This dish is often served at celebrations and festivals.

Preheat the oven to 350°F (180°C / Gas Mark 4). Season the lamb with salt and pepper, put it into an ovenproof dish, dot with the butter, and pour in the hot water. Bake for about 1 hour, until lightly browned and half cooked. Remove the dish from the oven, spread the rice evenly around the meat, and pour in the boiling water. Return to the oven and bake, adding a little more water if necessary, for 1 hour more, or until all the liquid has been absorbed and the rice is fluffy. Beat the eggs with flour in a bowl, beat in the yogurt, and spread the mixture over the surface of the meat and rice. Drizzle with the melted butter and bake for 10–15 minutes more, until the top is golden brown. Serve hot.

Serves 4
Preparation time 10 minutes
Cooking time 2¼ hours

☐ p 440

- 3¼ lb (1.5 kg) young stewing lamb, trimmed and cut into serving pieces
- salt and pepper
- 4 tablespoons (50 g / 2 oz) butter, cut into pieces
- ½ cup (120 ml / 4 fl oz) hot water
- 2½ cups (500 g / 1 lb 2 oz) long-grain rice
- 4 cups (1 litre / 1¾ pints) boiling water
- 2 eggs, lightly beaten
- 2 tablespoons all-purpose (plain) flour
- 4 cups (1 litre / 1¾ pints) strained plain or thick Greek yogurt
- 5 tablespoons melted clarified butter

LAMB AND VEGETABLE CASSEROLE FROM CYPRUS
ΤΑΒΑΣ ΛΕΥΚΑΡΙΤΙΚΟΣ
Tavas lefkaritikos

Preheat the oven to 400°F (200°C / Gas Mark 6). Cut 3 of the tomatoes into chunks and thinly slice the fourth. Combine the lamb, rice, onion, zucchini, artichoke hearts, and tomato chunks in a large bowl. Sprinkle the sliced potato and sliced tomato with half the cumin or coriander and a little oil. Add the remaining cumin or coriander and oil to the lamb mixture in the bowl, season with salt and pepper, and pour in 1 cup (250 ml / 8 fl oz) water. Mix well and pour the mixture into an ovenproof dish. Make a layer of the sliced potato, top with the sliced tomato, season with a little salt, and drizzle with the oil. Bake for about 2 hours. If the top browns too quickly, cover with aluminum foil and continue baking until the meat is tender. Serve hot.

Serves 6
Preparation time 20 minutes
Cooking time 2 hours

- 4 large tomatoes
- 1¾ lb (800 g) boneless spring lamb, cut into pieces
- 1 cup (200 g / 7 oz) long-grain rice
- 1 onion, coarsely chopped
- 2 zucchini (courgettes), cut in bite-size pieces
- 2 artichoke hearts, quartered
- 1 large potato, thinly sliced
- 1 teaspoon ground cumin or coriander
- ½ cup (120 ml / 4 fl oz) olive oil, plus extra for sprinkling
- salt and pepper

- 7 tablespoons olive oil, plus extra for brushing
- 1 garlic clove, thinly sliced
- 1½ lb (700 g) boneless lamb, cut into 1-inch (2.5-cm) cubes
- salt and pepper
- pinch of dried oregano
- 2 tablespoons freshly squeezed lemon juice
- 1¼ cups (150 g / 5 oz) peas (optional)
- 3 carrots, cut into ½-inch (1-cm) cubes
- 2 large potatoes, cut into ½-inch (1-cm) cubes
- 8 thick tomato slices
- 8 sheets of phyllo dough (filo pastry)
- 5 oz (150 g) kefalotiri, regato, or pecorino cheese, cut into ½-inch (1-cm) cubes

LAMB KLEFTIKO
ΑΡΝΙ ΚΛΕΦΤΙΚΟ
Arni kleftiko

Heat 3 tablespoons of the oil in a heavy skillet or frying pan. Add the garlic and cook over medium heat, stirring frequently, for a few seconds. Add the meat and cook, stirring frequently, for about 8 minutes, until lightly browned all over. Season with salt and pepper, sprinkle with the oregano and lemon juice, and remove from the heat. Blanch the peas, if using, and carrots in lightly salted boiling water for 5 minutes and drain. Heat the remaining oil in another skillet or frying pan. Add the potatoes and cook over medium heat, stirring frequently, for 5–8 minutes, until lightly browned. Remove with a slotted spoon and drain on paper towels. Add the tomato slices to the skillet and cook for 2–3 minutes on each side. Remove from the heat. Preheat the oven to 350°F (180°C / Gas Mark 4) and brush an ovenproof dish with oil. Cut the sheets of phyllo into 12-inch (30-cm) squares and make 4 equal stacks, brushing each sheet with oil. Divide the cubes of lamb, vegetables, and cheese among the stacks, placing them in the center of the squares. Top each with 2 tomato slices, sprinkle with oregano, and season with pepper. Gather the edges of the dough together over the filling to form 4 pouches. Tie loosely with kitchen string and brush lightly with oil. Put the pouches into the prepared dish, cover loosely with aluminum foil, and bake for about 40 minutes, until lightly browned. Serve immediately.

Serves 4
Preparation time 1 hour
Cooking time 40 minutes

Note: *Kleftiko* has a long history in Greek cooking. The name means "stolen meat," and it refers to the tradition of Greek freedom-fighters hiding in the mountains from the Ottoman authorities. They baked their lamb wrapped it in its own hide and buried it beneath their campfire so that the smell wouldn't give them away. This updated version wraps the lamb in phyllo (filo) to replicate the effect—a culinary memorial of Greece's fight for independence. For a traditional *kleftiko*, omit the peas and wrap the lamb in baking parchment instead of phyllo.

Roast lamb with rice and yogurt, p 438

Kid, onion, and potato casserole from Cyprus, p 443

WRAPPED MEAT PIE FROM SMYRNA
ΣΜΥΡΝΕΙΚΗ ΣΑΡΜΑΔΟΠΙΤΑ
Smirneiki sarmadopita

- butter, for greasing
- 2 tablespoons fresh bread crumbs
- 1 lamb's liver and lights (lungs), about 2¼ lb (1 kg)
- 5 tablespoons olive oil
- 1½ cups (10–12) finely chopped scallions (spring onions)
- 5–6 romaine lettuce leaves, finely chopped
- ½ cup (100 g / 3½ oz) long-grain rice
- ½ cup (15 g / ½ oz) finely chopped fresh dill
- 4 tablespoons finely chopped fresh mint
- salt and pepper
- 1 cup (250 ml / 8 fl oz) hot water
- 1 lamb's caul, soaked in cold water
- 1 egg

Preheat the oven to 400°F (200°C / Gas Mark 6), grease an oven-proof dish with butter, and sprinkle with the bread crumbs. Cook the liver and lights for 5 minutes in boiling water, then drain, let cool slightly, and chop into small pieces. Heat the oil in a large pan. Add the meat and cook over medium heat, stirring frequently, for 5 minutes. Add the scallions and lettuce and cook, stirring constantly, for 2–3 minutes more, until the scallions are softened and the lettuce has wilted. Stir in the rice, dill, and mint, season with salt and pepper, and cook for 1–2 minutes more. Add the hot water and remove from the heat. Spoon the rice and liver mixture into the prepared dish and cover with the lamb's caul. Beat the egg with 2 tablespoons water in a bowl and brush the top of the pie with the mixture. Bake for about 45 minutes, or until the top is nicely browned.

Serves 6
Preparation time 30 minutes
Cooking time 45 minutes

Vefa's secret: While you are preparing the filling, rinse the caul well and soak it in a bowl of cold water. This will soften it and prevent it from tearing.

GOAT WITH SORREL FROM CRETE
ΖΙΓΟΥΡΙ ΜΕ ΞΥΝΟΛΑΠΑΘΑ
Zigouri me xinolapatha

- 4½ lb (2 kg) year-old goat or lamb leg or shoulder, cut into serving portions
- salt and pepper
- 2¼ lb (1 kg) sorrel leaves, coarse stalks removed, blanched, and cut into large pieces
- 2¼ cups (500 ml / 18 fl oz) strained plain or thick Greek yogurt
- 5 tablespoons olive oil

FOR THE MARINADE
- 4 cups (1 litre / 1¾ pints) red wine
- 1 cup (250 ml / 8 fl oz) red wine vinegar
- 2 bay leaves
- 4–5 garlic cloves
- 2 onions, sliced
- 10 black peppercorns

A *zigouri* is a fully grown goat or sheep. Its meat is very tasty, but can be tough, and it needs marinating to tenderize it.

Combine all the marinade ingredients in a bowl. Put the meat into a nonmetallic dish and pour the marinade over it. Cover and let marinate in the refrigerator for 24 hours. Transfer the meat and marinade to a large pan, bring to a boil, reduce the heat, and simmer for about 2 hours, or until the meat is tender. Meanwhile, preheat the oven to 350°F (180°C / Gas Mark 4). Remove the pan from the heat. Using a slotted spoon, transfer the meat to an ovenproof dish. Pour in ½ cup (120 ml / 4 fl oz) of the cooking liquid and season with salt and pepper. Spread the sorrel leaves over the meat. Combine the yogurt and oil in a bowl, season with salt and pepper, and pour the sauce evenly over the sorrel. Bake for 45 minutes, or until the top is browned. Serve hot.

Serves 6
Preparation time 24 hours (including marinating)
Cooking time 2¾ hours

- ¾ cup (175 ml / 6 fl oz) olive oil
- 3¼ lb (1.5 kg) potatoes, cut into wedges
- 9 oz (250 g) pearl (pickling) onions or shallots
- 2¼ lb (1 kg) young goat (kid) or lamb leg or shoulder, cut into serving pieces
- 1 cup (250 ml / 8 fl oz) dry red wine
- pinch of ground cinnamon or allspice
- salt and pepper
- 2 tablespoons tomato purée
- 2 bay leaves

KID, ONION, AND POTATO CASSEROLE FROM CYPRUS
ΚΑΟΥΡΜΑΣ
Kaourmas

Heat the oil in a large heavy pan. Add the potatoes and cook over medium heat, stirring frequently, for 6–8 minutes, until golden. Remove with a slotted spoon and drain. Add the onions to the same pan and cook, stirring frequently, for 8 minutes, until golden. Remove the onions, add the meat to the pan and cook, turning occasionally, for 8–10 minutes, until lightly browned. Pour in the wine, add the cinnamon or allspice, and season with salt and pepper. Mix the tomato paste with 2 cups (450 ml / 16 fl oz) water, pour into the pan, and add the onions and bay leaves. Cover and simmer for 1 hour. Add the potatoes and simmer for 1 hour more, until all the ingredients are tender and the liquid has reduced to a thick and glossy sauce. Serve immediately.

Serves 4
Preparation time 40 minutes
Cooking time 2 hours

☐ p 441

- 2¼ lb (1 kg) Spanish oyster plant or salsify (see note)
- 2 tablespoons freshly squeezed lemon juice
- ½ cup (120 ml / 4 fl oz) olive oil
- 1 onion, sliced
- 1 cup (7–8) finely chopped scallions (spring onions)
- ½ cup (120 ml / 4 fl oz) dry white wine
- 2 very small lemons
- 3¼ lb (1.5 kg) young goat (kid) or lamb shoulder, cut into serving pieces
- salt and pepper
- 2 garlic cloves, finely chopped and beaten with 1 tablespoon olive oil
- 1 lb 2 oz (500 g) small potatoes
- 1 large carrot, sliced
- 4 tablespoons finely chopped fresh dill

KID WITH SPANISH OYSTER PLANT
ΚΑΤΣΙΚΙ ΜΕ ΑΣΚΟΛΙΜΠΡΙ
Katsiki me askolimbri

Preheat the oven to 350°F (180°C / Gas Mark 4). Scrub the root and trim the leaves of the oyster plant, then blanch for a few minutes in boiling water mixed with the lemon juice. Drain and cut into pieces. Heat the oil in a pan. Add the sliced onion and scallions and cook over low heat, stirring occasionally, for 5 minutes, until softened. Add the oyster plant and cook, stirring occasionally, for 3 minutes more. Pour in the wine and cook for a few minutes until the alcohol has evaporated. Scrape the skin of the lemons and blanch them in hot water for 1–2 minutes. Lightly season the meat with salt and pepper and place in a deep earthenware casserole. Put the oyster plant, onion, and scallions around the meat, with the garlic mixture, potatoes, carrot, dill, and whole lemons, and season with salt and pepper. Cover and bake, adding a little hot water if necessary, for 2 hours, or until the meat is very tender. Serve hot.

Serves 6
Preparation time 15 minutes
Cooking time 2¼ hours

Note: Spanish oyster plant or askolimbri (Scolymus hispanicus) is a kind of thistle that grows in the Mediterranean. It is similar to salsify, which can be used as a substitute.

GAME

-

ΚΥΝΗΓΙ

-

Kinigi

Game is fairly abundant in Greece, especially in the north of the country, and it is always considered a treat. Game birds are cooked in more or less the same way as chicken, and chicken can be substituted for feathered game in any of these recipes. Some birds require special preparation before cooking. For example, the skin of domestic ducks and geese should be pricked with a sharp fork to allow excess fat to drain off, while the upper part of the tail should be removed from wild ducks, as the oil glands located there have an unpleasant smell. Most game birds larger than quail will benefit from marinating. Several hours of soaking in a marinade of wine and herbs will improve the flavor, tenderize the flesh, and eliminate any strong odors.

Furred game should also be marinated before cooking, usually for several days, because the meat is apt to be tough. Here, too, aromatic herbs in the marinade enhance the flavor of the meat. All game, furred or feathered, is remarkably lean, so it must always be well protected with fat to prevent it from drying out. This can be done in several ways, including wrapping in caul, barding (covering the meat with a layer of fat), or larding (threading strips of fat through the meat with a larding needle) with bacon or pork fat. The extra fat melts during cooking and the meat remains succulent. Sautéing and broiling (grilling) are the quickest ways to cook game. Young birds and tender cuts of meat can be simply cooked in a little olive oil. Once they have been browned, a liquid (water, stock, or wine) should be added to the hot pan to dissolve the sediment on the base of the pan and create a sauce. The pieces of meat should be of uniform thickness so they cook evenly and in the same time. Small birds should be butterflied (split open and flattened), or cut in half.

Broiling (grilling) requires more attention and careful timing, but works well for venison cutlets, loin chops, and medallions from the tenderloin, as well as cuts of rabbit. Trim the meat, drizzle with olive oil and mixed dried herbs, such as thyme, oregano, and marjoram, and let marinate for 1 hour. Preheat the broiler (grill) so that the meat sears when placed on the broiler pan. Young game birds are also good for broiling. They should be butterflied first, then brushed generously with olive oil before being placed under the broiler, and should be basted with more herbed olive oil during cooking.

All types of game can be roasted, from small birds, such as snipe and quail, to a haunch of venison. Roasting requires careful control of the temperature and timing for meat that is golden brown and crusty on the outside and juicy inside. Large birds can simply be barded, but smaller ones, such as partridge and quail, should be spread with butter and wrapped in grape (vine) leaves before barding. Depending on size, pheasant will require about 25 minutes, partridge and quail about 15 minutes.

The most common way to cook game in Greece, however, is braising or stewing. After browning in olive oil, the pan should be deglazed with wine, and the meat should be simmered over a low heat with herbs, vegetables, and a small amount of liquid in a covered pan. As it gradually softens and absorbs the flavors of the other ingredients, it becomes delectably tender and the liquid becomes concentrated into a rich sauce. All mature game is suitable for braising. In the famous dish *stifado*, pieces of wild rabbit are combined with small onions and flavored with allspice, bay leaves, and garlic. The types of game and the flavorings can be varied according to seasonal availability and your own preferences.

- 3¼ lb (1.5 kg) wild boar shoulder, cut into serving pieces
- ½ cup (120 ml / 4 fl oz) olive oil
- 1 onion, sliced
- 1 large carrot, sliced into rounds
- 1 celery stalk, sliced
- 2 garlic cloves
- 1 cup (250 ml / 8 fl oz) dry red wine
- 1 cup (250 ml / 8 fl oz) meat stock
- 2 bay leaves
- salt and pepper
- 3 – 4 tablespoons heavy (double) cream (optional)
- egg noodles (pasta), to serve

FOR THE MARINADE
- ½ cup (120 ml / 4 fl oz) olive oil
- 2 small carrots, sliced
- 2 shallots
- 2 scallions (spring onions), sliced
- 2 garlic cloves, sliced
- 1 celery stalk, finely chopped
- 3 fresh parsley sprigs
- 10 black peppercorns
- 2 bay leaves
- 2 cloves
- salt
- 3 cups (750 ml / 1¼ pints) white wine
- ½ cup (120 ml / 4 fl oz) red wine vinegar

WILD BOAR IN RED WINE FROM THRACE
ΑΓΡΙΟΓΟΥΡΟΥΝΟ ΚΟΚΚΙΝΙΣΤΟ ΚΡΑΣΑΤΟ
Agriogourouno kokinisto krasato

To make the marinade, heat the oil in a pan. Add the carrots, shallots, scallions, garlic, celery, and parsley and cook over high heat, stirring constantly, for 10 minutes, until lightly browned. Add the peppercorns, bay leaves, and cloves and season with salt. Pour in the wine and vinegar, reduce the heat, cover, and simmer for 30 minutes. Remove from the heat and let cool. Remove and discard the shallots, bay leaves, and cloves. Put the meat into a large nonmetallic dish, pour in the marinade, and toss well to coat. Cover and let marinate in the refrigerator, turning occasionally, for 24 hours. Drain the meat and discard the marinade. Heat the oil in a large pan. Add the meat and cook over medium heat, turning occasionally, for 8 – 10 minutes, until lightly browned all over. Remove from the pan with a slotted spoon. Add the onion, carrot, celery, and garlic to the pan, reduce the heat, and cook, stirring occasionally, for 5 minutes, until slightly softened. Return the meat to the pan, pour in the wine and stock, add the bay leaves, and season with salt and pepper. Cover and simmer, adding a little water if necessary, for 1½ hours, or until the meat is tender and the sauce has reduced to about 1 cup (250 ml / 8 fl oz). Using a slotted spoon, transfer the meat to a warm platter and keep warm. Remove and discard the onion, bay leaves, and garlic cloves and strain the sauce into a clean pan, pressing down on the remaining vegetables with the back of a spoon to extract their juices. Bring the sauce to a boil, add the heavy cream (if using), skim off the scum, and pour it over the meat. Serve immediately with egg noodles.

Serves 4
Preparation time 25 hours (including marinating)
Cooking time 1¾ hours

DUCKLING WITH KUMQUATS FROM CORFU

ΠΑΠΑΚΙ ΜΕ ΚΟΥΜΚΟΥΑΤ

Papaki me koumkouat

Prick the skin of the duckling in several places with a sharp knife and season it inside and out with salt and pepper. Combine a few of the kumquats with half the garlic in a bowl. Stuff the duckling with the mixture and sew up the opening with trussing thread. Melt half the butter in a heavy pan. Add the duckling and cook, turning frequently, for about 15 minutes, until it has released most of its fat. Transfer the duckling to a roasting pan. Preheat the oven to 350°F (180°C / Gas Mark 4). Discard the fat and melt the remaining butter in the same pan. Add the onion and the remaining garlic and cook over low heat, stirring occasionally, for 5 minutes, until softened. Pour in the liqueur and cook, scraping up the sediment from the base of the pan with a wooden spoon, for 1–2 minutes, or until the alcohol has evaporated. Add the stock and bay leaves, bring to a boil, and simmer for 5 minutes. Remove and discard the bay leaves. Pour the stock mixture over the duckling and arrange the remaining kumquats around it. Roast for about 1 hour, or until the skin is crisp and the duckling is thoroughly cooked. Add the rice and the boiling water to the roasting pan. Shake the pan to distribute the rice evenly and when the liquid returns to a boil, turn off the oven. Leave the pan in the oven for 10 minutes more, until the rice is tender and the liquid has been absorbed. Serve immediately, sprinkled with parsley.

Serves 4
Preparation time 30 minutes
Cooking time 1½ hours

Note: Kumquats are not native to Corfu, but were introduced to the island in the nineteenth century. Since then they have become a local specialty in various forms including crystallized, preserved, and as the basis for kumquat liqueur. If you cannot find fresh kumquats, substitute tangerine or mandarin segments.

☐ p 450

- 1 oven-ready duckling, about 3¼ lb (1.5 kg)
- salt and pepper
- 1 lb 2 oz (500 g) kumquats, quartered
- 2 garlic cloves, finely chopped
- ½ cup (120 g / 4 oz) butter
- 1 onion, grated
- 4 tablespoons orange liqueur
- 1 cup (250 ml / 8 fl oz) chicken stock
- 2 bay leaves
- generous 1 cup (225 g / 8 oz) basmati rice
- 1 cup (250 ml / 8 fl oz) boiling water
- 2 tablespoons finely chopped fresh parsley

- 2 small ducklings or wild ducks, 4½–5½ lb (2–2.5 kg) total weight
- salt and pepper
- 2 tablespoons (25 g / 1 oz) butter
- 2 tablespoons all-purpose (plain) flour
- 3 tablespoons heavy (double) cream (optional)
- clarified butter, for frying
- 2¼ lb (1 kg) tart apples, peeled, cored, and sliced

FOR THE MARINADE
- ½ cup (120 ml / 4 fl oz) olive oil
- 2 small onions
- 2 cloves
- 2 small carrots, sliced
- 1 small celery stalk, chopped
- 2 garlic cloves
- 3 fresh parsley sprigs
- 10 black peppercorns
- 2 scallions (spring onions), chopped
- 2 bay leaves
- 3 cups (750 ml / 1¼ pints) white wine
- ½ cup (120 ml / 4 fl oz) red wine vinegar

ROAST DUCKLING WITH APPLES
ΠΑΠΑΚΙΑ ΨΗΤΑ ΜΕ ΜΗΛΑ
Papakia psita me mila

Trim off the excess fat at the base of the tail and inside the ducklings. Rub inside and out with salt and pepper, prick the skin in several places with the point of a knife, and tie the legs together. Put the ducklings into a large nonmetallic bowl. To make the marinade, heat the oil in a pan. Stud 1 of the onions with the cloves. Add the carrots, onions, celery, garlic, parsley, peppercorns, scallions, and bay leaves to the pan and cook over low heat, stirring occasionally, for about 10 minutes, until lightly browned. Pour in the wine and vinegar, cover, and simmer for 30 minutes. Remove from the heat and let cool. Remove the onions, garlic cloves, and bay leaves. Pour the marinade over the ducklings, cover, and let marinate in the refrigerator, turning occasionally, for about 24 hours. The next day, preheat the oven to 350°F (180°C / Gas Mark 4). Remove the ducklings from the marinade and place on a rack in a roasting pan. Add 1 cup (250 ml / 8 fl oz) water to the pan and roast the ducklings for about 40 minutes, or until the skin is golden brown and the ducklings are cooked through. Remove from the oven, cut each duckling in half, and place on a warm platter. Keep warm. Strain the cooking juices into a bowl, then skim off and discard the fat. This should leave about 1½ cups (350 ml / 12 fl oz) cooking liquid. Melt the butter in a pan. Add the flour and cook stirring constantly, for 2–3 minutes, until the mixture begins to bubble. Gradually pour in the duckling juices and stir vigorously to blend together. Simmer, stirring occasionally, for about 15 minutes, until the sauce has thickened. Stir in the cream, if using, then remove from the heat, season to taste with salt and pepper, and keep warm. Melt 1 tablespoon clarified butter in a large skillet or frying pan. Add the apples in batches and cook for about 5 minutes, until lightly browned on both sides. Drain and arrange the apples around the ducklings. Serve immediately, passing the sauce separately.

Serves 4
Preparation time 25 hours (including cooling and marinating)
Cooking time 1¼ hours

Duckling with kumquats from Corfu, p 448

PHEASANT WITH ALMONDS AND PINE NUTS
ΦΑΣΙΑΝΟΣ ΜΕ ΑΜΥΓΔΑΛΑ ΚΑΙ ΚΟΥΚΟΥΝΑΡΙΑ
Fasianos me amigdala ke koukounaria

Rinse the pieces of pheasant, pat dry with paper towels, season lightly with salt and pepper, and coat with flour, shaking off any excess. Heat the oil with the butter in a heavy pan. Add the almonds and pine nuts and cook over low heat, stirring constantly, for 1–2 minutes, until lightly golden. Remove with a slotted spoon and set aside. Add the pieces of pheasant to the pan, increase the heat to medium, and cook, turning occasionally, for about 10 minutes, until lightly browned all over. Pour in the wine and 2–3 tablespoons water, add the orange zest, cover, and simmer for about 45 minutes, or until the meat is tender and the sauce has thickened. Using a slotted spoon, transfer the pheasant to a warm platter. Add the almonds and pine nuts to the pan and pour in the vinegar and orange juice. Stir well, cover, and simmer until the sauce has thickened. Pour a little of the sauce over the pheasant and serve hot with rice pilaf or potato purée topped with the remaining sauce. Garnish with orange slices, if using.

Serves 4
Preparation time 45 minutes
Cooking time 45 minutes

⬚ p 451

- 1 pheasant, about 3¼ lb (1.5 kg), cut into serving pieces
- salt and pepper
- all-purpose (plain) flour, for coating
- 4 tablespoons olive oil
- 4 tablespoons (50 g / 2 oz) butter
- ½ cup (50 g / 2 oz) blanched almonds
- ½ cup (50 g / 2 oz) pine nuts
- ½ cup (120 ml / 4 fl oz) dry white wine
- ½ teaspoon grated orange zest
- 1 tablespoon balsamic vinegar
- ½ cup (120 ml / 4 fl oz) freshly squeezed orange juice
- orange slices, to garnish (optional)
- rice pilaf or potato purée, to serve

- 1 pheasant, about 3¼ lb (1.5 kg)
- 1 celery stalk
- 1 carrot
- 2 bay leaves
- 10 peppercorns
- 2 cloves
- 6 tablespoons (80 g / 3 oz) butter
- 2¼ lb (1 kg) pearl (pickling) onions or shallots
- 1 teaspoon dried thyme
- salt and pepper
- 2 tablespoons finely chopped fresh parsley

FOR THE SAUCE
- 2 tablespoons (25 g / 1 oz) butter
- 1 tablespoon all-purpose (plain) flour
- salt and pepper
- pinch of ground mace

ROAST PHEASANT WITH ONIONS
ΦΑΣΙΑΝΟΣ ΜΕ ΚΡΕΜΜΥΔΙΑ ΣΤΟ ΦΟΥΡΝΟ
Fasianos me kremidia sto fourno

Put the pheasant into a large pan, pour in water to cover, and add a pinch of salt. Bring to a boil, skimming off the scum that rises to the surface. Add the celery, carrot, bay leaves, peppercorns, and cloves, cover, and simmer for 30 minutes. Meanwhile, melt the butter in a wide pan. Add the onions and cook over low heat, stirring constantly, for 5 minutes. Transfer them to an ovenproof dish. Preheat the oven to 350°F (180°C / Gas Mark 4). Lift out the pheasant from the pan, drain, and place in the ovenproof dish with the onions. Reserve the cooking liquid. Sprinkle the pheasant with the thyme, season with salt and pepper, and pour in half the reserved cooking liquid. Cover with aluminum foil and bake, adding more of the reserved cooking liquid if necessary, for about 1½ hours, or until the pheasant and onions are tender. Strain the remaining cooking liquid through a cheesecloth- (muslin-) lined strainer into a pan and cook over high heat until it has reduced to 1 cup (250 ml / 8 fl oz). To make the sauce, melt the butter in a pan. Add the flour and cook over medium heat, stirring constantly, for 1 minute. Gradually stir in the reduced cooking liquid and simmer, stirring constantly, until the sauce has thickened. Season with salt and pepper and stir in the mace. Remove the dish from the oven and pour the sauce over the pheasant and onions. Sprinkle with chopped parsley and carve into serving portions immediately.

Serves 4
Preparation time 30 minutes
Cooking time 2 hours

FRIED QUAIL
ΟΡΤΥΚΙΑ ΤΗΓΑΝΙΤΑ
Ortikia tiganita

- 8 quail or other small game birds
- 5 tablespoons olive oil, plus extra for rubbing
- salt and pepper
- pinch of dried oregano
- 5 tablespoons (65 g / 2½ oz) clarified butter
- 4 scallions (spring onions), finely chopped
- 1 lb 2 oz (500 g) fresh mushrooms, sliced
- 2 tablespoons finely chopped fresh parsley
- 1 teaspoon freshly squeezed lemon juice
- 2 tablespoons dry white wine
- watercress sprigs, to garnish

Using a pair of kitchen scissors or poultry shears, slit the birds along the backbones from the neck to the tail. Place them, breast side up, on a flat work surface, press down with the palm of your hand, and break the breastbones. With a knife, make a slit in the skin in the lower part of the breast cavity between the legs. Fold the legs carefully and slip them under the slit. Alternatively, ask your butcher to spatchcock the birds for you. Rub the birds with oil, season with salt and pepper, and sprinkle with oregano. Cover and let stand for 1–2 hours. Heat the oil with the butter in a deep, heavy skillet or frying pan. Add the birds, a few at a time, and cook over medium heat for about 8 minutes on each side, or until the birds are golden brown and cooked through. Remove with a slotted spoon and keep warm in a low oven. Strain the fat from the skillet into a pan and reheat. Add the scallions and cook over low heat, stirring occasionally, for 5 minutes, until softened. Add the mushrooms, increase the heat to high, and cook, stirring frequently, for 7–8 minutes, until their liquid evaporates. Add the parsley, lemon juice, and wine, stir well, and cook for 1 minute. Slide the mushrooms and sauce into the middle of a warmed platter and arrange the birds around them. Garnish with watercress sprigs and serve immediately.

Serves 4
Preparation time 1½–2½ hours (including standing)
Cooking time 30 minutes

QUAIL ROASTED IN GRAPE (VINE) LEAVES
ΟΡΤΥΚΙΑ ΣΤΟ ΦΟΥΡΝΟ ΜΕ ΚΛΗΜΑΤΟΦΥΛΛΑ
Ortikia sto fourno me klimatofila

- 8 quails
- salt and pepper
- pinch of dried thyme
- softened butter, for spreading
- 8 large grape (vine) leaves, rinsed and drained
- 8 thin slices of lard or bacon
- toasted garlic bread and Lemon-roasted potatoes (p 222), to serve

Preheat the oven to 425°F (220°C / Gas Mark 7). Rub the birds all over with salt, pepper, and thyme. Spread a thin layer of butter over the breast of each bird and place a grape leaf on top. Cover the grape leaves with a slice of lard or bacon and secure with kitchen string. Arrange the birds side by side in an ovenproof dish, add ½ cup (120 ml / 4 fl oz) water, and roast for 15 minutes. Remove the birds from the oven, then remove and discard the string, lard, and grape leaves. Return the dish to the oven and roast for 5–10 minutes more, or until the breasts are golden brown. Serve on toasted garlic bread, accompanied by Lemon-roasted potatoes.

Serves 4
Preparation time 30 minutes
Cooking time 25 minutes

- 8 quails
- 3½ cups (800 ml / scant 1½ pints) dry white wine
- 4 bay leaves
- 3 teaspoons mixed peppercorns
- 10 allspice berries
- ½ cup (120 g / 4 oz) clarified butter
- 1½ teaspoons mixed dried herbs
- 1 teaspoon dried thyme
- salt and pepper
- red currant, blackberry, or blueberry jelly, to serve
- cooked basmati rice, to serve

ROAST QUAIL WITH WINE
ΟΡΤΥΚΙΑ ΣΤΟ ΦΟΥΡΝΟ ΜΕ ΚΡΑΣΙ
Ortikia sto fourno me krasi

Put the quails into a bowl, pour in 2 cups (450 ml / 16 fl oz) of the wine, add 2 bay leaves, half the peppercorns, and half the allspice berries, and let marinate in the refrigerator for 12 hours or overnight. Drain the birds, discarding the marinade. Preheat the oven to 350°F (180°C / Gas Mark 4). Melt the butter in a large skillet or frying pan. Add the birds, in batches, and cook over medium heat, turning occasionally, for about 8 minutes, until golden all over. Transfer to an ovenproof dish just large enough to hold them, sprinkle with the herbs, and season with salt and pepper. Add the remaining bay leaves, peppercorns, and allspice berries. Pour the remaining wine and the cooking juices from the skillet over the birds, cover the dish with aluminum foil, and bake for about 40 minutes. Serve immediately on warmed plates, accompanied by red currant, blackberry, or blueberry jelly and cooked basmati rice.

Serves 4
Preparation time 12 hours (including marinating)
Cooking time 50 minutes

□ p 456

- olive oil, for brushing
- 6 large quails
- 6 slices of bacon

FOR THE STUFFING
- 5 tablespoons olive oil
- 2 tablespoons grated onion
- scant 4½ cups (300 g / 11 oz) sliced small white mushrooms
- 2 tablespoons blanched almonds, toasted and coarsely chopped
- 3 tablespoons pine nuts
- 1 tablespoon currants
- 6 prunes, pitted (stoned) and finely chopped
- salt and pepper
- 4 tablespoons dry red wine

FOR THE SAUCE
- 3 tablespoons (40 g / 1½ oz) clarified butter
- 1 lb 2 oz (500 g) seedless grapes
- 4 tablespoons dry white wine
- 1 teaspoon red wine vinegar

QUAIL STUFFED WITH DRIED FRUIT
ΟΡΤΥΚΙΑ ΓΕΜΙΣΤΑ ΜΕ ΞΕΡΑ ΦΡΟΥΤΑ
Ortikia gemista me xera frouta

To make the stuffing, heat the oil in a heavy skillet or frying pan. Add the onion and mushrooms and cook over low heat, stirring occasionally, for 5 minutes, until softened. Stir in the almonds, pine nuts, currants, and prunes and season with salt and pepper. Increase the heat to high, pour in the wine, and cook for 1–2 minutes until the alcohol has evaporated. Remove from the heat and let cool. Meanwhile, preheat the oven to 400°F (200°C / Gas Mark 6) and brush a roasting pan with oil. Season each bird inside and out with salt and pepper and put 2–3 tablespoons of the stuffing into the cavity of each. Secure the opening with a wooden toothpick and put the birds into the prepared pan. Place a slice of bacon on each and roast for 30 minutes. Meanwhile, make the sauce. Melt the butter in a pan. Add the grapes and cook over low heat, stirring occasionally, for 5 minutes. Pour in the wine and vinegar, increase the heat to high, and cook for 1–2 minutes until the alcohol has evaporated. Remove and discard the toothpicks from the quail and serve them on warm plates with the sautéed grapes.

Serves 6
Preparation time 45 minutes (including cooling)
Cooking time 35 minutes

Roast quail with wine, p 455

Rabbit with walnut sauce from the Peloponnese, p 459

HARE STIFADO
ΛΑΓΟΣ ΣΤΙΦΑΔΟ
Lagos stifado

Combine the ingredients for the marinade in a large glass dish, add the pieces of hare or rabbit, and turn to coat. Let marinate in the refrigerator for 24 hours (2–4 days if using hare), turning 3–4 times. Remove the meat from the marinade and drain. Strain the marinade into a bowl, reserving the flavorings and the liquid separately. Heat the oil in a large heavy pan. Add the onions or shallots and cook over low heat, stirring occasionally, for 5 minutes, until softened. Remove with a slotted spoon. Add the pieces of meat and cook, turning occasionally, for 8–10 minutes, until lightly browned. Pour in the reserved marinade and season with salt and pepper. Add 2 bay leaves, 6 peppercorns, and 6 allspice berries from the marinade with the tomatoes. Cover and bring to a boil, then simmer for 30 minutes. Add the onions and garlic cloves and simmer for another 1½ hours, until the meat and onions are tender and the sauce has reduced. If they are cooked but the sauce has not reduced, strain it into another pan and simmer until it thickens. Serve hot.

Serves 6
Preparation time 25 hours (including marinating)
Cooking time 2 hours

- 3¼ lb (1.5 kg) hare or rabbit, cut into serving pieces
- ⅔ cup (150 ml / ¼ pint) olive oil
- 4½ lb (2 kg) pearl (pickling) onions or shallots, blanched and peeled (see p 358)
- salt and pepper
- 3 cups (750 ml / 1¼ pints) puréed peeled fresh or canned tomatoes

FOR THE MARINADE
- 5 tablespoons olive oil
- 1 cup (250 ml / 8 fl oz) dry red wine
- 2 tablespoons red wine vinegar
- 3 bay leaves
- 20 black peppercorns
- 10 allspice berries
- 4 garlic cloves, sliced

RABBIT WITH PRUNES FROM MACEDONIA
ΛΑΓΟΣ ΜΕ ΔΑΜΑΣΚΗΝΑ
Lagos me damaskina

Combine the ingredients for the marinade in a large bowl. Add the pieces of meat and let marinate overnight in the refrigerator. Drain the meat, reserving the marinade, pat dry with paper towel, rub with salt and pepper, and coat with flour. Melt the butter in a large pan. Add the meat and cook over medium heat, turning occasionally, for 10 minutes, until lightly browned all over. Meanwhile, fry the bacon in a nonstick skillet or frying pan for 6–7 minutes, until crisp, then remove from the skillet, and drain on paper towels. Add the bacon and shallots to the pan and strain in 2 cups (450 ml / 16 fl oz) of the reserved marinade. Reduce the heat, cover, and simmer for about 1 hour. Add the prunes, and simmer for 30 minutes more, or until the meat, shallots, and prunes are tender and the sauce has thickened. Serve immediately.

Serves 4
Preparation time 12½ hours (including marinating)
Cooking time 1¾ hours

- 1 rabbit, about 3¼ lb (1.5 kg), cut into serving pieces
- salt and pepper
- ¼ cup (25 g / 1 oz) all-purpose (plain) flour
- 4 tablespoons (50 g / 2 oz) clarified butter
- scant 1 cup (150 g / 5 oz) finely chopped bacon
- 1 lb 2 oz (500 g) shallots, blanched
- 8 oz (225 g) prunes, pitted (stoned)

FOR THE MARINADE
- 4 cups (1 litre / 1¾ pints) dry red wine
- 1 teaspoon black peppercorns
- 6 allspice berries
- 2 garlic cloves, thinly sliced
- 2 bay leaves
- 1 teaspoon dried sage
- 1 teaspoon dried thyme

- 1 large rabbit, about 5½ lb (2.5 kg), cut into serving pieces
- red wine vinegar, for soaking
- all-purpose (plain) flour, for coating
- ½ cup (120 ml / 4 fl oz) olive oil
- ½ cup (120 ml / 4 fl oz) dry white wine
- ½ cup (120 ml / 4 fl oz) hot water
- salt and pepper
- pinch of ground allspice
- 1 quantity Walnut garlic sauce (p 154)
- buttered vegetables, to serve

RABBIT WITH GARLIC SAUCE
ΛΑΓΟΣ ΣΚΟΡΔΑΤΟΣ
Lagos skordatos

Rinse the rabbit and place in a large bowl. Add equal parts vinegar and water to cover the meat and let soak in the refrigerator for 24 hours. Preheat the oven to 350°F (180°C / Gas Mark 4). Drain the meat, pat dry, and coat with flour. Heat the oil in a skillet or frying pan. Add the rabbit and cook over medium heat, turning occasionally, for 10 minutes, until lightly browned. Transfer to a casserole. Pour the wine and hot water into the skillet and cook, scraping up any sediment from the base with a wooden spoon, then pour the mixture over the rabbit, season with salt and pepper, and add the allspice. Cover tightly and bake for 2 hours, or until the meat is tender. Remove from the oven, spread the walnut garlic sauce over the meat, and bake, uncovered, for 15 minutes more, until lightly browned. Serve hot with buttered vegetables.

Serves 6
Preparation time 24 hours (including soaking)
Cooking time 2¼ hours

- 1 rabbit, about 4½ lb (2 kg), cut into serving pieces
- 1 cup (250 ml / 8 fl oz) red wine vinegar
- ½ cup (120 ml / 4 fl oz) olive oil
- 1 onion, finely chopped
- ½ cup (120 ml / 4 fl oz) dry red wine
- 2 tablespoons tomato paste
- 1 cup (250 ml / 8 fl oz) tomato juice
- ¼ teaspoon ground cinnamon
- ¼ teaspoon ground cloves
- 10 allspice berries
- 3 bay leaves
- salt and pepper
- ½ cup (120 ml / 4 fl oz) hot water
- 1 cup (120 g / 4 oz) coarsely chopped walnuts
- mashed potatoes or rice pilaf, to serve

RABBIT WITH WALNUT SAUCE FROM THE PELOPONNESE
ΛΑΓΟΣ Η ΚΟΥΝΕΛΙ ΚΑΡΥΔΑΤΟ
Lagos i kouneli karidato

Put the meat into a bowl. Combine the vinegar with 1 cup (250 ml / 8 fl oz) water in a pitcher (jug) and pour the mixture over the meat. Turn to coat, then cover, and let marinate in the refrigerator for 12 hours overnight. Drain the meat, rinse in plenty of cold running water, and pat dry with paper towels. Heat the oil in a large pan. Add the pieces of rabbit and cook over medium heat, turning occasionally, for about 10 minutes, until lightly browned. Add the onion, reduce the heat, and cook, stirring occasionally, for 5 minutes, until softened. Pour in the wine and cook for 1–2 minutes, or until the alcohol has evaporated. Combine the tomato paste and tomato juice in a bowl and add to the pan, together with the cinnamon, cloves, allspice berries, and bay leaves. Season with salt and pepper, pour in the hot water, cover, and simmer for about 45 minutes, or until the meat is almost tender (wild rabbit will take longer to cook than farmed rabbit). Add the walnuts and simmer for 15 minutes more, until the sauce has thickened. Serve immediately with mashed potatoes or rice pilaf.

Serves 4
Preparation time 12 hours (including marinating)
Cooking time 1¼ hours

▢ p 457

RABBIT LEGS WITH ROSEMARY
ΜΠΟΥΤΑΚΙΑ ΚΟΥΝΕΛΙΟΥ ΜΕ ΔΕΝΤΡΟΛΙΒΑΝΟ
Boutakia kouneliou me dedrolivano

- 4 rabbit legs
- 2 tablespoons capers
- 2 garlic cloves, finely chopped
- 2 tablespoons finely chopped fresh rosemary, thyme, or marjoram
- salt and pepper
- 4 tablespoons olive oil
- ½ cup (120 ml / 4 fl oz) dry white wine
- ½ cup (120 ml / 4 fl oz) freshly squeezed orange juice

Ask your butcher to slit open and remove the bones from the thighs, and to leave the lower legs intact. Flatten the opened thighs with a meat bat. Combine the capers, garlic, and rosemary in a bowl and season with salt and pepper. Spread a quarter of the mixture on each flattened thigh. Roll up and tie with trussing thread or secure with wooden toothpicks. Heat the oil in a pan. Add the legs and cook over medium heat, turning occasionally, for 8 minutes, until lightly browned all over. Pour in the wine and cook, scraping up the sediment from the base of the pan with a wooden spoon, for 5 minutes, until the alcohol has evaporated. Season with salt and pepper and pour in the orange juice. Bring to a boil, cover, and simmer, adding ½ cup (120 ml / 4 fl oz) water, a little at a time, for about 1 hour, or until the meat is tender and the sauce has reduced. Transfer the legs to individual plates and cut a few slices of each to reveal the stuffing. Drizzle with the sauce and serve immediately.

Serves 4
Preparation time 30 minutes
Cooking time 1 hour

◻ p 462

WOODCOCK BRAISED IN WINE
ΜΠΕΚΑΤΣΕΣ ΚΡΑΣΑΤΕΣ
Bekatses krasates

- 8 woodcocks, partridges, or quails
- salt and pepper
- pinch of dried oregano
- olive oil, for brushing
- ½ cup (120 g / 4 oz) clarified butter
- 1 cup (250 ml / 8 fl oz) dry white wine
- 1 tablespoon freshly squeezed lemon juice
- 1 cup (250 ml / 8 fl oz) peeled puréed tomatoes (optional)
- buttered vegetables and salad greens (leaves), to serve

Rub the birds all over with salt, pepper, and oregano and brush them with oil. Set aside for about 30 minutes. Melt the butter in a heavy pan. Add the birds and cook over medium heat, turning occasionally, for 8–10 minutes, until browned all over. Pour in the wine and lemon juice, cover, and simmer for about 40 minutes, or until the birds are tender and the cooking liquid has reduced to ½ cup (120 ml / 4 fl oz). Remove the birds and keep warm. Add the tomatoes (if using) to the sauce and simmer gently until the sauce is very thick. Transfer the birds to a platter and spoon the sauce over them. Serve immediately with buttered vegetables and salad greens.

Serves 4
Preparation time 30 minutes
Cooking time 50–60 minutes

◻ p 463

- 3¼ lb (1.5 kg) leg or saddle of venison in one piece
- 1 tablespoon freshly squeezed lemon juice or red wine vinegar
- 1 medium or 2 small onions
- 1 celery stalk
- 2 carrots
- 3 fresh parsley sprigs
- 2 bay leaves
- 10 black peppercorns
- 3 cloves
- 5 tablespoons olive oil
- 2¼ lb (1 kg) shallots
- 1 large lamb's caul or 8 strips of bacon
- salt and pepper
- 1 tablespoon finely chopped fresh parsley

FOR THE SAUCE
- 2 tablespoons (25 g / 1 oz) butter
- 2 tablespoons all-purpose (plain) flour
- 2 egg yolks
- 3 tablespoons heavy (double) cream

VENISON WITH ONIONS AND WHITE SAUCE
ΕΛΑΦΙ ΜΕ ΚΡΕΜΜΥΔΙΑ ΚΑΙ ΑΣΠΡΗ ΣΑΛΤΣΑ
Elafi me kremidia ke aspri saltsa

Put the venison into a large pan, pour in water to cover, and add a pinch of salt. Bring to a boil over medium heat, skimming off the scum that rises to the surface. Add the lemon juice or vinegar, onion, celery, carrots, parsley, bay leaves, peppercorns, and cloves, cover, and simmer for 30 minutes. Meanwhile, heat the oil in a skillet or frying pan. Add the shallots and cook over medium heat, stirring frequently, for 4–5 minutes, until slightly translucent. Transfer them to an ovenproof dish. Preheat the oven to 350°F (180°C / Gas Mark 4). Remove the venison from the pan and reserve the cooking liquid. Let the venison cool slightly, then wrap it in the caul or bacon strips and put it into the dish with the onions. Add 1 cup (250 ml / 8 fl oz) of the reserved cooking liquid and season with salt and pepper. Cover with aluminum foil and roast for 1 hour, or until the meat is cooked through. Meanwhile, strain the remaining cooking liquid into a pan, bring to a boil, and simmer until reduced to 2 cups (450 ml / 16 fl oz). To make the sauce, melt the butter in a pan. Add the flour and cook over medium heat, stirring constantly, for 1 minute. Remove the pan from the heat, and slowly pour in the reduced cooking liquid, stirring continuously. Return the pan to the heat, cover, and simmer for about 10 minutes, or until thickened. Lightly beat the egg yolks with the cream and gradually pour the mixture into the sauce, stirring constantly, then remove from the heat. Taste and adjust the seasoning if necessary. Slice the venison and transfer to a platter, surround with the shallots, pour the sauce over the meat, and sprinkle with parsley. Serve immediately.

Serve 4
Preparation time 20 minutes
Cooking time 1½ hours

Rabbit legs with rosemary, p 460

Woodcock braised in wine, p 460

PIES

-

ΠΙΤΕΣ

-

Pites

The art of making the thin sheets of flour-and-water pastry known as phyllo (filo) is ancient, probably as old as bread-making itself. In fact, it is thought to have evolved directly from flatbreads baked on the sides of clay ovens, hot flat stones, and, later, metal griddles. These ancient techniques are still used over a wide area around the Mediterranean and the Middle East, extending as far as the Indian subcontinent, and are still visible in Turkish *pides*, Arabic flatbread, Jewish *matzo*, Italian focaccia, and Indian *chapatis*. The word "phyllo" is derived from the ancient Greek word for leaf, suggesting a connection with the age-old culinary technique of cooking food wrapped in edible fresh leaves, which prevented it from being scorched or dried out by direct contact with fire. As wheat varieties improved and the gluten content of wheat flour increased, cooks were able to make their doughs as thin and pliable as the fig, cabbage, or grape (vine) leaves that they had never forgotten how to use. The convergence of these two ancient culinary concepts resulted in phyllo pastry. The phyllo *pita*, or pie, is to the Greeks what pizza is to the Italians, pie is to the Americans, strudel is to the Austrians, and tarts are to the French. It is said in Greece that just about anything edible can be used in a pie, from artichokes to fish, and from greens to zucchini (courgettes). There is even a pie made from watermelon. Pies form the very backbone of Greek culinary tradition, and there is virtually no town or village in the country that doesn't have its own special version.

GENERAL INSTRUCTIONS

Greek pies usually contain fillings of vegetables, meat, cheese, or other ingredients baked between sheets of oiled or buttered phyllo (filo) pastry in large, round, flat metal pans. They can also be rolled, folded, twisted, or coiled, and small pies are often fried just before serving. Phyllo dough is not difficult to make by hand. It is a simple mixture of flour, water, salt, baking powder, a little olive oil, and vinegar that can be rolled and stretched into paper-thin sheets on a surface dusted with cornstarch (cornflour), with the help of a long, narrow rolling pin or *plasti*. Many home cooks, however, now prefer to use ready-made phyllo, sometimes referred to as strudel pastry. In Greece, there are usually at least two or three types available: very thin phyllo for making desserts and cakes such as baklava, all-purpose phyllo, and rustic, thicker phyllo suitable for making pies. However, any type of phyllo can be used in these recipes with very acceptable results—just layer up the sheets if you can only find the very thin variety.

Large pies are generally around 14 inches (35 cm), and can be cut into 12–16 pieces. This is because a 1 lb 2-oz (500-g) package of phyllo (filo) is exactly the amount required for this size of pie and it must all be used up once the package has been opened. Unused fresh phyllo cannot be frozen because it crumbles when thawed. If fewer servings are required, it is better to divide the ingredients in half and make two smaller pies. Bake one and freeze the other one, uncooked, for future use. Leftover pieces of cooked pie can also be frozen and reheated.

Homemade phyllo (filo) sheets are more easily rolled out if the work surface and surface of the dough are lightly dusted with cornstarch (cornflour). Let freshly made phyllo sheets rest and dry slightly before using. Brush them generously with olive oil or melted clarified butter, as they need more fat than ready-made phyllo. To make a rustic "puff" pastry, stack 4–5 small rounds of homemade phyllo dough, each brushed with oil or butter, on top of each other. Roll them out into one large sheet. The layers will separate during baking. Use a flat, wide brush such as a 2-inch (5-cm) pastry brush or an atomizer to apply the oil or melted clarified butter. For the best flavor, use olive oil or a mixture of olive oil and melted clarified butter.

Keep ready-made phyllo (filo) frozen until you are ready to use it and thaw it in the refrigerator in its original wrapping. Remove from the refrigerator 15–20 minutes before it is required to let it come to room temperature. It dries out quickly, making it too brittle to use, so keep any sheets not being used covered with plastic wrap (cling film) with a damp towel on top, but do not let water come into contact with the dough. If you need to cut strips, simply cut off the width required from one end of the phyllo roll, keeping the rest covered.

Prepare vegetable fillings just before making the pie. The vegetables should be blanched before they are drained and chopped, or chopped, then rubbed with salt and drained. Either way, the excess liquid should be squeezed out by hand before they are combined with other ingredients for the filling. Adding bread crumbs, semolina, or *trahana* to the filling will also help prevent the pie from becoming soggy. The filling should be no deeper than 1–2 inches (2.5–5 cm) so that it cooks evenly. A traditional Greek pie is best baked in a large pan made from anodized aluminum—a 14-inch (35-cm) round pan or a 12 x 14-inch (30 x 35-cm) rectangular pan is ideal. Ovenproof glass dishes can also be used. Ready-made phyllo (filo) is sold in rectangular sheets, so these are easier to use in rectangular baking pans. If using homemade round phyllo sheets, roll them out, spread them in the rectangular pan, trim the edges, and use the trimmings to fill in between the layers. Score the pie into serving pieces with a sharp knife before baking to let the steam escape and ensure thorough cooking. The papery texture of ready-made phyllo can be reduced by sprinkling the pie with club soda (soda water) after the first 15 minutes of baking. Alternatively, before baking, brush the surface of the pie with a mixture of water, olive oil, and 2–3 tablespoons all-purpose (plain) flour.

Bake phyllo (filo) pies at around 350–400°F (180–200°C / Gas Mark 4–6) until golden brown. For the best flavor, always bake them just before serving. To maintain a crisp top on cooked pies, do not cover them tightly. Just drape paper towels or a clean dish towel loosely over the pan. Reheat pieces of pie in a nonstick skillet or frying pan, or in the oven, but do not microwave, as this makes them soggy.

CHARD AND CHEESE PIES FROM NAXOS
ΜΠΟΥΡΕΚΙΑ ΝΑΞΟΥ
Bourekia naxou

Sift together the flour, baking powder, and salt into a bowl, make a well in the center, and pour in the olive oil, vinegar, and lukewarm water. Gradually incorporate the dry ingredients into the liquid and knead to a smooth pliable dough, adding more water if necessary. Gather the dough into a ball, cover and let rest for 1 hour. Meanwhile, prepare the filling. Heat the oil in a pan. Add the scallions and cook over low heat, stirring occasionally, for 5 minutes, until softened. Add the chard and cook for 5 minutes more, until wilted. Add the dill and rice, cover, and simmer for 15 minutes, until the rice has absorbed all the liquid. Remove from the heat, add the cheese, and season with pepper and salt if necessary. Let the mixture cool. Divide the dough into 10 pieces and roll out into 8-inch (20-cm) rounds. To make small pies, roll out 20 rounds, 4 inches (10 cm) in diameter. Divide the filling among the rounds, placing it in the center of each, and then spreading it to cover half of the dough to within ½ inch (1 cm) of the edge. Moisten the edges, fold the uncovered half over the filling to form a half-moon, and pinch the edges together. Heat the vegetable oil in a deep-fryer to 350–375°F (180–190°C). Fry the pies in batches for about 5 minutes on each side, until golden brown. Drain on paper towels and serve hot or cold.

Makes 10 large or 20 small pies
Preparation time 2 hours (including resting and cooling)
Cooking time 15 minutes

- 4½ cups (500 g / 1 lb 2 oz) all-purpose (plain) flour
- 2 teaspoons baking powder
- ½ teaspoon salt
- 2 tablespoons olive oil
- 1 tablespoon red wine vinegar
- 1 cup (250 ml / 8 fl oz) lukewarm water
- vegetable oil, for deep-frying

FOR THE FILLING
- 4 tablespoons olive oil
- 4 scallions (spring onions), finely chopped
- 2¼ lb (1 kg) chard, coarse stalks removed, chopped
- ½ cup (15 g / ½ oz) finely chopped fresh dill
- ¼ cup (50 g / 2 oz) long-grain rice
- generous 1 cup (250 g / 9 oz) grated kefalotiri, regato or Parmesan cheese
- salt and pepper

AEGEAN ISLAND CHEESE PIES
ΚΟΠΑΝΙΣΤΟΠΙΤΕΣ
Kopanistopites

Combine the flours in a bowl and add the oil and enough warm water to make a soft pliable dough. Knead until it loses its stickiness and comes away from the side of the bowl. Divide the dough into 12 balls, cover with a damp towel, and let rest for 30 minutes. Roll out into thin, round sheets about the size of the pan to be used for cooking the pies. Spread a thin layer of the soft cheese on half the rounds, leaving a narrow margin around the edges. Moisten the edges, place another round on top, and press with your fingers to seal. Dust with flour. Heat a nonstick, heavy skillet or frying pan and brush with oil. Add a pie and cook over medium-low heat for 5–7 minutes on each side, or until lightly browned. Drain on paper towels and sprinkle with grated cheese. Cook the remaining pies, brushing the skillet with oil each time. Serve hot.

Makes 6 large pies
Preparation time 45 minutes (including resting)
Cooking time 15 minutes

- 1½ cups (175 g / 6 oz) all-purpose (plain) flour, plus extra for dusting
- 6 oz (175 g) whole-wheat (wholemeal) flour
- 5 tablespoons olive oil, plus extra for brushing
- lukewarm water, for binding
- 12 oz (350 g) kopanisti, mizithra, or ricotta cheese
- grated kefalotiri, regato, or Parmesan cheese, for sprinkling

- ½ cup (120 ml / 4 fl oz) melted clarified butter
- 2 egg whites
- ½ cup (120 ml / 4 fl oz) light (single) cream or evaporated milk
- 1½ lb (700 g) feta cheese, crumbled
- 1 lb 2 oz (500 g) ready-made phyllo (filo) sheets or Homemade phyllo dough (filo pastry), p 46, rolled into 12 x 16-inch (30 x 40-cm) sheets
- pepper

CHEESE PIE FROM THESSALONIKI
ΜΠΟΥΓΑΤΣΑ ΜΕ ΤΥΡΙ
Bougatsa me tiri

Preheat the oven to 350°F (180°C / Gas Mark 4) and brush a large rectangular baking pan with butter. Beat the egg whites with the cream or evaporated milk in a bowl, then stir in the cheese. Carefully place half the phyllo sheets one on top of the other in the prepared pan, brushing each sheet with melted butter. Spread the filling evenly on top and season with pepper. Cover with the remaining phyllo sheets, brushing each with melted butter. Score the pie into wide strips and bake for 40 minutes, or until the top is golden brown. Serve hot, cut into bite-size pieces if you want to eat it the way they do in Thessaloniki.

Note: You can substitute puff pastry for the phyllo.

Makes 16 small squares
Preparation time 35 minutes
Cooking time 40 minutes

□ p 470

FOR THE DOUGH
- 3 cups (350 g / 12 oz) all-purpose (plain) flour
- 2 teaspoons baking powder
- ½ teaspoon salt
- ½ cup (120 ml / 4 fl oz) olive oil
- ½ cup (120 ml / 4 fl oz) melted clarified butter, plus extra for brushing
- ½ cup (120 ml / 4 fl oz) plain yogurt
- 1 egg yolk

FOR THE FILLING
- 2 eggs, lightly beaten
- 9 oz (250 g) feta cheese, crumbled
- scant 1 cup (100 g / 3½ oz) grated kaseri or Gruyère cheese
- 3 tablespoons light (single) cream or evaporated milk

SHORTBREAD CHEESE PIES FROM MACEDONIA
ΚΟΥΡΟΥΜΠΟΥΓΑΤΣΕΣ
Kouroubougatses

To make the dough, sift together the flour, baking powder, and salt into a large bowl. Add the oil and butter and work into the dry ingredients with a pastry blender or a table knife until coarse crumbs are formed. Add the yogurt, mix lightly, and gather the dough into a ball. Cover and let rest in the refrigerator for 30 minutes. Preheat the oven to 350°F (180°C / Gas Mark 4) and brush a cookie sheet (baking tray) with melted butter. Roll out the dough into a ⅛-inch (3-mm) thick sheet and stamp out 4½-inch (12-cm) rounds with a plain cookie cutter. Lightly combine all the filling ingredients in a bowl. Place 1 tablespoon of the filling on each round and fold in half, pressing the edges together to seal. (At this point, you can wrap and freeze the pies. Thaw before baking.) Put the pies onto the prepared cookie sheet. Lightly beat the egg yolk with 1 teaspoon water in a bowl and brush the glaze over the pies. Bake for 35 minutes, or until golden brown. Serve hot or cold.

Makes 20–25 small pies
Preparation time 1 hour (including resting)
Cooking time 35 minutes

Cheese pie from Thessaloniki, p 469

Cornmeal pie with greens from Epirus, p 472

FENNEL PIES FROM CRETE
ΜΑΡΑΘΟΠΙΤΕΣ
Marathopites

To make the dough, sift together the flour and salt into a large bowl and make a well in the centre. Pour in the 4 tablespoons oil and the water, mix and knead to a soft pliable dough. Form into a ball, cover, and let rest for 30 minutes. Meanwhile, prepare the filling. Combine the fennel, leek, garlic, and 3 tablespoons oil in a pan, season with salt and pepper, and cook over medium heat, stirring frequently, for about 5 minutes, until soft and translucent. Sprinkle with the flour and remove from the heat. Divide the dough into 24 balls about the size of a lime. Roll out the balls into 8-inch (20-cm) rounds. Place 4–5 tablespoons of the filling onto half the rounds and cover them with the remaining rounds. Moisten the edges and press together to seal. Trim off any excess dough with a pastry wheel or knife. Brush a nonstick pan with oil and heat. Add the pies, one at a time, and cook for 5–8 minutes on each side, until golden. Brush the pan with oil before cooking each pie. Serve hot, topped with a little grated cheese.

Makes 12 small pies
Preparation time 1 hour (including resting)
Cooking time 30–40 minutes

FOR THE DOUGH
- 4½ cups (500 g / 1 lb 2 oz) all-purpose (plain) flour
- ½ teaspoon salt
- 4 tablespoons olive oil, plus extra for brushing
- 1 cup (250 ml / 8 fl oz) lukewarm water
- grated kefalograviera or other semi-hard cheese such as Gruyère, for sprinkling

FOR THE FILLING
- 1 lb 2 oz (500 g) tender fennel branches or fennel bulbs, coarsely chopped
- 1 large leek, finely chopped
- 2 garlic cloves, finely chopped
- 3 tablespoons olive oil
- salt and pepper
- 1 tablespoon all-purpose (plain) flour

CORNMEAL PIE FROM EPIRUS
ΜΠΑΤΣΑΡΙΑ Η ΚΑΛΑΜΠΟΚΟΠΙΤΑ
Batsaria i kalabokopita

Preheat the oven to 400°F (200°C / Gas Mark 6) and brush a 16-inch (40-cm) round baking pan with oil. Blanch the greens in boiling water for 1 minute and drain in a colander. Mix the greens with the herbs, scallions, and feta, if using, in a bowl. Combine the eggs, yogurt, and the olive oil in another bowl, stir in the cornmeal, and add enough water—about 1 cup (250 ml / 8 fl oz)—to make a thick batter. Pour half the batter into the prepared pan and sprinkle the greens mixture evenly over the top. Carefully cover with the remaining batter and bake for about 1 hour, or until the top is golden brown. Let the pie stand for 10 minutes before serving.

Makes 1 large pie
Preparation time 30 minutes
Cooking time 1 hour

Note: You can make a lighter pie by combining 1½ cups (175 g / 6 oz) all-purpose (plain) flour with 1½ cups (175 g / 6 oz) cornmeal and 3 teaspoons baking powder.

- ⅔ cup (150 ml / ¼ pint) olive oil, plus extra for brushing
- 1½ lb (700 g) assorted greens, such as spinach, sorrel, and chard, coarse stalks removed, chopped
- 5 tablespoons finely chopped fresh parsley
- 5 tablespoons finely chopped fresh dill
- 5 tablespoons finely chopped fresh mint
- 8 scallions (spring onions), finely chopped
- 9 oz (250 g) feta cheese, crumbled (optional)
- 2 eggs, lightly beaten
- 1 cup (250 ml / 8 fl oz) plain yogurt
- 3 cups (350 g / 12 oz) coarse cornmeal

☐ p 471

- ⅔ cup (150 ml / ¼ pint) olive oil
- 1 lb 2 oz (500 g) ready-made phyllo (filo) OR Homemade phyllo dough (filo pastry), p 46

FOR THE FILLING
- 4½ lb (2 kg) eggplants (aubergines)
- ½ cup (120 ml / 4 fl oz) olive oil
- 1 large onion, grated
- 1 tablespoon balsamic vinegar
- 4 oz (120 g) feta cheese, crumbled (optional)
- ½ cup (25 g / 1 oz) finely chopped fresh parsley or mint
- ½ cup (120 ml / 4 fl oz) light (single) cream or evaporated milk
- 4 eggs, lightly beaten
- 2 tablespoons bread crumbs
- salt and pepper

EGGPLANT (AUBERGINE) SPIRALS
ΜΕΛΙΤΖΑΝΟΠΙΤΕΣ ΣΤΡΙΦΤΕΣ
Melitzanopites striftes

First, make the filling. Preheat the broiler (grill). Broil (grill) the eggplants, turning frequently, for 5–8 minutes, or until the skins are charred and the flesh is softened. Remove from the heat and hold each eggplant briefly under cold running water until cool enough to handle, then peel. Do not let the unpeeled eggplants cool completely or the flesh will turn black. Cut the eggplant flesh into pieces and transfer to a bowl. Heat the oil in a pan. Add the onion and cook over low heat, stirring occasionally, for 5 minutes, until softened. Add the eggplants, vinegar, cheese, if using, parsley or mint, cream or evaporated milk, eggs, and bread crumbs. Season with salt and pepper, mix well, then remove from the heat. Preheat the oven to 350°F (180°C / Gas Mark 4) and brush a large cookie sheet (baking tray) with oil. Divide the dough into 12 pieces and roll out each into a thin sheet. Lay out 1 sheet of phyllo with the short edge nearest to you. Brush the top half with oil, fold over the bottom half, and brush with oil again. Put 3–4 tablespoons of filling on the long edge and roll up. Wind the roll into a loose spiral. Make more spirals in the same way until all the phyllo and filling are used. Arrange the spirals on the prepared cookie sheet, seam side down. Brush the rolls with the remaining oil and bake for 40–50 minutes, or until golden brown. Serve immediately or at room temperature.

Makes 12 spirals
Preparation time 1 hour
Cooking time 40–50 minutes

🖵 p 474

Eggplant (aubergine) spirals, p 473

Mount Pelion bell pepper and onion pie, p 477

LEEK AND CHEESE PIE
ΠΡΑΣΟΤΥΡΟΠΙΤΑ
Prasotiropita

Preheat the oven to 350°F (180°C / Gas Mark 4) and brush a 14-inch (35-cm) round baking pan with melted butter. Roll out or cut the phyllo into 12 x 16-inch (40-cm) rounds. Blanch the leeks for 1–2 minutes in boiling water, drain, and put in a pan. Add the milk and simmer for 10 minutes, or until the leeks are tender and the liquid has thickened. Remove from the heat, add the parsley, 2 tablespoons of the melted butter, and the cheese, and season with salt and pepper. Fold in the eggs. Combine the remaining melted butter with the oil. Put 5 phyllo sheets on the base of the baking pan, brushing each with the butter and oil mixture, and sprinkle with half the bread crumbs. Spread half the leek filling on top and cover with 2 more sheets of phyllo, brushed with butter and oil. Sprinkle with the remaining bread crumbs and spread the remaining filling on top. Cover with phyllo sheets and brush with the remaining butter and oil. Moisten the edges, press together and pinch together to crimp the edges. Score into serving pieces with a sharp knife. Sprinkle a little water on top of the pie and bake for 1 hour, or until golden brown. Serve hot or cold.

Makes 12–16 pieces
Preparation time 40 minutes
Cooking time 1 hour 10 minutes

- 6 tablespoons melted clarified butter
- 1 lb 2 oz (500 g) ready-made phyllo (filo) or Homemade phyllo dough (filo pastry), p 46
- 2¼ lb (1 kg) leeks, sliced
- 1 cup (250 ml / 8 fl oz) milk
- 4 tablespoons chopped fresh parsley or mint
- 1 lb 2 oz (500 g) feta cheese, crumbled
- salt and pepper
- 4 eggs, lightly beaten
- ½ cup (120 ml / 4 fl oz) olive oil
- 2 tablespoons fine bread crumbs

MACARONI, SPINACH, AND CHEESE PIE
ΜΑΚΑΡΟΝΟΠΙΤΑ ΜΕ ΤΥΡΙ ΚΑΙ ΣΠΑΝΑΚΙ
Makaronopita me tiri ke spanaki

Preheat the oven to 350°F (180°C / Gas Mark 4) and brush a 10 x 14-inch (25 x 35-cm) ovenproof dish with melted butter. Line the dish with half the phyllo sheets, brushing each with melted butter. Bring a large pan of water to a boil, stir in salt and 2 tablespoons of the oil, add the macaroni, and cook for 8–10 minutes, or until al dente, then drain. Blanch the spinach for 1 minute in boiling water and drain. Let cool and squeeze out the excess water. Heat the remaining oil in a pan. Add the onion and cook over low heat, stirring occasionally, for 5 minutes, until softened. Add the spinach and cook for 5 minutes more, then remove from the heat. Beat the eggs with the milk, cornstarch, and nutmeg in a bowl, season with salt and pepper, and add the spinach mixture, macaroni, and both types of cheese. Spoon the mixture into the dish and cover with the remaining phyllo sheets, brushing each with butter. With a sharp knife, score the pie into large squares. Bake for 1 hour, or until the top is golden brown. Let stand for a few minutes before serving.

Makes 1 large pie
Preparation time 40 minutes (including cooling)
Cooking time 1 hour

- 5 tablespoons melted clarified butter
- 10 sheets ready-made phyllo (filo)
- 5 tablespoons olive oil
- 2¼ cups (250 g / 9 oz) elbow macaroni
- 9 oz (250 g) spinach, coarse stalks removed
- 1 onion, grated
- 3 eggs
- ⅔ cup (150 ml / ¼ pint) milk
- 1 tablespoon cornstarch (cornflour)
- ¼ teaspoon grated nutmeg
- salt and pepper
- 3 cups (350 g / 12 oz) grated Gruyère cheese
- ½ cup (50 g / 2 oz) grated kefalotiri or Parmesan cheese

- 1 lb 2 oz (500 g) ready-made phyllo (filo) Or Homemade phyllo dough (filo pastry), p 46
- ⅔ cup (150 ml / ¼ pint) olive oil

FOR THE FILLING
- 4 tablespoons olive oil
- 1 large red bell pepper, seeded and cut into thin strips
- 1 large yellow bell pepper, seeded and cut into thin strips
- 1 large green bell pepper, seeded and cut into thin strips
- 2 large onions, thinly sliced
- ½ cup (4) finely chopped scallions (spring onions)
- 4 tablespoons finely chopped fresh parsley
- 2 tablespoons dried bread crumbs
- 9 oz (250 g) feta cheese, crumbled
- 3 eggs, lightly beaten
- ¼ teaspoon cayenne pepper
- salt and pepper
- 1 large tomato, sliced

MOUNT PELION BELL PEPPER AND ONION PIE
ΠΙΠΕΡΟΠΙΤΑ ΠΗΛΙΟΥ
Piperopita piliou

Preheat the oven to 350°F (180°C / Gas Mark 4). Cut 10 of the phyllo sheets into 16-inch (40-cm) rounds, or if using homemade, roll out into 10 thin 16-inch (40-cm) rounds. Lay half of them in the base of a 14-inch (35-cm) round baking pan, brushing each with oil. Let the excess phyllo ruffle around the side of the pan. To make the filling, heat the 4 tablespoons oil in a pan. Add the bell peppers, onions, and scallions and cook over medium heat, stirring frequently, for 5 minutes, until softened. Remove from the heat and stir in the parsley, bread crumbs, feta, eggs, and cayenne, and season with salt and pepper. Spoon the filling into the phyllo-lined pan and put the tomato slices on top. Cover with the remaining phyllo sheets, brushing each with oil and letting the edges ruffle around. Brush the top and ruffled edges with oil. Score the pie into 8 or 10 serving pieces and bake for about 50 minutes, or until golden brown. Serve immediately.

Makes 8–10 pieces
Preparation time 30 minutes
Cooking time 50 minutes

▢ p 475

- 1 lb 2 oz (500 g) ready-made phyllo (filo) Or Homemade phyllo dough (filo pastry), p 46
- ⅔ cup (150 ml / ¼ pint) olive oil

FOR THE FILLING
- 2¼ lb (1 kg) onions, sliced
- 4 eggs, lightly beaten
- ½ cup (25 g / 1 oz) finely chopped fresh mint
- 5 tablespoons light (single) cream or evaporated milk
- 2¾ cups (300 g / 11 oz) grated kefalotiri, pecorino, or regato cheese
- 7 oz (200 g) feta cheese, crumbled
- salt and pepper

ONION PIE FROM THESSALY
ΚΡΕΜΜΥΔΟΠΙΤΑ
Kremidopita

Preheat the oven to 400°F (200°C / Gas Mark 6). If using homemade phyllo, roll out into thin sheets roughly 12 x 16 inches (30 x 40 cm). Brush a baking pan that is slightly smaller than the size of the phyllo sheets with oil. To make the filling, cook the onions in a pan with a little water for 15 minutes, then drain well. Combine the onions, eggs, mint, cream or evaporated milk, grated cheese, and feta in a bowl and season with salt and pepper. Place half the phyllo sheets on the base of the prepared pan, brushing each with oil. Spread the filling on top and cover with the remaining phyllo sheets, brushing each with oil. Roll and crimp the overhanging phyllo neatly around the edge and score the pie into 12 or 16 serving pieces with a sharp knife. Brush the top with the remaining oil and sprinkle with a little water. Bake for about 1 hour, or until golden brown. Serve immediately.

Makes 12–16 pieces
Preparation time 30 minutes
Cooking time 1 hour

SPINACH AND CHEESE PIE
ΣΠΑΝΑΚΟΠΙΤΑ
Spanakotiropita

Preheat the oven to 350°F (180°C / Gas Mark 4) and brush a 14-inch (35-cm) baking pan with oil. If using homemade, roll the phyllo dough into thin 18-inch (46-cm) rounds. Sprinkle the spinach with a little salt and rub with your fingers. Rinse, drain, and squeeze out the excess water. Alternatively, blanch it for 1 minute, drain, and squeeze out the excess water. Combine the spinach, scallions, dill, parsley, cheese, milk, eggs, and melted butter in a bowl and season with pepper. Lay half the phyllo sheets in the prepared pan, one on top of the other, brushing each with oil. Spread the spinach filling evenly on top and cover with the remaining phyllo sheets, brushing each with oil. Roll up the over-hanging phyllo neatly around the pan. Score into 12 serving pieces, and brush the top with oil. Sprinkle with a little water and bake for 1 hour, or until golden brown. Serve warm or at room temperature.

Makes 12 pieces
Preparation time 30 minutes
Cooking time 1 hour

□ p 480

- ½ cup (120 ml / 4 fl oz) olive oil
- 1 lb 2 oz (500 g) ready-made phyllo (filo) or Homemade phyllo dough (filo pastry), p 46
- 2¼ lb (1 kg) spinach, coarse stalks removed, chopped
- 1 cup (7–8) finely chopped scallions (spring onions)
- ½ cup (15 g / ½ oz) finely chopped fresh dill
- ½ cup (25 g / 1 oz) finely chopped fresh parsley
- 1 lb 2 oz (500 g) feta cheese, crumbled
- 4 tablespoons milk
- 3–4 eggs, lightly beaten
- 4 tablespoons melted clarified butter
- salt and pepper

BEAN CRESCENTS FROM ASIA MINOR
ΠΙΤΑΚΙΑ ΜΕ ΚΟΚΚΙΝΑ ΦΑΣΟΛΙΑ
Pitakia me kokina fasolia

To make the dough, sift the flour and salt into a bowl, stir in the yeast, and make a well in the center. Add the water and the 2 tablespoons olive oil and incorporate the dry ingredients to form a stiff dough. Knead until smooth and no longer sticky. Cover with a damp cloth and let rise for 1 hour, or until doubled in volume. Meanwhile, put the beans into a pan, cover with water, and bring to a boil. Cook for 40 minutes or until very soft, then drain. Heat the 5 tablespoons olive oil in a pan. Add the onion and cook over low heat, stirring occasionally, for 5 minutes, until softened. Add the beans and parsley, season with pepper, and cook for 5 minutes more. Remove from the heat and mash with a fork, or process to a purée in a food processor. Divide the dough into 20 balls and roll out 4-inch (10-cm) rounds. Place 1–2 tablespoons of the filling on each round, moisten the edges and fold in half, sealing to form crescents. Let rise for 30 minutes. Heat the vegetable oil in a deep-fryer to 350–375°F (180–190°C). Cook in batches for 5 minutes, or until golden. Remove, drain and serve hot or at room temperature.

Makes 20 small crescents
Preparation time 13½ hours (including soaking and rising)
Cooking time 20 minutes

FOR THE DOUGH
- 4½ cups (500 g / 1 lb 2 oz) all-purpose (plain) flour
- ½ teaspoon salt
- 1 tablespoon rapid-rise (fast-action) dried yeast
- 1 cup (250 ml / 8 fl oz) lukewarm water
- 2 tablespoons olive oil
- vegetable oil, for deep-frying

FOR THE FILLING
- 1¾ cups (300 g / 11 oz) dried red beans (such as red kidney or borlotti beans), soaked overnight in water to cover and drained, and blanched for 10 minutes
- 5 tablespoons olive oil
- 1 onion, grated
- 4 tablespoons finely chopped fresh parsley
- salt and pepper

FOR THE DOUGH

- 3 cups (350 g / 12 oz) all-purpose (plain) flour
- 1 teaspoon salt
- ½ cup (120 ml / 4 fl oz) olive oil
- 4 tablespoons raki, tsikoudia, or white wine
- 1 egg yolk
- 2 tablespoons milk

FOR THE FILLING

- 2¼ lb (1 kg) zucchini (courgettes), thinly sliced
- salt and pepper
- 5 tablespoons olive oil
- 1 lb 2 oz (500 g) anthotiro or ricotta cheese
- 4½ cups (500 g / 1 lb 2 oz) grated tyromalama or mozzarella cheese
- 5 tablespoons finely chopped fresh mint
- all-purpose (plain) flour, for coating
- sesame seeds, for sprinkling

CRETAN ZUCCHINI (COURGETTE) CHEESE PIE FROM CHANIA
ΧΑΝΙΩΤΙΚΟ ΜΠΟΥΡΕΚΙ
Haniotiko boureki

To make the dough, sift together the flour and salt into a bowl and make a well in the center. Add 4 tablespoons of the oil, the raki, and ½ cup (120 ml / 4 fl oz) water, and gradually incorporate the dry ingredients. Knead to a smooth elastic dough. Divide the dough into 6 pieces, cover with plastic wrap (cling film), and let rest for 1 hour. Meanwhile, prepare the filling. Sprinkle the zucchini slices with a little salt and let drain in a colander for 30 minutes. Preheat the oven to 400°F (200°C / Gas Mark 6) and brush a 14-inch (35-cm) round baking pan with oil. Combine both types of cheese and the mint in a bowl, season with salt and pepper, and set aside. Roll the pieces of dough into 6-inch (15-cm) rounds. Stack 3 rounds on top of each other, brushing each one with some of the remaining olive oil. Repeat with the other 3 rounds to create a second stack. Roll out each stack into a 14-inch (35-cm) diameter round. Place 1 round in the prepared pan. Rinse and drain the zucchini slices, pat dry, and coat with flour. Spread out half the slices in the pastry-lined pan. Spread the cheese mixture on top and cover with the remaining zucchini slices. Sprinkle with the olive oil and lay the second phyllo sheet on top. Crimp the edges around the rim. Score the pie into 16 serving pieces with a sharp knife. Beat the egg yolk with the milk in a bowl and brush the glaze over the pie. Sprinkle with sesame seeds and bake for about 1 hour, or until golden brown. Serve hot.

Makes 1 large pie
Preparation time 1½ hours (including resting)
Cooking time 1 hour

Spinach and cheese pie, p 478

Imond pastry triangles from Chios, p 486

MOUNT PELION MONASTERY VEGETABLE PIE
ΧΟΡΤΟΠΙΤΑ ΜΟΝΑΣΤΗΡΙΑΚΗ
Hortopita monastiriaki

Preheat the oven to 400°F (200°C / Gas Mark 6) and brush a 16-inch (40-cm) round baking pan with oil. Blanch the greens in boiling water for 1 minute and drain well in a colander, pressing out the excess water. Heat 5 tablespoons of the oil in a pan. Add the onion, scallions, and leeks and cook over low heat, stirring occasionally, for 5 minutes, until softened. Add the greens, fennel, parsley, and bread crumbs, season with salt and pepper, mix well, and remove from the heat. Divide the dough into 12 pieces and roll out each into a thin sheet. Lay 5 phyllo sheets on the base of the prepared pan, brushing each with oil. Spread half the filling evenly on top and season with pepper. Brush 2 phyllo sheets with oil and put them on top. Spread the remaining filling over them and cover with the remaining phyllo sheets, brushing each with oil. Roll the overhanging phyllo neatly around the edge of the pan and score the pie into 12 or 16 serving pieces. Brush the surface with the remaining oil and bake for about 1 hour, or until golden brown. Serve hot or at room temperature.

Makes 12–16 pieces
Preparation time 1 hour
Cooking time 1 hour 10 minutes

- 1 cup (250 ml / 8 fl oz) olive oil, plus extra for brushing
- 2¼ lb (1 kg) assorted greens, such as dandelions, nettles, chard, and spinach, coarse stalks removed
- 1 onion, grated
- 3–4 scallions (spring onions), finely chopped
- 2 leeks, white parts only, finely chopped
- ½ cup (15 g / ½ oz) finely chopped fresh fennel fronds
- ½ cup (25 g / 1 oz) finely chopped fresh parsley
- 2 tablespoons bread crumbs
- salt and pepper
- 1 lb 2 oz (500 g) ready-made phyllo (filo) or Homemade phyllo dough (filo pastry), p 46

FISH PIE FROM LEFKADA
ΜΑΡΙΔΟΠΙΤΑ ΛΕΥΚΑΔΑΣ
Maridopita lefkadas

Preheat the oven to 400°F (200°C / Gas Mark 6) and brush a 14-inch (35-cm) round baking pan with oil. Heat half the remaining oil in a pan. Add the onions and cook over low heat, stirring occasionally, for 5 minutes, until softened, then remove from the heat. Line the prepared pan with half the phyllo, brushing each sheet with oil. Arrange the fish in a single layer on top of the phyllo. Spread the onions over the fish, season lightly with salt and pepper, and cover with the tomato slices. Sprinkle with the crumbled feta and oregano and season with pepper. Cover with the remaining phyllo, brushing each sheet with oil. Score into serving pieces with a sharp knife and cut a vent in the center of the lid. Beat the egg with the evaporated milk and brush the pie with the glaze. Bake for about 1 hour, or until the top is well browned. Serve immediately.

Makes 1 large pie
Preparation time 30 minutes
Cooking time 1 hour

- 1 cup (250 ml / 8 fl oz) olive oil
- 2 large onions, thinly sliced
- 11 oz (300 g) ready-made phyllo (filo)
- 2¼ lb (1 kg) whitebait or tiny smelt, cleaned
- 2 tomatoes, thinly sliced
- 11 oz (300 g) feta cheese, crumbled
- pinch of dried oregano
- 1 egg, lightly beaten
- 5 tablespoons evaporated milk
- salt and pepper

- 2¼ lb (1 kg) salt cod, skinned and cut into pieces
- scant ½ cup (80 g / 3 oz) short-grain rice
- ½ cup (120 ml / 4 fl oz) olive oil, plus extra for brushing
- 1 onion, chopped
- 1 cup chopped scallions (spring onions)
- ½ cup (15 g / ½ oz) finely chopped fresh dill
- ½ cup (25 g / 1 oz) finely chopped fresh marjoram
- salt and pepper

FOR THE PHYLLO DOUGH (FILO PASTRY)

- 4½ cups (500 g / 1 lb 2 oz) all-purpose (plain) flour
- 2 teaspoons baking powder
- ½ teaspoon salt
- ½ cup (120 ml / 4 fl oz) olive oil
- ½ cup (120 ml / 4 fl oz) white wine

SALT COD PIE FROM KEFALLONIA
ΜΠΑΚΑΛΙΑΡΟΠΙΤΑ
Bakaliaropita

Put the salt cod in a bowl, pour in water to cover, and let soak for 12–14 hours, changing the water several times. To make the dough, sift together 3 cups (350 g / 12 oz) of the flour, the baking powder, and salt into a bowl and make a well in the center. Pour in the oil, wine, and 2–3 tablespoons water and gradually incorporate the dry ingredients. Knead until the dough is soft and pliable, adding more flour as necessary. Divide the dough in half and let rest for 30 minutes. Meanwhile, prepare the filling. Bring 1 cup (250 ml / 8 fl oz) water to a boil. Add the rice and cook for about 15 minutes, until all the liquid has been absorbed. Remove from the heat. Heat the oil in a pan. Add the onion and scallions and cook over low heat, stirring occasionally, for 5 minutes, until softened. Remove the pan from the heat. Preheat the oven to 350°F (180°C / Gas Mark 4) and brush a 14-inch (35-cm) round baking pan with oil. Drain the cod, remove the bones, and flake the flesh. Combine the fish, rice, onion mixture, and herbs in a bowl and season with pepper and salt if necessary. Stir in ½ cup (120 ml / 4 fl oz) water to form a soft mixture. Roll out the dough into two 14-inch (35-cm) rounds. Put 1 round on the base of the prepared pan and stretch to cover the base and side. Spread the filling evenly on top and cover with the second phyllo round. Crimp the edges together. Score the pie into serving pieces with a sharp knife and bake for about 50 minutes, or until the top is golden brown. Serve hot or at room temperature.

Makes 1 large pie
Preparation time 15 hours (including soaking and resting)
Cooking time 50 minutes

CHICKEN PIE OF THE VLACHS
ΒΛΑΧΙΚΗ ΚΟΤΟΠΙΤΑ
Vlahiki kotopita

To make the filling, blanch the onions and leeks for 2–3 minutes in boiling water and drain. Melt the butter in a large pan. Add the chicken pieces and cook over medium heat, turning frequently, for 10–15 minutes, until lightly browned all over. Add the onions, leeks, allspice berries, peppercorns, and bay leaf and season with salt and pepper. Cover and simmer for 30–40 minutes, until the chicken is cooked through. Remove the chicken from the pan and discard the bay leaf and allspice. Let the chicken cool. Meanwhile, preheat the oven to 350°F (180°C / Gas Mark 4) and grease a 16-inch (40-cm) round baking pan with butter. Remove and discard the bones from the chicken and shred the meat. Return the meat to the pan, together with the beaten eggs, and the leeks and onions, and mix well. If using homemade phyllo, divide the dough into 10 balls, then roll out into 8-inch (20-cm) rounds. Brush each generously with oil, stack 5 together, one on top of the other, and roll out each stack into an 18-inch (46-cm) diameter sheet. Lay 1 phyllo sheet on the base of the prepared pan, scrunching it up to fit. Spread the filling over it and cover with the other phyllo sheet, scrunching it up to fit. Moisten the excess phyllo with water and roll neatly around the edge of pan. If using ready-made phyllo, lay half the sheets on the base of the baking pan and the other half on top of the filling, brushing each with oil (reduce the total quantity by 4 table-spoons). Score the pie into serving pieces with a sharp knife. Bake for 1 hour, or until golden brown. Serve hot.

Makes 1 large pie
Preparation time 1¼ hours (including cooling)
Cooking time 1 hour

- butter, for greasing
- 1 lb 2 oz (500 g) ready-made phyllo (filo) or Homemade phyllo dough (filo pastry), p 46
- ¾ cup (175 ml / 6 fl oz) olive oil

FOR THE FILLING
- 3 large onions, sliced
- 3 leeks, white parts only, cut into short lengths
- 4 tablespoons (50 g / 2 oz) butter
- 1 large chicken, about 3¼ lb (1.5 kg), skinned and jointed into quarters
- 10 allspice berries
- 10 black peppercorns
- 1 bay leaf
- salt and pepper
- 6 eggs, lightly beaten

FOR THE DOUGH

- olive oil, for brushing
- 4½ cups (500 g / 1 lb 2 oz) self-rising flour
- ½ teaspoon salt
- 1 cup (250 ml / 8 fl oz) olive oil or 8 oz (225 g) chilled butter, cut into pieces
- 1 cup (250 ml / 8 fl oz) strained plain or thick Greek yogurt
- 1 egg, lightly beaten
- 1 tablespoon sesame seeds

FOR THE FILLING

- 2¼ lb (1 kg) leg of lamb, in pieces
- 20 black peppercorns
- 2 bay leaves
- 1 lb 2 oz (500 g) malaka or mozzarella cheese
- 7 oz (200 g) anthotiro or ricotta cheese
- 2 tablespoons olive oil
- 1 cup (7–8) finely chopped scallions (spring onions)
- ½ cup (25 g / 1 oz) finely chopped fresh mint
- ½ cup (120 ml / 4 fl oz) staka or heavy (double) cream or 4 tablespoons olive oil
- salt

CHANIA MEAT PIE FROM CRETE
ΧΑΝΙΩΤΙΚΗ ΚΡΕΑΤΟΠΙΤΑ
Haniotiki kreatopita

To make the filling, put the meat into a pan, pour in 2 cups (450 ml / 16 fl oz) water, and add the peppercorns, bay leaves, and a pinch of salt. Bring to a boil and cook for about 1 hour, or until the meat is very tender. Remove with a slotted spoon and let cool slightly. Reserve ½ cup (120 ml / 4 fl oz) of the cooking liquid. Remove the meat from the bone and cut into small pieces, then mix with both types of cheese in a bowl. Heat the 2 tablespoons oil in a skillet or frying pan. Add the scallions and cook over low heat, stirring occasionally, for 5 minutes, until softened. Add them to the meat mixture, together with the mint and reserved cooking liquid. Preheat the oven to 350°F (180°C / Gas Mark 4) and brush a 12-inch (30-cm) round baking pan with oil. To make the dough, sift together the flour and salt into a large bowl. Add the oil or butter and rub in with your fingertips or a pastry blender until crumbly. Lightly knead in the yogurt, a little at a time, to a smooth, pliable dough. You may not need all the yogurt. Divide the dough into 2 balls, one slightly larger than the other. Roll out the larger ball into a sheet large enough to cover the base and sides of the prepared baking pan. Spread the filling over the dough and dot with the staka or heavy cream or drizzle with oil. Roll out the second ball of dough and use it to cover the filling. Moisten and crimp the edges. Brush with the beaten egg and sprinkle with the sesame seeds. Bake for 1 hour, or until golden. Serve hot.

Makes 1 large pie
Preparation time 1½ hours
Cooking time 1 hour

PORK AND LEEK PIE FROM FLORINA
ΠΙΤΑ ΜΕ ΧΟΙΡΙΝΟ ΚΑΙ ΠΡΑΣΑ
Pita me hirino ke prasa

To make the filling, blanch the leeks and celery separately in boiling water, then drain. Heat 4 tablespoons of the oil or lard and oil mixture in a pan. Add the meat and cook over medium heat, stirring frequently, for 6–8 minutes, until lightly browned. Add 1 cup (250 ml / 8 fl oz) water, cover, and simmer for 25 minutes, until the meat is tender. Meanwhile, preheat the oven to 350°F (180°C / Gas Mark 4) and brush a 14-inch (35-cm) round baking pan with olive oil or melted butter. Add the leeks and celery to the pork, season with salt and pepper, and remove from the heat. Spread 5 sheets of phyllo in the prepared pan, brushing each with oil or melted butter and allowing the excess to hang over the sides. Spread the filling over the phyllo, sprinkle the cheese on top, and cover with another 5 phyllo sheets, brushing each with oil or melted butter. Roll up the overhanging pastry to form a rim around the edge of the pie. Score into 8 or 10 serving pieces, brush with the remaining oil or melted butter, and sprinkle lightly with water. Bake for 50 minutes, or until the top is golden. Serve hot.

Makes 1 large pie
Preparation time 1 hour
Cooking time 50 minutes

- 1 cup (250 ml / 8 fl oz) olive oil or melted clarified butter
- 1 lb 2 oz (500 g) ready-made phyllo (filo)

FOR THE FILLING
- 4 leeks, sliced
- 2 celery stalks with leaves, chopped
- ¾ cup (175 ml / 6 fl oz) olive oil or a mixture of ½ cup (120 ml / 4 fl oz) melted lard and 4 tablespoons olive oil
- 1 lb 2 oz (500 g) lean boneless pork, cut into very small pieces
- salt and pepper
- ½ cup (50 g / 2 oz) grated kefalotiri, regato or Parmesan cheese

ALMOND PASTRY TRIANGLES FROM CHIOS
ΤΡΙΓΩΝΑΚΙΑ ΧΙΩΤΙΚΑ
Trigonakia hiotika

Preheat the oven to 350°F (180°C / Gas Mark 4) and brush a baking pan with melted butter. Combine the ground almonds, sugar, and mastic in a bowl. Add the lemon juice, orange flower water, and beaten eggs and fold in to make a loose but not runny batter, adding more orange flower water, if necessary. Spread out the phyllo sheets and cut into 2-inch (5-cm) wide strips. Brush each strip with melted butter. Put 1 tablespoon of the filling at 1 end of each strip, lift the bottom corner over to the side and continue to fold into small triangles. Put the triangles side by side into the prepared pan, brushing each with melted butter. Bake for 15–20 minutes, or until golden. Dust with confectioners' sugar and let cool.

Makes 25–30 triangles
Preparation time 30 minutes
Cooking time 15–20 minutes

- 5 tablespoons melted clarified butter
- 3 cups (375 g / 13 oz) finely ground almonds
- generous 1 cup (225 g / 8 oz) superfine (caster) sugar
- ¼ teaspoon ground mastic
- 1 tablespoon freshly squeezed lemon juice
- 2 teaspoons orange flower water
- 1 egg plus 1 yolk, lightly beaten
- 9 oz (250 g) ready-made phyllo (filo)
- confectioners' (icing) sugar, for dusting

⬚ p 481

SWEET CHEESE PIE FROM CYPRUS
ΑΝΑΡΟΠΙΤΑ ΓΛΥΚΙΑ
Anaropita glikia

FOR THE PIE

- 1 lb 2 oz (500 g) ricotta or drained cottage cheese
- 2 teaspoons ground cinnamon
- ½ cup (100 g / 3½ oz) superfine (caster) sugar
- 5 tablespoons rosewater
- 1 lb 2 oz (500 g) ready-made phyllo (filo) or Homemade phyllo dough (filo pastry), p 46
- ½ cup (120 ml / 4 fl oz) melted clarified butter or corn oil

FOR THE SYRUP

- generous 1½ cups (350 g / 12 oz) superfine (caster) sugar
- 1 tablespoon freshly squeezed lemon juice
- 1 cinnamon stick
- 5 cloves

Preheat the oven to 350°F (180°C / Gas Mark 4). To make the pie, mash the cheese with a fork in a bowl, add the cinnamon, sugar, and rosewater, and mix well. Line a baking pan with half the phyllo sheets, brushing each with melted butter or oil. Spread the cheese mixture evenly over the base and cover with the remaining sheets of phyllo, brushing each with melted butter or oil. Score the pie into long 2-inch (5-cm) wide strips and bake for 40 minutes, until golden brown. Meanwhile, combine all the ingredients for the syrup in a pan, add 2 cups (450 ml / 16 fl oz) water, and cook over low heat, stirring constantly, for about 5 minutes. Remove the cinnamon stick and cloves and let cool. Remove the pie from the oven, cut crosswise into squares, and pour the cold syrup on top. Let cool completely, then serve.

Makes 14–16 squares
Preparation time 15 minutes
Cooking time 40 minutes

☐ p 488

APPLE-FILLED ROLLS
ΜΗΛΟΠΙΤΕΣ
Milopites

- ⅔ cup (150 ml / ¼ pint) olive oil, melted clarified butter, or a mixture
- 1 cup (225 g / 8 oz) superfine (caster) sugar
- 4 tablespoons fine bread crumbs
- 1½ teaspoons ground cinnamon, plus extra for sprinkling
- pinch of grated nutmeg
- 2¼ lb (1 kg) tart apples, peeled and coarsely grated
- 1 cup (120 g / 4 oz) coarsely chopped walnuts
- generous ½ cup (80 g / 3 oz) raisins (optional)
- 1 tablespoon freshly squeezed lemon juice
- 4 tablespoons melted clarified butter
- 1 lb 2 oz (500 g) ready-made phyllo (filo)
- confectioners' (icing) sugar, for sprinkling

Preheat the oven to 350°F (180°C / Gas Mark 4) and brush a 10 x 14-inch (25 x 35-cm) cookie sheet (baking tray) or a 14-inch (35-cm) round baking pan with some of the oil, melted butter, or the mixture of both. Combine the sugar, bread crumbs, cinnamon, and nutmeg in a small bowl. Combine the apples, walnuts, and raisins, if using, in another bowl, sprinkle with lemon juice, and toss. Add the dry ingredients and mix lightly. Pour the melted butter over the apple mixture and toss, then set aside. Brush the top half of each phyllo sheet widthwise with the oil, or butter, or the mixture. Fold the bottom half over it and brush again. Place 3–4 tablespoons of the apple filling on the long edge of each sheet and roll up. Arrange the rolls side by side on the cookie sheet or wind the rolls end to end to form a large coil in the baking pan. Brush the rolls with the remaining oil or butter and sprinkle with 2–3 tablespoons confectioners' sugar. (At this stage the rolls may be wrapped and frozen. Thaw before baking.) Bake for about 40 minutes, or until golden brown. Cool slightly before cutting into pieces. Sprinkle with confectioners' sugar and ground cinnamon and serve while still slightly warm.

Makes 10–12 rolls
Preparation time 40 minutes
Cooking time 40 minutes

Sweet cheese pie from Cyprus, p 487

Ruffled milk pie, p 492

FRIED RICOTTA PIES FROM SFAKIA, CRETE
ΣΦΑΚΙΑΝΟΠΙΤΕΣ
Sfakianopites

Sift together the flour and salt into a large bowl and make a well in the center. Pour in the oil and raki and knead, gradually adding enough water—about 1 cup (250 ml / 8 fl oz)—to make a soft dough. Divide the dough into 12 balls, cover with a damp cloth, and let rest for 30 minutes. Roll out each ball of dough into a 7-inch (18-cm) round. Divide the cheese into 12 equal balls. Place a cheese ball in the center of each round, . gather the edges of the dough, and wrap over the cheese. Pinch them firmly together to enclose the cheese and seal. Put the balls onto a lightly floured surface, seam side down, and flatten, first with the palm of your hand and then with a rolling pin, into 8-inch (20-cm) rounds. Brush a nonstick skillet or frying pan with oil and heat. Add the pies, 1 at a time, and cook for a few minutes on each side until golden brown. Brush the pan with oil before adding the next pie. Serve hot, drizzled with honey.

Makes 12 pies
Preparation time 1 hour (including resting)
Cooking time 30 minutes

- 4½ cups (500 g / 1 lb 2 oz) all-purpose (plain) flour, plus extra for dusting
- ½ teaspoon salt
- 2 tablespoons olive oil, plus extra for brushing
- 4 tablespoons raki or dry white wine
- 1½ lb (700 g) mizithra, ricotta or cream cheese
- honey, to serve

HONEY AND CHEESE TART FROM SIFNOS
ΜΕΛΟΠΙΤΑ ΣΙΦΝΟΥ
Melopita sifnou

To make the dough, sift together the flour and salt into a bowl and stir in the sugar. Add the butter to the dry ingredients, then rub in with your fingers or work with a pastry blender until the mixture resembles coarse bread crumbs. Sprinkle with 1–2 tablespoons water and knead lightly until the mixture comes away easily from your fingers. Form the dough into a ball, cover, and let rest for 30 minutes in the refrigerator. Meanwhile, prepare the filling. Beat the cheese with milk in a bowl using an electric mixer at medium speed for 1–2 minutes, until smooth. Add the eggs, honey, lemon zest, sugar, and salt and beat for 1 minute more. Preheat the oven to 350°F (180°C / Gas Mark 4). Roll out the dough into a 14-inch (35-cm) round and line the base and sides of a 10-inch (25-cm) tart pan. Roll and crimp the edges around the rim. Pour the filling into the pie shell and bake for about 50 minutes, or until the filling has set and the pastry is golden. Drizzle with honey and sprinkle with cinnamon before serving warm or cold.

Makes 1 large tart
Preparation time 1 hour (including resting)
Cooking time 50 minutes

FOR THE DOUGH
- 1 cup (120 g / 4 oz) all-purpose (plain) flour
- ¼ teaspoon salt
- 1 teaspoon sugar
- 6 tablespoons (80 g / 3 oz) clarified butter, chilled and cut into pieces

FOR THE FILLING
- 12 oz (350 g) mizithra or ricotta cheese
- 2 tablespoons milk
- 2 eggs, lightly beaten
- 4 tablespoons honey, plus extra for drizzling
- 1 tablespoon grated lemon zest
- 2 tablespoons superfine (caster) sugar
- pinch of salt
- ground cinnamon, for sprinkling

- 4 cups (1 litre / 1¾ pints) milk
- ¾ cup (175 ml / 6 fl oz) melted clarified butter
- ⅔ cup (120 g / 4 oz) semolina or cream of wheat
- ⅔ cup (150 g / 5 oz) superfine (caster) sugar
- 2 eggs
- 2 egg yolks
- 1 teaspoon vanilla extract
- 1 lb 2 oz (500 g) ready-made phyllo (filo)
- confectioners' (icing) sugar and ground cinnamon, for dusting

VANILLA PIE FROM THESSALONIKI
ΜΠΟΥΓΑΤΣΑ ΜΕ ΚΡΕΜΑ
Bougatsa me krema

Pour the milk into a pan, bring to just below boiling point, and remove from the heat. Heat 2 tablespoons of the butter in a pan. Add the semolina or cream of wheat and cook for 1–2 minutes. Pour in the hot milk, stirring constantly, then add the sugar, and cook for a few minutes, stirring constantly, until smooth and thick. Remove the pan from the heat and let cool for 5 minutes. Meanwhile, lightly beat the eggs with the egg yolks and vanilla in a bowl and pour into the semolina mixture, stirring constantly until smooth. Put a sheet of plastic wrap (cling film) on the surface to prevent a skin from forming and set aside. Preheat the oven to 400°F (200°C / Gas Mark 6) and brush a shallow baking pan, the same size as the sheets of phyllo, with some of the remaining melted butter. Lay half the phyllo sheets on the base of the prepared pan, brushing each with melted butter. Spread the semolina evenly over them and cover with the remaining phyllo, brushing each sheet with melted butter. Bake for 30–40 minutes, or until the pastry is golden brown. Cut into bite-size squares and serve warm, sprinkled with confectioners' sugar and ground cinnamon.

Makes 1 large pie
Preparation time 30 minutes
Cooking time 30–40 minutes

- 5 ready-made phyllo (filo) sheets
- 4 tablespoons melted clarified butter
- generous 1 cup (225 g / 8 oz) short-grain rice
- ¼ teaspoon salt
- 6 cups (1.5 litres / 2½ pints) milk
- generous 1 cup (225 g / 8 oz) superfine (caster) sugar
- 5–6 eggs, lightly beaten
- 1 tablespoon butter
- 2 teaspoons vanilla extract
- ground cinnamon, for sprinkling

MILK PIE WITH RICE
ΓΑΛΑΤΟΠΙΤΑ ΜΕ ΡΥΖΙ
Galatopita me rizi

Line the base of a 10 x 14-inch (25 x 35-cm) baking pan with the phyllo sheets, brushing each one with melted butter. Bring 2 cups (450 ml / 16 fl oz) water to a boil in a large pan. Add the rice and salt, stir well, cover, and simmer for 15 minutes, or until all the water has been absorbed. Preheat the oven to 350°F (180°C / Gas Mark 4). Pour the milk into another pan and bring to just below boiling point, then remove from the heat, and stir it into the rice, together with the sugar. Re-cover the pan and simmer for 15 minutes more. Stir 2–3 tablespoons of the hot rice mixture into the beaten eggs, then return to the pan, and stir in the butter and vanilla. Pour the mixture into the phyllo-lined pan and bake for 40–50 minutes, until the top and edges of the phyllo are golden brown. Remove from the oven and let cool slightly before cutting into pieces. Serve sprinkled with ground cinnamon.

Makes 1 large pie
Preparation time 30 minutes
Cooking time 40–50 minutes

RUFFLED MILK PIE
ΓΑΛΑΤΟΠΙΤΑ ΣΟΥΡΩΤΗ
Galatopita souroti

Preheat the oven to 350°F (180°C / Gas Mark 4) and brush a 14-inch (35-cm) round baking pan with some of the melted butter. Lay 1 sheet of phyllo on a work surface with the long edge toward you. Loosely ruffle it by pushing the short ends toward each other with your hands to create a long concertina shape, then place it upright in a loose spiral in the center of the prepared pan. Ruffle the remaining sheets of phyllo in the same way and continue the spiral until the base of the pan is filled with phyllo ruffles. Using a pastry brush, dab the melted butter on all the surfaces of the phyllo. Sprinkle with the ground cinnamon and bake for 25–30 minutes, or until golden brown. Meanwhile, pour the milk into a pan and bring to just below boiling point, then remove from the heat. Beat the eggs with the sugar in a bowl. Gradually pour in the milk, a little at a time, beating constantly. Add the vanilla. Remove the pan from the oven and spoon the egg mixture over the baked phyllo, covering all the surfaces evenly. Return the pan to the oven and bake for 25–30 minutes more, or until the filling has set. Dust with confectioners' sugar and extra ground cinnamon, and serve immediately.

Makes 1 large pie
Preparation time 15 minutes
Cooking time 1 hour

□ p 489

- 6 tablespoons melted clarified butter
- 8–9 ready-made phyllo (filo) sheets
- ¼ teaspoon ground cinnamon, plus extra for dusting
- 3 cups (750 ml / 1¼ pints) milk
- 6 eggs
- generous 1 cup (225 g / 8 oz) superfine (caster) sugar
- 1 teaspoon vanilla extract
- confectioners' (icing) sugar, for dusting

PUMPKIN CRESCENTS FROM CYPRUS
ΚΟΛΟΚΟΤΕΣ
Kolokotes

Combine all the filling ingredients in a bowl, cover, and let stand for 4–5 hours. To make the dough, sift together both types of flour, the baking powder, and salt into a bowl and make a well in the center. Pour in the oil and rub in with your fingertips. Gradually add 1 cup (250 ml / 8 fl oz) water and knead to a firm pliable dough. Form the dough into a ball, cover, and let rest for 30 minutes. Preheat the oven to 350°F (180°C / Gas Mark 4). Pinch off pieces of dough about the size of a large walnut and roll out into 4-inch (10-cm) rounds. Put 1 tablespoon of the filling in the center of each and fold in half to form a half-moon shape. Moisten the edges and press to seal. Put the crescents on a cookie sheet (baking tray) and bake for 30 minutes, or until golden. Serve hot or at room temperature.

Makes 30 crescents
Preparation time 4½–5½ hours (including standing and resting)
Cooking time 30 minutes

FOR THE DOUGH
- 3 cups (350 g / 12 oz) whole-wheat (wholemeal) flour
- 1 cup (120 g / 4 oz) all-purpose (plain) flour
- 3 teaspoons baking powder
- ½ teaspoon salt
- ½ cup (120 ml / 4 fl oz) olive oil

FOR THE FILLING
- 4 cups (650 g / 1 lb 7 oz) grated pumpkin
- scant ½ cup (80 g / 3 oz) superfine (caster) sugar
- 1 teaspoon salt
- generous ½ cup (100 g / 3½ oz) bulgur wheat
- 1 cup (150 g / 5 oz) raisins
- ½ cup (120 ml / 4 fl oz) olive oil
- 1 teaspoon ground cinnamon

PUMPKIN PIE FROM STEREA ELLADA
ΚΟΛΟΚΥΘΟΤΥΡΟΠΙΤΑ ΣΤΡΙΦΤΗ
Kolokithotiropita strifti

- 3¼ lb (1.5 kg) pumpkin or white or yellow winter squash, peeled and cut into pieces
- ½ teaspoon salt
- generous 1 cup (225 g / 8 oz) superfine (caster) sugar
- scant ½ cup (80 g / 3 oz) short-grain rice, parboiled
- 1 small onion, grated and blanched
- 1 tablespoon ground cinnamon, plus extra for dusting
- ⅔ cup (150 ml / ¼ pint) olive oil or melted clarified butter, or a mixture
- 1 lb 2 oz (500 g) ready-made phyllo (filo) or Homemade phyllo dough (filo pastry), p 46
- confectioners' (icing) sugar, for dusting

Grate the squash and toss with the salt, then let drain in a colander overnight. Squeeze out the remaining liquid and mash the squash with a fork in a bowl. Add the sugar, rice, onion, cinnamon, and 4 tablespoons of the melted butter, oil, or mixture. Preheat the oven to 350°F (180°C / Gas Mark 4) and brush a 14-inch (35-cm) round baking pan with melted butter or oil. If using homemade phyllo dough, divide it into 12 equal pieces and roll out into very thin sheets. Brush half of each sheet with melted butter or oil, fold the other half over it, and brush it again. Spread 3–4 tablespoons of the filling along the long edge and roll it up into a cylinder. Coil the roll into a spiral in the center of the baking pan. Repeat with the other phyllo sheets to form a large spiral. Brush with melted butter or oil and bake for 1 hour, or until golden. Sprinkle with confectioners' sugar and cinnamon and serve warm or cold.

Makes 1 large pie
Preparation time 12½ hours (including draining)
Cooking time 1 hour

□ p 494

FRIED SWEET PASTRIES FROM PONTUS
ΓΛΥΚΑΔΙΑ ΤΗΓΑΝΙΟΥ
Glikadia tiganiou

FOR THE PHYLLO (FILO)
- 3 cups (350 g / 12 oz) all-purpose (plain) flour
- scant 1 cup (100 g / 3½ oz) cornstarch (cornflour)
- 1 tablespoon baking powder
- ¼ teaspoon salt
- 1 egg
- 4 tablespoons ouzo
- 4 tablespoons olive oil, warmed
- 4 tablespoons lukewarm water

FOR THE FILLING
- 1 cup (120 g / 4 oz) walnuts, chopped
- 1 cup (150 g / 5 oz) blanched almonds, chopped
- scant 1 cup (175 g / 6 oz) superfine (caster) sugar
- 1 teaspoon ground cinnamon
- ½ teaspoon ground cloves
- 1 teaspoon ground mastic
- 1 cup (250 ml / 8 fl oz) olive oil
- 3 tablespoons melted clarified butter
- confectioners' (icing) sugar, for sprinkling

To make the dough, sift together the flour, cornstarch, baking powder, and salt into a bowl and make a well in the center. Add the egg, ouzo, and oil and gradually incorporate the dry ingredients, adding warm water to form a soft pliable dough. Knead until smooth and elastic. Cover and let rest for 30 minutes in the refrigerator. Meanwhile, combine the nuts, sugar, and spices for the filling in a bowl. Pinch off pieces of dough the size of a large walnut, and roll out into 4-inch (10-cm) rounds. Put 1 tablespoon of the filling in the center of each, moisten the edges, and fold in half, pinching the edges together with your fingers or a fork. Heat the oil and butter in a large skillet or frying pan. Add the pastries, a few at a time, and cook for 5–10 minutes, turning occasionally, until golden brown all over. Remove with a slotted spatula (fish slice), drain on paper towels, sprinkle with confectioners' sugar, and serve hot.

Makes 30 pastries
Preparation time 1 hour (including resting)
Cooking time 30 minutes

Pumpkin pie from Sterea Ellada, p 493

esame pies, p 496

SESAME PIES
ΣΟΥΣΑΜΟΠΙΤΕΣ
Sousamopites

Grind the sesame seeds to a rough paste in a food processor, then mix with the sugar, cinnamon, and cloves in a bowl. Preheat the oven to 350°F (180°C / Gas Mark 4). If using homemade phyllo, divide the dough into 12 pieces. Roll out on a lightly floured work surface into 8 x 12-inch (20 x 30-cm) rectangles. Brush with oil and place 4 tablespoons of the sesame mixture along a long edge. Roll up into a long cylinder, cut in half, and wind each part into a loose spiral. Put the pies on a cookie sheet (baking tray), brush with olive oil, and bake for about 45 minutes, or until lightly browned. To make the syrup, put the sugar and cinnamon stick into a pan, pour in 3 cups (750 ml / 1¼ pints) water, and bring to a boil, stirring until the sugar has dissolved. Boil without stirring for 5 minutes, then add the lemon juice, remove from the heat, and remove the cinnamon. Carefully pour the hot syrup over the pies when they come out of the oven. Let cool in the syrup.

Makes 24 pies
Preparation time 1 hour (including resting)
Cooking time 45 minutes

□ p 495

- 1 lb 2 oz (500 g) ready-made phyllo (filo) or Homemade phyllo dough (filo pastry), p 46
- all-purpose (plain) flour, for dusting
- olive oil, for brushing

FOR THE FILLING
- 2¼ cups (500 g / 1 lb 2 oz) sesame seeds, toasted
- 1 cup (200 g / 7 oz) superfine (caster) sugar
- 1 teaspoon ground cinnamon
- 1 teaspoon ground cloves

FOR THE SYRUP
- 5 cups (1 kg / 2¼ lb) superfine (caster) sugar
- 1 cinnamon stick
- 2 teaspoons freshly squeezed lemon juice

TANGERINE FLUTES FROM CHIOS
ΧΙΩΤΙΚΕΣ ΦΛΟΓΕΡΕΣ ΜΕ ΜΑΝΤΑΡΙΝΙ
Hiotikes flogeres me madarinia

Peel the tangerines, put the rinds into a pan, add water to cover, and cook until very soft. Drain and process to a purée in a food processor. Heat 4 tablespoons of the butter in a pan, stir in the sugar, almonds, tangerine rind purée, and tangerine juice, and cook over low heat for about 15 minutes, until thickened. Remove from the heat and let cool, then stir in the egg white, if using. Preheat the oven to 350°F (180°C / Gas Mark 4) and brush a cookie sheet (baking tray) with melted butter. Spread out a phyllo sheet with the long side toward you and cut across the width into 3 strips. Brush each strip with melted butter, fold in half, and place 1 tablespoon of the filling along the long edge. Roll up into long thin flutes or cigars and place on the prepared cookie sheet. Repeat until all the phyllo and filling is used. Brush the tops with the remaining melted butter and bake for about 20 minutes, or until golden. Do not overcook or they will dry out. Remove from the oven and sprinkle with confectioners' sugar while still hot. Let cool before serving.

Makes 60 flutes
Preparation time 30 minutes
Cooking time 20 minutes

- 2¼ lb (1 kg) tangerines
- 1 cup (250 ml / 8 fl oz) melted clarified butter
- generous 1½ cups (350 g / 12 oz) superfine (caster) sugar
- 3 cups (350 g / 12 oz) blanched, finely chopped almonds
- 5 tablespoons tangerine juice
- 1 egg white (optional)
- 1 lb 2 oz (500 g) ready-made phyllo (filo)
- confectioners' (icing) sugar, for sprinkling

- 3¼ lb (1.5 kg) zucchini (courgettes), coarsely grated
- ½ teaspoon salt
- generous 1 cup (225 g / 8 oz) superfine (caster) sugar
- scant 1 cup (100 g / 3½ oz) chopped walnuts
- 2 eggs (optional)
- 1½ teaspoons ground cinnamon, plus extra for dusting
- pinch of grated nutmeg
- 4 tablespoons bread crumbs
- generous ½ cup (130 ml / 4½ fl oz) melted clarified butter
- 5 tablespoons olive oil
- 1 lb 2 oz (500 g) ready-made phyllo (filo)
- confectioners' (icing) sugar, for dusting

SWEET ZUCCHINI (COURGETTE) TWISTS
ΣΤΡΙΦΤΑΡΙΑ ΜΕ ΚΟΛΟΚΥΘΙ
Striftaria me kolokithi

Sprinkle the zucchini with the salt and rub with your fingers, set aside for 30 minutes, then drain well in a colander. Combine the zucchini, sugar, walnuts, eggs, if using, cinnamon, nutmeg, bread crumbs, and 4 tablespoons of the melted butter in a bowl. Mix the remaining melted butter with the oil in another bowl. Preheat the oven to 350°F (180°C / Gas Mark 4) and brush a cookie sheet (baking tray) with the butter and oil mixture. Lay out a sheet of phyllo with the short edge toward you, brush the top half with the butter and oil, and fold over the bottom half. Brush again with the butter and oil, place 3–4 tablespoons of the filling along the long edge, and roll up into a long thin roll. Wind the roll around itself into a spiral. Repeat with the remaining phyllo sheets and filling. Put the rolls, flat sides down, on the prepared cookie sheet and brush with the remaining butter and oil. Bake for about 50 minutes, or until golden brown. Remove from the oven and dust with confectioners' sugar and cinnamon. Serve hot or at room temperature. Alternatively, prepare a syrup by boiling 2 cups (400 g / 14 oz) superfine (caster) sugar with 1½ cups (350 ml / 12 fl oz) water and 1 tablespoon lemon juice for 5 minutes. Carefully pour the syrup over the zucchini twists while they are still hot and let cool to absorb all the syrup before serving.

Makes 12–14 twists
Preparation time 1 hour (including draining)
Cooking time 50 minutes

BREAD

-

ΨΩΜΙ

-

Psomi

The history of bread is as old as civilization itself, commencing about 10,000 years ago with the beginning of the cultivation of wheat and barley. This turning point in the history of the eastern Mediterranean was commemorated in the ancient Greek myth of Demeter, the goddess of grain, who taught Triptolemos, a young prince of Eleusis and also a shepherd, the secrets of agriculture. The transition from meat-eating nomad to grain-eating farmer was celebrated at the ancient festivals of the Eleusinia and the Athenian Thesmophoria, and a relic of this ancient symbolism survives today in the memorial offering of *koliva*, a mixture of boiled wheat berries or kernels, nuts, parsley, and pomegranate seeds, prepared to commemorate the anniversary of a loved one's death.

Bread was being baked from as early as the sixth millennium BC. The first flour was made by grinding the inner core of the grain between two stones after removing the outer husk. Mixing this rough flour with water to make a grain paste provided nourishing, palatable, and filling food. Perhaps by accident, it was found that cooking the grain paste on the hearth improved the flavor. Soon, cereals comprised some 90 percent of the ancient Mediterranean diet. Bread and grains were not just an accompaniment, but formed the basis of every meal. The first breads were not at all like the loaves we eat today: They were made with coarse barley, millet, or garbanzo bean (chickpea) flour mixed with water and baked on hot flat stones or on the sides of large clay ovens. Bread made from wheat flour (*artos*) was a rare and expensive treat.

In the Christian era, bread was elevated to the ultimate symbol of salvation and eternal life, and there are still many special breads associated with religious festivals and rites of passage. Every neighborhood in Greece has at least one bakery, but many people, especially in rural areas, still make the week's bread at home. It is baked in outdoor ovens, and great pride is taken in the traditional sourdough *horiatiko* (village bread), for which a piece of dough left over from the previous week's batch is used as a starter. Another historic bread is the twice-baked barley rusk, known as *paximadia,* said to have been named after an ancient cook, Paximos, who discovered this method of preserving bread for soldiers on the march. Sweet, rich breads or *tsourekia* are usually associated with Easter, but are good at any time with coffee. Sesame bread rings (*simitia*) are delicious snacks sold by street vendors all over Greece. There are also many other breads with traditional Greek ingredients such as cheese, olives, nuts, raisins, herbs, and spices.

GENERAL INSTRUCTIONS

The quantity of liquid needed will vary according to the strength of the flour. Greek flours are, in general, not as strong as those found elsewhere, which have a higher gluten content. When following the recipes given here, start with two thirds of the liquid quantity listed and gradually add more as needed. Kneading gives the bread a better texture, and well-kneaded bread will have many small holes of a uniform size. Bread that has not been kneaded properly has large, uneven holes.

To prevent the surface of the dough from drying out and forming a crust while it rises, brush the top lightly with oil or melted butter. If the dough is too stiff to shape or roll out, let it rest for 5–10 minutes.

To start the bread rising well, warm the ingredients first. Yeast needs a warm environment to be activated, but it will start to die at temperatures over 100°F (38°C). To check that yeast, whether fresh or dried, is active, dissolve it in a small quantity of water with a little flour and let rise. If bubbles do not form on the surface after 10–15 minutes, discard it. If your dough rises slowly it will have a better flavor, and the ideal temperature is 70–85°F (21–29°C) in a draft-free place.

To check whether the bread is cooked, turn it out of the pan and tap the bottom; if it sounds hollow and the base is firm, the bread is cooked. Most home-baked bread keeps well in the freezer wrapped in an airtight bag. If you wish to keep your bread for many days or weeks, it is practical to slice it and freeze it, so that you can use as much as you need at a time. Sliced bread thaws quickly. If frozen whole, thaw and then reheat the bread in a hot oven before serving.

- ∘ butter, for greasing
- ∘ 1 oz (25 g) fresh yeast or 1 tablespoon dried yeast
- ∘ 1 cup (250 ml / 8 fl oz) lukewarm water
- ∘ ¼ cup (50 g / 2 oz) sugar
- ∘ 11 cups (1.25 kg / 2¾ lb) strong white bread flour, plus extra for dusting
- ∘ 1 tablespoon salt
- ∘ ½ cup (120 ml / 4 fl oz) lukewarm milk
- ∘ 3 eggs, lightly beaten
- ∘ 5 tablespoons melted clarified butter
- ∘ 1 egg yolk
- ∘ sesame or onion seeds, for sprinkling

WHITE BREAD
ΨΩΜΙ ΠΟΛΥΤΕΛΕΙΑΣ
Psomi politelias

Grease 3 cookie sheets (baking trays) with butter. If using fresh yeast, mash it with the lukewarm water in a bowl to a smooth paste. If using dried yeast, mix the lukewarm water with 1 teaspoon of the sugar in a bowl, sprinkle the yeast over the surface, and let stand for 10–15 minutes, until frothy, then stir to a smooth paste. Sift together the flour and salt into a bowl, stir in the sugar, and make a well in the center. Pour in the yeast mixture, milk, eggs, and melted butter. Mix all the ingredients together, gradually incorporating the dry ingredients, until a sticky dough is formed. Knead the dough well on a lightly floured work surface for about 10 minutes, until it loses its stickiness and becomes smooth and elastic. Cover and let rise in a warm place for 1½–2 hours, until it has tripled its volume. Punch down the dough and divide it into 3–4 pieces. Shape each piece into a long cylindrical loaf or make spirals from long strands of dough. You could also braid (plait) together 2–3 strands of dough to make decorative loaves. Preheat the oven to 400°F (200°C / Gas Mark 6). Place the loaves on the prepared cookie sheets, cover, and let rise until they have nearly doubled in volume. Beat the egg yolk with 1 teaspoon water in a bowl, brush the tops of the loaves with the glaze, and sprinkle with sesame or onion seeds. Bake for 25–30 minutes. Remove the loaves from the oven and let cool on wire racks.

Makes 3 loaves
Preparation time 2–3 hours (including rising)
Cooking time 25–30 minutes

BROWN BREAD
ΨΩΜΙ ΗΜΙΛΕΥΚΟ
Psomi imilefko

- butter, for greasing
- 1 oz (25 g) fresh yeast or
  1 tablespoon dried yeast
- 3 cups (750 ml / 1¼ pints)
  lukewarm water
- 9 cups (1 kg / 2¼ lb) strong white
  bread flour, plus extra for dusting
- 2¼ cups (250 g / 9 oz) whole-
  wheat (wholemeal) flour
- 2 teaspoons salt
- 4 tablespoons olive oil
- 4 tablespoons evaporated milk
- 3 tablespoons honey
- milk, for brushing (optional)
- sesame or onions seeds, for
  sprinkling (optional)

Grease 2 or 3 cookie sheets (baking trays) with butter. If using fresh yeast, mash it with ½ cup (120 ml / 4 fl oz) of the lukewarm water in a bowl to a smooth paste. If using dried yeast, put the lukewarm water into a bowl, sprinkle the yeast over the surface, and let stand for 10–15 minutes, until frothy, then stir to a smooth paste. Sift together both kinds of flour and the salt into a bowl and make a well in the center. Pour in the yeast mixture, oil, evaporated milk, honey, and remaining water. Gradually incorporate the dry ingredients until a sticky dough is formed. Turn out the dough onto a floured work surface and knead well for about 15 minutes, until elastic and glossy. Cover and let rise in a warm place for 1½–2 hours, until doubled in volume. Knead the dough again for 5 minutes, shape into 2 large loaves or 3 smaller ones, and put on the prepared cookie sheets. Preheat the oven to 400°F (200°C / Gas Mark 6). Cover and let rise until doubled in volume. You can slash the tops of the loaves in decorative patterns with a sharp knife, or simply brush with a little milk and sprinkle with sesame or onion seeds. Bake for 25–30 minutes. Remove from the oven and let cool on wire racks.

Makes 3 small loaves
Preparation time 2–3 hours (including rising)
Cooking time 25–30 minutes

HERBED BREAD
ΨΩΜΙ ΜΕ ΜΥΡΩΔΙΚΑ
Psomi me mirodika

- butter, for greasing
- ½ quantity White bread
  dough (p 501)
- 1 tablespoon anise seeds,
  plus extra for sprinkling
- 1 tablespoon onion seeds,
  plus extra for sprinkling
- 1 tablespoon dried oregano,
  plus extra for sprinkling
- 1 tablespoon dried mint, plus
  extra for sprinkling
- ¼ cup (40 g / 1½ oz)
  chopped pimientos
- 1 teaspoon garlic powder
- 1 egg white, lightly beaten
- pimiento or chili flakes and
  sesame seeds, for sprinkling

Grease a cookie sheet (baking tray) with butter. Let the dough rise, then punch down, and divide into 6 equal pieces. Knead each piece with 1 of the spices, herbs, or flavorings and shape it into a ball. Place the balls in a circle on the prepared cookie sheet, spaced about ½ inch (1 cm) apart, to make a daisy-shaped loaf. Preheat the oven to 400°F (200°C / Gas Mark 6). Cover and let rise for about 45 minutes, or until doubled in volume. Brush the tops of the dough balls with a little egg white and sprinkle each one with the spice, herb, or flavoring that has been used in it. Sprinkle the pimiento-flavored ball with dry pimiento or chili flakes and the garlic-flavored ball with sesame seeds. Bake for about 35 minutes, then remove from the oven, and let cool on a wire rack.

Makes 10 rolls
Preparation time 2–3 hours
Cooking time 35 minutes

☐ p 504

- 2¼ cups (250 g / 9 oz) whole-wheat (wholemeal) flour
- 2¼ cups (250 g / 9 oz) strong white bread flour, plus extra for dusting
- ½ teaspoon salt
- 1 tablespoon rapid-rise (fast-action) dried yeast or ¾ oz (20 g) fresh yeast
- ½ teaspoon garlic powder
- 1 tablespoon dried oregano
- 1½ cups (350 ml / 12 fl oz) lukewarm water
- 3 tablespoons superfine (caster) sugar or honey
- 2 tablespoons olive oil
- 1 cup (120 g / 4 oz) pitted (stoned) Kalamata olives, finely chopped
- sesame seeds, for sprinkling (optional)

OLIVE BREAD
ΕΛΙΟΨΩΜΟ
Eliopsomo

Line 1–2 cookie sheets (baking trays) with baking parchment. Sift together both types of flour, the rapid-rise yeast, if using, garlic powder, salt, and oregano into a large bowl. If using fresh yeast, mash it with ½ cup (120 ml / 4 fl oz) of the lukewarm water in a bowl to a smooth paste and sift the dry ingredients into a bowl. Make a well in the center of the dry ingredients and add the sugar or honey, oil, water, and fresh yeast mixture, if using. Gradually incorporate the dry ingredients to form a soft dough. Knead lightly, adding water or flour as needed, until the dough easily pulls away from your fingers and the side of the bowl. Knead vigorously for about 15 minutes on a lightly floured work surface until smooth and elastic. Cover and let rise in a warm place for about 2 hours, until doubled in volume. Punch down and divide the dough in half. Roll out each piece of dough into an 8 x 16-inch (20 x 40-cm) rectangle. Sprinkle the surface with the chopped olives and roll up tightly from the long edge. Dampen the edge to seal and place the rolls, seam side down, on the prepared cookie sheets. Alternatively, cut the rolls into 5-inch (13-cm) pieces and put on the cookie sheets, spaced well apart. Cover and let rise for 15 minutes. Meanwhile, preheat the oven to 400°F (200°C / Gas Mark 6). Brush the loaves or rolls with water, sprinkle with sesame seeds, if using, and bake for 20–25 minutes. Let cool on wire racks.

Makes 2 small loaves or 20 rolls
Preparation time 3 hours (including rising)
Cooking time 20–25 minutes

Note: You can substitute coarsely chopped walnuts for the olives if you like. If so, omit the garlic powder and oregano and add ¼ teaspoon grated nutmeg. Use walnut oil instead of the olive oil.

Herbed bread, p 502

Mount Pelion cheese bread, p 507

BREAD WITH POTATOES OR PUMPKIN
ΨΩΜΙ ΜΕ ΠΑΤΑΤΑ Η ΚΟΛΟΚΥΘΙ
Psomi me patata i kolokithi

Brush an 8-inch (20-cm) round baking pan or an 8 x 4 x 2½-inch (20 x 10 x 6-cm) rectangular pan with melted butter. Sift together the flour and salt into a large bowl and stir in the sugar and yeast. Make a well in the center, add the mashed potato or pumpkin, milk, and melted butter and incorporate the dry ingredients, gradually adding as much of the cooking liquid as necessary to make a smooth, pliable dough that comes away from your fingers. Knead for about 10 minutes. Lightly brush the bowl with melted butter and return the dough to it, then cover, and let rise in a warm place for 1 hour, until doubled in volume. Preheat the oven to 400°F (200°C / Gas Mark 6). Press the dough into the prepared pan. Brush with melted butter, cover loosely with plastic wrap (cling film), and let rise until the dough reaches the rim of the pan. Beat the egg with 1 teaspoon water, brush the glaze over the top of the loaf, and sprinkle with sunflower or pumpkin seeds. Bake for 20 minutes, reduce the oven temperature to 350°F (180°C / Gas Mark 4) and bake for 20 minutes more, covering the top with aluminum foil for the last 10 minutes so that it doesn't burn. Turn the bread out onto a wire rack to cool.

Makes 1 large loaf
Preparation time 2½ hours (including rising)
Cooking time 40 minutes

- 2 tablespoons melted butter, plus extra for brushing
- 3½ cups (400 g / 14 oz) strong white bread flour
- 1 teaspoon salt
- 2 tablespoons sugar
- 1 scant tablespoon rapid-rise (fast-action) dried yeast
- 1 cup (80 g / 3 oz) hot mashed potato or pumpkin
- 2 tablespoons milk
- 1 cup (250 ml / 8 fl oz) potato or pumpkin cooking liquid
- 1 egg
- sunflower or pumpkin seeds, for sprinkling

- 1¼ cups (150 g / 5 oz) all-purpose (plain) flour, plus extra for dusting
- 1¼ cups (150 g / 5 oz) strong white bread flour
- 1 teaspoon salt
- 1 scant tablespoon rapid-rise (fast action) dried yeast or 1 oz (25 g) fresh yeast
- 5 tablespoons lukewarm water
- 1 tablespoon sugar or honey
- 4 tablespoons olive oil, plus extra for brushing
- ½ cup (120 ml / 4 fl oz) lukewarm milk
- 1 egg white
- melted butter, for brushing
- 14 oz (400 g) feta cheese, crumbled
- 1 egg yolk
- 2 tablespoons sesame seeds

MOUNT PELION CHEESE BREAD
ΤΥΡΟΨΩΜΟ
Tiropsomo

Sift together both kinds of flour and the salt into a large bowl and stir in the dried yeast, if using. If using fresh yeast, mash it with the lukewarm water in a bowl to a smooth paste. Make a well in the center of the dry ingredients and add the sugar or honey, oil, milk, egg white, and water or yeast mixture. Incorporate the dry ingredients to form a soft, sticky dough. Turn out onto a floured surface and knead until the dough is smooth and elastic. Brush a bowl with oil, shape the dough into a ball, put it into the bowl, and brush the surface with oil. Cover and let rise in a warm place for about 1 hour, or until doubled in volume. Brush a 10-inch (25-cm) round baking pan or a cookie sheet (baking tray) with melted butter. Divide the dough into 4 pieces. Roll out each piece on a lightly floured work surface into a strip ⅛ inch (3 mm) thick and 2½ inches (6 cm) wide. Place a quarter of the cheese along the center of each strip lengthwise. Dampen, fold, and pinch the edges together around the cheese to form 4 long rolls. With the seam side down, wind the rolls end to end to form a large coil in the prepared baking pan. Alternatively, coil the rolls in individual spirals and place, spaced well apart and seam side down, on the cookie sheet. Preheat the oven to 400°F (200°C / Gas Mark 6). Brush the tops of the rolls with melted butter, cover, and let rise for 40 minutes, or until doubled in volume. Beat the egg yolk with 1 teaspoon water in a bowl, brush the loaf with the mixture, and sprinkle with the sesame seeds. Bake for 30–35 minutes, or until the top is golden brown. Let cool on a wire rack and serve warm.

Makes 4 small loaves
Preparation time 2 hours (including rising)
Cooking time 30–35 minutes

☐ p 505

CHEESE BREAD FROM CYPRUS
ΧΑΛΟΥΜΟΠΙΤΕΣ
Haloumopites

If using fresh yeast, mash it with some of the lukewarm water in a bowl to a smooth paste. If using dried yeast, mix ½ cup (120 ml / 4 fl oz) of the lukewarm water with 1 teaspoon of the sugar in a bowl, sprinkle the yeast over the surface, and let stand for 10–15 minutes until frothy, then stir to a smooth paste. Sift together the flour and salt into a bowl, stir in the mint, and make a well in the center. Add the oil, yeast mixture, and any remaining water and mix well. Knead the dough until soft and elastic. Cover with a damp cloth and let rise for 30 minutes, or until doubled in volume. Line a 12-inch (30-cm) baking pan or cookie sheet (baking tray) with baking parchment and brush with melted butter. Work the 4 tablespoons melted butter into the dough, gently kneading until it is completely absorbed. Add the cheese and knead until it is evenly distributed throughout the dough. Divide into 10 pieces, roll out small rounds on a floured work surface and place on the prepared cookie sheet, or evenly spread all the dough into the prepared baking pan. Brush with melted butter and let rise for about 30 minutes, or until doubled in volume. Meanwhile, preheat the oven to 400°F (200°C / Gas Mark 6). Bake the bread for about 20 minutes, or until golden. Serve warm.

Makes 10 rolls or 1 large loaf
Preparation time 2 hours (including rising)
Cooking time 20 minutes

- 1 oz (25 g) fresh yeast or 1 tablespoon dried yeast
- 1¼ cups (300 ml / ½ pint) lukewarm water
- 1 tablespoon sugar
- 4 cups (450 g / 1 lb) all-purpose (plain) flour
- 1 teaspoon salt
- 1 tablespoon dried mint or 4 tablespoons finely chopped fresh mint
- 4 tablespoons olive oil
- 4 tablespoons melted butter, plus extra for greasing
- 1 lb 2 oz (500 g) halloumi or provolone cheese, grated

CORN BREAD
ΚΑΛΑΜΠΟΚΟΨΩΜΟ
Kalabokopsomo

Preheat the oven to 400°F (200°C / Gas Mark 6) and grease an 8 x 4 x 2½-inch (20 x 10 x 6-cm) loaf pan with butter. Sift together the cornmeal, flour, sugar, baking powder, and salt into a large bowl. Add the milk, oil, and egg and beat with an electric mixer on medium speed for 1 minute. Fold in the corn kernels or golden raisins. Spread the batter in the prepared loaf pan and bake for 20–25 minutes, or until the top is golden. Turn out onto a wire rack and let cool slightly. Serve the corn bread while slightly warm.

Makes 1 large loaf
Preparation time 15 minutes
Cooking time 20–25 minutes

- butter, for greasing
- 1 cup (120 g / 4 oz) cornmeal
- 1 cup (120 g / 4 oz) all-purpose (plain) flour
- 2 tablespoons superfine (caster) sugar
- 4 teaspoons baking powder
- ½ teaspoon salt
- 1 cup (250 ml / 8 fl oz) milk
- 4 tablespoons olive oil
- 1 egg
- 1 cup (175 g / 6 oz) canned corn (sweet corn) kernels, drained and chopped, or golden raisins

- 6 tablespoons (80 g / 3 oz) butter, chilled and diced, plus extra for greasing
- 1¼ cups (300 ml / ½ pint) sheep's yogurt
- scant 1 cup (100 g / 3½ oz) grated kaseri or Gruyère cheese
- scant 1 cup (100 g / 3½ oz) grated kefalotiri, romano, or Parmesan cheese
- ½ cup (120 ml / 4 fl oz) corn oil
- 2 eggs, lightly beaten
- 2 tablespoons freshly squeezed lemon juice
- 3 cups (350 g / 12 oz) cornmeal
- 1 teaspoon baking soda (bicarbonate of soda)
- 3 teaspoons baking powder
- ½ teaspoon salt
- 4 oz (120 g) feta cheese, crumbled

CORN BREAD WITH CHEESE
ΜΠΟΜΠΟΤΑ ΜΕ ΤΥΡΙ
Bobota me tiri

Preheat the oven to 350°F (180°C / Gas Mark 4) and grease a 12-inch (30-cm) round baking pan with butter. Combine the yogurt, both types of grated cheese, oil, eggs, and lemon juice in a large bowl. Sift together the cornstarch, baking soda, baking powder, and salt into another bowl. Gradually add the dry ingredients to the cheese mixture, kneading lightly to form a soft dough. Spread the dough into the prepared pan, sprinkle the crumbled feta over the surface, and dot with the diced butter. Bake for about 40 minutes, or until the top is golden. Serve warm. Keep leftover bread in the refrigerator and reheat before serving.

Makes 1 large loaf
Preparation time 30 minutes
Cooking time 40 minutes

- 2¼ oz (60 g) fresh yeast or 2 tablespoons dried yeast
- 2½ cups (600 ml / 1 pint) lukewarm water
- 3 tablespoons honey or sugar
- 9 cups (1 kg / 2¼ lb) strong white bread flour, plus extra for dusting
- 2 teaspoons salt
- 4 tablespoons olive oil, plus extra for brushing
- 4 tablespoons sesame seeds

FLATBREAD
ΛΑΓΑΝΕΣ
Laganes

If using fresh yeast, mix it with 1 cup (250 ml / 8 fl oz) of the water in a bowl and mash it well with a fork. Stir in the honey or sugar. If using dried yeast, stir the honey or sugar into 1 cup (250 ml / 8 fl oz) of the water and sprinkle the yeast over the surface, then let stand for 10–15 minutes, until frothy. Stir well until smooth. Add enough flour to the yeast mixture to form a thick batter. Cover with plastic wrap (cling film) and let stand overnight. Sift the remaining flour and salt into a large bowl and make a well in the center. Pour in the yeast mixture, oil, and the remaining lukewarm water. Incorporate the flour from the sides of the well into the liquid. Knead the dough vigorously until soft, smooth, and elastic. Divide the dough into four balls. Brush each with a little oil, cover with a damp cloth, and let rise for 10 minutes. Roll out each ball on a lightly floured surface into a ½-inch (1-cm) oval or round. If the dough doesn't roll out easily, cover and let rest for 5–10 minutes. Brush two cookie sheets (baking trays) with oil, place the flatbreads on them, brush with a little oil, cover, and let rise until doubled in volume. Preheat the oven to 400°F (200°C / Gas Mark 6). Using 2 fingers, make indentations all over the dough, brush with a little water, and sprinkle with the sesame seeds. Bake the breads for 15–20 minutes. Remove from the oven and let cool slightly, then serve warm.

Makes 4 large flatbreads
Preparation time 12 hours (including rising)
Cooking time 20 minutes

FLATBREAD WITH ANCHOVIES AND ONIONS
ΛΑΓΑΝΑ ΜΕ ΑΝΤΖΟΥΓΙΕΣ ΚΑΙ ΚΡΕΜΜΥΔΙΑ
Lagana me antzougies ke kremidia

Sift together the flour and salt into a large bowl and stir in the yeast, ¼ teaspoon of the oregano, and the basil. Make a well in the center, pour in the honey, lukewarm water, and melted butter, and incorporate the dry ingredients. Knead until the dough is soft and pliable. Cover with plastic wrap (cling film) and let rise in a warm place for 1 hour, or until doubled in volume. Meanwhile, combine the oil, onions, garlic, thyme, rosemary, and remaining oregano in a pan, cover, and cook over low heat, stirring occasionally, for about 5 minutes, until softened, then remove from the heat. Brush a 12-inch (30-cm) pizza pan with oil. Pat the dough into the base of the pan and spread the onion mixture evenly over the surface, leaving a generous ¾-inch (2-cm) margin around the edge. Preheat the oven to 400°F (200°C / Gas Mark 6). Top with the anchovies and olives and let rise for 30 minutes. Bake the flatbread for 30 minutes, or until the edges are browned. Serve immediately.

Makes 1 large flatbread
Preparation time 2 hours (including rising)
Cooking time 30 minutes

- 2¼ cups (250 g / 9 oz) strong white bread flour
- ½ teaspoon salt
- 1½ teaspoons rapid-rise (fast-action) dried yeast
- ¾ teaspoon dried oregano
- ¼ teaspoon dried or 1 teaspoon chopped fresh basil
- 1 tablespoon honey
- ½ cup (120 ml / 4 fl oz) lukewarm water
- 1 tablespoon melted butter
- 3 tablespoons olive oil, plus extra for brushing
- 2¼ lb (1 kg) onions, sliced lengthwise
- 2 garlic cloves, thinly sliced
- ½ teaspoon dried thyme
- ½ teaspoon dried rosemary
- 18 canned anchovy fillets, drained
- 10 Kalamata olives, pitted (stoned)
- 10 pimiento-stuffed green olives, sliced

TOMATO FLATBREAD
ΛΑΓΑΝΑ ΜΕ ΝΤΟΜΑΤΕΣ ΚΑΙ ΒΟΤΑΝΑ
Lagana me domates ke votana

Sift together the flour and salt into a bowl, stir in the yeast and mixed herbs, and make a well in the center. Add the honey, 1 tablespoon of the oil, and the lukewarm water and incorporate the dry ingredients to form a soft elastic dough. Brush with oil, cover, and let rise in a warm place for 30 minutes, or until doubled in volume. Meanwhile, heat the remaining oil in a pan. Add the garlic and cook over low heat for 1–2 minutes. Mix the tomato paste with 4 tablespoons water. Add the tomato paste mixture, tomatoes, ketchup, and mustard to the pan, season with salt and pepper, increase the heat to medium, and cook for 3 minutes, or until slightly thickened. Preheat the oven to 400°F (200°C / Gas Mark 6). Roll out the dough on a lightly floured work surface and pat into a 12-inch (30-cm) pizza pan. Spread the tomato sauce evenly over the surface, leaving a generous ¾-inch (2-cm) margin around the edge. Sprinkle with the dried herbs and let rise for 10 minutes. Bake for 15–20 minutes, or until browned. Serve immediately.

Makes 1 large flatbread
Preparation time 1¼ hours (including rising)
Cooking time 20–25 minutes

- 1¼ cups (250 g / 9 oz) all-purpose (plain) flour, plus extra for dusting
- ½ teaspoon salt
- 1½ teaspoons rapid-rise (fast-action) dried yeast
- 1 teaspoon mixed dried herbs, such as oregano, thyme, or mint
- 1 tablespoon honey
- 5 tablespoons olive oil, plus extra for brushing
- ½ cup (120 ml / 4 fl oz) lukewarm water
- 4 garlic cloves, thinly sliced
- 2 tablespoons tomato paste
- 2¼ lb (1 kg) tomatoes, peeled, seeded, and coarsely chopped
- 2 tablespoons tomato ketchup
- 1 teaspoon Dijon mustard
- salt and pepper
- 1 teaspoon dried oregano
- 1 teaspoon dried thyme

⊡ p 512

- 1 quantity Flatbread dough (p 509)
- olive oil, for frying
- anthotiro or ricotta cheese, to serve
- honey, to serve

FRIED BREAD
ΤΗΓΑΝΟΨΩΜΟ Η ΤΗΓΑΝΙΤΕΣ
Tiganopsomo i tiganites

Divide the dough into 6–8 pieces. Flatten each into a ½-inch (1-cm) thick round and let rise for 30 minutes, or until doubled in size. Heat enough oil to cover the base of a heavy skillet or frying pan and fry the flatbreads for 5–8 minutes on each side, or until lightly browned. Serve immediately with anthotiro or ricotta cheese and honey.

Makes 6–8 flatbreads
Preparation time 1 hour
Cooking time 5–8 minutes

- 3 cups (350 g / 12 oz) all-purpose (plain) flour, plus extra for dusting
- ½ tablespoon rapid-rise (fast-action) dried yeast
- 2 tablespoons honey
- 2 tablespoons olive oil, plus extra for frying
- 1 cup (250 ml / 8 fl oz) lukewarm water
- 1 cup (120 g / 4 oz) Kalamata olives, pitted (stoned) and finely chopped

FRIED OLIVE BREAD FROM CYPRUS
ΤΗΓΑΝΟΨΩΜΟ ΜΕ ΕΛΙΕΣ
Tiganopsomo me elies

Sift the flour into a large bowl, stir in the yeast, and make a well in the center. Pour in the honey, oil, and lukewarm water, incorporate the dry ingredients and knead to a soft pliable dough, adding more flour if necessary. Cover the dough with plastic wrap (cling film) and let rise for about 1 hour, or until doubled in volume. Roll out the dough on a lightly floured work surface to a rectangle about ½ inch (1 cm) thick and sprinkle the olives on top. Roll up tightly. Using a floured knife, cut the roll crosswise into 20 pieces, ½ inch (1 cm) thick. Flatten each piece with the rolling pin to about ¼ inch (5 mm) thick. Let rise for about 15 minutes. Heat oil in a skillet or frying pan. Add the bread slices, in batches, and cook for 5–8 minutes on each side, until lightly browned. Alternatively, you can bake the breads in an oven preheated to 350°F (180°C / Gas Mark 4), for 15 minutes. Serve immediately.

Makes 20 pieces
Preparation time 1¾ hours
Cooking time 20 minutes

□ p 513

Tomato flatbread, p 510

ied olive bread from Cyprus, p 511

ONION BREAD FROM ASIA MINOR
ΜΙΚΡΑΣΙΑΤΙΚΕΣ ΚΡΕΜΜΥΔΟΠΙΤΕΣ
Mikrasiatikes kremidopites

If using fresh yeast, mash it with the lukewarm water in a bowl to a smooth paste. If using dried yeast, pour the lukewarm water into a bowl, sprinkle the yeast over it, and let stand for 10–15 minutes until frothy, then stir to a smooth paste. Sift 3 cups (350 g / 12 oz) of the flour into a bowl and make a well in the center. Pour in the yeast, milk, and oil and incorporate the flour. Knead well, adding extra flour as necessary to form a soft, smooth dough. Divide the dough into eight 6 inch (15 cm) long ovals. To make the filling, heat the oil in a pan. Add the scallions and cook over low heat, stirring occasionally, for 5 minutes, until softened. Stir in the dill and feta, season with salt and pepper, and remove from the heat. Place one eighth of the filling along the center of each oval and brush the edges with beaten egg. Lift up the edges and seal together to enclose the filling. Pinch together at each end to make boat shapes. Preheat the oven to 400°F (200°C / Gas Mark 6). Brush a cookie sheet (baking tray) with oil, put the breads on it, and let rise for 30 minutes. Beat the egg yolk with 1 teaspoon water in a bowl and brush over the breads. Bake for 30 minutes, or until golden. Brush with melted butter, cover and let cool slightly. Serve hot or cold.

Makes 8 pieces
Preparation time 1¼ hours (including rising)
Cooking time 30 minutes

FOR THE DOUGH
- 1 oz (25 g) fresh yeast or 2 teaspoons dried yeast
- 5 tablespoons lukewarm water
- 3–4 cups (350–450 g / 12–16 oz) all-purpose (plain) flour
- 5 tablespoons lukewarm milk
- 2 tablespoons olive oil, plus extra for brushing
- 1 egg yolk
- 4 tablespoons melted butter, for brushing

FOR THE FILLING
- 4 tablespoons olive oil
- 9 oz (250 g) finely chopped scallions (spring onions)
- 5 tablespoons finely chopped fresh dill
- 1¼ cups (150 g / 5 oz) crumbled feta cheese
- salt and pepper
- 1 egg, lightly beaten

PITA BREAD FOR SOUVLAKI
ΠΙΤΕΣ ΓΙΑ ΣΟΥΒΛΑΚΙ
Pites gia souvlaki

Combine the flour, salt, yeast, and sugar in a large bowl. Add the oil and water and knead lightly until the dough comes away from the sides of the bowl. Leave in a warm place to rise for about 30 minutes. Divide into 6 pieces and roll out into 8-inch (20-cm) rounds ¼ inch (5 mm) thick. Dust lightly with cornmeal, cover, and let rise for 5 minutes. Score the pita breads crosswise with the tines of a fork or a pastry wheel, taking care not to cut through. Brush a heavy nonstick skillet or frying pan with oil and fry the breads over high heat for 3 minutes on each side, until browned in several places but not completely cooked. Remove and immediately place in airtight bags to keep them moist. Let cool completely and broil (grill), bake in a hot oven, or fry to reheat.

Makes 6 pita breads
Preparation time 2 hours (including rising)
Cooking time 15 minutes

- 3 cups (350 g / 12 oz) all-purpose (plain) flour
- 1 teaspoon salt
- 1 tablespoon dried yeast
- 2 teaspoons sugar
- 2 tablespoons olive oil, plus extra for brushing
- ¾ cup (175 ml / 6 fl oz) lukewarm water
- cornmeal, for dusting

◻ p 516

- 2 teaspoons rapid-rise (fast-action) dried yeast
- 1 cup (250 ml / 8 fl oz) lukewarm water
- 2¾ cups (300 g / 11 oz) all-purpose (plain) flour
- 1 tablespoon superfine (caster) sugar
- 4 tablespoons olive oil, plus extra for brushing
- 1 teaspoon salt
- 1 teaspoon dried mint
- 1 tablespoon chopped fresh basil
- ½ teaspoon dried oregano
- ½ teaspoon dried thyme
- ½ teaspoon dried or finely chopped garlic

BREAD ROLLS WITH AROMATIC HERBS
ΨΩΜΑΚΙΑ ΜΕ ΑΡΩΜΑΤΙΚΑ ΒΟΤΑΝΑ
Psomakia me aromatika votana

Put the yeast into a bowl and stir in half the lukewarm water until yeast is dissolved, then stir in 1 tablespoon of the flour and the sugar. Let stand for 5 minutes. Put half the oil, the remaining flour, the remaining luke-warm water, the salt, herbs, and garlic into a bowl, add the yeast mixture, and knead with an electric mixer fitted with a dough hook until the dough forms a ball around the hook. Alternatively, knead by hand until the dough is soft and pliable. Brush the dough with the remaining oil and put it into a large bowl. Cover and let rise for about 1 hour. Meanwhile, brush a 12-cup muffin pan with oil. Punch down the dough and roll into a long cylinder. Cut it into 12 pieces, roll them into balls, and put them into the prepared pan. Let rise for 15 minutes. Meanwhile, preheat the oven to 350°F (180°C / Gas Mark 4). Bake the rolls for 15–20 minutes, until golden. Let cool and serve on the day they are made.

Makes 12 rolls
Preparation time 1½ hours (including rising)
Cooking time 15–20 minutes

Pita bread for souvlaki, p 514

Cinnamon twists, p 522

MEAT PIES FROM CYPRUS
ΕΜΠΑΣΚΙΕΣ ΠΑΦΟΥ
Ebaskies paphou

To make the filling, heat the oil in a pan. Add the meat and onion and cook over medium heat, stirring frequently, for about 8 minutes, until lightly browned. Add 1 cup (250 ml / 8 fl oz) water, cover, and simmer for 1–1½ hours, or until the meat is tender and the sauce has thickened. Let cool, then chop the meat and return to the pan. Combine the cheese, flour, eggs, and sugar and stir into the meat. Season with salt and pepper. To make the dough, sift together the flour, baking powder, if using, salt, mahlab, mastic, and sugar into a bowl. Add the butter and rub in with your fingers until the mixture is crumbly. Add the milk and knead until the dough is soft and pliable. Cover and let rest for 30 minutes. If using yeast, stir 1 teaspoon of the sugar into the milk in a bowl and sprinkle the yeast on the surface, let stand for 10–15 minutes, until frothy, then stir to a smooth paste. Sift the dry ingredients into a bowl and add the yeast mixture with the butter. Knead to a smooth and pliable dough, then cover, and let rise for 1 hour in a warm place until doubled in volume. Preheat the oven to 350°F (180°C / Gas Mark 4) and brush 2 cookie sheets (baking trays) with oil. Divide the dough into 8 pieces and roll out into 8-inch (20-cm) rounds. Spoon 2–3 tablespoons of the meat filling onto each round, moisten the edges, fold in half, and pinch to seal. Slightly flatten the folded edge. Put the pies on the prepared cookie sheets, seam side down. Beat the egg with 1 teaspoon water in a bowl and brush the pies with the glaze. Sprinkle with sesame seeds and bake for about 40 minutes, or until lightly browned. Serve hot or at room temperature.

Makes 8–10 pies
Preparation time 1¾ hours (including rising)
Cooking time 40 minutes

FOR THE FILLING
- 3 tablespoons olive oil
- 1 lb 2 oz (500 g) boneless leg of lamb, cut into small pieces
- 1 large onion, grated
- 2 cups (225 g / 8 oz) grated Gruyère cheese
- scant 1 cup (100 g / 3½ oz) grated halloumi or provolone cheese
- 1 tablespoon all-purpose (plain) flour
- 2 eggs, lightly beaten
- 1 teaspoon sugar
- salt and pepper

FOR THE DOUGH
- 2¾ cups (300 g / 11 oz) all-purpose (plain) flour
- 3 tablespoons baking powder or 2 teaspoons dried yeast
- ¼ teaspoon salt
- ¼ teaspoon ground mahlab
- ¼ teaspoon ground mastic
- 2 teaspoons superfine (caster) sugar
- scant ½ cup (100 g / 3½ oz) butter
- ⅔ cup (150 ml / ¼ pint) lukewarm milk
- olive oil, for brushing
- 1 egg
- sesame seeds, for sprinkling

TRADITIONAL SOURDOUGH STARTER
ΠΡΟΖΥΜΙ
Prozimi

If using fresh yeast, mix it with 1 cup (120 ml / 4 fl oz) of the water in a bowl and mash it well with a fork. If using dry yeast, mix it with the flour. Combine all the ingredients in a bowl and beat to a very thick, sticky batter. Cover loosely with plastic wrap (cling film) and let stand in a warm place for at least 24 hours (2–3 days for the best results). Stir, pour into a screw-top glass jar, and seal. Store in the refrigerator for up to 1 week. It is ready when clear liquid rises to the top. Mix well before using. To reactivate, stir in more flour and warm water, cover and set aside in a warm place for 12 hours.

Preparation time 2–3 days (including fermentation)

- ½ oz (15 g) fresh yeast or 2 teaspoons rapid-rise (fast-action) dried yeast
- 2 cups (450 ml / 16 fl oz) lukewarm water
- 3 cups (350 g / 12 oz) strong white bread flour
- 1 tablespoon sugar or honey

- ⅓ quantity Traditional sourdough starter (p 518)
- 13¼ cups (1.5 kg / 3¼ lb) strong white bread flour, plus extra for dusting
- 2 cups (450 ml / 16 fl oz) lukewarm water
- 3 tablespoons honey
- 1 tablespoon salt
- 3 tablespoons olive oil

TRADITIONAL SOURDOUGH BREAD
ΨΩΜΙ ΖΥΜΩΤΟ ΠΑΡΑΔΟΣΙΑΚΟ
Psomi zimoto paradosiako

First, reactivate the starter. Mix it in a bowl with one quarter of the flour and enough lukewarm water to form a thick batter. Cover and set aside in a warm place for at least 12 hours. Line a large cookie sheet (baking tray) with baking parchment. Stir the honey into the remaining lukewarm water in a bowl. Sift together the remaining flour and the salt into a large bowl and make a well in the center. Pour in the sourdough mixture, oil, and water and honey mixture and incorporate the dry ingredients to form a soft, sticky dough. Knead the dough on a lightly floured work surface for about 15 minutes, until smooth and elastic. Return the dough to the bowl, cover with plastic wrap (cling film), and let rise for 1½–2 hours, or until doubled in volume. Divide the dough into 3 pieces and shape each into a ball, then cover with a damp dish towel, and let rest for 10 minutes. Shape each ball into an oblong loaf. Arrange the loaves, spaced well apart, on the prepared cookie sheet and cover with a dry dish towel and then a damp dish towel. Let rise for 45–60 minutes, or until doubled in volume. Meanwhile, preheat the oven to 425°F (220°C / Gas Mark 7). Using a very sharp knife, make a few long shallow slashes across the top of each loaf. Bake the bread on the center shelf of the oven with a heatproof bowl of hot water on the floor of the oven for 20 minutes. Remove the bowl of water, reduce the oven temperature to 400°F (200°C / Gas Mark 6), and bake for 25–40 minutes more, until the top is golden brown and the loaves sound hollow when tapped underneath. Remove from the oven and brush the tops with a little water, then let cool on wire racks before slicing.

Makes 3 small loaves
Preparation time 14½–15½ hours (including activating the starter and rising)
Cooking time 45–60 minutes

NATURAL SOURDOUGH BREAD
ΨΩΜΙ ΕΦΤΑΖΥΜΟ
Psomi eftazimo

- 1 cup (225 g / 8 oz) dried garbanzo beans (chickpeas), coarsely crushed
- 2 teaspoons salt
- 3 cups (750 ml / 1¼ pints) boiling water
- 4 tablespoons superfine (caster) sugar, plus extra for sprinkling
- 6 cups (700 g / 1½ lb) strong white bread flour
- 2 tablespoons olive oil, plus extra for brushing
- ¾ cup (175 ml / 6 fl oz) lukewarm water
- 1 egg yolk

Many domestic cooks in Greece still bake *eftazimo*—a white, aromatic bread with a golden brown crust—using a natural yeast cultivated by combining garbanzo beans and water. When it is brought home, fresh from the oven, its aroma fills the house. Cultivating the yeast is not always successful, so they mix the garbanzo beans and water in three jars and use the frothiest one with the best sour flavor. The yeast and the dough must be kept warm, so the kitchen door stays closed from the moment the kneading starts to when the bread is baked. Cultivating natural yeast is not always successful, and failures are sometimes superstitiously attributed to the "evil eye" given to the bread by a friend or neighbor. Even today, some Greek village women will not tell anyone that they are baking *eftazimo*. In parts of Macedonia, flavorings such as a sprig of dried basil, a small hot chile, bay leaves, or anise seeds are infused in the water before mixing the dough.

Put the garbanzo beans and ¼ teaspoon salt into a tall, sterilized jar, pour in the boiling water, and stir well. Cover the jar, wrap it in a blanket, and leave in a very warm place for 24–48 hours, until the beans puff up and the froth on top of the liquid measures about 1½ inches (4 cm). If there is no froth and the liquid has turned orange, discard it and make a new batch. (To speed up the procedure, place the jar in a preheated oven at its lowest setting for 4–6 hours.) Transfer the froth from the top of the jar to a bowl with a wooden spoon and strain the liquid into the same bowl. Discard the garbanzo beans. Add 1 tablespoon of the sugar and enough flour to the liquid to make a light paste, cover, and let stand in a warm place overnight. The mixture is ready when it is spongy and has a pleasant sour smell.

Sift together the remaining flour and remaining salt into a large bowl and make a well in the center. Add the remaining sugar, the oil, yeast mixture, and lukewarm water. Incorporate the dry ingredients and knead for about 15 minutes to an elastic and pliable dough. Shape the dough into a cylindrical or round loaf. Generously brush a loaf pan twice as large as the unrisen dough with oil and put the loaf in it. Cover with wax (greaseproof) paper and a blanket and let rise in a warm place for about 2 hours, or until doubled in volume. Meanwhile, preheat the oven to 425°F (220°C / Gas Mark 7). Beat the egg yolk with 1 teaspoon water in a bowl, brush the top of the loaf with the glaze, and sprinkle with a little sugar. Bake the bread for 10 minutes, then reduce the oven temperature to 400°F (200°C / Gas Mark 6), and bake for 20 minutes more. Turn out onto a wire rack and let cool. *Eftazimo* stays fresh longer than ordinary bread, and does not turn moldy.

Makes 1 large loaf
Preparation time up to 3 days (including yeast cultivation and rising)
Cooking time 30 minutes

- 1 quantity Traditional sourdough starter (p 518) or 1 oz (25 g) fresh yeast or 1 tablespoon dried yeast
- 2½–3 cups (600–750 ml / 1–1¼ pints) lukewarm water
- 11 cups (1.25 kg / 2¾ lb) country or yellow flour (see note)
- 1 tablespoon salt
- 2 tablespoons vegetable oil
- 2 tablespoons honey
- 2 tablespoons milk

YELLOW VILLAGE BREAD
ΨΩΜΙ ΧΩΡΙΑΤΙΚΟ
Psomi horiatiko

If using chilled sourdough starter, reactivate it the evening before (see p 518). If using yeast, prepare it the evening before and let it stand in a warm place overnight. To prepare the yeast, mash it with 1 cup (250 ml / 8 fl oz) of the lukewarm water in a bowl and mix in enough flour to form a thick paste. Sift together the remaining flour and salt into a bowl and make a well in the center. Pour in the sourdough starter or yeast mixture, oil, honey, milk, and remaining water and incorporate the dry ingredients to a soft, sticky dough. Turn the dough out onto a cool work surface and knead for about 15 minutes, until elastic and glossy. Return it to the bowl, cover with plastic wrap (cling film) and let rise in a warm place for 1–1½ hours, or until doubled in volume. The dough is ready when a finger pressed into it leaves a dent that only very slowly fills out. Punch down the dough, knead for a few minutes, and divide into 3 pieces. Shape each piece into a tapered cylindrical loaf and place them, spaced slightly apart, on a cookie sheet (baking tray). Cover with a damp dish towel and let rise for 45–60 minutes, until doubled in volume. Meanwhile, preheat the oven to 425°F (220°C / Gas Mark 7). Using a sharp knife, make several ½-inch (1-cm) deep slashes across the tops of the loaves. Place a wide heatproof bowl filled with hot water on the oven floor and bake the loaves for 20 minutes. Remove the bowl of water, reduce the oven temperature to 400°F (200°C / Gas Mark 6), and bake for 20–25 minutes longer, until golden brown. Remove the loaves from the oven, brush the tops with water using a pastry brush, and let cool on a wire rack.

Makes 3 small loaves
Preparation time 15 hours (including reactivating the starter and rising)
Cooking time 40–45 minutes

Note: This traditional Greek village bread is made with country flour or, as also it is called, yellow flour. This is a white wheat flour enriched with 1–1¼ oz (25–35 g) finely ground semolina.

CINNAMON TWISTS
ΨΩΜΑΚΙΑ ΣΤΡΙΦΤΑ ΜΕ ΚΑΝΕΛΑ
Psomakia strifta me kanela

For the dough, put the evaporated milk, butter, sugar, and salt into a small pan and cook over medium heat, stirring occasionally, until the butter has melted and the sugar has dissolved. Remove from the heat and let cool slightly. If using fresh yeast, mash it with the lukewarm water in a bowl to a smooth paste. If using dried yeast, pour the lukewarm water into a bowl, sprinkle the yeast over the surface, and let stand for 10–15 minutes until frothy, then stir to a smooth paste. Beat the eggs and stir them into the butter mixture, together with the dissolved yeast and half the flour, stirring until the batter is smooth. Gradually add more flour and knead until the dough is pliable and smooth. It should be slightly softer than regular bread dough. Divide it into 3 pieces, cover, and let rise in a warm place for 1½ hours, or until doubled in volume. Roll out each piece of dough on a lightly floured work surface into an 8 x 12-inch (20 x 30-cm) rectangle. For the filling, combine the cinnamon and sugar in a bowl. Spread half the softened butter on 1 dough rectangle and sprinkle with half the cinnamon and sugar mixture. Put the second sheet of dough on top of the first, spread with the remaining softened butter, and sprinkle with the remaining cinnamon and sugar mixture. Put the third sheet of dough on top and brush with melted butter. Cover and let rise for 10 minutes. Meanwhile, brush a cookie sheet (baking tray) with melted butter. Cut the stacked dough lengthwise into generous ¾-inch (2-cm) strips with a pizza cutter. Twist each strip 2–3 times, roll into spirals, and place on the prepared cookie sheet. Brush with melted butter, cover, and let rise until doubled in volume. Meanwhile, preheat the oven to 400°F (200°C / Gas Mark 6). Brush the twists with melted butter and bake for 15–20 minutes, or until lightly golden. Serve warm.

Makes 8–10 twists
Preparation time 2¾ hours (including rising)
Cooking time 15–20 minutes

□ p 517

FOR THE DOUGH
- 4 tablespoons evaporated milk
- 4 tablespoons (50 g / 2 oz) butter
- 4 tablespoons superfine (caster) sugar
- ½ teaspoon salt
- 1 oz (25 g) fresh yeast or 1 tablespoon dried yeast
- 5 tablespoons lukewarm water
- 2 eggs
- 4½ cups (500 g / 1 lb 2 oz) strong white bread flour
- 2–3 tablespoons melted butter, plus extra for brushing

FOR THE FILLING
- 2 tablespoons ground cinnamon
- 4 tablespoons superfine (caster) sugar
- 4 tablespoons (50 g / 2 oz) butter, softened

- 1½ cups (350 g / 12 oz) butter, chilled and diced, plus extra for greasing
- 6 cups (700 g / 1½ lb) all-purpose (plain) flour, plus extra for dusting
- 1½ teaspoons baking soda (bicarbonate of soda)
- 1 teaspoon cream of tartar
- 2 tablespoons brandy
- 5 tablespoons milk
- 1 tablespoon vanilla extract
- 3 eggs
- 1½ cups (300 g / 11 oz) superfine (caster) sugar
- 1 egg yolk

NEW YEAR'S BREAD
ΒΑΣΙΛΟΠΙΤΑ ΤΡΙΦΤΗ
Vasilopita trifti

New Year's Day, the Feast of Saint Basil, is the main occasion for family get-togethers over the festive period, with Agios Vasilis (Saint Basil) bringing the gifts. The centerpiece of the Greek New Year's festivities is the *vasilopita,* in which a lucky coin is concealed. There are many versions, including a pie made with cheese or meat or whatever else is abundant, and a sweet yeast-risen bread. Nowadays, the most common version is a bread resembling a pound cake. Whoever finds the lucky coin will be blessed throughout the coming year.

Preheat the oven to 350°F (180°C / Gas Mark 4). Line a 12-inch (30-cm) round baking pan with baking parchment and grease with butter. Sift the flour into a large bowl, add the butter, and rub in with your fingertips until the mixture resembles coarse bread crumbs. Combine the baking soda, cream of tartar, and brandy in a bowl. Lightly beat together the milk, vanilla extract, eggs, and sugar in another bowl. Pour into the flour, together with the brandy mixture, and knead gently to a soft dough. Avoid over-kneading. Reserve a small piece of dough. Push a coin wrapped in aluminum foil into the remaining dough and press it into the prepared baking pan. Beat the egg yolk with 1 teaspoon water in a bowl. Roll out the reserved dough on a lightly floured work surface. Using tiny cookie cutters, stamp out seasonal shapes and stick them on the top of the bread, brushing with a little of the egg yolk mixture. Brush the top of the bread with the remaining egg yolk mixture and bake for 30–35 minutes, or until golden brown. Transfer to a wire rack to cool. Store the bread covered with plastic wrap (cling film).

Makes 1 loaf
Preparation time 45 minutes
Cooking time 35 minutes

□ p 524

New Year's bread, p 523

Lenten sweet bread with pumpkin, p 526

LENTEN SWEET BREAD WITH PUMPKIN
ΝΗΣΤΙΣΙΜΑ ΤΣΟΥΡΕΚΙΑ ΜΕ ΚΟΛΟΚΥΘΙ
Nistisima tsourekia me kolokithi

If using fresh yeast, mash it with the lukewarm water in a large bowl to a smooth paste. If using dried yeast, mix the lukewarm water with 1 teaspoon of the sugar in a large bowl, sprinkle the yeast over the surface, and let stand for 10–15 minutes, until frothy, then stir to a smooth paste. Sift together 2–3 tablespoons of the flour and the salt into the bowl with the yeast and stir to a thick batter. Let the mixture rise for about 30 minutes. Put the pumpkin, remaining sugar, orange juice, oil, orange zest, and vanilla into another bowl and beat with an electric mixer on high speed for 5 minutes, until the sugar has blended with the pumpkin purée. Sift together half the remaining flour and the mahlab, if using, into a large bowl and make a well in the center. Pour in the yeast mixture and the pumpkin mixture. Gradually knead together, adding the remaining flour, to make a smooth dough that comes away from the side of the bowl. Cover and let rise for 1 hour, or until doubled in volume. Divide the dough into 3 balls and divide each ball into 3 strips. Braid (plait) the strips together, pressing the ends to seal. Preheat the oven to 350°F (180°C / Gas Mark 4). Brush 1–2 cookie sheets (baking trays) with oil, put the loaves on them, and let rise for 30 minutes. Bake the loaves for about 45 minutes, or until golden. Let cool on wire racks, then store wrapped in plastic wrap (cling film).

Makes 2 loaves
Preparation time 3 hours (including rising)
Cooking time 45 minutes

□ p 525

- 3½ oz (100 g) fresh yeast or 1½ tablespoons dried yeast
- 4 tablespoons lukewarm water
- 1¾ cups (350 g / 12 oz) superfine (caster) sugar
- 9 cups (1 kg / 2¼ lb) strong white bread flour
- ½ teaspoon salt
- 1 lb 2 oz (500 g) pumpkin, cooked and well drained
- 4 tablespoons freshly squeezed orange juice
- ½ cup (120 ml / 4 fl oz) corn oil, plus extra for brushing
- grated zest of 1 orange
- 1 teaspoon vanilla extract
- ½ tablespoon ground mahlab or mastic (optional)

- 1 oz (25 g) fresh yeast or
  2½ teaspoons dried yeast
- ½ cup (120 ml / 4 fl oz)
  lukewarm water
- 4½ cups (500 g / 1 lb 2 oz)
  strong white bread flour, plus
  extra for dusting
- scant ½ cup (80 g / 3 oz)
  superfine (caster) sugar
- ½ cup (120 ml / 4 fl oz) milk
- 2 tablespoons melted butter,
  plus extra for brushing
- 1 tablespoon grated lemon
  zest (optional)
- ½ teaspoon salt
- 1 teaspoon baking powder
- 1 egg white, lightly beaten
- 1 cup (150 g / 5 oz) raisins
- 1 egg yolk

RAISIN BREAD
ΣΤΑΦΙΔΟΨΩΜΑ
Stafidopsoma

If using fresh yeast, mash it with the lukewarm water in a bowl to a smooth paste, then stir in enough flour to make a thick batter. Cover and let rise for about 10 minutes. If using dried yeast, mix the lukewarm water with 1 teaspoon of the sugar in a bowl, sprinkle the yeast over the surface, stir in enough flour to make a thick batter, cover, and let stand for 10–15 minutes. Meanwhile, pour the milk into a pan and bring to just below boiling point, then remove from the heat, and stir in the butter, remaining sugar, lemon zest, if using, and salt. Sift together the remaining flour and the baking powder into a large bowl and make a well in the center. Pour in the yeast mixture, milk mixture, and egg white and incorporate the flour to form a soft, sticky dough. Turn out onto a lightly floured work surface and knead for about 10 minutes, until smooth and elastic. Brush a bowl with melted butter, put the dough in it, cover, and let rise in a warm place for 1½–2 hours, or until doubled in volume. Meanwhile, brush a loaf pan or cookie sheet (baking tray) with melted butter. Punch down the dough and roll out on a lightly floured work surface into ½-inch (1-cm) thick square. Sprinkle with the raisins, roll up tightly, and put into the prepared loaf pan. Alternatively, divide the dough and shape into 12 cigar-shaped rolls. Put the rolls onto the prepared cookie sheet, spaced well apart. Preheat the oven to 400°F (200°C / Gas Mark 6). Cover with a damp dish towel and let rise for about 30 minutes, or until doubled in volume. Beat the egg yolk with 1 teaspoon water in a bowl and brush the glaze over the loaf or rolls. Bake for about 20 minutes, or until lightly browned. Let cool on a wire rack before serving.

Makes 1 large loaf or 12 rolls
Preparation time 3 hours (including rising)
Cooking time 20 minutes

SESAME BREAD RINGS
FROM THESSALONIKI
ΣΙΜΙΤΙΑ
Simitia

Dissolve half the yeast in ½ cup (120 ml / 4 fl oz) of the warm water and stir in 3–4 tablespoons of flour. Cover and set aside in a warm place for 24 hours. Shortly before making the dough, dissolve the remaining yeast in ½ cup (120 ml / 4 fl oz) warm water, stir in 3–4 tablespoons of flour and let rise for 15 minutes. Sift the remaining flour with the salt into a large mixing bowl and make a well in the center. Pour in both yeast mixtures, the sugar, oil, and remaining water. Gradually incorporate the flour into the liquid until a sticky dough forms. Knead the dough on a floured work surface for about 15 minutes, until smooth and elastic. Cover and leave to rise until doubled in size. Punch down and roll out into an oblong about ¾-inch (1.5-cm) thick. With a sharp, floured knife, cut the dough lengthwise into ¾-inch (1.5-cm) strips. Roll the strips evenly into 14-inch (35-cm) strands. Brush with water and roll in sesame seeds until completely coated. Pinch the ends together to form rings and arrange on cookie sheets (baking trays) lined with baking parchment. Cover and let rise for about 20 minutes. Meanwhile, preheat the oven to 425°F (220°C / Gas Mark 7). Bake for 10–15 minutes, or until golden brown on the outside, but soft on the inside. Cool on a wire rack and serve warm, preferably on the same day.

Makes 20–25 rings
Preparation time 24 hours (including rising)
Cooking time 15 minutes

☐ p 530

- ½ oz (15 g) fresh yeast or 1½ teaspoons dried yeast
- 1¼ cups (300 ml / ½ pint) warm water
- 4 cups (500 g / 1 lb 2 oz) all-purpose (plain) flour
- 1 teaspoon salt
- ¼ cup (50 g / 2 oz) superfine (caster) sugar
- 2 tablespoons vegetable oil
- 1 cup (175 g / 6 oz) sesame seeds

- 4 cups (500 g / 1 lb 2 oz) strong white bread flour, plus extra for dusting
- 1½ tablespoons rapid-rise (fast-action) yeast
- ½ teaspoon salt
- 4 tablespoons superfine (caster) sugar
- 2 tablespoons grated orange zest
- 4 tablespoons lukewarm water
- 5 tablespoons lukewarm milk
- 2 eggs, lightly beaten
- 5 tablespoons melted butter, plus extra for brushing
- 1 egg yolk
- slivered almonds, for sprinkling

FOR THE FILLING
- 1 egg, lightly beaten
- ½ cup (50 g / 2 oz) blanched almonds, roasted
- 1 cup (175 g / 6 oz) semisweet (plain) chocolate chips

EASTER BREAD WITH CHOCOLATE AND ALMONDS
ΤΣΟΥΡΕΚΙ ΜΕ ΣΟΚΑΛΑΤΑ ΚΑΙ ΑΜΥΓΔΑΛΑ
Tsoureki me sokolata ke amigdala

Easter is the most important traditional feast in Greece. On Easter Sunday, the fires are lit early for the spit-roasting of the Easter lamb, which is often a community affair. After the long fast, all types of food can be eaten during the week after Easter, even on Wednesday and Friday. Special breads, pies, desserts, and dishes with young goat (kid) and lamb all form part of the festivities.

Sift together the flour, yeast, and salt into a large bowl and make a well in the center. Add the sugar, orange zest, lukewarm water, lukewarm milk, and eggs and gradually incorporate the dry ingredients, kneading to a soft dough. Gradually pour in the melted butter and gently knead it into the dough. Cover and let rise in a warm place for 1–2 hours, until doubled in volume. Brush a cookie sheet (baking tray) with melted butter. Divide the dough in half and roll out each piece into a 12 x 16-inch (30 x 40-cm) rectangle. Cut each rectangle widthwise into 3 strips. Brush each strip with the beaten egg and divide the roasted almonds and chocolate chips among them, sprinkling them evenly. Roll into long ropes and pinch the edges to seal. Lay 3 ropes next to each other and braid (plait) them, pressing the ends to seal. Repeat with the remaining 3 ropes. Put the braids (plaits) on the prepared cookie sheet and cover with buttered plastic wrap (cling film). Let rise for about 20 minutes, or until doubled in volume. Meanwhile, preheat the oven to 400°F (200°C / Gas Mark 6). Beat the egg yolk with 1 teaspoon water in a bowl, brush the tops of the loaves with the mixture, and sprinkle with the slivered almonds. Bake for 20–25 minutes, until golden. Let cool and store covered.

Makes 2 loaves
Preparation time 3 hours (including rising)
Cooking time 20–25 minutes

□ p 531

Sesame bread rings from Thessaloniki, p 528

Easter bread with chocolate and almonds, p 529

COOKIES (BISCUITS)

-

ΚΟΥΛΟΥΡΙΑ

-

Koulouria

There are three basic methods for making cookie (biscuit) dough. In one method, the butter is first beaten alone, and then beaten vigorously with sugar so that air bubbles are trapped in the mixture. This light mixture is then mixed gently with eggs and flour. The resulting dough can be rolled out and the cookies can be stamped out with a cookie cutter or shaped by hand. The cookies can be rolled in chopped nuts before baking, or sandwiched together with a filling before or after baking. In the second method, the chilled and diced butter is rubbed into the flour and sugar until the mixture resembles coarse crumbs. Then just enough liquid is added to make the dough come together. The dough is not as pliable as the first type and should be covered and chilled in the refrigerator for 30 minutes before using. It can then be rolled out and stamped out with cookie cutters. The rolled-out dough can also be sprinkled with sweet or savory ingredients, such as ground walnuts or grated cheese, rolled up, and sliced into thin cookies or crackers. In the third method, the ingredients are rubbed lightly by hand until they come together. Honey and syrup-based cookies usually are made in this way.

GENERAL INSTRUCTIONS

For light, crisp, and crumbly cookies (biscuits), follow the quantities in the recipe carefully, keep the ingredients cool, and mix them together gently. Overworking the dough strengthens the gluten in the flour and makes the cookies tough. The dough is easier to handle if it is rolled out between two sheets of nonstick baking parchment. Roll it out to an even thickness to ensure even baking. Use shallow cookie sheets (baking trays), preferably made from anodized aluminum, and line them with baking parchment. All ovens vary, so it is important to pay attention to cooking times. Preheat the oven, set the timer for the shortest time suggested in the recipe, and check the cookies to see if they need more cooking, or have started browning too much. Condensation can make cookies soggy, so leave them to cool completely on a wire rack before storing. Store cooled cookies in an airtight container in a cool, dry place. Nearly all cookies can be frozen successfully if they are tightly wrapped in plastic wrap (cling film).

- 7 tablespoons olive oil
- 1 small leek, white part only, grated
- 2 tablespoons grated onion
- ½ cup (80 g / 3 oz) frozen spinach purée, thawed, or 9 oz (250 g) spinach, coarse stalks removed, cooked and puréed
- 4 tablespoons finely chopped fresh dill
- ¼ teaspoon pepper
- 5 tablespoons melted clarified butter
- 3 cups (350 g / 12 oz) self-rising flour
- 1 teaspoon salt
- ½ teaspoon baking soda (bicarbonate of soda)
- 1½ teaspoons superfine (caster) sugar

SPINACH CRACKERS
ΑΛΜΥΡΑ ΚΟΥΛΟΥΡΙΑ ΜΕ ΣΠΑΝΑΚΙ
Almira koulouria me spanaki

Preheat the oven to 350°F (180°C / Gas Mark 4) and line a cookie sheet (baking tray) with baking parchment. Heat 2 tablespoons of the oil in a small pan. Add the leek and onion and cook over low heat, stirring occasionally, for 5 minutes, until softened. Put the leek and onion into a food processor, add the spinach, dill, pepper, butter, and remaining oil, and process until thoroughly blended. Sift together the flour, salt, baking soda, and sugar into a large bowl and make a well in the center. Pour in the spinach mixture and gradually incorporate the dry ingredients to make a smooth dough. Do not overwork the dough or the crackers will be tough. Pinch off pieces of dough the size of a walnut and roll into ropes ½ inch (1 cm) thick. Twist into rings, bows, or knots, and put them on the prepared cookie sheet, spaced well apart. Bake for 15–20 minutes. Transfer to wire racks and let cool completely. Store in an airtight container.

Makes 30 crackers
Preparation time 1½ hours
Cooking time 15–20 minutes

Note: You can make carrot crackers in the same way by substituting 4 cooked, puréed carrots for the spinach.

- 1 cup (250 ml / 8 fl oz) melted butter, plus extra for brushing
- 3½ cups (400 g / 14 oz) self-rising flour
- 1 lb 2 oz (500 g) feta cheese, crumbled
- 4½ cups (500 g / 1 lb 2 oz) grated Gruyère, kaseri, or Emmenthal cheese
- 2 eggs, lightly beaten
- 2 egg yolks
- ⅓ cup (80 g / 3 oz) sesame seeds

SMALL CHEESE COOKIES (BISCUITS)
ΕΥΚΟΛΑ ΤΥΡΟΠΙΤΑΚΙΑ
Efkola tiropitakia

Preheat the oven to 350°F (180°C / Gas Mark 4). Line a large cookie sheet (baking tray) with baking parchment and brush with melted butter. Combine the flour, both types of cheese, the beaten eggs, and melted butter in a large bowl. Knead gently to form a soft, pliable dough. Pinch off pieces of the dough about the size of an egg, and roll into balls. Put the balls onto the prepared cookie sheet and flatten lightly with the palm of your hand. Beat the egg yolks with 2 teaspoons water in a bowl, brush the glaze over the pies, and sprinkle with the sesame seeds. Bake for about 25 minutes, or until golden. Transfer to wire racks to cool and serve the same day. Store leftovers in the freezer.

Makes 30 cookies
Preparation tine 15 minutes
Cooking time 25 minutes

BREADSTICKS WITH ANISE
ΚΡΙΤΣΙΝΙΑ ΜΕ ΓΛΥΚΑΝΙΣΟ
Kritsinia me glikaniso

Sift together the flour, anise seeds, salt, and baking powder into a bowl and stir in the sugar. Combine the wine, evaporated milk, and oil in another bowl, then add to the flour mixture, and mix using an electric mixer fitted with a dough hook to make a soft dough that pulls away from the side of the bowl and clings around the hook. Do not overwork the dough. Leave it to rest for 10 minutes. Preheat the oven to 350°F (180°C / Gas Mark 4). Line 2 cookie sheets (baking trays) with baking parchment. Roll out the dough into an 8 x 12-inch (20 x 30-cm) rectangle on a lightly floured work surface. Brush the surface with egg white and sprinkle with the seeds of your choice. Using a pizza wheel or sharp knife, cut the dough into thin strips, twist into long sticks, and place on the prepared cookie sheets. Bake for 15–20 minutes. Transfer to wire racks to cool and store in an airtight container. They keep well for up to 1 month.

Makes 30 breadsticks
Preparation time 40 minutes (including resting)
Cooking time 15–20 minutes

□ p 538

- 3 cups (350 g / 12 oz) all-purpose (plain) flour, plus extra for dusting
- 1 teaspoon anise seeds, ground
- 1 teaspoon salt
- 3 teaspoons baking powder
- 3 tablespoons superfine (caster) sugar
- ¾ cup (175 ml / 6 fl oz) white wine
- 2 tablespoons evaporated milk
- 5 tablespoons olive oil
- 1 egg white, lightly beaten
- 4 tablespoons sesame, poppy, dill, or mustard seeds

BREADSTICKS WITH TAHINI
ΚΡΙΤΣΙΝΙΑ ΜΕ ΤΑΧΙΝΙ
Kritsinia me tahini

Sift together the flour, baking powder, and salt into a bowl. If using fresh yeast, mash it to a smooth paste with the lukewarm water and let stand for 5 minutes. If using dried yeast, pour the lukewarm water into a bowl, sprinkle the yeast over the surface, and let stand for 10–15 minutes until frothy, then stir to a smooth paste. Stir the tahini, honey, and oil into the yeast mixture, then gradually add as much flour as necessary to form a soft, pliable dough. Cover and let rise in a warm place for 1½ hours, or until doubled in volume. Grease a cookie sheet (baking tray) with butter. Punch down the dough and roll it out on a lightly floured work surface into an 8 x 16-inch (20 x 40-cm) rectangle. Brush the top with water and sprinkle with sesame seeds. Preheat the oven to 350°F (180°C / Gas Mark 4). Using a pizza wheel or sharp knife, cut into ½-inch (1-cm) wide strips and put on the cookie sheet, spaced well apart. Let rise for 15 minutes. Bake the breadsticks for about 40 minutes, or until fully dried out. Transfer to a wire rack to cool and store in an airtight container.

Makes 40 breadsticks
Preparation time 2 hours (including rising)
Cooking time 40 minutes

- 4 cups (450 g / 1 lb) all-purpose (plain) flour, plus extra for dusting
- 2 teaspoons baking powder
- ½ teaspoon salt
- 1½ oz (40 g) fresh yeast or 1½ tablespoons dried yeast
- 1 cup (250 ml / 8 fl oz) lukewarm water
- 4 tablespoons tahini
- 4 tablespoons honey
- 2 tablespoons sesame oil or corn oil
- butter, for greasing
- black and white sesame seeds, for sprinkling

- 2 cups (225 g / 8 oz) all-purpose (plain) flour or strong white bread flour, plus extra for dusting
- 2 tablespoons dried yeast
- 2–3 cups (450-750 ml / 16-25 fl oz) lukewarm water
- 6 cups (700 g / 1½ lb) barley flour
- 1 tablespoon salt
- 4 tablespoons honey
- ½ cup (120 ml / 4 fl oz) olive oil
- butter, for greasing

CRETAN BARLEY RUSKS
ΚΡΙΘΙΝΑ ΠΑΞΙΜΑΔΙΑ ΚΡΗΤΗΣ
Krithina paximadia kritis

Combine the white flour and yeast in a bowl and add enough lukewarm water to make a thick batter. Let rise in a warm place until doubled in volume. Sift together the barley flour and salt into a large bowl and make a well in the center. Mix the honey with a little of the remaining lukewarm water in a bowl and pour into the well, together with the oil and the yeast mixture. Incorporate the dry ingredients, adding enough of the remaining lukewarm water to form a soft, sticky dough. Knead until the dough comes away from the side of the bowl and is smooth and elastic. Cover with plastic wrap (cling film) and let rise in a warm place for about 2 hours, or until doubled in volume. Meanwhile, grease 2 or 3 large cookie sheets (baking trays) with butter. Punch down and knead the dough for 6–7 minutes on a lightly floured work surface. Divide it into 16–20 pieces and roll each piece into a rope about 10 inches (25 cm) long. Join the ends together, overlapping slightly, and pinch together to form rings. Put them, spaced well apart, on the prepared cookie sheets. Cover with a dish towel and let rise for 1 hour, or until doubled in volume. Meanwhile, preheat the oven to 400°F (200°C / Gas Mark 6). Using a sharp knife, score a line horizontally around the rings so that later they can be easily divided in half. Bake for 1 hour. Remove from the oven and let cool. Cut the rolls in half horizontally along the scored lines. Preheat the oven to its lowest setting and bake the split rolls for 2–3 hours to dry out fully. Let cool and store in airtight containers.

Makes 16–20 rusks
Preparation time 3½ hours (including rising)
Cooking time 3–4 hours

☐ p 539

Breadsticks with anise, p 536

Cretan barley rusks, p 537

539

ALMOND AND RAISIN RUSKS
ΠΑΞΙΜΑΔΙΑ ΜΕ ΑΜΥΓΔΑΛΑ
Paximadia me amigdala

Preheat the oven to 350°F (180°C / Gas Mark 4). Line a 12-inch (30-cm) square baking pan with baking parchment and grease with butter. Sift together the flour and baking powder into a bowl. With an electric mixer, whisk the egg whites with the cream of tartar in a grease-free bowl on high speed until soft peaks begin to form, then gradually whisk in half the sugar, and continue whisking for a few minutes until smooth and glossy. Beat the egg yolks with the remaining sugar in another bowl until thick and pale. Gradually add the brandy and vanilla. With the speed on low, add the flour mixture, a little at a time, alternating with a spoonful of egg whites. Stop beating and gently fold in the remaining egg whites, taking care not to knock out the air. Carefully fold in the raisins and almonds. Pour the batter into the prepared pan and smooth the surface with a metal spatula. Bake for about 45 minutes, or until the top is golden and feels springy. Remove from the oven and let stand for 12 hours, then turn out. Preheat the oven to 300°F (150°C / Gas Mark 2). Using a sharp knife, cut the square into 4 lengths and cut each one crosswise into 10–12 slices. Put them on a large cookie sheet (baking tray) and bake for 15–20 minutes, or until dried out. Let cool, then store in an airtight container.

Makes 40–50 rusks
Preparation time 12½ hours (including standing)
Cooking time 1 hour

▢ p 542

- butter, for greasing
- 2¼ cups (225 g / 9 oz) all-purpose (plain) flour
- 2½ teaspoons baking powder
- 4 eggs, separated
- ½ teaspoon cream of tartar
- scant 1 cup (175 g / 6 oz) superfine (caster) sugar
- 2 tablespoons brandy
- 1 teaspoon vanilla extract
- 1¾ cups (250 g / 9 oz) raisins
- 2¼ cups (250 g / 9 oz) roasted and chopped almonds

ALMOND COOKIES (BISCUITS)
ΜΠΙΣΚΟΤΑ ΑΜΥΓΔΑΛΟΥ
Biskota amigdalou

Preheat the oven to 350°F (180°C / Gas Mark 4) and grease a cookie sheet (baking tray) with butter. Beat together the butter and sugar with an electric mixer until pale and fluffy. Beating constantly, add the eggs, one at a time, then add the almond extract. Sift together the flour and baking powder into another bowl and fold gently into the creamed mixture, a little at a time, alternating with the ground almonds. Knead lightly until smooth and soft, like choux pastry dough in consistency. Place the dough in a pastry (piping) bag fitted with a ½-inch (1-cm) plain tip (nozzle) and pipe into large rosettes on the prepared cookie sheet. Bake for about 15 minutes, or until lightly golden. Transfer to a wire rack to cool. Store in an airtight container.

Makes 40–50 cookies
Preparation time 20 minutes
Cooking time 15 minutes

- 1 cup (225 g / 8 oz) butter, softened, plus extra for greasing
- 2¼ cups (250 g / 9 oz) confectioners' (icing) sugar
- 2 eggs
- ½ teaspoon almond extract
- 3 cups (350 g / 12 oz) all-purpose (plain) flour
- 3 teaspoons baking powder
- 2 cups (225 g / 8 oz) roasted and ground almonds

- 4 cups (450 g / 1 lb) all-purpose (plain) flour, plus extra for dusting
- ½ teaspoon baking soda (bicarbonate of soda)
- 1 teaspoon baking powder
- ¾ cup (175 ml / 6 fl oz) olive oil
- 4 tablespoons (50 g / 2 oz) butter, softened
- ½ cup (100 g / 3½ oz) superfine (caster) sugar
- ½ cup (120 ml / 4 fl oz) freshly squeezed orange juice
- 2 tablespoons brandy
- 1 tablespoon grated orange zest
- 1 cup (120 g / 4 oz) walnuts, finely chopped
- 1 teaspoon ground cinnamon
- ¼ teaspoon ground cloves

FOR THE SYRUP
- 1 cup (250 ml / 8 fl oz) honey
- 1 cup (200 g / 7 oz) superfine (caster) sugar

CHRISTMAS HONEY-DIPPED COOKIES (BISCUITS)
ΜΕΛΟΜΑΚΑΡΟΝΑ
Melomakarona

Sift together the flour, baking soda, and baking powder into a bowl and make a well in the center. Put the oil, butter, sugar, orange juice, brandy, and orange zest into a food processor and process at high speed. Pour the mixture into the well and gradually incorporate the dry ingredients. Mix gently to combine, without kneading, to form a soft dough. Preheat the oven to 350°F (180°C / Gas Mark 4). Roll out the dough on a lightly floured work surface to ½ inch (1 cm) thick and stamp out rounds, ovals, or squares with cookie cutters. Put the cookies onto ungreased cookie sheets (baking trays) and crosshatch the tops with the tines of a fork. Bake for about 30 minutes, or until golden brown. Meanwhile, make the syrup. Put the honey and sugar into a large pan, pour in 1 cup (250 ml / 8 fl oz) water, and bring to a boil, stirring until the sugar has dissolved. Simmer for 5 minutes, skimming off the froth. Pour the syrup over the cookies as soon as they come out of the oven. When all the syrup has been absorbed, turn them over, and let cool completely. Combine the walnuts, cinnamon, and cloves in a bowl and sprinkle the mixture over the cookies. Transfer to a platter and cover with plastic wrap (cling film) until ready to serve. They keep well, covered, at room temperature for up to 3 weeks.

Makes 20–25 cookies
Preparation time 30 minutes
Cooking time 30 minutes

□ p 543

Almond and raisin rusks, p 540

Christmas honey-dipped cookies (biscuits), p 541

CINNAMON RUSKS FROM CRETE
ΠΑΞΙΜΑΔΙΑ ΚΑΝΕΛΑΤΑ
Paximadia kanelata

Preheat the oven to 350°F (180°C / Gas Mark 4) and grease a baking pan with butter. Put the oil, wine, cinnamon, orange zest, sugar, cloves, baking soda, and baking powder into a food processor and process until thoroughly combined. Transfer the mixture to a large bowl and stir in the hazelnuts. Gradually add as much flour as required to make a smooth, pliable dough. Divide the dough into 3 pieces and, using your hands, roll each piece on a lightly floured work surface into long cylinders about 1½ inches (4 cm) thick. Roll the cylinders in the sesame seeds to coat and put them in the prepared pan. Cut into ½-inch (1-cm) wide slices, without cutting all the way through. Bake for about 40 minutes. Remove from the oven, let cool for 5 minutes, separate the slices, and lay them flat on a cookie sheet (baking tray) lined with baking parchment. Reduce the oven temperature to 300°F (150°C / Gas Mark 2) and bake for 15 minutes longer. Turn the rusks over and bake for another 15 minutes, or until crisp. Transfer to wire racks to cool and store in an airtight container. They will remain crisp for several months.

Makes 30–40 rusks
Preparation time 30 minutes
Cooking time 1 hour 10 minutes

- butter, for greasing
- ¾ cup (175 ml / 6 fl oz) corn oil
- ½ cup (120 ml / 4 fl oz) dry white wine
- 1½ teaspoons ground cinnamon
- 2 tablespoons grated orange zest
- ¾ cup (150 g / 5 oz) superfine (caster) sugar
- ¼ teaspoon ground cloves
- ½ teaspoon baking soda (bicarbonate of soda)
- 1 tablespoon baking powder
- ½ cup (50 g / 2 oz) hazelnuts, roasted and finely chopped
- 4 cups (450 g / 1 lb) all-purpose (plain) flour, plus extra for dusting
- ⅓ cup (80 g / 3 oz) sesame seeds

ANISE-FLAVORED HAZELNUT COOKIES (BISCUITS)
ΚΟΥΛΟΥΡΑΚΙΑ ΜΕ ΓΛΥΚΑΝΙΣΟ ΚΑΙ ΦΟΥΝΤΟΥΚΙΑ
Koulourakia me glikaniso ke foudoukia

Preheat the oven to 350°F (180°C / Gas Mark 4). Sift together the flour, baking soda, baking powder, and salt into a large bowl. Combine the orange juice, olive oil, corn oil, sugar, ouzo, and anise extract in another bowl. Pour the mixture into the dry ingredients, add the ground hazelnuts, and mix to a soft, pliable dough. Roll out the dough between 2 sheets of baking parchment to ½ inch (1 cm) thick and stamp out round, square, or heart-shaped cookies with a cookie cutter. Put them on a cookie sheet (baking tray) and bake for about 20 minutes, or until lightly golden. Let cool and store in an airtight container. They keep for several months.

Makes 30 cookies
Preparation time 30 minutes
Cooking time 20 minutes

- 2½–3 cups (275–350 g / 10–12 oz) all-purpose (plain) flour
- ½ teaspoon baking soda (bicarbonate of soda)
- 1 tablespoon baking powder
- ¼ teaspoon salt
- 4 tablespoons freshly squeezed orange juice
- ½ cup (120 ml / 4 fl oz) olive oil
- ½ cup (120 ml / 4 fl oz) corn oil
- ½ cup (100 g / 3½ oz) superfine (caster) sugar
- 4 tablespoons ouzo
- 1 teaspoon anise extract or finely ground anise seeds
- ½ cup (50 g / 2 oz) ground hazelnuts

FOR THE DOUGH

- 3½ cups (400 g / 14 oz) self-rising flour
- 1 cup (225 g / 8 oz) butter, chilled and diced
- 4–5 tablespoons plain yogurt
- butter, for greasing
- confectioners' (icing) sugar, for dusting

FOR THE FILLING

- 4 large apples, peeled and coarsely grated
- 2 tablespoons freshly squeezed lemon juice
- 4 tablespoons superfine (caster) sugar
- ½ teaspoon ground cinnamon, plus extra for dusting
- ½ teaspoon ground cloves
- ½ teaspoon freshly grated nutmeg
- 1 cup (120 g / 4 oz) walnuts, coarsely chopped

APPLE-FILLED COOKIES (BISCUITS)
ΜΗΛΟΠΙΤΑΚΙΑ
Milopitakia

Sift the flour into a large bowl. Add the diced butter and rub it in with your fingertips until the mixture resembles coarse crumbs. Lightly stir in the yogurt and mix until the dough just begins to come together. It should feel crumbly. Do not knead, just gather all the crumbs from the side of the bowl into a ball, pressing them together with your hands. Cover and chill in the refrigerator for 30 minutes. Meanwhile, make the filling. Put the apples, lemon juice, and sugar into a small pan and cook over low heat, stirring constantly, until all the liquid has evaporated. Remove from the heat and stir in the spices and walnuts. Preheat the oven to 350°F (180°C / Gas Mark 4) and grease 1 or 2 large cookie sheets (baking trays) with butter. Divide the dough into 30 pieces. Roll each piece into a ball, then press your thumb into the ball to form a large hollow. Spoon the filling into the hollows and press the dough over it to seal. Pat them down very gently. Put the balls, seam side down, on the prepared cookie sheets and bake for about 35 minutes, or until lightly golden. Remove from the oven and sift a little confectioners' sugar and cinnamon on top, then let cool. They can be kept for 2–3 days at room temperature and for several months in the freezer.

Makes 30 cookies
Preparation time 1 hour (including chilling)
Cooking time 35 minutes

▢ p 546

Apple-filled cookies (biscuits), p 545

sweet cheese tarts from Sifnos, p 548

SWEET CHEESE TARTS FROM SIFNOS
ΜΕΛΙΤΙΝΙΑ ΣΙΦΝΟΥ
Melitinia sifnou

Sift together the flour and salt into a large bowl and make a well
in the center. Add the melted butter and lukewarm water and gradually
incorporate the dry ingredients, adding more flour if necessary, to make
a smooth elastic dough. Divide the dough into 20 small balls, put them
on a floured work surface, cover with a damp dish towel, and let rest for
1–2 hours. Meanwhile, prepare the filling. Put both types of cheese and
the confectioners' sugar into a bowl and beat until thoroughly blended.
Add the eggs, 1 at a time, then add the mastic or vanilla. Gradually
fold in the flour. Preheat the oven to 350°F (180°C / Gas Mark 4)
and brush 2 cookie sheets (baking trays) with melted butter. Roll out the
dough balls on a lightly floured work surface to 4-inch (10-cm) rounds.
Put 1 tablespoon of the filling in the center of each and spread it evenly,
leaving a ½-inch (1-cm) margin all around. Using your thumb and index
finger turn up the margin to make a rim, then pinch the rim to flute. Put
the tarts on the prepared cookie sheets and bake for about 20 minutes,
until the tops are golden. Transfer to wire racks to cool and store in an
airtight container in the refrigerator. They keep for 1 week in the refrigerator and for several months in the freezer.

Makes 40 tarts
Preparation time 1½–2½ hours (including resting)
Cooking time 20 minutes

☐ p 547

☐ p 547

FOR THE DOUGH
- 2 cups (225 g / 8 oz) all-purpose (plain) flour, plus extra for dusting
- ¼ teaspoon salt
- 2 tablespoons melted butter, plus extra for brushing
- ½ cup (120 ml / 4 fl oz) lukewarm water

FOR THE FILLING
- 8 oz (225 g) mizithra or drained cottage cheese
- 8 oz (225 g) ricotta cheese
- 3½ cups (400 g / 14 oz) confectioners' (icing) sugar
- 2 eggs, lightly beaten
- ¼ teaspoon ground mastic or 1 teaspoon vanilla extract
- 1 cup (120 g / 4 oz) self-rising flour

FOR THE DOUGH

- butter, for greasing
- 1¾ cups (200 g / 7 oz) all-purpose (plain) flour
- pinch of salt
- 2 tablespoons superfine (caster) sugar
- 1½ tablespoons olive oil
- ½ tablespoon grated lemon zest
- ½ teaspoon vanilla extract
- 1½ teaspoons ammonium bicarbonate or baking soda (bicarbonate of soda)
- equal quantities olive and corn oil, for deep-frying
- finely chopped walnuts, for sprinkling

FOR THE SYRUP

- 1¼ cups (250 g / 9 oz) superfine (caster) sugar
- ½ cup (120 ml / 4 fl oz) honey

PHOENICIAN HONEY COOKIES (BISCUITS)
ΦΟΙΝΙΚΙΑ
Finikia

It has been said that the Phoenicians introduced these delicious honey-dipped cookies to the people of Greece.

Preheat the oven to 400°F (200°C / Gas Mark 6) and grease 2 cookie sheets (baking trays) with butter. Sift together the flour and salt into a large bowl and make a well in the center. Add the sugar, oil, lemon zest, and vanilla. Stir the baking soda into 5 tablespoons water in a bowl and pour into the well. Using a spoon, gradually incorporate the dry ingredients, then knead gently to a soft and pliable dough, adding a little more water if necessary. Break off small pieces of dough and roll into cylinders the size of your thumb, then press lightly to flatten. Put them onto the prepared baking sheet, spaced well apart, and bake for 20–25 minutes, or until lightly golden. Remove from the oven. To make the syrup, put the sugar, honey, and 1¼ cups (300 ml / ½ pint) water into a pan and bring to a boil. Boil for 5 minutes, then remove from the heat. Pour a mixture of equal parts olive and corn oil into a heavy pan to a depth of 3 inches (7.5 cm) and heat it to 375°F (190°C), or until a cube of bread browns in 30 seconds. Carefully drop batches of the cookies into the hot oil and fry for a few minutes, until golden brown. Remove with a slotted spoon, drain well, and drop into the hot syrup. Let absorb syrup for 3–4 minutes. Remove with a slotted spoon, transfer to a serving platter, and sprinkle with finely chopped walnuts.

Makes 40–45 cookies
Preparation time 30 minutes
Cooking time 35 minutes

▢ p 550

Phoenician honey cookies (biscuits), p 549

Lenten marzipan cookies (biscuits) from Thessaloniki, p 552

LENTEN MARZIPAN COOKIES (BISCUITS) FROM THESSALONIKI
ΣΚΑΛΤΣΟΥΝΙΑ ΘΕΣΣΑΛΟΝΙΚΗΣ
Skaltsounia thessalonikis

Put the almonds, potato, sugar, rosewater or brandy, and vanilla or almond extract into a bowl and mash with a pastry blender or a fork to make a firm, pliable mixture. Cover and chill for about 2 hours. Meanwhile, make the filling. Combine the walnuts, golden raisins, crystallized fruit, and jam in a bowl. Preheat the oven to 350°F (180°C / Gas Mark 4) and line a cookie sheet (baking tray) with baking parchment. Roll out the dough on a lightly floured work surface into 4-inch (10-cm) rounds, about ⅛ inch (3 mm) thick. Spoon 1 table-spoon of the filling onto one half of each round and fold the other side over to form a crescent. Dip your fingertips into confectioners' sugar and lightly press the edges to seal. Place the crescents on the cookie sheet and bake for 10–15 minutes, until lightly golden. Let cool for 5 minutes. Carefully transfer the cookies to a sheet of wax (greaseproof) paper dusted with confectioners' sugar. Sift plenty of confectioners' sugar over them and dust with ground cinnamon. Store in an airtight container.

Makes 22–24 cookies
Preparation time 2½ hours (including chilling)
Cooking time 15 minutes

⬜ p 551

- 4 cups (450 g / 1 lb) blanched almonds, finely ground
- 1 small cooked and peeled potato, about 3½ oz (100 g)
- 2¼ cups (250 g / 9 oz) confectioners' (icing) sugar
- 1 teaspoon rosewater or brandy
- ½ teaspoon vanilla or almond extract
- all-purpose (plain) flour, for dusting
- confectioners' sugar and ground cinnamon, for dusting

FOR THE FILLING
- ½ cup (50 g / 2 oz) walnuts, coarsely chopped
- ⅔ cup (80 g / 3 oz) golden raisins
- ½ cup (80 g / 3 oz) finely chopped crystallized apricots and orange
- 2 tablespoons apricot jam

EASTER COOKIES (BISCUITS)
ΚΟΥΛΟΥΡΑΚΙΑ ΠΑΣΧΑΛΙΝΑ
Koulourakia paskalina

Preheat the oven to 400°F (200°C / Gas Mark 6) and grease a cookie sheet (baking tray) with butter. Beat together the butter and sugar with an electric mixer. Beating constantly, add the eggs and 2 of the egg yolks, 1 at a time, then add the vanilla. Fit the mixer with a dough hook. Combine the baking soda and milk in a bowl. Beating constantly, add the milk mixture in 2–3 batches, alternating with the flour. Knead the mixture, adding flour as necessary to form a smooth, easy-to-handle dough. Roll pieces of the dough into 8-inch (20-cm) long, finger-thick cylinders. Fold in half, twist and put them on the cookie sheet, spaced well apart. Beat the remaining egg yolks with 2 teaspoons water in a bowl and brush the cookies with the mixture. Bake for 20–30 minutes.

Makes 60–80 cookies
Preparation time 30 minutes
Cooking time 20–30 minutes

⬜ p 554

- 1 cup (225 g / 8 oz) butter, softened, plus extra for greasing
- 1½ cups (300 g / 11 oz) superfine (caster) sugar
- 4 eggs
- 4 egg yolks
- 3 teaspoons vanilla extract
- 1 oz (25 g) baking soda (bicarbonate of soda)
- ½ cup (120 ml / 4 fl oz) milk
- 9 cups (1 kg / 2¼ lb) all-purpose (plain) flour

FOR THE FILLING

- 1 cup (120 g / 4 oz) walnuts, ground
- 1¼ cups (150 g / 5 oz) blanched almonds, roasted and ground
- 4 tablespoons raisins
- ½ teaspoon ground mastic
- 2–3 tablespoons honey or jam

FOR THE DOUGH

- butter, for greasing
- 3 cups (350 g / 12 oz) all-purpose (plain) flour, plus extra for dusting
- 2 teaspoons baking powder
- ½ teaspoon baking soda (bicarbonate of soda)
- ½ teaspoon ground mastic
- ¼ teaspoon salt
- 1 cup (250 ml / 8 fl oz) sesame oil or vegetable oil
- ⅔ cup (150 ml / ¼ pint) freshly squeezed orange juice
- 4 tablespoons superfine (caster) sugar

TO DECORATE

- 1 cup (250 ml / 8 fl oz) rosewater
- 1⅓ cups (160 g / 5½ oz) confectioners' (icing) sugar

MASTIC-FLAVORED MARZIPAN COOKIES (BISCUITS)
ΣΚΑΛΤΣΟΥΝΙΑ ΜΕ ΜΑΣΤΙΧΑ
Skaltsounia me mastiha

Preheat the oven to 350°F (180°C / Gas Mark 4) and grease 2 cookie sheets (baking trays) with butter. To make the filling, combine the walnuts, almonds, raisins, and mastic in a bowl. Stir in enough honey or jam to bind the mixture together. To make the dough, sift together the flour, baking powder, baking soda, mastic, and salt into a large bowl and make a well in the center. Put the oil, orange juice, and sugar into a blender and process for 1–2 minutes, then pour into the dry ingredients. Gradually incorporate the dry ingredients to make a soft, pliable dough (avoid overworking). Roll out the dough on a lightly floured work surface to a ⅛-inch (3-mm) thick sheet. Stamp out rounds with a plain 4-inch (10-cm) cookie cutter. Place 1 tablespoon of the filling in the center of each round and fold in half to create a crescent shape. Press the edges with your fingers to seal and put the cookies on the prepared cookie sheets. Bake for 25–30 minutes, or until lightly golden. Remove from the oven and while still warm, quickly dip them, one at a time, in the rosewater and roll in the confectioners' sugar. Store in an airtight container.

Makes 24 cookies
Preparation time 30 minutes
Cooking time 30 minutes

- 1 lb (450 g) unsalted mizithra or ricotta cheese
- 2–3 tablespoons heavy (double) cream (optional)
- ½ teaspoon vanilla extract (optional)
- vegetable oil, for deep-frying
- honey, grape syrup, or confectioners' (icing) sugar, to serve

FOR THE BATTER

- 1 egg
- 1 cup (250 ml / 8 fl oz) milk
- ½ teaspoon baking powder
- 2 cups (225 g / 8 oz) all-purpose (plain) flour

LITTLE MIZITHRA BALLS FROM CRETE
ΜΑΛΕΒΙΖΙΩΤΙΚΑ ΜΥΖΗΘΡΟΠΙΤΑΚΙΑ
Maleviziotika mizithropitakia

To make the batter, beat the egg with the milk and baking powder in a bowl and gradually add as much flour as necessary to make a thick batter. Let the batter rest for 1 hour. Pinch off pieces of cheese and shape them into balls about the size of a walnut. If the mizithra crumbles and is hard to shape, add the cream and vanilla and work in until the cheese holds together. Heat the oil in a deep-fryer to 350–375°F (180–190°C). Dip the cheese balls in the batter to coat, draining off the excess. Add to the hot oil, a few at a time, and cook until golden. Transfer to a platter with a slotted spoon and serve drizzled with honey or grape syrup, or sprinkled with confectioners' sugar.

Makes 30 balls
Preparation time 1¼ hours (including resting)
Cooking time 15 minutes

Easter cookies (biscuits), p 552

Walnut tarts, p 559

MAHLAB COOKIES (BISCUITS)
ΚΟΥΛΟΥΡΑΚΙΑ ΜΕ ΜΑΧΛΕΠΙ
Koulourakia me mahlepi

Preheat the oven to 400°F (200°C / Gas Mark 6) and lightly grease
2 cookie sheets (baking trays) with butter. Sift together the flour and
mahlab into a bowl. Beat together the butter and sugar in another bowl
using an electric mixer on high speed. Fit the dough hook and, beating
constantly on low speed, add the flour, a little at a time, alternating with
the yogurt. Add enough flour to make a soft, pliable dough. Roll small
pieces of the dough into a short, broad cigar shape, then turn the
tapered ends in opposite directions to form the letter S. Put the cookies
on the prepared cookie sheet. Beat the egg yolk with 1 teaspoon water
in a bowl, brush the tops of the cookies with the mixture, and sprinkle
with sesame seeds. Bake for 15 minutes, or until golden. Let cool and
store in an airtight container. They keep well for up to a week.

Makes 45–50 cookies
Preparation time 20 minutes
Cooking time 15 minutes

- butter, for greasing
- 3½ cups (400 g / 14 oz) self-rising flour
- 1 teaspoon (225 g / 8 oz) ground mahlab
- 1 cup (225 g / 8 oz) soft butter
- scant 1 cup (175 g / 6 oz) superfine (caster) sugar
- ⅔ cup (150 ml / ¼ pint) plain yogurt
- 1 egg yolk
- sesame seeds, for sprinkling

PISTACHIO COOKIES (BISCUITS)
ΚΟΥΛΟΥΡΑΚΙΑ ΜΕ ΦΥΣΤΙΚΙ ΑΙΓΙΝΗΣ
Koulourakia me fistiki eginis

Preheat the oven to 400°F (200°C / Gas Mark 6). Line 1 or 2 cookie
sheets (baking trays) with baking parchment and grease with butter.
Sift together the flour, cornstarch, baking powder, and salt into a bowl.
Using an electric mixer, beat together the butter and sugar in another
bowl until smooth and fluffy. Beating constantly, add the egg. Gently
stir in the lemon zest, then gradually fold in the flour, a little at a time,
alternating with the finely ground pistachio nuts. Knead gently until the
dough is soft and pliable. Pinch off pieces of dough the size of a small
egg, and roll into 2-inch (5-cm) long strips the thickness of your thumb.
Brush with the egg white and roll them in the coarsely ground pistachios
to coat. Put them on the prepared cookie sheets, spaced well apart,
and flatten lightly, pressing with your fingers. Bake for about 15 minutes.
Cool and store in an airtight container. They keep well for up to 1 month.

Makes 30–35 cookies
Preparation time 30 minutes
Cooking time 15 minutes

- 1 cup (225 g / 8 oz) butter, plus extra for greasing
- 2 cups (225 g / 8 oz) all-purpose (plain) flour
- ½ cup cornstarch (cornflour)
- 2 teaspoons baking powder
- ¼ teaspoon salt
- 1 cup (120 g / 4 oz) confectioners' (icing) sugar
- 1 egg
- 1 teaspoon grated lemon zest
- 1 cup (120 g / 4 oz) pistachio nuts, roasted and finely ground
- 1 egg white, lightly beaten
- ½ cup (50 g / 2 oz) pistachio nuts, coarsely ground

- butter, for greasing
- 1½ cups (300 g / 11 oz) superfine (caster) sugar
- 2 tablespoons unsweetened cocoa powder
- 2 tablespoons all-purpose (plain) flour
- ½ teaspoon ground cinnamon
- 2 cups (225 g / 8 oz) walnuts, ground
- 3 egg whites, lightly beaten
- Chocolate frosting (icing), p 53 (optional)

WALNUT MACAROONS
ΚΑΡΥΔΑΤΑ ΤΗΣ ΦΩΤΙΑΣ
Karidata tis fotias

Line a cookie sheet (baking tray) with baking parchment and grease with butter. Sift together the sugar, cocoa powder, flour, and cinnamon into a heatproof bowl. Add the walnuts and egg whites, set the bowl over a pan of barely simmering water, and cook, stirring constantly, until hot and thoroughly mixed. Remove from the heat and let cool slightly. The mixture thickens as it cools, so as soon it is thick enough to pipe, spoon it into a pastry (piping) bag fitted with a ½-inch (1-cm) plain tip (nozzle). Pipe 1½-inch (4-cm) rounds, spaced about 1 inch (2.5 cm) apart, onto the prepared cookie sheet. Preheat the oven to 400°F (200°C / Gas Mark 6). Let the piped macaroons stand for about 10 minutes, until cooled and set. Bake the macaroons for 15–18 minutes. Let cool on the cookie sheet for 5 minutes, then remove carefully with a spatula, and transfer to a wire rack to cool completely. Sandwich pairs of macaroons together with chocolate frosting if you like. Store in an airtight container.

Makes 20 macaroons
Preparation time 45 minutes (including cooling)
Cooking time 15–18 minutes

- ½ cup (120 ml / 4 fl oz) melted butter, plus extra for brushing
- ⅓ cup (80 g / 3 oz) sesame seeds
- 3½ cups (400 g / 14 oz) self-rising flour
- ½ cup (120 ml / 4 fl oz) vegetable oil
- ½ cup (120 ml / 4 fl oz) white wine
- ½ cup (100 g / 3½ oz) superfine (caster) sugar
- 1 egg white, lightly beaten
- sesame seeds, to coat

WINE COOKIES (BISCUITS)
ΚΟΥΛΟΥΡΑΚΙΑ ΜΕΘΥΣΜΕΝΑ
Koulourakia methismena

Preheat the oven to 350°F (180°C / Gas Mark 4) and brush 2 cookie sheets (baking trays) with melted butter. Spread out the sesame seeds in a baking pan and toast lightly in the oven, then remove, and let cool. Sift the flour into a bowl and stir in the sesame seeds. Put the oil, wine, sugar, and butter into a food processor or blender and process for 1–2 minutes, until thoroughly combined. Pour the mixture into a large bowl, gradually stir in the dry ingredients, and knead lightly to a pliable dough. Avoid over-kneading. Roll out to ¼ inch (5 mm) thick on a lightly floured work surface and stamp out shapes with cookie cutters or cut out by hand. Brush the cookies all over with the beaten egg white and roll them in sesame seeds until well coated. Put them on the prepared cookie sheets and bake for about 15 minutes. Let cool and store in an airtight container. They keep well for up to 1 month.

Makes 30–40 cookies
Preparation time 20 minutes
Cooking time 15 minutes

CRETAN RAISIN CAKES
ΣΤΑΦΙΔΩΤΑ ΚΡΗΤΗΣ
Stafidota kritis

Preheat the oven to 350°F (180°C / Gas Mark 4) and brush 2 or 3 cookie sheets (baking trays) with oil. Spread out the sesame seeds in a baking pan and toast in the oven until just golden. To make the dough, put the oil, sugar, orange juice, raki or brandy, and orange zest into a food processor and process until thoroughly blended. Sift together the flour, baking soda, and baking powder into a bowl and make a well in the center. Pour in the liquid ingredients and gradually incorporate the dry ingredients to make a smooth dough that comes away easily from your fingers. Do not overwork. Gather into a ball and let rest for 30 minutes. Meanwhile, make the filling. Put the raisins, golden raisins, and sesame seeds into the food processor and process to a paste. Transfer the mixture to a bowl and stir in the ground almonds, ground walnuts, spices, and honey. Divide the dough into 35–40 pieces and roll them out on a lightly floured work surface into rectangular sheets ¼ inch (5 mm) thick. Place 1 tablespoon of the filling down the center of each and wrap the dough around the filling to form oblong cookies (biscuits). Brush with a little water and roll in sesame seeds to coat. Put them on the prepared cookie sheets, flatten with the palm of your hand, and bake for about 40 minutes, or until golden.

Makes 40 cookies
Preparation time 1 hour (including resting)
Cooking time 40 minutes

FOR THE DOUGH
- 1 cup (250 ml / 8 fl oz) olive oil, plus extra for brushing
- ½ cup (100 g / 3 ½ oz) superfine (caster) sugar
- 5 tablespoons freshly squeezed orange juice
- 3 tablespoons raki or brandy
- 1 tablespoon grated orange zest
- 3 cups (350 g / 12 oz) all-purpose (plain) flour, plus extra for dusting
- ½ teaspoon baking soda (bicarbonate of soda)
- 1 teaspoon baking powder

FOR THE FILLING
- 2 tablespoons sesame seeds
- generous ½ cup (80 g / 3 oz) raisins
- 1⅔ cups (225 g / 8 oz) golden raisins
- 4 tablespoons finely ground blanched almonds
- ⅔ cup (65 g / 2 ½ oz) walnuts, finely ground
- 2 teaspoons ground cinnamon
- ½ teaspoon ground cloves
- 2 tablespoons honey
- sesame seeds, for coating

SESAME SEED HONEY BARS
ΠΑΣΤΕΛΙ ΜΕ ΜΕΛΙ
Pasteli me meli

Preheat the oven to 350°F (180°C / Gas Mark 4) and generously oil a marble slab or other work surface. Spread out the sesame seeds in a baking pan and toast in the oven until just golden. Meanwhile, combine the honey and sugar in a heavy, nonstick pan and cook for about 10 minutes, until a candy (sugar) thermometer registers 475°F (240°C). Turn off the heat and stir in the sesame seeds. Stir the mixture well, carefully pour it onto the oiled surface, and spread it with an oiled rolling pin into a ¼-inch (5-mm) thick rectangle. While it is still warm, score with a sharp knife into pieces and then let cool completely. Break apart by placing a knife in the score marks and tapping it gently with a spoon. Wrap the pieces in plastic wrap (cling film) and store in a cool dry place. It keeps for up to 1 year.

Makes 56 pieces
Preparation time 1 hour (including cooling)
Cooking time 10 minutes

- corn oil, for greasing
- 2¼ cups (500 g / 1 lb 2 oz) sesame seeds
- generous 1 cup (250 g / 9 oz) honey
- 1 cup (200 g / 7 oz) superfine (caster) sugar

- butter, for greasing
- 4 eggs
- 1½ cups (300 g / 11 oz) superfine (caster) sugar
- 1 teaspoon vanilla extract
- 2¾ cups (300 g / 11 oz) walnuts, coarsely ground
- ⅔ cup (65 g / 2½ oz) finely ground rusks
- ⅓ cup (65 g / 2½ oz) grated semisweet (plain) chocolate
- ½ teaspoon baking powder

WALNUT COOKIES (BISCUITS)
ΚΑΡΥΔΑΤΑ
Karidata

Preheat the oven to 350°F (180°C / Gas Mark 4). Line a cookie sheet (baking tray) with baking parchment and grease with butter. Beat together the eggs and sugar in a bowl with an electric mixer on high speed until thick and pale, then stir in the vanilla. Combine the ground walnuts and rusks, grated chocolate, and baking powder in another bowl and gently fold into the egg mixture. The batter should be thick enough to be shaped, so it may be necessary to add 1–2 extra tablespoons of ground rusks or nuts. Shape the dough into balls the size of a small walnut and place them on the prepared cookie sheet, spaced well apart. Bake for 10 minutes. Transfer to wire racks to cool and store in an airtight container.

Makes 30 cookies
Preparation time 30 minutes
Cooking time 10 minutes

- 1 cup (250 ml / 8 fl oz) melted clarified butter, plus extra for brushing
- 6 sheets of ready-made phyllo (filo)
- ½ cup (120 ml / 4 fl oz) orange marmalade
- 6 eggs
- 1 cup (200 g / 7 oz) superfine (caster) sugar
- 2 cups (225 g / 8 oz) walnuts, chopped
- 2 tablespoons grated orange zest
- 2 tablespoons bread crumbs
- confectioners' (icing) sugar, for dusting

WALNUT TARTS
ΦΟΡΜΑΚΙΑ ΜΕ ΚΑΡΥΔΙΑ
Formakia me karidia

Preheat the oven to 400°F (200°C / Gas Mark 6) and brush two 12-cup muffin pans with melted butter. Stack 3 sheets of phyllo, one on top of the other, brushing each with melted butter. Stamp out 4½-inch (12-cm) rounds with a cookie cutter and use to line the prepared muffin pans. Put 1 teaspoon of marmalade in each. Beat together the eggs and sugar in a bowl until pale and fluffy. Stir in the walnuts, orange zest, and bread crumbs. Spoon the mixture into the tarts and bake for about 30 minutes, until lightly browned. Remove the tarts from the pans and drain on paper towels. Let cool, then dust with confectioners' sugar. Store in an airtight container.

Makes 24 tarts
Preparation time 30 minutes
Cooking time 30 minutes

□ p 555

CAKES

-

KEIK

-

Keik

Successful results in cake-making depend upon all the ingredients being measured accurately. Always use standard measuring cups and spoons. For standard cake batters made with butter, sugar and eggs, whisk in as much air to the batter as possible before adding the flour. This air expands during baking and causes the cake to rise. The ingredients of eggless cakes should be lightly and quickly mixed together by rubbing the fat into the flour by hand. Overworking the batter will make the cake tough.

Pour the batter into the size of cake pan specified in the recipe, filling it to around two-thirds full. The cooking time will vary according to the size of the pan. The same quantity of batter poured into a deep pan requires longer cooking time than if it were spread out into a wide, shallow pan. Always preheat the oven to the correct temperature. To test whether a cake is cooked, insert a wooden toothpick or skewer into the center, and if it comes out clean, the cake is cooked. You can also press very gently on the top of the cake in the center to check whether it feels firm, or look to see if it has shrunken away from the sides if the pan. Both are signs that the cake is cooked.

Glazing or frosting (icing) a cake not only adds flavor, but also helps to keep it moist. The simplest glaze is made with confectioners' (icing) sugar and a little warm water. Stir the water, a little at a time, into the sugar until a thick mixture forms. The glaze can be flavored by adding a little vanilla extract or grated orange or lemon zest. It should be spread on top of the cake while the cake is still warm.

ALMOND CAKE
ΚΕΙΚ ΑΜΥΓΔΑΛΟΥ
Keik amigdalou

Preheat the oven to 350°F (180°C / Gas Mark 4) and grease an 8-cup (2-litre / 3½-pint) turban or ring mold with butter. Sift together the flour, almonds, baking powder, and salt into a large bowl. Whisk the egg whites in a grease-free bowl with an electric mixer on high speed until soft peaks form. Add the sugar, 1 tablespoon at a time, and continue to whisk until the meringue becomes firm and glossy. Put the oil, orange juice, and almond extract into a food processor or blender and process until thoroughly combined and slightly thickened. Pour the mixture into the dry ingredients and fold them in. Stir a few spoonfuls of the beaten egg whites into the batter to loosen it, then gently fold in the remainder. Pour it into the prepared mold, filling it two-thirds full, and bake for about 50 minutes. Let the cake cool completely before cutting it. Store it in an airtight container for 3–4 days. It freezes well for several months.

Makes 1 large cake
Preparation time 20 minutes
Cooking time 50 minutes

- butter, for greasing
- 1½ cups (175 g / 6 oz) all-purpose (plain) flour
- 1½ cups (175 g / 6 oz) finely ground almonds
- 3 teaspoons baking powder
- pinch of salt
- 6 egg whites
- 1½ cups (300 g / 11 oz) superfine (caster) sugar
- ⅔ cup (150 ml / ¼ pint) light olive oil or corn oil
- ½ cup (120 ml / 4 fl oz) freshly squeezed orange juice
- ¼ teaspoon almond extract

FOR THE FILLING

- 8 large tart apples, coarsely grated
- ½ cup (100 g / 3 ½ oz) superfine (caster) sugar
- pinch of salt
- 2 tablespoons freshly squeezed lemon juice
- 1 teaspoon ground cinnamon

FOR THE CAKE

- 1 cup (225 g / 8 oz) soft butter or margarine, plus extra for greasing
- 3 cups (350 g / 12 oz) self-rising flour, plus extra for dusting
- 1½ cups (300 g / 11 oz) superfine (caster) sugar
- 1 teaspoon vanilla extract
- 5 tablespoons milk
- 5 eggs

TO DECORATE

- 1 cup (250 ml / 8 fl oz) apple juice (optional)
- 1 tablespoons cornstarch (cornflour)
- 1 teaspoon powdered gelatin
- 20 walnut halves

APPLE CAKE
KEIK ME MHAA
Keik me mila

For the filling, combine the apples, sugar, salt, and lemon juice in a colander set over a bowl and let drain for about 2 hours. Press lightly with your hands to expel all the juice. Reserve the apples and the juice separately. Preheat the oven to 350°F (180°C / Gas Mark 4) and grease a 12-inch (30-cm) round cake pan, then sprinkle it lightly with flour. Put all the cake ingredients in a bowl, stir to mix, then beat with an electric mixer on high speed for 4 minutes, until the batter is light and fluffy. Spread half the batter over the base of the prepared pan and spoon the apple mixture on top. Sprinkle with the cinnamon and spoon the remaining batter over the apple to cover. Smooth the top with a spatula and bake for about 1 hour 10 minutes. Let the cake stand for 5 minutes, then invert onto a serving dish and let cool completely. For the decoration, measure the reserved apple juice and make up to 1 cup (250 ml / 8 fl oz) with commercial apple juice. Mix the cornstarch to a paste with 2 tablespoons of the juice. Pour the remaining juice into a small pan and sprinkle the gelatin on the surface. Let soften for 5 minutes, then stir in the cornstarch mixture. Heat gently, stirring with a wooden spoon until clear and slightly thickened. Remove from the heat and let cool completely. Spread the apple gelatin over the cake and let set. Cut the cake into diamond-shaped pieces and top each piece with a walnut half.

Makes one 12-inch (30-cm) cake
Preparation time 4½ hours (including draining, cooling and setting)
Cooking time 1 hour 10 minutes

CHOCOLATE AND WAFER MOSAIC
ΜΩΣΑΙΚΟ ΣΟΚΟΛΑΤΑΣ
Mosaiko sokolatas

Melt the chocolate in a heatproof bowl set over a pan of barely simmering water, then remove from the heat, and let cool. Combine the milk and brandy in a bowl. Beat together the butter, sugar, and salt in another bowl with an electric mixer on medium speed. Beating constantly at low speed, gradually add half the milk mixture and then the melted chocolate. Stir in the almonds. Sprinkle the wafers with the remaining milk mixture, then stir into the chocolate mixture. Chill in the refrigerator until thickened. Roll the mixture into a thick cylinder, wrap in plastic wrap (cling film), and return to the refrigerator until ready to serve. Serve in slices. It keeps well for 1 week in the refrigerator and for 6 months in the freezer. To make the chocolate glaze, put the chocolate and butter into a pan and melt over very low heat or in a heatproof bowl set over a pan of barely simmering water. Stir in the sugar, vanilla, and as much milk as necessary to obtain a thin glaze, then spread it on the chocolate mosaic.

Serves 12
Preparation time 2 hours (including chilling)

☐ p 566

- 8 oz (225 g) semisweet (plain) chocolate, broken into pieces
- 5 tablespoons milk
- 5 tablespoons brandy
- 1 cup (225 g / 8 oz) butter, softened
- 1 cup (120 g / 4 oz) confectioners' (icing) sugar
- ¼ teaspoon salt
- 1 cup (120 g / 4 oz) blanched almonds, chopped and roasted
- 14 oz (400 g) vanilla wafers, coarsely chopped
- 1 cup (120 g / 4 oz) coarsely ground walnuts

FOR THE GLAZE (OPTIONAL)
- 8 oz (225 g) semisweet (plain) chocolate, broken into pieces
- 2 tablespoons butter
- ½ cup (60 g / 2¼ oz) confectioners' (icing) sugar
- 1 teaspoon vanilla extract
- ½ cup (120 ml / 4 fl oz) milk

CHOCOLATE CAKE
ΚΕΙΚ ΣΟΚΟΛΑΤΑΣ
Keik sokolatas

Preheat the oven to 350°F (180°C / Gas Mark 4) and grease an 8-cup (2-litre / 3½-pint) turban or ring mold with butter or margarine. Lightly mix all the cake ingredients in a bowl, then beat with an electric mixer on high speed for 4 minutes, until doubled in volume and fluffy. Pour the batter into the prepared mold, filling it to two thirds of its depth. Bake for 1 hour. Remove from the oven and let cool for 5 minutes in the mold, before inverting it onto a serving dish. Let cool completely. Meanwhile, make the frosting. Melt the chocolate in a heatproof bowl set over a pan of barely simmering water. Add the remaining ingredients all at once, stirring vigorously with a spoon. Remove from the heat. Spread the frosting evenly all over the cake and let set.

Makes 1 large cake
Preparation time 1 hour (including cooling)
Cooking time 1 hour

FOR THE CAKE
- ¾ cup (175 g / 6 oz) soft butter or margarine, plus extra for greasing
- 2 cups (225 g / 8 oz) self-rising flour
- ¾ cup (80 g / 3 oz) unsweetened cocoa powder
- 2 cups (400 g / 14 oz) superfine (caster) sugar
- 6 eggs
- ½ cup (120 ml / 4 fl oz) milk
- ¼ teaspoon almond extract
- 1 teaspoon vanilla extract
- ¼ teaspoon baking soda (bicarbonate of soda)

FOR THE CHOCOLATE FROSTING (ICING)
- 4 oz (120 g) semisweet (plain) chocolate, broken into pieces
- 1⅓ cups (160 g / 5½ oz) confectioners' (icing) sugar
- 2 egg yolks
- 2 tablespoons brandy
- 1 tablespoon milk
- 2 tablespoons (25 g / 1 oz) butter

- butter, for greasing
- 1 quantity Sponge cookie (biscuit) dough (p 52)
- confectioners' (icing) sugar, for dusting
- 1 quantity Whipped cream (p 53) or ½ quantity Pastry cream (p 51)
- 1 quantity Chocolate frosting (icing) (p 53)

CREAM-FILLED SPONGE COOKIES (BISCUITS)
ΚΩΚ
Kok

Preheat the oven to 400°F (200°C / Gas Mark 6). Line a cookie sheet (baking tray) with baking parchment and grease with butter. Spoon the sponge cookie dough into a pastry (piping) bag fitted with a ½-inch (1-cm) plain tip (nozzle). Pipe 2-inch (5-cm) rounds onto the prepared cookie sheet, spaced well apart. Sift a generous quantity of confectioners' sugar over each cookie and bake for about 10 minutes, or until lightly browned. Transfer to a wire rack and let cool. Sandwich pairs of cookies together with a thick layer of whipped cream or pastry cream and place on a serving dish. Spread the chocolate frosting over the tops. Store in the refrigerator until ready to serve.

Vefa's secret: To make cookies come out evenly sized, draw circles on the underside of the baking parchment before greasing it, and pipe the dough inside the circles.

Makes 12 cookies
Preparation time 1 hour (including cooling)
Cooking time 10 minutes

▢ p 567

- butter, for greasing
- 2 tablespoons all-purpose (plain) flour
- 1 tablespoon unsweetened cocoa powder
- ½ teaspoon ground cinnamon
- pinch of salt
- 2 cups (350 g / 12 oz) pitted (stoned) and chopped dried dates
- 2 cups (225 g / 8 oz) walnuts, coarsely ground
- 10 egg whites
- ¾ teaspoon cream of tartar
- 1 cup (200 g / 7 oz) superfine (caster) sugar

TO DECORATE
- 1 cup (250 ml / 8 fl oz) whipping cream
- 1 teaspoon vanilla extract
- 16 dried dates, pitted (stoned)
- crystallized fruit or preserved orange

DATE AND WHIPPED CREAM MERINGUE CAKE
ΓΛΥΚΙΣΜΑ ΜΕ ΧΟΥΡΜΑΔΕΣ
Glikisma me hourmades

Preheat the oven to 350°F (180°C / Gas Mark 4). Line a 10-inch (25-cm) round cake pan with baking parchment and grease with butter. Sift together the flour, cocoa powder, cinnamon, and salt into a bowl and stir in the dates and walnuts. Whisk the egg whites with the cream of tartar in a grease-free bowl until soft peaks form. Gradually add the sugar, beating constantly on the highest speed, until a thick and glossy meringue forms. Gently fold the nut mixture into the meringue. Spread the mixture evenly into the prepared pan and bake for 45 minutes. Let the cake cool in the pan for 5 minutes, then invert it onto a serving dish, and let cool completely. Meanwhile, whip the cream with the vanilla until thick and fluffy. Spoon it into a pastry (piping) bag and decorate the top of the cake. Decorate with the dates and crystallized fruit or preserved orange. Serve immediately or store in the refrigerator.

Makes one 10-inch (25-cm) cake
Preparation time 1 hour (including cooling)
Cooking time 45 minutes

Chocolate and wafer mosaic, p 564

Cream-filled sponge cookies (biscuits), p 565

FIG CAKE
ΚΕΙΚ ΜΕ ΣΥΚΑ
Keik me sika

Preheat the oven to 300°F (150°C/Gas Mark 2). Line a 10 x 5-inch (25 x 12-cm) loaf pan with baking parchment and grease with butter. Sift together the cinnamon, flour, and baking powder into a large bowl. Beat the egg whites in a grease-free bowl with an electric mixer until soft peaks form. Gradually add the sugar, beating constantly, until stiff peaks form. Add the egg yolks, 1 at a time, and beat until smooth and glossy. Gradually fold in the flour mixture with a spatula, alternating with the milk. Gently fold in the chopped walnuts, almonds, golden raisins, and figs, taking care not to knock out the air. Pour the batter into the prepared pan and bake for about 1 hour. Remove from the oven and let cool, then transfer to a platter, and decorate the top with walnut halves stuck on with a little jam.

Makes one 10-inch (25-cm) loaf cake
Preparation time 1 hour (including cooling)
Cooking time 1 hour

☐ p 570

- butter, for greasing
- 1 teaspoon ground cinnamon
- 1½ cups (175 g/6 oz) all-purpose (plain) flour
- 3 teaspoons baking powder
- 3 eggs, separated
- ¾ cup (150 g/5 oz) superfine (caster) sugar
- 4 tablespoons milk
- 1 cup (120 g/4 oz) walnuts, coarsely chopped
- 1 cup (120 g/4 oz) almonds, roasted and coarsely chopped
- 1 cup (150 g/5 oz) golden raisins
- 1 cup (120 g/4 oz) dried figs, finely chopped
- walnut halves and jam, to decorate (optional)

FRUIT CAKE
ΚΕΙΚ ΦΡΟΥΤΟΥ
Keik froutou

Preheat the oven to 350°F (180°C/Gas Mark 4) and grease a deep 10-inch (25-cm) round cake pan with butter or margarine. Sift together the flour, salt, and baking soda into a bowl. Beat together the butter or margarine and sugar in another bowl with an electric mixer on medium speed until light and fluffy. Beating constantly, add the eggs, 1 at a time, alternating with 1 tablespoon of the flour mixture to prevent the mixture from curdling. Lower the speed of the mixer and add the remaining flour mixture, a little at a time, alternating with the milk. Fold in the grated zest, dried fruit, and walnuts. Pour the batter into the prepared pan to two thirds of its depth. Bake for about 1 hour, or until a skewer inserted in the center of the cake comes out clean. Invert the cake onto a wire rack to cool.

Makes one 10-inch (25-cm) cake
Preparation time 30 minutes
Cooking time 1 hour

- 1 cup (225 g/8 oz) soft butter or margarine, plus extra for greasing
- 2¾ cups (300 g/11 oz) self-rising flour
- ¼ teaspoon salt
- ½ teaspoon baking soda (bicarbonate of soda)
- 1¼ cups (250 g/9 oz) superfine (caster) sugar
- 4 eggs
- ½ cup (120 ml/4 fl oz) milk
- 1 tablespoon grated orange or lemon zest
- 1 cup (120 g/4 oz) chopped dried apricots, prunes, or candied orange
- ½ cup (50 g/2 oz) walnuts, coarsely chopped

HAZELNUT CAKE
ΚΕΪΚ ΦΟΥΝΤΟΥΚΙΟΥ
Keik foudoukiou

- 1 cup (225 g / 8 oz) soft butter or margarine, plus extra for greasing
- 3 cups (350 g / 12 oz) self-rising flour, plus extra for dusting
- 2 cups (400 g / 14 oz) superfine (caster) sugar
- 2 teaspoons vanilla extract
- ⅔ cup (150 ml / ¼ pint) milk
- 5 eggs
- 1 cup (120 g / 4 oz) hazelnuts, roasted and ground
- confectioners' (icing) sugar or Chocolate frosting (icing), p 53

Preheat the oven to 350°F (180°C / Gas Mark 4). Grease a 10-inch (25-cm) turban or ring mold with butter or margarine and lightly dust with flour. Put the margarine, flour, superfine sugar, vanilla, milk, and eggs into a bowl and mix lightly with a spoon, then beat with an electric mixer on high speed for 4 minutes, scraping the sides of the bowl frequently with a spatula, until doubled in volume and fluffy. Add the ground hazelnuts, a little at a time, lightly sprinkling them on the batter and folding in. Pour the batter into the prepared mold, filling it to two thirds of its depth. Bake for 1 hour, or until a wooden toothpick inserted into the center of the cake comes out clean. Let cool in the mold for 5 minutes, then turn out onto a serving dish. Dust with confectioners' sugar or spread with chocolate frosting while it is still warm. Store in an airtight container or freeze it.

Makes one 10-inch (25-cm) cake
Preparation time 15 minutes
Cooking time 1 hour

🖵 p 571

JAM TART
ΠΑΣΤΑ ΦΛΩΡΑ
Pasta flora

- 3 cups (350 g / 12 oz) all-purpose (plain) flour, plus extra for dusting
- 1 teaspoon baking powder
- 1 cup (225 g / 8 oz) butter
- scant ½ cup (80 g / 3 oz) superfine (caster) sugar
- 2 egg yolks
- 2 tablespoons brandy
- 1 tablespoon grated lemon zest or 1 teaspoon vanilla extract
- 1¾ cups (500 g / 1 lb 2 oz) apricot jam, or other flavors as desired

This is a very popular treat in Greece with coffee or tea.

Preheat the oven to 350°F (180°C / Gas Mark 4). Sift together the flour and baking powder into a bowl. Beat together the butter and sugar in another bowl with an electric mixer until pale and fluffy. Beat in the egg yolks, brandy, and lemon zest or vanilla, then fold in the flour, and knead until smooth. Avoid overworking the dough. Roll out two-thirds of the dough on a lightly floured work surface into a circle to fit the base and sides of a 10-inch (25-cm) tart pan. Spread the jam over the dough. Roll out the remaining dough, cut into strips, and lay them over the top of the jam in a lattice pattern. Bake for 30–35 minutes, or until lightly golden. Serve warm or at room temperature. Store, uncovered, in a cool, dry place for up to 1 week.

Makes one 10-inch (25-cm) tart
Preparation time 20 minutes
Cooking time 30–35 minutes

🖵 p 574

Fig cake, p 568

Hazelnut cake, p 569

LENTEN TAHINI CAKE
ΤΑΧΙΝΟΠΙΤΑ
Tahinopita

Preheat the oven to 350°F (180°C / Gas Mark 4). Brush a 12-inch (30-cm) round cake pan with vegetable oil and dust with flour. Sift together the flour, baking soda, cream of tartar, cinnamon, and cloves into a bowl. Combine the walnuts, raisins, and 2 tablespoons of the flour mixture in another bowl. Put the tahini, orange juice, honey, and sugar in a food processor and process for 2–3 minutes, then pour the mixture into the dry ingredients and gently fold together. Stir in the walnut mixture. Spoon the batter into the prepared pan, spreading it out evenly, then bake for about 1 hour. Let cool in the pan for 5 minutes, then turn out onto a serving dish, sprinkle with the brandy, and let cool completely. Cut the cake into wedges and dust with confectioners' sugar. Store in an airtight container.

Makes one 12-inch (30-cm) cake
Preparation time 1 hour (including cooling)
Cooking time 1 hour

☐ p 575

- vegetable oil, for brushing
- 3½ cups (400 g / 14 oz) self-rising flour, plus extra for dusting
- 2 teaspoons baking soda (bicarbonate of soda)
- 1 teaspoon cream of tartar
- 1 teaspoon ground cinnamon
- ½ teaspoon ground cloves
- ½ cup (50 g / 2 oz) walnuts, coarsely chopped
- generous ½ cup (80 g / 3 oz) golden raisins
- generous ½ cup (80 g / 3 oz) raisins
- 1 cup (225 g / 8 oz) tahini
- 1 cup (250 ml / 8 fl oz) freshly squeezed orange juice
- ½ cup (120 ml / 4 fl oz) honey
- ½ cup (100 g / 3½ oz) superfine (caster) sugar
- 4 tablespoons brandy
- confectioners' (icing) sugar, for dusting

LENTEN APPLE AND CARROT CAKE
ΚΕΙΚ ΜΕ ΚΑΡΟΤΑ ΚΑΙ ΜΗΛΑ
Keik me karota ke mila

Preheat the oven to 350°F (180°C / Gas Mark 4). Brush a 10-inch (25-cm) cake pan with oil and dust with flour. Mix the carrots and apples with the lemon juice in a bowl. Sift together the flour and baking soda into a large bowl and stir in the sugar, oil, brandy, orange zest, and carrot and apple mixture. Beat with an electric mixer on medium speed for 4 minutes. Gently stir in the walnuts with a spoon. Pour the batter into the prepared pan and bake for 50 minutes, or until a wooden toothpick inserted into the center of the cake comes out clean. Transfer to a wire rack to cool, then transfer to a dish, and dust with confectioners' sugar.

Makes one 10-inch (25-cm) cake
Preparation time 1 hour (including cooling)
Cooking time 50 minutes

- ¾ cup (175 ml / 6 fl oz) corn oil, plus extra for brushing
- 2½ cups (275 g / 10 oz) self-rising flour, plus extra for dusting
- 3 large carrots, grated
- 2 small apples, grated
- 2 tablespoons freshly squeezed lemon juice
- 2 teaspoon baking soda (bicarbonate of soda)
- 1 cup (200 g / 7 oz) superfine (caster) sugar
- 4 tablespoons brandy
- 1 tablespoon grated orange zest
- 1 cup (120 g / 4 oz) walnuts, coarsely chopped
- confectioners' (icing) sugar, for dusting

- butter, for greasing
- 3½ cups (400 g / 14 oz) self-rising flour
- 1½ teaspoons baking soda (bicarbonate of soda)
- 1 teaspoon cream of tartar
- 1 tablespoon ground cinnamon
- ½ teaspoon ground cloves
- ½ cup (50 g / 2 oz) walnuts, coarsely chopped
- generous ½ cup (80 g / 3 oz) raisins
- ⅓ cup (80 g / 3 oz) currants
- 1 cup (250 ml / 8 fl oz) olive oil
- 1 cup (250 ml / 8 fl oz) grape syrup (petimezi)
- 1 cup (250 ml / 8 fl oz) freshly squeezed orange juice
- 1 tablespoon red wine vinegar
- ½ cup (100 g / 3½ oz) superfine (caster) sugar
- 4 tablespoons brandy (optional)

MUST CAKE
ΜΟΥΣΤΟΠΙΤΑ
Moustopita

In September, the month of the grape harvest, wine-making is celebrated with *moustalevria* (grape must dessert) and *moustopita* (grape must cake). The grape must is simmered for a long time until it is reduced to a molasses-like syrup called *petimezi*.

Preheat the oven to 350°F (180°C / Gas Mark 4) and grease a 10-inch (25-cm) round cake pan with butter. Sift together the flour, baking soda, cream of tartar, cinnamon, and cloves into a bowl. Combine the walnuts, raisins, and currants in another bowl and stir in 2 tablespoons of the flour mixture. Put the olive oil, grape syrup, orange juice, vinegar, and sugar into a food processor or blender and process for 3 minutes. Pour the mixture into the dry ingredients and mix to a smooth, soft batter. Gently stir in the dried fruit and pour the mixture into the prepared cake pan. Bake for 50 minutes, or until a skewer inserted into the center of the cake comes out clean. Let stand for 5 minutes before turning out into a platter. Sprinkle with the brandy, if using.

Makes one 10-inch (25-cm) cake
Preparation time 30 minutes
Cooking time 50 minutes

- 1 cup (225 g / 8 oz) soft butter or margarine, plus extra for greasing
- 3½ cups (400 g / 14 oz) self-rising flour, plus extra for dusting
- 2 cups (400 g / 14 oz) superfine (caster) sugar
- ⅔ cup (150 ml / ¼ pint) freshly squeezed orange juice or milk
- 5 eggs
- 4 teaspoons grated orange, lemon or tangerine zest
- 3–4 tablespoons confectioners' (icing) sugar or orange frosting (icing), to decorate (see note)

ORANGE, LEMON, OR TANGERINE CAKE
ΚΕΙΚ ΠΟΡΤΟΚΑΛΙΟΥ, ΛΕΜΟΝΙΟΥ Η ΜΑΝΤΑΡΙΝΙΟΥ
Keik portokaliou, lemoniou i madariniou

Preheat the oven to 350°F (180°C / Gas Mark 4). Grease a 10-inch (25-cm) turban or ring mold with butter or margarine and dust with flour. Put all the cake ingredients into a bowl and mix lightly, then beat with an electric mixer on medium speed for 4 minutes, scraping the sides of the bowl, until doubled in volume, light, and fluffy. Pour the batter into the prepared mold and bake for about 1 hour. Let cool in the mold for 5 minutes, then turn out onto a serving dish. Dust with confectioners' sugar or spread orange frosting over the top. Store in an airtight container for up to 1 week. Stored in the freezer, it keeps for several months.

Makes one 10-inch (25-cm) cake
Preparation time 10 minutes
Cooking time 1 hour

Note: To make the orange frosting (icing), beat together 2 tablespoons (25 g / 1 oz) softened butter, 1⅓ cups (160 g / 5½ oz) confectioners' (icing) sugar, 1 teaspoon finely grated orange zest, and 1–2 tablespoons freshly squeezed orange juice in a small bowl. Spread the frosting over the cake as soon as you take it out of the oven.

Jam tart, p 569

lenten tahini cake, p 572

FRESH PLUM CAKE
ΚΕΪΚ ΜΕ ΦΡΕΣΚΑ ΔΑΜΑΣΚΗΝΑ
Keik me freska damaskina

Preheat the oven to 350°F (180°C / Gas Mark 4). Grease a 14-inch (35-cm) round cake pan with butter and dust with flour. Beat together the eggs and sugar in a bowl with an electric mixer on high speed until thick and pale. Lower the speed and, beating constantly, add the melted butter and milk, a little at a time, alternating with the flour. Fold in the lemon zest. Pour the batter into the prepared pan, spreading it evenly, and arrange the plums on top, cut sides up. Bake for 1 hour 10 minutes. Serve the cake slightly warm, preferably on the day it is made. Keep leftovers in the freezer. Reheat before serving.

Makes one 14-inch (35-cm) cake
Preparation time 30 minutes
Cooking time 1 hour 10 minutes

- 1 cup (225 g / 8 oz) butter, melted, plus extra for greasing
- 4 cups (450 g / 1 lb) self-rising flour, plus extra for dusting
- 5 eggs
- 2 cups (400 g / 14 oz) superfine (caster) sugar
- ½ cup (120 ml / 4 fl oz) milk
- 2 tablespoons grated lemon zest
- 2¼ lb (1 kg) plums, pitted (stoned) and quartered

SAINT FANOURIOS CAKE
ΦΑΝΟΥΡΟΠΙΤΑ
Fanouropita

Saint Fanourios is believed to be the finder of lost objects, as well as being able to reveal the destiny of unmarried girls. His saint's day is on August 27. To petition the saint, a ceremonial cake known as *fanouro-pita* must be presented along with the votive offering and a silver effigy of the lost object.

Preheat the oven to 350°F (180°C / Gas Mark 4). Grease a 10 x 12-inch (25 x 30-cm) baking pan with butter and dust with flour. Combine the flour, walnuts, cinnamon, and cloves in a large bowl. Put the oil, orange juice, and brandy into a blender and process until combined. Beat the eggs with the sugar in another bowl until light and fluffy. Pour the liquid ingredients over the nut mixture and stir to mix, then gradually add the egg mixture, gently folding it in until thoroughly incorporated and the mixture is light and fluffy. Pour it into the prepared pan and bake for 45 minutes. Remove from the oven and let rest for 5 minutes before inverting onto a platter. When it is completely cold, dust with confectioners' sugar.

Makes one 10-inch (25-cm) cake
Preparation time 15 minutes
Cooking time 45 minutes

- butter, for greasing
- 1½ cups (175 g / 6 oz) self-rising flour, plus extra for dusting
- 1½ cups (175 g / 6 oz) walnuts, coarsely chopped
- 1 ground teaspoon cinnamon
- ½ teaspoon ground cloves
- ½ cup (120 ml / 4 fl oz) olive or vegetable oil
- ½ cup (120 ml / 4 fl oz) freshly squeezed orange juice
- 4 tablespoons brandy
- 4 eggs
- 1½ cups (300 g / 11 oz) superfine (caster) sugar
- confectioners' (icing) sugar, for dusting

WALNUT CAKE
ΚΕΙΚ ΜΕ ΚΑΡΥΔΙΑ
Keik me karidia

- 1 cup (225 g / 8 oz) soft butter or margarine, plus extra for greasing
- 2 cups (225 g / 8 oz) finely chopped walnuts
- ½ cup (120 g / 4 oz) grated bittersweet (plain) chocolate
- 1½ cups (300 g / 11 oz) superfine (caster) sugar
- 1½ cups (175 g / 6 oz) all-purpose (plain) flour
- 3 teaspoons baking powder
- 1 teaspoon ground cinnamon, plus extra for dusting
- 6 eggs
- 3–4 tablespoons brandy or light syrup (see note)
- confectioners' (icing) sugar, for dusting

Preheat the oven to 350°F (180°C / Gas Mark 4). Line a 12-inch (30-cm) round cake pan with baking parchment and grease with butter or margarine. Combine the walnuts and grated chocolate in a bowl. Put the sugar, flour, baking powder, cinnamon, and eggs into a large bowl and stir to mix, then beat with an electric mixer on medium speed for 4 minutes until light and fluffy. Gently fold in the walnut and chocolate mixture. Spoon the batter into the prepared pan, spreading it evenly, and bake for 1 hour, or until a wooden toothpick inserted into the center of the cake comes out clean. Remove from the oven and sprinkle with the brandy or syrup. Let cool, then dust with confectioners' sugar and a little cinnamon.

Makes one 12-inch (30-cm) cake
Preparation time 30 minutes
Cooking time 1 hour

Note: To make the syrup, put 1½ cups (300 g / 11 oz) superfine (caster) sugar and 1½ cups (350 ml / 12 fl oz) water into a pan and cook over medium heat, stirring until the sugar has completely dissolved. Add 1 tablespoon lemon juice and bring to a boil. Boil, without stirring, for 5 minutes, then remove from the heat and let cool slightly. Stir in 2–3 tablespoons brandy, pour the syrup over the cold cake, and leave to absorb.

YOGURT CAKE
ΓΙΑΟΥΡΤΟΠΙΤΑ
Giaourtopita

- 1 cup (225 g / 8 oz) soft butter or margarine, plus extra for greasing
- 3 cups (350 g / 12 oz) all-purpose (plain) flour, plus extra for dusting
- 1½ cups (300 g / 11 oz) superfine (caster) sugar
- 5 eggs
- 3½ teaspoons baking powder
- ½ teaspoon salt
- 1 cup (250 ml / 8 fl oz) strained plain or thick Greek yogurt
- 1 teaspoon vanilla extract
- confectioners' (icing) sugar, for dusting

Preheat the oven to 350°F (180°C / Gas Mark 4). Grease a 10 x 14-inch (25 x 35-cm) cake pan with butter or margarine and dust with flour. Put all the ingredients into a large bowl and stir lightly to mix, then beat with an electric mixer on high speed for 4 minutes. Pour the batter into the prepared pan, spreading it evenly with a spatula, and bake for about 1 hour. Dust with confectioners' sugar and let the cake cool. Cut into squares or diamond-shaped pieces. Cover leftover cake with plastic wrap (cling film) and store at room temperature for 3–4 days or in the refrigerator for 1 week. The cake may be frozen for several months.

Makes one 10-inch (25-cm) cake
Preparation time 15 minutes
Cooking time 1 hour

SYRUP PASTRIES

-

ΓΛΥΚΑ ΣΙΡΟΠΙΑΣΤΑ

-

Glika siropiasta

At the end of Book 10 of *The Odyssey*, the sorceress Circe gives Odysseus a recipe that he must prepare in the Underworld in order to receive directions from the ghost of Teiresias for his safe passage home. She first advises him to dig a trench, and then to pour honey, milk and wine into it as an offering to the dead. Finally he must sprinkle barley meal over the top. The components of Odysseus' sweet ticket home are the basic ingredients still used in modern recipes for syrup pastries today. The only differences are that wheat flour has now replaced barley and that honey is generally used sparingly, often combined with sugar, which was unknown to the Greeks until around the third century BC. In fact, pastries and sweets still figure importantly in religious and funerary rituals to this day.

Greek tavernas usually serve a fairly limited range of sweet dishes, and people often forsake the taverna for a stop at their favorite *zaharoplastio*—literally "sugar-plasterer"—for coffee and ice cream or a pastry. It is in Greek homes that the art of preparing sweet treats really comes into its own. Many home cooks like to exhibit their own specialties, the culmination of heritage and skill, with different types of confection. The most traditional sweet dishes are the *siropiasta*, or syrup cakes and pastries, which still bear witness to the ancient use of honey and spices. Most traditional Greek pastries and confections are flavored with spices such as cinnamon, mahlab, mastic from Chios, cloves, and nutmeg. Allspice, vanilla, and chocolate are newer flavors, introduced to the Mediterranean from the New World in the sixteenth century. The syrup pastries here represent cherished customs that continue to serve as a connection with the past, and the traditions that will never be lost.

GENERAL INSTRUCTIONS

A large part of the success in making a syrup pastry depends on the good quality and fresh flavor of the ingredients used. Nuts often go rancid, so buy them just before using. Otherwise, seal them in plastic bags or airtight jars and keep them in the refrigerator or freezer until used. Phyllo (filo) pastry should be fresh and soft so that it can be used easily without crumbling. While working with phyllo sheets, cover the ones that you are not using with plastic wrap (cling film) and a slightly damp dish towel to keep them from drying out until you are ready to use them. Treat *kataifi* pastry dough in the same way. The multiple layer effect of a phyllo pastry dessert is achieved by layering or folding the sheets with a light hand so that they will barely touch each other, allowing room for the syrup to penetrate them thoroughly. Cut the phyllo dough to the right size to fit in your baking tray and layer the sheets, generously brushing with melted butter. Intersperse the layers with the dough trimmings, also brushed with butter. After finishing the layering, score and sprinkle the surface with a few drops of warm water to prevent the phyllo from curling up during baking.

Clarified butter is a fundamental ingredient in most Greek pastries, and is very simple to make. Melt the butter over low heat, cool, and chill in the refrigerator overnight. The next day, lift off and reserve the solid butter and discard the water and white solids. To speed up the procedure, freeze the butter for 1–2 hours after it cools.

What really makes a syrup pastry perfect is making sure the syrup is the correct consistency. A light syrup is used for pouring over cakes, *ravani*, and sponge cakes, or for dipping cookies (biscuits), such as walnut macaroons, before they are rolled in confectioners' (icing) sugar. On a candy (sugar) thermometer, a light syrup consistency occurs at 220°F (105°C). A medium syrup consistency occurs at 225°F (107°C), and is used for pouring over nut cakes, *diples*, honey cookies (biscuits), and *finikia*. A heavy syrup occurs at 228°F (109°C), and is used for pouring over phyllo (filo) pastries, such as baklava, *saragli* rolls, *galaktoboureko*, or *kataifi*. To avoid crystallization, the sugar must be completely dissolved before the syrup comes to a boil. Stir it constantly over low heat, brushing down the sugar crystals from the side of the pan with a pastry brush dipped in cold water. Alternatively, put a lid on the pan for a minute to allow the steam to dissolve any sugar crystals on the sides of the pan. When a boiling point is reached, boil the syrup for the time specified without stirring at all. Add 1–2 tablespoons freshly squeezed lemon juice, corn syrup or glucose to the syrup a few minutes before removing it from the heat. To mantain crispness, do not cover a syrup pastry after pouring the syrup over it. Most syrup pastries can be frozen successfully before baking. They should be thawed before use.

- melted butter, for brushing
- 9 oz (250 g) ready-made puff pastry or ½ quantity Homemade puff pastry (p 48)
- all-purpose (plain) flour, for dusting
- 1 egg yolk

FOR THE FILLING
- ¾ cup (80 g / 3 oz) blanched almonds, ground
- ½ tablespoon superfine (caster) sugar
- 2 tablespoons milk
- 1 tablespoon melted butter
- ¼ teaspoon almond extract or 1 teaspoon vanilla extract
- 1–2 egg yolks

FOR THE SYRUP
- 1 cup (200 g / 7 oz) superfine (caster) sugar
- 4 tablespoons corn syrup or liquid glucose

ALMOND CREAM TURNOVERS
ΤΡΙΓΩΝΑΚΙΑ ΜΕ ΑΜΥΓΔΑΛΑ
Trigonakia me amigdala

Preheat the oven to 400°F (200°C / Gas Mark 6) and brush a cookie sheet (baking tray) with melted butter. Roll out the pastry dough on a lightly floured work surface to an ⅛-inch (3-mm) thick sheet and cut into 2-inch (5-cm) squares. Combine the filling ingredients in a bowl—the mixture should be firm. Add 1 egg yolk and mix well, adding the second if necessary. Place 1 teaspoon of the filling on each square, dampen the edges, fold in half to form a triangle, and press to seal. Place the triangles on the prepared cookie sheet. Beat the egg yolk with 1 teaspoon water and brush the triangles with the mixture. Bake for 20 minutes, or until golden brown. Meanwhile, prepare the syrup. Put the sugar, corn syrup or glucose and ¾ cup (175 ml / 6 fl oz) water in a pan and bring to a boil, stirring to dissolve the sugar. Boil, without stirring, for 5 minutes, then remove from the heat. Pour the hot syrup over the turnovers and let them absorb the syrup and cool completely.

Makes 16–20 turnovers
Preparation time 1 hour (including cooling)
Cooking time 20 minutes

ALMOND-SEMOLINA CAKE
ΧΑΛΒΑΣ ΤΗΣ ΡΗΝΑΣ
Halvas tis rinas

Preheat the oven to 350°F (180°C / Gas Mark 4) and grease a
10 x 14-inch (25 x 35-cm) baking pan with butter. Beat together the butter
and half the sugar in a bowl until light and fluffy. Add the egg yolks, 1 at
a time, beating well after each addition, then add the milk and almond
or vanilla extract. Combine the semolina and baking powder and
gradually fold into the mixture, then add the ground almonds. Whisk
the egg whites with the remaining sugar in a grease-free bowl to a soft
meringue and fold into the batter. Pour the batter into the prepared
pan and bake for about 35 minutes, until golden brown. Let cool slightly,
then cut into diamond shapes. To make the syrup, put the sugar and
lemon juice into a pan, pour in 2 cups (450 ml / 16 fl oz) water, and
bring to a boil, stirring until the sugar has dissolved. Boil, without stirring,
for 5 minutes, then remove from the heat, and ladle over the cake. Cover
and let it absorb the syrup and cool completely. Transfer the pieces to
a serving dish and garnish with maraschino cherry halves and almonds.

Makes 20 pieces
Preparation time 30 minutes
Cooking time 35 minutes

- 1 cup (225 g / 8 oz) butter,
  softened, plus extra for greasing
- ¾ cup (150 g / 5 oz) superfine
  (caster) sugar
- 6 eggs, separated
- 5 tablespoons milk
- ¼ teaspoon almond extract or
  1 teaspoon vanilla extract
- 1 teaspoon grated lemon zest
- 2 cups (350 g / 12 oz) fine
  semolina
- 2 teaspoons baking powder
- 1 cup (120 g / 4 oz) ground almonds
- maraschino cherry halves and
  almonds, to garnish

FOR THE SYRUP
- 2 cups (400 g / 14 oz) superfine
  (caster) sugar
- 1 tablespoon freshly squeezed
  lemon juice

ALMOND FLUTES
ΦΛΟΓΕΡΕΣ ΜΕ ΑΜΥΓΔΑΛΑ
Flogeres me amigdala

Preheat the oven to 400°F (200°C / Gas Mark 6) and brush a cookie
sheet (baking tray) with melted butter. Combine the almonds, sugar,
cream, melted butter, egg, almond or vanilla extract, and semolina in
a bowl and mix to make a stiff filling. If it is too stiff, add the egg yolk; if
it is too thin, add a little more semolina. Stack the phyllo sheets and cut
into 3 strips lengthwise. Lightly brush each strip of phyllo with melted
butter and fold in half widthwise, and brush again. Place 1 tablespoon
of the filling on the center of the short edge, fold in the sides, and roll
up loosely to make a cigar shape. Repeat with the remaining strips and
filling. Put the rolls on the prepared cookie sheet, spaced ½ inch (1 cm)
apart, and brush with melted butter. Bake for 35 minutes, until crisp and
golden brown. Meanwhile, put the sugar and corn syrup or glucose into
a pan, pour in 1 cup (250 ml / 8 fl oz) water, and bring to a boil, stirring
until the sugar has dissolved. Boil, without stirring, for 5 minutes and
add the lemon juice, then remove from the heat. Carefully ladle the syrup
over the flutes immediately. Cover loosely.

Makes 20 flutes
Preparation time 30 minutes
Cooking time 35 minutes

- 1 tablespoon melted clarified
  butter, plus extra for brushing
- 1¼ cups (175 g / 6 oz) blanched
  almonds, finely ground
- 2 tablespoons superfine
  (caster) sugar
- 2 tablespoons heavy
  (double) cream
- 1 egg
- 1 teaspoon almond or
  vanilla extract
- 1 tablespoon fine semolina
- 1 egg yolk (optional)
- 9 oz (250 g) ready-made phyllo
  dough (filo pastry)
- ½ cup (120 ml / 4 fl oz) melted
  clarified butter

FOR THE SYRUP
- 1½ cups (300 g / 11 oz) superfine
  (caster) sugar
- 2 tablespoons corn syrup or
  liquid glucose
- ½ tablespoon freshly squeezed
  lemon juice

- 1½ cups (350 g / 12 oz) clarified butter, melted, plus extra for brushing
- 1 lb 2 oz (500 g) ready-made phyllo (filo) or Homemade phyllo dough (filo pastry), p 46
- 2 cups (225 g / 8 oz) almonds, coarsely chopped
- 2 cups (225 g / 8 oz) walnuts, coarsely chopped
- 2 teaspoons ground cinnamon
- ½ teaspoon ground cloves
- cloves, to decorate (optional)

FOR THE SYRUP
- 3 cups (600 g / 1 lb 5 oz) superfine (caster) sugar
- ½ cup (120 ml / 4 fl oz) corn syrup or honey
- grated zest of 1 lemon or 1 teaspoon vanilla extract
- 2 tablespoons brandy (optional)

BAKLAVA
ΜΠΑΚΛΑΒΑΣ
Baklavas

Brush a baking pan exactly the same size as the sheets of phyllo with melted butter. Alternatively, cut the sheets of phyllo to fit your baking pan and brush it with melted butter. Combine the nuts, cinnamon, and cloves in a bowl. Preheat the oven to 350°F (180°C / Gas Mark 4). Lay 4 sheets of phyllo on the base of the prepared baking pan, brushing each with melted butter. Sprinkle some of the nut mixture evenly over them. Continue layering the sheets of phyllo, 1 at a time and brushing each with melted butter, and sprinkling with some of the nut mixture until all of it has been used and only 4 sheets of phyllo remain. (If it has been necessary to trim the phyllo, brush the trimmings with melted butter and place between the layers.) Top with the remaining sheets of phyllo, brushing each one with melted butter. Score the top layers with a sharp knife into small diamond-shaped or triangular pieces. Stick a clove in the center of each piece, if you like. Brush with the remaining melted butter and sprinkle lightly with warm water to prevent the phyllo from curling. Bake for 30–40 minutes, or until golden brown. Meanwhile, make the syrup. Put the sugar, corn syrup or honey, and lemon zest, if using, into a small pan, pour in 2 cups (450 ml / 16 fl oz) water, and bring to a boil, stirring constantly until the sugar has dissolved. Simmer, without stirring, for 5 minutes. Stir in the lemon zest or vanilla, if using, and brandy, if using, and remove from the heat. Ladle the hot syrup carefully and evenly over the baklava as soon as you take it out of the oven. Let it absorb the syrup and cool completely. Baklava keeps, covered loosely with a cloth, at room temperature for 1–2 weeks.

Makes 30 pieces
Preparation time 1¼ hours
Cooking time 40 minutes

p 584

Baklava, p 583

COPENHAGEN
ΚΟΠΕΓΧΑΓΗ
Kopenhagi

This tasty dessert was created in 1863 in honor of the Danish Prince George upon his coronation as King George I of Greece.

Preheat the oven to 400°F (200°C / Gas Mark 6) and grease a 10-inch (25-cm) round or square baking pan with butter. Roll out the pie dough on a lightly floured work surface to fit the prepared pan. Pat evenly and smoothly into the pan and prick all over with a fork. Bake for 10–15 minutes, or until lightly golden, then remove from the oven, and let cool. Preheat the oven to 350°F (180°C / Gas Mark 4). To make the filling, combine the rusk crumbs, baking powder, spices, and almonds in a bowl. Beat together the eggs and sugar in another bowl with an electric mixer on high speed until thick and fluffy. Gently fold in the dry ingredients and pour the mixture into the pie shell. Cut the phyllo sheets to the same size as the baking pan and stack them, one on top of the other, brushing each with melted butter. Cut them lengthwise into 4 strips, without cutting through the edges. Carefully place them on top of the filling. Bake for about 45 minutes, or until the top is golden brown. Remove from the oven and let cool. To make the syrup, put the sugar and lemon juice into a pan, pour in 1 cup (250 ml / 8 fl oz) water, and bring to a boil, stirring until the sugar has dissolved. Boil, without stirring, for 5 minutes, then remove from the heat, and carefully ladle the syrup slowly and evenly over the cake. Let cool completely before cutting the cake into pieces.

Makes 10–12 pieces
Preparation time 2 hours (including cooling)
Cooking time 1 hour

□ p 585

FOR THE TART
- butter, for greasing
- ½ quantity Rich pastry dough (p 48)
- all-purpose (plain) flour, for dusting

FOR THE FILLING
- 1 cup (50 g / 2 oz) rusk crumbs
- ½ tablespoon baking powder
- ¼ teaspoon ground cloves
- 1 teaspoon ground cinnamon
- ¾ cup (80 g / 3 oz) almonds, coarsely ground
- 4 eggs
- ½ cup (100 g / 3½ oz) superfine (caster) sugar
- 2 sheets of phyllo dough (filo pastry)
- 4 tablespoons melted clarified butter

FOR THE SYRUP
- 1½ cups (300 g / 11 oz) superfine (caster) sugar
- 1 tablespoon freshly squeezed lemon juice

- 4 cups (1 litre / 1¾ pints) milk
- 3 eggs
- 2 egg yolks
- ½ cup (100 g / 3½ oz) superfine (caster) sugar
- ½ cup (65 g / 2½ oz) fine semolina
- 2 teaspoons vanilla extract
- ½ cup (120 ml / 4 fl oz) hot melted clarified butter, plus extra for brushing
- 8 oz (225 g) ready-made phyllo dough (filo pastry)

FOR THE SYRUP
- 1½ cups (300 g / 11 oz) superfine (caster) sugar
- 1 tablespoon freshly squeezed lemon juice
- 1 teaspoon vanilla extract

CUSTARD PASTRY
ΓΑΛΑΚΤΟΜΠΟΥΡΕΚΟ
Galaktoboureko

Pour the milk into a pan and bring to just below boiling point, then remove from the heat, and let cool slightly. Lightly beat together the eggs, egg yolks, and sugar in a bowl until thoroughly blended. Stir in the semolina. Transfer the mixture to a large heavy pan and pour in the hot milk, stirring constantly. Simmer over low heat, stirring constantly, for about 10 minutes, until smooth and thick. Remove from the heat and stir in the vanilla and 3–4 tablespoons of the melted butter. Preheat the oven to 375°F (190°C / Gas Mark 5) and brush a 9 x 12-inch (23 x 30-cm) ovenproof glass dish with melted butter. Cut the phyllo sheets to fit the prepared dish and spread half of them on the base, brushing each with melted butter. Brush the trimmings with melted butter and place them between the phyllo layers. Pour in the custard and spread it evenly over the phyllo. Stack the remaining phyllo sheets, one on top of the other, brushing each with melted butter. With a sharp knife or pizza wheel, cut them lengthwise into 4 strips, without cutting through the edges. Carefully place the strips on the custard, brush with melted butter, and sprinkle with warm water. Bake for 15 minutes, then reduce the oven temperature to 325°F (160°C / Gas Mark 3), and bake for 35 minutes more, or until the top is golden brown and crisp. To make the syrup, put the sugar and lemon juice into a pan, pour in 1 cup (250 ml / 8 fl oz) water, and bring to a boil, stirring until the sugar has dissolved. Boil, without stirring, for 7 minutes, then remove from the heat, stir in the vanilla, and carefully ladle the syrup over the pastry as soon as you remove it from the oven. Let the pastry cool and absorb the syrup, then cut into squares or rectangles, and serve warm or at room temperature, preferably the same day. Store any leftovers uncovered in the refrigerator for 1–2 days.

Makes 10–12 pieces
Preparation time 30 minutes
Cooking time 50 minutes

☐ p 588

Custard pastry, p 587

Honey puffs, p 594

CUSTARD PIE

ΓΑΛΑΚΤΟΜΠΟΥΡΕΚΟ ΜΕ ΡΥΖΑΛΕΥΡΟ

Galaktoboureko me rizalevro

Stir the rice flour with 1 cup (250 ml / 8 fl oz) of the milk in a bowl. Pour the remaining milk into a pan, add the butter, salt, and vanilla, and bring to just below boiling point. Stir in the rice flour mixture and cook over low heat, stirring constantly, until thickened, then remove from the heat. Beat together the eggs, egg yolks, and sugar in a bowl with an electric mixer on high speed for 4 minutes, until light and fluffy. Stir in a little of the warm milk and rice flour mixture, then gently mix it into the pan. Preheat the oven to 350°F (180°C / Gas Mark 4). Lay half the phyllo sheets in a baking pan the same size as the sheets, brushing each with melted butter. Pour the custard over them. Stack the remaining phyllo sheets on top of each other, brushing each with melted butter. Cut the stack lengthwise into 4 strips, without cutting through the edges. Carefully place them on top of the custard. Brush with melted butter and sprinkle with warm water. Bake for 45 minutes, or until it is dark golden. To make the syrup, put the sugar, corn syrup or glucose, cinnamon stick, and lemon zest into a pan, pour in 1 cup (250 ml / 8 fl oz) water, and bring to a boil, stirring until the sugar has dissolved. Boil, without stirring, for 8 minutes, until the syrup is thick, then remove from the heat. Discard the flavorings and carefully ladle the hot syrup evenly over the pie as soon as it comes out of the oven. Let cool before serving.

Makes 10–12 pieces
Preparation time 30 minutes
Cooking time 45 minutes

- 1 cup (120 g / 4 oz) rice flour
- 6¼ cups (1.5 litres / 2½ pints) milk
- 3 tablespoons (40 g / 1½ oz) butter
- ¼ teaspoon salt
- 3 teaspoons vanilla extract
- 2 eggs
- 2 egg yolks
- 1 cup (200 g / 7 oz) superfine (caster) sugar
- 1 lb 2 oz (500 g) ready-made phyllo dough (filo pastry)
- melted clarified butter, for brushing

FOR THE SYRUP
- 1 cup (200 g / 7 oz) superfine (caster) sugar
- 2 tablespoons corn syrup or liquid glucose
- 1 cinnamon stick
- 1 strip of thinly pared lemon zest

LENTEN DONUTS FROM CRETE

ΚΟΥΜΠΑΝΙΑ ΝΗΣΤΙΣΙΜΑ

Koubania nistisima

Sift together the flour, salt, and spices into a bowl and stir in the yeast, sugar, and lemon zest. Add the olive oil, orange juice, and wine and knead by hand, or with an electric mixer with a dough hook, to make a soft pliable dough, adding a little water if necessary. Cover and let rise. Roll out the dough on a lightly floured work surface into thick 1-inch (2.5-cm) cylinders. Cut into 1-inch (2.5-cm) pieces. Heat the oil in a deep-fryer to 350–375°F (180–190°C). Fry the donuts in batches for 4–5 minutes, then drain well. Meanwhile, dissolve the sugar in ½ cup (120 ml / 4 fl oz) water, bring to a boil, and simmer, without stirring, for 5 minutes. Stir in the honey and pour the syrup over the donuts. Leave for 3 minutes, remove the donuts, and sprinkle with nuts and sesame seeds.

Serves 8–10
Preparation time 1 hour
Cooking time 15 minutes

- 4 cups (500 g / 1 lb 2 oz) all-purpose (plain) flour
- ½ teaspoon salt
- ½ teaspoon ground cinnamon
- ¼ teaspoon ground cloves
- 1 tablespoon rapid-rise (fast-action) yeast
- 3 tablespoons superfine (caster) sugar
- 1 tablespoon grated lemon zest
- 4 tablespoons olive oil
- 4 tablespoons freshly squeezed orange juice
- 4 tablespoons white wine
- oil, for deep-frying
- 1 cup (200 g / 7 oz) superfine (caster) sugar
- 2 cups (250 ml / 8 fl oz) honey
- finely chopped walnuts and sesame seeds, for sprinkling

- 3 cups (600 g / 1 lb 5 oz) superfine (caster) sugar, plus extra for sprinkling
- 2 cups (225 g / 8 oz) cornstarch (cornflour)
- 2 teaspoons vanilla extract
- ⅔ cup (150 ml / ¼ pint) melted clarified butter or vegetable oil
- ½ cup (50 g / 2 oz) blanched almonds, halved
- ground cinnamon, for sprinkling

HALVA FROM FARSALA
ΧΑΛΒΑΣ ΦΑΡΣΑΛΩΝ
Halvas farsalon

Mix 2 cups (400 g / 14 oz) of the sugar with the cornstarch and vanilla in a large bowl. Pour in 5 cups (1.2 litres / 2 pints) water and stir until thoroughly blended. Heat 1 tablespoon of the butter or oil in a 10-inch (25-cm) wide heavy pan, add the almonds, and cook over low heat, stirring constantly, until browned. Remove with a slotted spoon and set aside. Gradually add the reserved sugar to the pan, stirring constantly with a wooden spoon, until it has all melted and a dark golden colored caramel has formed. Remove from the heat and gradually stir in the cornstarch mixture. Return to the heat and cook over medium heat, stirring constantly, until the mixture is thick and comes away easily from the side of the pan. Stir in the almonds, increase the heat, and gradually add the remaining butter or oil, a little at a time, stirring constantly until it is all incorporated. Continue to stir until the mixture begins to fry and forms a crust. Smooth the surface and cook for 5–6 minutes, without stirring, until a thick, glistening caramelized crust forms on the bottom. Remove from the heat and let cool slightly. Invert a baking tray over the pan and, holding them together, carefully turn the pan over. Let cool completely, then cut into squares. Serve sprinkled with a little sugar and cinnamon. It keeps well at room temperature for up to 1 week.

Makes 40–50 pieces
Preparation time 15 minutes
Cooking time 1½ hours

HALVA CAKE FROM LEFKADA
ΛΑΔΟΠΙΤΑ ΛΕΦΚΑΔΑΣ
Ladopita lefkadas

Put the sugar, cloves and cinnamon in a pan, add 3 cups (750 ml / 1¼ pints) water and cook, stirring, on medium heat until the sugar has dissolved and the syrup begins to boil. Reduce heat, cover and simmer for 10 minutes, until it thickens. Preheat the oven to 475°F (240°C / Gas Mark 9). Pour the oil into a large, deep, heavy-bottomed pan and warm thoroughly over a high heat. Lower the heat and add the flour a little at a time, stirring constantly with a wooden spoon, until you have a smooth batter. Gradually add the syrup, stirring carefully, until the mixture thickens and comes away from the spoon without leaving a trace. This process demands slow, careful stirring and will take about 30 minutes. Empty the mixture into a deep 12-inch (30-cm) baking pan, smooth the surface with a spatula and scatter the sesame seeds over the top. Press down lightly on the surface with nonstick baking parchment to push the sesame seeds into the cake. Using a blunt knife, divide the cake into diamond-shaped portions and place half a blanched almond in the center of each (or, if you prefer, sprinkle with almond flakes). Bake for about 35 minutes, or until the surface is golden and the edges are crisp. Allow to rest for 6–7 hours to cool before serving. The cake will keep for 1 month, covered. There is no need to refrigerate it. It is even more delicious when made with a syrup containing ½ cup (120 ml / 4 fl oz) honey, ½ cup (120 ml / 4 fl oz) grape syrup (*petimezi*) and 1 cup (200 g / 7 oz) superfine (caster) sugar.

Serves 15
Preparation time 6½–7½ hours (including cooling)
Cooking time 35 minutes

- 2 cups (400 g / 14 oz) superfine (caster) sugar
- ½ teaspoon ground cloves
- 1 teaspoon ground cinnamon (optional)
- 4 cups (1 litre / 1¾ pints) olive oil
- 8⅓ cups (1 kg / 2¼ lb) all-purpose (plain) flour
- ½ cup (80 g / 3 oz) sesame seeds
- 20 blanched almond halves

- 9 oz (250 g) ready-made phyllo dough (filo pastry)
- 5 tablespoons melted clarified butter
- vegetable oil, for deep-frying

FOR THE SYRUP
- 1 cup (200 g / 7 oz) superfine (caster) sugar
- ½ cup (120 ml / 4 fl oz) honey
- 1 teaspoon vanilla extract
- 1 tablespoon freshly squeezed lemon juice

HONEY-DIPPED PASTRY BITES
ΚΟΥΡΚΟΥΜΠΙΝΙΑ
Kourkoubinia

Stack 2 phyllo sheets, one on top of the other, brushing each with melted butter. Brush the surface with melted butter, fold in half, and roll up tightly into a long thin cylinder, moistening the edge to seal. Repeat with the remaining phyllo sheets. Put them onto a large plate, cover, and chill in the refrigerator until firm. Heat the oil in a deep-fryer to 350–375°F (180–190°C). Meanwhile, cut the phyllo cylinders into generous ¾-inch (2-cm) lengths. Carefully add them to the hot oil, in batches, and fry until golden brown. Remove with a slotted spoon and drain on paper towels. To make the syrup, put the sugar, honey, vanilla, and lemon juice into a pan, pour in ⅔ cup (150 ml / ¼ pint) water, and bring to a boil, stirring until the sugar has dissolved. Boil, without stirring, for 5 minutes, then remove from the heat. Skim off the froth and carefully pour the syrup over the pastries. Let stand until all the syrup has been absorbed and they are completely cold. Alternatively, put the pastry bites into the syrup immediately after frying. Let them absorb syrup for a few minutes, then remove with a slotted spoon. Place on a serving dish. They keep well for several weeks at room temperature.

Serves 10
Preparation time 1 hour (including chilling)
Cooking time 15 minutes

HONEY PUFFS
ΛΟΥΚΟΥΜΑΔΕΣ
Loukoumades

If using fresh yeast, mash it to a smooth paste with the lukewarm water in a large bowl. If using dried yeast, mix the lukewarm water with 1 teaspoon of the sugar in a large bowl, sprinkle the yeast over the surface, and let stand for 10–15 minutes, until frothy, then stir to a smooth paste. Add the milk, flour, remaining sugar, salt, and olive oil and beat with an electric mixer on high speed until smooth and thick. Cover and let rise in a warm place for 1–2 hours, or until tripled in volume. Heat the vegetable oil in a deep-fryer to 350–375°F (180–190°C). Moisten one of your hands, take a handful of the dough, clench your fist, and squeeze out a small ball of dough the size of a walnut. Cut off the dough with a wet spoon and carefully drop it into the hot oil. Wet the spoon every time before cutting the dough to prevent it sticking. (You could also use a donut maker.) Fry a few puffs at a time, pushing them into the oil with a slotted spoon, until crisp and golden brown all over. Remove with the slotted spoon and transfer to a serving dish. Drizzle warm honey over them, dust with cinnamon, and sprinkle with chopped walnuts or pistachios. Serve immediately. If the honey is too thick, add a little water and heat for 1 minute. Skim off any scum before using.

Makes 40
Preparation time 1½–2½ hours (including rising)
Cooking time 30–40 minutes

□ p 589

□ p 589

FOR THE DOUGH
- 1 oz (25 g) fresh yeast or 1 tablespoon dried yeast
- ½ cup (120 ml / 4 fl oz) lukewarm water
- ½ tablespoon sugar
- ½ cup (120 ml / 4 fl oz) lukewarm milk
- 1½ cups (175 g / 6 oz) all-purpose (plain) flour
- ½ teaspoon salt
- 2 tablespoons olive oil
- vegetable oil, for deep-frying

TO DECORATE
- honey, warmed
- ground cinnamon
- finely chopped walnuts or pistachio nuts

- ½ cup (120 ml / 4 fl oz) melted clarified butter, plus extra for brushing
- 3 cups (350 g / 12 oz) walnuts, coarsely ground
- 2 teaspoons ground cinnamon
- 1 teaspoon ground cloves
- 9 oz (250 g) ready-made phyllo dough (filo pastry)

FOR THE SYRUP
- 1½ cups (300 g / 11 oz) superfine (caster) sugar
- 1 tablespoon freshly squeezed lemon juice
- 4 tablespoons corn syrup or liquid glucose

NUT PASTRY PINWHEELS
ΣΑΡΑΓΛΙ
Saragli

Preheat the oven to 350°F (180°C / Gas Mark 4) and brush 1 or 2 cookie sheets (baking trays) with melted butter. Combine the ground walnuts, cinnamon, and cloves in a bowl. Stack 3 phyllo sheets, one on top of the other, brushing each with melted butter. Sprinkle some of the walnut mixture over the surface and lay another 2 sheets of phyllo on top, brushing each with melted butter. Sprinkle with a little more of the walnut mixture and lay another 2 phyllo sheets on top, brushing each with melted butter. Repeat the procedure once more. Starting at the short end, roll up tightly into a thick cylinder. Dampen the edge and press to seal. Using a sharp knife, cut the cylinder into 1½-inch (4-cm) slices. Put the pinwheels on the prepared cookie sheet, side by side, cut sides up. Make more pinwheels in the same way with the remaining phyllo. Brush the tops with the remaining melted butter and bake for about 40 minutes, or until golden brown. Meanwhile, make the syrup. Put the sugar, lemon juice, and corn syrup or glucose into a pan, pour in 1½ cups (350 ml / 12 fl oz) water, and bring to a boil, stirring until the sugar has dissolved. Boil, without stirring, for 5 minutes, then remove from the heat. Ladle the syrup over the pinwheels as soon as they are removed from the oven. Let them absorb the syrup and cool completely. Transfer to a serving dish. They keep well uncovered at room temperature for 1–2 weeks.

Makes 16–18 pinwheels
Preparation time 1 hour
Cooking time 40 minutes

☐ p 596

Nut pastry pinwheels, p 595

ied dough ribbons, p 598

ORANGE PIE
ΠΟΡΤΟΚΑΛΟΠΙΤΑ
Portokalopita

Brush a 14-inch (35-cm) round baking pan with melted butter. Crumple each phyllo sheet by gathering all the edges around and pressing between your hands to form a rose-shaped ball. Place them in the pan and let stand at room temperature for a few hours to dry. Meanwhile, make the filling. Beat together the eggs, sugar, oil, orange zest, and vanilla with an electric mixer on high speed until smooth and foamy. Sprinkle the baking powder over the yogurt in another bowl, mix well, and stir into the egg mixture. Ladle the mixture evenly over the dried phyllo and set aside for 10 minutes. Preheat the oven to 350°F (180°C / Gas Mark 4). Bake the pie for 30 minutes, or until golden. Meanwhile, make the syrup. Put the sugar, orange juice, and zest into a pan, pour in 1½ cups (350 ml / 12 fl oz) water, bring to a boil, and stir until the sugar has dissolved. Simmer, without stirring, for 5 minutes, then remove from the heat. Ladle the hot syrup carefully over the warm pie and let stand for several hours to absorb the syrup and cool.

Makes one 14-inch (35-cm) pie
Preparation time 3½ – 4½ hours (including drying)
Cooking time 30 minutes

- melted clarified butter, for brushing
- 1 lb 2 oz (500 g) ready-made phyllo dough (filo pastry)

FOR THE FILLING
- 4 eggs
- ½ cup (100 g / 3½ oz) superfine (caster) sugar
- 1 cup (250 ml / 8 fl oz) corn oil
- 3 tablespoons grated orange zest
- 2 teaspoons vanilla extract
- 2 tablespoons baking powder
- ¾ cup (175 ml / 6 fl oz) strained plain or thick Greek yogurt

FOR THE SYRUP
- 2½ cups (500 g / 1 lb 2 oz) superfine (caster) sugar
- 1 cup (250 ml / 8 fl oz) orange juice
- 3 tablespoons grated orange zest

FRIED DOUGH RIBBONS
ΛΑΛΑΓΓΙΑ
Lalagia

Lalagia are prepared in many areas of Greece when a baby is born, and at Christmas to celebrate the newborn Christ.

If using fresh yeast, mash it with half the lukewarm water in a bowl to a smooth paste. Sift together the flour, salt and dried yeast, if using, into a bowl, add the remaining water, olive oil, honey, and vanilla, and beat with an electric mixer fitted with a dough hook on medium speed to make a soft, pliable dough. Cover and let rise for about 1 hour, or until doubled in volume. Oil your hands, roll out small pieces of dough into long, thin ribbons and fold into different shapes. Heat oil in a deep-fryer to 350–375°F (180–190°C). Carefully add the dough ribbons in batches to the hot oil and cook for 2–3 minutes, until golden brown. Remove with a slotted spoon and drain on paper towels. Transfer to a platter and dust with confectioners' sugar or drizzle with honey.

Serves 10–12
Preparation time 1¼ hours (including rising)
Cooking time 15 minutes

- 1 oz (25 g) fresh yeast or 1 tablespoon dried rapid-rise (fast-action) yeast
- 1 cup (250 ml / 8 fl oz) lukewarm water
- 4½ cups (500 g / 1 lb 2 oz) all-purpose (plain) flour
- ½ teaspoon salt
- 2 tablespoons olive oil, plus extra for oiling
- 2 tablespoons honey
- 1 teaspoon vanilla extract
- oil, for deep-frying
- confectioners' (icing) sugar, for dusting, or thyme honey, for drizzling

▢ p 597

- 2½–3 cups (500–600 g / 1 lb 2 oz–1 lb 5 oz) **superfine** (caster) sugar, according to taste
- 1 cinnamon stick
- thinly pared zest of 1 lemon
- 6–8 cloves
- 1 cup (250 ml / 8 fl oz) melted clarified butter or corn oil
- 2 cups (350 g / 12 oz) coarse semolina
- ½ cup (50 g / 2 oz) almonds, coarsely chopped, or pine nuts, plus extra to decorate
- 1 teaspoon grated lemon zest
- ground cinnamon, for sprinkling

SEMOLINA HALVA
ΧΑΛΒΑΣ ΣΙΜΙΓΔΑΛΕΝΙΟΣ
Halvas simigdalenios

This typical Greek dessert is a taverna favorite all over the country.

Pour about 4 cups (1 litre / 1¾ pints) water (check the semolina package for the correct quantity) into a large pan, add the sugar, and cook over medium heat, stirring until the sugar has dissolved. Add the cinnamon, lemon zest, and cloves, cover the pan, and simmer, without stirring, for 5 minutes. Meanwhile, heat the butter or oil in a large deep pan over medium heat. Add the semolina and cook, stirring constantly, until it begins to change color. Add the almonds or pine nuts and cook, stirring constantly, until the semolina is golden brown. Remove and discard the lemon zest and spices from the syrup. Stirring constantly, add the semolina mixture to the hot syrup, together with the grated lemon zest. Cook over medium heat, stirring constantly, until the semolina has absorbed all the syrup and slides easily off the spoon and the side of the pan. Remove the pan from the heat, cover with a dish towel placed between the lid and the pan, and let cool for 8–10 minutes. Spoon into individual fluted molds or a single 6-cup (1.5-litre / 2½-pint) mold and smooth the surface with the back of the spoon. Turn out onto a plate, sprinkle with ground cinnamon, and decorate with more almonds or pine nuts. Serve warm or cold.

Serves 15–20
Preparation time 5 minutes
Cooking time 15–20 minutes

☐ p 600

Semolina halva, p 599

Kataifi pastry rolls, p 606

CONSTANTINOPLE SEMOLINA DESSERT
ΣΑΜΑΛΙ ΠΟΛΙΤΙΚΟ
Samali politiko

Brush an 11 x 15-inch (28 x 38-cm) baking pan or 14-inch (35-cm) round cake pan with melted butter. Combine the semolina, sugar, baking powder, and mastic, if using, in a large bowl and make a well in the center. Combine the yogurt and baking soda in another bowl and pour into the well, together with the vanilla, if using. Gradually incorporate the dry ingredients until thoroughly blended. Pour the mixture into the prepared pan, smooth the surface with a wet spatula, and let stand for 2–3 hours to swell. Preheat the oven to 350°F (180°C / Gas Mark 4). Score the surface of the semolina, marking it into 30 pieces, and place an almond half on each. Bake for 35–40 minutes, until golden brown. Meanwhile make the syrup. Put the sugar, corn syrup or glucose, and lemon juice into a pan, pour in 1½ cups (350 ml / 12 fl oz) water, and bring to a boil, stirring until the sugar has dissolved. Boil, without stirring, for 5 minutes, then remove from the heat, and stir in the vanilla or mastic. Remove the cake from the oven, brush the top with the melted butter, and carefully ladle the hot syrup evenly over the surface. Let cool thoroughly before transferring the pieces to a platter. Covered with plastic wrap (cling film), leftovers keep for several days at room temperature.

Makes 30 pieces
Preparation time 2½–3½ hours (including standing)
Cooking time 35–40 minutes

- 4 tablespoons melted butter, plus extra for brushing
- 2½ cups (425 g / 15 oz) coarse semolina
- 1½ cups (300 g / 11 oz) superfine (caster) sugar
- 1 teaspoon baking powder
- ½ teaspoon ground mastic or 1 teaspoon vanilla extract
- 2 cups (450 ml / 16 fl oz) plain yogurt
- 1 teaspoon baking soda (bicarbonate of soda)
- 48 blanched almond halves

FOR THE SYRUP
- 2½ cups (500 g / 1 lb 2 oz) superfine (caster) sugar
- 5 tablespoons corn syrup or liquid glucose
- 2 tablespoons freshly squeezed lemon juice
- 1 teaspoon vanilla extract or pinch of ground mastic

LENTEN SEMOLINA DESSERT
ΣΑΜΑΛΙ ΝΗΣΤΙΣΙΜΟ
Samali nistisimo

Combine both kinds of semolina, the baking powder, sugar, and mastic in a large bowl. Add the club soda and stir to a thin mixture. Pour the mixture into a 12 x 8-inch (30 x 20-cm) rectangular or 12-inch (30-cm) round baking pan and let stand until the semolina has absorbed all the liquid and plumped up. Preheat the oven to 400°F (200°C / Gas Mark 6). Put the almonds on the top of the semolina mixture and bake for 50 minutes, or until the top is golden brown. Meanwhile, make the syrup. Put the sugar, lemon juice, lemon zest, and cinnamon stick into a pan, pour in 1 cup (250 ml / 8 fl oz) water, and bring to a boil, stirring until the sugar has dissolved. Boil, without stirring, for 5 minutes, then remove from the heat. Remove and discard the cinnamon stick. Cut the dessert into pieces. Carefully pour the syrup over it and let cool. Cover and store at room temperature for up to 1 week.

Makes 20–25 pieces
Preparation time 15 minutes
Cooking time 50 minutes

- 1 cup (175 g / 6 oz) coarse semolina
- ½ cup (80 g / 3 oz) fine semolina
- 3 teaspoons baking powder
- 1 cup (200 g / 7 oz) superfine (caster) sugar
- ½ teaspoon ground mastic
- 1½ cups (350 ml / 12 fl oz) club soda (soda water)
- 25 almond halves

FOR THE SYRUP
- 2 cups (400 g / 14 oz) superfine (caster) sugar
- 1 teaspoon freshly squeezed lemon juice
- 1 teaspoon grated lemon zest
- 1 small cinnamon stick

- 4 cups (1 litre / 1¾ pints) milk
- ⅔ cup (150 ml / ¼ pint) melted clarified butter, plus extra for brushing
- ⅔ cup (120 g / 4 oz) semolina or cream of wheat
- ¾ cup (150 g / 5 oz) superfine (caster) sugar
- 2 eggs
- 2 egg yolks
- 1 teaspoon vanilla extract
- 1 lb 2 oz (500 g) ready-made phyllo (filo)
- confectioners' (icing) sugar and ground cinnamon, for dusting

CUSTARD PIE FROM THESSALONIKI
ΜΠΟΥΓΑΤΣΑ ΜΕ ΚΡΕΜΑ
Bougatsa me krema

Pour the milk into a pan and bring to just below boiling point, then remove from the heat. Heat 3 tablespoons of the butter in another pan, add the semolina or cream of wheat, and cook, stirring constantly, for 1 minute. Stirring vigorously, pour in the hot milk all at once. Add the sugar and cook, stirring constantly, until smooth and thick. Remove from the heat and let cool slightly, stirring occasionally to prevent a skin from forming on the surface. Meanwhile, lightly beat together the eggs, egg yolks, and vanilla in a bowl, then stir into the semolina. Press a sheet of plastic wrap (cling film) on the surface to prevent a skin from forming and set aside. Preheat the oven to 400°F (200°C / Gas Mark 6) and brush a baking pan the same size as the phyllo sheets with melted butter. Layer half the phyllo sheets in the base of the prepared pan, brushing each with melted butter. Spread the semolina custard evenly on top and cover with the remaining sheets of phyllo, brushing each with melted butter. Bake for 30–40 minutes, or until golden brown. Cut into bite-size squares and serve warm, sprinkled with confectioners' sugar and ground cinnamon.

Serves 8–10
Preparation time 30 minutes
Cooking time 30–40 minutes

- butter, for greasing
- 4 tablespoons all-purpose (plain) flour, plus extra for dusting
- 1¼ cups (215 g / 7½ oz) fine semolina
- 2 tablespoons baking powder
- 1 teaspoon ground cinnamon
- 3 teaspoons unsweetened cocoa powder
- 6 eggs
- 1 cup (200 g / 7 oz) superfine (caster) sugar
- 4 tablespoons olive or vegetable oil
- 1 cup walnuts, finely chopped

FOR THE SYRUP
- 2 cups (400 g / 14 oz) superfine (caster) sugar
- 1 tablespoon freshly squeezed lemon juice

WALNUT SEMOLINA CAKE
ΜΕΛΑΧΡΙΝΗ
Melahrini

Preheat the oven to 350°F (180°C / Gas Mark 4). Grease a 12-inch (30-cm) round cake pan with butter and dust with flour. Combine the flour, semolina, baking powder, cinnamon, and cocoa powder in a bowl. Beat together the eggs and sugar in another bowl with an electric mixer on high speed until thick and light. Gently fold in the dry ingredients, then lightly sprinkle the oil and walnuts over the surface, and fold in. Pour the mixture into the prepared pan, spreading it evenly, and bake for about 30 minutes. Remove from the oven and let cool slightly, then cut into squares. To make the syrup, put the sugar and lemon juice into a pan, pour in 2 cups (450 ml / 16 fl oz) water, and bring to a boil, stirring until the sugar has dissolved. Boil, without stirring, for 5 minutes, then remove from the heat, and carefully pour it over the cake while it is still warm. Let cool completely before transferring to a serving plate. It keeps well for up to 1 week at room temperature.

Serves 20
Preparation time 40 minutes
Cooking time 30 minutes

GATHERED WALNUT PHYLLO (FILO) ROLLS
ΣΑΡΑΓΛΙ ΣΟΥΡΩΤΟ
Saragli souroto

Preheat the oven to 375°F (190°C / Gas Mark 5) and brush a cookie sheet (baking tray) with melted butter. Combine the ground walnuts, cinnamon, and cloves in a bowl. Spread out a sheet of phyllo. Place a medium-thick wooden dowel rod widthwise at one end of the sheet and fold the edge over the rod. (The rod should be slightly longer than the width of the phyllo.) Brush the entire surface of the phyllo above the rod with melted butter and sprinkle with some of the nut mixture. Loosely roll up the sheet around the rod. Slowly pull out the rod by pushing the phyllo in the opposite direction, letting it wrinkle or gather. Repeat with the remaining phyllo and walnut filling. Place the gathered rolls on the prepared cookie sheet, brush with more melted butter, and bake for 40 minutes, or until golden brown. Meanwhile, make the syrup. Put the sugar, lemon juice, and honey into a pan, pour in 1½ cups (350 ml / 12 fl oz) water, and bring to a boil, stirring until the sugar has dissolved. Boil, without stirring, for 5 minutes, then remove from the heat. Carefully ladle the hot syrup over the rolls as soon as they come out of the oven. Let them absorb the syrup and cool completely before sprinkling with the ground nuts. Cut the rolls into 2½-inch (6-cm) pieces and arrange on a plate. They keep at room temperature for 1–2 weeks.

Makes 40 pieces
Preparation time 1 hour
Cooking time 40 minutes

- 1 cup (250 ml / 8 fl oz) melted clarified butter, plus extra for brushing
- 6 cups (700 g / 1½ lb) walnuts, finely ground
- 4 teaspoons ground cinnamon
- 2 teaspoons ground cloves
- 1 lb 2 oz (500 g) ready-made phyllo dough (filo pastry)
- finely ground walnuts or pistachio nuts, to decorate

FOR THE SYRUP
- 3 cups (600 g / 1 lb 5 oz) superfine (caster) sugar
- 1 tablespoon freshly squeezed lemon juice
- ½ cup (120 ml / 4 fl oz) honey

- ½ oz (15 g) fresh yeast or ½ tablespoon dried yeast
- ½ cup (120 ml / 4 fl oz) lukewarm milk
- 1 teaspoon superfine (caster) sugar
- pinch of salt
- ½ cup (120 ml / 4 fl oz) olive oil or corn oil
- 1 egg, lightly beaten
- 2 cups (225 g / 8 oz) all-purpose (plain) flour, plus extra for dusting
- butter, for greasing
- 1 tablespoon grated lemon zest

FOR THE FILLING
- 1 tablespoon unsweetened cocoa powder
- ½ cup (50 g / 2 oz) walnuts, chopped
- 1 cup (50 g / 2 oz) fresh bread crumbs
- 4 tablespoons raisins (optional)
- 2 tablespoons superfine (caster) sugar
- 1 teaspoon ground cinnamon
- ¼ teaspoon ground cloves
- pinch of baking soda (bicarbonate of soda) dissolved in 1 teaspoon water

FOR THE SYRUP
- 3 cups (600 g / 1 lb 5 oz) superfine (caster) sugar
- 1 tablespoon freshly squeezed lemon juice

WALNUT-STUFFED PUFF ROLLS
POΞΑΚΙΑ
Roxakia

If using fresh yeast, mash it with the lukewarm milk in a large bowl to a smooth paste. If using dried yeast, mix the lukewarm milk with the sugar in a large bowl, sprinkle the yeast over the surface, and let stand for 10–15 minutes, until frothy, then stir to a smooth paste. Add the sugar, if not already used, salt, oil, egg, and as much flour as necessary to make a soft dough. Remove about one sixth of the dough and mix with the cocoa powder until thoroughly combined, then mix with the remaining filling ingredients. Chill in the refrigerator until firm. Preheat the oven to 400°F (200°C / Gas Mark 6) and grease 2 or 3 cookie sheets (baking trays) with butter. Add the lemon zest to the remaining dough, and as much flour as necessary to make a stiff, smooth dough, kneading until no longer sticky. Roll out the lemon dough on a lightly floured work surface into a rectangle about ½ inch (1 cm) thick. Roll the chocolate dough into a long cylinder about 1 inch (2.5 cm) thick, and place on the center of the light-colored dough. Dampen the long edges, lift them up to face each other, and press to seal, enclosing the chocolate cylinder. Cut the roll crosswise into generous ¾-inch (2-cm) slices and place, cut sides up, on the prepared cookie sheets, spaced well apart. Press lightly to flatten and bake for about 25 minutes, until well browned. Meanwhile, make the syrup. Put the sugar and lemon juice into a pan, pour in 2 cups (450 ml / 16 fl oz) water, and bring to a boil, stirring until the sugar has dissolved. Boil, without stirring, for 5 minutes, then remove from the heat, and carefully pour over the rolls as soon as they come out of the oven. Let stand to absorb all the syrup, then transfer to a platter.

Makes 30–35 rolls
Preparation time 2 hours
Cooking time 25 minutes

KATAIFI PASTRY ROLLS

ΚΑΤΑΪΦΙ
Kataifi

Combine the chopped walnuts, rusk crumbs, cinnamon, lemon zest, and cloves in a bowl and sprinkle with the brandy. Fluff up the kataifi and divide it into 15–18 pieces. Cover with a damp dish towel while you are working, as it dries quickly. Tease out 1 section into a 4 x 8-inch (10 x 20-cm) strip. Put 1 tablespoon of the nut mixture at one end and roll up loosely. Make more rolls in the same way. Preheat the oven to 350°F (180°C / Gas Mark 4) and brush a baking pan with melted butter. Arrange the rolls in the prepared pan and drizzle the melted butter evenly over them. Cover the pan with aluminum foil and bake for 30 minutes. Remove the foil and bake for 30 minutes more, or until crisp and golden. Meanwhile, make the syrup. Put the sugar, corn syrup or glucose, and cinnamon stick or lemon zest into a pan, pour in 2 cups (450 ml / 16 fl oz) water, and bring to a boil, stirring until the sugar has dissolved. Boil, without stirring, for 5 minutes, then remove from the heat and discard the cinnamon. Carefully ladle the syrup over the rolls, letting them absorb it before adding more. Let cool, then sprinkle with chopped pistachios. Keep uncovered at room temperature for 1–2 weeks.

Makes 15–18 rolls
Preparation time 1 hour
Cooking time 1 hour

□ p 601

- 2¼ cups (250 g / 9 oz) walnuts, chopped
- 2 tablespoons rusk crumbs
- 1 tablespoon ground cinnamon
- 1 teaspoon grated lemon zest
- 1 teaspoon ground cloves
- 1 tablespoon brandy
- 9 oz (250 g) kataifi pastry
- 1 cup (250 ml / 8 fl oz) melted clarified butter, plus extra for brushing
- chopped pistachio nuts, to decorate

FOR THE SYRUP
- 3 cups (600 g / 1 lb 5 oz) superfine (caster) sugar
- 4 tablespoons corn syrup or liquid glucose
- 1 cinnamon stick or 1 teaspoon grated lemon zest

RAVANI WITH ALMONDS

ΡΑΒΑΝΙ ΜΕ ΑΜΥΓΔΑΛΑ
Ravani me amigdala

Preheat the oven to 350°F (180°C / Gas Mark 4) and grease a 12-inch (30-cm) round baking pan with butter. Combine the semolina and ground almonds in a bowl. Beat together the eggs and sugar in another bowl with an electric mixer on high speed for about 10 minutes, until thick and fluffy. Add the vanilla. Carefully fold in the semolina and almond mixture. Pour the mixture into the prepared pan and smooth with a spatula. Bake for 35–40 minutes. Remove from the oven and let cool. To make the syrup, put the sugar in a pan, pour in 1½ cups (350 ml / 12 fl oz) water, and bring to a boil over medium heat, stirring until the sugar has dissolved. Boil, without stirring, for 5 minutes, stir in the lemon juice, and ladle the syrup carefully over the lukewarm cake. Let cool completely, then cut into pieces. Store in the refrigerator.

Makes 10–12 pieces
Preparation time 20 minutes
Cooking time 40 minutes

- butter, for greasing
- 1 cup (175 g / 6 oz) fine semolina
- 1 cup (120 g / 4 oz) finely ground almonds
- 5 eggs
- ¾ cup (150 g / 5 oz) superfine (caster) sugar
- 2 teaspoons vanilla extract

FOR THE SYRUP
- 1½ cups (300 g / 11 oz) superfine (caster) sugar
- 1 tablespoon freshly squeezed lemon juice

- 9 oz (250 g) kataifi pastry
- ⅔ cup (150 ml / ¼ pint) melted clarified butter
- 8 oz (225 g) mizithra or ricotta cheese
- ½ cup (120 ml / 4 fl oz) heavy (double) cream
- 4 tablespoons confectioners' (icing) sugar
- 1 teaspoon vanilla extract
- 1 cup (120 g / 4 oz) walnuts, coarsely chopped
- 1 teaspoon ground cinnamon
- ¼ teaspoon ground cloves

FOR THE SYRUP
- 1½ cups (300 g / 11 oz) superfine (caster) sugar
- 1 tablespoon freshly squeezed lemon juice
- pinch of ground mastic

TO DECORATE
- scant 1 cup (250 ml / 8 fl oz) heavy (double) cream, whipped
- ½ cup (50 g / 2 oz) pistachio nuts, finely chopped

KATAIFI PASTRY TORTE
ΤΟΥΡΤΑ ΚΑΤΑΙΦΙ
Tourta kataifi

Preheat the oven to 350°F (180°C / Gas Mark 4). Untangle the kataifi pastry and spread half on the base of a 10-inch (25-cm) round baking pan. Drizzle with half the melted butter. Put the cheese, cream, confectioners' sugar, and vanilla extract into the food processor and process to a smooth cream. Spread the mixture evenly over the pastry. Combine the walnuts, cinnamon, and cloves in a bowl and sprinkle the mixture over the cream. Cover the filling with the remaining pastry and drizzle the remaining melted butter over it. Bake for 20 minutes, or until golden. Remove from the oven and let cool. To make the syrup, put the sugar, lemon juice, and mastic into a pan, pour in 1 cup (250 ml / 8 fl oz) water, and bring to a boil, stirring until the sugar has dissolved. Boil, without stirring, for 5 minutes, then remove from the heat, and carefully pour the syrup over the pastry. Let stand for 2 hours to absorb the syrup before serving. Decorate with whipped cream rosettes, if you like, and sprinkle with chopped pistachios.

Makes one 10-inch (25-cm) torte
Preparation time 2½ hours (including standing)
Cooking time 20 minutes

- 1 cup (200 g / 7 oz) superfine (caster) sugar
- 1½ cups (250 g / 9 oz) coarse semolina
- ½ teaspoon baking soda (bicarbonate of soda)
- 1 tablespoon brandy
- 1 cup (250 ml / 8 fl oz) natural yogurt
- 1 tablespoon grated orange zest or 2 teaspoons vanilla extract
- 5 tablespoons melted clarified butter, plus extra for brushing
- flour, for dusting
- 3 eggs
- ½ cup (50 g / 2 oz) thinly sliced blanched almonds

FOR THE SYRUP
- 1½ cups (300 g / 11 oz) superfine (caster) sugar
- 1 tablespoon freshly squeezed lemon juice

YOGURT RAVANI
PABANI ME ΓΙΑΟΥΡΤΙ
Ravani me giaourti

Combine half the sugar and the semolina in a bowl. Stir the baking soda into the brandy and add to the semolina mixture with the yogurt and orange zest or vanilla. Mix well and let stand for 1 hour. Preheat the oven to 400°F (200°C / Gas Mark 6). Brush a 10-inch (25-cm) round cake pan with melted butter and dust with flour. Stir the melted butter into the semolina mixture. Beat the eggs and remaining sugar in a bowl until thick and pale, then gently fold them into the semolina mixture. Pour the mixture into the pan and sprinkle with the almonds. Bake for 30 minutes, or until firm and golden. Let cool for 5–10 minutes, then cut into diamond-shaped pieces. To make the syrup, put the sugar and lemon juice into a pan, pour in 1 cup (250 ml / 8 fl oz) water, and bring to a boil, stirring until the sugar has dissolved. Boil, without stirring, for 5 minutes, then carefully ladle over the cake. Let cool completely, then transfer to a serving dish. Store, covered, in the refrigerator.

Makes 20 pieces
Preparation time 1¼ hours (including standing)
Cooking time 30 minutes

CANDIES (SWEETS) AND PRESERVES

-

ΓΛΥΚΑ ΚΑΙ ΚΟΜΠΟΣΤΕΣ

-

Glika ke kobostes

SPOON SWEETS
ΓΛΥΚΑ ΤΟΥ ΚΟΥΤΑΛΙΟΥ
Glika tou koutaliou

Spoon sweets have always played an important role in the cultural and social life of Greeks. Initially, small fruit such as grapes and figs were preserved in sugar syrup to prolong their season, and subsequently other ingredients such as almonds, pistachios, apples, cherries, rose petals, and citrus fruits were treated the same way. Spoon sweets are served according to a formal etiquette to welcome visitors into the home. A small amount of the sweet is placed on a small spoon on a delicate glass plate, or several varieties can be presented in an decorative dish on a silver tray. A glass of water, in which the spoon is placed after eating the sweet, is always served alongside.

Hard-skinned fruits, such as figs, walnuts, Temple or Seville oranges, and kumquats, should be pierced in several places before soaking in acidulated water. This is necessary to prevent crystallization. To proceed, pit (stone) or core the fruit, then weigh it, and allow the same weight of sugar, unless otherwise specified. Dissolve the sugar in water, stirring over low heat. Cover the pan for 1 minute to let the steam dissolve any sugar splashed on the side of the pan. When the sugar has dissolved completely, cook for 5–10 minutes, without stirring, to make a thick syrup. To prevent the syrup from crystallizing you can also add a little corn syrup or liquid glucose. Add the fruit and cook, skimming occasionally, for 15 minutes. Remove from the heat and let the fruit stand in the syrup overnight. The next day, cook over medium heat, stirring occasionally to prevent burning, until the fruit is soft and translucent and the syrup has set. If the fruit is tender before the syrup has set, transfer it to jars with a slotted spoon and continue to cook the syrup until setting point is reached. Pour the syrup over the fruit in the jars. This procedure keeps the fruit intact and preserves the aroma.

To test for setting, dip a tablespoon into the syrup and hold it vertically, letting the syrup drip back into the pan. Let the final drops drip over a small dish. If they hold their shape and remain intact, the syrup has set. On a candy (sugar) thermometer, setting point is reached when it registers 220°F (105°C). Let the preserve cool slightly, shaking the pan occasionally to keep the fruit covered by the syrup. This helps it plump up and distributes it evenly. Carefully ladle the warm preserve into hot sterilized jars, cover tightly, and leave upside down until cool. This creates a vacuum and prevents mold from forming. Label the jars and store in a cool dark place. Once the jar has been opened, keep it in the refrigerator. If the syrup thins, drain it into a small pan, simmer until it sets again, and pour it over the fruit. If it crystallizes, empty the contents of the jar into a pan, bring to a boil with 2–3 tablespoons of corn syrup or glucose and a little water. Simmer until setting point is reached. If mold forms on the surface, carefully remove and discard it. Simmer the remaining preserve to reset the syrup. Usually the reason for mold forming is that the syrup was not properly set.

- 4½ cups (500 g / 1 lb 2 oz) blanched almonds, dried (see note)
- 2¼ cups (500 g / 1 lb 2 oz) honey
- 2 tablespoons brandy

ALMONDS IN HONEY FROM SANTORINI
ΓΛΥΚΟ ΚΟΥΦΕΤΟ
Gliko koufeto

This spoon sweet is traditionally served at weddings, engagement parties, and baptisms in Santorini and other islands.

Combine the almonds and half the honey in a pan and cook over medium heat, stirring constantly, until golden. Stir in the brandy and the remaining honey and cook for 10 minutes more. Do not overcook. Carefully transfer to a shallow glass bowl and let cool. Serve in small glass dishes with demitasse spoons.

Serves 10
Preparation time 1 hour (including cooling)
Cooking time 30 minutes

Note: The almonds must be completely dry. Let them dry in the sun for 2–3 days, or dry them in a very low oven for 10 minutes.

□ p 612

- 2¼ lb (1 kg) sour cherries
- 5 cups (1 kg / 2¼ lb) superfine (caster) sugar
- ½ teaspoon citric acid or 2 tablespoons freshly squeezed lemon juice
- ½ cup (120 ml / 4 fl oz) corn syrup or liquid glucose

SOUR CHERRIES IN SYRUP
ΒΥΣΣΙΝΟ Η ΚΕΡΑΣΙ ΓΛΥΚΟ
Visino i kerasi gliko

Pour ½ cup (120 ml / 4 fl oz) water into a bowl. Using a cherry pitter (stoner), remove the pits (stones) from the cherries, working over a bowl to catch the juice. Drop the pits into the water, stir, and drain over the cherries in a bowl. Make alternating layers of the cherries and sugar in a heavy pan, pour in the juice, cover, and let stand overnight. The next day, set the pan over low heat and gradually bring to a boil. Increase the heat and boil, stirring occasionally and skimming off any scum that rises to the surface, for 35 minutes. Reduce the heat, add the citric acid or lemon juice and corn syrup or glucose, and simmer, stirring occasionally, until setting point is reached (see p 610). Remove from the heat and let cool, shaking the pan several times to help the fruit absorb syrup and plump up. Carefully ladle into sterilized jars, seal, label, and store in a cool, dark place, or in the refrigerator.

Makes 2¼ lb (1 kg)
Preparation time 24 hours (including standing and cooling)
Cooking time 45 minutes

□ p 613

Almonds in honey from Santorini, p 611

Sour cherries in syrup, p 611

FRESH FIGS IN SYRUP
ΜΕΛΩΜΕΝΑ ΣΥΚΑ
Melomena sika

- 4½ lb (2 kg) fresh figs
- 5 cups (1 kg / 2¼ lb) superfine (caster) sugar
- 2 teaspoons vanilla extract

The figs left on the trees at the end of the season, which have started to shrivel and dehydrate, are perfect for this recipe. Arrange a layer of figs on the base of a large pan and sprinkle with one third of the sugar. Make 2 more layers with the remaining figs and sugar. Let stand for several hours, preferably overnight. Gradually bring to a boil over low heat and simmer for about 30 minutes. Remove from the heat and let stand for 12 hours. Cook over medium heat until a thick syrup forms. Stir in the vanilla shortly before removing from the heat. Let cool, carefully ladle into sterilized jars, cover, and seal. Label and store in a cool, dark place, or in the refrigerator.

Makes 4½ lb (2 kg)
Preparation time 24 hours (including standing)
Cooking time 1 hour

▢ p 617

GRAPES IN SYRUP
ΣΤΑΦΥΛΙ ΓΛΥΚΟ
Stafili gliko

- 2¼ lb (1 kg) firm Rozaki, Italian Regina, Tokay, or Muscat grapes, seeded
- ½ cup (120 ml / 4 fl oz) freshly squeezed lemon juice
- 5 cups (1 kg / 2¼ lb) superfine (caster) sugar

Spread out the grapes in a single layer in a glass dish, sprinkle with lemon juice, and let stand for 2–3 hours. Pour 2 cups (450 ml / 16 fl oz) water into a wide pan, add the sugar, and bring to a boil, stirring constantly until the sugar has dissolved. Boil, without stirring, for about 5 minutes, or until setting point is reached (see p 610). Add half the grapes and simmer over low heat for 10 minutes. Remove the pan from the heat and, using a slotted spoon, transfer the grapes to a colander set over a bowl. Repeat with the remaining grapes. Add the syrup that has drained from the grapes to the pan and cook until setting point is reached. Gently stir in the grapes and simmer over low heat for 5 minutes more, or until setting point is reached again. Remove from the heat and let cool in the syrup, shaking the pan carefully several times. Store in large wide glass container with an airtight seal.

Makes 2¼ lb (1 kg)
Preparation time 3 hours (including standing and cooling)
Cooking time 45 minutes

- 4½ lb (2 kg) kumquats
- 15 cups (3 kg / 6 lb 10 oz) superfine (caster) sugar
- 2¼ cups (500 ml / 18 fl oz) corn syrup or liquid glucose

KUMQUATS IN SYRUP
ΚΟΥΜΚΟΥΑΤ ΓΛΥΚΟ
Koumkouat gliko

Prick the kumquats all over, put them into a large pan, pour in water to cover and cook for 40 minutes, then drain. Return the kumquats to the pan, pour in 8¾ cups (2 litres / 3½ pints) water, and let stand for 24 hours. Remove with a slotted spoon and set aside. Add half the sugar to the soaking water and bring to a boil, stirring until the sugar has dissolved. Boil, without stirring, for 5 minutes. Add the kumquats, remove from the heat, and let stand for 24 hours. The next day, remove the kumquats and set aside. Add one quarter of the remaining sugar to the pan and bring to a boil, stirring until the sugar has dissolved. Remove from the heat and add the kumquats, then let stand for another 24 hours. Repeat this procedure another 4 times, adding the same quantity of sugar to the syrup each time and cooking for 5 minutes. On the final day, do not remove the kumquats, just add the corn syrup or glucose, and cook until the syrup sets (see p 610). Remove from the heat and let the kumquats cool in the syrup, occasionally shaking the pan carefully. Ladle the fruit and syrup into sterilized glass jars and seal.

Makes 6 lb 10 oz (3 kg)
Preparation time 7 days (including standing and cooling)
Cooking time 1¼ hours

☐ p 616

- 3¼ lb (1.5 kg) thick-skinned oranges
- 10¼ cups (2 kg / 4½ lb) superfine (caster) sugar
- 2 tablespoons freshly squeezed lemon juice
- ½ cup (120 ml / 4 fl oz) corn syrup or liquid glucose

ORANGE RIND ROLLS
ΠΟΡΤΟΚΑΛΙ ΡΟΛΑ
Portokali rola

Lightly rub the oranges with a fine grater. Score the rinds into 4, 6, or 8 segments, depending on the size of the fruit, and remove them carefully. Roll up each piece tightly and thread onto cotton, like a necklace, with a needle. Place the rinds in a pan, pour in 3 cups (750 ml / 1¼ pints) water, and let stand for 24 hours. The next day, set the pan over medium heat and cook for about 40 minutes, until tender. Slide the rinds off the cotton, add the sugar, and cook until the syrup is thick. Remove from the heat and let stand overnight. The next day, add the lemon juice and corn syrup or glucose and cook until setting point is reached (see p 610). Let the rinds cool in the syrup, then place in sterilized jars. Seal, label, and store in a cool, dark place, or in the refrigerator.

Makes 3¼ lb (1.5 kg)
Preparation time 2 days (including standing and cooling)
Cooking time 45 minutes

☐ p 618

Kumquats in syrup, p 615

Orange rind rolls, p 615

Carrot jam, p 624

PISTACHIO SWEETMEAT
ΑΙΓΙΝΙΤΙΚΟ ΦΥΣΤΙΚΙ ΓΛΥΚΟ
Eginitiko fistiki gliko

- 2¼ lb (1 kg) green, unripe pistachio nuts
- 7½ cups (1.5 kg / 3¼ lb) superfine (caster) sugar
- 2 tablespoons freshly squeezed lemon juice
- 1 teaspoon vanilla extract

Prick the pistachios with a thin metal skewer or a thick needle, pushing it from one end through the middle. Put them into a large pan, pour in water to cover, and bring to a boil, then simmer until they begin to soften. If their shells have begun to harden, they must be removed. Drain and set aside in a colander. Put the sugar into a pan, pour in 1 cup (250 ml / 8 fl oz) water, and bring to a boil, stirring until the sugar has dissolved, then simmer until the syrup has reached soft-ball stage, or 234–240°F (112–116°F) on a candy (sugar) thermometer. Add the pistachios and simmer, carefully skimming the surface, until setting point is reached (see p 610). Stir in the lemon juice and vanilla extract shortly before removing the pan from the heat. Let stand at room temperature for 24 hours. Let cool, then store in sterilized jars.

Makes 3¼ lb (1.5 kg)
Preparation time 24 hours (including standing)
Cooking time 1 hour

GRATED QUINCE IN SYRUP
ΚΥΔΩΝΙ ΤΡΙΦΤΟ
Kidoni trifto

- 2 tablespoons freshly squeezed lemon juice
- 2¼ lb (1 kg) quinces
- 3¾ cups (750 g / 1 lb 10 oz) superfine (caster) sugar
- ½ cup (120 ml / 4 fl oz) corn syrup or liquid glucose
- 2 lemon-scented geranium or lemon leaves, washed

Pour 3 cups (750 ml / 1¼ pints) water into a pan and stir in the lemon juice. Peel the quinces and grate them very coarsely to the core over the pan so that the fruit drops straight into the acidulated water. If a very coarse grater is not available, slice and then cut the quinces into strips with a pair of scissors. Set the pan over medium heat, cover, and cook until the fruit is soft and almost all the water has evaporated. Stir in the sugar and let stand overnight. The next day, simmer over low heat, stirring frequently, for about 15 minutes, or until the fruit is soft and translucent and the syrup is set (see p 610). Add the corn syrup or glucose and geranium or lemon leaves 5 minutes before the end of the cooking time. Carefully ladle into sterilized jars, cover, label, and seal. Store in a cool, dark place, or in the refrigerator.

Makes 2¼ lb (1 kg)
Preparation time 24 hours (including standing)
Cooking time 30 minutes

- 8 oz (225 g) rose petals
- 5 cups (1 kg / 2¼ lb) superfine (caster) sugar
- 2 tablespoons freshly squeezed lemon juice or ½ teaspoon citric acid
- ½ cup (120 ml / 4 fl oz) corn syrup or liquid glucose
- 1 tablespoon glycerin

ROSE PETAL PRESERVE
ΤΡΙΑΝΤΑΦΥΛΛΟ ΓΛΥΚΟ
Triantafilo gliko

This preserve is made with just one special variety of rose—an early pink rose that blooms at the end of April and the beginning of May in Greece. Remove the petals and cut off the white bottom part with a pair of scissors. Rinse the petals in cold water several times and drain them thoroughly. Weigh the petals and use 5 cups (1 kg / 2¼ lb) sugar for every 8 oz (225 g) trimmed petals. Rub the petals with the sugar between your palms until they look wilted, then let stand for 2–3 hours. Put the petals into a heavy pan, add 1 cup (250 ml / 8 fl oz) water, and cook over low heat, stirring constantly, until the syrup has almost set (see p 610). Add the lemon juice or citric acid, corn syrup or glucose, and glycerin. Remove from the heat and let cool, shaking the pan occasionally to distribute the petals and keep them covered by the syrup. Carefully ladle into jars, cover, and seal. Label and store in a cool dark place or in the refrigerator.

Makes 2¼ lb (1 kg)
Preparation time 4½ hours (including standing and cooling)
Cooking time 15–20 minutes

- 2¼ lb (1 kg) large, under-ripe strawberries, hulled
- ½ cup (120 ml / 4 fl oz) freshly squeezed lemon juice
- 5 cups (1 kg / 2¼ lb) superfine (caster) sugar

STRAWBERRIES IN SYRUP
ΦΡΑΟΥΛΕΣ ΓΛΥΚΟ
Fraoules gliko

Put the strawberries into a large, shallow dish, sprinkle with the lemon juice, and let stand for 2–3 hours. Put the sugar into a wide, heavy pan, pour in 2 cups (450 ml / 16 fl oz) water, and bring to a boil over medium heat, stirring constantly until the sugar has dissolved. Cook the syrup for 5 minutes, until it reaches setting point (see p 610), then add half the strawberries, and simmer over low heat, skimming frequently, for 10 minutes. Remove the pan from the heat. Using a slotted spoon, carefully transfer the strawberries to a large strainer set over a bowl. Bring the syrup back to setting point and repeat with the remaining strawberries. Add the juice that has drained off the strawberries to the syrup and cook until it reaches setting point again. Return the strawberries to the pan and cook for 5 minutes more, or until the syrup coats the fruits and setting point is reached. Remove from the heat and let cool, shaking the pan carefully several times to help the strawberries absorb syrup. Carefully transfer to wide shallow jars, distributing the strawberries and syrup equally. Cover the jars when the preserve is completely cool.

Makes 2¼ lb (1 kg)
Preparation time 4½ hours (including standing and cooling)
Cooking time 45 minutes

PRESERVES
ΚΟΜΠΟΣΤΕΣ
Kobostes

Many fruits can be preserved by cooking them with sugar. If prepared and stored correctly, they will keep for months. The proportion of sugar to fruit can vary from 12 oz (350 g) to 16 oz (450 g) sugar for every 1 lb (450 g) fruit, depending on the quality and sweetness of the fruit. Sugar also helps preserves to set, along with pectin (a natural gelling agent) and acid, both of which occur naturally in fruit. The pectin and acid content can vary considerably—even the same variety of fruit will have varying levels of pectin and acid, depending on its age. The acidity of the fruit can be adjusted by adding freshly squeezed lemon juice. About 2 tablespoons freshly squeezed lemon juice should be added to 1¼ cups (600 ml / 1 pint) low-acid fruit or juice at the beginning of the cooking to help the fruit release its natural pectin. Low-pectin fruits, such as apricots, peaches, pineapples, cherries, and kiwis, can be combined with high-pectin fruits, such as apples, quinces, or grapes. Commercial or homemade natural pectin (p 50) can also be added: ½ cup (120 ml / 4 fl oz) natural pectin is enough to set 5 cups (1.2 litres / 2 pints) low-pectin fruit. It is added at the end of cooking.

To test for setting, dip a spoon into the jam and lift it up, letting the jam drop back into the pan. The mixture is ready when the jam forms two large, distinct drops that fall off the spoon cleanly. Alternatively, carefully spoon a little of the jam onto a chilled plate and let cool for 2–3 minutes. Setting point has been reached if a skin forms on the surface that is firm enough to wrinkle when you push it with your finger, or when a candy (sugar) thermometer registers 220°F (105°C). Once the jam has reached setting point, skim off the froth from the surface and carefully ladle it into hot, sterilized jars, leaving a ½-inch (1-cm) gap at the top. Seal them and turn upside down. Let cool, then label, and store in a cool, dark place. To sterilize jars, put them into boiling water for 5 minutes, then remove, and leave upside down to dry on paper towels.

When preserving whole fresh fruit, it must be heat-processed in a hot water bath to retain its quality and aroma for up to 1 year. Pack the fruit into glass preserving jars, leaving a ½-inch (1-cm) gap at the top, and seal the lids (rubber gaskets or seals must be renewed every time the jar is used.) Following the manufacturer's instructions, heat the jars in water at the specified temperature and for the specified time. Use a large pan with a tight-fitting lid—it should be 3 inches (7.5 cm) taller than the jars. Put a trivet on the base of the pan to protect the jars from direct heat and wrap each jar in a cloth to prevent cracking. Cover the jars with water, cover the pan, bring the water to a boil, and simmer for as long as specified, counting from the moment the water begins to boil. Acidity is also an important factor in safe sterilization. Because the acidity of fruits can vary, it is advisable to add 2–3 teaspoons freshly squeezed lemon juice to each 1¼-cup (600-ml / 1-pint) jar of sweet fruits, such as figs and pears, or any overripe fruit.

- 6 tablespoons (80 g / 3 oz) butter, softened, plus extra for greasing
- 4 large apples
- 2 tablespoons freshly squeezed lemon juice
- ½ cup (100 g / 3½ oz) superfine (caster) sugar
- 5 tablespoons coarsely chopped walnuts
- 1 teaspoon ground cinnamon
- ½ teaspoon ground cloves
- 5 tablespoons brandy
- whipped cream, to serve

BAKED APPLES
ΜΗΛΑ ΨΗΤΑ
Mila psita

Preheat the oven to 300°F (150°C / Gas Mark 2) and grease an ovenproof dish with butter. Cut a horizontal slice from the top of each apple and core them. Rub the cut surfaces with lemon juice. Arrange the apples close together in the prepared dish and pour in 5 tablespoons water. Combine the sugar and butter in a small bowl, then add the nuts, cinnamon, cloves, and half the brandy, and mix well. Spoon the filling into the cavities in the center of the apples, reserving the unused mixture. Sprinkle the remaining brandy on top and bake, basting frequently with the cooking juices, for 1½ hours. As the filling shrinks during cooking, use the surplus mixture to refill the cavities until all of it has been used up. Serve the apples warm, with whipped cream.

Serves 4
Preparation time 30 minutes
Cooking time 1½ hours

- 3¼ lb (1.5 kg) firm apples or pears
- 2 tablespoons freshly squeezed lemon juice
- 1 cup (200 g / 7 oz) superfine (caster) sugar
- 1 teaspoon vanilla extract, or 1 cinnamon stick and 3 – 4 cloves, or thinly pared lemon zest

APPLE OR PEAR COMPOTE
ΜΗΛΟ Η ΑΧΛΑΔΙ ΚΟΜΠΟΣΤΑ
Milo i ahladi kobosta

Peel and core the fruit. Cut each fruit in half and plunge into a bowl of cold water mixed with the lemon juice to prevent discoloration. Put the sugar into a pan, pour in 1 cup (250 ml / 8 fl oz) water, and bring to a boil over low heat, stirring constantly until the sugar has dissolved. Boil, without stirring, for 5 minutes. Stir in the flavoring of your choice, then add the fruit, draining it with a slotted spoon. Simmer for 5 – 15 minutes, until just tender (avoid overcooking). Transfer the fruit to a bowl or jar with a slotted spoon. Boil the syrup until it has thickened slightly, then carefully ladle it over the fruit. Serve the compote warm or cold. It keeps in the refrigerator for about 1 week. If you want to keep the compote longer, it must be heat-processed after bottling (see p 622).

Serves 4
Preparation time 15 minutes
Cooking time 30 minutes

Note: If you like, add 1 cup (250 ml / 8 fl oz) sweet red wine to the syrup along with the fruit.

CARROT JAM
ΜΑΡΜΕΛΑΔΑ ΚΑΡΟΤΟ
Marmelada karoto

- 10⅔ cups (1.5 kg / 3¼ lb) grated tender young carrots
- 7½ cups (1.5 kg / 3¼ lb) superfine (caster) sugar
- grated zest and strained juice of 6 lemons

Put the carrots into a heavy nonstick pan and pour in water to cover. Simmer over medium heat, until the carrots are soft and the water has evaporated. Add the sugar, lemon zest, and lemon juice and cook, stirring frequently, for about 30 minutes, or until setting point is reached (see p 622) and the jam is thick and glossy. Remove from the heat, skim, and carefully ladle into warm, sterilized jars. Seal and leave the jars upside down to cool. Label and store in a cool, dark place.

Makes 4½ lb (2 kg)
Preparation time 20 minutes
Cooking time 1 hour

☐ p 619

SOUR CHERRY LIQUEUR
ΛΙΚΕΡ ΜΕ ΒΥΣΣΙΝΑ
Liker me visina

- 2¼ lb (1 kg) sour cherries
- 5 cups (1 kg / 2¼ lb) superfine (caster) sugar
- 10 cloves
- 2 cinnamon sticks, crushed
- 2¼ cups (500 ml / 18 fl oz) brandy

Put the cherries into a wide-mouthed bottle and add the sugar and spices. Cover tightly, shake well, and let macerate in a sunny place, shaking the bottle once or twice a day, for about 2 months. Drain the cherry juice and mix with the brandy, then bottle, and cork. Store in a cool place.

Makes about 4 cups (1 litre / 1¾ pints)
Preparation time 2 months

DAMSON COMPOTE IN WINE
ΔΑΜΑΣΚΗΝΑ ΣΕ ΚΡΑΣΙ
Damaskina se krasi

- 2¼ lb (1 kg) under-ripe damsons
- 2½ cups (600 ml / 1 pint) dry red wine
- 2 cinnamon sticks
- 20 cloves
- 1½ cups (300 g / 11 oz) superfine (caster) sugar
- 2 tablespoons freshly squeezed lemon juice

Put the damsons into a wide, shallow pan in a single layer and add the wine and spices. Bring to a boil, reduce the heat, cover, and simmer for 15 minutes. If any of the skins split, lift the fruit out with a slotted spoon, carefully remove the skin, then return to the pan. Stir in the sugar and lemon juice and cook for 30 minutes more, or until the syrup has thickened. Remove from the heat and let cool, then store in the refrigerator. Stored in a container with a tight-fitting lid, they will keep for up to 1 year.

Makes 3¼ lb (1.5 kg)
Preparation time 5 minutes
Cooking time 45 minutes

- 12 fresh figs
- ⅔ cup (150 g / 5 oz) thyme honey
- 1 cup (250 ml / 8 fl oz) sweet red wine
- 1 tablespoon grated lemon zest
- 1 cinnamon stick
- 10 cloves
- 1 lb 2 oz (500 g) anthotiro or ricotta or 2¼ cups (500 ml / 18 fl oz) strained plain or thick Greek yogurt
- 2–3 tablespoons heavy (double) cream (optional)
- 4 tablespoons chopped walnuts (optional)
- fresh mint sprigs, to decorate (optional)

FIGS WITH RICOTTA OR YOGURT
ΣΥΚΑ ΜΕ ΑΝΘΟΤΥΡΟ Η ΓΙΑΟΥΡΤΙ
Sika me anthotiro i giaourti

Put the unpeeled figs in a pan with the honey, wine, 1 cup (250 ml / 8 fl oz) water, lemon zest, and spices. Cook over high heat for 20 minutes, or until the syrup thickens. Remove the spices with a slotted spoon and discard. Let the figs cool completely in the syrup. Mash the cheese with a fork in a bowl or lightly beat the yogurt with a fork. If it is stiff, add the heavy cream. Divide among 4 small dessert bowls, place 3 figs on top of each bowl, and drizzle with the syrup. Store in the refrigerator until ready to serve. Serve sprinkled with the chopped nuts and decorate with mint sprigs, if using.

Serves 4
Preparation time 1 hour (including cooling)
Cooking time 20 minutes

- 2 tablespoons grated lemon zest
- 5 cups (1 kg / 2¼ lb) superfine (caster) sugar
- 3–3½ cups (750–850 ml / 1¼–1½ pints) freshly squeezed lemon juice, strained

LEMON SYRUP FOR LEMONADE
ΛΕΜΟΝΑΔΑ
Lemonada

Bring 2 cups (450 ml / 16 fl oz) water to a boil in a small pan with the lemon zest, cover, and simmer for 10–15 minutes. Strain through a fine strainer into a larger pan. Add the sugar and cook over low heat, stirring constantly until the sugar has dissolved. Increase the heat and simmer, without stirring, for 5–8 minutes, or until the syrup reaches the soft-ball stage, 234–240°F (112–116°C) on a candy (sugar) thermometer. To test for soft-ball stage, plunge a teaspoon of syrup into a small bowl of cold water and roll the syrup between your finger and thumb. If it makes a soft, pliable ball, it is ready. Add the lemon juice, stir, and immediately remove from the heat. Let cool slightly. Carefully pour the lemon syrup into sterilized bottles and store in the refrigerator. To serve, put about 4 tablespoons syrup and 3–4 ice cubes into a tall glass, fill with cold water, and stir. Serve with a twisted strip of lemon zest.

Makes about 6¼ cups (1.5 litres / 2½ pints)
Preparation time 10 minutes
Cooking time 15–20 minutes

ORANGE MARMALADE
ΜΑΡΜΕΛΑΔΑ ΠΟΡΤΟΚΑΛΙ
Marmelada portokali

- 2¼ lb (1 kg) oranges, carefully washed
- 1 lemon
- 8¾ cups (2 litres / 3½ pints) water
- 5 cups (1 kg / 2¼ lb) superfine (caster) sugar

Slice each orange and lemon into 8 wedges, and separate the flesh from the rind, removing all traces of pith. Using a pair of scissors, remove the seeds and membranes from the flesh and put them into a small bowl. Pour in enough of the water to cover. Finely chop the flesh with a sharp knife and cut the rind into thin strips. Put the chopped flesh and strips of rind into a heavy pan with the remaining water and let the pan and the bowl soak for 24 hours. Bring the contents of the pan to a boil over medium heat. Strain the water from the seeds into the pan, tie the seeds in a cheesecloth (muslin) bag, and add it to the pan. Cover and simmer for about 40 minutes. Remove the cheesecloth-wrapped seeds, squeeze out the liquid into the pan, and discard. Add the sugar and cook over low heat, stirring constantly until dissolved. Increase the heat to medium and cook, uncovered and stirring occasionally with a wooden spoon, for about 1½ hours, or until the marmalade is translucent and at setting point (see p 622). Remove from the heat and let cool slightly, shaking the pan occasionally to distribute the rind. Carefully ladle the warm marmalade into hot, sterilized jars, cover tightly, and leave upside down to cool. Label and store in a cool, dark place.

Makes 3¼ lb (1.5 kg)
Preparation time 24½ hours (including soaking)
Cooking time 2 hours

Note: You can follow the same procedure for any citrus fruit, or combine 2–3 fruits, according to taste and availability.

PEARS WITH SAMOS SWEET WINE
ΑΧΛΑΔΙ ΜΕ ΣΑΜΙΩΤΙΚΟ ΚΡΑΣΙ
Ahladi me samiotiko krasi

- 8 cooking pears
- 2 cups (450 ml / 16 fl oz) Samos sweet white wine
- scant ½ cup (80 g / 3 oz) superfine (caster) sugar
- 1 cinnamon stick

Peel the pears, put them into a pan with the wine, sugar, and cinnamon, and bring to a boil, stirring until the sugar has dissolved. Cook over medium heat for about 15 minutes, or until the pears are tender. Carefully transfer the pears with a slotted spoon to a shallow platter. Continue cooking the syrup for 5–10 minutes, or until it has thickened. Carefully pour it over the pears and serve warm or chilled.

Serves 8
Preparation time 10 minutes
Cooking time 20 minutes

- ¾ cup (150 g / 5 oz) superfine (caster) sugar
- 4 large peaches or 1½ lb (700 g) apricots, peeled, halved, and pitted (stoned)
- 4 tablespoons brandy

PEACH OR APRICOT COMPOTE
ΡΟΔΑΚΙΝΑ Η ΒΕΡΥΚΟΚΑ ΚΟΜΠΟΣΤΑ
Rodakina i verikoka kobosta

Put the sugar into a pan, pour in 1 cup (250 ml / 8 fl oz) water, and bring to a boil, stirring constantly until the sugar has dissolved. When the syrup is clear, add the peaches or apricots, and simmer for about 8 minutes, until they are just tender. Avoid overcooking. Transfer the fruit to a bowl with a slotted spoon. Boil the syrup until slightly thickened, stir in the brandy, and carefully pour it over the peaches. Serve the compote warm or cold.

Serves 4
Preparation time 10 minutes
Cooking time 15 minutes

Note: Compotes will keep for up to a year if they are heat-processed after bottling (see p 622).

- 4½ lb (2 kg) ripe plums, halved and pitted (stoned)
- 5 cups (1 kg / 2¼ lb) superfine (caster) sugar
- 1 teaspoon almond extract

PLUM JAM
ΜΑΡΜΕΛΑΔΑ ΔΑΜΑΣΚΗΝΟ
Marmelada damaskino

Put the plums into a pan, pour in 1½ cups (350 ml / 12 fl oz) water, and simmer for about 40 minutes, until very soft. Remove the pan from the heat and stir in the sugar until it has dissolved. Return the pan to the heat and cook rapidly, stirring occasionally with a wooden spoon, for about 15 minutes, until setting point is reached (see p 622). Add the almond extract and remove from the heat. Skim the froth off the surface, let cool slightly, and carefully ladle into warm, sterilized jars. Seal tightly and leave the jars upside down to cool. Label and store in a cool, dark place for up to 1 year.

Makes 4½ lb (2 kg)
Preparation time 30 minutes
Cooking time 55 minutes

Note: Red wine can be substituted for half the water, and 1 cinnamon stick and 10 cloves can be added instead of the almond extract. Add the spices at the beginning and remove before adding the sugar.

QUINCE OR APPLE JELLY
ΠΕΛΤΕΣ ΚΥΔΩΝΙ Η ΜΗΛΟ
Peltes kidoni i milo

- 4½ lb (2 kg) under-ripe quinces or apples, rinsed
- 7½ cups (1.5 kg / 3¼ lb) superfine (caster) sugar
- 2 tablespoons freshly squeezed lemon juice
- 1 teaspoon vanilla extract or 2–3 lemon-scented geranium leaves

Cut the quinces or apples into pieces, without peeling or coring. Put them into a large pan, pour in water to cover, cover, and simmer for about 30 minutes, or until the fruit is soft. Remove from the heat and let stand overnight. The next day, pour the fruit into a strainer lined with a double thickness of cheesecloth (muslin) and let the juice drip into a bowl, without pressing or squeezing the fruit, as this will cloud the liquid. Measure the juice and add 3¾ cups (750 g / 1 lb 10 oz) sugar for every 4 cups (1 litre / 1¾ pints) juice. Pour into a pan and bring to a boil, stirring until the sugar has dissolved, then boil rapidly for about 10 minutes, or until setting point is reached (see p 622). Stir in the lemon juice and vanilla or geranium leaves. Carefully ladle the warm jelly into sterilized jars and seal when completely cooled. Store in a cool, dark place or in the refrigerator for up to 1 year.

Makes 3¼ lb (1.5 kg)
Preparation time 24½ hours (including standing)
Cooking time 1 hour

QUINCES BAKED IN WINE WITH YOGURT
ΚΥΔΩΝΙΑ ΨΗΤΑ ΣΕ ΚΡΑΣΙ ΜΕ ΓΙΑΟΥΡΤΙ
Kidonia psita se krasi me giaourti

- 2¼ lb (1 kg) quinces
- 2 tablespoons freshly squeezed lemon juice
- 2 cups (450 ml / 16 fl oz) sweet red wine
- 10 cloves
- 2 cinnamon sticks
- 1½ cups (300 g / 11 oz) superfine (caster) sugar
- 2¼ cups (500 ml / 18 fl oz) strained plain or thick Greek yogurt

Preheat the oven to 350°F (180°C / Gas Mark 4). Rub the quinces to remove the fuzz on the skin, rinse, and cut into quarters. Remove the cores, put the pieces of fruit into a baking dish, and sprinkle with the lemon juice. Put the cores into a pan with the wine, cloves, and cinnamon, cover, and simmer for 10 minutes. Strain and reserve the wine. Sprinkle the quinces with the sugar and reserved wine, cover with aluminum foil, and bake for 1 hour. Remove the aluminum foil, turn the pieces of quince over, and reduce the oven temperature to 225°F (110°C / Gas Mark ¼) and bake for 30 minutes more, until they are well glazed with the wine sauce. Serve hot or cold with the yogurt.

Serves 6
Preparation time 15 minutes
Cooking time 1½ hours

▢ p 630

BONBONS
ΜΙΚΡΑ ΓΛΥΚΙΣΜΑΤΑ
Mikra glikasmata

The ancient Greeks and Romans, like their modern descendants, had a weakness for candies (sweets) and confections. The first professional candy-makers were Greeks, first in Athens, and later in the wealthy Greek colonies of southern Italy. The Byzantines, who pursued the spice trade links the Romans had forged with the East, developed them to even greater advantage, ensuring the legendary wealth and power of their Empire. Elegant confections made from rare and precious ingredients including sugar not only appeared on the tables of the Byzantine elite, but were also given as gifts on special occasions, which is still a custom in modern Greece.

- butter, for greasing
- 4 tablespoons corn syrup or liquid glucose
- ½ teaspoon red food coloring
- 1 teaspoon liquid baking ammonia or 1 teaspoon baking powder
- 2 teaspoons vanilla extract
- 5 cups (1 kg / 2¼ lb) superfine (caster) sugar
- 4½ cups (500 g / 1 lb 2 oz) almonds

ALMOND CLUSTERS FROM KEFALLONIA
ΜΑΝΤΟΛΕΣ
Madoles

Madoles are the traditional sweetmeats of Kefallonia. They were given to guests at the church after the marriage ceremony.

Grease a large cookie sheet (baking tray) or marble slab with butter. Combine the corn syrup or glucose with ½ cup (120 ml / 4 fl oz) water in a pan and bring to a boil. Dissolve the food coloring in the ammonia and stir into the pan, or add the baking powder and the food coloring to the pan, then remove from the heat. Let cool slightly, then stir in the vanilla. Put 3¾ cups (750 g / 1 lb 10 oz) of the sugar into a large heavy pan, pour in 1 cup (250 ml / 8 fl oz) water, and bring to a boil over medium heat, stirring constantly. Add the almonds and stir constantly until they are thoroughly coated. Remove from the heat and stir for 5 minutes. Return the pan to the heat, add the remaining sugar, and cook, stirring constantly, until thoroughly combined. Remove from the heat, add the red mixture, and stir vigorously to distribute it evenly. Spread the mixture onto the prepared cookie sheet or marble slab and let cool completely. Break into pieces and store in an airtight container in a cool, dry place.

Makes 3¼ lb (1.5 kg)
Preparation time 10 minutes
Cooking time 50–60 minutes

Quinces baked in wine with yogurt, p 628

Carrot truffles, p 632

CARROT TRUFFLES
KAPOTENIA
Karotenia

- 1 lb 2 oz (500 g) medium carrots
- 1 cup (200 g / 7 oz) superfine (caster) sugar
- finely grated zest of 1 large lemon
- 1 teaspoon vanilla extract
- 2⅓–3⅔ cups (200–300 g / 7–11 oz) dried unsweetened (dessicated) coconut

Parboil the carrots for 20 minutes, then remove from the heat, drain, let cool, and grate coarsely. Combine the grated carrots, sugar, and lemon zest in a pan and cook, stirring frequently, for 20 minutes. Remove from the heat and let cool slightly, then add the vanilla and half the coconut, and mix well. Let cool completely, then chill in the refrigerator for 30 minutes. Shape the mixture into 1-inch (2.5-cm) balls and roll each one in the remaining coconut. If they do not hold their shape after chilling, add a little more coconut. Put the truffles in candy (petit fours) cases and store in an airtight container in the refrigerator until ready to serve.

Makes about 36 truffles
Preparation time 1½ hours (including chilling)

□ p 631

ALMOND "PEARS" FROM HYDRA
ΑΜΥΓΔΑΛΩΤΑ ΑΧΛΑΔΑΚΙΑ
Amigdalota ahladakia

- 9 cups (1 kg / 2¼ lb) almonds, blanched and finely ground
- 5 tablespoons coarse semolina, plus extra for sprinkling
- 2½ cups (500 g / 1 lb 2 oz) superfine (caster) sugar
- 4 tablespoons rosewater, plus extra for dipping
- 3 tablespoons honey
- ½ teaspoon almond extract
- 80 whole cloves
- confectioners' (icing) sugar, for coating

These almond treats made on Hydra, Spetses, and Andros are often served at christenings. A tiny bow, pink for girls and blue for boys, is pinned to the top of each pear with a clove.

Combine the ground almonds, semolina, sugar, and rosewater in a bowl and knead into a smooth pliable paste that holds its shape. Cover with a dish towel and let stand overnight. The next day, knead the paste, gradually incorporating the honey and almond extract. If the paste is too stiff and dry, add a little more rosewater. Preheat the oven to 350°F (180°C / Gas Mark 4). Line a cookie sheet (baking tray) with baking parchment and sprinkle with semolina. Shape small pieces of the marzipan into pears and insert 1 clove in the top of each for a stalk. Put the pears onto the prepared cookie sheet and bake for 15–20 minutes. Let cool on a wire rack. Dip quickly in rosewater and roll in confectioners' sugar to coat. Let dry for 1–2 hours, then roll in confectioners' sugar again so that they are thickly coated and completely white.

Makes 80 "pears"
Preparation time 14 hours (including standing, cooling, and drying)
Cooking time 20 minutes

□ p 634

- 2¼ lb (1 kg) tangerines
- 1 cup (250 ml / 8 fl oz) freshly squeezed tangerine juice
- 3 cups (350 g / 12 oz) blanched almonds, finely ground
- 3 cups (600 g / 1 lb 5 oz) superfine (caster) sugar
- confectioners' (icing) sugar, for dusting

TANGERINE BONBONS FROM CORFU
ΜΠΙΑΝΚΕΤΑ ΚΕΡΚΥΡΑΙΚΗ
Bianketa kerkiraiki

Peel the tangerines, removing as much white pith from the rind as possible with a sharp knife. Put the rinds into a bowl, pour in water to cover, and let soak for 6 hours. Drain, transfer to a pan, pour in water to cover, and cook over high heat for about 1 hour, or until soft, then drain well and let cool slightly. Put the rinds into a food processor or blender, add 2–3 tablespoons of the tangerine juice, and process to a purée. Add the ground almonds and process until thoroughly combined. Pour the remaining tangerine juice into a heavy nonstick pan, add the sugar, and cook, stirring until the sugar has dissolved. Boil, without stirring, for about 5 minutes, until the syrup is slightly thickened. Add the tangerine mixture, reduce the heat to low, and simmer, stirring constantly, for about 15 minutes, or until the mixture pulls away from the side of the pan. Remove from the heat and let cool. Line 2 cookie sheets (baking trays) with baking parchment. Dampen your hands and shape the mixture into balls the size of a small walnut. Arrange them on the prepared cookie sheets and let dry for 1–2 days. Roll the tangerine bonbons in confectioners' sugar and put them in candy (petit fours) cases. Store them in an airtight container, as they tend to dry out.

Makes about 60 bonbons
Preparation time 2½ days (including soaking and drying)
Cooking time 1½ hours

▢ p 635

- ½ cup (120 ml / 4 fl oz) milk
- 8 oz (225 g) semisweet (plain) chocolate, broken into pieces
- 2 tablespoons brandy
- ½ cup (120 g / 4 oz) butter
- ½ cup (50 g / 2 oz) confectioners' (icing) sugar, plus extra for dusting
- 2 egg yolks
- 2 cups (120 g / 4 oz) graham cracker (sweet biscuit) crumbs
- 1¼ cups (150 g / 5 oz) walnuts, coarsely chopped
- brandy or liqueur, for shaping
- ½ cup (120 g / 4 oz) chocolate sprinkles

SMALL TRUFFLES
ΤΡΟΥΦΑΚΙΑ
Troufakia

Pour the milk into a pan and bring to a boil. Add the chocolate and stir over low heat until the chocolate has melted and the mixture is thoroughly blended. Remove from the heat and let cool. Stir in the brandy. Beat together the butter and sugar in a bowl with an electric mixer until pale and fluffy. Add the egg yolks, 1 at a time, beating constantly. Gradually pour the chocolate mixture into the bowl and mix gently. Fold in the graham cracker crumbs and walnuts. Chill in the refrigerator for a few hours, until firm. Dampen the palms of your hands with a little brandy or liqueur and shape the mixture into small balls. Roll them in the chocolate sprinkles and place in candy (petit fours) cases. Arrange on a serving dish and dust the tops with confectioners' sugar. Store in the refrigerator for up to 1 week. They will keep for several months in the freezer.

Makes 30 truffles
Preparation time 4 hours (including chilling)

Almond "pears" from Hydra, p 632

Tangerine bonbons from Corfu, p 633

MENUS
FROM CELEBRATED
GREEK CHEFS

-

ΜΕΝΟΥ ΑΠΟ
ΓΝΩΣΤΟΥΣ
ΕΛΛΗΝΕΣ ΣΕΦ

-

Menu apo gnostous Ellines sef

The following pages contain menus from some of the world's best chefs cooking Greek-influenced food. The emphasis on high quality and full-flavored ingredients cooked simply, which is characteristic of Greek cuisine, has translated into exceptional modern Greek cooking at restaurants from Melbourne to Detroit. These chefs have built on the traditions of Greek food to create delicious dishes that both celebrate and diversify Greek cuisine, and by doing so have helped to spread its popularity around the world.

GREECE: THE COOKBOOK'S GUEST CHEFS

Jim Botsacos — New York, NY, USA

- Scallop marinato
- Ouzo-cured salmon with fennel and dill
- Karidopita (walnut cake) with Greek yogurt and orange spoon sweet

George Calombaris — Melbourne, Australia

- Saganaki martini
- Yogurt and mastic-braised neck of lamb with olive oil pomme purée
- Baklava soufflé with smoked chocolate ice cream

Theo Kostoglou — Gold Coast, Australia

- Scallops with bulgur wheat, greens, avgotaraho, and saffron butter sauce
- Kataifi shrimp (prawns) on a zucchini (courgette) fritter with yogurt and feta sauce
- Manouri mousse with thyme honey and walnuts

Theodore Kyriakou — London, UK

- Fig, manouri, and pastourma sandwich
- Artichoke, potato, anchovy, and sourdough bread crumb salad
- Omelet with honey and sesame seeds

Michael Psilakis — New York, NY, USA

- Anthos Greek salad
- Spicy shellfish giouvetsi
- Anthos chocolate mousse

Michael Symon — Cleveland, OH, USA

- Shaved beet (beetroot) salad
- Skordalia with garbanzo beans (chickpeas)
- Braised lamb shanks

JIM BOTSACOS

Restaurants:
Molyvos, New York, NY, USA

Jim Botsacos had a long career in some of New York's best restaurants before opening his award-winning modern Greek restaurant, Molyvos, in 1997. He aims to challenge the conventional boundaries of Greek cuisine, while staying true to its origins. He has made many appearances to promote Greek food on television and in magazines.

SCALLOP MARINATO

- 5–6 shucked sea (king) scallops, sliced into 4 or 5 ⅛-inch (3-mm) rounds
- 1¼ cups (300 ml / ½ pint) freshly squeezed lemon juice
- pinch of salt
- 1 red onion, thinly sliced
- ½ Fresno chile or other large chile, sliced
- ⅔ cup (150 ml / ¼ pint) freshly squeezed orange juice
- pinch of superfine (caster) sugar
- ¼ cup (25 g / 1 oz) cucumber, peeled, seeded, and finely diced
- 1 tablespoon capers
- 1 tablespoon chopped fresh basil
- 2 tablespoons finely chopped scallions (spring onions)
- salt and pepper
- 2 tablespoons extra-virgin olive oil
- fresh basil sprigs, to serve

Put the scallops in a chilled stainless steel bowl with the lemon juice and a pinch of salt. Add the onion and chile, and toss gently until well combined. Let sit for 1–2 minutes. Add the orange juice and sugar, then divide the mixture among 6 chilled serving bowls. Sprinkle with the cucumber, capers, basil, and scallions, and season with salt and pepper. Drizzle with the oil and garnish with a sprig of basil. Serve immediately.

Serves 6
Preparation time 5–10 minutes

OUZO-CURED SALMON WITH FENNEL AND DILL

Using a sharp knife, fillet the salmon to create 2 whole fillets with the skin attached. You can ask your fish store (fishmonger) to do this for you. Wrap the fillets in a large piece of cheesecloth (muslin) and set aside. Combine the brown sugar, salt, fennel pollen, fennel seeds, dill, and pepper in a medium bowl, stirring well to combine. Set aside. Unwrap the fillets and lay them out on a work surface, skin side down. Using tweezers, carefully remove and discard any pinbones remaining in the flesh. Using a sharp knife, trim off the thin belly meat, leaving an almost perfect rectangle of fish. Place a double layer of cheesecloth on a clean work surface. Sprinkle half the sugar and salt mixture down the center, spreading it out evenly. Lay the fillets skin side down in the center of the sugar-salt cure with the interior edges touching. Coat the top of each fillet with the remaining sugar and salt mixture, then drizzle with half of the ouzo. Place one fillet on top of the other to put the fish back together. Wrap the fish packet with the cheesecloth to enclose it. Drizzle the remaining ouzo on the cheesecloth until it is almost saturated. Working carefully so that you don't lose too much of the curing mixture, tightly wrap the packet in plastic wrap (cling film). Place the wrapped fish in a dish or on a platter large enough to hold it flat, and with a rim to hold the liquid that will seep out as the fish cures. Place a heavy object, such as a cutting (chopping) board, on top of the fish and refrigerate for 2 days, turning every 12 hours or so. After 36 hours, unwrap the fish and separate the fillets. Quickly rinse off any remaining curing mixture under cool water. Do not soak. Pat dry with paper towels. If not serving immediately, individually wrap each fillet in plastic wrap and refrigerate until ready to serve. The cured fish may be stored, refrigerated, for a week or so. When ready to serve, using a sharp slicing knife, cut each fillet crosswise against the skin, into very thin skinless slices. Serve with warmed pita bread, thinly sliced lemon, and a glass of ouzo.

Serves 16
Preparation time 36 hours (including curing)

Note: To toast the fennel seeds, heat a skillet or frying pan and cook the seeds in a single layer over medium-low heat until lightly browned. Alternatively, toast in a baking pan in an oven preheated to 300°F (150°C / Gas Mark 2). Stir frequently to prevent them from burning and turning bitter. It should take no more than 5 minutes, as seeds are quite oily and will brown quickly.

Fennel pollen is collected from wild fennel flowers and it is available from specialist online retailers.

- 1 salmon, about 10–12 lb (4½–5½ kg) total weight, cleaned
- 3 cups (650 g / 1 lb 7 oz) light brown sugar
- 3 cups (650 g / 1 lb 7 oz) coarse salt
- 2 tablespoons fennel pollen (see note)
- 1 tablespoon fennel seeds, toasted and crushed (see note)
- 6 cups (350 g / 12 oz) chopped fresh dill, including stems
- ½ cup (50 g / 2 oz) freshly ground black pepper
- 3 cups (750 ml / 1¼ pints) ouzo
- pita bread and thinly sliced lemon, to serve

- vegetable oil, for greasing
- ½ cup (120 ml / 4 fl oz) Frangelico (see note)
- 1 teaspoon baking soda (bicarbonate of soda)
- 1 cup (175 g / 6 oz) fine semolina
- 1 cup (100 g / 3½ oz) coarsely chopped walnuts
- ⅓ cup (65 g / 2½ oz) superfine (caster) sugar
- 1 teaspoon baking powder
- 1 teaspoon ground cinnamon
- ¼ teaspoon ground cloves
- ½ cup (120 ml / 4 fl oz) freshly squeezed orange juice
- grated zest of 2 oranges
- ¼ cup (60 ml / 2¼ fl oz) olive oil
- generous ¼ cup (60 ml / 2¼ fl oz) Greek yogurt

FOR THE CITRUS SYRUP
- 3 cups (350 g / 12 oz) superfine (caster) sugar
- ½ cup (120 ml / 4 fl oz) honey
- zest of 1 orange, cut in large strips
- zest of 1 lemon, cut in large strips
- 1 cinnamon stick
- 1 tablespoon freshly squeezed lemon juice

FOR THE ORANGE SPOON SWEET
- 4 oranges, preferably organic, scrubbed and dried
- 2 cups (400 g / 14 oz) superfine (caster) sugar
- ¼ cup (60 ml / 2¼ fl oz) white wine

KARIDOPITA (WALNUT CAKE) WITH GREEK YOGURT AND ORANGE SPOON SWEET

To make the citrus syrup, pour 4 cups (850 ml / 1½ pints) water into a heavy pan. Stir in the sugar, honey, orange zest, lemon zest, cinnamon stick, and lemon juice, and bring to a boil over medium heat, stirring to dissolve the sugar. Lower the heat and simmer without stirring, skimming occasionally to remove any foam that rises to the top, for about 30–35 minutes, or until the liquid has reduced to a light syrup consistency. Remove from heat, let cool, and strain through a fine sieve, then set aside. To make the orange spoon sweet, put the oranges in a pan with water to cover, bring to a boil and cook for 1 minute. Drain well. Repeat this blanching process 3 times and let cool. Halve the oranges and remove the seeds. Arrange the orange halves on a cutting (chopping) board, cut side down. Using a sharp knife, cut each orange half vertically into very thin slices. Put them in a large bowl, add the sugar, and toss to coat evenly. Combine 1½ cups (350 ml / 12 fl oz) of water with the wine in a nonstick pan and bring to a boil, then carefully add the orange slices and sugar. Lower the heat and simmer for 1½ hours, or until quite thick. Remove from the heat, let cool, and set aside.

To make the karidopita, preheat the oven to 325°F (160°C / Gas Mark 3) and grease six ½-cup (120-ml / 4-fl oz) soufflé molds. Place the molds on a cookie sheet (baking tray) lined with baking parchment and set aside. Pour the Frangelico into a small bowl, add the baking soda, stir, and set aside. Combine the semolina, walnuts, sugar, baking powder, cinnamon, and cloves in another bowl and make a well in the center. Pour the orange juice into the Frangelico mixture, add the orange zest, and stir until well blended. Pour the liquid into the well and gradually incorporate the dry ingredients until thoroughly blended. Stir 2 spoonfuls of the olive oil into the batter to loosen it, then gently fold in the remainder of the oil. Pour ¾ cup (200 ml / 7 fl oz) of the batter into each of the prepared molds. Place in the oven and bake for 20 minutes, or until a toothpick inserted in the middle of a cake comes out clean. Remove from the oven and let cool slightly. Drizzle orange syrup evenly over each cake, using about half of the syrup in total. Serve warm, drizzled with the remaining orange syrup, and accompanied with a tablespoon each of yogurt and orange spoon sweet in the center of each cake.

Note: Frangelico is a widely available hazelnut-flavored liqueur. The citrus syrup and orange spoon sweet can be made in advance and stored, covered and refrigerated, for up to 2 weeks.

Serves 6
Preparation time 12 hours (including cooling)
Cooking time 20 minutes

GEORGE CALOMBARIS

Restaurants:
The Press Club, Melbourne, Australia
The Belvedere Club, Mykonos, Greece
Hellenic Republic, Melbourne, Australia
Mastic, Melbourne, Australia
Gazi, Melbourne, Australia
Jimmy Grants, Melbourne, Australia

One of Australia's top young chefs, George Calombaris opened his
flagship restaurant, The Press Club, at the age of 27. Serving up modern
twists on classic Greek cuisine, it has won many accolades, and has
now been followed by new modern Greek restaurants The Belvedere
Club and Hellenic Republic. He has been a Masterchef Australia host
and judge since it first aired in 2009 and has published several
cookbooks. The rich and varied culinary heritage of his Greek
upbringing has contributed to his success in creating a new style
of modern Greek cuisine.

SAGANAKI MARTINI

Preheat the oven to its lowest setting (around 175°F or 80°C). Place
the diced olives on a tray lined with wax (greaseproof) paper. Lightly
dust with the sugar and cook in the oven for 12 hours. To make the
tomato gin tea, combine all the ingredients except the gin in a blender
and pulse for 1 minute, or until smooth. Pour the liquid into a paper
coffee filter or cheesecloth (muslin) placed in a strainer over a bowl,
and let drain for 10–12 hours. To make the saganaki martini, combine
the tomatoes, cucumbers, olives, and chives into a bowl, mix well, and
divide evenly among 4 martini glasses. Stir the gin into the tomato gin
tea and fill each glass three-quarters full with the resulting liquid. Thread
the halloumi cheese cubes onto 4 skewers. Heat the oil in a heavy skillet
or frying pan, add the halloumi skewers and cook over medium-high heat
for 3–4 minutes, or until golden brown on each side. Rest 1 skewer over
the top of each martini glass and serve garnished with red kale leaves.

Serves 4
Preparation time 12½ hours (including preparing the olives)
Cooking time 5 minutes

- 1¾ cups (200 g / 7 oz)
  Kalamata olives, pitted (stoned),
  and finely diced
- 1 tablespoon superfine
  (caster) sugar
- 2 oz (50 g) ripe tomatoes, peeled,
  seeded, and diced into ⅛-inch
  (3-mm) squares
- ¾ oz (20 g) cucumber, peeled,
  seeded, and diced into ⅛-inch
  (3-mm) squares
- 1 tablespoon fresh chives,
  finely chopped
- 7 oz (200 g) halloumi cheese,
  cut into ½-inch (1-cm) cubes
- olive oil
- red kale leaves, to garnish

FOR THE TOMATO GIN TEA
- 2¼ lb (1 kg) very ripe tomatoes
- 10 fresh basil leaves
- ½ small red onion, chopped
- 1 garlic clove
- 1⅓ tablespoons (20 ml / 1 fl oz)
  Worcestershire sauce
- 5 drops Tabasco sauce
- 4 tablespoons gin

- Makes 4 cups (1 litre / 1¾ pints)

- 4 tablespoons olive oil
- 4 lamb neck fillets
- 8 shallots, roughly diced
- ¼ teaspoon ground mastic
- 1 clove garlic, crushed
- 6 sprigs fresh thyme
- 4 tablespoons white wine
- grated zest of 1 lemon
- 4 tablespoons Greek honey
- 12 cups (3 litres / 5¼ pints) chicken stock
- 2¼ cups (525 ml / 19 fl oz) thick Greek yogurt

FOR THE OLIVE OIL POMME PURÉE
- 2¼ lb (1 kg) rock salt
- 6 lb 10 oz (3 kg) Desiree potatoes
- 7 oz (200 g) butter
- 4 tablespoons olive oil
- ¾ cup (200 ml / 7 fl oz) milk

YOGURT AND MASTIC-BRAISED NECK OF LAMB WITH OLIVE OIL POMME PURÉE

Preheat the oven to 250°F (120°C / Gas Mark ½). Heat the oil in a heavy skillet or frying pan. Add the meat and cook over medium-high heat for 8–10 minutes until well browned all over. Remove the meat from the pan and place it in a large, deep, ovenproof dish. Add the diced shallots, mastic, garlic, thyme, and sprinkle with the wine and lemon zest. Drizzle the honey over the meat and pour the chicken stock into the dish until the lamb is just covered. Carefully spread the yogurt over the top and cover with wax (greaseproof) paper, then cover the whole dish with foil. Cook in the oven for 10 hours, or until tender. Remove the meat from the oven and let cool slightly. To make the olive oil pomme purée, cover the bottom of a large ovenproof dish with rock salt and arrange the potatoes on top. Bake at 325°F (160°C / Gas Mark 3) for 2 hours, or until the potatoes are tender. Let cool slightly and pass them through a fine strainer while still warm. Heat the butter in a frying pan with the oil and milk, and whisk until thoroughly combined. Add the sieved potatoes to the pan, whisk until smooth, and season with salt. Keep warm. To make the sauce, strain the lamb-cooking liquid through a fine strainer into a pan, bring to a boil over medium heat, and simmer until reduced to a sauce-like pouring consistency. Pour over the lamb and serve hot, accompanied by the pomme purée.

Serves 4
Preparation time 30 minutes
Cooking time 12¼ hours

BAKLAVA SOUFFLÉ WITH SMOKED CHOCOLATE ICE CREAM

To make the smoked chocolate ice cream, line a heavy, lidded pot with foil and place the hickory chips on top of the foil. Put the chocolate in a stainless steel bowl, place it inside the pot, and cook over high heat to smoke for 30 minutes. Meanwhile, combine the egg yolks, sugar, and cocoa powder in a bowl and beat with an electric mixer on medium speed. Remove the chocolate from the pot, and melt it in a heatproof bowl set over a pan of barely simmering water. Pour the milk and glucose into another pan and heat it to just below boiling point (do not allow to boil). Pour a third of the milk over the yolk mixture and beat together, then pour back into the pan, and cook until the temperature reaches 180°F (82°C), stirring continuously. Add the melted chocolate, mix well, then stir in the cream. Pass through a fine strainer and chill in the refrigerator for one day, then freeze in a Pacojet (see note), or in a domestic ice cream machine.

To make the baklava soufflé, grease 4 individual soufflé molds and dust them with sugar. Pour the milk into a large pan and bring to a boil. Meanwhile, combine the cornstarch, ¼ cup (50 g / 2 oz) of the sugar, the egg, and egg yolks in a bowl and mix to make a smooth paste. Pour the hot milk into the paste, stirring constantly, until smooth. Return the mixture to the pan, bring to a gentle simmer, and whisk continuously for 5–6 minutes, until thickened. Remove from the heat and pour into a bowl, cover with plastic wrap (cling film), and let cool slightly. Once cooled, beat with an electric mixer on medium speed, until smooth. Preheat the oven to 340°F (175°C / Gas Mark 3½). Whisk the egg whites in a grease-free bowl until foamy and gradually add the remaining sugar, whisking continuously, until stiff peaks form. Pour a third of the egg white mixture into the milk mixture, and whisk vigorously. Add the rest of the egg whites and carefully fold in. Pour into the prepared soufflé molds and bake for 13 minutes, or until the soufflé has risen to 1 inch (2.5 cm) above the rim of its mold. Serve warm, accompanied by the smoked chocolate ice cream.

Serves 4
Preparation time 24 hours (including chilling and freezing)
Cooking time 13 minutes

Note: A Pacojet is a type of food processor that makes fine-textured mousses, purées, sorbets, and ice creams.

- butter, for greasing
- ¾ cup (190 ml / 6½ fl oz) low-fat (semi-skimmed) milk
- 1½ tablespoons (20 g / ¾ oz) cornstarch (cornflour)
- ⅔ cup (145 g / 4¾ oz) superfine (caster) sugar, plus extra for dusting
- 1 egg
- 2 egg yolks
- 6 egg whites

FOR THE SMOKED CHOCOLATE ICE CREAM
- 7 oz (200 g) hickory chips
- ¾ cup (140 g / 4¾ oz) semisweet (plain) chocolate, grated
- 5 egg yolks
- ¾ cup (160 g / 5½ oz) superfine (caster) sugar
- generous ½ cup (65 g / 2½ oz) unsweetened cocoa powder
- 1½ cups (375 ml / 13 fl oz) whole milk
- 2 tablespoons liquid glucose
- 1½ cups (375 ml / 13 fl oz) heavy (double) cream

THEO KOSTOGLOU

Restaurants:
Greek Street Grill, Gold Coast, Australia

Theo Kostoglou spent many years working in Greece before returning to Australia to open his first restaurant in 1993. In 2006 he opened Mykonos, with an interior specially designed to enable diners to escape to the islands of Greece. His flagship restaurant, Kouzina, opened the following year, and showcased an innovative new approach that raised the bar for modern Greek cooking. He has since opened the Greek Street Grill in Surfer's Paradise with his son, John.

- 4 tablespoons olive oil
- 1¼ cups (100 g / 3½ oz) baby spinach leaves
- 1¼ cups (100 g / 3½ oz) chard, stalks removed
- freshly squeezed juice of 1 lemon
- salt
- 16 sea (king) scallops, shucked, roe removed
- 30 g (1¼ oz) cured fish roe (avgotaraho), to serve

FOR THE BULGUR WHEAT
- 1½ tablespoons (20 g / ¾ oz) butter
- 3 tablespoons olive oil
- ½ onion, finely diced
- 1 cup (175 g / 6 oz) boneless pork loin diced in ¼-inch (5-mm) squares
- 1 cup (175 g / 6 oz) bulgur wheat
- 1¼ cups (320 ml / 11 fl oz) chicken stock
- salt and pepper
- ¼ teaspoon ground nutmeg

FOR THE SAFFRON BUTTER SAUCE
- ½ teaspoon saffron threads, crushed
- 2 tablespoons ouzo
- grated zest of ½ lemon
- freshly squeezed juice of ½ lemon
- grated zest of ½ orange
- freshly squeezed juice of ½ orange
- 4 tablespoons (50 g / 2 oz) butter
- 1 clove garlic, finely chopped
- ½ teaspoon chopped fresh parsley
- ½ teaspoon ground fennel seeds
- salt and pepper

SCALLOPS WITH BULGUR WHEAT, GREENS, AVGOTARAHO, AND SAFFRON BUTTER SAUCE

To make the bulgur wheat, heat the butter and oil in a pan and add the onion. Cook over low heat, stirring occasionally, for about 5 minutes, until softened and translucent. Add the pork and cook for 2 minutes, then add the bulgur, and cook for 2 minutes more, stirring continuously. Pour in the stock and bring to a boil. Reduce the heat and simmer for 15–20 minutes, stirring occasionally, until the bulgur has absorbed all the liquid. Remove from the heat and season with salt, pepper, and the nutmeg. To make the saffron butter sauce, combine the saffron and ouzo in a small heatproof bowl and let soak for 5 minutes, set the bowl over a pan of barely simmering water, add the rest of the ingredients, and stir until thoroughly combined. Season with salt and pepper, and set aside. Heat half the oil in another pan and add the spinach and chard in small batches. Cook over medium heat, stirring frequently, for a few minutes, until wilted. Remove from the heat and put in a bowl. Add the lemon juice, toss, and season with salt. Set aside. Heat the remaining oil in a nonstick pan and add the scallops. Cook for 2 minutes on one side and 1 minute on the other. Remove from the heat and dip them in the sauce. Serve them immediately on top of the bulgur wheat and the cooked greens arranged in piles, sprinkled with shavings of the fish roe, and drizzle with more sauce.

Serves 4
Preparation time 30 minutes
Cooking time 30 minutes

KATAIFI SHRIMP (PRAWNS) ON A ZUCCHINI (COURGETTE) FRITTER WITH YOGURT AND FETA SAUCE

Preheat the oven to 375°F (190°C / Gas Mark 5). To make the white sauce, melt the butter in a heavy nonstick pan, and add the onion, garlic, chile, and shallot. Cook over low heat, stirring occasionally, for about 5 minutes, until softened. Stir in the flour, and cook, stirring frequently, for 1 minute. Remove the pan from the heat and gradually pour in the milk, stirring constantly with a whisk until the mixture is smooth. If lumps form, strain the sauce into another pan. Return the sauce to high heat and simmer, stirring constantly, for 5 minutes, until thickened and smooth. Remove from the heat and season with nutmeg, salt, and white pepper. Sprinkle with the parsley. To make the kataifi shrimp, season the shrimp with salt and pepper in a bowl. Tease out the kataifi pastry and divide into 8 x 2-inch (5-cm) strips. Keep the sections covered with a damp cloth to keep them moist. Take one section of kataifi and brush it with the melted butter, then season with salt and pepper. Dip a shrimp in the white sauce, place it at the end of one section, and roll it tightly until wrapped and covered entirely. Continue until all the sections of kataifi are rolled. Arrange on a wire rack and cook in the oven for 10–12 minutes, or until golden brown. Keep warm. To make the zucchini fritters, put the zucchini, mint, dill, and scallion in a cheesecloth (muslin) or a dish towel, and squeeze out the excess liquid. Combine the mixture with the eggs, feta, and flour in a bowl, and mix well. Add the lemon juice and season with salt and pepper. The mixture should be firm enough to hold its shape. Heat the vegetable oil in a deep-fryer to 350–375°F (180–190°C), shape the mixture into ½-inch (1-cm) patties, then deep-fry for about 5 minutes, or until golden brown on both sides. Meanwhile, make the yogurt and feta sauce. Put all the ingredients in a blender and process until smooth and thick. Serve each zucchini fritter topped with 2 shrimps, and the yogurt and feta sauce, sprinkled with sumac, and, if desired, garnished with a parsley sprig.

Serves 4
Preparation time 45 minutes
Cooking time 25 minutes

- 8 jumbo shrimp (king prawns), peeled and deveined
- salt and pepper
- 3½ oz (100 g) ready-made kataifi pastry
- 8 tablespoons (100 g / 3½ oz) butter, melted
- 1 tablespoon ground sumac
- 1 parsley sprig, to serve (optional)

FOR THE WHITE SAUCE

- 3½ tablespoons (1¾ oz / 45 g) butter
- 1 tablespoon diced onion
- 1 garlic clove, crushed
- 1 red chile, thinly sliced
- 1 tablespoon diced shallot
- 2 tablespoons (30 g / 1¼ oz) all-purpose (plain) flour
- ¾ cup (200 ml / 7 fl oz) milk
- pinch of ground nutmeg
- salt and white pepper
- 2 tablespoons chopped fresh parsley

FOR THE ZUCCHINI (COURGETTE) FRITTERS

- 3⅓ cups (550 g / 1 lb 4 oz) grated zucchini (courgettes)
- 1 tablespoon chopped fresh mint
- 1 tablespoon chopped fresh dill
- 1 finely chopped scallion (spring onion)
- 2 eggs
- 1¾ cups (100 g / 3½ oz) feta cheese
- ½ cup (60 g / 2¼ oz) all-purpose (plain) flour
- freshly squeezed juice of ½ lemon
- salt and pepper
- vegetable oil, for deep-frying

FOR THE YOGURT AND FETA SAUCE

- 1¾ cups (100 g / 3½ oz) crumbled feta cheese
- ¼ cup (50 ml / 2 fl oz) sheep's milk yogurt
- 2 tablespoons virgin olive oil
- freshly squeezed juice of ½ lemon
- 1 teaspoon ground sumac
- salt and pepper

- 3 sheets gelatin
- 1 cup (250 ml / 8 fl oz) warm water
- 2 tablespoons orange blossom water
- 8⅓ cups (1 kg / 2¼ lb) manouri cheese, or other soft cheese such as mascarpone
- ⅔ cup (150 ml / ¼ pint) Greek honey
- 2 cups (450 ml / 16 fl oz) heavy (double) cream, whipped

FOR THE SAUCE
- ¼ cup (50 ml / 2 fl oz) water
- ¾ cup (200 ml / 7 fl oz) Greek thyme honey
- ½ teaspoon chopped fresh mint

TO DECORATE
- 1 cup (120 g / 4 oz) finely chopped walnuts, toasted
- 1 piece of honeycomb (optional)
- 1 tablespoon Persian fairy floss (optional)
- 1 mint sprig

MANOURI MOUSSE WITH THYME HONEY AND WALNUTS

Dissolve the gelatin sheets in a bowl with the water and orange blossom water. Combine the cheese and honey in another bowl and beat together with an electric mixer until thoroughly combined. Fold in the cream and the gelatin. Pour the mixture into individual molds and refrigerate for 3 to 4 hours. To make the sauce, combine the water, honey, and mint in a pan, bring to a boil and simmer for 8–10 minutes. Remove from the heat and let cool. Serve the manouri mousse with the honey sauce, sprinkled with the walnuts, and, if desired, garnished with the honeycomb, Persian fairy floss, and mint sprig.

Serves 6–8
Preparation time 5 hours (including chilling)
Cooking time 10 minutes

Note: Persian fairy floss is a type of flavored cotton candy (candyfloss), available from specialty food shops.

THEODORE KYRIAKOU

Restaurants:
The Greek Larder, London, UK

Theodore Kyriakou trained as captain in the Greek navy before taking
to the kitchen. He has lived in England for many years and was head
chef of the award-winning The Real Greek restaurant in London from
1999. The restaurant was instrumental in popularizing modern Greek
cooking in the UK and, after expanding the chain throughout London
and subsequently selling it, he opened The Greek Larder, a restaurant
and delicatessen.

FIG, MANOURI, AND PASTOURMA SANDWICH

Mash the manouri and feta cheeses on a cutting (chopping) board
with a knife or fork. Put in a bowl, add the yogurt and pepper, and
mix well. Cut off the ends of the unpeeled figs and cut them into 3 slices
lengthwise. Spread the cheese mixture on all the bread slices. Build
up a layer of arugula, pastourma, and figs on half of the slices. Sprinkle
with a few drops of vinegar and cover it with the other piece of bread.
Heat the butter in a heavy skillet or frying pan over medium heat, until
foamy. Add the sandwiches, pressing them onto the pan, and slowly
fry over medium heat, making sure that the butter does not burn. Once
lightly brown, turn them over, and press down with a spatula to compress
all the layers together slightly. Remove from the heat and serve immediately.

Serves 5
Preparation time 20 minutes
Cooking time 10–15 minutes

Note: Pastourma is a Greek cured and spiced beef product similar
to pastrami.

- 11 oz (300 g) manouri cheese, or other soft goat's milk cheese
- 3½ oz (100 g) feta cheese
- 2 tablespoons thick Greek yogurt
- freshly ground pepper
- 10 fresh figs
- 10 slices sourdough bread, or any other good bread
- arugula (rocket) leaves, washed, to garnish
- 9 oz (250 g) sliced pastourma
- 2 teaspoons aged red wine vinegar or balsamic vinegar
- clarified butter, for frying

- 12 young globe artichokes
- 4 lemons, halved, and their freshly squeezed juice
- ½ tablespoon (10 g / ¼ oz) black peppercorns
- salt
- 1 lb 2 oz (500 g) small new potatoes, peeled
- ½ cup (120 ml / 4 fl oz) aged red wine or balsamic vinegar
- 2 oz (50 g) anchovies, chopped coarsely
- 3½ oz (100 g) arugula (rocket) leaves, coarsely chopped
- 5 oz (150 g) Cretan barley rusks (p 537) or dry sourdough bread, roughly crushed

FOR THE DRESSING
- ¾ cup (200 ml / 7 fl oz) extra-virgin olive oil
- ¼ cup (50 ml / 2 fl oz) Vin Santo wine, or other sweet white wine
- 4 tablespoons (50 g / 2 oz) finely chopped shallot

ARTICHOKE, POTATO, ANCHOVY, AND SOURDOUGH BREAD CRUMB SALAD

To prepare the artichokes, break off the stems, trim the bases, and remove the tough dark green leaves and the chokes, leaving the tender cup-shaped bases. As you prepare each artichoke, put it into a medium pan of water mixed with the lemon juice to prevent discoloration. Add the lemon halves, peppercorns, and salt. Bring to a boil, then reduce the heat and simmer for 10 minutes, until the artichokes are tender but retain some bite. Remove the artichokes with a slotted spoon (reserving the cooking liquid) and drain, top down, on paper towels. Put them in the refrigerator until completely cold and dry, then remove any fuzz. To prepare the potatoes, put them in the artichoke water and bring to a boil. Cover and simmer for 15 minutes, or until tender. Drain well and set aside. To prepare the dressing, combine the oil, wine, and shallot in a small bowl, and whisk well until thoroughly blended. Pour the vinegar in small saucepan and bring to a boil. Reduce the heat and let simmer for a few minutes, until the vinegar has reduced enough to coat the back of spoon. Transfer the artichokes and potatoes to a large salad bowl. Add the chopped anchovies, dressing, vinegar reduction, and chopped arugula. Toss very gently. Sprinkle with the rusks or dry sourdough bread, and serve warm.

Serves 6
Preparation time 30 minutes
Cooking time 20 minutes

Note: Choose artichokes with tight, dark green leaves. If the leaves appear too open, the artichoke is past its best.

- 10 eggs
- ¼ cup (50 ml / 2 fl oz) milk
- salt and black pepper
- ½ cup (120 ml / 4 fl oz) olive oil
- 7 oz (200 g) tomatoes, peeled, seeded, and coarsely chopped
- ½ bunch fresh mint, finely chopped
- 7 oz (200 g) feta cheese, crumbled
- sesame seeds, for sprinkling
- ⅔ cup (150 ml / ¼ pint) Greek thyme honey
- freshly squeezed juice of 1 lemon
- bread and sweet cured black olives, to serve

OMELET WITH HONEY AND SESAME SEEDS

Lightly whisk the eggs with the milk in a bowl until combined, and season with salt and pepper. Heat the oil in a heavy, nonstick skillet or frying pan over medium heat. Add the chopped tomatoes and the mint and stir for 3–4 minutes. Add the feta, the pour the egg mixture into the pan and cook for a few minutes, shaking gently to mix. Reduce the heat and cook for about 4–5 minutes, until the eggs have set. Remove from the heat and sprinkle with the sesame seeds, then drizzle the honey over the top, and finally fold over to make a half-moon shape. Drizzle the lemon juice on top and serve immediately, accompanied with warm bread and sweet cured black olives.

Serves 5
Preparation time 15 minutes
Cooking time 10–15 minutes

MICHAEL PSILAKIS

Restaurants:
Kefi, New York, NY, USA
MP Taverna, New York, NY, USA
Fishtag, New York, NY, USA
The Hall, Brooklyn, NY, USA

Michael Psilakis won many awards for the pioneering signature Greek
cuisine he developed at his previous flagship restaurant, Anthos (meaning "rebirth" or "blossoming"), including a Michelin star. Taught to cook
by his Greek mother, who remains his greatest influence in the kitchen,
he continues to take Greek cuisine in new directions while incorporating
his experiences of modern American cooking.

ANTHOS GREEK SALAD

Blanch the beans and peas in a large pan of boiling water for 3–4
minutes, or until tender. Drain well and let cool. Cut the beans into
½-inch (1-cm) squares and set aside. Preheat the oven to 375°F
(190°C / Gas Mark 5). Toss the beets in the oil in a roasting pan and
cook in the oven for 20 minutes, or until tender. Let cool slightly, then
peel, quarter, and season with salt and pepper. To make the vinaigrette,
combine the vinegar, lemon juice, mustard, and garlic in a blender,
season with salt and pepper, and process until puréed. Slowly drizzle
in the oil, processing all the time, until well blended. To assemble the
salad, combine all ingredients in a large bowl, and toss together with
one eighth of the dressing, until the vegetables are all evenly coated.

Serves 1
Preparation time 30 minutes
Cooking time 20 minutes

- ½ cup (25 g / 1 oz) yellow wax beans or green (French) beans
- ½ cup (25 g / 1 oz) shelled peas
- ½ cup (25 g / 1 oz) tender young beets (beetroots)
- extra-virgin olive oil, for roasting
- salt and pepper
- ¼ head small romaine lettuce, washed and trimmed
- ¼ head Belgian endive, washed and trimmed

- ½ oz (15 g) feta cheese, cut into ¼-inch (5-mm) cubes
- 5 black olives, quartered and pitted
- 1 tablespoon mixed fresh herbs, such as chives, dill, parsley, and basil

FOR THE VINAIGRETTE
- 7 tablespoons red wine vinegar
- freshly squeezed juice of ½ lemon
- 2 tablespoons Dijon mustard
- 3 cloves of garlic, slow-roasted
- salt and pepper
- 1 cup (250 ml / 8 fl oz) extra-virgin olive oil

- Makes enough for 8 servings

SPICY SHELLFISH GIOUVETSI

- 4 tablespoons olive oil
- 6 shallots, sliced
- 1 garlic clove
- piment d'espelette or black pepper
- sherry vinegar, for deglazing
- 2 cups (450 ml / 16 fl oz) fish or chicken stock
- 1 cup (200 g / 7 oz) orzo pasta
- salt
- 2 tablespoons fish sauce
- 2 shrimps (prawns)
- 6 mahogany or soft-shelled clams, scrubbed (see pp 323–4)
- 8 mussels, scrubbed (see p 324)
- 1 tablespoon finely chopped fresh dill
- 1 tablespoon finely chopped fresh parsley
- 2 tablespoons freshly squeezed lemon juice

Preheat the oven to 350°F (180°C / Gas Mark 4) and place a giouvetsi, or ceramic cooking pot, in it. Combine 2 tablespoons of the oil, the shallots, garlic, and pepper in a deep heavy skillet or frying pan, and cook over medium heat for 5–8 minutes, or until softened. To deglaze, pour the vinegar into the pan, stir, and scrape up the residue from the bottom and sides of the pan with a spoon. Add the stock, orzo, salt, and fish sauce. Bring to a boil and cook for 8–10 minutes, or until the pasta is al dente. Remove from the heat and transfer to the giouvetsi, cover with a lid, and bake for 10 minutes, stirring every 2 minutes. Add the shellfish, mix well, cover, and cook for 8–10 minutes, or until all mussels and clams have opened. Add the fresh herbs, lemon juice, the remaining oil, and season with salt and pepper. Serve warm.

Serves 4
Preparation time 45 minutes
Cooking time 20 minutes

Note: Piment d'espelette is a variety of small, fairly mild chile pepper from the Basque country.

ANTHOS CHOCOLATE MOUSSE

- 1 scant cup (215 g / 7½ oz) grated semisweet (plain) chocolate
- ½ cup (120 ml / 4 fl oz) milk
- 1 cup (250 ml / 8 fl oz) heavy (double) cream

FOR THE HALVA
- oil, for greasing
- ¾ cup (150 g / 5 oz) superfine (caster) sugar
- 1 cup (175 g / 6 oz) tahini
- 1¼ teaspoons salt

FOR THE CARAMEL SAUCE
- 1 cup (200 g / 7 oz) superfine (caster) sugar
- ⅓ cup (80 ml / 3 fl oz) water
- 1 cup (250 ml / 8 fl oz) heavy (double) cream
- ½ teaspoon salt

To make the chocolate mousse, put the chocolate in a heavy-based pan with the milk and melt over very low heat, stirring until smooth. Pour the cream into a bowl and whip it until it holds soft peaks. Using a spatula, gently fold the whipped cream into the chocolate. Pour the mousse into 4 martini glasses and let set in the refrigerator for at least six hours. To make the halva, combine the sugar and ¼ cup (60 ml / 2¼ fl oz) water in a pan, and cook for about 10 minutes, or until a candy (sugar) thermometer registers 257°F (125°). Meanwhile, mix the tahini and salt with an electric mixer on medium speed for 5 minutes. Add the hot sugar syrup and mix on low speed until combined, then pour into an oiled roasting pan to cool. To make the caramel sauce, put the sugar and water in a large pan, and cook over high heat until the sugar has dissolved and a dark golden caramel has formed. Meanwhile, heat the cream in a pan over low heat. Remove the caramel from the heat and very carefully add the hot cream, stirring with a wooden spoon. Season with salt and let cool. Remove the mousse from the refrigerator and spoon the caramel sauce over it. Crumble the halva over the mousse.

Note: You can make the mousse a day in advance and store it in the refrigerator, covered with plastic wrap (cling film).

Serves 4
Preparation time 6 hours (including setting)
Cooking time 20 minutes

MICHAEL SYMON

Restaurants:
Lola, Cleveland, OH, USA
Lolita, Cleveland, OH, USA
Roast, Detroit, MI, USA
Mabel's BBQ, Cleveland, OH, USA
The B Spot, OH, MI & IN, USA
Bar Symon, Coraopolis, PA, USA
Symon's Burger Joint, Austin, TX, USA

Award-winning chef Michael Symon is the owner of the popular
Lola and Lolita restaurants in Cleveland, Ohio, which serve modern
Greek-Italian food to much critical acclaim. He has also made many
television appearances and published several cookbooks.

SHAVED BEET (BEETROOT) SALAD

To make the dressing, combine the shallot, garlic, and salt in a bowl.
Whisk in the vinegar, oil, honey, and dill until well blended. Set aside.
To make the salad, combine the beets and radishes in a large bowl, and
toss together with the dressing until the vegetables are all evenly coated.
Sprinkle with the crumbled feta cheese and mint. Serve immediately.

Serves 4
Preparation time 20 minutes

- 4 oz (120 g) tender young beets (beetroots), very finely sliced
- 4 oz (120 g) golden beets (beetroots)
- 4 oz (120 g) tender young candy-striped beets (beetroots)
- 4 oz (120 g) radishes
- 4 oz (120 g) feta cheese, crumbled
- 1 oz (25 g) finely chopped fresh mint

FOR THE DRESSING
- 1 grated shallot
- 1 garlic clove, finely chopped
- salt
- ¼ cup (50 ml / 2 fl oz) red wine vinegar
- ½ cup (120 ml / 4 fl oz) extra-virgin olive oil
- 1 tablespoon honey
- 2 tablespoons chopped fresh dill

SKORDALIA WITH GARBANZO BEANS (CHICKPEAS)

- 1 cup (250 g / 9 oz) dried garbanzo beans (chickpeas), soaked for 12 hours in cold water to cover with 1 tablespoon salt
- 2 cups (150 g / 5 oz) day-old bread, crust removed, cut into ½-inch (1-cm) cubes
- 1 cup (250 ml / 8 fl oz) milk
- 4 garlic cloves
- freshly squeezed juice of 1 lemon
- grated zest of 1 lemon
- 1 cup (120 g / 4 oz) toasted almonds
- ¾ cup (175 ml / 6 fl oz) extra-virgin olive oil
- salt
- 3 tablespoons chopped fresh parsley

Drain and rinse the garbanzo beans, put them into a pan, add water to cover, and cook for 1–2 hours, or until very soft. Drain and set aside. Put the bread cubes in a bowl, cover with the milk and let soak for 30 minutes. Squeeze the bread dry, reserving the milk, and put it in a blender with the garlic, lemon juice and zest, almonds, and oil. Season with salt. Blend to a purée, and gradually pouring in the remaining milk. Finally, add the garbanzo beans and parsley, and process until smooth.

Serves 4
Preparation time 1 hour
Cooking time 1–2 hours

BRAISED LAMB SHANKS

- 2 tablespoons olive oil
- 4 lamb shanks
- 1 teaspoon ground coriander
- 1 teaspoon black pepper
- ½ teaspoon chili flakes
- 1 tablespoon salt
- ½ cup (50 g / 2 oz) flour
- 3 garlic cloves, finely sliced
- 3 leeks, white and tender green parts, roughly chopped
- 3 carrots, peeled and roughly chopped
- 2 cups (450 ml / 16 fl oz) chicken stock
- freshly squeezed juice of 2 lemons
- ½ oz (15 g) arugula (rocket), cleaned and trimmed
- 2 egg yolks
- Skordalia with garbanzo beans (chickpeas), to serve (see above)

Preheat the oven to 300°F (150°C / Gas Mark 2). Heat the oil in a large Dutch oven (casserole dish). Season the meat with the coriander, pepper, chili flakes, and ½ tablespoon salt, and dredge with the flour. Place the meat in the Dutch oven and cook for 2 minutes on each side until browned all over. Remove the meat and set aside. Add the garlic, leeks, carrots, and the remaining salt, and cook over medium heat for 5 minutes, or until caramelized. Add the stock and bring to a simmer. Return the meat to the Dutch oven and cover. Place in the preheated oven and cook for 4–5 hours, or until the meat and vegetables are tender. Remove the meat from the dish and sprinkle with the lemon juice. Add the arugula to the dish and let it wilt for 1 minute. Strain the liquid through a sieve, reserving the vegetable and arugula mixture. Pour the liquid into a pan, beat in the egg yolks, and slowly bring to a simmer. Arrange the vegetables into 4 bowls and top with the lamb shanks. Ladle the egg and lemon broth over the meat. Serve accompanied by Skordalia with garbanzo beans.

Serves 4
Preparation time 30 minutes
Cooking time 4–5 hours

GLOSSARY

-

ΓΛΩΣΣΑΡΙΟ

-

Glosario

RECIPE NOTES

1. Oil always means olive oil, preferably extra-virgin olive oil, which should be used for everything except deep frying.

2. Butter should always be sweet (unsalted).

3. Pepper is always freshly ground black pepper, unless otherwise specified.

4. Eggs, fruit, and vegetables are assumed to be medium size, unless otherwise specified.

5. Milk is always whole, unless otherwise specified.

6. Thyme and oregano are dried, unless otherwise specified. Parsley always means fresh flat-leaf parsley.

7. Mustard means prepared mild mustard, such as Dijon, unless otherwise specified.

8. When a recipe calls for strained yogurt, commercial thick Greek yogurt can be used. Alternatively, hang ordinary yogurt in cheese-cloth (muslin) overnight in the refrigerator, with a bowl underneath to catch the liquid, and it will become much thicker.

9. Garlic cloves are assumed to be large; use two if yours are small.

10. Cup, metric, and imperial measurements are given throughout. Follow one set of measurements, not a mixture, as they are not interchangeable.

11. Cooking and preparation times are for guidance only, as individual ovens vary. If using a convection (fan) oven, follow the manufacturer's instructions concerning oven temperatures.

12. To test whether your deep-frying oil is hot enough, add a cube of stale bread. If it browns in thirty seconds, the temperature is 350–375°F (180–190°C), about right for most frying. Exercise caution when deep frying: add the food carefully to avoid splashing, wear long sleeves, and never leave the pan unattended.

13. Some recipes include raw or very lightly cooked eggs. These should be avoided particularly by the elderly, infants, pregnant women, convalescents, and anyone with an impaired immune system.

14. All spoon measurements are level. 1 teaspoon = 5 ml; 1 tablespoon = 15 ml. Australian standard tablespoons are 20 ml, so Australian readers are advised to use 3 teaspoons in place of 1 tablespoon when measuring small quantities.

AL DENTE

Literally meaning "to the tooth," used to describe the texture of cooked pasta or vegetables when they are tender but still firm to the bite.

ALMONDS

The *Prunus dulcis* or almond tree was one of the earliest trees to be cultivated in the eastern Mediterranean, around 3,000 BC. There is evidence that wild or bitter almonds were being collected in Greece in around 10,000 BC. The almond is the first tree to bloom at the end of the winter, its lovely flowers coming to life on the leafless branches. This phenomenon was explained in the beautiful Greek myth of Phyllis, a wood nymph, and the young prince of Athens, Akamas. Having sworn his undying love for her, he sailed off to fight in the Trojan War. On the way back his ship was beset by violent storms and was delayed for repairs. The faithful Phyllis went to the sea-shore eight times, hoping to catch sight of Akamas's ship. On her ninth fruitless trip, she perished from a broken heart. Out of pity, the goddess Athena turned her into an almond tree. When Akamas returned soon after and learned what had happened, he threw his arms around the barren tree and immediately it burst into blossom. In ancient Greece, almonds were served as dessert with the wine because it was believed that eating them pre-vented drunkenness. The Italians called the almond the "Greek nut" and served them roasted and honey-coated at wedding feasts. Similar candy- (sugar-) coated almonds (*koufeta*) are still traditional and are given as favors at Greek weddings and baptisms

as symbols of joy, strength, and good luck. Greek island cuisine is famous for its *amygdalota*, a marzipan-type confection, and an almond drink known as *soumada*.

AMARANTH

Leafy green vegetable with large pointed leaves, similar to beet greens (beetroot leaves).

ANARI

A white, creamy cheese, pro-duced in Cyprus, with a very soft consistency. It is a by-product of the whey that drains during the making of halloumi. It is eaten as a table cheese. Ricotta or cottage cheese may be used as a substitute.

ANEVATO

A soft white cheese from sheep's or goat's milk made in the area of Kozani and Grevena in Macedonia. It is intended to be eaten fresh; the name literally means "to rise to the surface," which is what happens when the curds separate from the whey.

ANISE

Native to Greece, this plant grows on most of the islands and in many places on the mainland. It blooms in summer, has whitish-yellow flowers, and fruit that consists of two small connected seeds. It is these seeds that produce the essential oil. Anise is valued for its diuretic properties and for helping to activate the milk glands in nursing mothers. The ancients also recognized its aphrodisiac qualities. Its intense licorice flavor finds its way into breads, pastries, and, of course, Greece's national drink, ouzo, which may have its origins in Byzantine aniseed wine.

ANTHOTIRO

A soft, white, sweet, and creamy cheese that is a by-product of the whey that drains away during the making of feta. It is served as a table cheese and also widely used in cooking. Ricotta or drained cottage cheese may be used as a substitute. It can be dried and grated over pasta to release its special aroma. The name means "flower of the cheese." It contains very little salt and is lower in fat than other cheeses. It is found all over Greece, but is particularly good in Crete, Macedonia, Thrace, Thessaly, the Peloponnese, and the islands of the Aegean and Ionian Seas.

ARTICHOKE HEART

The tender cup-shaped part of a young globe artichoke that remains when the hard parts and leaves have been removed.

ARUGULA (ROCKET)

A salad green popular in Europe for its slightly bitter, peppery taste and bright green color.

ASPIC

A transparent gelatin prepared by reducing clarified meat or fish stock that is rich in natural gelatin.

AVGOLEMONO

An egg and lemon sauce made with freshly squeezed lemon juice and eggs beaten and mixed with hot stock or sauce.

AVGOTARAHO

The cured roe of the gray mullet, enjoyed around the Mediterranean ever since the Pharaohs first banqueted upon it. Called *bottarga* in Italian, *boutargue* in French, the Greek name means "pickled eggs," but that barely conveys the pleasure of eating an amber slice of this rare and delicious ingredient. The lingering, slightly piquant flavor is difficult to describe, and evokes the sea without tasting fishy. In Greece, the production of *avgotaraho* is most associated with the lagoons of Missolonghi and Aitoliko on the south-western mainland. These lagoons, shallow and rich in nutrients, attract all kinds of fish, which swim in to feed and are prevented from returning to the open sea by a series of corral-like traps. The mullet season lasts from late August to mid-October, depending on the weather. After scooping them from the traps with long-handled nets, the fishermen separate the males from the females. Then, they dexterously slit open the stomach cavities of the females and remove the double-lobed, bright yellow egg sacs that constitute about eighteen percent of the weight of the fish. Traditionally, they would have been salted and laid out on racks to dry in the sun until they formed hard, brick-colored rods. Now they are rinsed, salted for a few hours, dried out in special ovens, and dipped into beeswax several times to create a coating that protects them from bacteria. Treated in this way, the roes are far less salty. *Avgotaraho* is usually eaten sliced thinly on buttered toast with a squeeze of lemon juice. When grated, it makes a fine sauce for pasta and adds flavor to omelets and salads. It goes well with strong drinks such as *tsipouro* or malt whisky.

BAIN-MARIE
See Double boiler.

BALSAMIC VINEGAR
A slightly sweet-tasting vinegar with origins dating back to eleventh-century Italy. The flavor and price vary according to how it is made. The traditional and most expensive is produced from the wines of either Modena or Reggio Emilia, provinces of northern Italy, and aged and mellowed in a varied series of wooden casks. The less expensive type is a blend of high-quality wine vinegar, young traditional balsamic vinegar, and caramel.

BARLEY RUSKS
Thick slices of twice-baked bread made from wheat and barley flour. Also known as hard tack or *paximadia*.

BASIL
The Greek name for basil has the same root as the word for king (*vasileus*), which shows the high regard the ancients had for this herb. Basil is perhaps the best-loved decorative plant in Greece, appearing in pots on almost every balcony or courtyard throughout the summer. It also features in many folk songs, rhymes, and poems. Greeks consider basil sacred because, according to tradition, it was found growing in the place where the True Cross was buried in Jerusalem. In the Orthodox Church, priests dip a branch of basil in Holy Water when they perform blessings. As a tisane, it is said to have many therapeutic properties. Its leaves produce a superb essential oil, which is used in aromatherapy. The use of basil in cooking is not widespread in Greece, except in the Ionian islands and Crete, but it is becoming more popular. Fresh basil goes especially well with tomato dishes.

BASTE
To moisten foods—particularly roast meats—with cooking juices, dripping, or a sauce during baking or broiling (grilling), using a spoon, bulb baster, or a brush, to prevent them from drying out.

BATTER
A mixture of flour, beaten egg, and a liquid, such as milk or water, that is used to make pancakes and to coat food for deep-frying. Raw cake mixture is called cake batter.

BATZOS
A historic Greek cheese, which was for centuries made by the nomads of the Pindos mountain range. The name means "sheep-fold cheese." Today is it made in Thessaly in central Greece and in western and central Macedonia. Made from sheep's milk, it is quite salty and fairly dry. It is ideal for frying or broiling (grilling) and good with red wine, ouzo, or *tsipouro*.

BAY
According to myth, the nymph Daphne was a beautiful priestess of the virgin goddess Artemis. She refused the amorous advances of Apollo, and her father, the river-god Penios, turned her into a bay tree (also known as laurel) to preserve her chastity. Apollo then cut some branches from the tree and wove them into a wreath in her memory. He also made the bay tree his sacred plant and ruled that a crown of bay leaves be awarded to winners at the Pythian Games at Delphi, the site of his best-known shrine. The traditional linking of bay with excellence continues today when we refer to Nobel Laureates, or "rest on our laurels." The tree grows mainly in high plains and

flowers from July to September. In cooking, bay leaves are used in moderation to give their intense flavor to soups, stews, and marinades.

BÉCHAMEL SAUCE

A white sauce made from milk thickened with a roux, or flour and butter paste.

BLANCH

To plunge food briefly into boiling water to part-cook or remove strong flavors, salt, or bitterness before further cooking; also to facilitate the removal of skins or shells.

BORLOTTI BEANS

Mottled red and beige-colored beans, also known as cranberry beans.

BRAISE

To cook meat, vegetables, or both at low heat in a covered pan or casserole with a small quantity of liquid.

BREADING

To coat foods by dipping into flour, beaten egg, and bread crumbs before frying. Breading or flouring seals the juices in and prevents foods from drying out while frying.

BREAM

Family of Mediterranean fish including red snapper, gilt-head sea bream, and porgy.

BROCHETTE

A skewer; also a dish made by threading meat or other ingredients onto a skewer and broiling (grilling).

BROIL (GRILL)

To cook food on a rack by direct heat under a flame or heating element.

BULGUR WHEAT

Wheat that has been soaked, cooked, and dried before the bran is removed. Widely used in the Mediterranean as a substitute for rice.

BUTTER

Despite the prevalence of olive oil, butter has a place in modern Greek cuisine, mostly in pastries and contemporary dishes. Dishes that originate in Asia Minor also make more use of butter, mainly because olive oil was not available there. European butters are now widely available in Greek supermarkets, but the traditional clarified sheep's milk butter, *voutiro galaktos*, is also sold in jars in supermarkets and groceries. It is the prized ingredient for making desserts and pastries for special occasions. Another kind of butter, known as *stakovoutiro*, is produced in Crete, but even there it is hard to find. It is rather like crème fraîche and is used in cooking, particularly in the famous *gamopilafo*, a rice dish served at weddings.

CANDIED FRUITS

Fruits that have been boiled and soaked in heavy syrup, then dried. When chopped, they can be mixed in fillings, cake batters, or sweet bread doughs. Whole candied fruits are used to garnish various cakes and tarts. Also referred to as glazed or crystallized fruit.

CAPERS

The buds of the caper bush, pickled in brine or vinegar. In some Greek islands, tender sprigs and leaves of the caper bush are also pickled or dried in a well-ventilated place and used in salads. These must be soaked in water and blanched three times

to remove any bitterness before using. Pickled caper buds should be rinsed under cold running water to remove excess salt.

CAPON

A castrated chicken, which is prized for its succulent white breast meat.

CASSEROLE

A metal, ovenproof glass or ceramic cooking dish with a lid. It is also the term for a dish prepared in such a container.

CAUL

The soft, fatty membrane surrounding an animal's intestines. Lamb's caul is most commonly sold fresh in Greek markets. It can be replaced with the salted caul sold elsewhere. It is used to enclose fillings or to hold meat on a skewer, preventing it from drying out.

CELERY

A vegetable that is inextricably linked with ancient Greece. It is mentioned in the Linear B tablets found at Mycenae, as well as by Homer and Dioscurides, who extolled its virtues, including its ability to sober up drunks. The Byzantines drank a brew known as *selinitis inos*, "celery wine," for urological complaints. The celery eaten by Greeks is quite different from the long white stalks consumed in other countries. The stalks are thinner, shorter, and the same dark green as the leaves. Both leaves and stalk have a pronounced flavor. It combines particularly well with pork, fish, leeks, and cabbage and is often added to soups and mixed salads. If you have only ordinary celery when preparing recipes from this book, add a handful of chopped leaves to intensify the flavor.

CELERY ROOT (CELERIAC)

A variety of celery with a thick root, also known as knob celery or celeriac. Celery stalks can be used as a substitute if celery root is not available, but the flavor is much less mild.

CHAMOMILE

From April to the end of June, this charming yellow and white flower carpets much of Greece, appearing in fields, forests, gardens, parks, roadsides, and even in town centers. During this season it emits an intense and distinctive aroma, and many people collect and dry it to make tea during the rest of the year. Its therapeutic properties are thought to cover a wide range of ailments. It is drunk as a tisane to soothe indigestion and to act as a mild sedative. Bathing the eyes in chamomile tea is thought to soothe and relax them. Chamomile has even been called the "plant doctor" because weak garden plants benefit if chamomile is planted around them.

CHARD

A leafy green similar to spinach. There are two types, Swiss chard and ruby chard, which is similar to beet greens (beetroot leaves). It is rarely eaten raw.

CHEESE

According to Greek mythology, the gods of Olympus sent Aristaios, son of the god Apollo, to teach the arts of cheese-making and beekeeping to the Greeks. Nobody knows when and where the first cheese was made, but it probably occurred by chance—perhaps in several places—when a shepherd used the stomach of a young lamb or kid to transport milk. The first written account of the art is found in Book Nine of *The Odyssey* when, in his cave, the one-eyed Cyclops makes cheese with the milk of his ewes. Even older evidence of cheese-making has been uncovered by archaeologists in Thessaly on the mainland and in Minoan Crete dating back to 3,000 BC. Throughout Greek history, references to the Greek love of cheese are many, from Aristophanes' plays to modern food writers and chefs who never cease trying to find new ways to use Greek cheese. Modern-day Greeks are champion consumers of cheese and more than 250,000 Greek families are engaged in producing milk, 80 percent of which is made into 300 different kinds of cheese. Greeks eat cheese every day at nearly every meal: fried as mezedes (*saganaki*), crumbled in *horiatiki* salads, grated on macaroni, baked in *tiropites*, with bread as a snack, dipped in or dribbled with honey for dessert. The extent to which cheese is used in Greek cuisine is impressive. The chief characteristic of Greek cheese is the use of sheep's and goat's milk, alone or in combination. Very few cheeses are made from cow's milk because the mountainous terrain of the Aegean archipelago is not suitable for large animals. However, sheep and particularly goats are easily herded from the lowland pastures to the high meadows dispersed among the huge rocky outcrops and boulders. It is in these areas that 90 percent of the Greek herds forage freely on 6,000 species of wild herbs, flowers, and other plants. The diverse aromas of these plants give Greek cheeses their unique flavor and excellent quality. Although more than 300 kinds of cheese are made in Greece, only twenty bear the PDO (Protected Designation of Origin) seal of the European Commission. These are cheeses produced using traditional recipes and methods without the use of antibiotics, preservatives, added milk proteins, food coloring, or any other additive. The quality control imposed on the production of PDO cheese is extremely rigid. There are also other cheeses in the category PGI (Protected Geographical Indication) with slightly less rigid regulations than the PDOs.

CHOKE

The inedible, fibrous part of the globe artichoke.

CILANTRO (CORIANDER)

A native herb of the parsley family. It resembles parsley in appearance, but has a very different flavor. Although it was one of the most popular herbs in antiquity, modern Greek cooks rarely use the leaves. The Cypriots, however, often add the crushed seeds to pork and vegetable dishes and the chopped leaves to salads and kabobs (kebabs). Cilantro leaves produce an essential oil used in aromatherapy, soaps, and cosmetics. In addition to giving foods its characteristic flavor, they also help preserve them.

CLARIFIED BUTTER

Butter from which the water, milk solids, and salt have been removed, usually by melting and skimming off the white solids.

COLANDER

A perforated metal or plastic basket for draining liquids.

CONCENTRATE
To reduce the quantity and thicken a liquid by simmering it.

COUSCOUS
Fine semolina that has been rolled and coated with wheat flour. It is steamed and served with meat and fish stews on the North African coast and elsewhere in the Mediterranean.

CRANBERRY BEAN
See Borlotti beans.

CREAM
Thirty or forty years ago heavy (double) cream could rarely be found in Greece and was never used in Greek cuisine, except for whipped (chantilly) cream or *santigi*, which could be bought at pastry shops and was used exclusively for cream cakes. The traditional *kaimaki* is a very rich cream whose fat content has been increased by heating to evaporate the liquid, a tradition that comes from the Greeks of Asia Minor. There is a popular ice cream flavored with mastic by the same name.

CRIMP
To seal the edges of pastry dough by pinching and pushing between thumb and middle finger to create a fluted edge.

CROQUETTES
Small pieces of chopped fish, shellfish, or vegetables bound with a sauce or batter, rolled in bread crumbs, and fried.

CRUDITÉS
Vegetables cut into strips or bite-size pieces and served raw with dips or sauces.

DEEP-FRY
To cook food immersed in a large quantity of hot oil, shortening, or fat.

DEGLAZE
To pour a liquid, such as wine, stock, or water, into the pan in which meat or vegetables have been fried or roasted to dissolve the sediment on the base of the pan into the sauce.

DEGREASE
To remove fat from cooking juices, stock, or broths.

DILL
This herb has a long history, both in folk medicine and cooking. The ancient Greeks called it *anison* and prepared an aromatic oil from its shiny yellow flowers, which they added to a wine known as *anithitis inos*. Athletes used to rub their bodies with oil from its seeds to tone their muscles. Dill plays a prominent role in Greek cuisine, appearing regularly in fish and vegetable dishes, and is almost always sprinkled on a winter salad of romaine lettuce and scallions (spring onions). It even finds its way into liqueurs and breads. It not only adds a pleasant flavor, but it is also thought to aid digestion.

DITTANY
This gray-green, velvety-leaved plant grows only in remote areas of Crete, but the ancients thought of it as a cure-all. Dioscurides mentions a certain wild goat, which, when it had been hit by an arrow, chewed dittany leaves and then licked the wound to heal it. The Cretans drink it instead of tea and call it the plant of love, since it is also said to be an aphrodisiac.

DOUBLE BOILER OR BAIN-MARIE
A cooking vessel consisting of two pans, one of them designed to rest on top the other, so that food can be cooked by the heat of the steam from a small amount of water simmering in the lower pan. Also used to keep sauces hot.

DREDGE
To coat food with flour, crumbs, or confectioners' (icing) sugar until the surface is completely covered.

DRESS
To pluck, draw, singe, trim, and truss a bird in preparation for cooking.

DRIZZLE
To pour a thin stream of liquid over the surface of a dish.

DUTCH OVEN
A deep metal or earthenware cooking pot with a lid, used for braises or pot-roasts.

FENNEL
A thick bulb vegetable with a licorice flavor, also called Florence fennel. Its fine leaves resemble dill. Wild fennel grows all over the coastal areas of the Aegean and eastern Mediterranean, where it is widely used as an herb and a vegetable, eaten raw or cooked. You will see the feathery, dill-like leaves of wild fennel along many a Greek roadside in spring and early summer. The leaves and bulbs have a more pronounced aniseed flavor than cultivated fennel. It is a popular seasoning in the cooking of the Aegean islands and Crete, where it appears in dishes with octopus and fish and in croquettes. It is almost interchangeable with dill. Wild fennel forms the basis of many natural cough medicines, while the essential oil made from its

tart-tasting seeds is used in making digestive drinks and liqueurs.

FETA

A Greek curd cheese made from sheep's or goat's milk, ripened in brine. The crumbly cheese that made Greece famous is made from pasteurized sheep's milk and up to 30 percent goat's milk, and is allowed to ripen for three months. The word *feta* means "a piece" or "a slice" and it is the only cheese used in authentic *horiatiki,* or Greek salad. There are several different types of feta, but officially they must be made in Macedonia, Thrace, Epirus, Thessaly, central Greece, the Peloponnese, or the island of Lesvos. The Greeks produce 115,000 tons of feta annually and consume 22 pounds (10 kg) per person per year. It is Greece's best-known table cheese, but is also widely used in cooking, mostly in pies. It is one of the few cheeses that goes with retsina wine. Feta is widely available worldwide, but only Greek feta is authentic.

FIGS

The ancient Greeks believed that the fig was the first fruit to be cultivated. Myths tell of Demeter, goddess of agriculture, teaching Phytalos how to cultivate the fig tree, or *sikia,* out of gratitude for his kindness during her long search for her daughter Persephone. There are thousands of references to figs and fig trees in ancient Greek literature, beginning with Homer. It was the branch of a fig tree that saved Odysseus from drowning when the vengeful Zeus destroyed his ship with a thunderbolt. Among the fruits ripening in King Alkinous's orchard that greeted Odysseus's hungry eyes were

luscious figs. Odysseus also witnessed the underworld torture of Tantalos, condemned to be eternally tormented by juicy ripening figs and other fruits hanging just out of reach. The ancient Greeks were well aware of the food value of their sacred figs. Succulent and juicy when fresh, they could also be dried and stored for the winter. In the era of Solon, Greece's first lawmaker, the export of figs was forbidden. Xerxes, the King of Persia, is said to have invaded Greece in order to access the supply of Attic figs. There are many kinds of figs growing in Greece, but the large, green, succulent *basilika* or royal figs, which ripen in August, are considered the best.

FOLD

To mix ingredients gently from the bottom of the bowl to the top, in an under-over motion that distributes ingredients without knocking out the air. It is best done with a large metal spoon or spatula.

FONDANT

When a sugar syrup is cooked to the soft-ball stage, cooled, and then worked or stirred constantly, tiny sugar crystals form in it and the syrup gradually becomes a firm, pure-white paste. This paste is known as fondant.

FORMAELA PARNASSOU

This hard, cylindrical cheese made from sheep's or goat's milk has an elastic texture that makes it excellent for frying or broiling (grilling). These are the only ways in which it is usually eaten, as it does not have much flavor uncooked. It is made in the ski resort region of Arachova on the slopes of Mount Parnassos.

FRICASSEE

In Greece, a braised dish in which the cooking liquid is thickened with a mixture of egg and lemon juice.

FRITTERS

Vegetables or other foods dipped in batter and fried.

GALOTIRI

A very soft, yogurt-like cheese made in Epirus and Thessaly from sheep's or goat's milk, it is considered one of the oldest traditional Greek cheeses. The locals roll small balls of the cheese in pepper, oregano, and dill and store them in jars of olive oil with a bay leaf and whole chiles for their winter mezedes. It is also used in pies.

GIBLETS

The organ meats (offal), neck, feet, and wing tips of a bird. (Feet and wing tips are not necessarily included in birds sold in all countries, and the organ meats may also vary.)

GIOUVETSI

A Greek clay or ceramic vessel used to cook food slowly directly on the stove top (hob) or in the oven. Also the name of the dish cooked in such a vessel.

GRAVIERA

Several *gravieras,* or Gruyère-style semi-hard table cheeses, are made in Greece, but only three are certified as PDOs. *Graviera Agrafon* is named after a mountain range in Epirus where it is used to make *tiropites. Graviera Kritis,* which was exported during the Turkish Occupation, is nowadays eaten on special occasions, dipped in honey as a meze, in cooked dishes, or with fruit for dessert. Naxos *graviera* is made with cow's milk, often mixed with up to 20 percent sheep's or goat's milk. It is said that the first cows were brought there by Catholic monks from Venice when the Venetians ruled the Cyclades. Gruyère-style cheeses are made elsewhere in Greece, all exceptionally tasty and of excellent quality.

GREENS, FIELD
Wild or cultivated fresh greens are eaten raw or cooked everywhere in the Mediterranean. They include, but are not limited to, amaranth, broccoli rabe, chard, collards, dandelions, escarole, endive, flowering kale, nettle, mustard, romaine lettuce, radicchio, arugula (rocket), spinach, sorrel, and watercress.

GRIND
To chop food very finely.

HALLOUMI
A traditional Cypriot cheese made from unpasteurized sheep's and goat's milk. It is white with a salty flavor and a distinctive layered texture, similar to mozzarella. It is flavored with mint and when it is fried it does not melt, so it is often served fried or broiled (grilled). The Cypriots also use it in other dishes such as pies and cooked pastas.

HAZELNUTS
Hazelnut trees, native to northeastern Asia Minor, are grown all over the Mediterranean. Hazelnuts were popular in classical Greece and Rome and were served, like other nuts, after the meal to accompany the wine. The ancients called them *karion Pontikon*, or nuts of the Pontus, from which they were imported. In Greece, hazelnuts are a popular accompaniment to wine or whisky,

but also in candies (sweets) and chocolate-covered bonbons.

HERBS, AROMATIC
The cuisine of the northern Mediterranean coast and the Aegean archipelago is characterized by its use of indigenous wild and cultivated herbs: basil, bay leaf, celery, chervil, cilantro (coriander), dill, fennel weed, marjoram, flat-leaf parsley, spearmint, rosemary, oregano, saffron, sage, savory, tarragon, thyme. The cuisine of the eastern and southern Mediterranean makes more use of spices. Greek plants are among the richest and rarest on the planet, and an enormous range of herbs, extending from the seashore to the tip of Mount Olympus, scents the air with an enchanting fragrance. Many of these plants are connected with the history, culture, and very essence of the Greek people. Myths, legends, and folklore surround them, creating the links of a long chain that connects mythology with fact, gods with humans, and the heavens with the Greek soil. Greece's long coastline, hundreds of mountains, and small number of valleys form a rare ecosystem suitable for plants characterized by hardiness, adaptability to extreme weather conditions, and the ability to store and preserve valuable nutrients in their leaves, and to develop special aromas and tastes. The peculiarities of the Greek landscape and climate have led many herbs to acquire unusual qualities as they struggle to survive. Summer tests their resistance to drought, intense sunlight, and high temperatures, while winter calls upon them to withstand freezing temperatures, as well as snow and ice in the

mountains. In self-defense they produce substances that protect them from dehydration and insect pests. These substances have tremendous pharmaceutical value and have been used since the fifth century BC, when Hippocrates began studying, recording, and prescribing them. Galen and Dioscurides followed, laying the foundations of pharmacology and aromatherapy. Modern research and analysis of Greek plants has recorded more than 6,500 species. Of these, 1,200 are found nowhere else in the world. Whether as a cure for their ailments, a relaxing drink, or an ingredient in cooking, herbs connect Greeks to the place where they were born and the traditions in which they were raised.

HLORI (MIZITHRA KIKLADON)
A traditional, white, soft, creamy, whey cheese. *Hlori* is served as a table cheese with honey and fresh or preserved fruits. Ricotta, mascarpone, or cottage cheese may be used as a substitute.

HONEY
Honey is one of the oldest and most legendary foods. Imagine the thrill our ancestors felt when they found a ready-to-eat food that was relatively easy to find, was a boundless source of energy, and miraculously did not spoil or rot. They even discovered that foods submerged in it could be preserved indefinitely. No wonder honey was thought of as a gift of the gods. There are many legends and myths associated with honey in Greek literature, beginning with the birth of almighty Zeus himself. Fearing the wrath of Father Kronos, who jealously swallowed his children as soon as they were born,

Mother Rhea had Zeus spirited away to the island of Crete where he was raised by the goat-nymph Amaltheia, who gave the infant her milk, and the nymph-princesses, Io and Adrasteia (daughters of King Melliseus of Crete) who fed him honey. Later, when he became king of the gods, he set Amaltheia's image in the heavens as the constellation Capricorn. He also took one of her horns and gave it to the honey-princesses, and it was this horn that became the Horn of Plenty or Cornucopia, always filled to overflowing with good things to eat and drink, the eternal symbol of wealth and bounty. The oldest evidence of honey in Greece was found in Crete. Moreover, the Greek word for honey, *meli*, was found on the famous Linear B tablets that were inscribed more than 3,500 years ago in Minoan Crete. Today Cretan honey is among the finest produced in Greece, mainly due to the unique varieties of flowers and aromatic herbs that grow there. More than 15,000 tons of honey is produced in Greece, with 60–70 percent of it coming from forest nectar and the rest from wild flowers. The most famous is the thyme honey from the Hymettos Mountains near Athens. This has been exported since the fifth century BC, and honey remains an important export for Greece. Large quantities are also consumed by the Greeks—about 2 pounds (1 kg) per capita annually—not just because they like it, but also because they believe it is good for their health. A favorite taverna dessert is yogurt or soft cheeses such as *anthotiro* or *manouri* topped with honey and nuts. Honey continues to play a very important role in the traditional cuisine of Greece.

JULIENNE STRIPS
Long, thin strips, a common way of cutting vegetables.

KAKAVIA
Greek fishermen's soup made with various small fish simmered with onions, tomatoes, and olive oil for a long time until the fish bones have disintegrated.

KALAMATA OLIVES
Greek, black, pointed olives preserved in brine. Meaty in texture yet fruity in flavor, they are considered to be the finest-quality eating olives.

KALATHAKI LIMNOU
This white cheese looks like a little basket (*kalathaki*), hence the name. It has roots in Byzantium, when it was first made by Orthodox monks on the island of Limnos. It is very similar to feta but has a pleasant slightly sour taste.

KASERI
One of the most popular of Greek table cheeses, this semi-hard yellow cheese is made from sheep's milk in Lesvos, Macedonia, and Thessaly, and sometimes includes 20 percent goat's milk. Because of its good melting qualities, it is often used in pizzas and *kaseropita*, a kind of *tiropita*, as well as fried as *saganaki*. Mozzarella can be used as a substitute. It is aged for between three and four months and the flavor of this rich cheese ranges from mild and sweet to slightly peppery and piquant.

KATIKI DOMOKOU
This soft spreading cheese comes from a very small area around Mount Othrys, near the town of Domokos. Usually made from goat's milk combined with a very small quantity of sheep's milk, it is soft, slightly sour, lightly salted, and mild-tasting and has become a favorite breakfast and snack cheese with bread or rusks. It is a good partner for olive oil, oregano, olives, and red bell peppers as a dip. *Katiki* bears some resemblance to ricotta, but is much tastier.

KEFALOGRAVIERA
A semihard sheep's milk cheese, sometimes with up to 10 percent goat's milk. This table cheese, a cross between the older *kefalotiri* and *graviera*, is quite salty and piquant, good by itself served with ouzo, *tsipouro*, and dry red wine. It is used widely in cooking. It is made in Kastoria (western Macedonia), Ioannina and Dodoni (Epirus) and Amfilochia (central Greece).

KEFALOTIRI
A hard cheese made all over Greece. Its name, meaning "head," refers to its shape. It is an aged salty, sharp-tasting cheese with a strong aroma, made from sheep's milk and up to 30 percent goat's milk. It is good for grating on pasta dishes, fried, and as an appetizer with wine and ouzo. The oldest of hard Greek cheeses, it is made all over the country. In Kefallonia it is also used in the island's famous meat pie.

KNEAD
To fold, press and stretch dough until it becomes smooth and elastic.

KOPANISTI KYKLADON
A salty, peppery-tasting soft cheese made in the Greek islands. This is one of the few Greek

cheeses that has not been commercialized, perhaps because unpasteurized milk is used to make it. Produced only in the Cyclades—the best being from Mykonos and Tinos—it also is one of the few cheeses which is made from sheep's, goat's, or cow's milk or a mixture of the three. Its piquant, peppery, salty taste, reminiscent of Roquefort or Stilton, is thought to result from the sparse vegetation the animals graze on and the hot sun to which it is exposed in the early part of the fermentation process. In a class all its own, this is a cheese not to be missed with ouzo, *tsipouro*, or very dry white or red wines.

LADOTIRI MYTILINIS

This is a hard cheese made from sheep's or goat's milk that takes its name from the olive oil (*ladi*) in which is stored and allowed to mature, giving it a rich, buttery taste and sometimes a piquant aroma. Used as a table cheese, it is also found in dishes from Lesvos.

LARD

To thread strips of pork fat through lean meat. The fat melts during the cooking and keeps it moist.

LATHOURI

Small dried legume (pulse), also known as vetch or Santorini island fava (broad) bean. It is difficult to find outside the Mediterranean. Yellow split peas are the best substitute.

LEMON BALM

This grows in dry, uncultivated areas. It has deliciously fragrant leaves and flowers and is believed to have many therapeutic properties. Its leaves have a sweet taste and delicate lemony scent and are added to wines and juices.

A glass of cold lemon balm tea in summer is refreshing and revitalizing.

LIME LEAF

Mythology relates that Philyra was the mother of the centaur Chiron, the wise doctor and teacher of many a hero. When she realized that her newborn son was half human and half horse, she was so ashamed that she begged Zeus to turn her into a tree. Philyra thus became a beautiful decorative tree, every part of which is believed to have important therapeutic properties. Lime tea is drunk in the evening as a relaxant for both nerves and arteries.

MACARONI

Hollow pasta tubes of various thicknesses and lengths. Macaroni for Greek pastitsio is made in 10-inch (25-cm) lengths that are cooked whole for the dish of the same name. It is available from Greek suppliers, or you can substitute Italian ziti.

MAHLAB

An aromatic spice, it is traditionally used in breads, cakes, traditional Greek cookies (biscuits), and Greek Easter bread (*tsoureki*) It is made from the ground kernels of a variety of cherry.

MALLOW

This relative of the hollyhock grows in fields and on roadsides from March to July. The doctors of ancient Greece considered it among the most important healing plants, prescribing it in cases of difficult childbirth. Hippocrates used to apply mallow poultices to edemas and inflammations, while Dioscurides found it helpful against bee stings, both for prevention and cure. Today many ointments contain mallow root,

and an aromatic tisane made from its lovely dried pink flowers is said to help detoxify the system. The leaves and shoots used in cooking combine well with legumes (pulses), meat, and rice and lend a special fragrance to confectionery.

MANOURI

This is the richest of Greece's soft curd cheeses. It has been well known since the Byzantine era but was first referred to in the nineteenth century as *vlastis*, the name of a village in Macedonia. Today it is made in central and western Macedonia and Thessaly from sheep's or goat's milk, or a combination. Its texture is similar to that of cream cheese, but its taste and aroma are quite different. Some consider this the best of the traditional Greek cheeses, an excellent accompaniment to the delicate white wines of Greece.

MARINADE

A seasoning mixture, usually a combination of oil, wine or vinegar, and herbs and spices. It is used to flavor and tenderize meat, game, fish, or other raw foods.

MARINATE

To steep raw food in flavoring ingredients, often a liquid mixture, before cooking, in order to impart flavor and, in the case of meat, to tenderize it.

MARJORAM

This herb grows wild in Greece but is often cultivated in courtyard flower pots. Marjoram leaves give a particularly pleasant taste to a tisane and its essential oil is used in making beverages. The leaves, more often dried than fresh, are added to the same types of dishes as thyme and its first cousin oregano—in other words, to soups, salads, vegetables such as eggplants (aubergines) and zucchini (courgettes), and meats. It also sometimes appears as a candy (sweet). However, it should be used sparingly, as too much marjoram can leave a bitter taste.

MASTIC

Little known and rarely used outside the Mediterranean, the aromatic gum resin *mastiha* or mastic, is a product of the *Pistachia lentiscus* tree found on the island of Chios. Although trees of the same species grow elsewhere in Asia Minor, mainland Greece, and even elsewhere on the same island, only the two million small, bushlike trees growing in southern Chios produce this unusual flavoring agent. Local legend holds that the trees miraculously began weeping during the martyrdom of Saint Issidoros. In reality, mastic is produced by tapping the trees with a special knife, the *kenditiri*, between July 15 and October 15. The sap oozes out and forms a greenish glutinous mass, which eventually hardens into brittle, opaque white "tears" as crystals form in the resin. After about fifteen days the mastic is scraped off the tree. It is so precious that even pieces that fall to the ground are gathered up. Some 5,000–6,000 people in and around the twenty-one mastic villages of southern Chios are involved in the production of 125,000 tons of mastic annually. It was an important and valuable commodity throughout history, and every civilization of the area—Greek, Roman, Byzantine, and Ottoman—chewed mastic to clean the teeth and sweeten the breath. Christopher Columbus

visited Chios in 1473, several years before embarking on his famous voyage in search of gold, spices, and mastic, which he later erroneously claimed to have found in Cuba. A natural gum, powdered mastic is also widely used as a spice in Middle Eastern, Turkish, and Greek cuisines, lending its resinous aroma to liqueur and ouzo from Chios, as well as *kaimaki* ice cream, cookies (biscuits), cakes, breads, desserts, and other confections, including the Greek "submarine," or *ipovrihio*, a chewy, taffy (toffee)-like spoon sweet served submerged in glasses of ice cold water during the summer.

MAVRODAPHNE

Mavrodaphne, or "Black Daphne," is a world-class, port-like wine named after the beautiful, dark-haired fiancée of the Bavarian raisin merchant Gustav Clauss, who founded Achaia Clauss, one of Greece's oldest wineries, in 1861. Daphne died before they were married, but her name lives on in this delicious wine. Mavrodaphne is produced from a variety of eponymous red grape which, when mature, acquires an aroma of cherry, vanilla, and dried fruit. The grape is pressed with Corinthian black currants, which can account for up to 45 percent of the blend, giving the wine a silken, raisin-like taste. The wine is left to mature in oak barrels for at least two years until its alcohol level reaches 16–19 percent, most of which derives from natural fermentation. Its average age is six years, but the vineyard has bottles from casks that date back to 1873. Mavrodaphne is an excellent dessert wine with a deep red color, medium acidity, a rich

aroma, and a ripe flavor that goes well with blue cheese, chocolate, nuts, and dried fruit. It is often added to dry wines, such as Cabernet Sauvignon, to make a richer-tasting blend. Mavrodaphne has become associated with Greek religious tradition, as it is drunk at Holy Communion.

METAXA BRANDY

There are other Greek brandies, but the name Metaxa is known worldwide. It originated in 1888 when the owner of a taverna in Piraeus was inspired to create an alcoholic drink that would conquer the world. His invention was considered a revolution in distilling. It is the result of a blend of distilled white and old Muscat wines. Production starts with the double distillation of three grape varieties, Savatiano, Black Corinthian, and Soultanina, which are aged from three to thirty years in small oak barrels with large pores that enable them to breathe. At the same time another wine is prepared from the Muscat grape of Samos, Limnos, and Patras for eventual blending with the first. This wine is aged for at least two years, during which it acquires a rich fragrance, a full sweet taste, and a caramel color. Meanwhile, an extract of aromatic plants, rose petals, and spices is prepared for eventual blending with the two wines, but its exact ingredients are a closely-guarded secret. Finally, the three liquids are mixed together and then stored in barrels for further aging of six months or longer. The number of stars on the label indicates the quality of the brandy, which improves with age. The best way to drink it is to sip it from a brandy glass at room temperature, but many people like it with ice or club soda (soda water).

METSOVONE

This semi-hard smoked cheese is named for the town of Metsovo in the Pindos Mountains, the only place in which it is made. It is made from cow's milk, but may include up to 10 percent sheep's or goat's milk. After ripening for between three and five months, it is hung and smoked over burning vine branches and other aromatic plants. It is an excellent table cheese, good when grilled over charcoal, and also in salads, and with dry white or red wines.

MINT

This herb grows all year round in courtyards and gardens and has an intoxicating aroma. Known since antiquity, it is said that in classical times Greeks used to rub their tables with the herb before they sat down to eat. Hippocrates referred to mint as the plant with the greatest pharmaceutical value, while Aristotle thought it an excellent aphrodisiac. Cooks use it either fresh or dried in both savory and sweet dishes, especially in Crete. Its essential oil is an important aromatic component in the making of soaps and perfumes. In Greece there are fourteen species of mint, and nine subspecies.

MIZITHRA

This traditional whey cheese is made almost everywhere in Greece. A white soft creamy cheese when it is fresh (*hlori*), it is also dried (*xeri*) and grated over pasta. There are several variations in different parts of Greece, notably *xinomizithra* or "sour" *mizithra*, a PDO cheese from Crete, *mastelo* from the island of Chios, and *anari* from Cyprus.

Mizithra is served as a table cheese with honey or fruit. Ricotta, mascarpone, or drained cottage cheese can be used as substitutes for the fresh version.

MOUNTAIN TEA

This name covers a wide variety of herbs that grow on hillsides and are gathered and dried to make tea. Each region has its own species, most of which are endemic. They share a similar aroma but differ in flavor and chemical composition. Some of the best grows on the peaks of Mount Idi in Crete. Analyses of the essential oils of five different kinds of mountain tea have isolated between seventy and ninety different chemical compounds.

MUSTARD

Known since ancient times as a wonderful aid to preserving foods, mustard is believed to stop bacterial activity. It flourishes in sunny, dry areas and Greeks love to eat its tender shoots, called *vrouves* or *mavrovrouves*, in spring, alone or with other greens. The best-known use of mustard seed is, of course, the familiar hot yellow or light brown condiment that commonly accompanies pork, cured ham, and sausages, although in Greece it is also an ingredient in broths, flour, and oils.

NETTLES

This plant grows just about everywhere and is chiefly known for its sting, which is removed by cooking. The irritation is caused by formic acid in the hairs on the leaves and stems. Nettle tips are collected to drink in tisanes, and mixed with other greens in pies and vegetable stews.

OIL GLANDS

A pair of sacs containing a bitter oil, situated above the tail of a duck or goose, which should always be removed before cooking. The oil sacs of commercial poultry are removed before sale.

OLIVE OIL

The oil of the olive fruit. Use natural cold-pressed (or first-pressed) extra virgin olive oil (less than .01 percent acidity) for salads, cooked vegetables, and instead of butter, margarine, or other fats (except for candies (sweets) and desserts). Light oils are often refined and lose their natural healthy properties. The color of olive oil ranges from pale gold to greenish-gold. Save expensive boutique olive oil for salads or to add at the end of cooking. The less expensive brands can be used for general cooking and frying.

OREGANO

This well-known aromatic shrub grows wild in mountainous and rocky areas all over Greece. In fact, its name means "jewel of the mountains." The fresh flowers are collected and then dried in special sheds or ovens. After drying, they are rubbed and sieved into tiny particles. Oregano is the most characteristic seasoning in Greek cooking; it gives a special flavor to roast meats and potatoes and is an indispensable ingredient in Greek salad. Greek oregano is of such exceptional quality that it is widely considered the best in the world.

ORGAN MEATS (OFFAL)

The edible internal organs of an animal, such as liver, heart, lungs, spleen, kidneys, and sweetbreads. The term may also include the extremities, such as head, feet, ears, and tail.

ORZO
A type of small pasta shaped like barley grains or rice. Rice or bulgur wheat are often substituted.

OUZO
A Greek anise or licorice-flavored alcoholic apéritif. It is a popular summer drink in the Aegean, drunk either on the rocks or with ice-cold water. It is also used in cooking. It is made from pure alcohol, at least one third of which must be distilled from the skins, seeds, and branches of grapes after they have been pressed for wine. The rest, however, may come from grains, potatoes, or other fruits. Giving ouzo its flavor is a complex art. The producer first selects the type and quality of anise and then macerates it for up to three days in the pure alcohol along with other herbs and spices. These may include cilantro (coriander), cinnamon, cloves, fennel seeds, and even rosemary, and the recipe is each individual distiller's well-kept secret. This mixture is then distilled and stored for several months. At this point it is 100 percent alcohol and must be diluted with water before being bottled and sold. Most ouzo contains 38–42 percent alcohol and most people dilute it further with ice or water when they drink it. The addition of more water turns the clear liquid cloudy because anithol, the essential oil in aniseed, breaks down in solutions where the water-alcohol ratio is less than 38 percent. Although wine-making is a very ancient art, the technique of distilling alcohol from its by-products is much more recent. Ouzo-making seems to have begun in the eighteenth century in Asia Minor (the Turks have a similar drink they call *raki* or *arak*) and moved to Greece about a century later. By the late nineteenth century, two great centers had evolved, Tyrnavo in Thessaly and Plomari on Lesvos, which is still considered to make the best. However, it had not yet acquired its name. The story goes that in Tyrnavos, where it was christened, labels reading *uso Massalias* ("for the use of Marseilles") were put on bales of locally-made silk to denote an extra-high quality level reserved for export to that discerning market. Apparently, when three citizens of that town (a silk merchant, a distiller, and an Armenian doctor who loved to drink) got together to taste the brew they had collaborated on, the silk merchant pronounced, "This is as good as *uso Massalias*." Somehow the verdict stuck and was rapidly Hellenized into "ouzo." Much later, ouzo was classified as uniquely Greek, and Greece is the only country permitted to produce it under that name. Sipping ouzo is a national pastime that almost always involves companions, fun, and food. Greeks rarely drink alone and invariably nibble on something to mitigate the effects of alcohol. This can range from a simple plate of olives and sliced tomatoes to a full meal served on a series of little plates. In restaurants known as *ouzeris* or *mezedopoleia*, eating mezedes with ouzo is raised to the level of a ritual, and the menu can list more than a hundred items.

PAN-FRY
To cook in a shallow pan over high heat in a small amount of oil or fat.

PARBOIL
To cook food briefly in boiling water or stock in order to soften it or to shorten its final cooking time.

PARE
To cut off the peel of fruits and vegetables.

PARSLEY, FLAT LEAF
Many people's favorite herb, parsley has been known to the Greeks since antiquity, when it was used as both a perfume and a drug. With its characteristic fresh but unobtrusive flavor, parsley goes with everything. Almost all savory dishes benefit from its presence.

PASTOURMA
A cured beef product similar to pastrami.

PEARL (PICKLING) ONIONS
Small round onions often used in braised dishes.

PHYLLO (FILO)
Thin, pliable sheets of fresh pastry dough made from flour and water. One of the world's most versatile culinary materials, phyllo is used in a variety of ways in Greek and other Mediterranean cuisines, especially as a wrapping for baklava and other desserts and for pies. Phyllo can be homemade (see page 46) or bought ready made.

PICKLE
To preserve in brine or vinegar solution.

PILAF
A popular rice dish prepared from long-grain rice in which the grains remain separate, not soft and glutinous.

PISTACHIOS

The pistachio tree, related to the terebinth tree (or turpentine), is native to Afghanistan, where it was used as food as long ago as the third millennium BC. The earliest European reference appears in Theophrastus in his fourth-century writings about an expedition of Alexander the Great. During the Hellenistic era that followed, the pistachio quickly spread throughout the Mediterranean, grafted onto terebinth rootstock, which it still is. In modern Greece, pistachio trees have been cultivated since 1860 on the island of Aegina, from where the high-yield variety *fistiki Eginis* or *kilarati* (meaning "round") spread to Attica and other areas of Greece. Although smaller than other types of pistachios, their uniquely mild, distinctive flavor puts them in a class of their own, recognized by many as the finest pistachios in the world. Only those grown and processed by the Agricultural Association of Pistachio Producers of Aegina bear the PDO (Protected Designation of Origin) seal of the European Commission. There are approximately 200,000 trees on the island, which produce a yearly average of 1,300 tons of nuts. Pistachios are used mainly as appetizer or dessert nuts served with drinks, but are also used in several desserts and are an excellent, if expensive, ingredient in baklava.

PITA

A Greek word referring to two entirely different dough products: either a round or oval flat bread also known as Arab pocket bread or any one of a number of flat (usually round) sweet or savory pies made in Greece with sheets of phyllo (filo) pastry.

POACH

To cook food gently in simmering liquid, usually water, stock, or milk.

POT-ROAST

To cook meat slowly in a covered pan with little or no added liquid.

POUND

To grind ingredients in a mortar with a pestle to make a powder or paste.

PRALINE

Blanched or unblanched almonds or other nuts caramelized in boiling sugar.

PURÉE

To blend or mash the pulp of ripe or cooked foods into a smooth uniform paste. Purées are often used to thicken sauces or soups.

PURSLANE

A salad green with shiny thick round leaves and a slightly bitter flavor, eaten raw in salads or used as a garnish. Use watercress or arugula (rocket) as a substitute.

RAISING OR RISING

The process of increasing the volume of baked goods by adding leavenings such as yeast, baking powder, or baking soda (bicarbonate of soda).

RAISINS, GOLDEN RAISINS, AND CURRANTS

All three are dried grapes, another traditional Greek product since at least 1,500 BC. Most raisins are dark in color; golden are paler, and currants are a special variety of small black grapes first grown near ancient Corinth. In fact, the word "currant" is a corruption of the name of the Greek city Corinth. They were then, and remain now, an important export of that region.

REDUCE

To boil down a liquid to concentrate its flavor and thicken it to the consistency of a sauce.

RETSINA

Another distinctively Greek product, retsina is white wine to which pine resin has been added. The story of retsina is thought to have begun in antiquity, when the sticky resin was used to seal the amphoras in which wine was stored and transported. The strong smell permeated the wine and eventually became inseparable from it. In time, Greeks came to appreciate the resinous taste so much that they added a tiny amount of powdered resin directly to their barrels. They discovered that it also helped preserve the wine. For generations, retsina was the table wine of choice in many parts of Greece. Tourists used to complain that it tasted like turpentine, but then acquired the taste themselves. When properly made, pale yellow retsina has only a light fragrance that seems just right on a summer evening in a taverna. The best retsina came from Ravatiano and Roditis grapes grown in Attica. Sadly, this traditional wine is dying out, as the present generation of wine-makers turn to French and Californian methods with excellent results for both Greek and imported grape varieties. There are signs that a revival may be on the way, however, as some vineyards are beginning to market bottled retsina. But for the moment, the taverna barrel of house retsina is on the verge of extinction.

RISSOLE

A meat, fish, or vegetable mixture shaped into rounds or ovals, covered with batter, bread crumbs, or pastry, and deep-fried or baked.

ROSEMARY

This herb grows naturally in dry, barren soil and needs very little water. Its needle-like leaves are dark green and in spring it is covered with tiny white flowers. Its essential oil is considered an exceptional tonic, an aid to memory, as Shakespeare reminds us in *Hamlet*. In cooking, it goes particularly well with roast pork, lamb, chicken, and broiled (grilled) fish. It is also added to some wines and vermouths. The ancient Greeks considered it a gift from Aphrodite, goddess of love, and they used to burn it on her altars (after all, the Greek word for rosemary, *dentrolivano* translates as "tree incense".)

ROSEWATER

Commercially produced flavoring from rose petals, available from supermarkets, pharmacies, and specialty stores.

ROUX

Cooked mixture of flour and butter used to thicken sauces.

RUSK CRUMBS

These are made by crushing rusks into fine crumbs.

RUSKS

Hard dried bread made by drying out in the oven or cooking under the broiler (grill).

SAFFRON

Stigmas from the *Crocus sativas* flowers, indigenous to the Aegean and other areas of the Mediterranean. Prized for thousands of years as a yellow dye, it has been used at least since the Byzantine period in cookery. Natural Greek red saffron is cultivated in Greek Macedonia near the town of Krokos. Eighty percent of the crop is exported to Spain, France, and Italy, where it is more widely used in cooking than in Greece. Saffron has several legends surrounding its origin and name. The Greek god Hermes is said to have accidentally killed his friend Krokos with his javelin while they were hunting. Three drops of Krokos' blood fell on some beautiful purple flowers, which the god turned into three red stamens, naming the flower *krokos* in his friend's memory. Another myth relates that the beautiful little purple flowers appeared in a meadow at the foot of Mount Idi in Crete in the aftermath of the passionate union between Zeus and his wife Hera. The mythical mingling of love, passion, gods, and death in these legends indicates the importance of the crocus to ancient life and religion. The purple crocus grows wild all over the eastern Mediterranean and Asia Minor, from southern Italy to Kashmir. Throughout its history, saffron has been one of the most expensive spices, used to dye both cloth and hair, as a medicine, and in cosmetics. There is little evidence that saffron was used in cooking before the Greek medieval or Byzantine period, although cooks in isolated areas of the Aegean may have used local wild saffron to add color and fragrance to their food before then. Today it is widely used all over the world, its beautiful yellow color and pleasant iodine aroma adding to the flavor and appearance of modern dishes of rice, seafood, pasta, meat, soups, sauces, and sweet dishes. It is also used in some liqueurs and in cheese making. In Greece *safrani* is an ingredient in the special breads and cheese pies baked in the islands at Easter time. Systematic cultivation of the plant began in Greece in the early seventeenth century when merchants from Kozani in Macedonia brought some *Crocus sativas* bulbs back from central Europe. The extremely labor-intensive efforts of Greek saffron growers—there are about 50,000 stamens, each plucked by hand, in 3½ oz (100 g) of pure saffron—were exploited by traders until 1971, when the Cooperative of Saffron Producers of Kozani was established, based in the town of Krokos. Today, some 1,500 member-families in about forty villages have the exclusive right to grow, collect, package, and market natural Greek red saffron. Some 2,500 acres are under cultivation, which produce, depending on the weather, 6–8 tons per year of pure red saffron.

SAGANAKI

A two-handled, shallow skillet or frying pan used for frying or braising small portions of food, such as cheese and shellfish. The dishes take their name from it.

SAGE

This hardy plant prefers high altitudes and needs little water. Its aromatic leaves play little part in Greek cooking, but are dried and made into tea throughout the country. It is believed to strengthen the immune system and relieve the symptoms of the common cold. In winter, sage tea is drunk hot and it warms the whole body, while in summer, iced sage tea is very refreshing, and it is another beverage beloved by the Cretans.

SALTED

Meat, fish, or other foods cured in vinegar, salt, or pickling brine.

SAMOS MUSCAT

A naturally sweet wine from Muscat grapes grown on the island of Samos, which was famous for its wines in antiquity. Its modern history began in 1562, when the Sultan awarded the island the right to produce sweet wine. By the eighteenth century it was famous throughout Europe and was the wine of choice of the Roman Catholic church, as well as the court at Versailles in France. A taste for Samos Muscat survived despite the fate of the French kings and, even today, it is the only Greek wine with a strong following in France. The full range of sweet Samos wines is produced by the island's cooperative, a union of all its growers, at two wineries where a small amount of good dry white wine is also made. After the harvest, specially selected Muscat grapes from low-yield vines are dried for several days in the sun to increase their sugar content before they are pressed. The wine is then aged for three years or more in oak barrels, where it develops its strong, characteristic aroma and a color that can range from gold to amber to dark mahogany. The older wines resemble oloroso sherry or Madeira; the younger ones have a crisp but aromatic flavor and can be drunk as an apéritif as well as after dinner. Any of these wines can be a memorable finale to a wonderful meal, complementing a rich dessert or strong cheese and fruit.

SAN MICHALI SIROU

An excellent cow's milk table cheese, it has been made using the same recipe for at least fifty years. Slightly piquant, it has a full-bodied flavor and delicate buttery aroma, and is good in soufflés and pies, or fried or broiled (grilled).

SAUSAGE CASING

The thin tubes of membrane of an animal's intestines provide a natural casing widely used in sausage-making. They are prepared before sale and can be bought fresh or dry-salted. Lamb's and pig's casings are generally used in Greece for thin sausages that can be broiled (grilled) or fried.

SAUTÉ

The method of quickly frying onions or other chopped vegetables in oil or butter until softened but not browned.

SAVORY

This intensely aromatic little shrub prefers dry stony areas. The ancients esteemed it for its therapeutic properties and its fragrance. Cretans use water in which savory has been boiled to clean and disinfect wine barrels in preparation for the new vintage. Cooks like its subtle, pleasant flavor with roast meats, salads, omelets, and soups, and it is also an ingredient in digestive liqueurs. The ancient Greeks added it to their wine, a tradition that continues today in some parts of the country.

SCALD

To dip foods quickly in boiling water or to heat milk or another liquid to just below boiling point.

SCALLION (SPRING ONION)

A long, thin member of the onion family with a mild flavor. Also known as green onions.

SCALLOP (ESCALOPE)

Meat cut in thin slices and then beaten flat.

SCORE

To make cuts across the surface of food before roasting or baking.

SEAR

To brown rapidly in a hot pan.

SEMOLINA

A coarse-milled flour of hard or durum wheat. It is similar to North American cream of wheat, which can be used as a substitute.

SESAME SEEDS

Tiny, flat, oily seeds used whole or ground in cakes and cookies (biscuits). Also sprinkled on top of breads, cakes, and cookies.

SFELA

This white cheese, also known as "fiery feta" because of its sharp, peppery taste, is made in Messinia and Lakonia in the Peloponnese. It is made from sheep's or goat's milk. The cheese is cut into *sfelides*, or rectangular strips, from which it takes its name. It is eaten as a table cheese or used in pitas and other dishes of the region.

SIMMER

To cook food slowly in a liquid over low heat.

SKEWER

A long thin rod of metal or small wooden or bamboo sticks used for threading food before broiling (grilling).

SKIM

To remove from the surface of the cooking liquid the froth or impurities that are released by meats and some other ingredients when they are heated.

SNAILS

These are plentiful in many regions of Crete. They are collected from February to April after the rains and they are kept alive in a cool place until September. They can be cooked in a variety of ways—with tomato sauce, vegetables, or rice. *Hohlioi boubouristi* (fried snails with vinegar and flavored with rosemary), is one of the most famous mezedes in Crete.

SOAK

To let food steep in liquid, usually water, for a specified period of time until becomes soft and moist.

SPIT-ROAST

To roast meat or birds on a rotating spit so that it cooks evenly.

STAKA

This traditional product of Crete is the roux made from the residue of clarified butter with added flour. The ingredients are cooked until thick, all the moisture has evaporated and the mixture turns a pale creamy color. It gives excellent flavour in pies, soups and omelets. It is also served as an appetizer with *tsikoudia*, and is very rich but delicious.

STAKA BUTTER

A dairy product made from the fresh cream from the top of unpasteurized ewe's or goat's milk, which is skimmed off and then combined with a small amount of salt and flour. It is stirred constantly over very low heat until the protein solids in the cream separate from the clear liquid fat. This fat is clarified butter, or *stakovoutiro*, as it is known in Crete. The curdled protein-flour mixture which resembles clotted cream is known as *staka*.

STIR-FRY

To fry small pieces of food, moving them around constantly so that they cook rapidly all over and do not stick.

STOCK

A base for sauces, soups, and stews, made by simmering the giblets and carcass of poultry or meat bones in water with vegetables, herbs, and seasoning.

STRAIN

To separate the liquid from solid ingredients, when the liquid is required for a further purpose.

STRAINER

A fine metal mesh for straining and draining foods.

SWEAT

To cook a vegetable in its own juices. Place in a pan over low heat and let it wilt in its juices and the water clinging to the leaves after washing.

TAHINI

A sesame seed paste used in many Greek and Middle Eastern dishes, such as hummus. It can be used as a substitute for olive oil in some Lenten recipes.

TARAMAS

Salt-preserved fish roe from cod, striped mullet, carp, herring, or other fish. The quality of *taramas* ranges from the full-flavored light beige roe, the most expensive, to the cheaper but less tasty pink roe. Some *taramas* is naturally light pink. The bright pink-colored type is artificially tinted. Many cooks combine the beige type for flavor with a small amount of pink roe to improve the appearance of taramosalata and other dishes made with *taramas*.

TENDERIZE

To marinate certain cuts of meat, especially game, for a specified length of time until tender.

THICKEN

To add cornstarch (cornflour), flour, egg, or fresh cream to make sauces, stock, or other liquids thicker.

THYME

There is virtually nowhere in rural Greece where this small bush does not grow. It loves the Mediterranean climate, with its spring showers and hot summers. When touched, its tiny flowers, leaves, and branches emit an enchanting scent, which is inextricably linked with Greece. It provides exceptional food for bees, and thyme honey is highly regarded by connoisseurs. The therapeutic attributes of thyme were known and recorded by Hippocrates, and the ancients used it as a substitute for expensive imported incense. There are many varieties of thyme, which, when dried, lend themselves to flavoring meats, stews, and salads.

TIMBALE

A dish cooked in a special round mold or bowl by steaming or baking.

TORTE

A sponge cake sliced horizontally and filled with whipped cream, pastry cream, or other filling. Chopped nuts or pieces of fruit are usually added to the fillings.

TRUFFLES

Edible white or black fungi that grow underground near oak trees. They are highly prized for their special flavor.

TRUSS

To tie a bird or a cut of meat with string to help it keep its shape during cooking. The string may be tied around by hand or, in case of poultry, threaded with a trussing needle.

TSIPOURO AND TSIKOUDIA

Known variously as *raki*, *tsikoudia* (in Crete), or *tsipouro* (in Macedonia, Epirus, and Thessaly), this apéritif is very similar to Italian *grappa*, a clear liquid to which different flavorings—walnut leaves in Crete, aniseed or fennel in Macedonia—can be added after distillation. From mid-October to mid-December in most of Greece's wine-producing districts, the air shimmers with the fumes of strong alcohol. With the grapes harvested, the wine bubbling in tanks and barrels, attention turns to the production of a potent brew from the residues—skins, seeds (*tsikouda*), and stems—after the must has been squeezed from the grapes. Until the 1960s, the making of *tsipouro* was exclusively a cottage industry, with the distillery—a large cauldron, furnace, and system of bronze pipes—often located in a basement or woodshed. Many households that still make their own wine also distil *tsipouro*, on the islands as well as the mainland. Recently some of the major vineyards have begun to produce and market high-quality *tsipouro* in a variety of subtle flavors. Nowadays no longer a rough beverage tossed down by peasants on cold nights, it has become a fashionable drink in Athens and Thessaloniki. It is Volos, though, where *tsipouro* is best loved. In the famed *tsipouradika* there, it has inspired many wonderful mezedes to accompany it.

VELOUTÉ SAUCE

A sauce consisting of a roux to which stock has been added.

WALNUTS

Widely used in Greek cookery, walnuts are known to have been cultivated at least since 1,200 BC. Evvoia was and is still famous for its walnuts, although they grow all over Greece in ravines near brooks and streams. Not only are the nuts collected and ground for use in desserts, the immature fruit is collected in late spring before the nut has hardened, soaked in water, and cooked in sugar syrup, creating a dark green preserve known as *karidaki gliko*. Walnuts are excellent with honey as a topping for yogurt (a popular taverna dessert) and they are also the main ingredient in another taverna favorite, *karidopita*, or walnut cake.

WHEAT BERRIES

Whole kernels of wheat, available from specialist and health food stores (shops).

WHIP

To beat rapidly, inflating the volume of the ingredients.

WHISK

To beat rapidly with a flexible tool to increase the volume and aerate ingredients such as egg whites and mayonnaise.

WHITE SAUCE

A roux-thickened sauce made with milk or cream. (See Béchamel sauce.)

WINE AND SPIRITS

Grapes were pressed and fermented on the island of Crete more than 4,000 years ago, and possibly much earlier. A Minoan wine press has been found above Knosos in an area that is still planted with vines, while the palace ruins contained many amphoras that modern analyses confirm to have once been filled with wine. Of course, we have no idea what it tasted like, but it was most likely to be sweet and red. Much later, from the Classical era onward, Greek warships were crossing the seas and taking wines and vine cuttings west to Italy, France, and Spain and east to the shores of Crimea. We know that the wines must have been very strong because they had to be diluted with water. The ancients called the former *akratos inos* "undiluted wine" and the modern word for wine, *krasi*, harks back to those days, although adding water is no longer necessary. At the legendary symposiums, wine was served at the end of the meal to stimulate good conversation. The Byzantines continued the winemaking tradition and one of the consequences of the fourth Crusade, in which the Venetians and other Westerners turned their energies to capturing Constantinople instead of liberating Jerusalem, was that the Crusaders rediscovered a taste for Greek wines. Once again, ships carrying casks of sweet red wine journeyed westward. Malmsey wine, of which the English were so fond, came originally from Monemvasia in the eastern Peloponnese, and the vines of Madeira are descended from cuttings taken from Cyprus and Crete. The Muscat and

Mavrodaphne dessert wines still enjoyed today are direct descendants of those legendary drinks. During the Ottoman occupation, wine ceased to be exported but villagers continued to make and enjoy their own. In some areas they would follow the ancient custom of preserving wine (and flavoring it) with resin to produce retsina, but this was by no means a universal practice and remained unknown in Crete, northern Greece, and the Ionian islands. In modern Greece, wine-making persisted as a cottage industry for generations and did not really begin to assimilate Western tastes and methods until the second half of the twentieth century. Two pioneering vineyards, Achaia Clauss and Cambas, were the exceptions to this rule. Founded in the nineteenth century, these firms bottled standardized and non-resinated red, white, and rosé wines, but even in the 1960s and 1970s, most people purchased their wine in wicker-wrapped bottles, which they filled at a local taverna or in the barrel-lined basement of a neighbor's house. Nothing was regulated, but most of the wine was very drinkable. Given this history, the changes in Greece's wine production are nothing short of revolutionary. Beginning in the late 1970s, the sons and daughters of traditional vintners went off to study oenology in France and California, returning with new ideas and knowledge. Membership of the European Union presented an entry to new markets (as long as the wine did not taste of turpentine). Almost overnight, wineries sprouted in traditional wine-producing areas, and also in new ones. In Nemea, for example, known for a rather deadly red

known as Lion's Blood—a reference to Herakles' first labor—the local Agiorgitiko grape was transformed into a superb series of wines that, depending on blending and aging, can rival those of almost any international vineyard. Drama, on the other hand, an area in the northern reaches of Macedonia blessed with a mild microclimate, has seen the creation in the last twenty years of at least five boutique wineries whose wines are among the best in Greece. According to EU legislation, Greece has twenty regions that have been awarded the coveted appellation of high-quality origin. Starting in the north, these are Naousa, Amyntaio, and Goumenissa, established wine-growing districts known for their dark red wines made from the Xinomavro grape, and Côtes de Meliton, a new district in Chalkidiki. Epirus produces the naturally bubbly Zitsa, while Rapsani and Anchialos near Olympus make rich reds. Apart from Nemea, the Peloponnese provides the delicious crisp whites from the Roditis and Moshofilero grapes at Patras and Mantineia. Crete has four appellations of high-quality origin districts, Kefallonia boasts Robola whites, while Limnos, Paros, Rhodes, and Santorini produce excellent wines. The latter's Asirtiko has been described as Greece's finest white by an eminent wine guide. Attica remains the country's largest wine-producer, even though the native Savatiano grape no longer goes into much retsina. In addition to using indigenous grapes, Greek wine-makers are also adapting to international tastes with more familiar grape varieties, such as Chardonnay, Sauvignon Blanc,

Cabernet, Merlot, Pinot Noir, and Syrah. Sometimes these are blended with local varieties to make completely new wines, but each grape reacts differently to the soil and weather of its local environment, as well as to the expertise and *meraki*, or loving care, expended on its collection, pressing, fermentation, and storage.

YOGURT
Made from either sheep's or cow's milk, Greek yogurt is thicker and creamier than the commercial yogurts of other countries. Plain yogurt is sold in plastic containers or sometimes in a brown ceramic dish; this type is usually better quality. Another type of yogurt is the thick, strained type known as *stragismeno* or *sakoulas*. It is widely eaten as dessert in tavernas with honey, walnuts, or fruit preserves. Strained yogurt is a good substitute for sour cream, which is not used in Greek cuisine. You can strain regular yogurt through a coffee filter or triple layers of cheesecloth (muslin) for several hours in your refrigerator, set over a bowl to catch the liquid.

INDEX

-

EYPETHPIO

-

Evretirio

VEFA ALEXIADOU

Vefa Alexiadou is the leading authority on Greek cookery. Since 1980 she has published dozens of best-selling cookbooks in Greece, many of which have won awards and have been published in other languages. Formerly a chemist, she also has her own television series, regularly writes articles for magazines and gives lectures and demonstrations on Greek recipes and gastronomic traditions. She has served on the board of the Centre for the Preservation of Traditional Greek Gastronomy, is a member of the International Association of Culinary Professionals, and has won many prizes for her contribution to Greek gastronomy.

ACKNOWLEDGEMENTS

I dedicate this book, which contains just a hint of the timeless fragrance, flavor and beauty of Greece, to the citizens of the world.

I had the great good fortune to grow up in a home where food preparation was of primary importance, where tantalizing aromas from the kitchen enhanced all our activities. Meals were not only a basic biological necessity, but also rituals connected with the seasons, vacations, fasting, and special occasions. I couldn't possibly imagine Christmas without honey-soaked *melomakarona*, Easter without a lamb turning on the spit, Annunciation Day without a dish of salt cod. My passion for cooking began in my childhood, and the greatest influence on me was unquestionably my mother, Angeliki Ioannidou. She conveyed the beauty of her own homeland, Constantinople, in the unforgettable tastes and aromas of food that transported me to heaven. She was an inexhaustible source of recipes, which she taught me to cook in her own inimitable way, emphasizing the need for each dish to look as attractive as it tasted. I believe she succeeded in transmitting her love and flair for cooking to me, and to her I owe whatever I managed to achieve in this life, especially the chance to pass on to millions of Greek men and women my own love of cooking through my books and television programs. In essence, they are all her work.

To my late husband, Konstantinos, Professor of Chemistry at Aristotle University in Thessaloniki, I owe inexpressible gratitude for all that he was: colleague, advisor, partner, source of inspiration, taster, and much more. Without his invaluable contribution to my 30-year career in writing and publishing, I would never have been able to produce this superb volume, the work of a lifetime. I am so sorry he is not here to share my joy.

I also thank my sister, Zenovia Georgitziki, for her tremendous help throughout. And I thank the friends who urged me to write my first book, using the wonderful recipes we shared over tea and coffee. They were my first source of new recipes and the spark that lit the fire.

I thank the friends from every corner of Greece who let me have the precious notebooks filled with handwritten recipes that belonged to their mothers and grandmothers. Those traditional recipes revealed the stories and customs of generations. I thank my co-worker and marvelous assistant, my colleague in chemistry, Dali Machaidze, who helped test countless recipes. I thank my dear friends and colleagues, Nikos and Maria Psilakis, who provided valuable background information.

Words are not adequate to express my thanks to the two major collaborators who worked with me on this book: Diana Farr Louis, for her work on the regions of Greece and Cyprus, and Linda Makris, for her work on the recipe chapter introductions and to the book itself. Both of them also translated many of the recipes. I cordially thank Evi Botsari, for her indefatigable and meticulous processing of the texts and their corrections, which required many hours and days, and for all her invaluable assistance and support in the course of this project.

I send a big thank you to Edouard Cointreau, who for years has recognized and promoted my work internationally. Once again he showed his confidence in me when he recommended me unequivocally as the best person for this difficult undertaking.

I owe infinite gratitude to my publisher, Richard Schlagman, who entrusted me with this job and embraced my efforts with warmth and enthusiasm. He is a unique individual, a professional in every sense, and working with him has been a wonderful experience, which unquestionably broadened my horizons. I also thank Amanda Renshaw for her contribution to the creation of this book.

I must give special mention to the praiseworthy job done by the whole team at Phaidon Press, who worked tirelessly to complete this book. They are talented people with unique abilities in their fields, who believed in and loved this project. Many of them hold a special place in my heart, not just as colleagues but as very close friends. My warmest thanks go to Emilia Terragni, who commissioned the book and stood by my side from the first moment as a valuable assistant and advisor; Laura Gladwin, who edited the book with such care and attention to detail; Olivia Roussel, who assisted in the book's supervision; Julia Hasting, who with her experience and innovative ideas created its attractive design; Gary Hayes, who with his enormous experience coordinated production so smoothly; and Edward Park, whose excellent photographs decorate the pages of this book and whet the appetite. Very warm thanks are also due to the chef, Alex Risdale, for his superb preparation of the dishes, and the food stylist, Chiyo Shimazaki, for their impeccable presentation. Without the knowledge and experience of this admirable team, the result would not have been the same.

Phaidon Press Inc.
65 Bleecker Street
New York, NY 10012

Phaidon Press Limited
Regent's Wharf
All Saints Street
London N1 9PA

www.phaidon.com

First published in 2009 as *Vefa's Kitchen*
Reprinted 2010, 2011, 2013, 2015
Reprinted in 2016 as *Greece: The Cookbook*
© 2009, 2016 Phaidon Press Limited

ISBN 978 0 7148 7380 0

A CIP catalog record of this book is available
from the British Library and the Library of Congress.

Photographs by Edward Park

Designed by Julia Hasting

Printed in China